Encyclopedia of
KEYBOARD INSTRUMENTS

VOLUME 1
THE PIANO

Garland Reference Library of the Humanities
(Volume 1131)

Encyclopedia of
KEYBOARD INSTRUMENTS

Robert Palmieri
General Editor

Advisory Board
Frank Cooper
Craig Cramer
Quentin Faulkner
Malcolm Frager
Maurice Hinson
Howard Scott

PIANO

Robert Palmieri, *Editor*
Margaret W. Palmieri, *Assistant Editor*

Encyclopedia of
KEYBOARD INSTRUMENTS

VOLUME 1
THE PIANO

Edited By
Robert Palmieri

Assistant Editor
Margaret W. Palmieri

Garland Publishing, Inc.
New York & London
1994

Library of Congress Cataloging-in-Publication Data

Encyclopedia of keyboard instruments / edited by Robert Palmieri.
    v. cm. — (Garland reference library of the humanities : vol. 1131,)
    Includes bibliographical references and indexes.
    Contents: v. 1. The Piano
    ISBN 0–8240–5685–X (v. 1 : alk. paper)
    1. Keyboard instruments—Dictionaries. I. Palmieri, Robert.
II. Palmieri, Margaret W. III. Series.
ML 102.K5E53   1994   93–4742
786' .03—dc20   CIP
                                           MN

Printed on acid-free, 250-year-life paper
Manufactured in the United States of America

In memory of the unassuming Paduan artisan, Bartolomeo Cristofori, who ultimately proved to be a giant among his contemporaries.

Contents

List of Illustrations

Preface

The *Encyclopedia of Keyboard Instruments (EKI)* was conceived and written in celebration of four major keyboard instruments: organ, clavichord, harpsichord, and piano. Each instrument bears a rich history and each volume of the encyclopedia chronicles this past in as much detail as possible. The editors hope that the reader will become immersed in the history and development of the instruments as he/she delves into the many facts and features of this unique encyclopedia.

The three volumes of the *EKI* contain up-to-date, useful data about the instruments, often presenting the results of recent research on the instruments that appear here for the first time. Experts in the field were invited to participate in this important project; therefore, the reader will find in the volumes articles by published authors who specialize in particular aspects of the instrument. The editors of the individual volumes of the *EKI* have utilized an international cadre of contributors. We, as editors, are indebted to these writers for stepping forward to present their work and findings in this encyclopedia. The contributing authors express in their work a deep love of their instrument, and it is here that they are the active celebrants in this commemorative work.

The *Encyclopedia of Keyboard Instruments* attempts to cover all aspects of the instruments in a comprehensive manner. Each of the instruments is observed as to its structure, history, science, national industry, innovations, builders/makers, companies, and contemporary and future profiles. Since the instruments are inherently different, each *EKI* volume is also different in its treatment of that particular instrument. A detailed explanation of each volume is presented by the pertinent editor in the Introduction.

The editors of the *EKI* wish to thank the members of the Advisory Board for their help in the implementation of this unique work. Their collaboration in this effort is greatly appreciated. We mourn the loss of board member Malcolm Frager, who was not only a fine performing artist but also a scholar in the history of the piano and its music.

As General Editor I would like to especially thank volume editors—Douglas Bush, editor of the organ volume, and Igor Kipnis, editor of the clavichord and harpsichord volume—for their diligence and fortitude in guiding their volumes through to successful completion. Their jobs, difficult and challenging though they were, were also rewarding in that each had the freedom to control the structure of the volume, and upon completion could readily view the total profile of the instrument. It is this inclusive overview that we hope the reader will perceive. The value of having an encyclopedic work that investigates solely one instrument in a comprehensive manner is immeasurable. We trust you will join us in celebrating these venerable keyboard instruments.

Robert Palmieri
General Editor

Introduction
Volume 1: The Piano

Little did the Paduan instrument maker, Bartolomeo Cristofori, realize when he devised his first pianoforte, that it would receive such universal acceptance. Since then the piano has experienced hard times, such as depressions and wars, but has always survived and retained its eminence in the concert world as well as in its social setting. This stamina shows us how important the instrument has been to our musical environment. In just a few years, at the turn of this century, we will be celebrating the piano's 300th anniversary, and to help honor the event, this volume has been compiled to acknowledge the piano's stature and universal influence. The piano volume of the *Encyclopedia of Keyboard Instruments* highlights the piano's long evolution up to the year 1992, when this volume was completed.

The style of this work is somewhat different from the usual encyclopedic format in that the topics (from A to Z) are not all covered in a concise manner. One will find many subjects that are explored in depth, and the resulting articles approach comprehensive monographs. On the other hand, there are subjects that warrant only simple definitions. An earnest attempt has been made to see that new information regarding the piano has been incorporated in the articles. In selecting the topics, every effort was made to be as comprehensive as possible; however, it is, of course, impossible to cover all piano companies, all piano makers/builders, all countries that produce pianos, etc. We did, however, attempt to include the most important builders and companies. The composer entries in the piano volume are included because those composers had a direct or indirect influence on the development of the instrument, not because they wrote piano music. This volume deals primarily with the instrument itself, although you will find a few ancillary topics, e.g., piano music, pedagogy, technic, touch, etc. The reader will find birth/death dates in the index for most persons mentioned in the volume. Dates were only entered in the text when pertinent to the article. The index will also be useful in locating the many minor piano builders/makers and piano companies that are mentioned in the text, as well as in finding the many individual parts of the piano and where they are discussed.

I would like to thank Garland for undertaking this ambitious project, my fellow editors Douglas Bush (Organ volume) and Igor Kipnis (Clavichord-Harpsichord volume), the advisory board members for their advice and guidance, the Research Council of Kent State University for granting me a Summer Research Fellowship for extra time to work on the encyclopedia, the many colleagues and specialists who offered their advice, and particularly the many contributors to this volume—all experts in their fields—who are devoted to the piano and its colorful history. They essentially produced this volume. May the piano continue to enrich our lives!

Robert Palmieri

Keyboard ranges specified in this volume follow this format:

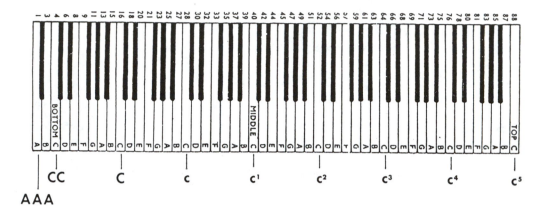

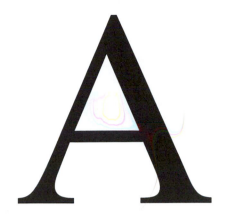

ACCOMPANYING

See Chamber Music and Accompanying.

ACOUSTICAL BLOCK

When cast-iron **frames** and **overstringing** became standard, it became obvious to more than one piano maker that significant areas of useable space were opening up within the framework of the piano in which a larger **soundboard** could be fitted. But, although piano design in general has always sought to incorporate the largest possible area of soundboard surface, these same makers soon discovered that there is such a thing as a soundboard that is too large. Prototypes of such instruments demonstrated that portions of the larger soundboard were not always under the strict control of the **strings**. In fact, a sort of booming, or semi-independent drum action, characterized the tone to such a degree that even the fall of the **dampers** could not immediately silence it.

Hence, the introduction of the acoustical block, a wooden structural member placed in the upper bass corner of the **grand piano** framework (or in one or more corners of the **upright** piano), the purpose of which is to limit the working area of the soundboard and to block out, or rather to prevent from ever getting started, unwanted vibrations and soundboard flutter. The acoustical block also serves an additional function in that it shortens several **ribs**, thereby allowing the **bridge** to sit more centrally upon them.

Two other commonly used terms for this wooden member are the harmonic trap and the dumb-bar.

See also Soundboard.

Nicholas Gravagne

ACOUSTICAL DISC

The acoustical disc is a small, hardwood disc approximately $3/4$ inch diameter by $3/8$ inch tall that is inserted into holes in the **soundboard**. These discs, which are located under the **bridges** at each place where a **rib** passes underneath, are sandwiched between the bridge and the rib, secured by a small diameter wooden dowel running through the three components. The result of this atypical plan on belly construction is to effectively extend the hardwood of the bridge down through the soundboard so that it makes direct contact with the ribs. Vibrations in the bridge are believed to more quickly energize the rib and to more completely intensify soundboard amplification where a disc is present. Most pianos, including the **Steinway**, do not employ the acoustical disc.

See also Soundboard.

Nicholas Gravagne

ACOUSTICS

Every musical action can be considered as the production of a chain of energy. The way this energy travels through the several parts of the system determines the final result, *in casu* the sound we hear. One very important phase in the process of making music on the piano is of course the instrument itself. Being an energy system of its own, the important moments of its acoustical chain of energy are:

1. the beating of the **hammer** on the **string** and the disturbance of the equilibrium of the latter,

2. the vibration of the string itself,

3. the floating of vibrational energy from the string to the **soundboard** via the **bridge**, and,

4. the radiation of sound from the body of the instrument to the surrounding air.

All of these moments are twofold: they are governed by general mathematical and physi-

1

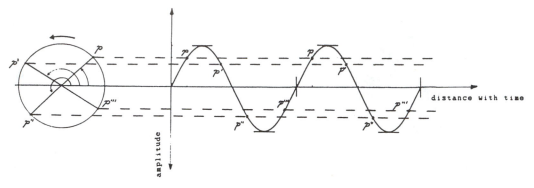

Fig. 1. _The generation of a sine wave._
The travelling of a point (p) around the circle, projected on a system of coordinates

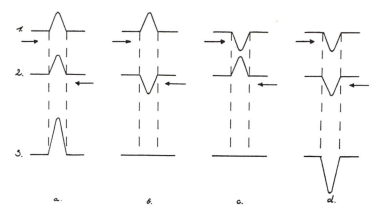

Fig. 2. _The principle of constructive and destructive interference._
Waves travelling in opposite directions with opposite senses (1b+2b and 1c+2c) interfere destructively when passing through each other (3b and 3c)
Waves travelling in opposite directions with equal senses (1a+2a and 1d+2d) interfere constructively when passing through each other (3a and 3d)

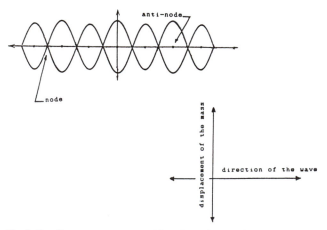

Fig. 3. _Standing transverse wave with nodes and antinodes._

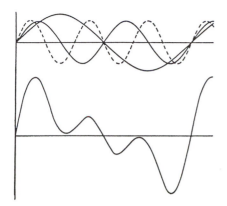

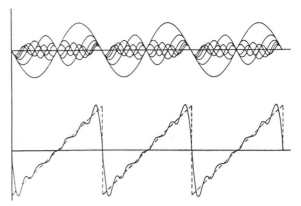

Fig. 4a. _Resultant wave form of the fundamental and first two overtones_ (third partial in dotted line).

Fig. 4b. _Resultant wave form of the first six partials of a tone._ The dotted line on the graph of the resultant represents the sawtooth wave, which results when a great number of partials are present (in theory only after an infinite number of partials).

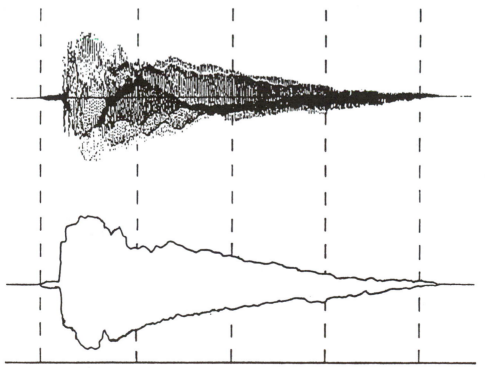

Fig. 5. _Oscillograph trace of a piano sound and the resulting envelope_ (the vertical dotted lines represent time units of 0.5 seconds).

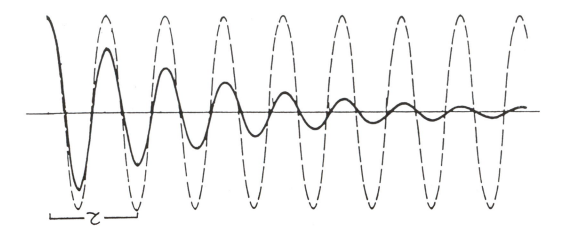

Fig. 6. _Damped vibration._
(The dotted curve represents the undamped vibration.)

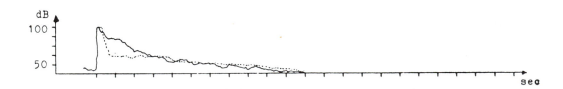

Fig. 7. _Decay curve for a¹ (trichord)._
(The dotted curve shows the result when the trichord is tuned pure.)

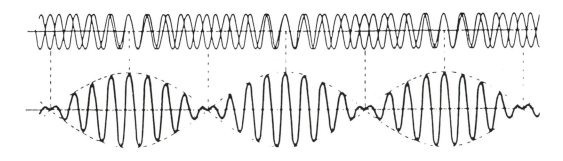

Fig. 8. _Beats._

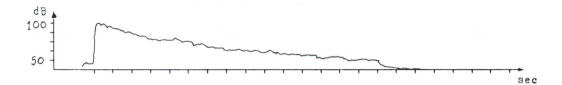

Fig. 9. _Decay curve for AAA (monochord)._

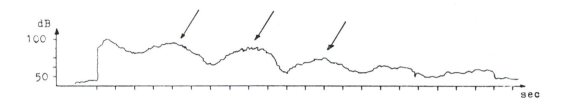

Fig. 10. _Decay curve AA (dichord)._
(Arrows indicate the wolf-resonance.)

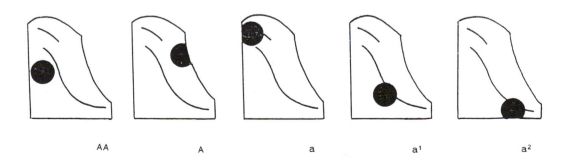

Fig. 11. _Resonance of the soundboard._
(Only the points of highest sympathy are marked.)

cal rules, but their actual behavior is determined chiefly by the nature and use of the building materials. A full understanding of the acoustical functioning of the piano is therefore only possible when the two levels (theory and actual realization) are both considered.

I. Generalities on Acoustics

Waves and their behavior. The greater part of acoustical events have to do with periodic motions. A periodic motion consists of the repetition of a basic movement in equal intervals of time, e.g., the swinging of the pendulum of a clock. The time that is needed for such a single motion is called the period T and is expressed in seconds. For the clock pendulum, this is the time it takes to go from its perpendicular position (equilibrium) to the right, back to the equilibrium, to the left, and back to the perpendicular position. The number of times such a single motion (or cycle) takes place in one second is called the frequency *f*:

$$\left(f = 1/T\right)$$

and is expressed in hertz (Hz). One hertz means one cycle per second.

We are also interested in the distance of the mass (*m*) from its equilibrium position. At every time *t*, this distance is called the displacement, or elongation *y* of the swinging mass. The maximum displacement is called the amplitude (*a*). Since the periodic motion takes place in two directions (e.g., to the right and the left), *y* fluctuates between -*a* and +*a*:

$$-a \leq y \leq +a$$

It is useful to represent periodic motion by a graph of displacement *y* vs. time *t*.

Some periodic motions have special characteristics. Of great importance in music is simple harmonic motion, which is characterized by the fact that the force that drives the mass to return to its equilibrium position is proportional to the displacement of this mass from its equilibrium. Simple harmonic motion can be represented by the projection of a point *p* travelling at constant speed around a circle. The projection is a sine wave (see fig. 1).

When a string is set to vibrate, it produces a simple harmonic motion and transverse waves result (fig. 1). In a transverse wave the medium (e.g., the string) through which the wave travels moves perpendicular to the wave's direction. Since strings are attached at both ends, the pulses that are generated at the starting point

are for the greater part reflected at the terminal point, and so they travel back in opposite directions. If pulses are continuously added to the string, the wave becomes a complex system of going and returning pulses at the same time. This might create a very chaotic situation, were it not that waves travelling in the same medium but in opposite directions can pass through each other. The principle of linear superposition determines the behavior of this passing: the elongations of pulses with the same sense are added, and those of pulses with opposite sense are subtracted. This adding or subtracting is called constructive or destructive interference, respectively (see fig. 2).

The continuous pulsation of a string gives birth to yet another phenomenon. The interference of initial and reflected pulses will create the impression that the wave no longer moves. The result is a standing transverse wave, having nodes at points of destructive interference with resulting displacement zero, and antinodes at points of constructive interference with the maximum displacement (see fig. 3).

The presence of nodes and antinodes allows the string to vibrate in several modes. For instance, if we consider a node that is in the middle, it divides the string in two halves, and the string will also vibrate as two halves, together with its basic vibration. This is called a mode of vibration. Typically, every mode produces its own frequency: the **partials**. It is obvious that the relative placement of the nodes and antinodes on a vibrating string follows from the character of the given pulse. Consequently, the pulse-shape is very important for the presence or absence of certain partials and their strengths.

Linear superposition is not only the creating force behind the standing of waves, it also rules the final shape of the wave. Indeed, since a musical tone consists of simultaneous modes of vibration, the elongation of all the resulting waves will add or substract. A quite complex resultant waveform may arise. This resultant waveform is of course determined by the relative presence of the constituent partials. It is the resultant waveform that defines the tone color (see figs. 4a and 4b).

The nature of strings and its implications. The behavior of strings described above is to a large extent determined by the nature of the string used and its application. Very important for stringed keyboard instruments is the relation that exists between length, tension, and mass of the string. These relations were formulated by Marin Mersenne (1588–1648). Mersenne stated that there exist ratios between the frequency of a vibrating string and:

1. its length L (f is inversely proportional to L),
2. its tension T (f is directly proportional to the square root of T),
3. its diameter D (f is inversely proportional to D),
4. its linear density e (f is inversely proportional to the square root of e).

Combining 1, 2, and 4 into one formula, we get:

$$\left(f = \tfrac{1}{2L}\sqrt{T/e'}\right)$$

where T is expressed in newton (and may sometimes well exceed 1 kN!), L in meters, and e in kilograms per meter. This has important implications for the stringing of the piano. If wire of the same kind were used (the mass stays the same) throughout the range of the instrument, with every descent of one octave the length of the string would have to double. An instrument with bass strings of an almost monstrous length (more than eight meters) would be the result. However, the frequency is inversely proportional to the square root of the density; thus there is no need to increase the length of the bass strings to impractical dimensions if we simply increase the diameter and consequently the mass of the lower strings. This implies a tempering of the stringing scale ratio from 2:1 per octave to ratios fluctuating between 1.88:1 and 1.94:1.

The tempering of the theoretical stringing scale ratio has a major inconvenience: the strings of the lower range may become so thick that they start to behave like rods, rather than like strings. There are several differences between vibrations of rods and those of strings. The most important difference in this context is the nonharmonic nature of the partials of a vibrating rod. Indeed, the ratio of the subsequent overtones is not 1:2:3:4: . . . as for strings, but 3.0112:5:7:9: . . . . The rod's partials are not only nonharmonic but do not match any interval on the musical scale. In other words, bass strings would be fundamentally unfit, unless

another solution is found to increase the mass without increasing the diameter too much. The solution is very simple: the strings are wrapped one or more times with copper wire. The wrapping of certain strings is only advantageous if further adjustments are made, since doing so changes the ratio between the mass of the string and its elasticity. For a full profit from the energy that is present in the vibrating string, the mass (and thus weight, dimensions, and strength) of the hammer has to increase. Moreover, the greater amount of energy in wrapped vibrating strings might create the desire to adjust the dimensions of the resonator (soundboard). The change is usually left aside and the actual dimensions of the soundboard become somewhat out of proportion to the amount of energy the heavy bass strings radiate. This results in a certain loss of higher partials (or their weakening), and the tone becomes darker and sounds very full.

The rules of Mersenne were conceived for ideal strings vibrating in an ideal way. In reality, the nature of the string, especially its degree of elasticity, causes some deviations. The natural stiffness of actual strings implies some restoring force, when the string is curved due to its vibration. This restoring force causes the partials to shift upwards as far as frequency is concerned. The frequency shift for the higher partials is inversely proportional to the length of the strings. This implies that this shift will be much more apparent for small uprights than for the **concert grand**.

II. The Striking of Strings

In order to start a chain of energy, some disturbance of an equilibrium is needed. For the piano the disturbing factor is the hammer beating a string or a string chorus. The way the beaten string vibrates is prescribed to a high degree by both mechanical and pure physical (acoustical) components. Important mechanical features are the nature and behavior of hammer and string and the relation between them. Major acoustical phenomena are the character and placement of the contact between hammer and string, and the reaction of the string to this contact. The hammer strikes the string at a certain angle and consequently produces a pulsation of the string. The shape of this pulse depends on the shape of the hammer and the angle at which it strikes the string. Indeed, the sharper the angle the more "rude" the disturbance of the equilibrium of the string and the more discontinuous the spread of the passed energy along the string. The more discontinuous and irregular the pulse shape is, the greater the number and strength of higher partials becomes, and the resulting sound becomes "sharper."

The shape of the hammer and its striking angle determine not only the degree of equality of the spread of energy throughout the string, but also its elasticity. Indeed, the soft surface felt allows the hammer to rest on the string during the whole process of giving its energy to the string. In this way, it tempers the violent disturbance of the string and forces the pulse-shape to be more regular. The resulting sound will comprise a more regular spreading of the strength and presence of overtones, especially the lower ones. The length of time the hammer rests on the string is directly proportional to the frequency of the string. Typically, this contact time varies between about one-fifth of a period for the bass strings and almost a whole period for the highest note (the actual contact time fluctuates between about 7 milliseconds for the lowest bass strings and about 0.2 milliseconds for the highest treble notes). Finally, there has to exist some constant ratio between the mass of the hammer and the mass of the string. This explains why the hammers of the lower strings are much more massive than their treble counterparts. Besides this difference in mass, hammers also differ in shape. The desire for more brilliance in the high notes has forced builders to make treble hammers harder and more pointed.

Hermann von Helmholtz (1821–1894; *Tonempfindungen*, p. 133) and many others following him stated that the ideal place for the hammer to strike the string was between one-seventh and one-ninth of its length, in order to avoid the seventh and ninth partials, for the simple reason that the seventh and ninth partials constitute the major second and minor seventh respectively, two notes that do not fit in the major chord. This theory, however, is not valid. The hammer does not strike the string at one precise point, but touches a segment of the string, and analyses of piano sounds have shown that the seventh and ninth partials are at times very clearly present. The beating of the string between one-seventh and one-ninth of its length

has merely practical reasons: empirically speaking it gives the best result.

III. The Sounding of Piano Strings and the Passing of Their Energy to the Body of the Instrument

Once the piano string is set in vibration, it leads a dynamic life of its own. The constant change in its quality emerges from the transfer of its energy via the bridge to the soundboard. Once the sound has been built up after the striking of the hammer, the process of decay (damping) starts. Both building up and decaying are processes of change in sound components and their strength, and are therefore called attack transient and decay transient states. In theory the transient states are separated by a steady state. The actual presence of this steady state, however, is quite restricted.

The easiest way to examine the composition of sounds is by using sound spectra. A sound spectrum is a linear image of the number and quality of the components of a sound, and is constructed after mathematical theories of Joseph Fourier (1768–1830). Typically for the piano, the spectrum changes over the wide range of the piano. The differences in strength of some partials are the result of formants (see below), but primarily of vibration coupling with the soundboard (see below). Remarkable is the shift of the quantity of partials from high in the bass range (in some cases up to 50 partials can be detected!) to very limited in the upper treble.

Attack transient. The attack transient consists of the gradual building up of the sound. For the piano, this building up happens quite fast: typically three to four milliseconds are needed to build up the whole spectrum of the sound.

However, the spectra of actual piano sounds also show some continuing noises (non harmonic components) that lie partially beneath the frequency of the fundamental. These additional noises result from some vibrations of the soundboard itself, the hammer, and the strings (see below), noises provoked by the mechanical action and irregularities of the vibration itself.

The initial non-periodicity of the vibration has to do with the gradual start of the several modes of vibration. This explains also why the maximum amplitude takes some time to establish, since the amplitude rises with the number of overtones. The envelope of the wave shows this clearly (the envelope is the curve indicating the change in amplitude with time: see Fig. 5).

The increase in the number of partials is also related to the time the hammer rests on the string. For average volume this change in complexity of the spectrum takes place gradually and is nondetectable audibly.

There exist outspoken differences in the number and kind of partials that are present in different sounds. In part, this can be explained by the character of the pulse shape given to the string by the hammer and the time the hammer rests on the string. On the other hand, resonance with the soundboard (see below) is also very important. For bass strings the cross stringing of the piano entails some enrichment of the number of partials following sympathetic coupling with the overlying string.

Decay transient. As explained, the sound that emanates from a vibrating string is very dynamic. Since the sole purpose of striking strings on a piano is to produce sounds, the way the energy propagates from a vibrating string to the listener is very important. The rate of transfer of vibration from a source to the air is determined by the surface of the vibrating body. For a string this surface is of course extremely limited.

It is obvious that some amplification of the vibration of the string is needed. Acoustical amplification of vibrations is produced by resonators, *in casu* the soundboard (see below). Need it be said that the transfer of the energy of the string to the soundboard has consequences for the behavior of both string and soundboard?

(a). Impedance: For a complete understanding of the way this transfer happens, the concept of impedance is quite important. In general, impedance is the ratio between a force exerted on a system and the response of the system to that force. This has some important implications: if transfer of energy from one system (the string) to another system (the body of the instrument) is meant to be optimal, the impedances of both systems ought to match each other.

Some degree of impedance match between the string and the bridge is needed to have transfer of energy. However, in order to have a standing transverse wave, reflection of the pulses at the endpoint of the string is also needed. This implies that the impedance match between the string and the bridge has to be imperfect to some degree. Were this match perfect the pulse would go straight to the bridge and no (standing) wave would arise. On the other hand, if the

impedance of the string and the bridge differ too much, no energy would transfer from the string to the bridge.

(b). Damping: Once a piano string has been set to vibrate, no further energy is added. Since there is a constant transfer of energy from the string to the soundboard, after some time the string will return to its position of equilibrium. This is the process of damping.

The reasons for damping are twofold. Primarily damping arises from both friction of the air and the characteristics of the several parts of the instrument and their construction. On the other hand, vibrating strings themselves damp because of their construction, their stiffness, and irregularities in diameter and straightness.

Damping can be considered in the first place as the gradual disappearance of the overtones, and the rate of damping diminishes with time. The rate of decrease of damping can be expressed by the decay halftime τ. This decay halftime is the time needed for the amplitude to reach one-half of its initial value, and is in reality very short (less than one second). Usually, the decay halftime factor is not dependent on the initial amplitude, nor does its value change in subsequent lapses of time (see fig. 6).

The decreasing character of damping is very important for instruments such as the piano, whose initial amplitude is very strong but dissipates at a high rate. Several experiments have shown that pianos with artificial damping at constant rate sound very hazy, especially when chords are played. Of some importance is the fact that the dying out of the distinct partials at different speeds provokes a constant change in tone color, since this color is determined by the presence and relative strength of certain overtones. This constant change in tone color constitutes the decay transient character of the sound. Typically, the decay transients of the piano show that its high frequency partials damp more slowly than the lower ones. This is largely due to the presence of the soundboard and the use of steel as material for strings.

The aim in piano construction has always been to create an instrument that is even in sound and quality for all ranges of its compass. The equalization of the degree and quality of damping throughout the compass of the instrument, however, can never be more than wishful thinking. The presence in one instrument of different species of strings (from very heavy and overspun to quite slim), and the need for both single strings and choruses of two or three strings, makes this equalization impossible. This leads to an exponential-like damping of some overtones, while others die out via beats (see below).

(c). Exponential damping: The exponential process takes place in the choruses. In general, the more pure the chorus is tuned, the higher the degree of damping. This (undesired) effect of pure tuned di- and trichords arises because of the equal phases of the vibration of the two or three strings. Phase can be thought of as the fraction of a cycle that has passed, calculated from some point of reference, e.g., the starting point of the wave. If the strings of the choruses are tuned pure, the waves they produce have the same phase, and the transfer of energy from the string chorus to the bridge is accentuated and accelerated. The sooner a vibrating system passes its energy to another system, the greater the damping effect becomes. It is therefore desirable not to tune di- and trichords pure. Of course, di- and trichords tuned too wide have other inconveniences, e.g., beats, (see below) where the result is that of the "barroom" piano, (see fig. 7).

It is important to realize that the piano can be thought of as a closed system. One may wish to alter the impedance match between bridge and strings or to tune choruses pure to increase the speed of the energy transfer from strings to soundboard, in order to have a louder sound. This cannot, however, be realized without increasing the damping. Diminishing the rate of damping, on the other hand, entails some loss of sound intensity.

(d). Damping with beats: The phenomenon of beats is yet another important feature of damping. Beats arise from the principle of constructive or destructive interference (see above). The sensation of beats occurs when two or more vibrations have frequencies that lie very close together (these vibrations can be fundamentals, but beating of overtones is also possible). The constant shifting of the two waves, one against the other, creates a new periodicity, determined by changes in amplitude and thus in sound intensity.

Beats are periodic and as such are easily recognizable. Moreover, they can be calculated with ease, which makes them a major support for the empirical piano tuner (see fig. 8).

Beats also appear as a damping factor, especially in the lower range of the piano. This type of damping arises when the frequency of the string comes close to one of the frequencies of the soundboard itself, so that it takes a few moments for this resonator to start its own vibration, accordingly taking away a maximum of energy from the string. One can easily explain why this particular kind of damping occurs especially in the bass range. First of all, the frequency of the soundboard lies in the same frequency region as that of the bass strings, and second — and most important — bass strings may behave awkwardly. Indeed, due to their greater mass and stiffness, bass strings show vertical, but also horizontal oscillations, unequal in strength. In other words, vibrating bass strings create beats within themselves. These internal beats reinforce the beats of the damping.

(e). Damping and strings: In the end, damping also has to do with the length of strings: long strings with smaller mass sound longer than shorter strings with higher mass. This explains why, for instance, a^2 on a concert grand may have a damping factor of 2.5 dB per second, while the same note on an upright may be damped at an average rate of 6.4 dB per second. (For comparison, the rustle of leaves has a sound-intensity of about 10 dB). (Compare fig. 9 with figs. 7 and 10.)

IV. Resonance of the Soundboard

Resonance is the state of a system (for the piano, the soundboard) in which a large vibration is produced at the natural frequency response to an external vibration stimulus (the string) of the same or nearly the same frequency. If the natural frequency of the resonator equals the stimulating vibration, the resonance amplitude is maximal.

As explained previously, the surface of a string is too limited to ensure an efficient radiation of the sound. For purposes of amplification, the vibration of the string is transferred to the soundboard via the bridge. Soundboards do not add any energy to the vibration, they enhance the transfer of acoustical energy to the air, producing more intensity for a shorter period of time.

It is obvious that the form, thickness, and ribbing are very important for the particular resonance and behavior of the soundboard. The response of the soundboard to the vibrating string determines which components (partials) of its complex vibrations will become prominent and what the rate of their radiation will be.

Formants and wolf-tones due to construction. Soundboards have their own natural frequencies, and concordance between the frequency (or partial frequency) of the string entails a string response to the soundboard. Particular features of all instrumental bodies are formants. Formants are frequency zones where the response is great. This explains partially why the spectrum of a piano sound shows differences in qualitative presence of some partials: the frequency of these predominant partials falls within the limits of a formant. The importance of formants in instruments is, however, not to be overestimated.

Present to an even lesser degree in pianos are wolf-tones due to construction. A wolf-tone (once described as resembling the howling of wolves) is not to be confused with its homonym used when speaking of **tuning** and temperaments. The kind of wolf-tone referred to in this context can be caused by either the increasing or the damping of certain frequencies, or by very strong resonances with frequencies a bit higher or lower than the frequency of the stimulus (see fig. 10).

Both kinds of wolf-tones result from irregularities in the wood used for the soundboard or in its construction. Sometimes, additional mechanisms (such as the tension resonator, see below) may also give birth to wolf-tones.

Sympathy of the soundboard. The actual response of a soundboard is very dependent on the particular instrument. In general, the points of greatest sympathy do not always coincide with the position of the vibrating string, neither are they always near the bridge (see fig. 11).

The phasing of the soundboard is also dependent on the particular construction of the instrument. Here it refers to whether or not the soundboard vibrates as a whole or rather in segments with constrasting phases (one segment moving upwards as the other moves downwards). Typically, piano soundboards do not react as a whole. There is, however, no connection between the pitch of the stimulating vibration and the division of the soundboard into several parts that are out of phase with each other. The only constant feature of the phasing is that the higher the stimulating pitch is, the more heterogeneous the reaction of the soundboard. A very scattered patchwork of small regions in or out of phase for the highest notes results.

Contrary to what one might expect, the bridge and ribs have no function in dividing the surface of the soundboard as far as phasing is concerned. Of further interest is that at several points the ribs react out of phase (the same is true for the bridge). Consequently, ribs seem to have no function as far as radiation of sound is concerned. Their meaning for phasing is therefore only to prohibit overly heterogeneous behavior.

V. Spatial Radiation

The way the sounds of the piano are passed to the surrounding area can only be studied in connection with room acoustics. Leaving aside that field of research, it will be clear that the degree of radiation (measured in loudness) depends on the energy level of the vibrations. In the grand piano, this level is high for the bass strings and will produce, therefore, a quite homogeneous sound emission at all sides of the instrument (front, back, left, and right). For high notes the best radiation takes place at the back/right, especially in the concave part.

VI. Important Changes in or Additions to Construction for Reasons of Acoustical Improvement

As one might expect, the important acoustical improvements of the piano have all had to do with the heightening of the acoustical strength (sound intensity and radiation) and the changing of the quality of the sound. The number of such additions is legion. Important are **aliquot scaling**, alterations of the soundboard, and registration.

Aliquot scaling is the adding of extra strings attached to the bridge (sometimes an additional bridge is constructed for the aliquot strings) and tuned to the same pitch (or one octave higher) of the string they accompany. They are not struck but start to vibrate sympathetically. In some cases they are muted when the dampers are not lifted.

The changing of the form, dimensions, or construction of the soundboard were historically all intended to increase the degree of resonance. In some cases additional mechanisms were devised.

Early pianos sometimes had registers that obtained their specific sound character from a change in constituent partials. Nowadays **pedals** are the only **stops** that are left.

More recently, the use of electronics has allowed fundamental changes in the concept of acoustical sound production of the piano. A very fine example of these kinds of evolutions is the Neo-**Bechstein**.

VII. Conclusion

The present form and function of the piano is the result of a very long and complicated evolution. Taking into consideration the actual acoustical characteristics of the instrument, it seems that the greater number of the components that have to do with the generation, amplification, and radiation of the sound are seen in the light of dynamics and quality. This becomes even more apparent when we compare the piano to, for instance, the harpsichord. The general evolution is that of a change from instruments with small dynamic range and great number of overtones to instruments with great dynamics and a sound structure focused on the fundamental tone. The foregoing analysis of the acoustical functioning of the piano illustrates this.

See also Tuning.

Peter G.C. van Poucke

Bibliography

Askill, John. *Physics of Musical Sounds.* New York: D. Van Nostrand Company, 1979.

Backus, John. *The Acoustical Foundations of Music.* London: John Murray, 1970.

Campbell, Murray, and Clive Greated. *The Musician's Guide to Acoustics.* New York: Macmillan, 1987.

Helmholtz, Hermann von. *Die Lehre von den Tonempfindungen als physiologische Grundlage für die Theorie der Musik.* Braunschweig: R. Wachsmuth, 1913. (Eng. trans.: *On the Sensations of Tone,* 1954).

Palmieri, Robert. *Piano Information Guide. An Aid to Research.* New York: Garland Publishing, 1989 (Music Research and Information Guides, 10 = Garland Reference Library of the Humanities, 806), pp. 118–23 (Bibliography).

Rossing, Thomas D. *The Science of Sound.* Reading: Addison-Wesley, 1982.

White, Harvey E., and Donald H. White. *Physics and Music. The Science of Musical Sound.* Philadelphia: Saunders College, 1980.

ACTIONS

The action mechanism of a piano consists of a combination of levers that transmit the mechanical impulse, initiated by the performer's finger, to the **hammers**. It is composed of key levers, transmitters, and intermediate levers. On its construction and efficiency depends the accuracy of conversion of mechanical impulses into sound. In contemporary actions (see fig. 1) finger pressure on the **key** raises the back end of the key lever, through the **capstan** screw (pilot) to the intermediate lever (**wippen**). The **jack** (hopper) fastened to the wippen pushes the hammer knuckle and propels the hammer to strike the **string**. When in the upper position, the jack's arm is stopped by the **let-off** (regulating) button, the jack slips out from the hammer **knuckle**, allowing the hammer to fall back after hitting the string (an effect called single **escapement**). If the key is still depressed, the hammer falls back only part way, resting on its knuckle on the repetition lever. A **back check**, fastened to the posterior part of the key lever, serves to moderate the backfall in order to avoid hammer-rebound and noise. A light release of the key results in the return of the jack—thanks to the jack spring pressure—to a position under the hammer knuckle in readiness for the next hammer stroke, from a distance shorter by half compared to the initial position (an effect called double escapement). The end of the key lever also raises the damper lever, which in turn raises the **damper**, allowing the string to vibrate freely as long as the key is depressed.

If one compares a contemporary action with preserved **Bartolomeo Cristofori** actions of 1720 and 1726 (see fig. 3 under Cristofori) we can see many similar elements (moveable jack, single escapement, intermediate lever, back check, upper damper) after almost 300 years. This is visible proof of Cristofori's genius. In the process of piano development there have been instances of "re-inventing" some of its parts that were used earlier by Cristofori. This evolution is reflected by a variety of actions used in different periods and in different types of pianos before the contemporary action became universal.

Anglo-German Action (Old English action).

In the Anglo-German action, which is a form of *Stossmechanik,* the hammer was not connected to the key lever (as it was in the English action), but rather hinged to a rail behind the key (see fig. 2). The hammer head pointed towards the keyboard (as in the Viennese [*Prellmechanik*] action). The Anglo-German action was used in

Europe in the eighteenth and first half of the nineteenth centuries. One of the oldest preserved examples is a Johann Söcher (of Allgäu) square piano from 1742; the latest are pianos of Johann Baptist **Streicher** of Vienna from the 1840s, with an action patented by him in 1831.

Double Repetition Action

English double action with double escapement.

Down-Strike Action

The action of a horizontal piano in which the hammers strike the strings from above, downwards towards the **soundboard**. This action was devised to overcome the tendency, in the up-striking action pianos, for the strings to be unseated from the **bridge**, thus losing the pitch. Furthermore, in up-striking action the soundboard has to be cut through to allow hammers to reach the strings. First attempts at a downstrike action are known from the early eighteenth century, e.g., by **Jean Marius** of Paris in 1716 and by **Christoph Gottlieb Schröter** of Dresden in 1721. From the end of that century there were many practical examples using this action. The main technical problem of the down-striking action was the return of the hammer to the rest position after striking the string. Two devices were used: a balancing counterweight of action components or a special returning spring. Actions with the spring were built as normal or repetition actions. Down-striking actions were built in the first half of the nineteenth century in Vienna by Nannette and Johann Streicher and **Matthias Müller**, in London by **Robert Wornum**, in Paris by **Jean-Henri Pape** and Jean-Georges Kriegelstein, in North America by **Thomas Loud**, Charles Saltonstall Seabury, and others. The most advanced was an action patented by Pape in 1839 (see fig. 3). Similar action was used in mass-produced pianos by Theodor Stöcker of Berlin in the 1850s–1860s. In the following years this type of action was discontinued.

English Action
(Stossmechanik/Striking Action)

Piano action in which the hammer is not connected to the key lever (as it is in the Viennese action), but is held in a rail and jacked up to the string with a strike of a key-lever projection or jack (hence, striking action). Used since the first decades of piano history, the oldest source is the drawing of Cristofori's action, published in 1711

by **Scipione Maffei**, who saw it in 1709 (see fig. 1 under Cristofori). This type of action, with double action or without intermediate lever (single action), was adopted first in the German-speaking lands. After 1860, it was used in England and intensively improved, thus gaining the name of "English action" still in use today.

English Double Action

The English double action, in which the stroke of the key-lever end is transmitted to the hammer through an intermediate lever (wippen), has been known since the birth of the piano and was used in the oldest preserved pianos of Cristofori, from 1720 and 1726. In the nineteenth century in almost all types of piano action, the jack was moved from the key lever to the intermediate lever. English double action is still used today in all types of pianos.

English Single Action

English action in which the strike of the key lever end is transmitted to the hammer directly (without an intermediate lever). (see fig. 4.) Known since the beginning of the eighteenth century in horizontal and vertical pianos, it has a projection on the key-lever (until the middle of the eighteenth century), and later, a secondary jack attached to this lever. This type of action went out of use by the end of the nineteenth century.

Erard Repetition Action

See Escapement, Repetition Action.

Escapement

A combination of devices that allows the hammer to fall back after striking the string, while the key is still depressed. Without this "fall-back," the hammer would remain in contact with the string. Some scholars give this name to the moveable jack, which is not precise. Escapement is the result of the particular shape of the jack (hopper), the element pushed by the jack (hammer knuckle, hammer **butt**, projection or end of intermediate lever), as well as the process by which the jack slides off this element. This kind of escapement is called single escapement and is always connected with a moveable type of jack. It is used in the earliest preserved pianos of Cristofori from 1720 and 1726. The later, simplified versions of an English action had immobile jacks and no escapement. The more

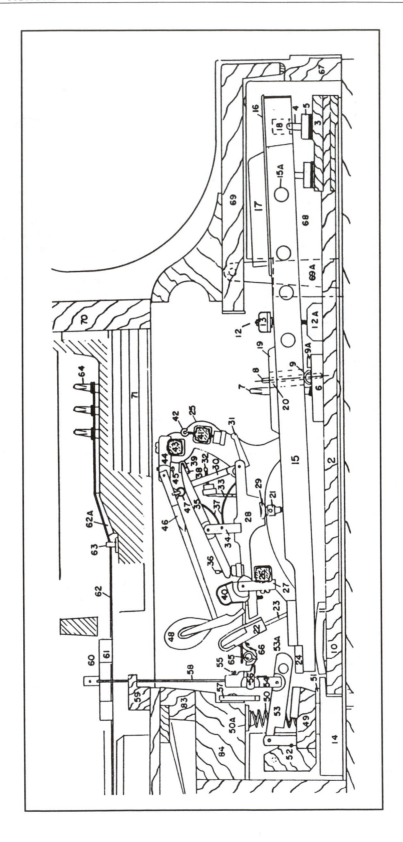

Fig. 1. *Grand Piano Action (contemporary) and surrounding parts by Steinway & Sons.*

2 - Keyframe
3 - Keyframe front rail
4 - Keyframe front rail pin
5 - Keyframe front rail punching
6 - Balance rail
7 - Balance rail stud
8 - Balance rail pin
9 - Balance rail bearing
9A - Balance rail bearing strip
10 - Back rail
11 - Back rail cloth
12 - Key stop rail prop
12A - Key stop rail prop block
13 - Key stop rail
14 - Dag (Keyframe stop)
15 - Key
15A - Key lead
16 - Key covering
17 - Sharp
18 - Front pin bushing
19 - Key button
20 - Balance pin bushing
21 - Capstan screw
22 - Back-check
23 - Back-check wire
24 - Underlever (damper lever) key cushion
25 - Action hanger
26 - Support (wippen) rail
27 - Support flange
28 - Support (wippen)
29 - Support cushion
30 - Fly (jack)
31 - Tender (jack toe)
32 - Fly (jack) regulating screw
33 - Spoon
34 - Support top flange
35 - Balancier
36 - Balancier regulating screw
37 - Repetition spring
38 - Repetition felt block
39 - Balancier covering
40 - Hammer rest
41 - Regulating rail
42 - Let-off screw
43 - Hammer rail
44 - Hammershank flange
45 - Drop screw
46 - Hammershank
47 - Knuckle
48 - Hammer
49 - Underlever frame
50 - Underlever frame spring
50A - Underlever frame spring punching
51 - Underlever frame cushion
52 - Underlever flange
53 - Underlever (damper lever)
53A - Underlever lead
54 - Underlever top flange
55 - Damper wire screw
56 - Tab (sostenuto tab)
57 - Damper stop rail
58 - Damper wire
59 - Damper guide rail
60 - Damper head
61 - Damper felts
62 - String
63 - Agraffe
64 - Tuning pins
65 - Sostenuto rod
66 - Sostenuto bracket
67 - Keyslip
68 - Keyblock
69 - Keylid (fallboard)
69A - Keylid pivot plate
70 - Case cornice
71 - Wrest plank (pinblock)

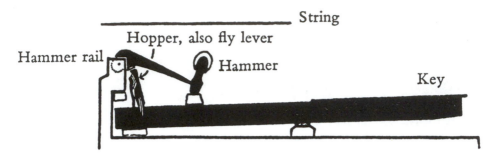

Fig. 2. *Anglo-German action (developed* Stossmechanik, *with escapement).*
(Courtesy of Da Capo Press [New York], agent for Franz Josef Hirt's Stringed Keyboard Instruments.)

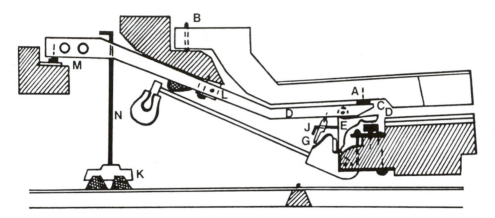

Fig. 3. *Down-strike action by Pape, 1839 (from the patent).*
A = Key; B = Lever; C = Hopper; D = Intermediate lever; E = Hammer spring; G = Moveable check; J = Hook; K,N = Dampers; M = Screw.
(Courtesy of Da Capo Press [New York], agent for Franz Josef Hirt's Stringed Keyboard Instruments.)

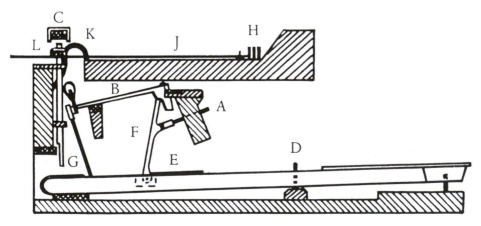

Fig. 4. *English Grand Action by John Broadwood & Sons, 1795.*
A = Screw to regulate escapement; B = Hammer shank attached to a screw for removal; C = Damper rail; D = Pivot; E = Spring; F = Escapement; G = Check; H = Tuning pins; J = String; K = Iron arc; L = Damper.
(Courtesy of Da Capo Press [New York], agent for Franz Josef Hirt's Stringed Keyboard Instruments.)

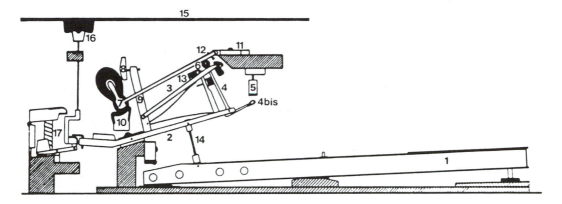

Fig. 5. Repetition Action with Double Escapement by Erard, 1822.
1 = Key; 2 = Intermediate lever; 3 = Escapement; 4 = Jack; 4bis = Projection on jack; 5 = Escapement pilot; 6 = Hammer shank head; 7 = Hammer head; 8 = Check; 9 = Check shank; 10 = Hammer rest; 11 = Hammer fork; 12 = Repetition screw; 13 = Regulating button (regulating the height of escapement); 14 = Hopper regulator (to guide the hammer); 15 = String; 16 = Damper; 17 = Pedal spring.
(Courtesy of Da Capo Press [New York], agent for Franz Josef Hirt's Stringed Keyboard Instruments.)

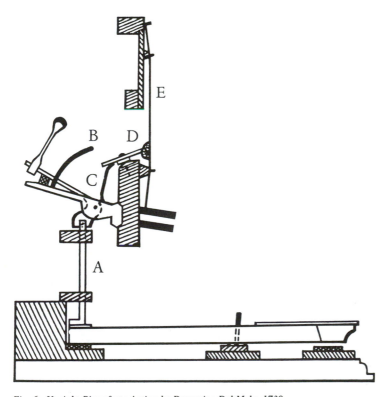

Fig. 6. Upright Pianoforte Action by Domenico Del Mela, 1739.
A = Sticker (jack); B = One of two guide wires; C = Damper spring; D = Damper; E = String.
(Courtesy of Da Capo Press [New York], agent for Franz Josef Hirt's Stringed Keyboard Instruments.)

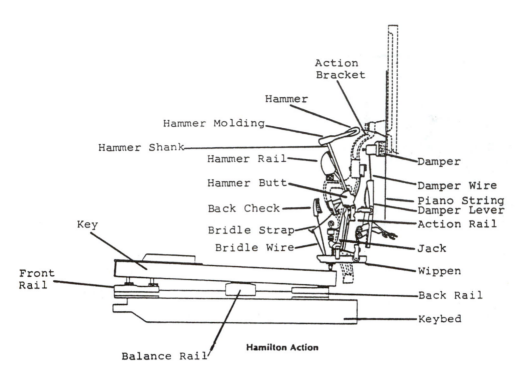

Fig. 7. Upright (Vertical) Piano Action (contemporary) by Baldwin.

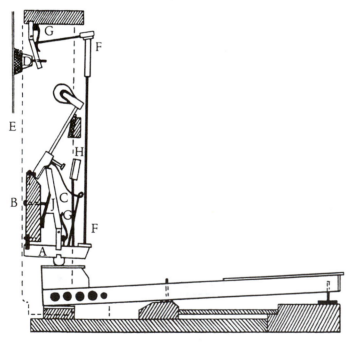

Fig. 8. Upright Tape-Check Action by Wornum, 1842–52.
A = Wippen; B = Escapement regulation screw; C = Leather tape connecting hammer butt with wire on wippen accelerating return of hammer; D = Damper; E = String; F = Damper lifter; G = Damper spring; H = Check; J = Escapement.
(Courtesy of Da Capo Press [New York], agent for Franz Josef Hirt's Stringed Keyboard Instruments.*)*

developed single and double actions with moveable jack and single escapement were made at the same time. Single English actions with single escapement were used until the end of the nineteenth century (although they were enhanced with a repetition device during that century). In the Viennese action, escapement is the result of a sliding moveable hook, which frees the hammer shank tail just before the string is struck by the hammer head. It was the only kind of escapement used in this type of action after it was first devised by **Johann Andreas Stein** around 1773. The growing dimensions of the piano and its strings, along with the size and weight of English action components, resulted in an action that was heavy and incapable of fast repetition. Construction of double escapement was the result of the search for a repetition device for English double action. It was an invention of **Sébastien Erard**, who patented the first version in 1808 and a second improved one in 1821 (patented by his nephew Pierre in England). This action (see fig. 5) became a prototype for the action used today with double escapement. It works by using the repetition lever (while the key remains depressed after the phase of single escapement), to stop the hammer after hitting the string, at less than half the distance from the starting point to the string. After lightly releasing the key, the jack, pushed by its spring, returns to its position under the hammer **knuckle**, ready for the next stroke, which can occur much more quickly, owing to the shorter distance. It offers the possibility of quick repetition. Since the 1920s and 1930s double escapement actions have been used in all grands.

German Action

See Viennese Action, below.

Hanging Viennese Action

A kind of Viennese action used mostly in the German-speaking world in upright pianos (**pyramid**, **giraffe**, **lyre**, and others) during the first half of the nineteenth century. The hammer shank is placed vertically, as in Standing Viennese Action, but beneath the level of the keyboard (as in the spinet), attached to the bent-down end of the key lever (see Harding, p. 233 for illustration).

Méchanique À double Échappement

See Double Repetition Action, above.

Old English Action

See Anglo-German Action, above.

Prellmechanik

See Viennese Action, below.

Repetition Action

An action that gives the possibility of quick repetition of hammer stroke.

Single Repetition Action

Single English grand action with added pushing and sliding units (besides the jack's spring) to accelerate the return of the jack under the hammer knuckle before the next strike to the string. Many types of this action were constructed in the 1840s as alternatives to the double repetition action. The most recent was an action patented in 1844 by Jean-Georges Kriegelstein of Paris, used in European pianos until World War I.

Standing English Action

An English action used in **uprights** since the beginning of the eighteenth century. The oldest preserved examples are: an anonymous piano from 1735, the piano of **Domenico del Mela** [di Gagliano] from 1739 (see fig. 6), and pianos of **Christian Ernst Friederici** of Gera from the 1740s. This type of action stems from the grand action invented by Cristofori around 1698–1700. The main development of Standing English Action took place in the first half of the nineteenth century. First, it was mainly a single action with jack attached to the key lever, similar to the action of **John Isaac Hawkins** of Philadelphia (1800), that of **Robert Wornum** of London (1811), and that of **Johann Christian Schleip** of Berlin (c. 1825). Next came double actions with the jack moved to an intermediate lever. Introduced simultaneously was a tape-check device (Hermann Lichtenthal of Brussels in 1832; Wornum, 1842). Together they provided the basis of today's upright piano action. However, today's upright action differs from the archetype, among other things by changing the jack feather spring to the spiral spring, used for the first time in the grand double escapement action patented by Antoine-Jean-Denis Bord of Paris in 1846. Until the last decades of the nineteenth century the Standing English Action was used with upper dampers; by the twentieth century with lower dampers only (see fig. 7).

Standing Viennese Action

A kind of Viennese action used mostly in the German-speaking world in upright pianos (pyramid, giraffe, lyre, and others) in the first half of the nineteenth century. The hammer shank is placed vertically, and the return of the hammer after striking the string is secured by a spring attached to the hammer shank's tail.

Sticker Action

A type of English action for the tall upright piano, with a **pinblock** in the upper part of the instrument. It was typical for **cabinet pianos**, made mostly in England from 1798, when it was patented by **William Southwell**, until the 1830s. Placed very high and far from the key levers, the hammers were jacked up by the stickers (rods), whose length reached up to 70 cm. In its primitive form, the 1798 action had no escapement (the sticker was used as a jack). In 1807 Southwell patented an improved action using a jack and an intermediate lever, which pushed the sticker, thus allowing escapement. In 1821, a hammer back check was added. A similar action was used by the French firm Pfeiffer et Cie in its upright called "Harmomelo." A type of sticker action has been used since the earliest preserved upright up to the high uprights of today, with stickers up to 20 cm. long.

Stossmechanik

See English Action, above.

Tangent Action

An action where the hammers are hung vertically in a kind of harpsichord box that allows them to slide and be jacked up by the back ends of the key levers (usually with intermediate levers), like harpsichord jacks (see illustration under Tangent Piano). The name is derived from the clavichord action, but the harpsichord affiliation is very clear and the sound of tangent pianos is similar to that of the harpsichord. Tangent action is associated with the oldest prototypes of piano action, for example "dulce melos," described by Heinrich Arnold von Zwolle in c. 1440. Jean Marius presented to the Paris Royal Academy of Science in 1716 a design of a hammer harpsichord action whose construction was related directly to the clavichord (wooden hammers attached vertically to the ends of the key levers). Christoph Gottlieb Schröter of Dresden designed a tangent action in 1717, and one with intermediate levers in 1739. In 1759 Weltman of Paris invented a clavecin with jacks (*marteaux*) that struck the strings. There are some preserved Italian tangent pianos, one from c. 1767–1773 and a harpsichord converted into a tangent piano at the end of the eighteenth century. In 1774 **John Joseph Merlin** in London patented a harpsichord with a second set of tangent hammers. About the same time Franz Jacob **Späth** of Ratisbon (Regensburg) constructed a tangent action. However, the date remains imprecise because the only preserved tangent pianos made by the Späth and Schmahl firm were made after 1790 by Späth's son-in-law and former partner, Christoph Friedrich **Schmahl**. There is a **square piano** with tangent action made in 1774 by Jan Skórski of Sandomierz (Poland), and a similar piano made c. 1780–1790, which is probably by Skórski or his pupil. In 1787, Humphrey Walton in England patented a tangent action for a grand. In Madrid, a type of square tangent piano was noted at a sale the same year, and another tangent piano was up for sale in 1797. Tangent pianos were made in Germany, Poland, and Italy in the last three decades of the eighteenth century. Because of their weak sound this action was discontinued.

Tape-Check Action

An action with a tape connecting the hammer butt with the intermediate lever to counteract hammer bounce after the string is struck and before the hammer head is caught by a check. This device was first used by Matthias Müller of Vienna in 1800 in his upright called *"Ditanaklasis."* Herman Lichtenthal of Brussels patented an upright piano action using **leather** tape in 1832. Tape-check action became popular thanks to Robert Wornum of London, who used it in grands in 1838 and in uprights in 1842 (see fig. 8). He changed the leather tape to fabric. This type of action is used in all uprights today. *See also* Wornum, Robert.

Viennese Action (Prellmechanik/German)

An action in which the hammer is connected directly to the key lever with a parchment hinge, a common axle or Kapsel (a kind of fork with beds for the hammer's axle). When pressed, the key lever goes up and simultaneously the hammer's tail is stopped by a fixed rail, thus flipping the hammer head to the string. This kind of action was used in the German-speaking world from about the middle of the eighteenth century. (For a detailed description and illustration of the Viennese action see the separate topic of *Prellmechanik*.)

Benjamin Vogel

Bibliography

Harding, Rosamond E.M. *The Piano-Forte: Its History Traced to the Great Exhibition of 1851.* Cambridge: Cambridge University Press, 1933. Reprints. New York: Da Capo Press, 1973; Old Woking, Surrey: Gresham Books, 1978.

Kenyon de Pascual, Beryl. "The five-octave compass in eighteenth-century harpsichords." *Early Music* 15 (February 1987): 74–75.

van der Meer, John Henry. "A curious instrument with a five-octave compass." *Early Music* 14 (August 1986):397–400.

———. "Observations." *Early Music* 15 (February 1987): 75–76.

Vogel, Benjamin. "Fortepiany tangentowe w Polsce" [The Tangent Pianos in Poland]. *Muzyka Fortepianowa* 7 (1987): 291–302.

ADLUNG, JAKOB (1699–1762)

Jakob Adlung was born in Bindersleben, Erfurt, on 14 January 1699 and died there 5 July 1762. He was an eclectic personality: theologian, scholar, musician, and musical instrument maker. In 1736 his house and all his belongings were destroyed by fire, including his workshop, the large storage of wood for musical instruments, and many of his books. In his autobiography he mentions, starting around 1728, having built sixteen instruments. After the big fire in Erfurt he gave up his former profession as an artisan because of the prejudices of scholars against musicians and artisans. He taught philosophy, mathematics, and philology. In 1755 he was awarded a degree as an ordinary member of the Erfurt Academy of Sciences. After that he contributed scientific, musical, and mathematical articles to the local periodicals.

His three surviving works in musical literature are:

Anleitung zur musikalischen Gelahrtheit. Erfurt, 1758, with a preface by Johann Ernst Bach; 2nd ed., after his death in 1777, by Johann Adam Hiller. This is a general encyclopedic treatise on musical knowledge, containing a large section about musical instruments, with didactic and informational purposes.

Musica Mechanica Organoedi, das ist: Gründlicher Unterricht von der Struktur, Gebrauch und Erhaltung der Orgeln, Clavicymbel, Clavichordien, und andere Instrumente, in zwey Theilen. Berlin, 1768, posthumous; two volumes on the structure, history, and **acoustics** of musical instruments, with the addition of a translation of the organ treatise by Bedos de Celles, and the autobiography of Adlung; additions by Johann Lorenz Albrecht and Johann Friedrich Agricola.

Musikalisches Siebengestirn, das ist: Sieben zur edlen Tonkunst gehörige Fragen. Berlin, 1768. The first two treatises reflect the intense contemporary research on keyboard instruments to conceive new models with the purpose of enriching the timbral effect. The author emphasizes the structural shape of the "instromento" (square instrument) and its vertical variant (clavicytherium); he describes the available mechanics of that time—plucked, with tangents, pipes, hammers, and pantaléon—and also examines the different registers.

In his *Musica Mechanica Organoedi*, chapter 529, Adlung describes the early piano invented in Florence by **Bartolomeo Cristofori**, using the article and drawing by **Scipione Maffei** (*Giornale de' Letterati d'Italia*, 1711) and the German version by Johann Ulrich König quoted in Johann Mattheson's *Critica Musica*. Adlung's concern is to focus on the structural features of the inverted wrestplank type of instrument. He writes that the sound is more agreeable at a certain distance from the instrument. The sound is stronger or weaker depending on the strength of the musician's touch. He points out the correct use of the instrument for *camera* music and not for *musica forte*, and that all the friction points of the instrument are damped by **leather** or fabric. Adlung also mentions the sympathetic effect of the string vibration.

Donatella Degiampietro and
Giuliana Montanari

Bibliography

Adlung, Jakob. *Anleitung zur musikalischen Gelahrtheit.* Erfurt: J.D. Jungnicol, 1758. Facs. Kassel und Basel: Bärenreiter, 1953.

———. *Musica Mechanica Organoedi, das ist: Gründlicher Unterricht von der Struktur, Gebrauch und Erhaltung der Orgeln, Clavicymbel, Clavichordien, und andere Instrumente, in zwey Theilen.* Berlin: Friedrich Wilhelm Birnstiel, 1768. Facs. Kassel und Basel: Bärenreiter, 1961.

Hiller, Johann Adam. *Lebensbeschreibungen berümter Musikgelehrten und Tonkünstler neuerer Zeit.* Leipzig: Verlage der Dytischen Buchhandlung, 1784. Reprint. Leipzig: Edition Peters, 1975.

Musik in Geschichte und Gegenwart. Kassel und Basel: Bärenreiter, 1949–79.

The New Grove Dictionary of Musical Instruments. Edited by Stanley Sadie. London: Macmillan ; Washington D.C.: Grove's Dictionaries, 1984.

AEOLIAN COMPANY

The Aeolian Company, an American manufacturer of organettes, reed organs, pianos, and **player pianos**, was created by William Burton Tremaine (1840–1907). He had entered the family piano business, Billings & Tremaine (later Tremaine Brothers), of New York in 1868 but left around 1876 when Mason J. Mathews, an inventor of small hand-cranked automatic reed organs, created a saleable product. Tremaine set up The Mechanical Orguinette Company to manufacture the small instrument, and in 1883 a small automatic reed organ was produced under the name Aeolian Organ. All these instruments played music from perforated paper rolls made by the Automatic Music Paper Company of Boston. Tremaine bought AMPC and its patents in 1888 and, four years later, acquired the Munroe Organ Reed Company of Worcester, a large manufacturer of not just organettes but the vibrating free reeds themselves.

In 1895 he introduced the Aeriol self-playing piano, but it was not until Edwin Scott Votey, inventor of the practical piano-player, joined the business in 1897 that serious work on piano players was begun, and later this was expanded to include player pianos, **reproducing pianos**, and reproducing pipe organs.

By 1903, a new company had been floated called the Aeolian, Weber Piano & Pianola Co., which was capitalized at $10,000,000. It comprised the amalgamation of a number of firms besides those already mentioned and included The Aeolian Co., New York; the Orchestrelle Co., London; the Choralion Co., Berlin; the Aeolian Co., Paris; the Pianola Company Pty. Ltd., Melbourne and Sydney; **Weber Piano Co.**; George Steck & Co.; Wheelock Piano Co.; Stuyvesant Piano Co.; Chilton Piano Co.; Technola Piano Co.; Votey Organ Co.; Vocalion Organ Co.; and the Universal Music Co., this last being a maker of perforated paper music rolls for pneumatically played pianos. These companies employed among them 5,000 people worldwide and, besides extensive piano factories in America, included the Steck factory at Gotha, Germany, and Weber at Hayes in Middlesex, England. This latter became the Aeolian Company's main British factory. The total capital under Tremaine's control was $15.5 million—more than the capital invested in the entire piano and organ industry in the United States in 1890.

William Tremaine was succeeded as president of the business by his son Henry Barnes Tremaine (born Brooklyn, 1866; died Washington, 1932). Henry was general manager until 1898 when he became president. It was he who perfected the AudioGraphic music roll, which provided the player with extensive written historical notes on the music, actually printed on the paper roll.

Aeolian was famed for its player piano, the **Pianola**, a name which to this day is the lay generic term for any make of player piano. From the Pianola it developed the **Duo-Art** reproducing piano. Aeolian's early prowess in reed organs was sustained in the self-playing Orchestrelle, developed using the technology of the Vocalion Organ Company (originally set up by Scotsman James Baillie-Hamilton), while the Duo-Art capability spawned the Aeolian Duo-Art Reproducing Pipe Organ.

After the Depression of the late 1920s, the fortunes of Aeolian deteriorated and the British company was forced to liquidate—a process that took almost twenty years to complete, due to the intervention of World War II. In 1932, Aeolian merged with its rival, the **American Piano Corporation**.

Arthur W.J.G. Ord-Hume

Bibliography

Bowers, Q. David. *Encyclopedia of Automatic Musical Instruments.* Vestal, N.Y.: Vestal Press, 1972.

Dolge, Alfred. *Pianos & Their Makers.* Covina, Cal.: Covina Publishing Co., 1911.

———. *Men Who Made Piano History.* [original title, *Pianos and Their Makers* Vol. 2, *Development of the Piano Industry in America Since the Centennial Exhibition at Philadelphia, 1876*] Covina, Cal.: Covina Publishing Co., 1913. Reprint. Vestal, N.Y.: Vestal Press, 1980.

Ord-Hume, Arthur W.J.G. *Pianola—History & Development.* . . . London: Allen & Unwin, 1984.

———. *Player Piano — History of the Mechanical Piano.* London: Allen & Unwin, 1970.

Roehl, Harvey. *Player Piano Treasury.* Vestal, N.Y.: Vestal Press, 1961 and 1973.

Spillane, Daniel. *History of the American Piano-forte: Its Technical Development and the Trade.* New York: D. Spillane, 1890. Reprint. New York: Da Capo Press, 1969.

AFTERTOUCH

Aftertouch is the term to describe the amount of keydip beyond the point of **let-off**. It is usually specified to be from .015" to .060". The absence of aftertouch in a piano **action** results in a **touch** that feels weak and sloppy.

See also Regulation; Touchweight.

Kent Webb

AGRAFFE

The agraffe is a brass guide that spaces and levels the **strings**. Agraffes are equipped with one, two, or three holes, corresponding to the number of strings in the unison. They are screwed into the metal plate at the tuning pin end of the stringing scale in most **grand pianos**. Invented by **Sébastien Erard** in 1808, the agraffe holds the strings in a fixed position, assuring counterpressure against the blow of the **hammer**, while permitting the strings to be moved laterally during **tuning**. The agraffe also provides **downbearing** and marks off the speaking length of the strings.

Edward E. Swenson

Agraffes.

Bibliography

Good, Edwin M. *Giraffes, Black Dragons, and Other Pianos.* Stanford Cal.: Stanford, University Press, 1982.

Harding, Rosamond E.M. *The Piano-Forte: Its History Traced to the Great Exhibition of 1851.* Cambridge: Cambridge University Press, 1933. Reprints. New York: Da Capo Press, 1973; Old Woking, Surrey: Gresham Books, 1978.

ALBRECHT, CHARLES (1759/1760–1848)

Charles Albrecht was the first important piano builder in the United States. He was a German immigrant who settled in Philadelphia in the 1780s. Albrecht worked as a joiner at first but by 1789 he began to build pianos. His shop was at 95 Vine Street until 1825 when he moved to 3 South Third Street. During the same year (1825) Christian L. Albrecht (1788–1843), whose relationship is uncertain, started his own piano business at 98 Sassafras (later renamed Race Street).

Charles Albrecht built **square pianos** with a five-octave to five-and-one-half-octave range. The younger Albrecht also built square pianos and **upright pianos**, each with a six-octave compass. Both men built high-quality instruments, excellent in **action** and **casework**. At least seven or eight pianos that Charles Albrecht built before 1800 are still in existence. One of these, built about 1785 with serial number 24, is in the Metropolitan Museum of Art collection. The Smithsonian collection contains Albrecht pianos built around 1790 and 1798.

The surviving Albrecht pianos show a surprising diversity in design. The most important difference is in the type of action they contain. Charles Albrecht built pianos with the English double action, the **Zumpe** second action, one with an intermediate lever, and the Viennese *Prellmechanik*. Other differences, in the damper mechanism, use of knee levers, foot **pedals** or hand stops, and alignment of **strings**, are copies of details that appeared in earlier pianos by other makers. Albrecht's main contribution to American piano making was his elevation of the standards of craftsmanship.

Jack Greenfield

Bibliography

Libin, Laurence. *American Musical Instruments in The Metropolitan Museum of Art.* New York: The Metropolitan Museum of Art and W.W. Norton and Company, 1985.

———. *Keynotes: Two Centuries of Piano Design.* New York: Metropolitan Museum of Art, 1985.

Spillane, Daniel. *History of the American Piano-forte: Its Technical Development and the Trade.* New York: D. Spillane, 1890. Reprint. New York: Da Capo Press, 1969.

Duplex Scale by Steinway & Sons.
a. Shows sectional view of capo d'astro bar and bearing of chilled Steinway steel, which forms the dividing point between the main scale and the added duplex scale.
b. Shows the added duplex scale.
c. Shows the fundamental vibrations (pulses) of the main scale in combination with its harmonic subdivisions, caused by the impulse of the added duplex scale.
d. Shows sectional view of the soundboard bridge, which transmits the transverse vibrations (pulses) of the strings to the soundboard, which vibrates (pulses) molecularly.
(*Steinway & Sons duplex scale from the 1888 Steinway Catalogue*)

ALIQUOT SCALING

Aliquot Scaling is a stringing arrangement for the piano whereby the power and beauty of the treble register is supposedly enhanced by adding overtone luster from the sympathetic vibrations of additional **strings** or by allowing the waste lengths of the strings, which are normally muted with cloth, to vibrate in sympathy with the speaking length. When a piano string vibrates it produces both a fundamental tone and overtones. The aliquot scale and the **duplex scale** seek to reinforce certain **partials** in the overtone series, particularly in the treble register where the strings are short and stiff. In 1873 the **Blüthner** Company invented a **grand piano** stringing **scale** with a separate, sympathetic aliquot string for each unison in the treble. In 1872 **Steinway** invented the duplex scale (U.S. Patent No. 126,848), in which "the front duplex scale assists mechanically in a more rapid subdivision of the usual speaking length into its segmental vibrations, strengthening the harmonic partials. In addition, the rear duplex scale vibrates in sympathy with its corresponding partial tones (in the main portion of the string), thus producing overtones that lend brightness and color to the fundamental tone." In the 1880s the short-lived Ithaca Piano Co. produced a few full duplex pianos with two metal **plates** and two complete sets of strings; one set sounded normally with the **hammer** action while the other strings, controlled by a long, continuous damper, were free to vibrate and reinforce the sound sympathetically.

Edward E. Swenson

Bibliography

Good, Edwin M. *Giraffes, Black Dragons, and Other Pianos*. Stanford, Cal.: Stanford University Press, 1982.

Steinway & Sons. *Pianoforte Catalogue*. New York: Steinway, 1888.

ALLEN, WILLIAM (FL. 1800–1840)

William Allen was a Scotsman who came to London and worked as a tuner for the Stodart firm of piano makers early in the nineteenth century. His importance in the history of piano making lies in his role in the introduction of metal to strengthen the **frame** of the wooden piano. With James Thom, the foreman at Stodart's, he devised a system of metal tubes running parallel to the **strings** with wooden bars at right angles, using brass above the bass brass strings and iron above the iron strings

(English Patent No. 4,431 of 15 January 1820). The aim, which succeeded, was to compensate for atmospheric changes affecting the **tuning**, because the tubes expanded or contracted at the same rate as the strings. **William Stodart**, who bought the **patent**, could have used it to block all the development of resistance bars by other manufacturers, but he let it be known that he did not intend to do so. Stodart's built many **grand pianos** with this frame and underdampers; the volume of these pianos was greater because the frame made thicker strings possible.

Allen patented a cast-iron frame (somewhat similar to **Alpheus Babcock's** 1825 design) on 20 July 1831 (Eng. Patent no. 6,140). It had dovetailed grooves that were intended to make the **tuning pins** less liable to slip so that the instrument would stay better in tune. Unfortunately this idea was not adopted.

See also Thom, James and William Allen.

Margaret Cranmer

AMERICAN PIANO COMPANY

The American Piano Company was formed in June 1908, an amalgamation of **Chickering & Sons** of Boston; **Wm. Knabe & Company** of Baltimore; the Haines Brothers; Marshall & Wendell; Foster & Company; Armstrong; Brewster; and J. B. Cook companies. The Foster-Armstrong Company had been formed in 1894 by George C. Foster and W. B. Armstrong; in 1899 it acquired the Marshall & Wendell Piano Company of Albany, and in 1906 built a new plant at East Rochester, New York. With the acquisition of the other firms noted above, it was incorporated with a capital of $12 million. With such a diverse array of piano names, the American Piano Company was able to offer a wide spectrum of instruments, from pianos of concert quality to those of a strictly commercial grade. Responding to the burgeoning interest in the **player piano**, the company established a special player-piano department in 1909, and a sophisticated reproducing mechanism with the name **Ampico** was later developed to meet competition from **Aeolian's Duo-Art**, and to a lesser extent, the **Welte** Mignon. In 1924 the company absorbed the **Mason & Hamlin Piano Company**, which was in turn sold to the Aeolian Company in 1930. In the same year the American Piano Company became the American Piano Corporation, and in 1932, after divesting itself of many of its holdings in the interests of economy, merged with its arch-rival, the Aeolian Company. In this much-reduced form, the Aeolian-American Company survived the depression of the 1930s, taking part in the resurgence of interest in the piano by producing the newly introduced **spinet** and **console** pianos. In 1959 the company was acquired by Winter and Company, and in 1961 the name "American" was dropped from the company's title. In 1985 the remanent Aeolian Corporation went out of business, and the American Piano Company's three leading piano names, Chickering, Knabe, and Mason & Hamlin, passed to other hands.

James Howard Richards

Bibliography

"Aeolian Corp. Shortens Name." *The Piano Trade Magazine* (July 1961): 71.

Dolge, Alfred. *Pianos and Their Makers*. Covina, Cal.: Covina Publishing Company, 1911. Reprint, New York: Dover, 1972.

The New Grove Dictionary of Musical Instruments. Edited by Stanley Sadie. S. v. "American Piano Co.," by Cynthia Adams Hoover. London: Macmillan; Washington D.C.: Grove's Dictionaries, 1984.

Roell, Craig H. *The Piano in America, 1890–1940*. Chapel Hill: The University of North Carolina Press, 1989.

AMPICO CORPORATION

The Ampico Corporation was established in New York by the **American Piano Corporation**, from whose name Ampico was derived. Ampico was created to develop and market a **reproducing piano** using a system first invented in 1913 by Charles Fuller Stoddard (born c.1879) and later improved upon by Dr. Clarence N. Hickman and John Anderson from Chickering (see **Jonas Chickering**). During 1925, Hickman developed a machine for recording the dynamics of the piano using a spark chronograph technique.

The first Stoddard-Ampico was introduced in 1916 and was also known at one time as the Ampico-Artigraphic. Although at first there was a foot-pedalled **upright** (called the Marque-Ampico), all subsequent Ampico reproducing pianos were electrically operated. The popular Model A, which exists in by far the greatest numbers, was introduced in 1920–21, and the Model B, whose production was virtually halted by the depression, came along in 1929.

The Ampico action was available for being fitted to a wide variety of **grand pianos**, including those made by companies within the American Piano Corporation's portfolio (such as **Knabe & Co.**, Haines Brothers, Franklin, **Mason & Hamlin**, Marshall & Wendell, Chickering, and J & C Fischer). It was also fitted in a variety of English makes, including **John Broadwood & Sons, Chappell & Co., Collard & Collard,** Marshall & Rose, and Rogers, while in Canada it was also installed in Willis instruments.

In 1932, the company merged with Aeolian.

Arthur W.J.G. Ord-Hume

Bibliography

Bowers, Q. David. *Encyclopedia of Automatic Musical Instruments*. Vestal, N.Y.: Vestal Press, 1972.

Ord-Hume, Arthur W.J.G. *Pianola—History & Development.* . . . London: Allen & Unwin, 1984.

ANCESTORS OF THE PIANO

The ancestors of the piano may be classified into two types: those played by plucking and those played by striking the strings. The development of both of these types of instruments can be traced through two distinct stages: those that do not have a **keyboard** and those that do.

The earliest ancestors of the piano were the harp and the lyre, found in various sizes and shapes in most early civilizations. The psaltery, a modification of these instruments, employs the same plucking method of activating the **strings**, but its invention introduced a different string-to-**soundboard** relationship. Instead of the strings being connected directly into the soundboard, the psaltery's strings are parallel to the soundboard, and the two are connected by a fixed **bridge** that transmits the vibrations of the string.

The dulcimer, similar in most ways to the psaltery, has an innovation that influenced the design of the piano centuries later. Rather than being activated by plucking, the strings are struck with small, hand-held mallets.

The development of the monochord during the sixth century B.C. had a direct effect on the design of the psaltery and the dulcimer. The monochord's construction is similar except that it has only one string, and the bridge is moveable rather than being in a fixed position. It was used by Greek philosophers, notably Pythagoras (c. 550 B.C.), for experiments regarding the math-

ematical relations of musical sounds, for the tuning of other instruments, and centuries later in churches as an instrument to give **pitches** for choral singing. The idea of the moveable bridge used in conjunction with a keyboard influenced the invention of the clavichord several centuries later.

The keyboard was first used on a stringed instrument, the organistrum, in the twelfth century A.D. Known today as the hurdy-gurdy, this ingenious instrument has several strings resting against a resined wheel, which is turned by a crank, setting the strings in motion. Some of the strings are open, providing a drone accompaniment to a melody played on a small keyboard that presses tangents against the other strings.

During the fourteenth century a keyboard was combined with a psaltery-like instrument, producing the clavicytherium. Its strings are stretched over a boxlike structure and are sounded by plectra fastened to the ends of the **keys.** Efforts to improve this instrument, along with the influence of the moveable bridge of the monochord, resulted in the invention of the clavichord during the fifteenth century.

The clavichord has strings that are made to vibrate not by plucking or by striking with mallets, but by being struck with a tangent that remains in contact with the string during the vibration. The tangent is a small metal blade fastened in the back of the key. Toward the end of the sixteenth century the clavichord was so much improved that it became the favorite keyed instrument of the period, and it maintained this popularity even during the eighteenth century. The damper principle of the clavichord, and its capability of being played expressively, were some of the improvements that were later incorporated into the piano.

The plucking method of the harp and psaltery, the plucking keyboard of the clavicytherium, and the rectangular design of the clavichord were combined during the sixteenth century to produce the spinet and the virginal, the first members of the harpsichord family. Although the shape and size of the spinet, virginal, and harpsichord are quite different, all three instruments function with the same principle of a plectrum mounted in a **jack** that rests on the rear end of each key. This unique feature of the harpsichord is also its disadvantage, because regardless of the manner in which a key is played, the timbre or the loudness of the sound cannot be affected.

Despite the continued popularity of the clavichord, dissatisfaction with its tiny sound and with the harpsichord's incapability of being played with full dynamic expression led to experiments in the modification of the harpsichord by harpsichord builders near the end of the sixteenth century. While the size, shape, and design of the harpsichord were virtually unchanged, the plucking action was replaced with a **hammer** action, making it possible to produce gradations of loudness ranging from *piano* to *forte*, and thus bringing into existence the first *gravecembalo col piano e forte*, or "harpsichord with soft and loud."

Danny L. Boone

Bibliography

Dobronic-Mazzoni, Rajka. *The Harp*. Zagreb, Yugoslavia: Grafici zavod Hrvatske, 1989.

Dolge, Alfred. *Pianos and Their Makers*. Covina, California: Covina Publishing Company, 1911. Reprint. New York: Dover, 1972.

Ehrlich, Cyril. "Introduction." In *The Piano: A History*. London: J.M. Dent & Sons, Ltd., 1976.

Good, Edwin M. "The Classic Piano." In *Giraffes, Black Dragons, and Other Pianos*. Stanford, Cal.: Stanford University Press, 1982.

Harding, Rosamond E.M. *The Piano-Forte. Its History Traced to the Great Exhibition of 1851*. Cambridge: Cambridge University Press, 1933. Reprints. New York: Da Capo Press, 1973; Old Woking, Surrey: Gresham Books, 1978.

Hollis, Helen Rice. *The Piano*. New York: Hippocrene Books, 1975.

Rimbault, Edward F. *The Pianoforte, Its Origin, Progress, and Construction*. London: Robert Cocks & Co., 1860.

Sumner, W.L. "Early Keyboard Instruments." In *The Pianoforte*. New York: St. Martin's Press, 1966.

Wainwright, David. "The First Experiments." In *The Piano Makers*. London: Hutchinson & Co. Ltd., 1975.

ANGLO-GERMAN ACTION

See Actions.

APYTHMOLAMPROTÉRIQUE

The *apythmolamprotérique* was an **upright piano** presented in 1834 at the Paris Exhibition. Its inventor remains unknown. A special feature of the *apythmolamprotérique* was its lack of a back; thus it was said that a much clearer sonority was obtained.

F.J. de Hen

Bibliography

Pontécoulant, L. de *Organographie*. Reprint. Amsterdam: Frits Knuf, 1972.

ASTOR & COMPANY

George Peter Astor (1752–1813) operated a shop in London that sold various musical merchandise and musical instruments, including pianos. Born in Germany, he emigrated to London about 1778 and was followed a year later by his brother, John Jacob Astor (1763–1848). The firm operated under the name "George & John Astor" and was located at 26 Wych Street until 1797. In 1783, early in the development of the firm, John Jacob Astor began travelling to the newly formed United States of America to sell pianos and flutes. He established a shop at 81 Queen Street (now Pearl Street) in New York City, which at the time was the heart of the music and furniture business, with many craftsmen residing in the area.

Having met a furrier on board ship on one of his journeys to the United States, John Jacob Astor subsequently became involved in the highly profitable fur trade, launching his business in 1784. In the late 1790s he phased out of the piano business and, aside from importing pianos occasionally to pay his bills, the fur trade became his main enterprise. He established fur trading stations in the north and northwestern parts of the United States and thereby amassed an immense fortune.

After his brother's departure, George Astor continued to develop his own dealership in London. In 1797 operations were moved from the Wych Street address to 79 Cornhill, after which time the company's instruments are marked either "George Astor "or "George Astor and Co." (occasionally "Astor & Co."). A second shop was opened at 27 Tottenham Street and the business expanded into publishing sheet music and instruction manuals for the flute. In 1815, still at the same locations, the name "Astor & Horwood" was adopted, and in 1822 "Astor & Co." In 1824 the name was changed again to "Gerock, Astor & Co.," continuing under that name until 1831.

It has been suggested that during his early years in London, Astor trained with the woodwind maker George Miller. Indeed, a large number of the surviving instruments bearing Astor's name are woodwinds. As business grew, it is likely that Astor became less involved with the production of individual instruments, employing other craftsmen to accomplish their manufacture. At the time it was not uncommon for a dealer to contract others to build the instruments that were sold at his shop. It is not known to what degree Astor himself was involved with the construction of his pianos. In his book, *Broadwood by Appointment*, David Wainwright recounts a transaction with the **Broadwood** firm, when on 16 July 1796 John Jacob Astor made a "purchase in bulk" of six Broadwood **square pianos** for which he paid 20 guineas each—a total of 129 pounds, 4 shillings. Before shipping the lot to the United States, Astor put his own name on the instruments.

Typical of the period's English piano trade, most of the surviving Astor pianos are of the square type. An advertisement does, however, mention Astor as a maker of **grand pianos**. Astor pianos after the late 1790s carry the words "New Patent" on the **nameboard**, although he is not known to have produced any particular innovations in piano design, patented or otherwise. The "patent" probably refers either to the employment of the piano **action** patented by **John Geib** in 1786 or the **damper** system patented by **William Southwell** in 1794.

Astor pianos usually possess a four-digit stamped **serial number**, the series apparently continuing with pianos produced under the "Astor and Horwood" name. The series of numbers and related dates cited in the *Pierce Piano Atlas* are not to be believed. The lowest known number from an extant Astor piano with the Cornhill address is 1314, while the lowest on an instrument with the "Astor and Horwood" name is 5134.

Thomas Jefferson, president of the United States and patron of the arts, owned an Astor square piano dated 1795. Another fine example of an early pianoforte inscribed with the nameplate "Astor & Co. 79 Cornhill (1795)" is in the Boehm-Kooper collection in New York City. Besides the unusual sustaining **pedal** found on the early square pianos of this type, the piano has a swell box manipulated by a foot lever.

Mary Louise Boehm and
Darcy Kuronen

Bibliography

Astor Foundation Archives–New York City.

Good, Edwin M. *Giraffes, Black Dragons, and Other Pianos*. Stanford, Cal.: Stanford University Press, 1982.

Kidson, Frank. *British Music Publishers, Printers and Engravers*. London, 1900.

Koster, John. *Catalogue of Keyboard Instruments*. Boston: Museum of Fine Arts, forthcoming.

Libin, Laurence. *American Musical Instruments in the Metropolitan Museum of Art*. New York-London: Norton, 1985.

The New Grove Dictionary of Musical Instruments. Edited by Stanley Sadie. London: Macmillan; Washington, D.C.: Grove's Dictionaries, 1984.

Spillane, Daniel. *History of the American Pianoforte*. New York: D. Spillane, 1890. Reprint. New York: Da Capo Press, 1969.

Wainwright, David. *Broadwood by Appointment, a History*. London: Quiller, 1982; New York: Universe Books, 1983.

AUSTRALIA, PIANO INDUSTRY IN

The first piano to arrive in Australia belonged to surgeon George Worgan, who arrived on the *Sirius* with the First Fleet in 1788. Pianos were valued possessions in the Colony and were serviced in the first half of the nineteenth century by a steadily increasing number of independent piano tuners and technicians. Major interference with the healthy growth of the piano industry in Australia had several causes: the first and second World Wars with their periods of boom and bust; the Great Depression of the 1930s; the commencement of radio and television transmission; and the high cost of a labor-intensive industry, which has not been able to successfully compete with imports since the mid-1970s. In 1926–1927, 24,000 pianos were sold. With the depression in 1931–1932 only 170 pianos were sold and 26 of these were imported.

Probably the first piano built in Australia was the product of John Benham (arrived in Australia 1831, died 1845). This instrument (preserved in the Old Mint Building, Sydney) has a wooden **frame** with overdamper **action** in an Australian red-cedar **case**.

Already around 1850, pianos were being made by John Williams of Hobart in Tasmania, and the brothers James and Jabez Carnegie of Melbourne in Victoria. *Sand's Sydney and N.S.W. Directory* lists piano makers in Sydney in 1858 and 1861: David Buirst and Son; Robert T. Buirst; Henry R. Hurford and Co.; George E. Young; and Charles James Jackson. It is difficult to ascertain whether these concerns involved the actual building of pianos or rather the repair and renovation of instruments. A government study lists only one piano manufacturer in N.S.W. in 1880 (T. Richards: *N.S.W. in 1881, 1882*. Sydney: Government Printer, 1882). A piano built by William Ezold received a First Degree of Merit at the 1879 Exhibition in Sydney, where judges recorded: "Well made, good workmanship and material, good tone and touch."

Joseph Kilner first arrived in Australia in 1850 and, after making his fortune in gold and returning to England to collect his family, he returned to Victoria. In 1854 he began making pianos from parts imported from **Broadwood's** in London, where he had served his apprenticeship. In 1862 Joseph Wilkie, also from Broadwood's, joined him, the firm becoming Wilkie, Kilner and Co. Between 1863 and 1866 they sold 305 pianos. Around 1870 this factory reverted to a family business and made wooden-frame pianos under the name of Joseph Kilner. The artisans used Australian timber such as blackwood and red gum for the construction of the tuning-plank (**pinblock**), but when these proved unsuitable they went back to beech. Under the new name of Frederick Kilner and Sons Pty. Ltd., a large factory was built at Auburn in 1915, where iron-frame pianos were made using the latest German techniques. All parts were made in Australia until it proved cheaper to import the actions. The firm continued business until 1969 when it was taken over by Brash's music business. The pianos were of good quality and they won several prizes: 1866–1867, Melbourne Intercolonial Exhibition; 1872, Intercolonial Exhibition of Victoria; 1876, Great Philadelphia Centennial Exhibition.

During the 1890s many piano manufacturers began business in Sydney and Melbourne, although some workshops only assembled imported parts. About 700,000 pianos were imported into Australia during the nineteenth century. The turn of the century saw the Australian piano market dominated by German instruments, which were thought to have a superior tone, stronger construction, and more attractive case work. German pianos could also be supplied more cheaply than the instruments of English manufacturers, who failed to meet delivery dates and gave poor service.

Octavius Charles Beale (born 1850, Ireland; died 1930, Australia) began importing pianos into Australia in 1893, the same year that he produced his first saleable Australian model. He founded the Beale Piano Factory in 1895 and

production proper commenced in 1900. On 9 November 1901 Octavius Beale took out a **patent** in Germany for his piano's most distinguishing feature: the use of a nut behind the wrest block to fasten the shaft of the **tuning pin**. This was supposed to ensure the stability of the tuning under the tremendous demands made by climactic extremes in Australia. In 1908 Beale tried to sell this idea to the following disinterested German makers: **Ibach**, **Blüthner**, Schwechten, **Bechstein**, and Duysen. After World War I, German imports were restricted and Fred Allan, member of the famous family music business in Melbourne, gained permission from the Thürmer factory in Germany to make pianos under license in Australia. The Beale piano factory in Sydney made about twenty- four Thürmer pianos, but as they were more expensive than the imported Thürmers, they were hard to sell. As part of their silver jubilee celebrations in 1925, Beale's, having produced some 52,000 **uprights** and **grands** to concert size, claimed to be the largest piano manufacturer in the British Empire. A 1927 publicity sheet claims that their factory showed "the largest proportional production of players of any factory in the world" and it built "more **Player-Pianos** each week than any three European factories combined." Beale continued to make player pianos until the 1950s. In 1927, after 30 years of production, some 60,000 Beale instruments had been sold. Their factory, the largest in the British Empire, covered 10 acres, with 43,000 square feet of floor space. Only three full-size **concert grands** were produced and one of them is in Government House in Sydney. Like most concerns, Beale's went through a troubled period in the depression of the 1930s and recovered around 1948 only to be severely hit by the transmission and sale of television in 1957. By 1951 the Beale factory had produced some 75,000 pianos. Its operations were reduced to four-and-a-half acres at Annandale, employing 250 workers, but it still claimed to be the largest self-contained piano factory in the British Commonwealth (*Melbourne Herald*, 3 February 1951). In 1960 the company traded under a new name: Beale Pianos Ltd. The only imported part was the action. Having produced around 95,000 pianos, Beale's was forced to cease production in 1975 because it could not compete with the low cost of Japanese and Chinese imports. Beale pianos were awarded

Gold Medals at the Franco-British Exhibition of 1908 and the Royal Agricultural Society of N.S.W. Exhibition, 1897 and 1898.

The Wertheim family, headed by Hugo Wertheim, began importing pianos into Australia in the 1890s. Around 1905 three piano builders were invited from the Lipp factory in Germany to assist in the building of pianos for the Wertheim family business. In 1908 a large piano factory employing the latest technology was built on four acres at Richmond in Melbourne. The factory covered some 52,000 square feet, employing about 300 workers. This new venture was so important to the establishment of industry in Australia that the prime minister, Alfred Deakin, laid the foundation stone for the factory. Practically all of the parts were manufactured at the plant, which included iron and brass foundries; timber-seasoning racks; woodworking equipment; and cabinetmaking, French polishing, and **soundboard** departments. The actions were largely made in Canada. The engine plant was underground and belt-drive was used to ensure the best possible working conditions. Ducted heating, "lavatories, luncheon rooms, and smokers' pavillions fitted in the most up-to-date manner" were provided for employees (*Australian Musical News*, 1908). The head of the new factory was Herbert Wertheim, son of Hugo, who had studied at the Boston Technological Institution and had visited leading European makers. Wertheim's made uprights and grands, including twelve grands with wide **hammers** (12mm) to strike four **strings** in the treble. At the height of their production they were producing around 2,000 units per year, whereas the Ronisch factory in Germany was producing only 500. The effects of the depression in 1930 forced Wertheim's, Allan's (Melbourne-based music business), Sutton's (Melbourne-based music house), and Paling's (Sydney-based music house) to join forces and create the Australian Piano Factory, using the Wertheim plant at Richmond. About 1935 the business failed.

Shortly after World War I, Wertheim's invited Paul Zenker to come from Germany to Australia and work in the action fitting and tuning sections of their plant. About 1923 he joined with Carl Schultes and, with the financial backing of Allan's Music Company, they began building pianos at Camberwell. They employed a staff of about forty. Their player pianos were quite satisfactory but their pianos

had many design problems. Allan's pulled out of the business in 1929, Zenker and Schultes becoming another victim of the depression a few years later. A. Macrow and Sons built two models ("Spencer" and "Cranford") in Melbourne between 1924 and 1928. Their product was so inferior that it became difficult to sell.

Around 1920, J. Carnegie and Son began building pianos in Richmond, Victoria. They produced two models using family names ("Francis Howard" and "Henry Randall") before buying the rights to use the "Rönisch," "Thalburg," "August Hyde," and "Gors and Kallmann" names. They made uprights, player pianos, and some **baby grands**, continuing to build until about 1950. In 1919 Sutton's moved to form the Concord Company in Melbourne to produce pianos and player pianos. The members of this concern were Sutton's, Nicholson and Company of Sydney, The Australasian Implement and House Furnishing Company of Adelaide, Buhler and Company of Perth, and Findlay's of Tasmania. Production ceased shortly after the end of World War II.

South Australia also supported a major piano producer in Furness Pianos. The company was formed by Herbert S. Furness (born 25 May 1859, Halifax, Yorkshire, England; died 1934, South Australia), his son, James Ross (born 1888, England; died 1962, South Australia), and Albert Behrndt, who had been employed in a piano factory in Germany and carried out the cabinet-making and French polishing. They began manufacturing pianos in 1908 with a workshop and showroom in Adelaide, South Australia. Herbert had worked for the English piano manufacturer, **Pohlmann** and Son, and had visited **Brinsmead**'s and Broadwood's before emigrating to South Australia in 1892. Special pianos used Australian red gum or Tasmanian blackwood but most had a walnut case. In 1922 Glen Furness, a family member, visited piano factories in England, Canada, and the U.S. in order to learn up-to-date techniques. Furness began to manufacture player pianos in 1923. On 24 June 1924 the company went public and became known as Furness Limited. In 1925 operations moved to Edwardstown, South Australia, and by 1925 production had reached almost a piano per day. About 600 units were manufactured in 1925–1926. In the 1930s Furness Ltd. sold about 1300 pianos and player pianos through agents in Australia and Papua New Guinea. In 1927 Furness diversified in order to survive the depression but in 1939, when so-called luxury items were discontinued in favor of munition work, piano production ceased. Their pianos won several prizes including: 1910, Adelaide Exhibition, Silver Medal for piano construction; 1925, South Australia Chamber of Manufacturers, All-Australian Exhibition, Silver Medal for player piano, Bronze Medal for piano; 1930, South Australian Chamber of Manufacturers, All-Australian Exhibition, Bronze Medals for piano, player piano, and piano and player-piano parts.

Carl von Heiden (born 13 April 1880, Berlin; died 1936, Australia) operated a music business until World War I, when because of his German background he was forced to close down. He had trained at the Bechstein factory in Berlin and in the early 1900s he worked with **Steinway** in New York. After the war he moved to Brisbane and between 1932 and 1936 he operated his Heiden Piano Factory. His pianos used iron frames cast at the Balmer and Crowthers foundry in Brisbane and later at Scott's foundry at Ipswich. Soundboards, wrest planks, and **bridge** timbers were imported along with **keyboard** and action parts from England (Schwander) and Canada (Otto Heygel). Heiden sold pianos under his own name but also manufactured pianos for Paling's (music house) using the name "Victor and Belling."

In the late 1930s Geoff Allan, of the Melbourne-based music house, decided that the time was right to put the failure of the Australian Piano Factory behind him and to investigate filling the growing demand for pianos. It was hard to get German and English models and the quality since World War I was thought to be inferior. Allan still had the license to use the Thürmer name, and rather than joining with Beale, who had not been able to compete with the price of the imported Thürmer, Allan approached Charles Davies, a Sydney manufacturer. World War II interfered with their work. The first piano by C.E. Davies made after the war was completed on 28 November 1946. C.E. Davies Pty. Ltd. won a government contract to make upright pianos for use in schools and institutions in Australia. Using the model name of "Symphony," they produced around 25,000 pianos, employing a staff of twenty five. They cast their own frames at Yagoona and made all parts by hand from imported materials. Canadian spruce was used for the soundboard and English beech for wrest

planks. Between 1946 and 1976 they produced on average twelve Symphony pianos each week. In 1978 C.E. Davies Pty. Ltd., Australia's last piano manufacturing concern, ceased production due to rising costs and cheaper imports. There is considerable interest among piano technicians in Australia to employ innovative technological improvements in piano design and to start new piano building concerns to cater to the domestic and international markets.

Keith T. Johns

Bibliography

Beale and Company Limited, archive materials held by Australia Music Limited, Sydney.

Game, Peter. *The Music Sellers*. Melbourne: Hawthorn, 1976.

Foulcher, Trevor. "Piano Building in Australia." *Sydney International Piano Competition Programme* (1988):51.

Furness, Rex, and Keith Furness. *The History of Furness Limited*. Printed by the Furness family, 1986.

Ottley, Brent L. *Piano Building in Victoria 1850–1950*. Private publication, 1987.

Sutton, George. *Richard Henry Sutton, Esq. 1830–1876*. Melbourne: Renwick Pride, 1954.

"The Symphony Lingers On." *Piano Action, Newsletter for Australian Piano Technicians* 18 (April 1985):1–2.

AUSTRIA, PIANO INDUSTRY IN

In the Austrian Empire there was a flourishing and widely known piano industry from the end of the eighteenth century until World War I. In addition to the capital and court city of Vienna, Prague and Budapest were of primary importance. The *gravecembalo col piano e forte* invented by **Bartolomeo Cristofori** around 1700, with its **Stossmechanik**, must have been known in Vienna by the first quarter of the eighteenth century. Austria had close contact with Italy and most of the court musicians in Austria were Italians since the time of Emperor Ferdinand III (r. 1637–1657).

In 1725 Johann Christoph Leo, organ maker in Augsburg, advertised his "Cimbalen ohne Kiel nebst anderen schönen Flügeln" [harpsichords without quills besides other beautiful **grands**] in the journal *Wiener Diarium*. The Kunsthistorisches Museum in Vienna possesses a harpsichord made in 1696 (KHM/SAM Inv.Nr.845), probably of Viennese origin, which was repaired by the Viennese organ maker Frantz

Walter in 1703 and later converted into a piano with *Stossmechanik* by Wenceslaus Dacfur in Prague in 1726. Most of the oldest preserved Viennese pianos—e.g., by Ignatz Kober, Johann Schantz, F.X. Christoph—are equipped with a *Stossmechanik* **action**. Further evidence of the importance of the piano in Austria is the fact that the earliest known recital on a fortepiano took place in Vienna (at the Burgtortheater) in 1763, played by Johann Baptist Schmid.

The ideas of the Enlightenment, the increasing significance of the bourgeoisie, and the reform-minded reign of Emperor Joseph II (r. 1780–1790) effected a generalized economic and social boom. From every area in the empire and neighboring countries there commenced a lively influx of tradespeople, craftsmen, and artists who primarily settled in the suburbs of Vienna. This led to very keen competition.

Until the Congress of Vienna (1815) approximately 200 instrument builders lived in the city and its environs, of which 137 were organ or pianoforte builders. Thirty years later the number of piano builders alone had nearly tripled to 387. Of course not each of these had his own firm. The workshops were for the most part small manufactures. For instance, **Ferdinand Hofmann**, who produced one piano a week with his eight journeymen, or **Anton Walter**, who in 1804 employed some twenty journeymen, were considered large-scale enterprises by contemporary standards.

Piano construction in Vienna before 1800 was determined by two "schools": the one direction, substantially influenced by Anton Walter, preferred a strong type of piano oriented toward volume and extroverted virtuosity; the other had as its representatives Nannette **Streicher** (née **Stein**) and her brother Matthäus Andreas Stein (André Stein), as well as **Johann Schantz**. The "Stein Siblings," who settled in Vienna in 1794 and worked together in the same shop until 1802, continued the tradition of their father, Johann Andreas Stein of Augsburg. The brighter, distinctive tone of the instruments of the Stein-Streicher dynasty was preferred by musicians of the Classical tradition as well as for chamber music. In the era of the "Wiener Klassik," besides the aforementioned masters, **Joseph Brodmann**, Johann Jakesch, Ignatz Kober, and **Michael Schweighofer** were important.

The nineteenth century was a very innovative epoch for the trend-setting Viennese piano

industry. Between 1821 and 1843, fifty-three inventions were patented for the piano industry alone. Austrian piano **wire** producers were able to prosper, despite duty-free import of foreign products. Steel piano wire produced by Martin Miller & Sohn of Vienna was famous in all parts of Europe and was even used by **Broadwood** at the Great Exhibition in London in 1851 (see Wire). While certain masters such as Johann Baptist Streicher, **Matthias Müller**, or Martin Seuffert were noted for willingness to experiment, others concentrated on the development of a few proven models (i.e., **Conrad Graf**), which nevertheless could vary drastically in external appearance.

The development in western Europe of ever-increasing volume of sound in the building of pianos was only hesitantly imitated by Austrian masters. Until the middle of the nineteenth century, most Austrian piano builders and pianists considered superfluous the case trusses and iron **frames**; **hammer felt** invented by **Jean-Henri Pape**; and **Sébastien Erard**'s repetition **action** with its double escapement, for reasons of **tone**, technique, and economics. Despite this "backwardness" — from a modern standpoint— Austria in the middle of the nineteenth century remained a net exporter. This is mainly due to very low production costs in relation to the high quality of the products.

A detailed and planned division of labor, from England primarily, was also practiced in Vienna, though divided at first among various smaller firms. Thus, in 1850 the Lower Austrian trade organization lists 105 piano builders, 21 **keyboard** makers, 17 **case** builders, 11 piano shank and **tuning pin** makers, 7 piano-leg makers, 5 **string** producers, 5 piano nameplate makers, 4 *Kapsel* makers, 3 bone workers, and 2 piano wire producers. When Johann Baptist Streicher visited the Broadwood Company a year later (1851), he was extremely impressed that this one company was able to produce in a year almost as many pianos as all 105 Viennese piano builders combined, namely 2,300 pianos (in Vienna 2,600).

Despite his admiration, Streicher preferred the indigenous method of production. The boss in a Viennese factory was at the same time the number-one worker. The result of this was very high quality (through continuous checking) combined with individual character. The accurate and even intonation of Austrian pianos is often singled out for mention. The leading

Viennese companies were decidedly against expansion of factory size for mass production. Ludwig **Bösendorfer**, for example, consciously limited the number of his co-workers to 120. It is true, however, that in doing so they missed becoming part of the world market. Several piano builders distinguished themselves by their significant musical capabilities (such as Nannette and Andreas Stein, Johann B. Streicher, Carl Stein, Ludwig Bösendorfer) and in part introduced their instruments to the public themselves. Eduard Seuffert furthered the development of the erect Viennese pianoforte (the **"giraffe** piano," **"pyramid piano"**) constructed by his father, which eventually evolved into the **"pianino"** (**upright** piano).

In addition to Seuffert, the most significant masters of this period were Ignaz Bösendorfer, Conrad Graf, Carl Stein, and Johann Baptist Streicher. From the middle of the nineteenth century, French, English, and American influence (which finally led to the modern piano) began to show itself. This brought about a great developmental impetus with respect to construction techniques as well as economics. Iron trusses and string plates and finally the cast-iron frame (first used in Vienna in 1862 by Friedrich **Ehrbar** [1827–1905]), hammer felt, crucible cast steel strings, and **overstringing** were incorporated into production. Sound intensity and tonal volume prevailed as the most important criteria of quality. Not a few contemporaries warned of the one-sidedness of this development. They had personally heard **Ludwig van Beethoven**, Johann Nepomuk Hummel, and Carl Czerny, and treasured the fortepiano as a poetic instrument of **chamber music**. They recognized that by gaining in sound intensity there was a loss of tonal beauty and the singing qualities for which **Viennese pianos** were famous at that time in all of Europe. The "Viennese action," once so valued for its lightness and subtlety, could not be reconciled with this development because of the increasing mass of moveable parts. Subsequently, this mechanism was considered sluggish and recalcitrant and was taken out of production by Bösendorfer, for example, starting in 1906.

The number of firms decreased while the productivity of individual firms greatly in-

Grand Pianoforte by Ludwig Bösendorfer, Vienna 1875, designed by Theophil Hansen (1813–1891), architect of the "Musikverein" in Vienna. From the possession of Emperor Franz Joseph I (1830–1916). Kunsthistorisches Museum, Sammlung alter Musikinstrumente, Inv. No. 387.

creased. Austrian firms, which primarily supplied local demand, found themselves increasingly pressured by cheaper imports from foreign countries (especially uprights from Germany). In order to withstand the price pressure of top-ranking factories, in 1873 several smaller builders joined together as the "First Viennese Production Cooperative."

The Austrian piano industry, as a consequence of the first industrial expositions of 1835, 1839, and 1845 in Vienna, documented its international and historical significance at the Vienna World's Fair in 1873 and at the International Music and Theater Exposition of 1892. At further large piano expositions abroad (1851 and 1862 in London; 1867, 1878, 1889, 1900 in Paris; 1876 in Munich and Philadelphia; 1881 in Sydney; 1893 in Chicago), Viennese firms were awarded numerous medals and honors. In addition to Streicher, Ehrbar, Bösendorfer, the firms Schweighofer's Sons (founded 1832), Dörr (founded 1817), Czapka (founded c. 1840), and Heitzmann (founded 1839) gained greater significance.

The euphoria of the so-called Gründerzeit (in 1909 Bösendorfer achieved a highpoint with 460 pianos a year) ended abruptly in 1914 with the disaster of World War I. With the dissolution of the Austro-Hungarian Empire in 1918, the former crown lands—the chief customers for Austrian piano builders—became foreign countries. The previous flourishing trade was hindered by high protective tariffs.

Many smaller firms, rendered uncompetitive in the European market because of obsolete production techniques, were forced into bankruptcy during the years of the depression. Their demise was also brought about by the ultimate success of radio and record players. Until after 1930, single examples of the Viennese mechanism were handmade. Annexation into "Großdeutschland" in 1938 brought about temporary economic recovery, which ended all too soon in the horrors of World War II. The Viennese piano industry was not able to achieve the recovery of the post-war era. After 1950 the import of inexpensive mass-produced wares, predominantly from East Asia, brought about the suspension of the last unprofitable piano manufacturers. Of the once-famous Viennese piano industry, only the Bösendorfer company maintained and was able to expand its international significance. The brands Ehrbar, Stingl, and Stelzhammer are produced sporadically on a small scale. In three workshops (Alfred Watzek, Vienna; Richard Koch, Tulln; Robert Brown, Salzburg) **Fortepianos** are being built according to historic principles.

In 1988 there were thirty-nine piano builders officially registered, whose prime areas of expertise were in repair, tuning, and trade.

Alfons Huber

Translated by David Anderson

Bibliography

Badura-Skoda, Eva. "Prolegomena to a History of the Viennese Fortepiano." *Israel Studies in Musicology* 2 (1980): 77–99.

Beschreibung der Erfindungen und Verbesserungen, für welche in den k.k. österreichischen Staaten Patente erteilt wurden. Wien: Hof- und Staats-Aerjarial-Druckerei 1841 bis 1845, I–III.Bd.

Fischhof, Joseph. *Versuch einer Geschichte des Clavierbaues.* Wien: Wallishausser, 1853.

Harding, Rosamond E.M. *The Piano-Forte: Its History Traced to the Great Exhibition of 1851.* Cambridge: Cambridge University Press, 1933. Reprints. New York: Da Capo Press, 1973; Old Woking, Surrey. Gresham Books, 1978.

Haupt, Helga. "Wiener Instrumentenbauer von 1791–1815." In: *Studien zur Musikwissenschaft,* vol. 24. Edited by Erich Schenk. Wien-Graz-Köln: Böhlau, 1960.

Huber, Alfons. "Deckelstützen und Schalldeckel an Hammerklavieren." *Studia Organologica.* Festschrift John Henry Van der Meer. (Edited by Friedemann Hellwig), Tutzing: Schneider, 1987.

Kraus, Gottfried., ed. *Musik in Österreich.* Wien: Brandstätter, 1989.

Kunsthistorisches Museum, ed. *Die Klangwelt Mozarts.* Katalog zur Ausstellung in der Neuen Burg April 1991–February 1992, Wien: Eigenverlag, 1991.

Luithlen, Victor. *Saitenklaviere.* Katalog der Sammlung alter Musikinstrumente des Kunsthistorischen Museums. Wien: Eigenverlag, 1966.

Mayer, Michael. *Bösendorfer. Historische Betriebsanalyse der Firma L. Bösendorfer Klavierfabrik AG.* Dissertation an der Wirtschaftswissenschaftlichen Universität; Wien, September 1989.

Ottner, Helmut. *Der Wiener Musikinstrumentenbau 1815–1833.* Tutzing: Schneider, 1970.

Prilisauer, Richard, ed. *Klavierland Wien.* Katalog zur Ausstellung des Bezirksmuseums Mariahilf, Gumpendorferstraße 4, 1060 Wien: Jänner, 1981.

Scholz, Helmut R., ed. *Ehrbar—Tradition der Wiener Klavierbaukunst.* Festschrift zum 185 jährigen Firmenjubiläum. Wien: Eigenverlag, 1986.

Streicher, Andreas. *Kurze Bemerkungen über das Spielen, Stimmen und Erhalten der Fortepiano,* welche von Nannette Streicher geborene Stein in Wien, verfertiget werden. Wien: Albertinische Schriften, 1802.

AUTOMATIC PIANO

See Player Piano.

B

BABCOCK, ALPHEUS (1785–1842)

Alpheus Babcock, a significant American piano maker and inventor, is best known for his invention of the one-piece metal **frame**, patented 17 December 1825, in Boston. Having learned his craft from **Benjamin Crehore** in Milton, Massachusetts, Babcock set up shop with his brother Lewis (1779–1814) in Boston in 1810, and after Lewis's death he carried on, both in partnerships and on his own. During the 1820s, he was financed by the Mackay family in Boston, one of whose members was John Mackay (d. 1841), later **Jonas Chickering**'s partner, and **nameboard** inscriptions referring to G. (George) D. Mackay and R. (Ruth) Mackay are common among surviving Babcock instruments. Babcock married Margaret Perkins (1789–1842) in 1822, and they had one son, John (1828–1847). In 1829, he moved to Philadelphia, where he worked in the shop of John G. Klemm and later for William Swift. In 1837, he returned to Boston and was employed by Jonas Chickering until his death, 3 April 1842.

The only known surviving exemplar of the 1825 **patent** for the frame is a **square** made at Swift's shop in Philadelphia, now in the Smithsonian Institution. The patent named several possible metals, though cast-iron came to be the metal of choice. Babcock took out three other patents. One (24 May 1830) was for a stringing mechanism that Babcock called "Cross-Stringing." Many authors, not having examined the patent, have credited Babcock with the invention of what is now called cross-stringing, but the patent called for looping the **string** over the **hitchpin** and had nothing to do with crossing planes of strings. A patent of 31 December 1833 was an **action** design with rolled **felt** for **hammer** heads, very much like **Bartolomeo Cristofori**'s roll of parchment as the hammer head. Babcock's last, U. S. Patent No. 1389 of 31 October 1839, described a new design of the fly (**jack**) that eliminated an action noise. How well known any of these patents were is uncertain. Chickering apparently used the last design, but the only known instance of the action patent is in a Babcock piano, and no examples of the stringing patent survive. Other makers certainly knew of Babcock's metal frame, and some were willing to imitate it. But the fact that Conrad Meyer (d. 1881) could later gain credence for his claim to have invented and patented the iron frame in 1832 indicates that Babcock's success was not well known. On the other hand, Jonas Chickering patented a one-piece metal frame for **grands** in 1843 shortly after Babcock's death, having unsuccessfully attempted to obtain a patent in 1840, and we may plausibly infer that, because Babcock had been working for Chickering since 1837, he assisted in the design.

A number of Babcock squares (he built nothing else) are to be found in American collections, and they are notable for superlative workmanship. Although not an outstanding success as a businessman, Alpheus Babcock holds an important place in the general history of the piano and in the American trade.

Edwin M. Good

Bibliography

Good, Edwin M. *Giraffes, Black Dragons, and Other Pianos*. Stanford, Cal.: Stanford University Press, 1982: 126–36.

Grafing, Keith G. "Alpheus Babcock: American Pianoforte Maker (1785–1842): His Life, Instruments, and Patents." D.M.A. dissertation, University of Missouri-Kansas City, 1972.

BABY GRAND

A baby grand is a **grand piano** between four feet nine inches and five feet four inches in length, generally used in small living rooms, conservatory practice rooms, and musicians' studios.
See also Grand Piano.

Camilla Cai

BACH, CARL PHILIPP EMANUEL (1714–1788)

Carl Philipp Emanuel Bach was the second surviving son of **Johann Sebastian Bach** and his first wife Maria Barbara. He was a brilliant keyboard performer, possibly because of his musical studies with his father (in his autobiography he says that in "keyboard playing I never had any other teacher than my father"), and he became harpsichordist to the court of **Frederick the Great**, King of Prussia. In this position he wrote a great number of works for solo keyboard. Living in a time when the harpsichord and the clavichord were slowly being replaced by the **fortepiano**, Bach did not cling to one instrument throughout.

In his essay *Versuch über die wahre Art, das Clavier zu spielen* [Essay on the True Manner of Playing Keyboard Instruments] (1st part 1753, 2nd part 1762), which was widely read during his lifetime, he discusses the pros and cons of the three keyboard instruments. He personally preferred the clavichord, which he brought to recognition and great reputation in Middle- and Northern Germany. Because of its dynamic possibilities it suited his style of musical expression best. Since he was the chief exponent of the *empfindsame Stil* [highly sensitive style], Bach wanted to "touch the hearts" of his audience. He writes that his "chief effort . . . has been . . . to play and compose as airlike as possible for the clavier [i.e., clavichord], not withstanding its lack of sustaining power." According to his opinion the harpsichord, because of its full sound, was best fitted for "strong music," for playing along with other instruments. As for the fortepiano, Bach states in his essay: "the new fortepianos, if they are made very well, have many advantages. . . . They are good for playing alone or for music that is not scored too heavily." Here he stresses the main problem of the early fortepiano: its small sound, which was softer than that of the harpsichord.

Bach's numerous sonatas, fantasias, and rondos (altogether about 170 pieces) are playable on any of the three keyboard instruments of his time, but a few of them can be classified either as harpsichord works or as music for the clavichord by comparing their musical "affects" with the description of the "affects" given in his essay.

Carsten Dürer

Bibliography

Bach, Carl Philipp Emanuel. *Versuch über die wahre Art, das Clavier zu spielen.* Facsimile-Reprint edition, Lothar Hoffmann-Erbrecht. Wiesbaden: Breitkopf & Härtel, 1986.

Barford, Philip. *The Keyboard Music of C. P. E. Bach, Considered in Relation to His Musical Aesthetic and the Rise of the Sonata Principle.* London: Barrie & Rockliff, 1965.

Clark, Stephen L., ed. *C. P. E. Bach Studies.* Oxford: Clarendon Press, 1988.

Kirkpatrick, Ralph. "C. P. E. Bach's *Versuch* Reconsidered." *Early Music* 4 (April 1976): 384–92.

Mitchell, William J. "C. P. E. Bach's Essay, An Introduction." *Musical Quarterly* 33 (1947): 460–80.

Newman, William S. "Emanuel Bach's Autobiography." *Musical Quarterly* 51 (1905): 363–72.

Ottenberg, Hans-Günter. *Carl Philipp Emanuel Bach.* München: Piper, 1988.

———. "Carl Philipp Emanuel Bach–Ein Komponist im Abseits?" *Concerto* 44 (June 1989): 9–13.

Schmidt, Christopher. "C. Ph. E. Bach und das Clavichord." *Schweizerische Musikzeitung* 92 (November 1952): 441–45.

Special issue in honor of the 200th anniversary of the death of C. P. E. Bach. *Early Music* 16 (April 1988).

Vrieslander, Otto. *Carl Philipp Emanuel Bach.* München: Piper, 1925.

Wotquenne, Alfred. *Thematisches Verzeichnis der Werke von Carl Philipp Emanuel Bach (1714–1788).* Leipzig: Breitkopf & Härtel, 1905.

BACH, JOHANN CHRISTIAN (1735–1782)

The youngest son of **Johann Sebastian Bach**, (1685–1750) Johann Christian was one of the most influential composers of the pre-Classical period. Following his early years of training in Berlin with his older brother **Carl Philipp Emanuel** (1714–1788), and then a period of study and employment in Italy, Johann Christian travelled to London in 1762. He made England his home for the remainder of his life and enjoyed a prominent reputation in London's musical circles. His keyboard compositions are mostly in the Italian galant style, the best-known works being two sets of sonatas, Op. 5 from about 1768 and Op. 17 from 1779.

As with the keyboard writing of many composers during this period, Bach's compositions present some questions as to performance medium. The two sets of sonatas both specify on the title page that they are "for the Harpsichord or Piano-forte," but this was a common marketing device during the period, especially in England where the two instruments coexisted comfortably for several decades. Bach is, however, considered by many to be one of the first to fully exploit the potential of the new pianoforte.

A notice in London's *Public Advertiser* on 2 June 1768 lists a concert of vocal and instrumental music "At the Large Room, Thatch'd House, St.-Jame's-Street," in which the last item mentioned is a "solo on the Piano Forte by Mr. Bach." Based on a supposition put forth by Terry in his biography of J. C. Bach, most historians since have asserted that this very early public performance of solo piano music was played on a small **square** piano purchased by Bach from the instrument maker **Johannes Zumpe** (1726–1791). Cole, however, has recently reexamined the facts and published a convincing argument that calls for other possible interpretations. London's *Morning Chronicle* of 5 April and 22 April 1774 makes mention of Bach's appearance in two London concerts playing "a new Concerto upon Mr. Merlin's lately-invented Harpsichord." **John Joseph Merlin**, an ingenious instrument builder among his many other talents, produced some harpsichords with an added piano **action**; perhaps it was one of these on which Bach performed.

Darcy Kuronen

Bibliography

Cole, Warwick Henry. "The Early Piano in Britain Reconsidered." *Early Music.* Vol. 14, No. 4. (November 1986), pp. 563–65.

Hess, A. G. "The Transition from Harpsichord to Piano." *Galpin Society Journal.* Vol. 6 (1953): 75–94.

Maunder, Richard. "J.C. Bach and the Early Piano in London." *Journal of the Royal Musical Association* 116 (1991): 201–210.

Schott, Howard. "From Harpsichord to Pianoforte: A Chronology and Commentary." *Early Music* Vol. 13, No. 1. (February 1985): 28–38.

Terry, Charles Sanford. *John Christian Bach.* London: Oxford University Press, 1929.

BACH, JOHANN SEBASTIAN (1685–1750)

Johann Sebastian Bach was born in Eisenach (21 March 1685) and died in Leipzig (28 July 1750).

For a long time it has been assumed that Johann Sebastian Bach came to know and to appreciate the pianoforte only towards the end of his life. However, recent research reveals the likelihood that Bach saw a *Hammerflügel* built by **Gottfried Silbermann** already in the 1720s, perhaps one of those *pantalone* instruments with moveable **keyboards** (*aufsetzbaren Tastaturen*) and **hammers** that fall from above onto the **strings.** Such an instrument for instance was offered for sale in a newspaper advertisement in Leipzig in 1731. In Volume 5 of Zedler's *Universal-Lexikon,* which appeared in 1733 in Leipzig, an article under the heading *"Cembal d'amour"* appeared, where at the end one reads that Gottfried Silbermann, the constructor of the *Cembal d'amour,* also invented another keyboard instrument, *"so er Piano Fort nennet"* [which he calls Piano Fort]. Such a *Piano Fort,* or Piano Forte (the missing letter "e" at the end might have been a printing error), for which Silbermann was heartily congratulated by the crown prince at the court in Dresden in 1732, may have been delivered to Leipzig in that year, too. It was probably J. S. Bach himself who was responsible for the wording of the following newspaper announcement, which appeared on 16 June 1733 in Leipzig:

> Es "soll morgen, 17 Juni . . . von dem Bachischen Collegio musico . . . der Anfang mit einem schönen Concert gemachet und wöchentlich damit continuieret werden, dabey ein neuer Clavicymbel, dergleichen allhier noch nicht gehöret worden," gespielt werden. [Tomorrow, 17 June . . . Bach's Collegio musico will give the first of its weekly concerts, and will start with a fine concerto using a new clavicymbel of a kind that so far has not been heard here.]

It is most likely that this "new clavicymbel" referred to Silbermann's *Hammerflügel,* which naturally was not immediately named by everybody "pianoforte" but for a rather long period of time was called *new clavecin, clavecin, clavecin à maillet,* or *cembalo (con martelli).* On this occasion in 1733 it is likely that Bach performed his (first?) harpsichord, *Concerto in D Minor* BWV 1052. Bach's pupil Johann Friedrich Agricola, who studied in Leipzig between 1738 and 1741, reported that he not only saw one of Silbermann's later pianofortes, which were built to the complete satisfaction of J. S. Bach, but also one of the earlier *Hammerflügel.* Thus, Bach must have had one of Silbermann's Pianofort instruments at his disposal by 1741 at the latest.

Perhaps he owned it and it is the same expensive *"fourniert clavecin, welches bey der familie so viel möglich bleiben soll"* that is mentioned in Bach's estate list. It is quite understandable that the scribe of this "Nachlaßverzeichnis" in 1750 did not know any other name for the piano than the generic term "clavecin."

Today, there can no longer be any doubt that in the 1740s Bach played on *"instruments piano et forte genandt"* (the name used in a document signed by Bach in 1749). That Bach in 1747 did not hesitate at all to perform for the Prussian king immediately after his arrival in Potsdam on a pianoforte by Silbermann attests to the probability that he was accustomed to such instruments, which were not easy to play for someone who had never practiced on them.

Eva Badura-Skoda

Bibliography

Badura-Skoda, Eva. "Komponierte Johann Sebastian Bach `Hammerklavier-Konzerte'?" In *Bach-Jahrbuch* 1991: 159f.

———."Besaitete Tasten-Instrumente um und nach 1700: Hämmer-Pantalone und Lautenwerke." (Unpublished, in preparation)

———. "Zur Frühgeschichte des Hammerklaviers." In *Florilegium Musicologicum Festschrift für Hellmut Federhofer zum 75. Geburtstag.* Tutzing, 1988: 37f.

Henkel, Hubert. "Bach und das Hammerklavier." In *Beiträge zur Bachforschung* 2 (1983).

BACK CHECK

The back check is the part of **grand** and vertical piano mechanisms that arrests the **hammer** after it rebounds from the **string**. In modern grand pianos, the back check is attached to the end of the **key**; in vertical **actions**, to the **wippen**. The back check prevents the hammer from repeatedly reflecting to and from the string with a single key stroke (called "bobbling") and was invented by **Bartolomeo Cristofori**, himself the inventor of the piano. Cristofori's first piano (c. 1698–1700) used crossed threads to cushion the rebounding hammer shank and prevent bobbling. By 1726, he had devised a padded wood back check like that used on grands today.

See also Actions.

Philip Jamison, III

BACKERS, AMERICUS (FL.1763–C.1781)

Americus Backers was one of the so-called **Twelve Apostles**. Backers played a seminal part in early experiments to develop the **action** for what came to be known as the pianoforte. He was born in the Netherlands and is believed to have worked in the **Silbermann** workshop for a time. The conditions that led to the departure of the Twelve Apostles suggest that he was among the first of the group to leave Germany, particularly as he was a foreigner in Saxony. It is thought that he arrived in London before 1760 and initially worked making spinets for John Hitchcock at 28 Fetter Lane. One such Hitchcock instrument survives—number 2,012, which is signed *"Backus No. 8."*

Backers lived in Jermyn Street under the name "Andrew Backus" from 1763 to 1778. This was also his workshop, where his main activity was the manufacture of harpsichords. He is described as "the young Dutchman" [Wainwright: *The Piano Makers*, p.27], yet no further reference to him is found after 1781, in which year he presumably died. At the time of his arrival, the piano was still considered to be a novelty: in 1767, a Covent Garden performance of *The Beggar's Opera* included a song that was advertised as being "accompanied on a new instrument called Piano Forte."

Backers worked on the design of the piano in his spare time, and the youthful **John Broadwood** and his apprentice **Robert Stodart** used to visit him at Jermyn Street in the evenings after their work was done, in order to assist him. Backers' new piano action, described as the **"English" pianoforte action**, was apparently completed some time late in the 1760s, although manuscript notes by James Shudi Broadwood variously give it as 1772 and 1776. Although the actions subsequently developed by **Pohlmann**, **Shudi**, and Broadwood were more practical, to Backers must go credit for his pioneering work.

Arthur W.J.G. Ord-Hume

Bibliography

Boalch, Donald H. *Makers of the Harpsichord & Clavichord, 1440–1840.* Oxford: Oxford University Press, 1974.

Ehrlich, Cyril. *The Piano: A History.* London: J.M. Dent & Sons, Ltd., 1976.

Harding, Rosamond E.M. *The Piano-Forte: Its History Traced to the Great Exhibition of 1851.* Cambridge: Cambridge University Press, 1933. Reprints. New York: Da Capo Press, 1973; Old Woking, Surrey: Gresham Books, 1978.

Wainwright, David. *Broadwood by Appointment, a History*. London: Quiller, 1982; New York: Universe Books, 1983.

———. Wainwright, David. *The Piano Makers*. London: Hutchinson, 1975.

BALANCIER

Balancier is another term for **repetition lever**. *See also* Repetition Lever.

Philip Jamison, III

BALDWIN PIANO AND ORGAN COMPANY

The Baldwin Company is a firm of musical-instrument builders that sprang from origins deep in nineteenth-century American musical culture. Dwight Hamilton Baldwin (1821–1899) was an itinerant music teacher in the singing school tradition, although he also taught violin and reed organ. Educated at Oberlin College, he moved to Cincinnati, Ohio, in 1857, becoming active in music instruction in the public schools. In the same year, Baldwin and Luther Whiting Mason, son of Lowell Mason and brother of Henry Mason (co-founder of the piano and organ manufacturing firm of **Mason & Hamlin**), published a *Book of Chants* for community singing, and in 1860, *The Young Singer, Part I*. Baldwin was also a minister, spending much of his time throughout his life in the activities of his church and church schools.

As the most prominent music educator of his area, Baldwin was frequently called upon for advice on the purchase of musical instruments. Capitalizing on his reputation, in 1862 or 1863 he became a retail dealer in pianos and organs, at the same time continuing his teaching activities. In 1866 Lucien Wulsin (1845–1912) was hired as a clerk, becoming a partner in 1873 with the formation of D. H. Baldwin Company. A branch at Louisville, Kentucky, was opened in 1877 under the charge of Robert A. Johnson (1838–1884), who also became a partner in 1880. After the death of Johnson in 1884, three other partners joined the firm: Albert A. Van Buren, George W. Armstrong, Jr. (1857–1932), and Clarence Wulsin (1855–1897), Lucien Wulsin's younger brother. The firm became one of the largest retailers of keyboard instruments in the Midwest, with franchises including **Steinway & Sons, Chickering & Sons, Decker Bros., J & C Fischer, Haines Bros., Vose,** and Estey organs, among others. By 1875 the firm was selling 2,500 pianos and organs annually. As the end of the century neared, the Baldwin Company found itself increasingly caught between territorial limitations imposed by eastern instrument-makers who supplied its goods, and potential increases in sales that might be afforded by wider geographical coverage. For several years Baldwin had contracted with the Ohio Valley Piano Company (est. 1871) to provide **square** and **upright** pianos that were labelled "built exclusively for D. H. Baldwin & Co." This firm was purchased and renamed the Valley Gem Piano Company, although Baldwin's actual manufacturing activities had begun in Chicago in 1889 with the production of Monarch and Hamilton reed organs. By 1891 the manufacture of low-priced upright pianos had begun at the Baldwin Piano Company in Cincinnati, and in 1893 the Ellington Piano Company was established for the production of moderately priced pianos. It was decided to develop a truly high quality piano, with John Macy, a talented piano technician in the employ of the company, being instrumental in its design and production. The piano, named the Baldwin, won the Grand Prix at the Paris Exhibition of 1900, thus establishing the company as a builder of genuinely first-class instruments.

In 1899 Dwight H. Baldwin died, leaving the bulk of his holdings in the business to the Presbyterian Church, and under the law the partnership of the D. H. Baldwin Company was dissolved. In 1903, after protracted negotiations, Lucien Wulsin and George Armstrong bought control of the company, with Wulsin serving as chief executive officer until 1912, Armstrong from 1912 to 1926, and Lucien Wulsin, Jr. (1889–1964) from 1926 to 1964.

In the 1920s Baldwin held its place in the automatic piano market with the Manualo player mechanism, available in all Baldwin-made pianos, as well as the Welte (Licensee) reproducing mechanism, which competed with the **Ampico** of the **American Piano Company** and the **Duo-Art** of **Aeolian**. It was also in the latter 1920s that Baldwin began a research and development program in conjunction with the physics department of the University of Cincinnati, which was to result in the introduction of the Baldwin electronic organ in 1946. This venture also laid the groundwork for Baldwin's extensive future involvement in electronics.

In 1936, in response to demand for the small piano, the thirty-six-inch Acrosonic **spinet** was introduced, followed shortly thereafter by the forty-inch Acrosonic **console** piano. In 1938, the forty-four-inch Hamilton studio upright, subsequently one of the most widely used pianos in the United States, was put into production. These and other developments helped the company recover from the depression to which many other manufacturers had succumbed. This recovery was halted by the advent of World War II. In addition to producing numerous wooden parts for aircraft, the company developed a leakproof gasoline tank for fighter planes and produced a top-secret proximity fuse for the U. S. Navy. Reconversion to the production of pianos began almost immediately after the cessation of hostilities, and in 1946 production was resumed.

By 1958 the need for decentralization was felt, as well as the need for additional room for increased production. In 1958 factory space at Conway, Arkansas, was acquired for the manufacture of the thirty-six-inch Howard spinet, and factories were opened at Fayetteville and Trumann, Arkansas, as well as at Greenwood, Mississippi. By 1972 only executive offices remained at Cincinnati.

The 1960s saw a further advance in company growth. The prestigious German piano-making firm of **Bechstein** (est. 1853) was acquired by Baldwin in 1963, and in 1965 Baldwin introduced its newly designed **concert grand** piano, designated the SD-10. In 1967 a factory was opened in Juarez, Mexico, for the manufacture of electronic equipment and piano **actions**. This period saw the increased acquisition of electronics firms, and, as profits increased, activities grew in the area of finance, including banks, savings and loan associations, leasing companies, and insurance companies. In all, forty-two separate acquisitions were recorded between 1968 and 1982. The Baldwin Piano and Organ Company was now reduced to a small division of a huge corporation called Baldwin United. In 1982–1983, after the acquisition of the Mortgage Guarantee Insurance Company, rising interest rates forced Baldwin United to file for Chapter 11 bankruptcy. The executive staff of the profitable piano and organ division, fearful that it might be sold to satisfy Baldwin United's debts, negotiated a leveraged buy-out

in 1984, and the Baldwin Piano and Organ Company again became privately owned. Two years previously Baldwin had joined with the South Korean piano maker Samick to form the Korean American Music Company for the production of the Howard grand piano, a piano which had been made in the 1970s by the Japanese maker **Kawai**. (Most recently [1992], Baldwin has decided to dispense with its affiliation with Asian piano manufacturers in the production of the lower end of its grand piano production, expanding its "Classic" line of grands to include competitively priced 4'9" and 5'7" instruments to be produced at the Conway, Arkansas, plant.)

In 1985 Baldwin gained control of the action-making firm at **Pratt, Read** (est. 1798) to form the Pratt-Win Corporation, and its piano action production was transferred to the Baldwin plant at Juarez, Mexico. In the same year, in an effort to diversify in an economic climate that saw several old-line piano companies go out of business, Baldwin began the manufacture of a full line of grandfather clocks. In 1987 Baldwin sold Bechstein, acquiring in 1988 the American piano and organ building firm of **Wurlitzer** (est. 1856) as a wholly owned subsidiary, with independent sales, marketing, and manufacturing operations. In 1989 Baldwin also acquired Chas. Pfriemer, Inc., a manufacturer of piano **felts** since 1870, and Baldwin's chief supplier of these materials.

In 1989 Baldwin could make the claim that all piano markets and categories were covered by its operations: grands for concert and artist use, a concert vertical, decorator-styled verticals for the home, studio uprights for schools, electronic pianos for lab and teaching systems, and a **player piano**, with electronic **keyboards** utilizing digital sampling technology. (Recently [1992] Baldwin has joined with Ensoniq Corp. to produce a line of digital keyboards, the first of which, a high-end digital piano housed in a grand-style case, has just been produced.) Advertising could claim twenty-nine different grand piano models, thirty-five vertical piano models, seventeen models of electronic and portable keyboards, and eight "classical" organs, comprising probably the widest diversity of pianos and organs offered by any domestic maker.

James Howard Richards

Bibliography

"Baldwin Acquires Wurlitzer Keyboard Business." *The Music Trades* 136 (February 1988): 20, 116–18.

"Baldwin Celebrates 125th With New Electronics and Aggressive Marketing." *The Music Trades* 135 (February 1987): 94–95.

"The D. H. Baldwin Company." Unpublished manuscript, The Baldwin Piano and Organ Company, 1987.

"Baldwin Expands Market Share." *The Music Trades* 130 (July 1982): 84, 86.

"Baldwin Piano and Organ Company." *The Purchaser's Guide to the Music Industries*. New York: The Music Trades, 1989.

"Baldwin Pursues New Markets with Digital Pianos & Low-End Grands." *The Music Trades* 140 (March 1992): 133.

"The Baldwin Story." *The Music Trades* (September 1962): 39–45.

Bowers, Q. David. *Encyclopedia of Automatic Musical Instruments*. Vestal, NY: Vestal Press, 1972.

Dolge, Alfred. *Pianos and Their Makers*. 2 vols. Covina, Cal.: Covina Publishing Company, 1911. Vol. 1, Reprint. New York: Dover Publications, Inc., 1972.

———. *Pianos and Their Makers*. 2 vols. Covina, Cal.: Covina Publishing Company, 1913. Vol. 2 reprinted as *Men Who Have Made Piano History*. New York: Dover Publications, Inc., 1980.

"Harrison & Smith Acquire Baldwin." *The Music Trades* 132 (February 1984): 19, 102–04.

The New Grove Dictionary of Musical Instruments. Edited by Stanley Sadie. S. v. "Baldwin," by Cynthia Adams Hoover. London: MacMillan; Washington DC: Grove's Dictionaries, 1984.

"Pratt-Read and Baldwin Form Pratt-Win Corp. to Manufacture Keys and Actions in Mexico." *The Music Trades* 133 (June 1985): 50.

Roell, Craig H. *The Piano in America, 1890–1940*. Chapel Hill: The University of North Carolina Press, 1989.

Roehl, Harvey. *Player Piano Treasury*. 2nd ed. Vestal, N.Y.: The Vestal Press, 1973.

Wulsin, Lucien. "A Piano Man Looks Back." *The Music Trades* (February 1963): 39–43.

BARREL PIANO

The barrel piano is a mechanically played piano in which the musical program is provided by a barrel or cylinder, most commonly of wood and very occasionally of metal, the surface of which is equipped with protrusions that operate the action of the instrument. In the case of the wooden barrel, these are in the form of "pins" resembling headless nails; metal cylinders have holes or slots into which the ends of metal levers may drop to sound a musical note. In all such instruments, the linkage to the strung back of the piano is via a series of simple hammer mechanisms, one for each note, mounted in a keyframe placed adjacent to the surface of the barrel so that its projections (or, very rarely, surface slots) can act on the hammer action.

The barrel is the earliest form of fixed musical program as applied to mechanical instruments, and its origins are to be found in the early mechanical organ or "barrel organ."

The use and development of barrel-played pianos proceeded along two parallel courses. First, it was seen as a way of providing a respectable performance from a piano without the services of a pianist, and makers such as John **Longman**, Thomas **Rolfe** and others incorporated such mechanisms into their instruments for use in the home. Longman, for example, made a number of drawing-room vertical barrel pianos that were intended only for self-playing: they had no **keyboard**. Rolfe made instruments that had both keyboard and barrel actions. Both these varieties were clockwork-driven when in automatic play, the driving force being the energy stored in a descending weight. The musical program was almost exclusively the dance or minuet. Combined barrel-and-finger instruments (the contemporary term used to indicate the dual capability) were made mainly in England (specifically in London), Germany, France, and the Low Countries.

The second line of development was in the instruments made for public use; there were two main types: the hand-turned, open-air piano, commonly known as the **street piano**, and the cafe or bar piano. These latter were always clockwork-driven, using either a descending weight or, most commonly, a large spring motor. These last two categories are the ones most closely associated with the Italians, both itinerant manufacturers and street musicians travelling to France, Germany, England, and America to produce them in large quantities. The barrels were replaceable and could be exchanged or re-pinned with new music as required to keep the program up-to-date. Paul Lochmann of Leipzig, Germany, used perforated metal cylinders to replace the heavy and awkward wooden barrel.

The barrel piano developed into the barrel-operated piano **orchestrion** where, in addition to piano **strings**, percussion instruments were added such as drums, triangle, wood blocks, and tambourine. The variety known as the cafe piano, produced mainly in Belgium, France, and Germany, was a popular interpreter of light music and dances for public places. It was superseded by the piano orchestrions produced in Germany and America, which operated on the pneumatic system and could offer more comprehensive music and the ready changing of tunes by substituting a small roll of perforated paper for the cumbersome barrel and its delicate musical pinning.

Arthur W.J.G. Ord-Hume

Bibliography

Harding, Rosamond E.M. *The Piano-Forte: Its History Traced to the Great Exhibition of 1851.* Cambridge: Cambridge University Press, 1933. Reprints. New York: Da Capo Press, 1973; Old Woking, Surrey: Gresham Books, 1978.

Ord-Hume, Arthur W.J.G. *Clockwork Music—An Illustrated History.* London: Allen & Unwin, 1973.

———.*Pianola.* London: Allen & Unwin, 1984.

———.*The Mechanics of Mechanical Music.* London: Ord-Hume, 1973.

BEATS

The term "beats" refers to the augmentation and diminution of sound resulting from two **strings** vibrating at slightly different frequencies. This phenomenon is the basis of piano **tuning**.

For example, if one string vibrating at 440 cycles-per-second (CPS) is sounded along with one at 441 CPS, one hears, instead of a pure, even tone, a distinct though brief increase in volume every second. This occurs when the unsynchronous pressure waves produced by each string periodically overlap, much as overlapping ocean waves combine and increase in power. By regulating the number of beats, the tuner can accurately adjust the **pitch** of each string.

See also Acoustics.

Philip Jamison, III

BEBUNG

"Bebung" is a German word indicating a vibrato played upon the clavichord from the eighteenth century onwards. Its aim was to give more expression and to sustain the notes. There is no mention of "bebung" before the eighteenth century. During the nineteenth century the term was sometimes used for *sostenente* pianos with repeating **hammers**. Another name for these instruments was "pianos with Italian Tremendo." Such a piano was patented in 1841 in Paris by Mrs. Girard-Romagnac (French Patent No. 12079).

F.J. de Hen

BECHSTEIN

For generations the name Bechstein has been synonymous with excellence in the art of piano construction. From the very beginning, composers such as **Franz Liszt**, **Richard Wagner**, and **Johannes Brahms** would express their pleasure in playing the instrument. A generation later, pianists such as Josef Hofmann and Artur Schnabel would declare the Bechstein as the "realization of an ideal in a piano," and a "triumph of touch and tone."

The founder of this symbol of approbation, Carl Bechstein (1826–1900), was born in the Thuringian town of Gotha (Germany). Years of travel and apprenticeships began in Erfurt, where he developed a passionate interest in piano building and where he worked with his brother-in-law, piano maker Johann Gleitz. From 1844 until 1852, Bechstein travelled considerably, working in Dresden with the Pleyel company, in Berlin with Perau, and in Paris with the firm of Pape and Kriegelstein. On returning to Berlin, Bechstein took over management of the Perau factory. Later, in Paris again, he was made superintendent of Pape and Kriegelstein's factory. At the conclusion of his travels, Bechstein settled down in Berlin to establish his own piano factory.

In 1853, at age 27, after a period of nine months Bechstein produced his first two pianos, followed three years later by his first **grand piano**. Learning that Liszt, with his remarkable strength, often broke the **strings** of certain pianos of his day, such as the **Erard**, Bechstein built an instrument that could withstand greater and more powerful virtuoso performances. Hans von Bülow proved the point by performing the Liszt B-Minor Sonata on the new Bechstein grand with great success. In the process of creating his new instrument, Bechstein employed **cross-stringing** on a cast-iron **frame** (as used in America), and combined the powerful tone of the **English action** with the repetition action of the French. At the Industrial and Art Exhibition in London in 1862, Bechstein won the silver medal. As a result of this success, and an even greater success at the Exposition Universelle of Paris in 1867, Bechstein began to secure a place among master piano builders of the day.

Orders for **upright** and grand pianos first came from England and Russia; once London was supplied with pianos, Australia and Canada, members of the Commonwealth, were also included. Annual output ran from 300 pianos, during the 1860s, to over 5,000 pianos by 1900. In 1879, the Bechstein firm sold its own pianos in London, and eventually the market opened worldwide, including dealerships, in the U.S., Europe, Asia, and South America.

Upon Carl Bechstein's death in 1900, his three sons, Edwin, Carl, and Johann, took over the company's management. In 1901, a London branch was established on Wigmore Street, where part of the building contained a 550-seat concert hall. Years later this "Bechstein Hall" was renamed the Wigmore Hall.

The two World Wars and the Great Depression had a profound effect on the fortunes of the firm. Moreover, in 1933, the sale of the "neo-Bechstein," an experimental piano using fewer strings per note, strung over an amplified **soundboard**, failed to gain public acceptance. During World War II the Bechstein factory was almost totally destroyed, and only after efforts were made to reassemble its workers did the firm begin to re-establish its former reputation. Grand piano building began again in 1951. In 1963 the company was acquired by the Baldwin Company.

In 1987 Baldwin sold its Bechstein unit to Karl Schulze, a well-known German master piano craftsman. Back in German hands, and under new management, the Bechstein company appears to have sustained its former quality and has regained a new vitality. Because of acquisitions in 1991 and 1992, the company has changed its name to "Bechstein Gruppe."

Frederic Schoettler

Bibliography

Burde, Wolfgang. *The House of Bechstein, A Chronicle — 1853 Up to the Present.* Berlin: C. Bechstein Pianofortefabrik, n. d.

Fine, Larry. *The Piano Book.* Boston: Brookside Press, 1987.

The New Grove Dictionary of Music and Musicians. Sixth edition, Vol. 2. Edited by Stanley Sadie. London: Macmillan, 1980.

BECK, FREDERICK (FL.1756–1798)

Frederick Beck was one of the so-called **Twelve Apostles.** Little is known of his life and work before his arrival in London, but one of two known surviving Beck instruments is a five-octave **cabinet piano**—there is no recess for the player's legs—in an outstandingly decorated **case.** This is dated 1775 and bears the serial number 2,000. Beck was at work at 4 Broad Street, Golden Square, from 1774, but in the last reference to his name (1794) his address is given as 10 Golden Square, Carnaby Market. There was a spinet maker of the same name at work in Lavenham, England, in 1741 but he is very unlikely to have been the same man.

Arthur W.J.G. Ord-Hume

Bibliography

Boalch, Donald H. *Makers of the Harpsichord & Clavichord, 1440–1840.* Oxford: Oxford University Press, 1974.

Ehrlich, Cyril. *The Piano: A History.* London: J.M. Dent, 1976.

Good, Edwin Marshall. *Giraffes, Black Dragons, and Other Pianos: A Technological History from Cristofori to the Modern Concert Grand.* Stanford, Cal.: Stanford University Press, 1982.

BECKER, JOHN CONRAD (FL. C.1801–1841)

John Conrad Becker was a Bavarian-born piano maker who worked in London for a short while at the start of the nineteenth century. In 1801 he was at Princes Street, Soho, and was granted British **patent** No. 2,551 of that year for "improvements in musical instruments, chiefly applicable to harps and pianofortes."

His invention was twofold. First, he proposed a system of producing sharps and flats from natural notes by a mechanism that turned the wrest pins to tighten or slacken the string slightly. The impracticability of this technique was later eradicated by **Sébastien Erard** in his important patent for the mechanism of the concert harp: in this, he rightly left the **tuning pins** alone and tightened the **strings**, using a mechanical toggle to adjust the speaking length of the string.

Becker's second proposition was the elimination of **hammers** to strike the strings. He replaced them with "one or more wheels" turned by a **pedal** to vibrate the strings. **John Isaac Hawkins** produced a similar instrument in Philadelphia in the following year. None of Becker's instruments is known to survive. He later returned to Germany and with his son Jacob subsequently moved to St. Petersburg in Russia, where together they founded the famous piano-making business that bore their name.

Arthur W.J.G. Ord-Hume

Bibliography

Grove Dictionary of Music & Musicians, first edition. Edited by Sir George Grove. London: Macmillan, 1879.

Harding, Rosamond E.M. *The Piano-Forte: Its History Traced to the Great Exhibition of 1851.* Cambridge: Cambridge University Press, 1933. Reprints. New York: Da Capo Press, 1973; Old Woking, Surrey: Gresham Books, 1978.

BECKET

The becket is the bend where the piano **string** passes through the **tuning pin**.

Philip Jamison, III

BEETHOVEN, LUDWIG VAN (1770–1827)

Because of his great musical prominence, because of the central role played by the piano in his *oeuvre*, and because he lived at a time when the piano was at an interesting and dynamic phase in its development, Ludwig van Beethoven exerted a powerful influence on the future direction of piano manufacture. By his constant demands for pianos that were more sturdy, more resistant, and had a stronger tone, Beethoven played an important role in encouraging builders to develop their instruments in this direction.

Beethoven's initial impact in Vienna was as a pianist playing primarily his own music or improvising, rather than solely as a composer. He astonished the Viennese, impressing them with the elemental force of his performances. One critic in 1791 commented on Beethoven's "fiery expression," saying that his playing "differs from the usual method of treating the piano, that it seems as if he had struck out on an entirely new path for himself." Although from the start his piano writing shows numerous features idiomatic to the Viennese **fortepiano**, in performance he often transcended that instrument's limitations, if con-

temporary reports can be credited. Anton Reicha recounted that when Beethoven was playing a **Mozart** concerto at court, instead of turning pages he (Reicha) was mostly occupied with wrenching out **strings** of the piano that had snapped, and disentangling the **hammers**! This intensity of playing required pianos that were more powerful in tone in order to accommodate the heightened level of expressivity, and instruments that were strung and built more sturdily in order to resist such powerful onslaughts.

Three pianos that actually belonged to Beethoven — the French **Erard** in the Vienna Kunsthistorisches Museum, the English **Broadwood** in the Budapest National Museum, and the Austrian **Graf** in the Bonn Beethovenhaus—are extant. However, these provide only a partial picture of the instruments the master actually used and, in and of themselves, give a one-sided and possibly misleading view of his preferences in pianos.

Beethoven's most enduring relationship with a piano manufacturer was with the firm associated with the names **Stein** and **Streicher**. As early as 1783 Beethoven is reported as preferring instruments manufactured by Johann Andreas Stein of Augsburg. The rapport with the Stein family continued after the elder Stein's death in 1792, when the company was taken over by Stein's two children; the removal of the firm's headquarters to Vienna in 1794 made it convenient for Beethoven to carry on dealings with them. Beethoven developed particularly close contacts with Stein's daughter Nannette (Anna Maria, Maria Anna) and her husband, Johann Andreas Streicher. Although Beethoven preferred pianos made by "Nannette Streicher née Stein" (the name under which their firm was known after 1802), he was extremely demanding in his requirements and made these requirements known to the Streichers on numerous occasions; they, for their part, did their best to comply.

Beethoven's admiration of the Streichers' instruments, coupled with a strong conviction that important changes in piano construction ought to be forthcoming, was expressed in the following letter to Johann Andreas from 1796.

> . . . I assure you in all sincerity, dear S[treicher], that this was the first time it gave me pleasure to hear my trio performed; and truly this experience will make me decide to compose more for the pianoforte than I have done hitherto. . . . There is no doubt that so

far as the manner of playing is concerned, the pianoforte is still the least studied and developed of all instruments; often one thinks that one is merely listening to a harp. And I am delighted, my dear fellow, that you are one of the few who realize and perceive that, provided one can feel the music, one can also make the pianoforte sing. I hope the time will come when the harp and the pianoforte will be treated as two entirely different instruments. . . .

Around 1802 (the year of the Heiligenstadt Testament), a new and complicating factor began to modify profoundly Beethoven's requirements in pianos — his deafness. Beethoven's deafness increased his exigencies for pianos in two principal ways. First, he had an exacerbated need for an instrument that would be as loud as possible, simply so that he could hear it. This was expressed in a letter to Nannette Streicher in 1817 in which he implores her to have her husband adjust one of his pianos to maximum loudness. Related to this, Beethoven required an instrument that would be even more sturdy than those he needed at the beginning of his career, because in his efforts to make his own playing audible to himself, he played with ever-increasing force on his instruments. The result of this can be seen in Beethoven's letter to Streicher in 1810, pleading with him to construct instruments that would not wear out so quickly.

Although Beethoven was certainly a special case, he was not the only musician asking Streicher for a sturdier, more powerful instrument. **Muzio Clementi**, among others, wanted to see the Viennese piano evolve in a direction that would make it more closely resemble the English piano, with its fuller tone and deeper, heavier action. Streicher at first resisted this notion mightily, as shown by a letter he wrote to Härtel (of the firm Breitkopf und Härtel, agents for Streicher's pianos) dated 1805. However by 1809 Johann Friedrich Reichardt was able to report significant changes in the way Streicher was manufacturing his instruments.

Streicher has left the soft, the yielding too easily, and the bouncing rolling of the older Viennese instruments, and — upon Beethoven's advice and request — has given his instruments more resistance and elasticity so that the virtuoso who performs with strength and significance has power over the instrument. . . . Through this [change] he has given his instruments a greater and more diverse character so that more than any other instruments they will satisfy the virtuoso who seeks more than easy glitter in performance.

Although the evidence of the surviving instruments is not so unequivocal, here is contemporary evidence that Beethoven had an influence upon what was to be the future course of piano manufacture.

Beethoven apparently never owned an instrument by Streicher, but would simply ask to borrow one when he needed it for use in a concert. In any case, Streicher was not the only Viennese builder with whom Beethoven had dealings. Early in his career he owned a piano by **Anton Walter**, upon which Carl Czerny played in 1801 at the age of ten, later calling it one of "the best ones made then." Beethoven was very interested in Walter's instruments, and wanted Walter to make for him a piano with an *una corda* stop, which was not available on Viennese pianos at that time. The letter of 1802 in which Beethoven expresses this request warrants quoting, for it shows Beethoven's influence and following among contemporary piano manufacturers, as well as his high opinion of Walter.

Well, my dear Zmeskall, you may give Walter, if you like, a strong dose of my affair. For, in the first place, he deserves it in any case; and what is more, since the time when people began to think that my relations with Walter were strained, the whole tribe of pianoforte manufacturers have been swarming around me in their anxiety to serve me — and all for nothing. Each of them wants to make me a pianoforte exactly as I should like it. For instance, Reicha has been earnestly requested by the maker of one of his pianofortes to persuade me to let him make me one; and he is one of the more reliable ones, at whose firm I have already seen some good instruments — so you may give Walter to understand that, although I can have pianofortes for nothing from all the others, I will pay him 30 ducats. . . . Furthermore, I want a stop built into it to give one string only [i.e., *una corda*] . . . .

Walter, unfortunately, was unable to comply with Beethoven's request on this occasion.

The other Viennese builder with whom Beethoven had a significant relationship was Conrad Graf. In 1825 Graf built Beethoven a special grand that was intended to compensate for the composer's deafness, insofar as this was possible. The instrument, now in the Beethovenhaus in Bonn, was provided with supplementary stringing throughout: trichord from CC to C#, and quadruple from D to f⁴, as well as fitted with a special resonator. Unfortunately, even such extraordinary measures failed to surmount the master's infirmity.

Viennese instruments were not the only ones associated with Beethoven's career. In 1803 he was presented with "un piano forme clavecin" by the well-known Parisian maker Sébastien Erard, a piano with a compass of five-and-a-half octaves (FF to c⁴). This instrument boasted four **pedals**, including the *una corda* that Beethoven had vainly requested of Walter the year before, as well as lute stop, damper, and *sourdine*. The **English-type action** with which this piano was equipped would have been heavier and deeper than the light, shallow, responsive touch of the Viennese grands to which Beethoven was accustomed. Nonetheless he evidently gave the instrument considerable usage, since by 1810 he wrote to Streicher asking for a new piano, his French piano no longer being of any use. On the other hand, it is possible that from the beginning Beethoven may never really have liked playing on the Erard. According to Streicher, "up to now he still is not able to manage his fortepiano received from Erard in Paris, and has already had it changed twice without making it the least bit better." Whether this judgment stemmed from professional jealousy at seeing his friend using the instrument of a foreign rival builder, or whether it was based on reasoned observation, remains an open question.

The other foreign instrument owned by Beethoven was a Broadwood, given to him in 1818 by Thomas Broadwood, head of the firm of **John Broadwood and Sons**, London, and having a range of six octaves (CC to c⁴). Beethoven was extremely susceptible to the honor of receiving this instrument, which had his name inscribed on a special plaque, and he wrote an effusive letter of thanks to Broadwood in which he stated, "I shall look upon it as an altar on which I shall place the most beautiful offerings of my spirit to the divine Apollo." Beethoven often showed off his Broadwood to visitors, pointing out the beauty of its **case** and lovely **tone**.

Beethoven both used and abused his Broadwood; at this advanced stage of his deafness he would have had to pound it mercilessly to hear anything at all. A visit in 1824 by the harp-maker Johann Andreas Stumpff produced a horrified report: "The upper registers are quite mute, and the broken strings in a tangle, like a thornbush whipped up by a storm." Ignaz Moscheles had borrowed the piano in late 1823 for a concert at the Kartnerthor Theater, when the piano was already seriously damaged; he used it alternately with a Graf, intending to show the good qualities of both instruments. Graf himself had done some restoration on the Broadwood, but this effected at best a partial improvement, and the Viennese public remained loyal to the local product.

The issue of whether Beethoven preferred Viennese pianos or his Broadwood deserves to be considered, in assessing his impact on piano manufacture. Most writers on the subject have attempted to show either that it was English pianos in general, with their fuller tone and deeper action, and the Broadwood in particular, that really corresponded to Beethoven's inner idea of what a piano ought to be, or, conversely, that the Broadwood represented to Beethoven at most a prestigious gift, and that the true vehicle of his musical thought remained the Viennese piano.

Neither argument is totally free of logical objections. Beethoven indeed was constantly searching for a more resilient instrument and, after the onset of his deafness, a louder one. The Broadwood certainly fulfilled at least some of these requirements. On the other hand, by 1810 the Streichers, by their modifications in construction, had also achieved some of the same results. Tragically, in his later years Beethoven was incapable of assessing accurately the tonal qualities of *any* instrument.

Beethoven's early success as a pianist was achieved on Viennese grands, and it was precisely during this period that he best heard the sounds he was actually writing. The first twenty sonatas (up to opus 53) were written within the five-octave compass of the Stein or Walter fortepiano, and performances on modern replicas or restored originals have shown the great beauty of this repertoire played on the appropriate instrument.

Beethoven's Broadwood arrived late in his life, after he had ceased performing on the piano in public and when only the last three of the thirty-two piano sonatas remained to be written. It is ironic that whatever its other qualities, the Broadwood proved no more resistant to Beethoven's heavy-handed onslaughts than previous pianos he had used. The main point is that Beethoven, a pragmatic man, had naturally been happy to receive a gift from Broadwood in 1818, as he had from Erard in 1803. For his ongoing needs, however, he could not possibly count on foreign builders. For this he had to remain in close contact with Viennese manufacturers, and he did precisely that.

Whichever type of instrument Beethoven may actually have preferred, his relationship to the piano must always be viewed with a certain degree of reserve. For him, the music, not the instrument, was at the center of his concern, and virtuosic display for its own sake was anathema. His frustration with the limitations of the piano is expressed in his statement in 1826, the year before his death, that the piano "is and remains an inadequate instrument."

Despite this frustration, Beethoven's impact on piano manufacture is undeniable. His career was part of a trend towards more public concerts, taking place in larger halls, for which more powerful pianos would be necessary. The piano during Beethoven's lifetime made considerable strides in the direction of what it eventually became.

Seth A. Carlin

Bibliography

Anderson, Emily, ed. *The Letters of Beethoven* 3 vols. New York: St. Martin's Press, 1961.

Clemen, Otto. "Andreas Streicher in Wien." [Andreas Streicher in Vienna] *Neues Beethoven-Jahrbuch* 4 (1930): 107–17.

Czerny, Carl. *On the Proper Performance of All Beethoven's Works for Piano.* London, 1839; Vienna, 1842. Reprint. Edited by P. Badura-Skoda. Vienna: Universal Edition, 1970.

———. "Recollections from my Life." Translated by Ernest Sanders from "Erinnerungen aus meinem Leben." *The Musical Quarterly* 42,3 (July 1956): 302–17.

Drake, Kenneth. *The Sonatas of Beethoven as He Played and Taught Them.* Edited by F. Stillings. Cincinnati: Music Teacher's National Association, 1972.

Forbes, Elliot, ed. *Thayer's Life of Beethoven.* Princeton: Princeton University Press, 1964.

Frimmel, Theodor von. "Von Beethovens Klavieren." [On Beethoven's Pianos] *Die Musik* 2,3 ([n.d.] 1903): 83–91.

Lutge, William. "Andreas und Nannette Streicher." *Der Bar (Jahrbuch von Breitkopf & Härtel)* 4 (1927): 53–69.

Melville, Derek. "Beethoven's Pianos." In *The Beethoven Reader.* Edited by D. Arnold and N. Fortune. New York: Norton, 1971.

Newman, William S. "Beethoven's Pianos Versus His Piano Ideals." *Journal of the American Musicological Society* 23,3 (Fall 1970): 484–504.

———. *Performance Practices in Beethoven's Piano Sonatas.* New York: Norton, 1971.

Sakka, Keisei. "Beethovens Klaviere — Der Klavierbau und Beethovens künstlerische Reaktion." [Beethoven's Pianos–Piano Construction and Beethoven's Artistic Reaction.] In *Colloquium Amicorum—Joseph Schmidt-Gorg zum 70. Geburtstag* [70th birthday offering to Joseph Schmidt-Gorg]. Edited by S. Kross and H. Schmidt. Bonn: Beethovenhaus, 1967: 327–37.

Schindler, Anton Felix. *Beethoven As I Knew Him.* Edited by D. MacArdle; translated by C. Jolly. Chapel Hill: The University of North Carolina Press, 1966.

Sonneck, O. G. *Beethoven: Impressions by his Contemporaries.* G. Schirmer, 1926. Reprint. New York: Dover, 1967.

BEHRENT, JOHN (FL. 1775)

John Behrent was the first builder of a piano in North America. The earliest pianos on this continent were probably small **square pianos** sent from England. A notice in the 7 March 1771 *Massachusetts Gazette* of a concert in Boston is the first record of the presence of a piano in the British Colonies. Newspaper reports from New York, Baltimore, and Philadelphia mentioned the presence of pianos in these cities soon afterward.

The first record of an American-made piano is the 1775 advertisement by John Behrent of "Third and Green Streets" offering "an extraordinary instrument by the name of piano-forte, in mahogany in the manner of the harpsichord." Since the instrument was a wing-shaped **grand piano**, it is likely that Behrent came from Germany, where grands were more common than in England; at this time few grands had yet been built in England. There is no further information on Behrent, whose piano-building evidently was halted by the start of the Revolutionary War later in 1775.

Jack Greenfield

Bibliography

Spillane, Daniel. *History of the American Pianoforte: Its Technical Development and the Trade.* New York: Da Capo Press, 1969. D. Spillane, 1890. Reprint. New York: DaCapo Pres, 1969.

BELGIUM, PIANO INDUSTRY IN

See Low Countries, Piano Industry in.

BELLYING

One of the most interesting terms used in the nomenclature of piano technology is that of the "belly." Anatomical designations for the various parts of constructed items, be they pianos or furniture, tend to surface (often unofficially) where the builder's involvement is personal and artistic. Probably borrowed from the violin maker's vernacular, the term "belly" refers to the **soundboard**, although the more complete system comprising the soundboard, **bridges**, and **rim** (or liner) has also been referred to as such. It is thought that the rounded and crowned shape of violin and piano soundboards suggested early on the appropriateness of the name belly. But beyond that, there is conjured up in the analogy the idea of the visceral — the guts, the deep seat of emotion, that boils and springs from the belly and nowhere else.

As a construction term, "bellying" refers to the process of building and crowning the soundboard, attaching bridges and other accouterments, fixing the soundboard assembly to the rim (or back, or liner), and finally, adjusting the cast-iron **plate** for proper **string** bearing. In the early days of piano making, and up through the early decades of the 1900s, the people who accomplished this work were called bellymen, and the equipment they used enjoyed kinship terms such as belly-jigs and bellying press. Although belly-related terms are still in use today, they are not as prevalent as in days past.

Nicholas Gravagne

BENTSIDE

The bentside of a **grand piano case** is on the right or treble side of the instrument when facing the **keyboard**. This graceful feature of both the grand piano and harpsichord design is a result of treble **strings** being shorter than the bass strings that run along the **spine**, or opposite side.

See also Spine.

Peggy Flanagan Baird

BEYER, ADAM (FL. 1774–1795)

Adam Beyer was one of the so-called **Twelve** **Apostles** and is considered to be one of the earliest inventors of the **upright piano action**. The Handel-Haus Collection in Halle claims that one of its instruments, a **square** by Adam Beyer of London dated 1777, is the earliest known piano provided with a **damper pedal**, although a London-made **grand** dated 1772 and made by Beyer's fellow "apostle" **Americus Backers** has what is thought to be the original pedal. Beyer's instrument certainly exhibits the earliest use of iron gap stretchers. In Rosamond E. M. Harding (p.387), this maker is listed as Adam Bleyer, Compton Street, Soho, fl.1774. This seems to be a confusion with a Viennese maker of the name Bleyer who is cited by Ernest Closson (p.105) as one of the early inventors of the upright piano action.

Arthur W.J.G. Ord-Hume

Bibliography

Closson, Ernest. *History of the Piano*. Translated by Delano Ames. London: Paul Elek, 1947. 1st ed. (*Histoire du piano*. Elek, London, n.d. [1973]. Bruxelles: Editions Universitaires, c.1944. 2nd ed., rev. and ed. by Robert Golding. London: Paul Elek, 1974.)

Good, Edwin Marshall. *Giraffes, Black Dragons, and Other Pianos: A Technological History from Cristofori to the Modern Concert Grand*. Stanford, Cal.: Stanford University Press, 1982.

Harding, Rosamond E.M. *The Piano-Forte: Its History Traced to the Great Exhibition of 1851*. Cambridge: Cambridge University Press, 1933. Reprints. New York: Da Capo Press, 1973; Old Woking, Surrey: Gresham Books, 1978.

Sasse, K. "Halle an der Salle." In *Katalog . . . des Handel-hauses in Halle*, Pt. 5. 1965: 139.

BLÜTHNER

Blüthner is a German piano-building company founded by Julius Blüthner, who was born in Falkenhain on 11 March 1824 and died on 13 April 1910 in Leipzig. Blüthner founded his own Leipzig-based firm in 1853, after having worked for the piano builders Hölling and Spangenberg. Just one year later his "repetition action" was patented. At first he built only **grand pianos**, by arrangement with the Feurich piano company (also of Leipzig) but from 1864 on, he also produced **upright pianos**.

In 1873 Blüthner obtained a **patent** for **aliquot scaling**, which he had invented. The principle of aliquot scaling is based on the aural effect of an additional **string**, tuned an octave higher, that is caused to vibrate by the vibrations of the other strings without being struck itself. Aliquot scaling produces a sound rich in overtones.

The first sales agency for the firm was founded in London in 1876. Blüthner's sons Max, Robert, and Bruno continued to run the firm and expanded it until World War II, when almost the entire company was destroyed. Later, the firm was rebuilt and expanded by Rudolf Blüthner-Haessler. Under the GDR regime, the company was run as a "Volkseigener Betrieb" [company owned by the people], which caused considerable organizational problems but no loss of quality, as the pianos are still largely hand-crafted. Since 1989 the firm has been run by the founder's great-great-grandson.

Jan Rademacher
Translated by Sandra Lustig

Bibliography

Blüthner, Julius Ferdinand, and Heinrich Gretschel. *Lehrbuch des Pianofortebaus in seiner Geschichte*. . . . Weimar: Bernhard Friedrich Voigt, 1872.

BÖHM (BOEHM), JOSEPH (1786–C.1850)

Joseph Böhm was a piano builder and a distinguished member of the Piano Builders Guild in Vienna. On 6 July 1821 he was granted citizenship rights of the City of Vienna, where his workshop was located at Mariahilf Nr.77. In 1835 he was named *Zweiter Repräsentant* of the Viennese Piano Builders Guild, and in 1836 he became *Vorsteher* [chairman or president]. Böhm was given the distinctive title of *Kaiserlich und Königlicher Hoff Kammer Klaviermacher* in Vienna.

Böhm invented a **transposing keyboard** that allowed a transposition shift over four-and-a-half tones, for which he received an Austrian **patent** in October 1823 (*Wiener Zeitung*, June 1823). **Beethoven** expressed interest in the transposing mechanism, according to a dialogue recorded in Volume 3 of his conversation books. Böhm also invented a mechanical page-turning device. In 1837 he was granted an Austrian patent for an instrument with a **pedal** keyboard of twenty-two keys connected to the ordinary finger **keyboard** by rods or trackers, making special **stringing** unnecessary, also

adding a five-and-a-half octave flute register. The instrument could be played as an organ, as a piano, or both.

Among his friends were the pianists Antonio Salieri, Adelbert Gyrowetz, and Joseph Weigl, all of whom played his pianos. Judging from several ornately decorated instruments and his use of fine woods, Böhm attracted a wealthy, aristocratic clientele. About sixteen Böhm pianos are known to exist in various collections. The Metropolitan Museum of Art in New York City owns a Böhm piano from about 1820, which is said to have belonged to Empress Marie Louise, Grand Duchess of Parma. Other Böhm pianos are found in the collection of Rien Hasselaar (Amsterdam), the collection of Georg Demus (Vienna), and the Böhm-Kooper collection in New York City. Of these only the piano in the Böhm-Kooper collection (built 1825, six-octave compass) has the original seven **pedals**: *una corda*, bassoon, **moderator** or mute, double moderator, sustaining, treble sustaining only, and "Turkish" (drum and bells). The pedals can be used in various combinations, resulting in more than a dozen different effects. Böhm-type Viennese pianos with five to seven pedals were built only from about 1815 to 1830. The pianos made by Joseph Böhm in the 1820s mark the highpoint of a trend, begun in the eighteenth century, to build pianos capable of producing a variety of different sonorities and tonal colors.

Mary Louise Boehm

Bibliography

Anderson, Emily. *The Letters of Beethoven*. New York: St. Martin's Press, 1961.

Beethovens Konversations. Vol.3. Leipzig, 1983: 331, 483.

Harding, Rosamond E.M. *The Piano-Forte: Its History Traced to the Great Exhibition of 1851*. Cambridge: Cambridge University Press, 1933. Reprints. New York: Da Capo Press, 1973; Old Woking, Surrey: Gresham Books, 1978.

Haupt, Helga. "Wiener Instrumentenbauer von 1791 bis 1813." *Studien zur Musikwissenschaft* 24 (1960).

Libin, Laurence. *Keynotes: Two Centuries of Piano Design*. New York: The Metropolitan Museum of Art (Exhibition Catalogues, Robert Ward Johnson, Jr.), 1985.

———. "Keyboard Instruments." *The Metropolitan Museum of Art Bulletin* 47 (Summer 1989).

The *New Grove Dictionary of Musical Instruments*. Edited by Stanley Sadie. London: Macmillan; Washington, D.C.: Grove's Dictionaries, 1984.

Ottner, Helmut. *Der Wiener Instrumentenbauer, 1815–1833*. Tutzing: Verlegt Bei Hans Schneider, 1977.

BÖSENDORFER

The Bösendorfer piano is usually identified as the piano with the extra keys in the bass end of the **keyboard**; it has also been one of the most distinguished and sought after instruments for a period of over 160 years.

After the death of Vienna's most successful early nineteenth-century piano maker, **Josef Brodmann**, his young apprentice, Ignaz Bösendorfer (1794–1859) took direction of the company. Tax records show that in 1828 Bösendorfer was granted a permit to start his own piano business. (This predates by twenty-five years the beginnings of the **Bechstein**, **Blüthner**, and **Steinway** piano companies.)

During its early years of piano manufacturing, the quality of the Bösendorfer piano was such that it earned gold medals and honors at the Vienna industrial exhibits of 1839 and 1845. Moreover, Emperor Ferdinand I of Austria in 1839 bestowed on Ignaz the title of "Piano Maker Appointed to the Royal and Imperial Court."

It was not long until concert pianists discovered the excellence of the instrument. **Franz Liszt**, who was known to have performed concerts on not only one, but a number of contemporary pianos, and who was known to have inflicted damage on an equal number of them with his sheer physical strength, performed on a Bösendorfer **grand piano** to great success. The fact that the piano was left intact at the close of one of the master's concerts served to enhance the Bösendorfer reputation and began a close personal relationship between Liszt and Ignaz Bösendorfer. After the death of Ignaz, his son, Ludwig (1835–1919), who worked in his father's workshop, took over management of the company.

Both Ignaz and his son were in an uncommon position, historically. Musical classicism was giving way to the romantic movement, Vienna was still the place to be as a composer, and, most significantly, the piano was to become the most popular instrument in both the concert hall and home. Thus, in 1860 Ludwig opened a new and larger factory and ten years later moved again to another location.

In 1872 Bösendorfer inaugurated a 200-seat concert hall adjacent to his new offices and salesrooms. The Bösendorfer-Saal, formerly a riding academy, was chosen by Ludwig himself because of its excellent acoustical qualities. It soon became the most popular concert hall in Vienna until it was closed in 1913. Among the scores of artists who performed in the hall were Ferrucio Busoni, Anton Rubinstein, Edvard Grieg, Ossip Gabrilowitsch, and Theodor Leschetitzky.

Ludwig not only managed his concert hall, but he also continually strove to improve his pianos (he was credited with having **patented** an improved piano **action**). The addition of extra **keys** was the result of an experiment with Busoni to reproduce the sound of a thirty-two-foot organ pipe on the pianos for Busoni's transcriptions of **Johann Sebastian Bach's** works. After Bösendorfer saw how this extension enriched the character of the rest of the piano, he put the design into production.

The "House of Bösendorfer" was prominently represented in the international **exhibitions** of London, Paris, and Vienna, and its pianos continued to be awarded the highest prizes. Ludwig Bösendorfer often accompanied Liszt and Anton Rubinstein on their concert tours, bringing along the necessary **concert grands**. He was one of the most colorful and respected figures in Vienna, and his love for horses was well known. In 1909 Ludwig sold the firm to his friend Carl Hutterstrasser. In 1919 Ludwig Bösendorfer died; he was twice married and left no heirs.

Hutterstrasser was obliged to experience World War I and its aftermath. During that period he wrote, with understatement, that it was not a pleasure to be a piano manufacturer. Particularly distressing was the deflation of the Austrian crown. In 1913, production went from over 434 pianos to 136 within a year. Between 1919 and 1929, yearly piano production rose again, from 250 to 310 pianos. It was in 1927 that the Bösendorfer name was honored with a Grand-Prix at the International Music Exhibition in Geneva.

The extension of the bass portion of the keyboard in 1891 was first applied to the Model 275, built to include four extra keys at the lowest end of the keyboard (ninety-two keys in all). In 1904, the largest grand piano built, the Model 290, Imperial, had a range of eight full octaves, with nine extra keys at the lowest end (ninety-seven keys in all). In length, the Model

275 was nine feet long, and the model 290, nine feet, six inches. There was also a seven-foot, four-inch Model 225—Halbkonzertflügel [half concert grand]—that was constructed using the four extra keys.

In the beginning, the company employed the lighter Viennese action. By the end of the nineteenth century, pianos with both the Viennese and **English actions** were constructed. When, during the first decade of the twentieth century, the general taste turned in favor of quicker key repetition, Bösendorfer built pianos with only the English action. In 1966 the company was taken over by the Jasper Corporation, a firm that also makes low-priced pianos under the **Kimball** name. At the present time, Kimball makes smaller grand pianos, the Models 170 and 200, and builds two **upright** pianos, Models 120 and 130, each in two cabinet styles.

A most recent development is the Bösendorfer Model 290-SE Computer-Based Piano Performance Reproducing System. This piano, an Imperial model, is essentially a very accurate **reproducing** instrument—**player piano**—that, by means of computer **electronics**, reproduces faithfully anything played on the keyboard. The solenoids that are placed beneath the key shaft nearest the hammer digitally register the slightest finger pressure, thereby "recording" on computer disk every nuance of a performance. The ability to edit, speed up, or slow down a performance is easily accomplished (and without change in pitch).

As indicated, Bösendorfer has kept pace with other piano makers in looking to the future; companies that do not realize the importance of adjusting to newer tastes do not survive. Bösendorfer remains an honored and respected instrument, sought after by classical and popular musicians alike.

Frederic Schoettler

Bibliography

Bösendorfer. Vienna: Gutenberg Ges. m.b.H., n.d.

Fine, Larry. *The Piano Book.* Boston: Brookside Press, 1987.

Good, Edwin M. *Giraffes, Black Dragons, and Other Pianos.* Stanford, Cal.: Stanford University Press, 1982.

The New Grove Dictionary of Music and Musicians. Sixth edition. Vol. 2. Edited by Stanley Sadie. London: Macmillan, 1980.

Robert, Walter. *One Hundred Years "Bösendorfer" 1828–1928.* Unpublished monograph.

BOUDOIR GRAND

A boudoir grand is a six- or seven-foot **grand piano** commonly found in a reasonably sized room of a home. The name is a nineteenth-century term, the boudoir being a private room in which a lady received intimate friends.
See Grand Piano.

Camilla Cai

BRACES

Braces form the structural support of the piano. Even early pianos with their thinner **strings** required a significant amount of wood (and sometimes metal) bracing to prevent the **case** from buckling under the string tension. With the invention of the cast-iron **plate** in the early nineteenth century, bracing was reduced considerably and heavier strings could be used.
See also Frame.

Philip Jamison, III

BRAHMS, JOHANNES (1833–1897)

Johannes Brahms owned only two pianos in his lifetime, first a **Graf** and then a **Streicher**. The 1839 Graf, which had been **Robert Schumann's** piano, was a gift from **Clara** Schumann after Robert's death in 1856. It had **leather**-covered **hammers**, single-escapement Viennese **action**, a wooden **frame**, and a range of six octaves and a fifth (CC–g^4), not sufficient for Brahms's Piano Concerto No. 1, Opus 15 (1854–58) or his Variations on a Theme by Paganini, Opus 35 (1862–63). The piano was moved first to his parents' home in Hamburg, then to the home of Frau Dr. Elisabeth Rösing, where Brahms stayed in 1861–62 and composed the Variations and Fugue on a Theme by Händel, Opus 24. The piano remained in Hamburg when he moved on. Brahms discussed its disposition in a letter to Clara in 1868, indicating that he had not had it with him in a long time. Brahms was no longer interested in having it as his house piano and thought of it only as a sentimental item. When the Graf was finally brought to Vienna, Brahms exhibited it in 1873 at the Vienna Exposition and then donated it to the Gesellschaft der Musikfreunde in Vienna. From there it travelled with their collection of instruments to the Kunsthistorisches Museum, Vienna, where it is today in poor condition.

In 1873 Brahms received an 1868 Streicher **grand** (no. 6713) as a gift from the company. Photographs exist of this piano in Brahms's apartment, covered with a cloth cover, piled with objects and music. He kept this piano as his studio instrument until his death in 1897. This Streicher had a frame that consisted of two cast-iron tension bars bolted to the metal string **plate**. This partial metal frame supported a straight-strung mechanism and the **soundboard**. The piano had a single-escapement Viennese action with soft, leather-covered hammers. Its range, AAA–a^4, would not have been limiting to Brahms, although his Opus 118, no. 1, does use the AAA. The piano was destroyed in World War II.

As a student and in his early concertizing, Brahms used a Baumgardten & Heins, a local make from Hamburg. He practiced in their establishment, and his first performance of the Opus 15 Piano Concerto in Hamburg (1858) was on their piano. Later he either rented or borrowed pianos when he stayed in one place for any length of time.

On his concert tours he played many different makes. In 1867 he used a Streicher in Graz (Nov. 11) and three days later in the same hall, a **Bösendorfer** (Nov. 14). On his later travels he played **Bechsteins**, **Blüthners**, and Steinweg Nachfolgerns most frequently. He also came to know the American **Steinway** and **Knabe**. Lesser-known pianos, Trau, **Ibach**, Lipp, and Jacobi, were pianos he played in other cities and towns. Brahms wrote positive comments about the German Bechstein, the American Steinway, the Austrian Bösendorfer, and the Swiss Jacobi. Although he played most often on German and Austrian pianos, because he travelled mainly in those areas, he also knew the French **Erard**. He had played an Erard as well as an English **Broadwood** at Clara Schumann's home.

Brahms's letters and communications suggest that he had his strongest leanings toward the conservative pianos of his day: the straight-strung, Viennese-action Streichers, Bösendorfers, and similar Viennese instruments. Brahms performed frequently at the J. B. Streicher Salon in his early years in Vienna (from 1862). In 1864 he told Clara Schumann, "I have a beautiful grand from Streicher [to practice on]. He [Streicher] wanted to share [his]

new achievements with me. . . ." (Litzmann, III, 167–68). In other concerts around Vienna, Brahms regularly chose Streichers as late as the spring of 1869; Brahms's last solo public performance on a Streicher seems to have been 29 November 1874, but he accompanied in public using a Streicher as late as 18 November 1880, when he played with the Hellmesberger Quartet.

Brahms performed on Bösendorfers as early as 1862, but only after 1880 did he change his public allegiance to them, possibly because Bösendorfer had taken control of the Viennese piano market by then, opening a new Bösendorfer-Saal in 1872. Viennese concert programs do not mention that Brahms played public concerts on other Viennese pianos, but he knew **Ehrbar** pianos well because he played many private recitals at their salon. He thought highly of the Viennese **Schweighofer**. His private devotion, however, remained with the Streicher, as witnessed by his retaining in his apartment until his death the conservative, straight-strung, Viennese-action Streicher.

One of the distinctive features of conservative nineteenth-century pianos (using Brahms's 1868 Streicher as the model) can be traced in Brahms's music in his exploitation of its three contrasting registers: treble, middle, and bass. Each register has a clear and separate sound quality or timbre, a feature in marked contrast to the prized even timbre of the modern piano. The distinctive middle range—around and below middle c^1—sounds full and mellow, and it can easily dominate both the treble and bass ranges. The separation of registral texture is apparent in Brahms's music in his frequent use of tenor melodies and in his balance of the voices. For example, a Brahms melody placed in the middle range (the central sections of Opus 116, No. 7; Opus 118, No. 2; and elsewhere) stands out with no special effort by the pianist. It requires only the knowledge of where the melody line lies to carve out a place for it; the nature of the instrument's sound will support the melody.

The bass **strings** of a mid- to late-nineteenth-century Streicher (or other similar piano) produce a clear, light sound that resembles the timbre of instruments from the 1820s more than that of a modern piano. Few interfering overtones thicken the tone quality, and the bass notes, though initially forceful, have a very fast decay rate. The strings, therefore, produce a purer, softer sound than the modern piano. Because a tone fades quickly, its sound cannot run into the next tone. This allows the notes to be heard individually. The resulting openness for these low **pitches** creates an illusion of sustained, connected sound, yet the listener can clearly identify which pitches have been played.

Brahms's written music has to the modern eye an apparent thickness of texture in the lower ranges. Such low-range sonorities feature prominently in Opus 118, No. 5, or Opus 119, No. 4, where Brahms used the low-placed third in his chords. The modern concern that these notes might not be clearly heard did not exist for a conservative piano from the second half of the nineteenth century. These notes in the low range, clear in pitch and without interfering overtones, could be subtly balanced within the low-range texture. As a result, harmonic implications, melodic imitations, and other effects that Brahms placed in these low ranges stand out in sharp relief. In Opus 118, No. 6 the low-range pitches that accompany the opening melody convey not an undifferentiated wash of sound, but rather are notes that stand out individually as unusual and well-balanced parts of the texture.

The conservative nineteenth-century pianos, with their clear, sweet, yet sustaining sound in the bass register, suggest that normal pedalling in Brahms's music, at both its best and worst, could be less than what the average twentieth-century pianist applies today. (Brahms himself, however, was notoriously heavy-footed in his later years.)

Closely connected to the characteristics of the conservative piano of this period are issues of **touch** and articulation in Brahms's piano music. The Streicher as well as the Ehrbar and Bösendorfer continued to use the Viennese action well into the last quarter of the century. This design, different from the double-escapement repetition actions of English pianos, produces an especially crisp attack followed by immediate and very rapid decay. Because this action is of lighter weight than a modern repetition action, the **key** feels very responsive. Further, the shallow key depth requires only a very short finger stroke. For a *pianissimo* effect this stroke may seem to require extra pressure, but in fact any change in dynamics needs only a minute adjustment of pressure. Overall, the key action seems to require the fingers to move with small, quick, or delicate motions even for the most vigorous of effects.

Such a **keyboard** easily permits Brahms's wide range of touch strokes and it allows the performer to produce realistic, audible contrasts among them. Brahms indicates these various styles of playing in his scores with three words for different touches—*legato*, *leggiero*, and *marcato*—and two markings for different articulations—slurs and staccatos. His 51 Exercises (1893) were to be used as the training ground for these various effects in his piano pieces.

The dynamic range of the conservative Austrian or German piano was much smaller than that of a twentieth-century piano, yet even Brahms's monumental Piano Concerto No. 1 and his bravura Paganini Variations were performed on such pianos. In Brahms's late piano pieces, Opp. 116–119 (1892–93), he asks even less of the piano's dynamic range. His markings hover around a norm of *p*. The extremes of range move away from this quiet level only to *pp* and *ff* markings. This range will seem smaller yet when considered on the nineteenth-century conservative piano. Even the loudest of these pianos, the popular Bösendorfers of the 1880s and 1890s that came in various models—**overstrung** or parallel strings, **English** or Viennese **action**—had a sound that remained soft and transparent. These pianos made significantly less sound than a modern piano, though a bit more than Brahms's old-fashioned, straight-strung Streicher. Brahms's preference for a narrow written dynamic range and for the light Streicher sound would suggest that he worked within a dynamic sphere significantly smaller than that produced on a modern piano.

Each dynamic level on a conservative nineteenth-century piano displays a characteristic timbre and quality of tone, and therefore Brahms used these differing levels to coloristic effect. Opus 118, No. 6, particularly exploits this expressive capability. The cantus-firmus-like melody speaks with a new character each time it returns at a new dynamic level. In addition, the changing octave levels for this melody provide further expressive coloring because each register produces a distinctive timbre.

Camilla Cai

Bibliography

Biba, Otto. *Johannes Brahms in Wien.* Exhibit catalog. Vienna, 1983.

Bozarth, George. "Brahms's Pianos." *The American Brahms Society Newsletter* 6/2 (Autumn 1988): 1–7.

Cai, Camilla. "Brahms's Pianos and the Performance of His Late Piano Works." *Performance Practice Review* 2 (1989): 58–72.

———. "Brahms' Short, Late Piano Pieces, Opus Numbers 116-119: a Source Study, an Analysis and Performance Practice." Ph.D. dissertation, Boston University, 1986.

Collection of the Kunsthistorisches Museum, Vienna, Austria. *Katalog der Sammlung alter Musikinstrumente.* Part I: *Saitenklaviere.* Vienna, 1966. Reprint, 1978.

Edmund Michael Frederick and Patricia Frederick Collection, Ashburnham, Massachusetts. (Further information on this collection in Edmund M. Frederick, "The Big Bang." *The Piano Quarterly* 126 [Summer 1984]: 33; Michael Boriskin, "They Prefer Pianos to Furniture." *The Piano Quarterly* 130 [Summer 1985]: 41–43; Andrew Porter, "Musical Events." *The New Yorker* [October 26, 1981]: 182–85.)

Finson, Jon W. "Performing Practice in the Late Nineteenth Century, with Special Reference to the Music of Brahms." *Musical Quarterly* 70 (1984): 457–475.

Good, Edwin M. *Giraffes, Black Dragons, and Other Pianos.* Stanford, Cal.: Stanford University Press, 1982.

Kalbeck, Max. *Johannes Brahms.* Vol. 2. Berlin, 1912–21. Reprint. Tutzing, 1976.

Litzmann, Berthold. *Clara Schumann, Ein Künstlerleben: Nach Tagebüchern und Briefen.* 3 vols. Leipzig, 1902, 1905, 1908.

BREAK

The break is a notch or cut in the treble **bridge** to allow room for the **plate**. Unless carefully designed, the break can result in tonal irregularities.

Philip Jamison, III

BRIDGE

The bridge is a strip of wood, usually maple, used to transmit the vibrations of the **strings** to the **soundboard**. The modern piano generally has two bridges; one for the tenor and treble strings, and a shorter one for the bass strings. The separate bridge (first patented in 1828 by **Jean-Henri Pape**) allowed the bass strings to be strung diagonally across the tenor strings. Thus, longer bass strings could be used and the bridge could be more centrally located on the soundboard.

See Bridge Pin; Soundboard.

Philip Jamison, III

BRIDGE PIN

Bridge pin is the name given to metal pins driven into the **bridge** to align **strings** and allow for efficient transmission of string vibrations.

Philip Jamison, III

BRIDLE STRAP

Sometimes called the "bridle tape," this strip of cloth connects the **hammer** butt to the **wippen** in the vertical piano mechanism. Thus connected, the weight of the wippen speeds the rebounding of the hammer as well as holding the wippen in place when the mechanism is removed for repair.

See also Actions.

Philip Jamison, III

BRINSMEAD, JOHN (1814–1908)

John Brinsmead was born in Devonshire. Apprenticed to a cabinetmaker, he went to London at the age of twenty-one and worked as a journeyman in pianoforte **case**-making. Through frugal living, by 1836 he had saved enough capital to start up in business as a pianoforte maker, initially with his elder brother, Henry (d. 1880), on the top floor of 35 Windmill Street off Tottenham Court Road.

In 1841 he moved to Charlotte Street and, twenty-two years later, to Wigmore Street. Quickly renowned for his quality instruments, his success was sealed with the receipt of the French Legion of Honor award following the 1878 Paris Exhibition, at which his highly acclaimed instruments were shown.

He was granted numerous **patents** for improvements: one in 1879 was for a "perfect check repeater action providing increased durability and perfection of touch."

Meanwhile, his brother and former partner, Henry, was making pianos in Rathbone Place; John Brinsmead ultimately acquired this business.

In 1868 John Brinsmead's youngest son, Edgar (d. 1907), wrote his *History of the Pianoforte*, a once-popular book, which ran to several editions. After the death of John Brinsmead, the business was run by his oldest son, Thomas Brinsmead (d. 1906). A man who demonstrated both acute xenophobia and puritanical attitudes towards his workers, Thomas became a somewhat contentious figure in London's piano industry at the outbreak of World War I. Largely through his inflexibility the business suffered and, as with many industries at that time, sapped of its expert labor force and management vitality, it was unable to adjust to the fresh conditions of the postwar years. In January 1920, John Brinsmead & Company was declared bankrupt, and the remaining stock of unsold instruments was found to be very substandard. Cramer acquired the business for a mere 4,000 pounds and subsequently revitalized the company as John Brinsmead Ltd. (1921). Within five years it had recouped much of its onetime reputation for quality instruments and, in a deal with the American makers of the Angelus player action, it also made some good quality **player pianos**.

Brinsmead pianos were produced up to 1960, when the business was acquired by Kemble Pianos, now Yamaha-Kemble, where the name remains purely as a brand name.

Arthur W.J.G. Ord-Hume

Bibliography

Ehrlich, Cyril. *The Piano: A History*. London: J.M. Dent & Sons, Ltd., 1976.

Wainwright, David. *Broadwood by Appointment, a History*. London: Quiller, 1982; New York: Universe Books, 1983.

BROADWOOD & SONS, JOHN

John Broadwood & Sons is the oldest firm of keyboard instrument makers in existence. The founder, John Broadwood (1732–1812), was born in Oldhamstocks on the border of Berwickshire and East Lothian, Scotland, on 6 October 1732. His father was a joiner and cabinetmaker, and John Broadwood learned that trade from him.

At the age of twenty-nine, he decided to better himself with work in England and so travelled to London in 1761. Through family connections, he took with him a letter of introduction to **Burkat Shudi** from the local laird. By mid-September, he was working for Shudi and began making harpsichords with him at Great Pulteney Street. On 2 January 1769, when he was thirty-six, he married Shudi's second daughter, Barbara. She was one month short of her twenty-first birthday.

After their marriage, John Broadwood and his bride took over the premises in Great Pulteney Street and the mews workshops at the back in Bridle Lane. Meanwhile, Burkat Shudi and his family moved to their new house in Charlotte Street, off Tottenham Court Road. In the following year, Broadwood formally became Shudi's partner and remained so until Shudi's death in 1773, when he became associated with Burkat Shudi, Jr.

On 7 March 1771, Shudi, Sr., leased to John Broadwood the premises in Great Pulteney Street as well as the Bridle Lane mews. At the same time, he licensed his son-in-law to continue the Shudi business and to make use of the Venetian Swell, with Broadwood agreeing to pay a royalty to Shudi for each harpsichord sold. After Shudi's death, John Broadwood became head of the business.

Throughout the 1760s, while devoting his time to the business of harpsichord-building, John Broadwood was becoming increasingly more interested in the pianoforte. This interest was aroused by his fellow workman at Shudi's, **Johannes Zumpe**, and their mutual friendship with **William Stodart** and **Americus Backers**, the last-named being the developer of the **grand** pianoforte. The three men more or less together devised what became known as the "**English Grand Action.**" While Backers produced an instrument (which still survives) as early as 1772, it was not until 1777 that **Robert Stodart** took out the first **patent** in which the term "grand" was used in association with the pianoforte.

During this formative time in John Broadwood's career, on 8 July 1776 his wife, Barbara, died in childbirth, at age twenty-seven. In December 1781, John Broadwood took a second wife, twenty-nine-year-old Mary Kitson from Doncaster.

John Broadwood's son, James Shudi Broadwood (1772–1851), joined the business as a partner in 1795, the firm being renamed John Broadwood & Son. In 1807 he took his other son, Thomas Broadwood (1786–1861), into the partnership as well, the company name now becoming John Broadwood & Sons.

By 1783, Broadwood's records show that the pianoforte began to surpass the harpsichord in popularity; in the following year he sold 133 pianofortes and 38 harpsichords. Sometime around 1793, the business ceased making harpsichords altogether.

John Broadwood had begun to manufacture the so-called **square piano** around the mid-1770s, initially producing an instrument after the style of Johannes Christoph Zumpe, but in 1780 he produced a square piano of his own, which he patented three years later (British Patent No. 1379 of 18 July 1783). In this prototype he strengthened the instrument and discarded the old harpsichord/clavichord disposition of the wrest plank [**pinblock**] and **tuning pins**, moving the wrest pins from the **soundboard** to the left side of the back of the **case**. He also added a second soundboard beneath the main one, linking the two with soundposts so as to improve the **tone**.

With the assistance of the polymath Dr. Edward Whittaker Gray, who established that the tone of the piano improved if the **strings** were struck at a point that he established as being approximately one-ninth of their vibrating length, John Broadwood now set about redesigning the grand piano. His major improvement was to divide the **bridge**, introducing a separate bass bridge. This was in 1788. John Broadwood's divided bridge became common throughout the piano-making industry in the years that followed. The earliest known date of a Broadwood grand is 1781.

The rapidly expanding business of Broadwood demanded a larger manufacturing area, in particular now that the grand pianoforte was assuming greater importance. Although the former Shudi workshops had been enlarged with the creation of extra room in the Bridle Lane mews behind, additional space was urgently needed, so in March 1787 John Broadwood took a twenty-one-year lease on a house at 14 Kensington Gore.

The Bohemian pianist Jan Ladislav Dussek suggested to Broadwood that the grand pianoforte might be improved by adding a further half-octave in the treble, above the then-usual five-octave compass. By 1793 these "additional keys" were commonplace, and John Broadwood wrote to a customer that: "We now make most of the Grand Pianofortes in compass to CC in alt. We have made some so for these three years past, the first to please Dussek . . . and we have begun to make some of the small Pianofortes [i.e., square] up to that compass."

Broadwood then extended the **keyboard** compass yet further by adding another half-octave in the bass, a measure now possible thanks to the provision of the separate, special bass bridge. This brought the total compass of the pianoforte up to six octaves. The first full six-octave grand was made early in the summer of 1794.

The output of the Broadwood business was prodigious. Between the year 1780 and 30 September 1867, the house of Broadwood manufactured 135,344 pianofortes, of which 30,481 were grands. Of that total, 86,966 were made between 1826 and 1867. In the year beginning October 1867 (the firm's fiscal year) until 11 July 1868, not quite ten months, 1,570 pianofortes were made, of which 471 were grands.

In 1795, a grand pianoforte sold for 70 guineas (73.5 pounds), a square with additional keys at 27.5 guineas (27.5 pounds), a square with inlaid case 25 guineas (26.25 pounds), and the cheapest square at 20 guineas (21 pounds).

John Broadwood retired in 1811 and died the following year. His two sons, James Shudi and Thomas, now assumed control.

By 1823 the new premises were once again too small, and James Shudi Broadwood and Thomas Broadwood leased a factory in Horseferry Road, Westminster. At that time, Broadwood was experimenting with the introduction of metal to strengthen the **frame**. **William Allen**, a tuner employed by **William Stodart**, had devised a system of parallel metal tubes to stabilize tuning and patented it in 1820 (British Patent No. 4431 of 15 January 1820). Its main benefit was that it allowed greater tension to be put on the frame, thus permitting thicker and heavier strings. Broadwood had applied "tension bars" (meaning, surely, "compression" bars to resist the string tension) as early as 1808 and used from three to five bars in grand pianofortes in 1821 (the present author restored an 1823 five-bar Broadwood grand in 1972). Thus, Broadwood was the first maker to apply steel bars to resist the tension of the strings.

An employee, **Samuel Hervé**, made the first metal **hitch-pin plate** for a square pianoforte and these were used from 1822 onwards. From this point, James Shudi Broadwood made many systematic improvements to the metal bracing of the pianoforte as a prelude to the metal plate.

In 1821, **Sébastien Erard** patented the "Double **Escapement** Action" and this invention was tightly guarded by its inventor. Its undoubted advantage lay in the improved speed of repetition. On many occasions, Broadwood had supplied his pianos to the king and was thus a holder of the Royal Warrant as piano maker to the king. However, one of the new Erards was ordered by King George IV, and the coveted Royal Warrant entitling the holder to claim that he was the royal piano-maker passed from Broadwood to Erard; Broadwood was very upset over this loss of face.

Henry Fowler Broadwood (1811–1893), the son of James Shudi Broadwood (who died on 8 August 1851), was in charge of the business at the time of the company's second humiliation at the hands of the Erard firm: the granting of the Gold Medal for pianos to Erard in 1851 at the Great Exhibition in London. Faced with declining sales, Henry Fowler sought advice from a team of experts (which included Charles Hallé) as to the differences between Erard and Broadwood grand pianofortes.

Sales were soon boosted by the rising popularity of the **cottage upright**, while the old "wall-climbing" **cabinet** upright was phased out in 1856. On 12 August of that year, fire destroyed the Horseferry Road plant and with it almost 1,000 instruments, as well as the tools of the workmen. By a strange coincidence, it was three years earlier, to the very hour, that fire had destroyed the factory of Broadwood's rival, the **Kirkman** firm.

The square piano, challenged by the cheap **upright** now being produced in increasing quantities by many makers, was phased out in the summer of 1860, although further examples were made for export for a few more years. The last one was made in 1866.

The dismay following the 1851 Exhibition award to Erard was ameliorated with the award of the 1862 International Exhibition's Gold Medal to the Broadwood firm for its instruments.

During the last decade of the nineteenth century, the company's fortunes waned, through cheap competition in the marketplace. New types of pianos were introduced (the Pianette of 1896 was described as "now with the full iron frame. . .with overstrung scale"), as well as an **overstrung** grand that was six feet, four inches long, said to be the finest short Grand ever offered to the public." In addition, management weaknesses developed, and the market for Broadwood's quality grands disappeared by 1900. In 1901 the firm became a Limited Liability Company and built a new factory on the outskirts of London at Old Ford, Hackney.

Around 1904, the company began making **player pianos** and later developed their own model. Faced with producing a player action for their grand piano, they devised a unit valve system fixed beneath the piano frame and operated by wire trackers. Fortunately for the company, production of this was halted by the start of World War I. By 1915, the Old Ford factory had been partially cleared for aircraft production. Like most pianoforte makers during the war, their workers' skills at woodwork were applied to wooden aircraft construction. The De Havilland DH9A, complete with undercarriage and bomb cells, earned the company 125 pounds apiece. As the end of the war approached, Broadwood was once more profitable and solvent. With the end of hostilities, though, this lucrative contract-work suddenly ceased.

Player-piano production restarted, this time using proven and reliable actions licensed from other manufacturers. Between 1920 and the decline of the player-piano business in 1930, players represented almost one-third of the company's total piano output.

The business underwent further tribulations and at one time it was decided to scrap upright production and concentrate only on grands. However, following extensive restructuring, the company still survives, marking an unbroken record of 250 years of achievement, varying fortunes, and reputation.

Arthur W.J.G Ord-Hume

Bibliography

Grove Dictionary of Music & Musicians. 1st ed. Edited by Sir George Grove. London: Macmillan, 1879.

Harding, Rosamond E.M. *The Piano-Forte: Its History Traced to the Great Exhibition of 1851*. Cambridge: Cambridge University Press, 1933. Reprints. New York: Da Capo Press, 1973; Old Woking, Surrey: Gresham Books, 1978.

Ord-Hume, Arthur W.J.G. *Pianola—History & Development*. . . . London: Allen & Unwin, 1984.

Wainwright, David. *Broadwood by Appointment, a History*. London: Quiller, 1982; New York: Universe Books, 1983.

BRODMANN, JOSEPH (1771–1848)

Born in Eichswald (Prussia) in 1771, Joseph Brodmann in 1796 became a citizen of Vienna, where he was soon established as one of the leading piano makers. His work was favored by notable musicians, including Carl Maria von Weber, who in 1813 purchased a grand piano (now in the Berlin Musikinstrumenten-Museum collection, cat. no. 312). A number of piano makers, most significantly Ignaz Bösendorfer, were trained by Brodmann, who died in Vienna on 13 May 1848.

Brodmann's early **grand pianos** bear some resemblance to the five-octave instruments of the older Viennese maker **Ferdinand Hofmann** in incorporating characteristics of both the school of Johann Andreas **Stein** (e.g., the S-curved **bentside**) and that of **Anton Walter** (e.g., the use of metal *Kapseln* to hold the **hammers**). Later Brodmann grand pianos (of five-and-a-half, six, and six-and-a-half octave compasses) are distinctive in having **cases** shaped like those of a few Walter instruments of the 1780s, i.e., with bentsides having a gentle reverse curve leading to a square **tail**. Brodmann advertised or **patented** a number of improvements, including, about 1800, a version of the *Querflügel* (i.e., a small piano in the form of the obsolescent harpsichord-action bent-side spinet; the nature of his improvement of this then well-established type is obscure) and, in 1825, a laminated **soundboard**. A magnificent **pedal piano** made by Brodmann about 1815 (now at the Kunsthistorisches Museum in Vienna) consists of a grand piano (with compass CC to f⁴) resting on an independent pedalboard piano (with compass C to a at 16' pitch).

Brodmann's business was taken over by Bösendorfer in 1828, and inscriptions on Bösendorfer pianos of that year (in the Vienna and Yale University collections) note that he was "Brodmann's pupil" or that the firm was "formerly Brodmann." Thus, Brodmann (who, however, according to Ottner, himself remained active as a piano maker until 1832) may be regarded as the forebear of the great Viennese firm.

John Koster

Bibliography

Droysen, Dagmar, and Sabine Stahnke, eds. *Das Musikinstrumenten-Museum des Staatlichen Instituts für Musikforschung: eine Einführung.* Berlin: Staatliches Institut für Musikforschung Preussischer Kulturbesitz, 1978.

Haase, Gesine. "Hammerklaviere." In *Tasteninstrumente des Museums* by Gesine Haase and Dieter Krickeberg, Berlin: Staatliches Institut für Musikforschung, 1981: 71–117.

Haupt, Helga. "Wiener Instrumentenbauer von 1791 bis 1815." *Studien zur Musikwissenschaft, Beihefte der Denkmäler der Tonkunst in Österreich* 24 (1960): 120–184.

Hirt, Franz Josef. *Meisterwerke des Klavierbaus: Geschichte der Saitenklaviere von 1440 bis 1880.* Olten, Switzerland: Urs Graf-Verlag, 1955.

Luithlen, Victor, and Kurt Wegerer. *Katalog der Sammlung alter Musikinstrumente, 1. Teil: Saitenklaviere.* Vienna: Kunsthistorisches Museum, 1966.

Ottner, Helmut. *Der Wiener Instrumentenbau 1815–1833.* Wiener Veröffentlichungen zur Musikwissenschaft. Vol. 9. Tutzing: Hans Schneider, 1977.

Renouf, Nicholas. *Musical Instruments in the Viennese Tradition: 1750–1850* (exhibition catalog). New Haven: Yale University Collection of Musical Instruments, 1981.

Sachs, Curt. *Sammlung alter Musikinstrumente bei der Staatlichen Hochschule für Musik zu Berlin: beschreibender Katalog.* Berlin: Julius Bard, 1922.

BURGER & JACOBI

This company was one of Switzerland's most renowned piano manufacturers. Christian Burger (1842–1925), born in Emmenthal, began building pianos in Burgdorf, canton Bern, in 1870. He moved to Biel/Bienne in 1875, where he was joined by Hermann Emil Jacobi (b. 1852). Jacobi, then a trained piano maker, was the son of Heinrich Christian Jacobi (1817–1879). The senior Jacobi had emigrated from Germany and had worked with a number of different piano makers in Switzerland before establishing his own company in Thun. The earliest existing works by both Burger and the younger Jacobi are **upright pianos** with a vertically oriented string bed.

In 1882 the firm's name became Burger & Jacobi. The annual production of the first decade was doubled by 1900 to about 400. While many smaller firms in Zürich and Bern had not survived the turn of the century, Burger & Jacobi grew steadily. Their annual output almost doubled again in the early 1920s to about 740. However, the depression of the 1930s brought production down again to pre-1900 figures. During World War II, production never stopped, but at the end of the war the company was not able to take advantage of its lead over German firms. Only in the 1960s and early 1970s did the output reach numbers of the pre-depression period.

The Burger & Jacobi pianos have always had a very good reputation. In 1888 Brahms had praised their quality, and since then every Burger & Jacobi piano has carried a small plaque commemorating this fact. Customers were, and remain to a large extent, Swiss, known for their extremely critical nature.

The major production has consisted of upright pianos, and since 1971 no **grand pianos** have been built. Burger & Jacobi has faced more turbulent times than any piano firm in Switzerland. In 1975 a strike was settled by offering the workers an extra month's salary per year, a practice common in Switzerland. Increasing competition from abroad led in 1981 to lay-offs of workers and to short shifts. In 1986 the factory in Biel was closed and the company sold. Barely avoiding bankruptcy, production came to a halt in 1991.

Under the same roof with Burger & Jacobi was the Swiss piano-building school, Schweizerische Lehrstätte für Klavierbau, founded in 1973. Unique in Switzerland, this school was moved in 1986 to the piano manufacturing firm **Sabel** in Rorschach.

Werner Iten

Bibliography

H.R. Herzog, *Europe Piano Atlas: Das Musikinstrument.* 4th edition. Frankfurt am Main, 1978.

Rindlisbacher, Otto. *Das Klavier in der Schweiz.* Bern and Munich: Francke Verlag, 1972.

Schlegel, Maria. "Ein trauriges Ende." *BielBienne* (weekly magazine) 9/10 January 1991.

BURNEY, CHARLES (1726–1814)

Dr. Charles Burney is described in the *Dramatis Personae* preface of Percy Alfred Scholes's *The Great Dr. Burney* as "Harpsichordist, Organist, Composer and Historian of Music, Encylopaedist, Reviewer and Poet, European Traveller, Student of Astronomy, Society Man, and Man of Universal Interests." Somewhat surprisingly, he is not described as "pianist," though it may be that by the time Burney first owned such an instrument (probably by 1768 when he was forty-two) his ability as a performer was not as great as his former ability as a harpsichordist,

which in his twenties was considerable. Indeed it was as a result of this ability, coupled with his charm and general education, that he first stepped into the society of the rich and influential persons of the day, when in about 1746, at the age of twenty, he was introduced through intermediacy of the harpsichord maker **Jacob Kirkman** to Fulke Greville. The latter, styled as "the finest gentleman about town," had considerable wealth and invited Burney to become his personal musical tutor. Burney accepted and went with Greville to Wilbury House in Wiltshire, where his fortunes changed dramatically, his life becoming much more that of a man of leisure, than that of a scholar and musician. At Wilbury, Burney met Samuel Crisp, a man twenty years his senior, who was to remain a lifelong friend, and who, according to Burney, was the first to introduce the piano to England. Whether this can be believed is doubtful, and the date is uncertain, for Burney related the event in 1805 when writing the article on "Harpsichord" for Abraham Rees's *Cyclopedia.*

In the beginning of the last century, hammer harpsichords were invented at Florence, of which there is a description in the Giornale d'Italia, 1711. The invention made but a slow progress. The first that was brought to England was made by an English monk at Rome, Father Wood, for an English friend, the late Samuel Crisp, esq. of Chesington, author of Virginia, a Tragedy, and a man of learning, and of exquisite taste in all the fine arts.

The tone of this instrument was so superior to that produced by quills, with the additional power of producing all the shades of *piano* and *forte* by the fingers, that though the touch and mechanism were so imperfect that nothing quick could be executed upon it, yet the dead March in Saul, and other solemn and pathetic strains, when executed with taste and feeling by a master a little accustomed to the touch, excited equal wonder and delight to the hearers. Fulke Greville, esq., purchased this instrument of Mr Crisp for two guineas, and it remained *unique* in this country for several years, till Plenius (the maker of the lyrichord, tuned by weights, and the tone produced by wheels) made a pianoforte in imitation of that of Mr Greville. Of this instrument the touch was better, but the tone very much inferior.

The fact that Burney had at least one, and probably two or more pianos by 1771 shows that he was impressed with the instrument, and his daughter Fanny describes in her diary an informal musical party at the Burneys' house in Poland Street in 1768 at which

> Cerveto, who plays the base very finely, and his son, came in and, to grace the whole set Mr Crisp. We had a charming concert— Hetty [Fanny's sister] play'd the piano forte, and Charles the violin, the two Cervetos the base, and papa the organ . . . and my cousin [Charles] shone in a lesson of papa's on the harpsichord.

Burney's compositions, in addition to his writings, were numerous and varied, but it is noteworthy that in England he was a relatively early composer specifically for the piano. His first works for solo keyboard date from 1761 (Six Sonatas or Lessons for the Harpsichord) though others, using the harpsichord as continuo, date from as early as 1748. A further set of Six Sonatas for the Harpsichord followed in 1766. By about 1770, however, he had produced Two Sonatas for the Harpsichord or Forte Piano with Accompanyment for a Violin and Violoncello (extant versions survive in the British Library, and possibly in Berlin), and this is the first mention of the piano in his compositions, two years after he had acquired one himself.

In 1775, Burney met the noted inventor **John Joseph Merlin**, and within a short time he was a favorite visitor to Burney's house, being especially liked by the ladies. In 1777 Merlin completed the piano mentioned in Burney's will as:

> my large Piano Forte with additional keys at the top and bottom . . . made by Merlin, with a compass of six octaves . . . constructed especially at my desire for duets à Quatre Mains.

Several writers have suggested that the performance of duets at the piano with the old standard compass of five octaves was difficult, or even impractical for two ladies of the day wearing hooped skirts. Clearly Burney was interested in this form of music, for in the same year that he acquired the Merlin piano he wrote Four Sonatas or Duets for Two Performers upon One Piano Forte or Harpsichord, most probably for performance by the family; a second set appeared in 1778.

Whether he wrote the sonatas to encourage Merlin to produce the piano or he was inspired to write the duets after receiving the instrument is not known. However, none of the duets does actually require the six-octave compass of the piano, and it may therefore be more likely that

the compositions preceded the instrument, and that in any case Burney, who would have wished to see the music sell, felt that there was little point in writing music that could most probably have been performed on only one instrument in the kingdom, namely the one to be found in his own home.

Around 1780, three years after the extended piano arrived, an interesting Sonata à Trois Mains by Burney appeared, of which only one copy seems to have survived (in the Bodleian Library, Oxford) and which, while according to Scholes was "for Harpsichord," is quite clearly conceived as piano music. Certainly this is not impractical for two ladies, for the performer of the upper part has only one line to contend with, and this may (with some degree of dexterity) be performed with the left hand, or more practically by the "primo" performer standing and using the right hand. Scholes notes that it was thirteen years later, in 1790, that **Broadwood** "put on the market what is usually spoken of as the first piano of five and a half octaves," and it was not until 1794 that Broadwood produced one like Burney's with six octaves. It is surprising to note the tardiness with which Broadwood introduced the extended compass of the piano, since **Shudi**, his predecessor, had extended the compass of the harpsichord down by half an octave to CC, thus offering five-and-a-half octaves from as early as 1765.

Charles Mould

Bibliography

Boalch, Donald H. *Makers of the Harpsichord and Clavichord 1440–1840*. 3rd Edition. To be published by Oxford University Press. 2nd Edition. Oxford University Press, 1974.

John Joseph Merlin — The Ingenious Mechanick. Catalogue of an Exhibition held in 1985 at the Iveagh Bequest, Kenwood, Hampstead, London. GLC, London, 1985.

Scholes, Percy A. *The Great Dr. Burney*. 2 vol. Oxford: Oxford University Press, 1948.

BURNING SHANKS

Burning shanks is a term describing the process of heating and twisting piano **hammer** shanks in order to set the angle of the hammers in relation to the **strings** and to the neighboring hammers. The heat may be either a small flame or hot air from an electric heat gun, and must be applied carefully to avoid burning or scorching the wood shank.

Danny L. Boone

Bibliography

Vagias, E. "Burning Shanks?" *The Piano Technicians Journal* (February 1988): 17.

BUSHINGS

Bushings are the cushioning material (usually wool **felt**) used in piano **action** flanges and **keys** to assure silent operation.
See also Actions.

Philip Jamison, III

BUTT

The butt is the central part of the **hammer** mechanism in **upright piano actions**. Hinged upon the hammer flange, the butt (more properly called the "hammer butt") is moved forward by the **jack** and returned to its original position by the butt spring and **bridle strap**.
See also Actions.

Philip Jamison, III

CABINET PIANOFORTE

The Cabinet Pianoforte, also called "Cabinet Grand" and "**Upright** Grand Pianoforte," is a tall upright **grand piano**. Its upper **case** forms a cupboard; two or three shelves were placed to the right of the **strings**. The cabinet grand rests on its **keyboard** side: literally a grand placed on end. The instrument is then placed in this seemingly precarious position on a four-legged stand.

See also Upright Piano.

Martha Novak Clinkscale

CABLE-NELSON PIANO COMPANY

Cable-Nelson Piano Company was a major midwestern piano manufacturer. In 1903, Fayette S. Cable, the youngest of three brothers prominent in the industry, left the Cable Company, Chicago, Illinois, after purchasing the Lakeside Piano Company and E. Sweetland Company and combining them to form the Fayette S. Cable Company in South Haven, Michigan. The name was changed to Cable-Nelson Company when Nelson joined the firm in 1905. The firm manufactured **upright** and **player pianos**, ranking among the leaders in total sales during the 1920s.

In 1926, Cable-Nelson acquired the **Everett Piano Company** in Boston, closed the Boston factory and moved Everett production to South Haven. The South Haven firm then adopted the name of "The Everett Piano Company," although Cable-Nelson was kept as a label name.

Jack Greenfield

Bibliography

Dolge, Alfred. *Men Who Made Piano History*. Vestal, N. Y.: Vestal Press, 1980. Covina, Cal.: Covina Publishing Company, 1913.

"Everett Marks 100th with Townwide Celebration." *The Music Trades* (September 1983): 38.

Presto Buyers Guide to Pianos. Vestal, NY: Vestal Press reprint (undated) of 1926 Presto edition.

CANADA, PIANO MANUFACTURING IN

Piano manufacturing was a thriving industry in Canada during the period 1880–1920, at its peak employing about 5,000 people in more than 100 companies.

To meet the demand of the growing population, pianos were imported from Europe in the early nineteenth century. However, if they did not suffer in the long transport, they were often unable to withstand the variable Canadian climate. Skilled German and British immigrant craftsmen such as Frederick Hund (Quebec City, fl. 1816) and John Thomas (Montreal, fl. 1832; Toronto, fl. 1839) first operated repair businesses and then began constructing pianos in their small workshops at a rate of one or two per month. According to early census figures, there were seventeen piano builders in Canada, all in Montreal, Quebec City, or Toronto.

At the time of Confederation (1867) larger firms were being established (listed geographically, east to west) in Halifax (W. Fraser & Sons, c. 1856–c. 1890), Montreal (Craig Piano Co., 1856–1930), Kingston (John C. Fox, 1862–1868—later Weber, 1871–1939), Toronto (**Heintzman & Co.,** 1866–1986), Hamilton (Ennis Co., 1863–1911), Ingersoll, Ontario (Evans Bros., c. 1871–1933), and Victoria (John Bagnall, c. 1871–1885—later Charles Goodwin & Co. to 1891).

By the turn of the century most of the firms that existed throughout the history of Canada's piano industry were actively operating. Many of them had begun in the late nineteenth century as manufacturers of reed organs. As piano production was introduced, reed-organ building began to wane and ceased altogether with many companies in the first decade of the century. The major firms, in addition to some of those mentioned above, were in Montreal and vicinity: **Lesage Pianos**, 1891–1987; Pratte Piano Co., 1889–1926; Willis & Co., c. 1900–1979; Ottawa: Martin-Orme Co., 1902–c. 1924; Bowmanville, Ontario: Dominion Organ & Piano Co., 1879–c. 1935; Toronto: Gourlay, Winter & Leeming, 1904–1924; Gerhard

Heintzman, 1877–1927; Mason & Risch, 1877–c. 1970; Nordheimer Piano and Music Co., 1890–1927; R.S. Williams, 1873–1930s; Guelph: Bell Piano and Organ Co., 1888–1934; Woodstock: Karn Piano Co., 1880s–1920; London, later Clinton: Sherlock-Manning Piano Co., 1902–; Clinton: Doherty Pianos, 1875–1920 (dates represent piano manufacture).

Although the industry was centered in the Montreal region and southern Ontario, pianos were shipped to retail outlets across the country after the completion of the railway in 1885. Import-export trade existed between other countries of the Commonwealth and with the United States (though tariffs in both countries stifled trade with the latter). In 1903 business statistics reported 367 pianos imported and 509 exported. **Hammers, actions, strings, keys**, etc., were imported at first, but gradually companies were formed to manufacture these accessory parts (Otto Higel Co., A.A. Barthelmes, D.M. Best, J.M. Loose, W. Bohne, Sterling Action and Keys). The Canadian Piano and Organ Manufacturers Association was formed in 1899 (to 1975) and a trade magazine, *Canadian Music Trades Journal*, was published c. 1899–c. 1933.

The industry recovered from the setback caused by World War I, but went into serious decline during the 1920s, owing to factors such as the decreasing popularity of the **player piano**, the increasing popularity of the radio and the phonograph, and the general economic instability of the time. Firms were taken over or amalgamated until only a few remained active by the end of the depression era, notably: Lesage, Willis, Heintzman, Sherlock-Manning, and Mason & Risch.

Stability returned during the next two decades, but production demand was never again as high as those peak years preceding World War I. The piano was displaced as the focus of home entertainment by more sophisticated home sound systems, the electronic organ, and the advent of television. Its importance in the field of music education was lessened to an extent by interest in other instruments, especially guitar and accordion.

Foreign manufacturers began to move into the Canadian market, first with the purchase of Mason & Risch by the U.S. **Aeolian** Corporation, and by the 1960s with the invasion of lower-priced, competitive-quality Asian imports. Most of the Canadian firms had been managed either by the families who founded them or by piano tradesmen (often employees) who acquired them. The oldest and most revered company, Heintzman, was sold to a furniture manufacturer and ceased production five years later (1986). The two other survivors during the 1980s, Sherlock-Manning and Lesage, were purchased by PSC Management in 1984 and 1986 respectively. Lesage closed the following year (1987); Sherlock-Manning has changed owners twice since then. In 1991 Sherlock-Manning remained as the last manufacturer of pianos in Canada, although it has suspended production pending refinancing of the firm.

Florence Hayes

Bibliography

Draper, D. Murray. *W.D.: The Story of Doherty and Sherlock-Manning*. Clinton, Ontario: the author, 1986.

Hayes, Florence. "Piano Building." In *Encyclopedia of Music in Canada*. Edited by Helmut Kallmann, Gilles Potvin, and Kenneth Winters. Toronto: University of Toronto Press, 1981.

Kelly, Wayne. *Downright Upright*. Toronto: Natural History, Natural Heritage, 1991.

Nixon, D.C. "Making Canadian Pianos." *Canadian Courier* (12 October 1912).

"The Piano and Organ Industry." *Industrial Canada* (February 1904).

Roback, Frances. "Advertising Canadian Pianos and Organs, 1850–1914." *Material History Bulletin* 20 (Fall 1984): 31–44.

CAPO TASTO/CAPO D'ASTRO/V-BAR

In the **grand piano**, the *capo tasto* is an integral part of the **plate** that forms one end of the speaking length of the **strings** (the **bridge** forms the other), typically in the treble section where the strings run perpendicular to the **keyboard**. As the strings fan out, **agraffes** may be used instead of a capo tasto. Normally the capo is cast as part of the plate, but there are some constructions (e.g., **Bösendorfer** of Vienna) that use a separate, adjustable piece that is finely positioned, then bolted into place. The strings run under this rounded V-shaped bar, the bottom of which should be hardened so that the strings do not easily indent into the relatively soft cast-iron. Some capo bars have a groove into which a hardened steel rod can be inserted. (See illustration under **Aliquot Scaling**.)

Joel and Priscilla Rappaport

CAPSTAN

Used on both vertical and **grand actions**, this screw adjusts the height of the **wippen** and, in the case of the grand action, the height of the **hammer**. The part is so called because one design resembles a ship's capstan.

See also Actions.

Philip Jamison, III

CARE AND MAINTENANCE

All musical instruments require maintenance in order to assure optimum playing efficiency. Most wind and string players are able to tune and maintain their own instruments. Because the pianist is compelled to rely on a professional technician for **tuning**, **voicing**, and repairs, the first and most important aspect of piano maintenance is to obtain the services of an experienced, reliable piano technician.

Temperature and humidity control are also critical elements in maintaining a valuable instrument. Central heating, without some kind of humidity control, poses a great danger for musical instruments made of wood. The worst possible environment for a piano is one with radical swings in humidity and temperature. In regions with hot, humid summers, and dry, cold winters, special attention must be given to humidifying in the winter and dehumidifying in the summer. Wood is hygroscopic and it expands and contracts across the grain with changes in humidity. The **pitch** of the **strings** depends to a certain extent on the amount of humidity present in the **soundboard**, which expands and contracts with changes in heat and relative humidity. If the environment is too dry, the soundboard will shrink beyond the dryness level at which the instrument was manufactured, causing cracks in the wood and even failure of glue joints. Extreme dryness can cause complete failure of the soundboard and **pinblock**. The loss of natural moisture in the soundboard also causes the pitch to go flat. In the winter, care must be taken to maintain a humidity of not less than 50 percent and a room temperature of not more than 65 degrees Fahrenheit. Conversely, too much humidity causes the soundboard to swell and bow upward, often causing pressure ridges in the soft, crushed fibers of the wood, increasing the tension of the strings and causing the instrument to go sharp. Too much moisture can ruin a piano, as it causes the wood in the **keys** and soundboard

to swell, resulting in sticking keys, loose **ivory**, and sluggish response in the mechanism. Excessive moisture may also cause the strings, **tuning pins**, and other metal parts to rust.

The **lid** of the piano should be completely closed when the instrument is not in use, in order to prevent the accumulation of dust and foreign objects in the **action** and on the soundboard. For instruments with ivory keys, however, the keyboard cover or **fallboard** should be kept open periodically, as ivory will turn yellow if it is not exposed to natural light. Care should be taken not to drop pencils, paper clips, and other foreign objects, which can cause noise and damage, into the piano. Foreign objects on the strings and soundboard will produce irritating vibrations. Never put objects on top of the piano as they also can cause noises and vibrations. Sometimes other objects in the room, even window panes, can cause sympathetic vibrations with the piano tone. Vases, flower pots, beverage glasses, or any vessel containing liquid, should never be placed on the piano.

No attempt should be made by the owner, without special instructions, to remove the action from the piano. To avoid personal injury and possible damage to the instrument, piano moving should only be entrusted to experienced pianomovers who are fully insured for liability. Moths were very destructive to the **felt** in pianos made before World War II, but most modern instruments are made with mothproof felt.

Finding an ideal location for a piano is often difficult. In the order of importance, the location should help preserve the instrument, be acoustically satisfactory, and be aesthetically pleasing. Ideally, a piano should be placed on an inside wall, away from the direct rays of the sun. Moreover, it should not be placed next to heaters, stoves, air conditioners, or near heat ducts or cold air returns. Drafty locations next to open windows or doors should also be avoided. Instruments that are placed directly beneath water pipes or emergency sprinkler systems should be protected with a waterproof cover from possible water damage. Finding the best location for a piano also includes acoustical considerations; usually a piano sounds best in a room without thick wall-to-wall carpeting or heavy, sound-absorbing draperies.

The frequency of tuning depends in part on the severity of the climate, the age and condition of the piano, and the extent to which it is used. In any case, pianos should be tuned at least twice a year to keep the pitch level from sagging below A=440. New instruments should be tuned three or four times a year during each of the first two years, because the new strings will continue to stretch during that period. For instruments in home use, two or three tunings a year are usually adequate to keep a piano at concert pitch. An experienced piano-tuner will thump the keys vigorously during tuning in order to encourage the strings to stretch and stabilize across their entire length. If piano tuning is neglected, the pitch of the piano will gradually go flat, often to the point where the tuner cannot raise it successfully in one tuning. Even after raising pitch, a neglected piano will not stay in tune as well as an instrument that is regularly maintained. Concert instruments are tuned before every concert, even if there are two on the same day, as the slightest inaccuracy in tuning cannot be tolerated in a concert.

Tuning a piano is not enough to ensure complete maintenance. Periodically the action and pedals should be regulated. The more an instrument is used, the more frequently it will require both tuning and **regulation**. Pianos that are in constant use, such as those in conservatory practice rooms and the studios of teachers and professional musicians, require much more frequent maintenance than instruments that are only used occasionally. In time the hammer felt will become grooved and flattened by the steel strings, necessitating reshaping, voicing, and eventual replacement of the hammers. Reshaping hammers by sanding is a possible, but imperfect, solution to hammer wear, because it also reduces the weight of the hammers and changes the blow distance between the striking point of the hammer and the string.

Voicing, or tone regulating, piano hammers should only be attempted by an experienced specialist. To regulate tone quality, the voicer first makes certain that the action is in perfect regulation and that the hammers have a proper acoustical shape. The hammers are also checked to ensure that they are striking all the strings of the unison squarely and simultaneously. Finally, the density of the hammer felt is regulated by needling the shoulders of the hammers so that they produce an even, homogenous tone quality throughout the scale. Voicing should only be entrusted to a seasoned professional, as it requires a thorough knowledge of the piano mechanism, a sensitive musical ear, and years of experience.

Most pianos are not regulated as often as they should be. A competent piano technician must check action and **pedal** function after each tuning and make recommendations for regulation and repairs. The piano action will function after a fashion, even if it is very badly out of regulation, but the piano will not provide satisfactory results and may even hinder the progress of an unsuspecting student.

Periodically, the piano technician should clean the action, keys, soundboard, and **keyframe**. Only the slightest amount of moisture should be used on ivory keys because dampness can penetrate the ivory and soften the glue that bonds it to the key.

Piano **cases** were finished with a variety of materials during different historical periods. Alcohol-soluble spirit varnishes were used on early instruments. Oil varnish was used for many instruments made after the mid-nineteenth century, and both lacquer and polyester finishes are currently in use. No single cleaning technique can be used for all of them. To clean a piano case it is best to remove dust with a feather duster. A bit of moisture from the breath in conjunction with a soft leather chamois skin can be used to remove stubborn smudges, although it is usually best to consult the manufacturer's instructions for maintaining the finish.

Edward E. Swenson

Bibliography

Fine, Larry. *The Piano Book*. Boston: Brookside Press, 1987.

Funke, Otto. *The Piano and How to Care for It*. Frankfurt am Main: Das Musikinstrument Publishers, 1961.

Schmeckel, Carl D. *The Piano Owner's Guide*. New York: Charles Scribner's Sons, 1971.

CASE

Present day pianos are built in either the "**grand**" or "**vertical**" styles. The grand piano case was directly derived from that of the harpsichord, as **Bartolomeo Cristofori**, inventor of the piano, was a harpsichord maker. Since Cristofori's time, numerous piano configurations have come and gone with changes in fashion, but the only types to seriously compete with the grand were the square and the vertical. The "**square**" piano (actually rectangular in shape) was derived from the clavichord, a predecessor of the piano, and from the virginal, a rectangular harpsichord. The earliest known square is one made by Johann Söcher in Upper Bavaria in 1742 (now in Germanisches Nationalmuseum, Nuremberg). Due to its somewhat smaller size and lower cost, the square piano enjoyed great popularity for over 150 years. In fact, squares outsold verticals *and* grands in the United States until the 1890s. The earliest known vertical piano, by an unknown maker, is dated 1735 (according to Harding) and looks much like a grand piano set vertically on four legs. It wasn't until the late nineteenth century that the vertical piano **action** was truly practicable. "Vertical" refers to the upright placement of the **strings** and **soundboard.** Such an arrangement could reduce the instrument's depth to about two feet. Even more economical with space than the square, the vertical is today's best-selling design.

The piano was as prone to fashion and novelty as any aspect of human endeavor, though some of these innovations lacked practicality. Pianos have been fashioned to double as desks, sewing tables, and bookshelves. They have been made as tiny as a small valise and longer than ten feet. Several makers offered "**duoclaves,**" pianos with opposing **keyboards** suitable for duets. Numerous makers incorporated other instruments into their piano cases; these included pipe and reed organs, drums, triangles, cymbals, and even phonographs. Certain styles gained a brief popularity, such as the classically inspired "**harp piano**" of the late 1850s. Similar in shape, the "**giraffe piano**" sometimes incorporated sculptural elements. The "pyramid piano" achieved its symmetrical appearance by an artful arrangement of the strings and, in at least one case, placement of the bass strings in the center of the scale. These instruments generally sacrificed the piano's **tone** and ease of maintenance for novelty, and soon passed into obscurity.

As mentioned previously, the piano case was based on that of the harpsichord and other related instruments that preceded it. Soundboards and case woods also were basically unchanged from harpsichord to piano. Well into the 1800s, it took little more than a good knowledge of cabinetmaking to produce an acceptable piano, at least for the home market. With the advent of cheaper mass production and the resulting increase in sales, piano making turned from little more than a cottage industry to an important segment of the Industrial Revolution. The intro-

duction of metal **plates** added foundrywork to the process. The resulting additional weight made the delicate and almost portable pianos of the past obsolete. Pianos became less varied as manufacturers agreed on standards for **key** size, **pedal** placement, international **pitch**, etc.

Piano makers have generally favored the use of thin wood veneer over a thicker wood core for most case parts. This construction approximates the qualities of today's plywood. Since wood shrinks and expands parallel to its grain, it is less likely to split or warp when made up of layers whose grain alternates in direction. Some pianos have been cased with plastic, metal, flakeboard, and even concrete, but veneered solid wood has proved the overwhelming favorite.

Certain problems are inherent in piano-case construction, and these took many generations to overcome. The foremost was the pull of the strings on the case, the result of which was a piano twisted like the neck of a cheap guitar. Lack of case rigidity also caused **tuning** instability and loss of **tone**. This quandary was resolved with the eventual use of the cast-iron plate in the mid- to late-nineteenth century.

The distinctively rounded case or "**rim**" of the grand piano is today made up of many thin wood layers glued together and bent around a form. Earlier grand rims were made of solid wood pieces that were fitted together and veneered. The latter method was used by European makers well into the twentieth century.

The **finish** on the piano is not a factor in its tone, except for the soundboard; on this, a thin, flexible coating is desired. Piano finishes have generally been the same as those used on other cabinets. Various resin formulations (shellacs and varnishes) were brushed or patted on until sprayed lacquer was developed in the 1930s. Polyester, a type of plastic resin, gained popularity in the 1980s due to its high solids content and durability.

The piano case is a marriage of **acoustics**, aesthetics, and engineering. To be successful, it must serve finger, ear, and eye.

See also Frame; Actions.

Philip Jamison, III

Bibliography

Bielefeldt, Catherine C. *The Wonders of The Piano:* Melville, N.Y.: Belwin-Mills Publishing, 1984.

Ehrlich, Cyril. *The Piano: A History*. London: J.M. Dent & Sons, Ltd., 1976.

Gaines, James R. *The Lives of the Piano*. New York: Holt, Rinehart and Winston, 1981.

Gill, Dominic, ed. *The Book of the Piano*. Ithaca, N.Y.: Cornell University Press, 1981.

Good, Edwin M. *Giraffes, Black Dragons, and Other Pianos*. Stanford, Cal.: Stanford University Press, 1982.

Harding, Rosamond E.M. *The Piano-Forte: Its History Traced to the Great Exhibition of 1851*. Cambridge: Cambridge University Press, 1933. Reprints. New York: Da Capo Press, 1973; Old Working, Surrey: Gresham Books, 1978.

Hollis, Helen Rice. *The Piano*. New York: Hippocrene Books, 1975.

Libin, Laurence. *Keyboard Instruments*, New York: Metropolitan Museum of Art, 1989.

Pierce, Bob. *Pierce Piano Atlas*. Long Beach, Cal.: Bob Pierce, 1982.

Roell, Craig M. *The Piano in America*. Chapel Hill, N.C.: University of North Carolina Press, 1989.

Schott, Howard. *Catalogue of Musical Instruments*. Vol. I: *Keyboards*. London: Victoria and Albert Museum, 1985.

White, William B. *Theory and Practice of Piano Construction*. New York: Dover Publications, 1975.

Wolfenden, Samuel. *A Treatise on the Art of Pianoforte Construction*. Oxfordshire, England: Gresham Books, 1982.

CASIO DIGITAL PIANOS

Casio, Inc. is a Japanese manufacturer of digital pianos, portable **keyboards, synthesizers, samplers,** and other electronic musical instruments. These products are marketed in the United States through the Electronic Musical Instruments Division and the Professional Music Products Division. Initially best-known as a maker of low-cost, aggressively marketed home consumer instruments, Casio has also developed a line of high-quality professional products. The CPS-series of digital pianos includes velocity-sensitive keyboards of 61–76 **keys**, five preset PCM sample voices, 16-note polyphonicity, **MIDI** compatibility, tuning controls, built-in stereo speakers, and sustain **pedals**. The CSM-10P is a rackmount version of the high-end CPS-700.

In 1991, the Professional Products Division began marketing the Celviano digital piano, which features a built-in CD player, a more advanced sampling process of tone generation known as "multiple point wave sampling" (MPWS), and an 88-key, velocity-sensitive, weighted keyboard. Interactive CDs played on the instrument provide background accompaniments for practice and study. RAM cards allow the musician to record and save performances.

See also Electronic Pianos.

Samuel S. Holland

CHALLEN AND SONS

English piano manufacturer Challen and Sons dated its founding to 1804, when Charles H. Challen built his first piano. Although several writers have echoed this date, in fact Challen seems not to have emerged as an independent entity until the 1830s. During the last quarter of the nineteenth and first quarter of the twentieth centuries, it occupied a secure place in the second tier of English builders, with annual output of around 500 instruments.

Challen's fortunes changed dramatically with the arrival of William Evans, who joined the company in 1926 and became managing director in 1931. Upon coming to Challen from the **Chappell** company, Evans designed a four-foot "**baby grand**," which by some accounts nearly displaced the **upright** as the compact home instrument of choice in England. Much of its success came about because Evans introduced modern mass-production techniques to what had been a traditional, conservative family concern; the resultant economies enabled him to reduce prices drastically. Thus, in the decade from 1925 to 1935, Challen's annual output rose fivefold to 2,500 instruments, even as many other English piano-makers experienced financial difficulties or went out of business entirely. Indeed, in 1932 Challen completed an agreement to take over all manufacturing for **Broadwood**, which found itself forced to restructure as a solely retail concern.

Although perhaps best known to the general public for its small **grands**, Challen produced a full range of pianos, including what it claimed to be the world's largest, a single one-ton eleven-foot, eight-inch instrument specially built for the Silver Jubilee of George V in 1935. Many more conventional Challen instruments found their homes in BBC broadcasting studios, beginning with contracts after a series of tests in 1936 (the other makers receiving contracts were **Bösendorfer** and **Steinway**).

Challen and Sons ceased independent existence upon the retirement of William Evans in

1959. The name was sold first to Brasted Brothers; then, upon Brasted's demise in 1970, it went to Barratt and Robinson, its current owners.

David R. Hoehl

Bibliography

Blom, Eric. *The Romance of the Piano*. New York: Da Capo Press, 1969.

Dolge, Alfred. *Pianos and Their Makers*. Covina, Cal.: Covina Publishing Co., 1911. Reprint. New York: Dover, 1972.

Ehrlich, Cyril. *The Piano: A History*. London: J.M. Dent & Sons, Ltd., 1976.

Grover, David S. *The Piano: Its Story from Zither to Grand*. London: Robert Hale, Ltd., 1976.

Michel, N. E. *Old Pianos*. Rivera, Cal.: N.E. Michel, 1954.

Sumner, W.L. *The Pianoforte*. London: Macdonald & Co., Ltd., 1966.

Wainwright, David. *Broadwood by Appointment: A History*. London: Quiller Press, Ltd., 1982.

———. *The Piano Makers*. London: Hutchinson & Co., Ltd., 1975.

CHAMBER MUSIC AND ACCOMPANYING

Despite its humble origins, the piano quickly established itself as an important participant in chamber-music literature—first in Classical compositions, then in a somewhat more limited number of Romantic and post-Romantic works. During the late eighteenth and early nineteenth centuries the piano also became the most important vehicle of musical accompaniment, especially in the realm of the art song. Less important since World War I, the piano has nevertheless figured significantly in vocal and chamber works by a host of composers from Paul Hindemith to Philip Glass. Initially extremely important in popular song and jazz, the piano has also declined in prestige as an accompanying instrument, although serious as well as popular composers continue to utilize it.

During the 1760s and 1770s the continuing tradition lost its iron grip on many European composers, including individuals associated with the Mannheim school. At the same time the piano began to replace the harpsichord as the most popular and versatile **keyboard** chamber instrument. Those compositional forms in which the piano tended to dominate winds or strings (e.g., the piano quintet) contributed to the evolution of the modern piano concerto, especially in the hands of **Johann Christian Bach**. Other forms, among them the accompanied solo sonata and trio sonata, gradually evolved into modern sonatas and piano trios, works written as much for the keyboard artist as for his or her "soloist" colleagues. By the 1790s, for example, **Joseph Haydn** had made the piano at least the equal of the violin in his excellent piano trios (although he often slighted the cello on the other instruments' behalf). **Wolfgang Amadeus Mozart**, however, was even more important as a composer of chamber works with piano; his enormous output includes dozens of violin and piano sonatas, piano trios, piano quartets, two especially important piano quintets (K. 386c and K. 581), a masterful sonata for two pianos (K. 375a), a quintet for piano and winds (K. 452, which Mozart himself proclaimed the finest of his life), and a host of other pieces, some of them for piano four-hands. **Ludwig van Beethoven** extended the piano-chamber literature along similar lines, writing sonatas and sets of variations for violin, cello, and flute (all with piano parts, many of which transcend what is often implied by "accompaniment") that rank among his finest works. He also completed several piano trios—among them the "Archduke" (Op. 97)—as well as a sonata for piano and horn (Op. 17), a quintet for piano and winds (Op. 16), and a variety of lesser works.

Chamber music was not always able to accommodate the demands made by Romantic composers for extremes of instrumental color and volume, and several important composers—**Franz Liszt** and Richard Wagner, to name but two—wrote almost nothing for small ensembles. Other Romantics specialized in chamber works for unusual combinations of instruments; Carl Maria von Weber, for instance, left a number of pieces for piano and clarinet. Those Romantics with a penchant for more traditional compositional forms and effects, however, produced volumes of chamber-music masterpieces, many of which featured the piano. Franz Schubert, for example, is remembered today not only as a composer of symphonies and songs, but as the author of the "Arpeggione" sonata (D. 821; generally performed today by violin and piano), two important piano trios (Opp. 99 and 100), larger works for piano and strings, and a considerable body of four-hands piano music. Felix Mendelssohn completed several solo sonatas with piano accompaniment, two important piano trios (Opp. 49 and 66), and a group of less important pieces. Even **Frédéric Chopin**, who limited himself almost exclusively to solo-piano music, wrote a sonata for piano and cello.

The most influential Romantic chamber-music composers, however, were **Robert Schumann** and **Johannes Brahms**. Always fascinated by the piano, Schumann produced a justifiably successful quintet for piano and strings (Op. 44), several two-piano works, solo sonatas, and collections of Phantasiestücke ("fantasy pieces") for clarinet or viola with piano. Brahms published piano trios and quartets, an impressive quintet (Op. 34) modelled to some extent on Schumann's composition for the same ensemble, a number of pieces for piano four-hands, solo sonatas for violin, cello, and clarinet with piano, a trio for violin, horn (or viola), and piano (Op. 40), and one of the cornerstones of the two-piano literature: the keyboard version of the Variations on a Theme by Haydn (Op. 56b). Antonin Dvořák, Edvard Grieg, Bedřich Smetana, and other post-Romantics with an inclination toward musical nationalism, also completed important chamber compositions, as did Peter Ilich Tchaikovsky, Vincent d'Indy, and Max Reger. Influenced by Schumann and Brahms, American composers—among them Edward MacDowell and Amy Beach—wrote a number of chamber works with piano; the Beach sonata for piano and violin (Op. 34) has recently become part of the standard concert repertory. The growth of chamber music outside nineteenth-century Germany and Austro-Hungary was gradual, however, and it is scarcely surprising that only shortly before World War I did France produce in César Franck and Claude Debussy two chamber composers of outstanding calibre. Best-known today for his sonata for violin and piano (1886), Franck also composed a piano quintet (1879). Debussy wrote rhapsodies for saxophone and cello with piano as well as smaller chamber pieces; his works for two pianos are frequently performed today. Like other composers of his generation, though, Debussy experimented with non-keyboard "accompanying" instruments in pieces like the sonata for flute, violin, and harp. The Viennese composers who developed twelve-tone compositional techniques also ignored the piano in chamber works, or employed it in unusual ensembles: Arnold Schönberg, for example, used the piano and other instruments in his Pierrot lunaire song cycle (Op. 21), while Alban Berg—who otherwise virtually ignored the piano—

included it in his Chamber Concerto for Fifteen Instruments (1925).

Twentieth-century composers have, by and large, continued to repudiate traditional instrumental forms, especially in chamber music, and the piano has played a less important role in recent chamber works than it did in compositions by Classic and Romantic figures. Igor Stravinsky, Charles Ives, and Richard Strauss, for instance, produced comparatively few pieces for piano and small ensembles; instead, Stravinsky employed the **cimbalom** in his Ragtime for eleven instruments. Hindemith, of course, composed a substantial (although aesthetically uneven) number of sonatas for orchestral instruments and piano, while Béla Bartók used the piano in three outstanding chamber compositions: the Contrasts for clarinet, violin, and piano (Op. 111), the Sonata for two pianos and percussion (Op. 110), and the very large "chamber" work entitled Music for Strings, Percussion, and Celeste (Op. 106). Since World War II the piano has perhaps been employed most characteristically either as a stabilizing influence (especially by composers who prefer a comparatively conventional harmonic vocabulary), or in highly experimental ways. John Cage, for example, pioneered the use of prepared pianos in several ensemble works; more recent figures, among them Philip Glass, have written for piano ensembles in pieces like Music in 5ths (1969), Music in Similar Motion (1969), and Music with Changing Parts (1970)—composed, respectively, for two, four, and six pianos. Even in the quasi-popular chamber works of George Crumb, the piano has either been abandoned in favor of other instruments (including the sitar), or utilized in untraditional ways (e.g., as an electrically amplified instrument in Vox balaenae [1971]).

One of the principal roles assigned to the piano (or the piano "part") in chamber and vocal works is that of accompanying melodies produced by other performers. Thus the term "accompaniment" has two principal meanings: it refers to the *function* of an instrument, performer, or piece of music relative to another (thus the piano, pianist, or piano part may be said to "accompany" a tune); and to the *character* of that instrument, performer, or piece relative to another (i.e., as less important).

During the Classical era the piano gained almost universal acceptance as the most suitable instrument for accompanying solo singers, small choral groups, and instrumental ensembles. (Only in church music did the organ maintain preeminence.) Haydn, Mozart, and Beethoven employed piano accompaniments in their original songs, as well as in certain transcriptions of traditional melodies. In more ambitious works, especially "An die ferne Geliebte" ("To the Distant Beloved"; Op. 98), Beethoven inaugurated the Romantic song cycle, complete with piano writing that transcended mere incidental support. Songs and song cycles by Schubert, Schumann, Liszt, Brahms, and Hugo Wolf included many brilliant, even extravagent piano "accompaniments"; the thundering octaves of Schubert's "Erlkönig" ("Elf-King"; D. 328) quickly became more famous than the vocal line they "support," while the extended codas that connect several of Schumann's songs in the cycle "Dichterliebe" ("Poet's Love"; Op. 16) establish the melancholy mood of that work as effectively as do Heinrich Heine's words. The piano also played a crucial role in the dissemination of early popular music, especially as an accompanying instrument, after about the 1860s. In turn-of-the-century European and American homes as well as in theaters and concert halls, pianos were employed to support vocalists and instrumentalists in works as diverse as Paolo Tosti's "Good-bye!," the tunes of Gilbert and Sullivan operettas, or the popular songs of Irving Berlin and George Gershwin. By the middle of the twentieth century, however, the piano had gradually come to be supplanted as an accompanying instrument—at least in popular music—by jazz ensembles, or by acoustic and electric guitars. Those twentieth-century pianists who have established reputations primarily as accompanying artists have thus concentrated their efforts on music of the eighteenth and especially the nineteenth centuries; of these individuals Gerald Moore is an outstanding example.

Michael Saffle

Bibliography

Hinson, Maurice. *Piano in Chamber Ensemble: An Annotated Guide.* Bloomington: Indiana University Press, 1978.

———. *Music for More than One Piano.* Bloomington: Indiana University Press, 1983.

King, A. Hyatt. *Chamber Music.* Westport, Connecticut: Greenwood Press, 1979.

———. *Mozart Chamber Music.* Seattle: University of Washington Press, 1969.

Mason, Daniel Gregory. *The Chamber Music of Brahms.* 2nd ed. New York: AMS Press, 1970.

Moore, Gerald. *The Unashamed Accompanist.* London: Macmillan, 1944.

Stein, Franz A. *Verzeichnis der Kammermusikwerke von 1650 bis zur Gegenwart* [A Catalog of Chamber Music Works from 1650 to the Present]. Bern: Francke, 1962.

Stuber, Robert. "Die Klavierbegleitung im Liede von Haydn, Mozart und Beethoven." ["Piano Accompaniment in the Songs of Haydn, Mozart, and Beethoven"]. Dissertation, University of Biel, 1958.

Webster, James. "Towards a History of Viennese Chamber Music in the Early Classic Period." *Journal of the American Musicological Society* 27 (1974): 212–247.

CHAPPELL & COMPANY

Founded in London by Samuel Chappell (d. 1834), Johann Baptist Cramer (1771–1858), and Francis Tatton Latour, Chappell & Company has flourished as a builder and seller of pianos and also as a music publisher since 1810. In the early days of the firm's existence it produced a large number of London concerts. Samuel Chappell's sons and their descendants have continued the business and are still music publishers and dealers in London, but Chappell pianos are now manufactured by Kemble in Milton Keynes. An unusual **square** glass piano built by Chappell & Company about 1815 is in the collection of the Victoria and Albert Museum. The tones of the instrument are produced by **hammers** that strike glass rods instead of strings.

Martha Novak Clinkscale

Bibliography

Clinkscale, Martha Novak. *Makers of the Piano: 1700–1820.* Oxford: Oxford University Press, 1992.

Ehrlich, Cyril. *The Piano: A History.* 2nd ed. Oxford: Oxford University Press, 1990.

Husk, W. H., and Peter Ward Jones. "Chappell." *The New Grove Dictionary of Music and Musicians* 4:153.

Schott, Howard. *Catalogue of Musical Instruments.* Volume 1: *Keyboard Instruments.* London: Her Majesty's Stationery Office, 1985.

The Piano. (New Grove Musical Instrument Series) New York: Norton, 1988.

CHICKERING, JONAS (1798–1853)

Jonas Chickering was the founder of Chickering & Sons, the largest American piano manufacturer of the nineteenth century. He was the first major piano builder to use a full metal **plate** in his instruments.

Born 5 April 1798 in New Ipswich, New Hampshire, Chickering first trained as a cabinet-maker. He moved to Boston about 1817 and became apprenticed to the piano maker **John Osborne** in nearby Milton. Osborne was himself a student of **Benjamin Crehore**, a noted piano and instrument maker originally from England. Crehore greatly influenced what became known as the Boston School of piano makers, and his apprentices included Lewis and **Alpheus Babcock**. Chickering studied with Osborne until 1823 when he opened a partnership with James Stewart. The Stewart & Chickering firm dissolved in 1826 when Stewart went to work for **Clementi** in London. In 1830, Chickering became partners with John MacKay, a successful international trader and ship owner. MacKay's business acumen proved invaluable to the young firm, then known as Chickering & MacKay.

Chickering's most important invention, the full iron plate, would appear to stem from Alpheus Babcock's 17 December 1825 **patent** for **square** grands. This introduced a continuous metal ring that held the tension of the **strings** more reliably than the wooden **frames** then in use. Babcock joined Chickering & MacKay in 1837, the same year Chickering developed his own iron plate for squares (the patent was granted in 1840). The same principle was used by Chickering in his 1843 patent for a full iron plate for **grands**. This scheme allowed heavier strings and **hammers** to be used, thus producing a louder, fuller tone. The rigid iron frame also improved **tuning** stability, since it didn't shrink and expand with humidity changes as wood does, nor did it bend as readily under tension. It was some time before the full iron plate was in general use by other piano makers, however. Most American manufacturers adopted the idea by the 1850s, following **Steinway's** lead in 1853. Some European makers didn't use full plates until the twentieth century.

By 1841, Chickering was the leading manufacturer of pianos in America, despite the loss of his partner MacKay at sea that year. In 1851, Chickering & Sons, along with Meyer of Philadelphia, **Nunns** & Clark of New York, and Gilbert & Company of Boston, became the first American piano manufacturers to exhibit in Europe (at the London Exhibition).

Sales of Chickering pianos continued briskly, thanks to sturdy construction and an unrelenting promotional campaign begun by MacKay and

surpassed only by Steinway. On 1 December 1852, the Chickering factory at 334 Washington Street in Boston burned to the ground. In a demonstration of the firm's success, the new plant on Tremont Street was not only the largest manufacturing facility in the United States, but the second-largest building, surpassed only by the U.S. Capitol. Jonas Chickering died 8 December 1853. His three sons, Thomas E. (1824–1871), C. Frank (1827–1891), and George H. (1830–1896), ran the business until the last of them died in 1896. Chickering & Sons was sold to the **American Piano Company** in 1908.

Chickering can be said to have established the modern American piano industry as well as having influenced the design of the modern piano. Although Steinway eventually gained superiority, it was Chickering who led the way.

Philip Jamison, III

Bibliography

Chickering & Sons. *The Romance of the Chickering.* East Rochester, N.Y.: Chickering & Sons (no date).

Dolge, Alfred. *Pianos and Their Makers.* Covina, Cal.: Covina Publishing Company, 1911 Reprint. New York, Dover, 1972.

Ehrlich, Cyril. *The Piano: A History.* London: J.M. Dent & Sons, Ltd.,1976.

Gill, Dominic, ed. *The Book of the Piano.* Ithaca, N.Y.: Cornell University Press, 1981.

Good, Edwin M. *Giraffes, Black Dragons, and Other Pianos.* Stanford, Cal.: Stanford University Press, 1982.

Harding, Rosamond E.M. *The Piano-Forte: Its History traced to the Great Exhibition of 1851.* Cambridge: Cambridge University Press, 1933. Reprints. New York: Da Capo Press, 1973; Old Woking, Surrey: Gresham Books, 1978.

CHINA, PIANO INDUSTRY IN

According to the recollections of living piano tuners who learned their craft from their fathers and grandfathers, the first firm to deal in the piano business in China was Moutrie & Company. It was a British firm in Shanghai that started business with the sale and maintenance of pianos and other musical instruments around 1850. Instead of shipping pianos from England, it turned to assembling imported parts from the home country around 1870. But no mention nor advertisements of it can be found in the 1874 *North China Daily News*, a leading English newspaper published in Shanghai from 1864 on, while in the first six months of 1890 the same newspaper carried advertisements of a Moutrie, Robinson & Co., for its sale of pianos of various types, featuring **Broadwood cases** and iron **frames** of different English and European makes. The assembling of pianos was sure to have been done by then, if not earlier. A more exact date could have been ascertained, had more of the archives been accessible.

All jobs at the Moutrie workshops were at first done by English workers. Soon they took on Chinese apprentices and workers. It is no exaggeration to say that all the early Chinese piano tuners and repairers came from the Moutrie staff. A few of them quit Moutrie and started smaller enterprises of their own. The first Chinese piano store, Xiangxing Qinhang, was owned and run by a carpenter named Huang from Moutrie. It dealt chiefly in **tuning** and repairing, and occasionally sold pianos assembled in the shop.

Instead of importing every component from abroad, Moutrie began to manufacture cases and **soundboards**, order cast-iron frames from local foundries, and make **keyboards** in Shanghai. For cases Moutrie used teak and other hardwood from South East Asia, and for soundboards, wood from America. Local frames were marked with the imprint "Moutrie Shanghai" or "Moutrie S." But the crucial parts of the piano — **actions**, **felt**, and **strings** — were all imported. Up to serial number 10,000, Moutrie used actions made in England, but later exclusively actions made by the Canadian firm Otto Higel. After number 10,000, the company began to make its own actions, which were not as good. In 1910 the factory had a staff of more than a hundred workers and produced 70 to 80 pianos a month, mostly **upright pianos**. It made several sizes of uprights, the largest of which—called the concert upright, with 88 keys—was the best. Moutrie also made **baby grand** and **parlor grand** pianos, though the quality did not match its uprights. Moutrie pianos enjoyed great popularity in China and were sold also to South East Asian countries.

Pianos made by other minor firms, both foreign and Chinese, bearing the brands Robinson, Lazaro, Mozart, Strauss and Kinear, etc., appeared in much smaller quantities.

Moutrie closed down in the early 1950s, as did other foreign enterprises. But Chinese-owned piano businesses lingered on until the socialist transformation of capitalist enterprises. In 1958 the government called for a merger of all joint state-private piano enterprises, other Western musical-instrument makers, and other businesses associated with the piano industry, and founded officially a self-sufficient piano manufacturing plant, the Shanghai Piano Factory.

Under the country's policy of self-reliance, intensive research was carried on after 1958 in the making of **hammers**, and in the 1970s many of its individual processes were automated or semi-automated. Nie-er pianos, the brand name Shanghai Piano Factory adopted for its products, with domestic hammers and action mechanisms, began to be produced in large quantities to meet the growing domestic demand, and a former brand, Strauss, has been recently restored to use. Both brands are now used for uprights and baby grands.

Concurrently with the development of piano manufacturing in Shanghai, the new Republic decided in the latter half of the 1950s to launch a centralized piano industry in the country with bases in Beijing (the capital), and Yingkou in the northeast, where timber is abundant and a new steel and iron industry was booming. Skilled master workers were transferred from Shanghai to the Beijing and Yingkou piano plants to lead the technological sections and to train new recruits and build a staff of skilled workers and technicians. Their products, Xing Hai (Beijing) and Xing Fu (Yingkou) pianos, were sold mostly to South East Asia, where they had a special appeal because of their low price and handsomely lacquered appearance. Shortly afterwards a fourth piano factory was established in the south, again with skilled staff from Shanghai. The Pearl River brand pianos made by the Guangzhou Pearl River Piano Corporation are better suited for humid tropical climates.

With the implementation of the national policy of free trade with the rest of the world, all four major piano manufacturing plants of the country have imported equipment and expertise from abroad. Foreign experts have been invited from England, Germany, Italy, Japan, South Korea, and Sweden to share their skills, giving lectures and demonstrations, and to help with the work. A **Steinway** manager from London visited Shanghai and Beijing in the early 1980s. Shortly afterwards the Austrian firm of **Bösendorfer** held short-term training courses in Beijing and Guangzhou. A German specialist has been working with the Beijing Piano Plant on a four-year contract. Besides Xing Fu pianos for domestic use, the Yingkou Piano Plant has been producing Nordiska pianos in cooperation with Sweden, its annual output of Nordiskas reaching 1,000 and more.

China is now making pianos not only to satisfy the growing demand at home, but for export as well. Chinese pianos have an international market in many countries and regions in the world. Not only is the annual output of pianos in the country soaring, the number of piano manufacturing plants is also on the increase. There have appeared Sino-foreign joint ventures in other cities of China in recent years, with investors from Sweden, Hong Kong, and the Philippines, and more such enterprises are expected to be launched.

Lianli Ku

Bibliography

Chen Qian. "Xi-yue-qi de chuan-ru he zai-wo-guo de fa-zhan" [The Introduction of Western Instruments to China and Their Development in China]. *Yue Qi* [*Musical Instruments*] 4 (August 1985): 28–29.

History of the Shanghai Piano Company (draft).

Lao Chang. "Foreign Help Boosts Piano Trade." *China Daily* (3 March 1991): 2.

North China Daily News. 1874 (January to December) and 1890 (January to June).

CHIPPING

Chipping refers to the initial **tuning** of a newly strung piano. After the **strings** are installed, but before the **action** is in place, the technician plucks each string with a wedge of wood or similar material, adjusting its **pitch** with a **tuning hammer**. The strings are thus brought roughly up to pitch (middle A vibrating 440 times per second). The piano may require two or three such tunings before the action is put into place and regulated. Following this, the piano is tuned normally several more times.

Philip Jamison, III

CHIROGYMNASTE

The *chirogymnaste* is a device invented by Casimir Martin in 1841 (Fr. **patent** 1842). Martin, a French piano maker, described the *chirogymnaste* as a "hand-director mechanism." Its aim was to extend the compass of the hand and to develop equal strength in the fingers. An improved version of the *chirogymnaste* was introduced by Martin in 1844. It consisted of a wooden board with fastened rings for the fingers. Adjustable springs made it more or less difficult to press the fingers down.

On the same board there was also a knob upon which to rest the hand (in order to correct its position), a screw to forcefully widen the distance between the fingers, an adjustable bridge with rollers bending the fingers backwards, etc.

The *chirogymnaste* was preceded by several similar devices such as the *dactylion* by Henri Herz (1836) and the *chiroplast* by Johann Bernhard Logier (1814). The *dactylion* consisted of a rail that was placed upon the front of the piano. Ten adjustable springs carrying brass wires, ending in rings for the fingers, were attached to the rail. The aim of the *dactylion* was to strengthen the fingers.

The *chiroplast* consisted of two parallel rails that prevented vertical wrist movements as well as thumb crossing. In 1820 Peter Hawkes invented a similar device, a handmold that was buckled to the wrists. The mold then slid along a supporting rod.

A device to exercise the third finger was proposed by William Prangley in 1856. Jacob Stolz made a *Doppel-Handleiter* for the same purpose (c.1860), as did William Hamilton with his "radial hand-guide" (1865) and Myer Marks with his *digitorium* (1866). In 1891 Gustave Lyon, of the **Pleyel** firm in Paris, devised a *digito-égaliseur* and *durcisseur*.

Due to justifiable criticism, all these devices fell into disuse by the beginning of the twentieth century.

See also Keyboard Practice and Exercise Aids.

F.J. de Hen

Bibliography

Logier, Johann. *An Explanation and Description of the Royal Patent Chiroplast or Hand-Director*. London: Clementi & Co., 1816. 1816.

Mahillon, Victor-Charles. *Catalogue descriptif et analytique du Musée Instrumental du Conservatoire Royal de Musique de Bruxelles*. Vol.1. Gand: Hoste, 1893.

CHOPIN, FRÉDÉRIC FRANÇOIS (1810–1849)

Frédéric François Chopin, a Polish-born pianist and composer of Polish and French parentage, was born in Zelazowa Wola, near Warsaw, on 1 March 1810, and died in Paris on 17 October 1849. After a childhood in which he displayed pianistic and compositional precocity (his first piece was published when he was seven), he trained at the Warsaw Conservatory from the ages of sixteen to nineteen, studying piano with Wojciech Zywny and composition with Joseph Elsner. Chopin lived most of his adult life in Paris, supporting himself primarily by teaching and composition, performing in public but rarely. For many musicians and music-lovers worldwide, his music has become virtually synonymous with the piano and its capabilities. Chopin is perhaps the only representative of the legions of pianist-composers associated with Paris in the middle fifty years of the nineteenth century whose music has remained consistently popular, enduring no period of disfavor with concert artists, amateurs, or students.

Chopin's preferred instrument was a **Pleyel** (which he nevertheless called "a perfidious traitor"), an instrument so sensitive that the pianist's slightest imperfection could be heard undisguised; he also owned an **Erard,** which he found easier to play when he wasn't feeling in full command. His student Emilie Gretsch quoted him on the subject of the Erard: "You can thump it and bash it, it makes no difference: the sound is always beautiful and the ear doesn't ask for anything more since it hears a full, resonant tone." By contrast, Chopin said of the Pleyel "But when I feel in good form and strong enough to find my own individual sound, then I need a Pleyel piano."

The design and capabilities of the Pleyel were perfectly suited to Chopin's needs and pianistic approach. As Robert Winter's research has shown, the Pleyel's action was of the single-**escapement** English **grand** variety, with regulation geared toward light fall-weight and as little **aftertouch** as possible. The **hammers**—made either entirely of **felt** or at least having a felt core—were relatively light in terms of mass, especially in the treble register, where the hammer was shaped so that it met the **string** at a point rather than along a curve. Like **Broadwood**s, Pleyels had regularized **strike-point** ratios, but the upper two octaves remained substantially different: while the bass and tenor approximate a ninth, and the alto and soprano up to g^2 evolve to an eighth, the remaining treble range moves from a ninth through a tenth and eleventh to a thirteenth at g^4. The combined characteristics of the hammers and strike points produced an otherworldly quality, ideal for Chopin's melodies and characteristic of contemporaries' descriptions of his playing, but wholly lacking in modern instruments.

With its single-escapement, light hammers, and light fall-weight, the touch of the Pleyel was far lighter than that of contemporary Erards and closer to such **Viennese pianos** as the **Graf**. A contemporary technician named **Claude Montal** went so far as to say that Pleyel had achieved a "facility, an evenness and a rapidity of repeated notes" previously thought to be unattainable by pianists and even piano manufacturers. Clearly, this conquest of **keyboard** stiffness was ideally suited to both the energy level and the refined aesthetic of the delicately constituted Chopin.

Chopin's exploitation of the Pleyel's resources is apparent in his music. Music which (on a modern instrument) might seem interpretively problematic could well be intended to produce a breathtaking effect arising from the different registral capabilities of a far less tonally homogeneous instrument than is used today. Winter cites the coda to the Nocturne in D-flat Major, Op. 27, No. 2, as an example: on a Pleyel the difference in character of sound between the high treble of the grace notes and the lower principal notes enable this passage to produce a far different and much more characteristic effect than the same passage played on a modern instrument. Similarly, a wispier high end wouldn't, as on a modern instrument, cover a primary train of musical thought proceeding in the tenor range, as in the Etude, Op. 25, No. 11 ("Winter Wind"; not Chopin's title) for instance. Interestingly, the recording of this piece by Raoul von Koczalski, who studied with Chopin's student Karol Mikuli and is a clear heir to the tradition, maintains some of the original balance: the piece is more a rhythmically vibrant but controlled march, with a background of glistening chromatic tracery, rather than the accustomed thundering, shrieking northern gale.

Intimately bound up with the question of registers is another area of pianism in which Chopin was generally held to be a master: the use of the **pedals**. His piano's unique registral make-up, its thinner tone, and its shorter sustain, enabled him to produce effects all but impossible today. That the sustain and resonance of his piano differed radically from ours is apparent from the pedal indications in the D-flat Nouvelle étude, to cite one example among many: the notated tonic-dominant blend of bars 59–60 almost certainly meant something other than what it produces today. Similarly, such pedal indications as that of the Nocturne in D-flat Major, Op. 27, No. 2, m.39, testify to a relatively rapid decay and an upper register much less inclined to cover other registers. The long pedal over a forte crescendo in mm.53–56 of the Etude in F Minor, Op. 10, No. 9, suggests that the accretion of sound in the bass registers would have been much less than it is today, and that the decay in the treble would have been sufficiently prompt for the half-steps in the melody not to conflict with each other. (This was composed while Chopin was still in Warsaw, and therefore probably on a Viennese instrument.)

It is beyond question that Chopin's repertoire of **touches** and articulations far exceeds those used today, and it is likely that the different capabilities of pianos are at least partly responsible. The old school of cantabile playing, of producing an Adagio *style* (as opposed to merely a "singing tone"), which would rival that of a singer, today is essentially a lost art. This kind of pianism was a constant goal of Chopin's, who continually exhorted his students to listen to and imitate singers, to "sing" at the keyboard ("It is necessary to sing with the fingers!"), to phrase and "breathe" with the wrist, and to evoke a singer's rhythmic freedom over the accompaniment of an operatic orchestra. The varieties of articulation he used are evident in his notation: in addition to the usual staccato, legato, phrase, and accent indications, he uses them in combinations, such as in the Nocturne in G Minor, Op. 37, No. 1, where accent indications appear under a legato phrase. The purely timbral indication *mezza voce* in the fourth Ballade and elsewhere, of course, bears clear testimony to the vocal timbre he sought to duplicate.

These varieties of articulation link Chopin, more by pianistic aesthetic than by actual lineage, to an older French School of pianism, that of Louis Adam and his students Frédéric Kalkbrenner and Pierre Zimmermann. Chopin's somewhat atypical long-over-short cantabile fingerings (i.e., third finger over fourth and fourth over fifth), it should be added, while also advocated by Johann Nepomuk Hummel, represent a further correspondence with the Parisian School. In all of these delicate areas the sensitivity of the Pleyel allowed Chopin to produce the effects he desired. The notation of his contemporaries, interestingly, does not seem to reflect the same interest in the varieties of articulation.

In sum, his music displays an imaginative utilization of the piano's different registers, which suggests that even at a variety of dynamic levels, the registers could easily be distinguished from one another. These registral differences could be manipulated with an extremely subtle pedal technique and a variety of articulative approaches that were characteristic of both Chopin's own native approach and the fast-disappearing Parisian piano aesthetic. The thick, overpedalled sonority that often results from a literal reading of his dynamic and pedal indications on today's instruments, therefore, seems unlikely to have been his intention.

Chopin's pianism was of a uniquely introverted variety in an age of extroverted virtuosi. Rather than titillate huge audiences, he consistently preferred to explore the piano's subtleties and delicate effects in his choice of instrument, his compositions, and in his performances, however few initiates happened to be present for them. That his works maintain their popularity in the face of today's radically different interpretive treatment of them testifies to their quality and almost universal appeal. Until more pianists take some of the historical considerations into account in their approaches to these works, however, some of Chopin's intended effects will remain obscure.

Jonathan Bellman

Bibliography

Bellman, Jonathan. "Chopin and the Cantabile Style." *Historical Performance* Vol. 2/2 (Winter 1989):63–71.

Chopin, Frédéric François. *Selected Correspondence of Fryderyk Chopin*. Ed. and trans. after Sydow, by Arthur Hedley. London: Heinemann, 1962.

Eigeldinger, Jean-Jacques. *Chopin: Pianist and Teacher* [1970]. Trans. Naomi Shohet et al. Cambridge: Cambridge University Press, 1986.

Temperley, Nicholas. "Chopin." *The New Grove Early Romantic Masters 1* (Revision of his entry on Chopin in *The New Grove Dictionary of Music and Musicians*.) New York: W. W. Norton & Company, 1985.

Winter, Robert. "The 19th Century: Keyboards." *Performance Practice: Music after 1600*. Edited by Howard Mayer Brown and Stanley Sadie. New York: W. W. Norton & Company, 1989.

CIMBALOM

Cimbalom is a Greek word designating a box zither of a type used in Hungary, but, in fact, related to the smaller versions of the German Hackbrett and Anglo-American dulcimer. During the Middle Ages the word *cimbalom* indicated several sorts of percussion instruments. It is not known with certainty when the word came to refer to the Hungarian instrument. One can distinguish two versions: the smaller, or *kiscimbalom*, and the larger *ornagycimbalom*. About 1870 Jozsef Schunda (Budapest) gave the cimbalom a standard size and design, that of the *pedalcimbalom*: four legs, **pedal**, **dampers**, and full chromatic range. Nowadays it is still used in folk music in Hungary (mainly by gypsies). Related instruments can be found in Rumania (*țambal*), Greece (*tsimbalo*), Poland (*cymbaly*), Ukraine (*tsymbaly*), and Latvia (*cimbole*).

F.J.de Hen

Bibliography

Sarosi, Balint. *Die Volksinstrumente Ungarns.* Leipzig: Deutscher Verlag für Musik, 1966.

CLARK (-STEINIGER), FREDERIC HORACE (1860–1917)

Frederic Horace Clark, American pianist, pedagogue, inventor, philosopher, theologian, and physiologist, was, according to Rudolf Breithaupt's *Handbuch der modernen Methodik und Spielpraxis*, 3rd ed. (1912), the first scholar to discuss and graphically illustrate the rolling movement of arm and wrist, in his *Lehre des einheitlichen Kunstmittels beim Klavierspiel* [The Doctrine of Unified Art of Piano Playing] (1885). This makes him the world pioneer in the physiological approach to piano playing. His *Harmonie-Piano*, built with two parallel **keyboards** with the pianist standing between them to play it, was an attempt to substantiate his intricate and highly speculative philosophic system in which religious (Christian) hierarchy and doctrine become a model for the coordination between internal and external parameters of artistic performance.

Clark was born near Chicago, and was essentially self-taught in piano playing until 1876, when he sailed to Germany. He proceeded on foot to Italy, just to see his idol, **Franz Liszt**. Clark allegedly spent some time with Liszt, and this experience was described in his book, *Liszts Offenbarung* [Liszt's Revelation] (1907). Clark then studied with Dr. Oscar Paul (author of a book on piano history) and later with Ludwig Deppe, in the interim returning for a while to the United States. In 1882 he married Anna Steiniger (1848–1890), a prominent Prussian pianist, who was probably the strongest exponent of Deppe's teaching method and was also Deppe's assistant. Clark and his wife arrived in Boston in 1885 but failed to arouse interest in their newly developed piano school. After his wife's death, Clark apparently moved to Valparaiso, Indiana, and by 1903 was again in Berlin. Always under extreme hardship and poverty, and rejected by the professors at the Berlin University as well, Clark spent his last years in Zürich. There he worked incessantly on his writing projects, dying before they were finished.

Clark's writings reveal a person of intense intellect, almost fanatical beliefs, and relentless drive. Wanting to persuade everyone to turn to his ideas on the true artistic spirit and its manifestations as a mirror of divine activity, he seems to have quite freely interpreted his conversations with Franz Liszt and **Johannes Brahms**, if they occurred at all. He even states that Brahms was the first one to experiment and build models of the *Harmonie-Piano*. To this day no existing proof of his claim to an intimate friendship with the two musicians has been discovered. However, he describes in detail Liszt's playing, observing with much more analytical and comprehending eyes than Amy Fay, who wrote a book that also deals partly with Liszt's teaching (*Music Study in Germany* [1880]). He seems to be among the first to understand the change in piano technique intro-

Frederic Horace Clark at the keyboards of his Harmonie-Piano.

duced by Liszt. Building on it, and acknowledging Liszt as a source and Hermann Helmholtz as an impetus, Clark, in his *Lehre*, tried to employ the pianist's body as a unit.

Clark's *Harmonie-Piano*, developed by 1913, bears the Royal German Patent Number 225,367. It consists of two parallel keyboards, elevated to shoulder level, with a forty-five degree inclination. The pianist stood between them with outstretched arms, thus eliminating all angles and establishing a general basis from finger-tips to the solar plexus, through arms, shoulders, and spine. (See illustration.) Recreating with this "Cherubim-doctrine" the old Greek principle of the "golden-mean," Clark thought that through this posture he had blended all extensors and flexors into one unbroken vortex-like motion. Under the keys there were springs to preserve the original key resistance in this inclination. Caps (faces) of the **keys** were slightly curved (concave), to allow the fingers to cling better. This position actually makes the thumb play more with its flat side, and certainly puts it closer and more even in respect to the other fingers. The pianist moved between the keyboards and there were several pairs of **pedals** that he could step on as he moved to and fro.

Clark apparently had a tendency to bend historical truth slightly, in order to prove his point and draw on authorities. Perhaps this could be justified by the amount of criticism and rejection he himself received. However, in the memory of his contemporaries he remained an extremely honest, direct, naïve, and childlike person, full of intense emotions, always somewhat detached from everyday life. Trying to systematize his approach and find a natural, logical, and unimpeded manner of playing, he assigned a specific meaning and place for each element in the material and ideal universe. His tendency towards absolute harmony with the surrounding world seems to have projected from his high social awareness. He was convinced that he had the means to teach humanity how to coexist better, how to understand Nature, and how to bring Art closer to the human soul. His renaissance approach, with a philosophy of total liberation of man's inner potential and its amalgamation with higher natural laws, is as much archaic as it is progressive in its message. Clark provided a significant link between the age of instinctive performance and the age of the scientific study of all parameters of playing.

Robert Andres

Bibliography

Andres, Robert. "Frederic Horace Clark: A Forgotten Innovator." *Journal of the American Liszt Society* 27 (January-June 1990): 3–16.

Breithaupt, Rudolf M. *Die natürliche Klaviertechnik.* Leipzig: C. F. Kahnt Nachfolger, 1912.

Clark, Frederic H. *Liszts Offenbarung.* Berlin: C. F. Vieweg, 1907.

———. *Pianistenharmonie.* Berlin: n.p., 1910.

———. *Brahms' Noblesse.* Zürich: Pianistenharmoniepresse, 1914.

Clark-Steiniger, Frederic H. *Iphigenia, Baroness of Styne.* London: Pure Music Society, private ed., 1896.

———. Frederic H. *Die Lehre des einheitlichen Kunstmittels beim Klavierspiel.* Berlin: Raabe & Plothow, 1885.

Cobb, John S. *Anna Steiniger.* Boston: G. Schirmer, 1886.

Fay, Amy. *Music Study in Germany.* Chicago: Jansen, McClurg, 1880.

Helmholtz, Hermann. "The Action of Arm Muscles." *Niederrh. Gesellsch. für Heilkunde*, 10 December 1857.

Die Musik in Geschichte und Gegenwart. S.v. "Clark, Frederic Horace," by Kurt Johnen.

CLAVICHORD'S INFLUENCE ON THE PIANO

The influence of the clavichord on the piano can be considered in four categories: 1. The term "clavier" was applied at first to both instruments; 2. Certain traits of sound generation are common to both instruments; 3. Some characteristics of construction are common to both instruments; 4. Piano playing **technique** originated from clavichord playing technique.

In early eighteenth-century German, the term "clavier" included organ, harpsichord, and clavichord, but later applied only to the clavichord. The term's usage is sometimes very confusing. **Johann Sebastian Bach** used the term both for any **keyboard** instrument (as in "The Well-Tempered Clavier") and for the keyboards of organ and harpsichord (see the introduction to the Goldberg Variations). When the "gravecembalo col piano e forte" was invented by **Bartolomeo Cristofori**, the term "clavier" was used for it as well.

Cristofori had tried to develop an instrument that had the volume and the fullness of **tone** of the harpsichord while also generating the differentiated tones of the clavichord.

The clavichord is a string instrument that uses a very simple **action** to make the **strings** oscillate. A tangent attached to the rear end of every **key** is in direct contact with the string. This tangent, a small metal plate approximately 1 to 1.5 cm long protruding from the end of the key, is pressed against the string. The sound produced in this way is very soft, but can easily be modulated because the player can control it directly.

Whereas the clavichord's tone is produced by pressing the tangent against the string, a **hammer** striking the string produces the fortepiano's sound (as the instrument was called in its early phase). The part of the clavichord string that oscillates is between the point where the tangent touches the string and the fret that transmits the vibrations to the **soundboard**. This means that the tangent's position determines the **pitch**. The shorter part of the string on the other side of the tangent is dampered by a piece of **felt**. The crucial common characteristic of the two instruments is the player's ability to influence the tone's volume and its quality by **touch**. Pressing the tangent against the string produces a very soft sound, between *p* and *ppp*, which can be varied after the key is struck. Applying more or less pressure produces a kind of vibrato. In contrast, the piano's tone remains unchanged and cannot be influenced after the key is struck; however, the tone's volume and quality can be modified up to the time that the hammer strikes the string.

Although significant outward construction characteristics of the harpsichord were applied to the early piano, for instance, the wing shape (**Flügel**) and the lengthwise arrangement of the strings, many outward characteristics of the clavichord were applied to the **square piano**. **Christian Ernst Friederici** was thought to have invented the square piano until a square by Johann Söcher, signed in 1742, was found. The square piano is rectangular, like the clavichord. Its **case** is a little larger than that of the late clavichords that were common during the time the piano was invented and developed. Clavichords made by leading producers, for example, Johann Heinrich Silbermann, Hironymus Albrecht Hass, or Christian Gottlob Hubert, are up to 150 cm wide, approximately 45 cm long, and up to 14.5 cm high. The square pianos of this time were about 170 cm wide, 55 cm long, and 19 cm high. The arrangement of the strings is identical in the clavichord and the square piano: parallel to the keyboard. This means that the point where the string is touched is in a different position on every string, whereas it is in the same position in harpsichords and **grand pianos**. The position of this point *does* influence the character of the tone, if only in a minor way. More important is the influence of generating a sound by striking two strings tuned identically. The two or more strings of the clavichord or the piano are struck simultaneously and sound the same, while the harpsichord's strings tuned to the same pitch produce different timbres. This action is closest to that of the unfretted clavichord. In contrast, the fretted clavichord uses one string to produce several tones, even though it is double-coursed.

In 1753 **Carl Philipp Emanuel Bach** published his essay *Versuch über die wahre Art das Clavier zu spielen*, wherein he applies some significant characteristics of clavichord playing technique to the fortepiano. The essay describes the musical and aesthetic views of its time. It has the following consequences for fortepiano playing technique: the clavichord key is struck only by a bent finger that touches the key before striking it. This produces a more or less perfect legato. The same hand position also produces a satisfactory legato on the early pianoforte. Another important common characteristic of clavichord and piano playing techniques at this time is the use of "light" and "heavy" fingers. Many sixteenth-century to eighteenth-century textbooks for keyboard instruments provide **fingering** that indicates which fingers were preferred and which ones were not used at all. Used on the organ and the harpsichord, this type of fingering creates a similar kind of melodic form as on the clavichord or the piano, but only on the two latter instruments are phrasings possible like ⌒ that sound loud-soft. This perfection of dynamic differentiation and the legato playing technique are the most important characteristics of clavichord playing technique that were taken over by the piano.

Jan Rademacher
Translated by Sandra Lustig

Bibliography

Bach, Carl Philipp Emanuel. *Versuch über die wahre Art das Clavier zu spielen, mit Exempeln und achtzehn Probestücken in sechs Sonaten erläutert.* 2 parts. Berlin 1753 and 1762. English edition. London and New York: W. J. Mitchell, 1949.

Couperin, Francois. *L'Art de toucher le clavecin.* Paris, 1717. Reprint. Wiesbaden, 1961.

Ehrlich, Cyril. *The Piano: A History.* 2nd ed., Oxford: Oxford University Press, 1990.

Haase, Gesine. "Clavichorde, Hammerklaviere." In *Tasteninstrumente.* Edited by Staatliches Institut für Musikforschung Berlin. Berlin, 1981.

Neupert, Hanns. *Das Klavichord.* Kassel, 1948. English edition. 1965.

Santa Maria, Tomás de. *Arte de tañer fantasia.* Valladolid. 1565. Reprint. 1973.

Sumner, William Leslie. *The Pianoforte.* London: Macdonald and Co., 1966.

CLAVIHARPE

Claviharpe was the name of an **upright piano** consisting of a gilded harp resting above a piano **keyboard**. The harp strings were plucked by hooks activated when the **keys** were pressed. Designed by the Johann Christian Dietz family, this instrument was an attractive addition to the nineteenth-century Parisian salon.

See also Harp-Piano.

Martha Novak Clinkscale

CLÉDI-HARMONIQUE

The *clédi-harmonique* was a piano invented by Jean Louis Boisselot of Marseille and shown at the Paris Exhibition of 1839. He obtained two perfectly unison-tuned **strings** by looping one string on a **hitch pin**. The advantages were precise unison, half the required **tuning** time, and half the number of **tuning pins** needed.

This idea had already been applied at the end of the eighteenth century by **Pascal Taskin** with his *crochet d'accord*. Also, previous to Boisselot, the Paris-based firm of **Pleyel** patented a similar idea in 1826.

F.J. de Hen

Bibliography

Description des Machines et Procédés spécifiés dans les Brevets d'Inventions, de Perfectionnement et d' Importation dont la Durée est expirée. Paris, no publisher named, 1811–1863.

CLEMENTI, MUZIO & COMPANY

Muzio Clementi (1752–1832) was born in Rome and at age fifteen moved to England, where he lived and worked until his death at the age of eighty. Well-known and honored during his lifetime as a composer, pianist, teacher, music publisher, and piano manufacturer, Clementi exerted considerable influence on musicians of his generation, most notably **Beethoven**. His lasting contribution was to the field of **keyboard** music, where his major works are *Gradus ad Parnassum*, published in three volumes (1817, 1819, 1826); and *Introduction to the Art of Playing on the Pianoforte* (1801).

In addition to his prominence as a musician, Clementi was also an entrepreneur, a surprising designation to those not aware of his extramusical achievements. In fact, his shrewd business dealings secured for his commercial enterprise a firm base for his piano division and numerous important publishing rights. Clementi was on friendly terms with every major composer and performer of his time, although his attention was invariably centered on whatever business opportunities these friendships might offer. In regard to Clementi's shrewd business sense, Leon Plantinga points out that to Clementi's admirers on the Continent his gradual conversion from art to business seemed like a degrading capitulation to materialism, yet in higher English society it would have been seen as a step towards respectability.

During the last decade of the eighteenth century Clementi was sufficiently affluent, through investments in publishing and instrument building, to be able to buy the bankrupt firm of **Longman & Broderip**, in which he had previously held a stake. The new firm, during several joint ownerships, became known as Clementi & Co., where music publishing and piano manufacturing existed under the same name. Together with his craftsman-partner, Frederick William Collard, Clementi formed an organization that would compete with the established English piano maker, **Broadwood & Sons**.

Clementi's artistic sense and technical ability as a performer led him to construct pianos of lighter **touch**, akin to the continental Viennese action (*Prellmechanik*) instruments, unlike those of Broadwood, which had the heavier **English action**. Clementi & Company produced **square pianos**, similar to those of Longman & Broderip, having a range of five-and-a-half octaves, with no hand stops or pedals. By 1810 the firm was producing pianos with a six-octave compass employing a damper **pedal**. From 1824 to 1832 the company manufactured **cabinet pianofortes**, **upright grand** pianofortes, and horizontal grand pianofortes, the last having a range of six-and-a-half octaves. W. J. G. Ord-Hume writes that during the years 1820 to 1825 Clementi also produced mechanical pianos, large upright instruments called "Self-Acting Pianofortes," or, more specifically, "Clock Work **Barrel Pianos**." The latter contained a pinned barrel, or cylinder, that, when wound, was capable of playing for half an hour without rewinding. This, combined with normal playing on the **keyboard**, produced surprising effects.

Clementi left matters of design and innovation to others in his company; however, he took an interest in choosing the **wires** used in **stringing** his pianos. Rosamond E. M. Harding lists nearly a dozen **patents** granted to F. W. Collard and James Stewart, Clementi's chief associates; however, Plantinga notes that only six patents were taken out during Clementi's lifetime "under the names of his business partners." From this information one can assume that additional patents were granted the pair either before or after their association with Clementi (Stewart was also a partner of **Jonas Chickering's** in Boston).

In addition to minor improvements in piano hinges, **checks**, and **hammers**, Collard's and Stewart's most important patents under the employ of Clementi are as follows: in 1821 Collard patented the "Harmonic Swell," also called "Bridge of Reverberation," whereby the construction of two **bridges** allowed extra undamped strings to produce rich and powerful sympathetic vibrations, thus increasing the clarity of the piano sound; in 1827 Stewart patented a stringing method—used to this day—whereby one continuous length of wire was looped around a **hitch pin** and attached to two wrest (**tuning**) **pins**, thereby creating two parallel unison strings.

As his popularity as a teacher grew, Clementi attracted many of the best talents of his time. Among pianist-composers who studied with Clementi, and who themselves went on to enjoy major careers, were Johann Baptist Cramer and John Field. (Friedrich Kalkbrenner is often included but must be considered a disciple, as no record of formal study with Clementi exists.) It was Clementi's habit to use his students to demonstrate the quality of his pianos to prospective buyers. During his extended sojourn to the Continent between 1802 and 1810, a journey designed primarily to cultivate European markets for his company's products, Cramer and Field were taken along to perform on Clementi's pianos. The itinerary included the cities of Paris, Vienna, Berlin, Prague, Zürich, Rome, and St. Petersburg. Con-

currently, Field was able to enhance his own stature as a performer, especially in Moscow and St. Petersburg.

Among pianists who spoke highly of Clementi's pianos was Ignaz Moscheles. Moscheles, who kept a diary throughout his career, wrote of his preference for Clementi's more supple mechanism to the heaviness of touch of the Broadwood piano—although he admired the latter's fullness and resonance of tone. Moscheles remained a devotee of the Clementi piano for many years, notably during much of the period when the firm of **Erard** was attempting to lure the pianist into committing himself solely to its own instrument. However, unlike Clementi & Company, the Erard firm continued to improve its pianos at a rapid rate, attempting to combine the best qualities of both the Viennese and English actions. As a result of Erard's development of the double **escapement**, or "repetition action"—which appealed to Moscheles' fondness for easily executed repeated notes—together with the firm's success in refining and enriching its piano sonority, the pianist chose to perform as a matter of course on Erard's instrument.

In addition to publishing new works of his own and those of Daniel Steibelt, Kalkbrenner, and other pianist-composers of his time, Clementi's resolve to publish the works of Beethoven was ultimately realized. His well-documented encounter with the Viennese master in 1807 secured for his publishing unit the British rights to a quantity of Beethoven's music. Included were the String Quartets: Opus 59, No. 1 in F Major; Opus 59, No. 2 in E Minor; Opus 59, No. 3 in C Major; and Opus 74 in E-Flat Major. Also included were the Concerto for Piano and Orchestra, Opus 73; the Symphony No. 4, Opus 60; the Fantasy for Piano, Chorus, and Orchestra, Opus 80; the Piano Sonata, Opus 81a; and the Concerto for Violin and Orchestra, Opus 61, along with its arrangement as a piano concerto.

"Father of the Pianoforte" was the title, with variants, given to Clementi during his lifetime. Indeed, his close association with the instrument as a composer and publisher of piano music, and as a piano manufacturer, lends truth to the description. In his role as composer, he is remembered today primarily for his sonatinas, an unfortunate circumstance since his many sonatas—of which there are over sixty—are artistically more substantial in scope, ranging in style from the pre-Classical galant to the dramatic, dynamic style of Beethoven. There are few performers today who include a Clementi Sonata in their concert repertoires; there are even fewer who have discovered the wealth of appealing material to be found in the original *Gradus ad Parnassum* (referring to the complete edition of 100 pieces, not the truncated version edited by Carl Tausig, which contains only the piano excercises). If he had not been overshadowed by his more celebrated contemporaries, Haydn, Mozart, and Beethoven, it would be interesting to speculate as to Clementi's present position in history. But regardless, as a teacher, composer, and mentor, Clementi's influence was felt throughout the pianistic world for many decades after his death.

Frederic Schoettler

Bibliography

Books

Colt, C. F. *The Early Piano*. London: Stainer & Bell, 1981.

Good, Edwin M. *Giraffes, Black Dragons, and Other Pianos*. Stanford, Cal.: Stanford University Press, 1982.

Harding, Rosamond E.M. *The Piano-Forte: Its History Traced to the Great Exhibition of 1851*. Cambridge: Cambridge University Press, 1933. Reprints. New York: Da Capo Press, 1973. Old Woking, Surrey: Gresham Books, 1978.

Ord-Hume, Arthur W. J. G. *Pianola: The History of the Self-Playing Piano*. London: Allen & Unwin, 1984.

Plantinga, Leon. *Clementi: His Life and Music*. Oxford: Oxford University Press, 1977.

Shedlock, J.S. *The Pianoforte Sonata: Its Origin and Development*. London: Methuen, 1895. Reprint. New York: Da Capo Press, 1964.

Tyson, Allen. *Thematic Catalogue of the Works of Muzio Clementi*. Tutzing: Hans Schneider, 1967.

Wainwright, David. *The Piano Makers*. London: Hutchinson, 1975.

Encyclopedias, Collections

Music Publishing in the British Isles. Edited by Charles Humphries and William C. Smith. London: Cassell and Co., 1954.

The New Grove Dictionary of Music and Musicians. Sixth edition. Edited by Stanley Sadie. S.V. "Clementi" (Volume IV). London: Macmillan, 1980.

The Science of Music in Britain, 1714–1830: A Catalogue of Writings, Lectures and Inventions. Edited by Jamie Croy Kassler. New York: Garland Publishing, 1979.

Music

Clementi, Muzio. *Gradus ad Parnassum*. Leipzig: C.F. Peters, 1817, 1819, 1826.

Recordings

Clementi, Muzio. *The Clementi Piano*. John Newmark playing a Clementi piano built in 1810. Clementi Sonatas: Opus 50, No. 3; Opus 40, No. 1. Pamphlet notes. Folkways Records, FM 3342.

CLUTSAM, FERDINAND (FL. c. 1900)

Ferdinand Clutsam was one of a number of inventors who devised concave **keyboards**. Clutsam received German **Patent** No. 211650 on 21 July 1907 for his innovation. Of the inventor himself, other than his Australian origin, no facts can be ascertained (**Alfred Dolge** even spelled his name Cludsam). The Kunsthistorisches Museum in Vienna possesses a **Bösendorfer grand** of 1895 equipped in 1910 with a Clutsam keyboard (Inventory No. 434 [9194]).

See also Keyboards.

Edwin M. Good

COCKED-HAT GRAND

Cocked-hat grands were a type of horizontal piano, designed and produced mainly by **Chickering & Sons**. The form is reminiscent, whether or not the Chickerings knew it, of the bentside spinet, an eighteenth-century type of harpsichord, and perhaps of the small late eighteenth- and early nineteenth-century horizontal piano the Germans called **Querflügel**. The nickname, of unknown origin, comes from the shape of the instrument as seen from directly above; the Chickering company called it a **Parlor Grand**. The instrument differs from a normal grand in having an acute angle, approximately forty-five degrees, between **keyboard** and **spine**. The **strings** run at the same acute angle as the spine, obliquely toward the right from the keyboard. **Hammers** must therefore be attached at an angle to their shanks.

A few magazine references in 1854–1855 suggest that **Jonas Chickering** himself designed the piano very shortly before his death in 1853. The company produced about four hundred of them from 1854 to 1863, when production stopped, 1856 being the year of greatest production, just over one hundred. **Serial numbers** range between 15,405 (a lost number book forbids certainty about any made before that) and 24,072. The **Mathushek** firm in New Haven, Conn., also made an unknown number.

The cocked-hat grand was intended to take a place midway between the **square** and the **grand**. Its length is about seventy-six inches, almost exactly the width of Chickering squares at the time, but it contained a grand **action**, often that designed by Edwin Brown. A major advantage was that the piano could be placed against a wall quite close to a corner, requiring less floor space than a normal grand, and **tuning pins** at the front made it much easier to tune than a large square.

Edwin M. Good

COIN-OPERATED PIANOS

Automatic pianos that were intended to be used in public places as a means of entertainment were normally set in play by the use of a coin or game token. These were called coin-operated or, occasionally, coin-freed pianos.

The coin-operated piano became a useful means of earning money for the keepers of bars, restaurants, clubs, and dancehalls, and was made possible by the introduction of instruments powered by clockwork spring motors and, later, by electricity, first provided from wet-cell accumulators and later from the public electricity supply.

The coin mechanism was of the sort devised for gaming machines, and makers sought similar protective devices to obviate the use of counterfeit coins or slugs.

While the first instruments of this type were the barrel-playing keyboardless pianos and, later, **barrel piano orchestrions**, the coin-operated piano came into its own with the dual perfection of perforated paper music (often in the form of multi-tune endless bands) and the independence offered by improved public electricity supply. There were many makers, and in America vast numbers of instruments were made in the key centers of New York, Philadelphia, Baltimore, and Chicago.

In Europe, German makers such as **Ludwig Hupfeld** produced prodigious numbers of such instruments for public places. Hupfeld was the first to produce a remote coin-box, which could be placed on a bar wall or table, so that the piano could be operated from a distance. This feature was soon taken up by the key American makers. The coin-operated piano was ousted by the jukebox, of which it was undoubtedly a progenitor.

Arthur W.J.G. Ord-Hume

Bibliography

Bowers, Q. David. *Encyclopedia of Automatic Musical Instruments*. Vestal, New York: Vestal Press, 1972.

Ord-Hume, Arthur W.J.G. *Pianola—History & Development* . . . . London: Allen & Unwin, 1984.

Roehl, Harvey. *Player Piano Treasury*. New York: Vestal Press, 1961 and 1973.

COLLARD & COLLARD

Among English piano manufacturers the London firm Collard & Collard (which continued Clementi's company) was second only to **Broadwood** in importance and production during the nineteenth century.

The roots of the business go back to James Longman's company, founded around 1767, which became the well-known **Longman & Broderip** (1776–1798), music publishers as well as piano builders. Bankruptcy in 1798 led to a partnership between John Longman and Muzio Clementi, from which—with a succession of members—Clementi, Collard & Collard evolved in 1822. William Frederick Collard (1776–1866) joined the firm around 1801; his brother, Frederick William Collard (1772–1860), became a partner in 1810. Clementi's death in 1832 left Collard and Collard, with F. W. Collard as senior partner. Thomas E. Purday took over the music publishing around 1834. Later, nephews Frederick William Collard and Charles Lukey Collard became partners, the latter heading the firm around 1877.

Clementi's genius helped shape the sound and quality of the pianos, but **patents** were filed in the names of F. W. Collard (in 1811, for an **upright** piano made by setting a **square** piano upwards on its long side) and W. F. Collard (in 1821, for a harmonic swell [pedal] and **bridge** of reverberation that increased the resonance). Around 1826 James Stewart, formerly of Chickering in Boston and an inventor in his own right, joined Clementi, Collard & Collard, where he served as foreman for thirty-five years. In 1827 he patented a technique that became the basis of modern **stringing**: in place of separate, adjacent strings, a double length of **wire** was passed around a larger, single **hitch pin** and back to an adjacent **tuning pin**. **Erard's** double **escapement action**, simplified by Henri Herz (1803–1888) around 1840, was further modified and adopted by Collard & Collard.

In England the **grand pianos** of Collard & Collard, along with those of Broadwood, were among the most highly regarded concert instruments in the first half of the nineteenth century. The firm also catered to clients of diverse economic strata. It made large instruments with six-and-a-half octave **keyboards** in **cases** of rose or other expensive woods highly ornamented with carving or inlaid work. But Rimbault (pp. 160–161) notes that Collard was also praised for "little Quaker-like pianos of white wood, fine tone and most moderate price" designed for those of limited means. These were small upright pianos of five-and-a-half octaves and one **pedal** in plain cases of inexpensive wood. These instruments displayed in the Crystal Palace Exhibition of 1851 cost 30 guineas, while a decorative grand piano cost 500 guineas. Collard exhibited two grand pianos, one large square, and three uprights. For comparison, Broadwood showed only four grands, and the London branch of Erard showed four grands and three upright instruments.

During the 1850s, after the construction of a new, efficiently organized factory, Collard & Collard produced approximately 1,500 pianos a year, surpassed only by Broadwood's approximately 2,500. (About a half-dozen English firms produced 300 to 500 and other companies far fewer.) By 1870 Collard's output rose to 2,500. Unfortunately, in the latter part of the century the firm was headed by men loath to accept the technological innovations of cast-iron **frames**, overstringing (see **Overstrung**), and the use of machinery in the manufacturing process. In 1888 John Clementi Collard (1844–1918) attacked the new stringing as acoustically inferior. At the same time, aggressive marketing of their modernized instruments by German companies caused sales of English pianos to decline and in 1929 the **Chappell Piano Company**, with an infusion of American capital, bought Collard & Collard, whose name, however, continued until 1971. A fire in Chappell's headquarters on 6 May 1964 destroyed all Collard records.

Sandra P. Rosenblum

Bibliography

Ehrlich, Cyril. *The Piano: A History.* London: J.M. Dent & Sons, Ltd. 1976.

Lamburn, Edward. *A Short History of a Great House—Collard & Collard.* London: Private printing, 1938.

Rimbault, Edward Francis. *The Pianoforte, Its Origin, Progress and Construction.* London: Cocks, 1860.

COLLECTIONS

This list includes only the largest of the many known private collections in the world. In the various public collections, there are significant differences in the numbers and choices of instruments. Patriotism often dominates a museum's selection of pianos. Whether according to plan or to coincidence, it is not unusual for a museum to concentrate its attention on pianos made domestically. Nevertheless, the world's greatest piano collections tend toward eclecticism, an aim achieved by occasional trade or purchase.

AUSTRALIA
Parkville
  University of Melbourne,
    Faculty of Music
Parkville
  University of Melbourne, Grainger
    Museum
Wornambool Downs
  Wornambool Museum

AUSTRIA
Baden-bei-Wien
  Beethovenhaus
Eisenstadt
  Burgenländisches Landesmuseum
Eisenstadt
  Haydn-Haus
Gneixendorf
  Johann van Beethoven-Haus
Graz
  Abteilung für Kunstgewerbe,
    Landesmuseum Joanneum
Graz
  Institut für Aufführungspraxis,
    Hochschule für Musik
Graz
  Stadtmuseum
Innsbruck
  Tiroler Landesmuseum
Linz
  Oberösterreichisches Landesmuseum
Salzburg
  International Stiftung Mozarteum,
    Mozart-Museum
Salzburg
  Museum Carolino-Augusteum
Vienna
  Jörg Demus Collection

Vienna
  Paul Badura-Skoda Collection
Vienna
  Bundes Mobilien Museum
Vienna
  Kunsthistorisches Museum
Vienna
  Museum der Stadt Wien
Vienna
  Niederösterreichisches Landesmuseum
Vienna
  Technisches Museum in Wien

BELGIUM
Antwerp
  Muziekconservatorium (Vleeshuis
    Museum)
Brugge (Bruges)
  Gruuthusemuseum
Brussels
  Musée Instrumental du Conservatoire
    Royal de Musique
Brussels
  Musées Royaux d'Art et d'Histoire
Brussels
  Institut Royal du Patrimoine Artistique

CANADA
Carillon, Québec
  Musée Historique d'Argenteuil
St. John, New Brunswick
  New Brunswick Museum
    Provincial Gallery
Toronto, Ontario
  Royal Ontario Museum, R. S. Williams
    Collection

CZECHOSLOVAKIA
Bratislava
  Slovenske Norodne Múzeum (Slovak
    National Museum)
Opava (Troppau)
  Schloss Hradec
Prague
  Bertramka, Mozart and Dusek Memorial
Prague
  City Museum
Prague
  Národni Muzeum (National Museum)

DENMARK
Copenhagen
  Carl Claudius' Musikhistoriske Samling
Copenhagen
  Musikhistorisk Museum

Copenhagen
  University of Copenhagen
EQUADOR
Quito
  Casa de la Cultura Ecuatoriana, Pedro
    Pablo Traversari Collection (Museo de
    Instrumentos Musicales)

FINLAND
Åbo (Turku)
  Sibeliusmuseum (Åbo Akademi)

FRANCE
Grasse
  Musée de Grasse
Lyon
  Musée Historique de Gadagne
Paris
  Musée de l'Opéra
Paris
  Musée Instrumental du Conservatoire
    National Supérieur de Musique
Paris
  Musée National des Techniques:
    Conservatoire National des Arts et
    Metiers
Paris
  Pleyel Collection
Versailles
  Château: Grand Trianon and Petit
    Trianon

GERMANY
Albstadt
  Musikhistorische Sammlung Jehle
Augsburg
  Mozartmuseum
Bad Krozingen
  Sammlung Fritz Neumeyer
Baden
  Stadtmuseum Schopfheim
Bayreuth
  Richard-Wagner-Museum, "Wahnfried"
Berlin
  Musikinstrumenten Museum der
    Staatliches Institut für
    Musikforschung, Preussischer
    Kulturbesitz
Berlin
  Sammlung Bradford Tracey (loan from
    Sammlung Neumeyer, Bad Krozingen)
Bingen
  Heimatmuseum
Bonn
  Beethovenhaus

Braunschweig
Braunschweigisches Landesmuseum
Braunschweig
Piano Museum und Sammlung
Schimmel
Braunschweig
Städtisches Museum, including the
Grotrian-Steinweg Collection
Bremen
Bremer Landesmuseum für Kunst- und
Kulturgeschichte
Cologne
Kölnisches Stadtmuseum
Cologne
Kunstgewerbemuseum
Cologne
Westdeutscher Rundfunk
Darmstadt
Hessisches Landesmuseum
Eisenach
Bachhaus
Erbdrostenhof (Münster)
Landesamt für Denkmalpflege
Erlangen
Universität Erlangen Musikwissenschaft
Seminar
Frankfurt am Main
Goethe Haus
Frankfurt am Main
Historisches Museum
Frankfurt am Main
Universitäts Bibliothek, Manskopfisches
Museum
Frankfurt an der Oder
Museum Viadrina und Musikkabinett
Freiburg
Universität Musikwissenschaftliches
Institut
Gelsenkirchen-Buer
Heimatmuseum
Göttingen
Georg-August Universität
Musikwissenschaftliches Seminar
Halle an der Saale
Händel-Haus
Hamburg
Altonaer Museum/Norddeutsches
Landesmuseum
Hamburg
Museum für Kunst und Gewerbe
Heidelberg
Universität Heidelberg
Musikwissenschaftliches Seminar

Leipzig
Universität Leipzig Musikinstrumenten-
Museum
Leipzig
Stadtgeschichtliches Museum (loan to
the MIM)
Lübeck
Museum für Kunst und
Kulturgeschichte der Hansestadt
Lübeck: St. Annen-Museum
Markneukirchen
Musikinstrumenten-Museum der Stadt
Munich
Bayerisches Nationalmuseum
Munich
Deutsches Museum von Meisterwerken
der Naturwissenschaft und Technik
Munich
Städtische Instrumentensammlung
Munich
Universität Musikwissenschaftliches
Institut
Nuremberg
Germanisches Nationalmuseum
Potsdam
Schloss Sans Souci
Stuttgart
Württembergisches Landesmuseum
Ulm
Museum der Stadt Ulm
Weimar
Goethe Museum
Weimar
Liszt Museum
Zwickau
Robert-Schumann-Haus

HOLLAND
The Hague
Haags Gemeentemuseum, including
several individual collections, such as
the Carel van Leeuwen Boomkamp,
the Dutch Royal Family, and the
Rijksmuseum Collections
Utrecht
Instituut voor Muziekwetenschap der
Rijksuniversiteit (University of Utrecht)

HUNGARY
Budapest
Iparmüvészeti Museum (Decorative
Arts Museum)
Budapest
Magyar Nemzeti Museum (Hungarian
National Museum)

Györ
János Xántus Museum
Kalocsa
Archbishop's Palace
Sopron
Liszt Ferenc Museum

ITALY
Bologna
Collezione L. F. Tagliavini
Florence
Museo degli Strumenti Musicali del
Conservatorio di Musica L. Cherubini
Milan
Museo degli Strumenti Musicali, Civico
Museo, Castello Sforzesco
Milan
Museo Teatrale alla Scala
Modena
Museo Civico di Storia e Arte
Medievale e Moderna
Naples
Conservatori`o di Musica San Pietro a
Maiella
Rome
Museo Strumentale Antico e Moderno
dell' Accademia nazionale di Santa
Cecilia, includes the Gorga Collection
Treviso
Museo Civico
Verona
Accademia Filarmonica, includes the
collection of the Musei Civici, Museo
di Castelvecchio

JAPAN
Tokyo
Kunitachi College of Music
Tokyo
Ueno Gakeun College

MONACO
Monaco
Prince Rainier, Royal Palace

NORWAY
Drammen
Austad Gård, Drammen Museum
Oslo
Norsk Folkemuseum
Trondheim
Ringve Museum

POLAND
Bendomin k. Gdańska
Muzeum Hymnu Narodowego
Brok
Parafia rzymsko-katolicka
Bydgoszcz
Kolekcja Zabytkowych Fortepianów
Filharmonii Pomorskiej
Kamienna Góra
Muzeum Tkactwa Dolnoslaskiego
Koz ówka k. Iubartowa
Muzeum Pa ac
Kraków
Muzeum Narodowe (National Museum)
Lańcut
Muzeum Zamek
Lublin
Muzeum Okregowe
Nieborów
Muzeum Narodowe
Opatówek
Muzeum Historii Przemys u
Poznań
Muzeum Instrumentow Muzycznych
Poznań
Palace in Arcugowo
Przemyśl
Muzeum Narodowe Ziemi Przemyskiej
Pszczyna
Muzeum Wnetrz Pa acowych
Warsaw
Muzeum Historyczne, Miastaw
Warszawy
Warsaw
Polskie Radio i Telewizja, Dyrekcja
Nagran
Warsaw
National Gallery
Warsaw
Towarzystwo im F. Chopina
W oc awek
Muzeum Historyczne Miasta Wloclawka
Zelazowa Wola
Chopin's Birthplace
Zgierz
Muzeum Miasta Zgierza

PORTUGAL
Lisbon
Museu Instrumental do Cónservatório
Nacional, including the Lambertini
collection

**RUSSIA AND THE UNIFIED STATES
(formerly Union of Soviet Socialist
Republics)**
Leningrad/St. Petersburg
  State Institute for Scientific Research:
    Institute for Theater, Music, and
    Cinematography
Moscow
  "Glinka, M.I.," State Central Museum of
    Musical Culture

SOUTH AFRICA
Cape Town
  University of Cape Town Faculty of
    Music

SPAIN
Barcelona
  Museo de la Música de Barcelona
El Escorial
  Palacio de El Escorial
Madrid
  Collección Hazen
Madrid
  Museo de Medallas y Música del Palacio
    Real de Madrid
Madrid
  Museo Municipal de Madrid
Madrid
  Museo Nacional del Pueblo Español
Madrid
  Real Academia de Bellas Artes de San
    Fernando
Murcia
  Museo de Bellas Artes de Murcia
Palma, Mallorca
  Monastery of Valldemosa
Seville
  Casa de Murillo Museum

SWEDEN
Göteborg
  Historiska Museet (Historical Museum)
Lund
  Kulturhistoriska Föreningen/Södra Sverige
Stockholm
  Musikhistoriska Museet (Museum of the
    History of Music)
Stockholm
  Stiftelsen Musikkulturens Främjande
Uppsala
  Upplandsmuseet

SWITZERLAND
Aarau
  Museum Schlössli

Basel
  Historisches Museum Basel, Sammlung
    alter Musikinstrumente
Bern
  Historisches Museum Bern
Bern
  Schloss Oberhofen Historisches Museum
Bischofszell
  Ortsmuseum
Bulle
  Musée gruérien
Burgdorf
  Historisches Museum, Rittersaalvereins
Frauenfeld
  Museum des Kantons Thurgau
Fribourg
  Musée d'Art et d'Histoire
Fribourg
  Musikwissenschaftliches Institut der
    Universität Fribourg
Geneva
  Conservatoire de Musique
Geneva
  Musée d'Art et d'Histoire
Geneva
  Musée d'Instruments Anciens de
    Musique de Geneva
Genf
  Musée d'art et d'histoire
Heiden
  Historisch-Antiquarischer Verein
La Sarraz
  Château La Sarraz
Laufen
  Heimatmuseum
Lausanne
  Musèe Historique de l'Évêché
Lichtensteig
  Toggenburger Heimatmuseum
Lucerne
  Richard-Wagner-Museum, Tribschen
Neuchâtel
  Musée d'Art et d'Histoire
Olten
  Historisches Museum Olten
Rapperswil
  Heimatmuseum Rapperswil
Sarnen
  Convent of St. Andreas
Sarnen
  Heimatmuseum
Scuol/Schuls
  Museum d'Engiadina bassa

Solothurn
   Historisches Museum, Schloss
    Blumenstein
Solothurn
   Museum der Stadt Solothurn
St. Gall
   Neues Museum
Thun
   Historisches Museum, Schloss Thun
Zürich
   Brogli Collection
Zürich
   Schweizerisches Landesmuseum

UNITED KINGDOM

England
Bath
   Holburne of Menstrie Museum
Bath
   Number 1 Royal Crescent
Bethersden, Kent
   Colt Clavier Collection
Brentford, Middlesex
   The British Piano Museum
Bristol
   Mobbs Keyboard Collection
Cambridge
   Emmanuel College
Cambridge
   Cambridge University Faculty of Music
County Durham
   Bowes Museum, Barnard Castle
Cranbrook, Kent
   Period Piano Co.
East Clandon, Surrey
   Hatchlands (Alec Cobbe Collection)
Exeter
   Royal Albert Museum
Goudhurst, Kent
   The Finchcocks Collection
Liverpool
   Liverpool Museum, includes the
   Rushworth and Dreaper Collection
London
   Her Majesty the Queen
London
   English Heritage, Ranger's House,
   Blackheath (part of the Dolmetsch
   Collection)
London
   English Heritage, The Iveagh Bequest,
   Kenwood

London
   Fenton House, Benton Fletcher
   Collection
London
   Horniman Museum, Dolmetsch Collection
London
   The Broadwood Collection
London
   The Royal Academy of Music, includes
   many pianos from the collection of
   John Broadwood & Sons, Ltd.
London
   The Royal College of Music
London
   Victoria and Albert Museum
Maidstone, Kent
   Maidstone Museums & Art Gallery
Manchester
   Heaton Hall
Manchester
   The Royal Northern College of Music
Oxford
   Faculty of Music, St. Aldate's, including
   The Bate Collection
Port Sunlight
   Trustees of the Lady Lever Collection
York
   Castle Museum

Scotland
Dundee
   City of Dundee Art Galleries and
   Museums
Edinburgh
   The Georgian House
Edinburgh
   Reid School of Music, University
   of Edinburgh, includes the Russell
   Collection
Edinburgh
   Royal Museum of Scotland (on loan to
   University of Edinburgh)

UNITED STATES OF AMERICA

California
Anaheim
   Mother Colony House (first house in
   Anaheim)
Berkeley
   University of California, Department of
   Music
Cherry Valley
   Edward-Dean Museum

City of Industry
  Workman-Rowland Ranch Reservoir
    Museum, Workman and Temple
    Homestead
Claremont
  Kenneth G. Fiske Museum
Los Angeles
  University of Southern California,
    Hancock Memorial Museum
Los Angeles
  Avila Adobe, Olvera Street
Los Angeles
  County Museum of Natural History
Los Angeles
  Lugo Family, Rancho San Antonio Lugo
Los Angeles
  Toller Ranch House
Los Angeles
  University of California, Department
    of Music
Mission Hills
  Eulegio de Celis family, Andres Pico
    Adobe
Montebello
  Adobe Sanchez Museum
Monterey
  Robert Louis Stevenson Home
Pomona
  Adobe de Palomares Museum
Riverside
  Mission Inn Foundation
San Francisco
  California Historical Society
San Francisco
  DeYoung Museum, Golden Gate Park
San Francisco
  Frank V. de Bellis Collection,
    San Francisco State University
San Francisco
  Society of California Pioneers
San Marino
  Henry E. Huntington Library,
    Art Gallery and Botanical Gardens
Santa Ana
  Bowers Museum
Santa Fe Springs
  Ogilvie Family, Sanford Adobe
Sonoma
  Governor Vallejo Home
Stanford
  Stanford University, Department
    of Music

Sunnyvale
  Bjarne B. Dahl Collection
Whittier
  Pio Pico's El Ranchito, Pio Pico
    State Park
Wilmington
  General Phineas Banning Residence
    Museum

Connecticut
New Haven
  Yale Collection of Musical Instruments,
    including the Skinner and Steinert
    Collections

Delaware
Winterthur
  The Henry Francis duPont Winterthur
    Museum

District of Columbia
Washington
  National Museum of American History
    (Smithsonian Institution), including
    the Hugo Worch Collection
Washington
  The White House

Florida
Jacksonville
  Cummer Gallery of Art
St. Augustine
  Lightner Museum
St. Augustine
  National Society of Colonial Dames,
    Ximenez-Fatio House
White Springs
  Stephen Foster Memorial

Hawaii
Honolulu
  Hanaiakamalama, Home of Queen
    Emma of Hawaii

Illinois
Chicago
  Chicago Historical Society
Galena
  Galena Museum

Indiana
Indianapolis
  Benjamin Harrison Home

Maine
Portland
  Henry Wadsworth Longfellow Home

Maryland
Baltimore
  Edgar Allan Poe Home
Frederick
  Historical Society of Frederick County

Massachusetts
Ashburnham
  E. Michael Frederick Collection
Boston
  Boston Public Library
Boston
  Museum of Fine Arts, Boston
Braintree (Quincy)
  John Adams Home, Peacefield
Cambridge
  Ruth and G. Norman Eddy Collection
Deerfield
  Frary House, Historic Deerfield
Deerfield
  Stebbins House, Historic Deerfield
Milton
  Milton Historical Society, Suffolk
    Resolves House
Newton
  The Marlowe A. Sigal Collection
Old Newbury
  Historical Society
Salem
  Essex Institute
Salem
  Pingree House
Salem
  The House of Seven Gables
Sharon
  Whaling Museum
Wellesley
  Wellesley College

Michigan
Ann Arbor
  University of Michigan, Stearns
    Collection
Dearborn
  Henry Ford Museum & Greenfield
    Village
Detroit
  Detroit Historical Society
Detroit
  Detroit Institute of Arts

Minnesota
Rochester
  Olmstead County Historical Society

St. Paul
  Minnesota Historical Society
St. Paul
  The Schubert Club

Nebraska
Lincoln
  Nebraska Historical Society

New Hampshire
Concord
  Franklin Pierce Home
Hillsborough
  Franklin Pierce Homestead

New Jersey
Caldwell
  Grover Cleveland Home
Newark
  Newark Museum

New York
Albany
  Albany Institute of History and Art
Buffalo
  Buffalo Museum of Science
New York
  Metropolitan Museum of Art, including
    the Crosby Brown Collection
New York
  Museum of the American Piano
Scarsdale
  Dorothy and Robert Rosenbaum
    Collection

North Carolina
Chapel Hill
  Ackland Art Museum
Greensboro
  Greensboro Historical Museum
New Bern
  New Bern Historical Society
Raleigh
  State of North Carolina, Executive
    Mansion
Raleigh
  Wake County Chapter, Colonial Dames,
    Haywood Hall
Winston-Salem
  Moravian Music Foundation
Winston-Salem
  Old Salem, Inc.
Winston-Salem
  Wachovia Historical Society, Old Salem,
    Inc.

Ohio
Cincinnati
  Cincinnati Art Museum
Cincinnati
  Taft Museum
Lima
  Allen County Historical Society
Niles
  William McKinley National Memorial
    Library
Toledo
  Museum of Fine Arts

Oregon
Hillsboro
  Washington County Pioneer Museum

Pennsylvania
Harrisburg
  State Museum of Pennsylvania
Harrisburg
  The Governor's Mansion
Lewisburg
  Bucknell University
Philadelphia
  American Catholic Historical Society
Philadelphia
  Historical Society of Pennsylvania

South Carolina
Charleston
  Charleston Museum: Aiken-Rhett House
Charleston
  Charleston Museum: Joseph Manigault
    House
Charleston
  Historical Charleston Foundation
Columbia
  Museum of Art
Salem
  Alumni House, Salem College

South Dakota
Vermillion
  The Shrine to Music Museum

Tennessee
Columbia
  James Knox Polk Home
Memphis
  Peabody Hotel
Nashville
  Andrew Jackson Home, The Hermitage

Virginia
Arlington
  Custis Lee Mansion, Arlington Cemetery
Charles City
  John Tyler Home, Sherwood Forest
Charlottesville
  James Monroe Home, Ash Lawn
Charlottesville
  Thomas Jefferson Home, Monticello
Clarksville
  Prestwood Plantation
Fredericksburg
  James Monroe Law Office and Memorial
    Library
Mount Vernon
  Woodlawn Plantation
Williamsburg
  College of William and Mary, Earl
    Gregg Swem Library
Williamsburg
  Colonial Williamsburg Foundation

West Virginia
Huntington
  Huntington Galleries

Wisconsin
Sturgeon Bay
  Door County Historical Society

Martha Novak Clinkscale

Bibliography

Few collections have printed catalogs available. The following bibliography contains a list of books and articles that describe some of the outstanding collections that do include pianos. The reader is referred to Laurence Libin's article, "Instruments, Collections of," in *The New Grove Dictionary of Music and Musicians*, vol. 9. pp. 248–254, for a helpful and extensive bibliography of general and specific musical instrument collections.

[Austria. Graz] Stradner, Gerhard. *Musik-instrumente in Grazer Sammlungen (Grazer öffentliche Sammlungen) (Tabulae Musicae Austriacae: Kataloge österreichischer Musik-überlieferung)*, ed. Othmar Wessely. Band XI. Vienna: Der Österreichischen Akademie der Wissenschaften, 1986.

[Austria. Vienna. Kunsthistorisches Museum] Luithlen, Victor. *Katalog der Sammlung alter Musikinstrumente. I. Teil: Saitenklaviere.* Vienna: Kunsthistorisches Museum, 1966.

[Belgium. Antwerp. Museum Vleeshuis] *Catalogus van de Muziekinstrumenten uit de verzameling van het Museum Vleeshuis.* Antwerp: Ruckers Genootschap, 1981.

[Belgium. Brussels. Conservatoire Royal de Musique] Mahillon, Victor-Charles. *Catalogue descriptif et analytique du Musée Instrumental du Conservatoire Royal de Musique de Bruxelles,* v. 5. Brussels: T. Lombaerts, 1922; repr. Brussels: Les Amis de la Musique, 1978.

[Canada. Toronto. Royal Ontario Museum] Cselenyi, Ladislav. *Musical Instruments in the Royal Ontario Museum.* Toronto: Thorn Press, 1971.

[Finland. Åbo (Turku). Sibeliusmuseum Musik-vetenskapliga Institutionen vid Åbo Akademi, Bibliotek & Arkiv] Dahlström, Fabian. *Finlänsk Klavertillverkning före år 1900 samt beskrivning av Sibeliusmuseets inhemska klaversamling.* Åbo (Turku): Abo Akademi, 1978.

[Germany. Berlin. Staatliches Institut für Musikforschung (Stiftung Preußischer Kulturbesitz). Musikinstrumenten-Museum] Haase, Gesine, and Dieter Krickeberg. *Tasteninstrumente des Museums.* Berlin: Staatliches Institut für Musikforschung, 1981.

[Germany. Nürnberg. Germanisches National-museum] Meer, John Henry van der. *Wegweiser durch die Sammlung historischer Musik-instrumente.* Nürnberg: Germanisches Nationalmuseum, 3rd ed., 1982.

[Germany. Eisenach. Bachhaus] Heyde, Herbert. *Historische Musikinstrumente im Bachhaus Eisenach.* Eisenach: Bachhaus Eisenach, 1976.

[Great Britain. East Clandon, Surrey. Hatchlands] Cobbe, Alec. *A Century of Keyboard Instruments 1760–1860.* Cambridge: Fitzwilliam Museum, 1983.

[Great Britain. Edinburgh. University] Newman, Sidney, and Peter Williams. *The Russell Collection and Other Early Keyboard Instruments in Saint Cecilia's Hall, Edinburgh.* Edinburgh: Edinburgh University Press, 1968.

[Great Britain. Goudhurst, Kent. Finchcocks] Dow, William. *Finchcocks Collection: Catalogue. The Richard Burnett Collection of Historical Keyboard Instruments.* Compiled by William Dow, with a Foreword by Richard Burnett. Goudhurst, Kent: Finchcocks, 1989.

[Great Britain. London. Victoria and Albert Museum] Schott, Howard. *Catalogue of Musical Instruments. Volume I: Keyboard Instruments.* London: Her Majesty's Stationery Office, 1985.

[Great Britain. London. Horniman Museum and Library] Palmer, Frances. *The Dolmetsch Collection of Musical Instruments.* London: Archway Press, Ltd., 1981.

[Netherlands, The. The Hague. Gemeente-museum] Gleich, Clemens von. *A Checklist of Pianos: Musical Instrument Collection Haags Gemeentemuseum. Checklists of the Musical Instrument Collection of the Haags Gemeente-museum, The Hague.* Rob van Acht, editor. Vol 1. The Hague: Haags Gemeentemuseum, 1986.

[Poland. Bydgoszcz. Filharmonia Pomorska] Vogel, Beniamin. *Kolekcja Zabytkowych Fortepianów Filharmonii Pomorskiej.* Bydgoszcz: Filharmonia Pomorska im. Ignacego Paderewskiego Osrodek Dokumentacji Zabytkow W Warszawie, 1987.

[United States of America. Oxford]Clinkscale, Martha Novak. *Makers of the Piano: 1700–1820.* Oxford: Oxford University Press, 1992.

[United States of America. Cambridge, Mass. The Ruth and G. Norman Eddy Collection] Good, Edwin M. *The Eddy Collection of Musical Instruments.* Berkeley: Fallen Leaf Press, 1985.

[United States of America. New York, NY. Metro-politan Museum of Art] Libin, Laurence. *American Musical Instruments in The Metropolitan Museum of Art.* New York: W. W. Norton & Company, Inc., and London: Thames and Hudson, 1985.

[United States of America. Washington, D.C. Smithsonian Institution] Odell, Scott, and Cynthia Adams Hoover, editors. *A Checklist of Keyboard Instruments at the Smithsonian Institution,* 2nd ed. Washington: Smithsonian Institution, 1975.

COMBINATION PIANOS

A combination or compound piano is a piano that is combined with another instrument. Unlike the piano **orchestrion**, it is generally an amalgamation with another **keyboard** instrument. The earliest examples were the combined harpsichord-spinets of the eighteenth century. When in 1716 **Bartolomeo Cristofori** catalogued the musical instrument collection in Florence of the Grand Duke Cosimo III of Tuscany, he listed an organ combined with a spinet, another with a harpsichord and two spinets, and a third combined with a clavichord. By the second half of the eighteenth century, harpsichord-pianos were popular. In 1759, the Amsterdam-born maker Weltman [Veltman] showed the Academy of Science in Paris a *Clavecin à maillets* that also included a full-compass carillon.

Numerous combinations of pianos with all sorts of other instruments have been constructed. The ingenuity of the builder was given full reign to explore the possibilities that lay ahead. Examples of various types of combination pianos are here listed.

Harpsichord-Piano: The oldest known harpsichord-piano was made in 1774 by **John Joseph Merlin**, who called his instrument "Claviorganum" (the title is in fact erroneous, this name being reserved for the combination of harpsichord and organ). Other similar combinations were invented or improved by **Robert Stodart** in 1777, Johannes Andreas **Stein** in his *vis-à-vis Flügel* of 1777, James Davis in 1792, and **Sébastien Erard** in 1809.

Clavichord-Piano: In 1792, **John Geib** invented a new musical instrument with two sets of keyboards, a piano joined together with a clavichord.

Double Piano: The combination of two pianos was also devised; in 1801 in Vienna, **Matthias Müller** constructed his *Ditanaklasis*, in which two **upright** pianos were placed back to back, with one instrument playing an octave above. In 1811, Sébastien Erard devised his *"piano à deux claviers en regard,"* a double piano with two opposing keyboards. The Mangeot Bros. **patented** a *"piano à claviers renversés"* in 1876. The idea came from Joseph Wieniawski, a famous pianist of the day. The instrument consists of two **grand pianos**, one being reversed and placed upon the other. The left hand plays the lower keyboard, which runs from the bass (left) to the treble (right), while the right hand plays on the upper keyboard, which runs the opposite way.

Piano-Violin: Gama of Nantes invented his *plectroeuphone* in 1827. The **strings** were struck with **hammers** or bowed with an endless bow. In 1865, a **patent** was obtained by Hubert Cyrille Baudet, represented by Leblanc, for a combination of keyboard instruments called *piano-violon*.

Piano-Cymbalom: This instrument was introduced in 1913 by Hideg (Hungary). It met no success, not even in its country of origin.

Piano with Three or More Instruments (or their imitation): Robert Worton made a combination of piano, harpsichord, and violin in 1861 called the *lyro-vis-piano*. Here, **jacks** and hammers were combined by joining the hammers with an arm equivalent to the harpsichord jack. The strings could also be bowed by means of a piece of wood in the shape of a quadrant, "which forms a rocking or reciprocating bow which partially revolves in contact with the strings and produces a kind of violin tone." Without the harpsichord stop this instrument was called *vispianoforte*. **Alexandre-François Debain**, a well-known Parisian instru-

ment maker, invented the *piano-concert* in 1877, which combined a harmonicorde, an organ, a harmonium, and a piano.

Piano-Organ: Both **square pianos** and grand pianos have been combined with positive organs. At the end of the eighteenth century there were several builders of these instruments: Johann Gottlob Horn from Dresden (1785), Thomas Kunz from Prague (1796), and Sébastien Pfeffel from Havre (1797). In 1800, Johann Heinrich Völler from Angersbach brought out the *Apollonion*, which was a piano with an eighteen-stop organ. In 1854, Edouard Alexandre presented a combination instrument with separate mechanisms. This instrument was made at the request of **Franz Liszt**. It had three keyboards and sixteen stops, as well as a pedal. Athanase Mathurin Pierre Airiau took provisional protection in 1862 for a "new musical instrument . . . permitting the simultaneous or alternate production of tones . . . of the piano and the organ." Here the organ part was added mainly below the keyboard. Some sources, though difficult to verify, mention that Christian Gottlob **Friederici** also made piano-organs at the beginning of the nineteenth century. In 1772, the organ builder to the king of France, L'Epine, displayed to the Academy of Science in Paris a "forte piano" to which was attached a pipe organ. By far the largest number of piano-organ combinations followed the development and subsequent refinement of the principles of the free-reed organ, or harmonium, and its design and construction. **Claude Félix Seytre** appears to have had such an instrument in mind: his patent of 1842 refers to incorporating in his piano "the music board of the organ, harmonica, or accordion which play in all keys and which accompany the piano or play solos." The first definitive reference to a piano-reed-organ combination appears to be that of Obed M. Coleman of Philadelphia, whose invention was covered by U.S. **patent** No. 3548 granted on 17 April 1844. Three years later, piano-organs built on Coleman's designs were being manufactured in Boston by T. Gilbert & Company. A similar instrument was designed in 1863 by a man from Buffalo, Lafayette Louis, who was granted a U.S. patent for his combined reed organ and piano. The popularity of the reed organ in the 1880s, particularly following the invention of the so-called American organ, which used suction instead of pressure (as used by the original melodeon and harmonium), spawned many attempts to unite reed organs with pianos. Makers in the United States, England, Germany, and France turned out pieces ranging from full-compass dual mechanisms down to small organ keyboards combined with the upper registers of the piano. The best-known of the former was the "Orgapian" made by Whomes of Bexleyheath, England, a number of which were produced in 1915. Another was the "Clavimonium," intended as an accompaniment instrument for silent pictures, a rather poor attempt at making a low-cost English **theater photoplayer**. All such combination pianos, whether reed organ or pipe, suffered from one inherent defect: that of keeping the two instruments in tune with each other.

F.J. de Hen and
Arthur W.J.G. Ord-Hume

Bibliography

Good, Edwin Marshall. *Giraffes, Black Dragons, and Other Pianos: A Technological History from Cristofori to the Modern Concert Grand*. Stanford, Cal.: Stanford University Press, 1982.

Harding, Rosamond E.M. *The Piano-Forte: Its History Traced to the Great Exhibition of 1851.* Cambridge: Cambridge University Press, 1933. Reprints. New York: Da Capo Press, 1973; Old Woking, Surrey: Gesham Books, 1978.

Ord-Hume, Arthur W.J.G. *Harmonium*. Newton Abbot: David & Charles, 1986; New York: Vestal Press, 1986.

———. *Pianola—History & Development*. London: Allen & Unwin, 1984.

Russell, Raymond. *The Harpsichord & Clavichord*. London: Faber, 1973.

COMPOSERS' INFLUENCE ON THE PIANO

Although influential primarily because of the music they created, composers from **Wolfgang Amadeus Mozart** through **Johannes Brahms** and Béla Bartók also encouraged—or at least responded to—developments in piano technology; in so doing they helped make the piano the most widely purchased and played instrument of the late nineteenth and early twentieth centuries. Other composers—John Cage and Karlheinz Stockhausen, to name but two—have to some extent been responsible for the relative decline of the piano's importance in serious music, especially since World War II.

Many of the finest Classical, Romantic, and post-Romantic composers of Europe and the United States were themselves pianists who wrote large amounts of music for their instrument. A complete list of these composers would fill pages; it merely begins with the names of **Johann Christian Bach, Joseph Haydn**, Mozart, **Ludwig van Beethoven**, Franz Schubert, John Field, **Frédéric Chopin**, **Robert Schumann**, **Franz Liszt**, Brahms, Peter Ilich Tchaikovksy, Edward MacDowell, Edvard Grieg, Antonin Dvořák, Claude Debussy, Alexander Scriabin, Charles Ives, Arnold Schönberg, and Bartók. These and other creative artists stimulated developments in piano technology, or at least made use of those developments, primarily through the piano music they wrote. More than a few of these composers were also performing artists of the highest caliber, whose concert appearances helped secure for the piano a position in nineteenth-century music analogous to the position held by the violin in the eighteenth century or by the lute in the seventeenth. Finally, a few composers—**Muzio Clementi** among them—were themselves piano manufacturers who used their own instruments to demonstrate the beauties of the pieces they composed.

The development of the piano concerto as a medium of musical expression called for instruments capable of projecting the quietest as well as the most violent passages Mozart—and later Beethoven—were capable of writing. These composers and others of their generations put an end to the harpsichord versus piano controversy that had raged during much of the late eighteenth century in certain musical circles. Beethoven, especially, wrote music that demanded the larger compass, stronger **frame**, and greater capacity for dynamic contrasts that pianos like those of **Broadwood**'s firm made available to purchasers by 1820; thus the designation "Hammerklavier" for Beethoven's Sonata in B-flat Major, Op. 106 (published in 1819), was utterly appropriate. Subsequently, Sigismond Thalberg, Chopin, and especially Liszt exploited the capacities of the even larger, even more flexible instruments manufactured by **Erard** and other French firms. Their compositions thus became associated with Parisian instruments of seven octaves and double-**escapement** actions, just as the compositions of Schubert, Schumann, and Brahms became associated with Viennese instruments manufactured by **Graf, Bösendorfer**, and **Streicher**. Even today many performers believe that **Viennese pianos** are uniquely suited to delicate passages like the opening of Schubert's posthumously published Sonata in B-flat Major (1828); that the rhapsodies and intermezzos of Brahms, pitched to a considerable extent in the middle and lower ranges of the modern piano, sound best on Bösendorfer instruments; and that Chopin and Liszt conceived at least some of their most spectacular keyboard effects on and for pianos manufactured by the firms in whose showrooms they regularly introduced their music to the world.

Piano pieces, especially of a somewhat simpler character, increased in popularity after the middle of the nineteenth century. Method books and collections of keyboard exercises, some of them composed or contributed to by the likes of Carl Czerny, Schumann, and Liszt, provided students of every background and taste with appropriate pedagogical material. The rise of the American piano industry, especially after 1865, was complemented by the compositions of Edward MacDowell and his New World successors, as well as by ragtime composers like Scott Joplin, who tailored piano pieces to amateur as well as professional talents. In Europe as in America, piano ownership became a *sine qua non* of financial as well as artistic respectability—and small wonder, since so much of the best (as well as the most entertaining) music was written for the piano. By 1914, when World War I began, the talents of the piano composers, combined with the increasing affluence of Western music-lovers, had made possible the mass production and widespread sales of iron-framed, seven-octave **Steinway**, **Chickering**, and Bösendorfer instruments (to mention but a few prominent names) on both sides of the Atlantic Ocean.

The piano began to decline in relative popularity only when composers like Debussy, Scriabin, and Schönberg began to write music either too technically demanding or too experimental in style to suit mass consumption. As the twentieth century progressed, the piano gradually became associated less often with new music, more often with the masterpieces of the previous century and with jazz, the earliest popular music of distinctive character. Comparative indifference on the part of composers like Igor Stravinsky, Paul Hindemith, and the Viennese serialists to solo piano music as an important vehicle for expression and experimentation contributed to that situation, as did growing fondness on the part of jazz enthusiasts for bigger bands and fewer keyboard solos. Bartók was an exception to this rule; his piano works, including the six-volume collection of Mikrokosmos pieces, have influenced the teaching of piano music and have found a place in the permanent keyboard repertory. Less "successful" than Bartók, avant-gardists of the 1930s, 1940s, and 1950s proved themselves more innovative in approaching the piano as a mechanism. In works like Metamorphosis (1938), for instance, John Cage experimented with **"prepared" pianos**, instruments outfitted with wedges and coins inserted between or placed on top of groups of **strings**. Explorations into the electrical amplifications of conventional instruments by Stockhausen and his followers failed satisfactorily to transform the standard piano into a "modern" instrument—although, since the late 1950s, electric keyboard instruments (including certain kinds of **synthesizers**) have begun to acquire composers and literatures of their own.

Michael Saffle

COMPOUND PIANOS

See Combination Pianos.

CONCERT GRAND

A concert grand is a nine- to twelve-foot **grand piano** used almost exclusively in medium to large concert halls. It is usually finished in ebony black. A piano this size is necessary for the concerto repertoire, in which the piano competes with a full-sized symphony orchestra. The largest sizes have usually been made at a customer's special request.

See also Grand Piano; see illustration under Steinway & Sons.

Camilla Cai

CONSOLE PIANO

Console Piano is a type of low **upright piano** about forty inches high, first introduced by **Jean-Henri Pape** in Paris in 1828. This instrument was the first to be built with **cross-stringing**, which was Pape's invention and which was quickly adopted by contemporary makers.

Console is also used as a synonym for the modern **spinet** piano.

See also Overstrung; Upright Piano.

Martha Novak Clinkscale

COTTAGE PIANO

The cottage piano was originally a small, low **upright** about four to five feet high and distinguished by vertical **stringing** that reaches to the floor. It was **patented** by the London builder **Robert Wornum** in 1811; the earliest models were built by Wornum and his partner, George Wilkinson. Wornum continued to improve his original design for the cottage piano until 1828, while other London builders lost no time in imitating the style. These include **John Broadwood & Sons, William Rolfe & Sons**, and **William Stodart**. During the 1830s cottage pianos by **Collard & Collard** reached a height of seven feet.

See also Upright Piano.

Martha Novak Clinkscale

COUPLERS

Couplers are seldom used in pianos. A series of experiments with octave couplers are to be found in the first half of the nineteenth century (**patented** variously by **Erard, Streicher**, Boisselot, Samuel Warren, et al). They also occur in some multimanual pianos, such as the **Moór** keyboard, to make keyboards play simultaneously.

See also Keyboards.

Edwin M. Good

CREHORE, BENJAMIN (1765–1831)

Benjamin Crehore was the first piano builder in New England. Apprentices trained by him became national leaders of the piano industry during the early nineteenth century.

Crehore was born and lived in Milton, Massachusetts, where he had an instrument making and repair shop for most of his life. He also travelled occasionally to Boston, New York, and Philadelphia, where he was well known as a stage carpenter.

After previous experience with other instruments (there are still several extant Crehore violoncelli), Crehore began to repair keyboard instruments by 1792. He started to build pianos a few years later and then entered into a business venture with Peter A. Von Hagen, a musical conductor at Federal Street Theater, Boston, who owned a music shop and gave music lessons also. The partnership dissolved after several years. Crehore continued to build pianos in Milton but his production never exceeded ten or twelve pianos annually. Crehore pianos were sold in New York as well as in New England. Unfortunately for Crehore, most wealthy buyers preferred the more prestigious imports. In his final years, he gave up his shop and went to work for others. All but one of the few Crehore pianos still in existence contain simple **Zumpe actions**. The Metropolitan

Museum of Art collection includes the Crehore **square piano** with a double action.

While Crehore was unsuccessful in his own business, he is credited with establishing the industry in New England. Prominent piano makers of the early nineteenth century, such as **John Osborne** and **Alpheus** and Lewis **Babcock**, received their training in Crehore's shop.

Jack Greenfield

Bibliography

Kuronen, Darcy. "The Musical Instruments of Benjamin Crehore." *Journal of the Museum of Fine Arts, Boston* 4 (1992): 52–79.

Libin, Laurence. *American Musical Instruments in the Metropolitan Museum of Art.* New York: The Metropolitan Museum of Art and W. W. Norton and Company, 1985.

*The New Grove Dictionary of Music and Musicians.*Vol. 5; 29–30. Edited by Stanley Sadie. S.V. "Benjamin Crehore," by Cynthia Adams Hoover. London: Macmillan; Washington, D.C.: Grove's Dictionaries, 1984.

Spillane, Daniel. *History of the American Pianoforte: Its Technical Development and the Trade.* New York: D. Spillane, 1890. Reprint. New York: Da Capo Press, 1969.

CRISTOFORI, BARTOLOMEO (1655–1732)

The inventor of the first pianoforte, Bartolomeo Cristofori, was born on 4 May 1655, in Padua, Italy. He was a builder of musical keyboard instruments, and after 1680 he concentrated on and experimented with the structural design and the **action** mechanism of harpsichords. Around 1698, during his early career as court instrument maker to Prince Ferdinando de' Medici at Florence, he invented the *arpicimbalo che fà il piano e il forte* (a harpsichord that produces soft and loud). He continued to experiment, design, and build this instrument—which to this very day has no name other than "quiet-loud," i.e., pianoforte— until the time of his death in Florence on 27 January 1732 [*stile fiorentino* 1731, based on the liturgical calendar]. There are at present only three surviving Cristofori instruments, all of which were completed during the second decade of the eighteenth century—in 1720, 1722, and 1726.

The church records of St. Luke's in Padua indicate that Bartolomeo was the son of Francesco Cristofori, a man of meager circumstances. The younger Cristofori began his career as a tuner and builder of lutes, bowed string instruments, and

Earliest extant Cristofori "Pianoforte" (1720).
(Metropolitan Museum of Art, The Crosby Brown Collection of Musical Instruments, 1889. [89.4.1219])

harpsichords (*clavicembali*). By 1687 Cristofori's impressive reputation as a fine harpsichord builder attracted the attention of Prince Ferdinando de' Medici, who, while travelling through Venice and Lombardy, stopped in Padua and invited Cristofori to move to Florence and work as an instrument builder at the royal court. The Prince was the eldest son of the reigning grand duke, Cosimo III of Toscana, and was himself a capable amateur harpsichord player. He was a dedicated patron of the arts who endeavored to establish an Italian center of intellectual affairs at Florence. Incidentally, he was not satisfied with the work of the Florentine harpsichord builders of the time.

The earliest documents recording Cristofori's activities in Florence are dated 12 August 1690, and are located in the Medici account files (1073 No. 35) requesting reimbursement for materials and services. Judging from the files 15 August 1690 to 12 October 1711, most of his duties for the Medici court involved the restoring, repairing, and general maintenance of various court instruments and the building of new harpsichords. Part of his duties included the purchasing of essential construction materials such as glue, brass and iron **wire**, vulture quills, various types of wood, **felt**, **leather**, nails, and transporting of the Medici

court instruments to and from the Royal Palace Theater.

There were very few court records or letters bearing Cristofori's name during the period 1690–1700. A letter written in 1693 from Florence, indicating that he hired a singer, only serves to locate his whereabouts. Of more importance is the fact that during the last decade of the seventeenth century he began work on his first **hammer** action **keyboard**. According to the court opera composer and music director, Francesco Mannucci, Cristofori began preliminary work on the "*arpicimbalo che fà il piano e il forte*" before 1698; and the Medici inventory of musical instruments states that he completed work on the instrument prior to 1700. Nevertheless, the Medici account files of August 1690 through October 1711 include no instrument of this description. Among the signed and unsigned keyboard instruments catalogued, we find seven harpsichords by Cristofori but no mention of a piano. On the other hand, the *Inventario di diverse sorti d'instrumenti musicali in proprio del serenissimo Sig. Principe Ferdinando di Toscana* (The Medici Inventory of Diverse Instruments [entry No. 30]) of 1700 includes Cristofori's invention, *un Arpicimbalo di*

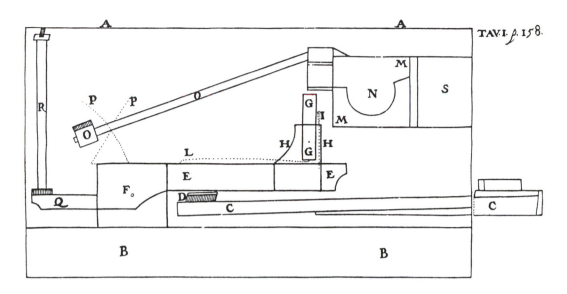

TAV. I. p. 158.

Fig. 1 <u>Scipione Maffei's diagram of the Cristofori action</u>, which Maffei published in 1711. (The explanation below is the first published English translation [1860] of the Maffei text.)

A. String.
B. Frame of the keyboard.
C. The key or first lever, which at its extremity raises the second lever.
D. The block on the first lever by which it acts.
E. The second lever, on each side of which is a jawbone-shaped piece to support the little tongue or hopper.
F. The pivot of the second lever.
G. The moveable tongue (hopper), which, being raised by the second lever (E), forces the hammer upwards.
H. The jawbone-shaped pieces between which the hopper is pivoted.
I. The strong brass wire pressed together at the top, which keeps the hopper in its place.
L. The spring of brass wire that goes under the hopper and holds it pressed firmly against the wire that is behind it.
M. The receiver, in which all the buts [butts] of the hammers rest.
N. The circular part of the hammers, which rests in the receiver.
O. The hammer, which, when pressed upwards by the hopper, strikes the string with the leather on its top.
P. The strings of silk, crossed, on which the stems, or shanks, of the hammers rest.
Q. The end of the second lever (E), which becomes lowered by the act of striking the key.
R. The dampers, which are lowered when the key is touched, leaving the string free to vibrate, and then returning to their places, atop the sound.
S. Part of the frame to strengthen the receiver.

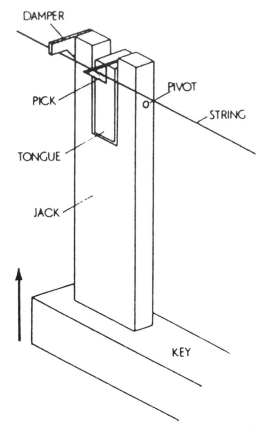

Fig. 2 Harpsichord Jack.

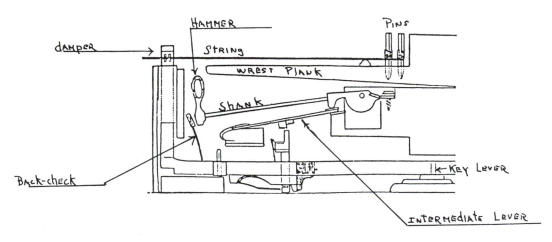

Fig. 3 Cristofori's action for his "pianoforte" of 1720.
(Courtesy Dover Publications [New York] — Alfred Dolge, Pianos and Their Makers.*)*

Bartolomeo Cristofori, di nuova inventione che fà il piano e il forte.

In all probability, the Prince, who was a passionate lover of music and who manifested great interest in technical advancement, discussed with Cristofori the idea of an instrument that could effectively produce various levels of intensity, an instrument that could clearly imitate the inflections and nuances of the human voice. Such an instrument could utilize a touch sensitive keyboard to satisfy the new expressive requirements of baroque opera. And initially at least, Cristofori attempted to achieve these ends by improving the sound-generating mechanism of the traditional Italian harpsichord (see Fig. 2) by replacing the **jacks** (*saltarelli*) with little **leather-covered hammers**. The new instrument had to be capable of producing, throughout the complete range of the keyboard, various levels of intensity and subtle gradations of nuance.

Cristofori's crowning achievement was his creation of a high-velocity sound-generating device that was not attached to any other part of the action mechanism (see Fig. 1), one that was a free-moving agent, not attached to the jack or to the key lever. Generally, when a relatively fixed or limited amount of energy was applied to a key lever, it and all other stationary parts affixed to it could only generate a low level of intensity. An example of just such a relatively slow-motion, low-level intensity, single-lever keyboard action is found in the clavichord. Historically this instrument, though very expressive, was characterized as being capable of producing an extremely narrow range of dynamics and very weak sonorities (at a distance of ten feet or more this instrument was practically inaudible). Cristofori created greater keyboard action speed by first increasing the tension and density of the **strings** and then by expanding the system of keyboard leverage. Thicker strings and higher string tension increased the intensity of sound and also drove the hammers back and away from the string (rebound) at a much higher speed. Obviously a faster hammer return immediately increased the speed of key repetition. Momentum was also substantially increased by the addition of intermediate levers, which greatly improved the ratio (of movement) from 1:1 to approximately 8:1.

In his quest for unencumbered action parts, Cristofori reduced the friction of at least two mechanical components by separating the sound-generating device (hammer assembly) from the key lever. He envisioned a free-moving hammer assembly that could somehow be controlled: a mechanism that would strike the string but once, not rebounding several times and repeating itself, and at the same time a mechanism that, when the key is depressed, would not lodge itself against the string and thus obstruct the vibration. Towards this end he engineered a separate sound-activator assembly consisting of a hammer head, **butt**, and shank. Then a *linguetta mobile* (see G. Fig. 1, moveable tongue), positioned directly in front of the key **rail** fulcrum, was inserted between the hammer butt and the key lever. This spring-loaded **escapement** lever (*spingitore*) directed all movement from the key lever directly to the hammer butt, and at that precise moment when the hammer made contact with the string the same lever would shift slightly forward, allowing the hammer to return once again to its original position. As a result, the entire hammer assembly (butt, flange, and shank) could freely move without being impeded by any other action part. This complicated interaction between and among parts is called escapement.

Other important features of Cristofori's first piano action were the **damper** and the hammer **back-check** mechanism. In Cristofori's 1700 keyboard action, each single damper was lowered when the front of the **key** was depressed, a design quite unlike the traditional harpsichord jack. The main difference was that the harpsichord damper raised when the key was pressed down and was a single, integral part of the jack and plectrum assembly (see Fig. 2). In the piano action the damper was attached instead to a second lever at the far end of the key and functioned on its own, as a separate entity. Furthermore, the back-check mechanism served to catch the hammer on its first rebound from the stretched string. Since the hammer could now travel at a high rate of speed, any rebound, depending upon the force applied and the momentum generated, could repeat the original impulse several times before coming to rest. In the initial action design (before 1720) Cristofori solved this problem by creating a back-check cradle made of crossed silk-threads, capable of catching and securing the hammer when it returned from the string, thereby preventing any further hammer rebound movement. Apparently sometime between 1700 and 1720 the back-check mechanism was redesigned and moved permanently (in the 1722 and 1726 extant pianos) to the far end of the key lever, where it now functioned as a leather-covered, wire-supported wedge that successfully secured the entire hammer assembly after only one single rebound (see Fig. 3).

Cristofori was confronted with still another engineering dilemma. His new piano action design, now an up-striking hammer assembly resting on its back in a horizontal position, simply did not fit very well into the traditional harpsichord **case**. The distance the hammer had to travel from its point of rest to the point of impact at the string was too great. (Later in his career Cristofori chose to solve this particular problem by elongating the hammer heads in order to reach the strings.) The inventor knew that in order to execute the infinite number and variety of nuances inherent in baroque musical art on a pianoforte, the performer's only control over the instrument would be limited to his/her control over the speed of the hammer from its point of rest to its point of contact at the string. And in fact, the shorter the distance from the hammer head (at rest) to the string, the greater the degree of control by the player. In a traditional Italian harpsichord the strings were located on top of the wrest plank (**pinblock**) and were transverse over the **soundboard** and soundboard **bridges**. This particular arrangement was not deemed satisfactory by Cristofori, since the pinblock (wrest plank) now almost completely dominated the space between the hammer heads and the overhead strings. Therefore, in order to resolve the problem, the inventor drove the pins through the wrest plank and strung the wires beneath, reducing the distance from the action parts to the strings by nearly half.

Cristofori was also thoroughly convinced that a vented opening near the front of a keyboard instrument was extremely important for acoustical reasons. While some Italian builders of the time omitted any type of acoustical vent, others did include such an aperture, but it was located in the center of the soundboard and inlaid with an ornamented rosette made of parchment and veneer. Cristofori was confident that this opening allowed the surrounding air to escape while the soundboard and strings freely vibrated. Without such an opening, he felt, the instrument would not have the capacity to sustain pitches over a long period of time. In short, the instrument would not be able to resonate. Therefore, he placed the vents in the belly rail on the inner case **frame**. This tradi-

tion was carried out by Cristofori and his apprentice workmen (Geronimo of Florence, Gherardo of Padua, and **Giovanni Ferrini**), becoming a trademark that clearly identified his instruments over all others.

In 1709 the prominent scholar-poet Marchese **Scipione Maffei**, along with Antonio Villisner and Apostolo Zeno, visited Prince Ferdinando in Florence to solicit monetary support for a *Giornale de' letterati d' Italia*. During their stay at the Medici court they saw Cristofori's workshop and were significantly impressed by his craftsmanship and in particular by his new invention—the pianoforte. Later in 1711 Maffei published an article in Vol. V of the *Giornale* (article IX) entitled "*Nuova Invenzione d'un Gravecembalo col piano, e forte; aggiunte alcune considerazioni sopra gli strumenti musicali*" ("New invention of a Harpsichord, with *Piano* and *Forte*; Also Some Remarks Upon Musical Instruments"), which thoroughly and articulately described the new instrument. Further, it included a rough sketch/diagram of the internal workings of the piano action (see Fig. 1). Maffei exclaimed,

"So bold an invention has been no less happily conceived than executed in Florence, by Signor Bartolomeo Cristofali, of Padua, harpsichord player . . . . He has already made three of the usual size of other harpsichords, and they have all succeeded to perfection. The production of greater or less sound depends on the degree of power with which the player presses on the keys, by regulating which, not only the piano and forte are heard, but also the gradations and diversity of power, as in a violoncello."

Later in the same text he mentions a fourth piano, "This invention has also been effected in another form, the inventor having made another harpsichord, with the piano and forte, in a different and somewhat more simple shape; but, nevertheless, the first has been more approved." This information, along with a detailed explanation of the diagram, was published in Venice in 1711.

It was very likely that many of the newly created pianofortes by Cristofori were located in his Uffizi Palace workshop in Florence prior to 1711. Therefore, Handel possibly knew of them and even may have played one while he was in residence at the Medici court for one year, composing and producing his first opera, *Rodrigo*, which was commissioned by Prince Ferdinand in 1708. Also, **Domenico Scarlatti** visited Florence in 1702 and 1705, where he probably first heard of and tried the instruments. Scarlatti's patroness, Queen Maria Barbara of Spain, owned five Florentine pianofortes. One or more of these was certainly built by Cristofori and at least one of the others was constructed in 1730 by Ferrini.

Prince Ferdinand died on 13 October 1713 but Cristofori remained in the service of the royal Medici family as instrument maker. On 23 September 1716 the reigning grand duke, Cosimo III, who had little or no interest in music himself, put Cristofori in charge of the musical instruments of his deceased son. The 1716 inventory of these instruments listed some 159 items, of which 48 were keyboard instruments by Giovanni Antonio Baffo, Domenico da Pesaro, Girolamo Zenti, Giuseppe Mondini, and Cristofori. Included were 20 harpsichords, 16 spinets, 3 clavichords, 2 small organs, and 3 organs with various combinations. It is somewhat baffling that the pianofortes of Cristofori, which were usually referred to as *col piano e forte*, are not listed in the inventory. However, it is very possible that these particular instruments had been either sold outright or were located elsewhere on or outside the Medici grounds; therefore, they were not included in the survey. Furthermore, the document of verification that certifies Cristofori's acceptance of the inventory contains several examples of his name: Cristofori, Cristofari, Cristofali, and Cristofani. It is also possible to find his name spelled Cristofoli and even Bortolo Padovano in other sources.

In addition to his duties as conservator and builder of instruments, Cristofori continued to experiment with hammer-action mechanics.

While it is not certain exactly how many pianos Cristofori actually built during his lifetime, some sources claim that by 1726 he had already completed twenty of them. However, only three pianos made by Cristofori are today extant: the first, dated 1720, originally belonged to Signora Ernesta Mocenni Martelli of Florence and was acquired in 1895 by Mrs. J. Crosby Brown of New York for presentation to the Metropolitan Museum of Art in New York City, where it now resides; the second, from 1722, was originally from Padua and is now located in the Museo degli strumenti musicali in Rome; the third, from 1726, was formerly in a Florence museum owned by Commendatore Alessandro Kraus but is now housed in the Musikinstrumenten-Museum of the University of Leipzig. An examination of the three existing pianos from the 1720s clearly indicates that Cristofori continued to gradually develop,

modify, and experiment with each succeeding generation of instrument. By comparing Maffei's action description and engraving of 1711 in the *Giornale* to the extant pianos, it may be concluded that sometime between 1709 and 1720 Cristofori dramatically altered and renovated the piano action. For example, both the escapement lever (jack) and the back-check mechanism were relocated onto the key lever (see Fig. 3). The thick intermediate lever found in the earlier piano action was removed and replaced with a much thinner and narrower lever, anchored with a leather hinge at the far end of the key lever, midway between the **keybed** and the hammer shank. These instruments were built in such a manner that they fitted into an outer case in the style of the Italian harpsichord; but while the early pianofortes may very well have resembled harpsichords externally, they were in fact totally new instruments internally.

The 1720 piano was the result of much experimentation (see Fig. 3). Additional keyboard and hammer action alterations were made after Cristofori's death and still later in 1875 by Cesare Ponsicchi in Florence and in 1938 by Curt Sachs at the New York Metropolitan Museum. As a result, it is extremely difficult to determine the precise original design of the instrument. Stewart Pollens' examination of this instrument in 1977 shed a great deal of light on the problem by revealing that originally the instrument had a keyboard range of fifty-four keys, extending from FF to c^3 with FF$^\#$ and GG$^\#$ being omitted; the present range of C to f^3 was an obvious alteration. The other two extant pianos have a keyboard range of only four octaves (forty-nine keys). However, the most incontestable and dramatic change of design in the 1720 instrument was Cristofori's utilization of a noninverted wrest plank. The reason for not inverting the plank was that it could be safely constructed at a thickness of 30 mm, so as to insure that the pins remained more or less seated and secure. Also, with a noninverted plank the dampers were now relocated above the strings, allowing for a more efficient mechanism using gravitational weight, as opposed to the previous design, which approached the strings from below. But with the noninverted plank design, when the piano wires were struck by the hammers, the vibrations tended to move the strings away from both the nut and the pin, which in effect put the instrument out of tune.

Maffei claimed that prior to 1711 Cristofori had built several pianos all with inverted wrest planks, and both the 1722 and the 1726 pianos are in the inverted wrest-plank form. One excellent reason for using an inverted wrest-plank design in the first place was that due to the constant impact of the hammers against the strings the piano wires were forced up towards the **downbearing** point (nut), thereby preventing excessive wire tension or movement on the pin. Also, the inverted design allowed space for an *una corda* stop. This particular stop made it possible to shift all hammers horizontally from a double to a single string unison, significantly altering the sound of the instrument. On the other hand, one of the disadvantages of the inverted plank design was that this unique arrangement greatly restricted the amount of space available for action parts, particularly the distance from the top of the hammer action assembly to the bottom surface of the string. Worse yet, the inverted construction required that the wrest plank itself be trimmed by one-half its original thickness to 15 mm, in order to have room to position the strings directly above the hammer action. Furthermore, due to the lack of space, a suitable damper mechanism simply had to be located beneath the strings, on an independent key lever. Nevertheless, Cristofori did continue to use the inverted wrest plank design with both the 1722 and the 1726 extant pianos.

A great deal of controversy was generated by the claim that Cristofori had, in fact, invented the first piano. From the first quarter of the eighteenth century, three builders stand out as probable candidates to challenge Cristofori. First, there was **Jean Marius**, a French manufacturer, who submitted four plans for *clavecins à maillets* (hammer harpsichords) for examination to the *Académie des Sciences* February 1716; then **Gottfried Silbermann** of Freiburg, who apparently read about Cristofori's invention in the third volume of the *Musikalische Kritik*, published by Johann Mattheson 1722–1725 in Hamburg. It had been translated into German by his friend König, who was poet of the Dresden Court. By 1726 Silbermann had built his first two pianos, which were followed later by several others. And finally, **Christoph Gottlieb Schröter**, born in Hohenstein in Saxony, constructed a model of a pianoforte that was exhibited at the Court in Dresden in 1717. Alfred Hipkins doubts that Marius ever made a pianoforte, and is certain that Schröter never did. He further states that "by proof I have been able to

bring forward that Frederick the Great's Silbermann pianos at Potsdam are copies which still exist of the Cristofori pianos. There is no other claim either English, French, or German that is now to be seriously considered."

During his lifetime Cristofori was bitterly disappointed by the realization that his invention, the pianoforte, had attracted little or no attention. At least in Italy it was not successful and was not produced in any quantity until after 1900. Shortly after Cristofori's death the instrument became the object of harsh criticism. In 1755 the Italian builder Giovanni Zempel disapproved of the pianoforte for "The insufferable noise made by the keys, the levers, and the hammers." And ironically enough, two pianos made by Cristofori (or possibly Ferrini), which were sold to Queen Maria Barbara of Spain prior to 1756, were finally changed back into harpsichords. In 1774 Voltaire wrote: "the piano is nothing but a smith's instrument (*instrument de Chaudronnier*) in comparison to the magnificent harpsichord." And generally speaking, music for keyboard fell out of favor in Italy for the remainder of the eighteenth century.

Nevertheless, Cristofori's influence and reputation spread into Germany through translations of Maffei's article in **Jakob Adlung's** *Musica Mechanica Organoedi*, Hamburg 1767, and in Walther's *Musikalisches Lexikon*, Leipzig 1732. Consequently, in Germany the pianoforte created great interest and was enthusiastically received and manufactured. A serious impetus for piano making was initiated by both Silbermann of Saxony and Schröter of Dresden.

A memorial plaque honoring Cristofori, with the inscription: "*A Bartolomeo Cristofori / Cembalaro da Padova / Che / in Firenze / Nell Anno MDCCXI / Invento / Il/ Clavicembalo Col Piano E Forte / Il/ Comitato Fiorentino / Cooperanti Italiani E Stranieri / Pose Questa Memoria / MDCCCLXXVI*," was placed in the Convent Church of Santa Croce walkway on 7 May 1876. For the same event a medal was created from drawings by P. Cavotis, modeled by A. Bertone and engraved by L. Gori. A painting of Cristofori from 1726, owned by Berlin State Music Instrument Society, was discovered by Schünemann in 1934. Aside from its aesthetic value, the painting is important because it also contains a sketch of his improved piano action.

It was nearly a century before Cristofori's invention was perceptibly altered. With the creation of his improved 1726 pianoforte, all the basic mechanical components of a modern piano action were in place: the extended leverage, the escapement, the back-check mechanism, the damper system, and the *una corda*. Furthermore, the basic **frame** of the traditional harpsichord, which had been structurally altered, reinforced and expanded to sustain greater string tension, had been transformed into a completely different medium. Nearly all vestiges of the traditional harpsichord design were mere shadows in the wake of the newly invented creation—the "soft and loud" of Cristofori.

See also Ferrini, Giovanni.

Ron Surace

Bibliography

Blume, Friedrich. *Die Musik in Geschichte und Gegenwart: Allgemeine Enzyklopädie der Musik.* 15 vols. Kassei and Basel: Bärenreiter, 1949–1973.

Casella, Alfredo. *Il Pianoforte.* Milan: Tumminelli & Co., 1954.

Dolge, Alfred. *Pianos and Their Makers: A Comprehensive History of the Development of the Piano from the Monochord to the Concert Grand Player Piano.* Covina, Cal.: Covina Publishing Co., 1911; New York: Dover Publications, Inc., 1972.

Gai, Vinicio. *Gli Strumenti Musicali Della Corte Medicea E Il Museo Del Conservatorio "Luigi Cherubini" Di Firenze. Firenze, 1969.*

Hipkins. Alfred J. *A Description and History of the Pianoforte and of the Older Keyboard Stringed Instruments.* Reprint. Detroit: Detroit Reprints in Music, 1975.

Kinsky, George. *Musikhistorisches Museum von Wilhelm Heyer in Cöln: Katalog. Vol I: Besaitete Tasteninstrumente, Orgeln und orgelartige Instrumente, Friktionsinstrumente.* Cologne, 1910.

Ponsicchi, Cesare. *Il Pianoforte, sua origine e sviluppo.* Firenze: Presso G. Guidi Editore Di Musica, 1876.

Sadie, Stanley, ed. *The New Grove Dictionary of Music and Musicians.* London: Macmillan, 1980.

Journals

Fabbri, Mario. "Il primo 'pianoforte' di Bartolomeo Cristofori." *Chigiana Rassegna Annuale di Studi Musicologici* 21 (1964): 162–72.

Greenfield, Jack. "Cristofori's Initial Piano Design." *Piano Technicians Journal* 28 (Sept. 1985): 22–24.

———. "Cristofori's Soundboard Design: Cristofori Becomes Curator of Medici Instrument Collection." *Piano Technicians Journal* 28 (Oct. 1985): 21–23.

———. "Cristofori's Last Work and His Successors." *Piano Technicians Journal* 28 (Dec. 1985): 15–17.

Maffei, Scipione. "Nuova invenzione d'un Gravecembalo col piano, e forte; aggiunte alcune considerazioni sopra gli strumenti musicali." *Giornale de' Letterati d'Italia* 2 (1711): 144–59.

Montanari, Giuliana. "Bartolomeo Cristofori." *Early Music* 19 (August 1991): 383–96.

Pollens, Stewart. "The Pianos of Bartolomeo Cristofori." *Journal of the American Musical Instrument Society* 10 (1984): 32–68.

Tagliavini, Luigi Ferdinando. "Giovanni Ferrini and His Harpsichord 'a Penne e a Martelletti'," *Early Music* 19 (August 1991): 399–408.

CROSS-STRINGING

Cross-stringing or cross-strung usually refers to the string layout of a modern piano, in which the strings overlap diagonally in order to allow the use of longer strings in the bass and also to enhance the tone quality of the instrument. **Overstrung** and overstringing are the more correct terms for this principle, although they are often used interchangeably with cross-strung and cross-stringing.

See also Overstrung.

R.P.

CROWN

Crown refers to the curvature of the piano **soundboard**. Much like a violin, the piano soundboard is curved outward toward the **strings**. This curvature is set so as to allow the strings to set firmly upon the **bridges**. Until the mid-nineteenth century, many piano soundboards were made with no crown, but the curved soundboard was found necessary to support the increased downward pressure of the heavier modern strings.

See also Downbearing; Soundboard.

Philip Jamison, III

CYCLOID GRAND

In 1860, the New York piano firm of Lindeman and Son introduced a style of piano that they called the Cycloid Grand. It was essentially like the large American **square pianos** of the time, but with the back of the **case** rounded to a wide arc. Supported by three legs, one at each of the front corners and a third at the center of the rounded back, the rounded design was apparently meant to create an instrument that was visually suited for placement in the center of a room. The action employed was the same single-**escapement**-action type used in most square pianos of the time. Lindeman was the only company to produce the Cycloid Grand, probably owing to the **patent** (U.S. No. 29,502) that was secured on the design 9 August 1860 by Hermann Lindeman, not his father William Lindeman (1795–1875), as stated in Spillane. According to Groce, it was William's son Henry Lindeman (b. 1838) who invented the Cycloid Grand.

The Cycloid Grand was briefly mentioned in *Frank Leslie's Illustrated Newspaper* on 21 January 1865 followed by a lengthy article on 14 October of the same year. The article indicates that a Cycloid Grand was exhibited at the "Fair of the American Institute" and goes on to say that the Lindeman factory had been enlarged specifically to meet the great demand for this new style of instrument. American pianist Louis Moreau Gottschalk is said to have tested and approved of the instrument, calling it the "finest of the square class." *Leslie's* also explains in some detail the advantages of the Cycloid's framing system and remarks at how well the instrument stays in tune.

Darcy Kuronen

Bibliography

Groce, Nancy. *Musical Instrument Makers of New York: A Directory of Eighteenth- and Nineteenth-Century Urban Craftsmen.* Stuyvesant, N.Y.: Pendragon Press, 1991.

Loest, Roland. "The Museum Collection—Two Oddities: Cocked-Hat and Cycloid Grands." *Museum of the American Piano Newsletter* No. 8, April–June 1990.

Spillane, Daniel. *History of the American Piano-forte.* New York: 1890: D. Spillane. New York: Da Capo Press, 1969. Reprint.

CZECHOSLOVAKIA, PIANO INDUSTRY IN

Of the pianos presently made in Czechoslovakia—Petrof, Weinbach, Rösler, and Scholze—Petrof dominates as the country's finest instrument for use in concert halls and as an export-quality instrument. Weinbach, Rösler, and Scholze are concerned with the production of **uprights**, whereas the building of **grand pianos** has always been central to the Petrof tradition. Scholze was founded in 1876 in Warnsdorf, Georgswalde, and moved to Liberec-Ruprechtice in 1949. Weinbach was founded in 1884, also in Georgswalde.

Antonín Petrof (born 1838 in Königgrätz; died 1915) trained as a carpenter in his father's business. In 1857 he moved to Vienna, where he served his apprenticeship with his uncle, Johann Heitzmann, a piano manufacturer. Petrof then worked for **Ehrbar** and for **Schweighofer.** In 1864 Antonín Petrof founded the Petrof factory in Königgrätz [Hradec Králové], building his first piano with a Viennese **action.** He travelled and collected innovative ideas and technical improvements. In 1875 he used a cast-iron **frame** and developed a new type of repetition mechanics based on the English model. In 1880 he began building upright pianos. By the turn of the century Petrof had sold some 13,000 units through agencies in his own country as well as in London (1918), Vienna (1895), and Hungary (1877). Shortly before his death Antonín divided the firm among his three sons: Jan, Antonín, and Vladimir. Up to 1915, the year of Antonín's death, 30,500 units had been sold.

During World War I there was a fall in production, but in 1920–1922 Petrof exported to China and Australia. Because of its firmly established name, Petrof weathered the depression, and in 1932 the third generation—Dimitrij, Eduard, and Evžen—took over leadership of the company. World War II again interfered with sales, Petrof exporting to Sweden, Switzerland, and Hungary.

In 1948 the Petrof company was nationalized and in 1965 became part of Czechoslovak Musical Instruments Hradec Králové. In 1966, upright production was moved to Liberec and Jihlava. A new assembly-line factory for the production of uprights was opened in Hradec Králové in 1970. The Petrof plant produces annually about 10,500 uprights and 800 grand pianos, exporting to some 70 countries. In 1989 a new grand piano production line opened in Hradec Králové and Petrof reached the serial number 450,000. Over the years the pianos have won many prizes including: 1877, Vienna; 1921, Barcelona; 1935, 1958, Brussels; 1937, Paris.

Other makers have included Gärtner, active in Tachau in 1763; Kalb, active in Prague around 1796; Johann and Thomas Still, active in Prague around 1796; Johann Joseph Muschel, active in

Prague at the end of the eighteenth century; Johann Zelinka, active in Prague at the end of the eighteenth century; Michael Weiss, known around 1807 in Prague; Leicht, active in Pilsen in the nineteenth century; Meiners, active in Prague during the first quarter of the nineteenth century; A. Proksch, established 1864 in Reichenberg; Carl Spira, established 1892 in Reichenberg; Koch & Korselt, 1893–1920 in Reichenberg; Karl J. Baroitus, established 1898 in Prague; V. Novák, c.1900–c.1910; Protze & Company, founded 1905 in Georgswalde; Fibich, 1949–1960 in Jihlava (Iglau).

Keith T. Johns

Bibliography

Dolge, Alfred. *Pianos and Their Makers*. Covina, Cal.: Covina Publishing Company, 1911. Reprint. New York: Dover, 1972.

Hirt, Franz Josef. *Meisterwerke des Klavierbaus*. Olten: Graf, 1955.

Joppig, Gunther. "Petrof — der Begründer der tschechischen Klavierbauschule." [Petrof—founder of the Czech school of piano construction] *Das Musikinstrument* 11 (November 1987): 49–54.

Brochures

"125 Years of Successful Tradition of Mark Petrof."

"Petrof Pianos Since 1864."

"Petrof Piano Made in Czechoslovakia"

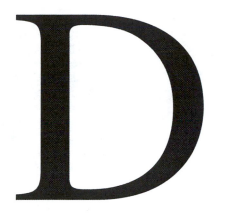

DAMPER

A damper is an **action**-related part that controls the damping of a **string**'s vibration. The damper is a small wooden block with an attached **felt** pad that comes in direct contact with the string. Without a damper system the strings would continue to vibrate freely, without any tonal control. The damper is activated (lifted from the string) whenever the **damper pedal** is depressed or when a **key** is depressed. Dampers can act either together or separately: the damper pedal lifts all of the dampers, whereas an individual key controls its own damper.

See also Pedals and Stops.

R.P.

DAMPER PEDAL

The damper pedal is usually the right pedal, which raises all of the **dampers** from the **strings**. In some eighteenth-century **squares**, dampers were raised by hand stops, and in German pianos of the same time, knee levers served the same function.

See also Pedals and Stops.

Edwin M. Good

DEBAIN, ALEXANDRE-FRANÇOIS (1809–1877)

Starting as a foreman, Alexandre-François Debain established his own factory in Paris in 1834. In 1836 he **patented** the metal **frame** in a single casting—four years before Conrad Meyer of Philadelphia. In the same year Debain pat-

ented the forged iron frame in a diminutive folding **upright**, called *piano-écran* (fire screen piano; 3'5" x 3'3" x 7" closed). In 1842 Debain started manufacturing an instrument he called the *harmonium*. It was a free-reed keyboard instrument, already existing in its primitive form, but Debain insisted on calling it *orgue expressif*, since he added the mechanical *grand jeu* and the expression stop to the original designs. In 1846 he invented the *clavi-harmonium*, a **combination** of piano and harmonium. In this instrument a piano was fitted with a second **keyframe** and played by pumping the air-levers with the knees, to free the feet for piano **pedals**. Sounds were produced by vibrating spring reeds. In the same year Debain patented the *antiphonel* and in 1848 its perfected form, the *piano mécanique*, capable of mechanical reproduction of music by means of a second set of **hammers** and springs fitted to a **cottage piano**. The *piano mécanique* was shown at the Great Industrial Exhibition in 1851 in London and was described as being capable of replacing the organ and harmonium in churches, while being less expensive.

Robert Andres

Bibliography

Constant, Pierre. *Les Facteurs d'instruments de musique, les luthiers et la facture instrumentale*. Paris, 1893.

Debain, Alexandre-François. *Antiphonal-harmonium suppléant de l'organiste*. Paris, 1873.

Harding, Rosamond E.M. *The Piano-Forte: Its History Traced to the Great Exhibition of 1851*. Cambridge: Cambridge University Press, 1933. Reprints. New York: Da Capo Press, 1973; Old Woking, Surrey: Gresham, 1978.

The New Grove Dictionary of Music and Musicians. Edited by Stanley Sadie. S.V. "Debain, Alexandre-François," by Marie Louise Pereyra; "Mechanical Instrument," by Alexandr Buchner; "Harmonium," by Alfred Berner. London: Macmillan, 1980.

Ord-Hume, Arthur W.J.G. *Player Piano*. London: Allen & Unwin, 1970.

Pole, William. *Musical Instruments in the Great Industrial Exhibition of 1851*. London, 1851.

DECKER BROTHERS

The Decker Brothers Piano Company was founded in New York City in 1862 by two brothers, David and John Jacob Decker, who had learned piano building in Germany before immigrating to the United States. In addition to being skilled craftsmen, the brothers were also inventors and skilled **scale** designers, who controlled numerous **patents** for innovations and improvements in their instruments. Although this company was described in 1890 by Spillane as a "large and leading house devoted to the production of first-class pianos," the company discontinued production in 1893. A Decker Brothers **upright piano** equipped with a **Jankó** keyboard (invented in 1882) is preserved at the Smithsonian Institution in Washington, D.C. The Decker brothers were apparently not related to the American-born piano builder Myron Decker, who founded the successful company Decker and Sons, which manufactured pianos from 1856 to 1949.

Edward E. Swenson

Bibliography

Spillane, Daniel. *History of the American Pianoforte: Its Technical Development and the Trade.* New York: D. Spillane, 1890. Reprint. New York: Da Capo Press, 1969.

Good, Edwin M. *Giraffes, Black Dragons, and Other Pianos.* Stanford, Cal.: Stanford University Press, 1982.

DEL MELA, DOMENICO (1683–C. 1751–72)

Domenico Del Mela (Gagliano Di Mugello, Florence), priest and school teacher in Gagliano, is considered by many as the inventor of the vertical pianoforte (a type that rises from a table). In 1739, he devised and constructed his first vertical piano, using the clavicytherium (vertical harpsichord) as a model. Del Mela followed the mechanical ideas and designs of **Bartolomeo Cristofori** in building his instrument. Just six years later (1745) **Christian Ernst Friederici**, the innovative instrument-maker from Gera, also built a vertical piano, again based on the clavicytherium. The Friederici instrument (now in the Musée Instrumental du Conservatoire Royale de Musique, Brussels) was shaped like a **pyramid**, had a triangular **soundboard**, and was equipped with small doors that opened from the front. This instrument was based on a principle similar to that of Del Mela's, i.e., with retro-percussion of the **hammer**, but was clearly devised later than the one invented by Del Mela, who, as Ponsicchi em-

Fig. 1. Upright Pianoforte (1739) by Domenico Del Mela in the Instrument Collection of the Conservatory of Music "Luigi Cherubini" in Florence.
(Courtesy of Da Capo Press [New York] agent for Franz Josef Hirt's Stringed Keyboard Instruments.)

phasizes in his book, warrants being considered the true father of the vertical piano.

The Del Mela piano consists of a solid wood rectangular supporting table with **keybed** bordered on three sides by a hand-worked **frame** with a band of trim beneath. The table has four curved legs that are reinforced by a turned column on one side and a plain column on the opposite side. A backdrop rises vertically from the mobile table keybed. The pianoforte, in the proper sense of the word, is installed in the cabinet above this and consists of a soundboard **case** with an inserted **keyboard** consisting of forty-five keys: twenty-seven of yellow wood with inlays on the front and eighteen black **keys.**

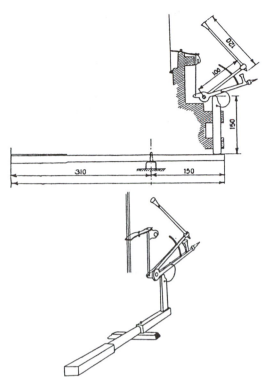

Fig. 2 <u>Vertical (Upright) Pianoforte Action by Domenico Del Mela, 1739.</u>
(*Courtesy of Vinicio Gai Gli* strumenti musicali della corte Medicea . . . *Firenze: Licosa, 1970.*)

In a small wood bar in front of the keyboard the following words have been carved: P. DOMINICUS DEL MELA DE GAGLIANO INVENTOR FECIT ANNO MDCCXXXIX. On the front surface of the **pinblock**/soundboard case there are (starting from the bass): 135 **tuning pins** with respective **strings** (three for each key), the **pressure bar** on which the strings rest from below, a finely worked horizontal trim covering the point at which the strings are struck, a pierced rosette with a fine inlaid decoration around the edge, the **bridge** (which rises diagonally from the right to left and upon which the strings rest), a red cloth strip, and the **hitch pins** for fastening the strings from above.

The instrument Del Mela built can presently be seen in the Museum of the Luigi Cherubini Conservatory in Florence. It was purchased by the museum in 1928 from a descendant of the builder, Ugo Del Mela. This unique example is

one of the most interesting and famous articles housed in the Florentine collection. It is not playable at the present time, as it is in need of repair. In order for the instrument to function as Del Mela intended, proper **restoration** is in order. Despite its condition it still is able to offer a clear image of its mechanical components and structure. (See Fig. 1.)

Of interest are the upright garland-shaped framework with an upper turn, perpendicular to the keyboard, and the jointed handles, which allow the instrument as such to be separated from the table on which it rests. The measurements of the Del Mela instrument are furnished in Vinicio Gai's book. The latest analyses and measurements of the instrument were made in the summer of 1989 by Stewart Pollens (conservator of New York's Metropolitan Museum of Art) and Donatella Degiampietro (Florence), who plan to publish their studies.

As for the action, Ponsicchi describes it as follows:

The keyboard and the action . . . consist of a key with axis at $2/3$ of the length (which obliged the maker to lighten it at the front and add lead at the back for agile movement), a jack-type rod channeled into two jack guides to bring the movement to the desired height, and two roller levers constituting the mechanical movement.

The first lever is connected to the rod, which we will call the **jack**, the other is free in its action but guided into the first by a thick arched brass **wire**, as later used by **Erard**. The first lever, besides being connected to the jack, is joined to it by another device similar to an arc, serving to brake the thrust.

After the thrust is applied to the key, the jack pushes the first lever and makes it describe part of an arc of a circle; when the desired movement has reached maximum, the leather-covered end of the jack touches the arc of the roller and is stopped.

The second lever, operating as a hammer and previously resting on the first lever, is transported by the movement of the latter and sent directly with its long horseshoe head onto the strings making them vibrate. A damper spring, acting on the roller, pushes the second lever back to rest again on the first. Note that the first lever, with its rotatory movement, hooks onto the damper located on the corner of the action **rail**, and during this movement it is detached from the string to return to its position when the player's finger is lifted from the key. Considered as a whole, two essential things are lacking in this mechanism: the **let-off** and the **back check**, which, applied earlier by Cristofori, were not restored until the end of the last century and very ably by Erard.

In addition, the unusualness of wanting to strike the strings from the back resulted in very remote action and it was necessary to give the hammer its curious form, thereby producing an oscillating action.(See Figure 2.)

In the same museum one can also see a wind instrument that unfortunately does not bear the maker's name; the museum catalog describes it as a bass clarinet and reports that it was found in Del Mela's house when the Musical Institute of Florence purchased his vertical pianoforte of 1739. Arnaldo Bonaventura attributed the instrument to Del Mela but up to the present this has not been proven.

Even if little remains regarding Del Mela's craftsmanship, it is certain that he is an important figure in the evolution of keyboard instruments. His masterful intuition contributed greatly to broadening the possibilities of the "gravecembalo col piano e forte," first invented by his illustrious predecessor Cristofori.

Daniele Mezzatesta

Bibliography

Bonaventura, Arnaldo. "Domenico Del Mela e il primo pianoforte verticale." *Bollettino della Società Mugellana di studi storici* 4 (1928): 1–10.

Conservatorio di Musica "Luigi Cherubini." *Antichi strumenti — Collezione dei Medici e dei Lorena,* pp. 26–27,93–94,97,103,114. Firenze: Giunti-Barbera, 1981.

Fabbri, Mario. *L'alba del pianoforte — verità storica sulla nascita del primo cembalo a martelletti,* p.23. Milano: N.E.M., 1968.

Gai, Vinicio. "Note storiche e descrittive sul più antico pianoforte verticale costruito da Domenico Del Mela." *La Zagalia* (Lecce) 40 (1968): 3–11.

———. *Gli strumenti musicali della corte Medicea e il Museo del Conservatorio "Luigi Cherubini" di Firenze,* p. 222. Firenze: Licosa, 1970.

Lamanna, Chiara Irene. *La storia del pianoforte dalle origini al '700,* pp. 179–181. Brindisi: Schena, 1984.

Ponsicchi, Cesare. "Il primo pianoforte verticale." *La Nuova Musica* 24 (December 1897): 3.

Schmidl, Carlo. *Dizionario universale dei musicisti,* p. 428. Vol. 1. Milano: Sonzogno, 1926.

DETTMER, GEORGE W. AND SON (FL. C.1810–C.1820)

George W. Dettmer was a London piano maker who is known to have been in partnership with his son during the second decade of the nineteenth century. Their earliest address was probably in Fitzroy Square. Harding lists them in Clipstone Street in 1848–1849; however, this date might have been meant as 1818–1819. Their extant instruments, which have been dated from c. 1810–1815, are finely crafted of mahogany with a compass of five-and-one-half octaves.

Martha Novak Clinkscale

Bibliography

Clinkscale, Martha Novak. *Makers of the Piano: 1700–1820.* Oxford: Oxford University Press, 1992.

Harding, Rosamond E. M. *The Piano-Forte: Its History Traced to the Great Exhibition of 1851.* Cambridge: Cambridge University Press, 1933; Reprint. New York: Da Capo Press, 1973; Old Woking, Surrey: Gresham Books, 1978.

DIP

Dip is the term used to describe the total distance the **key** travels from its full up position to the fully depressed position. Manufacturers usually specify from .375" to .428".

See also Regulation; Touchweight.

Kent Webb

DITANAKLASIS

The *Ditanaklasis* (also "Dittanaclasis" or "Ditaleloclange"), one of the earliest **uprights** constructed (with **frame** to floor), was invented by the Viennese builder **Matthias Müller** in 1800. **John Isaac Hawkins** of Philadelphia also built an upright (with frame to floor) at this same time and thus shares the credit with Müller for producing the first upright piano whose frame was not placed on a table but rather rested on the floor. The first Ditanaklasis built by Müller had two **keyboards** for two players (vis-à-vis), but in 1803 he built a cheaper model with one keyboard. The sound of the Ditanaklasis, whose **strings** were struck close to the middle of the vibrating length, was said to be similar to the sound of the basset horn.

Alfons Huber

Bibliography

Fischhof, Joseph. *Versuch einer Geschichte des Clavierbaues*. Wien: Wallishausser, 1853.

Harding, Rosamond E.M. *The Piano-Forte: Its History Traced to the Great Exhibition of 1851*. Cambridge: Cambridge University Press, 1933. Reprints. New York: Da Capo Press, 1973; Old Woking, Surrey, 1978.

Haupt, Helga. "Wiener Instrumentenbauer von 1791–1815." In: *Studien zur Musikwissenschaft*. vol. 24 Edited by Erich Schenk. Wien-Graz-Köln: Böhlau, 1960.

DOLGE, ALFRED (1848–1922)

Alfred Dolge was an American entrepreneur, a manufacturer of piano **felts** and **soundboards**, and author. Born in Leipzig, Dolge emigrated to the U.S. in 1866 and worked for two years (1867–1869) for **Frederick Mathushek**, then set up in New York as an importer and later as a maker of hammer felts. Maintaining a supply house on East 13th Street, New York City, he established in 1874 a large factory for felts and soundboards at Brockett's Bridge, N.Y. (renamed Dolgeville in 1887). The company incorporated innovative ideas of worker compensation and pensions. Bankrupted in 1898, Dolge moved to California, at first growing oranges and grapes and later making felt and soundboards in Dolgeville, California. In 1911 and 1913 he published the two volumes of *Pianos and Their Makers*, remarkably accurate accounts of piano history and technology.

Dolge **patented** a hammer-covering machine in 1887 and improved it in 1910. He was an early entrant in the business of supplying parts, such as **hammers**, soundboards, and **cases**, to manufacturers. His books described the people in the piano industry generously, though he opposed "stencilling," in the interests of high-quality instruments. His *Pianos and Their Makers* (1911) praised the development of the **player** piano and accurately predicted its later success.

Edwin M. Good

Bibliography

Dolge, Alfred. *Pianos and Their Makers*. Covina, Cal.: Covina Publishing Company, 1911. Reprint. New York: Dover, 1972.

———. *Pianos and Their Makers*, Vol. II. Covina, Cal.: Covina Publishing Company, 1913. Reprint. 1980 as *Men Who Have Made Piano History*, Vestal Press, Vestal, N.Y.).

Franz, Eleanor. *Dolge*. Herkimer, N.Y.: Herkimer County Historical Society, 1980.

DOUBLE ESCAPEMENT

See Actions.

DOWNBEARING

Downbearing is the term used for the force with which the **strings** press upon the **bridge**. This is determined by the height of the strings in relation to the height of the bridges. Downbearing will be reduced if the **soundboard** loses its **crown**. Both excessive and insufficient downbearing affect the clarity of **tone**.

Philip Jamison, III

DOWN-STRIKE ACTION

See Actions.

DOWNWEIGHT

See Touchweight.

DROP

Drop is the term that describes the distance that the **hammer** in a **grand piano** drops, in addition to **let-off**. Drop must be present so that the **wippen** does not cause the hammer to block against the **string**; it is also required for efficient repetition. In a well-regulated grand **action**, the **jack** makes contact with the let-off button at the same time that the repetition arm makes contact with the drop screw.

See also Regulation; Touchweight.

Kent Webb

DUO-ART

Duo-Art was the name given to the **reproducing piano** marketed by the **Aeolian Company**. Developed from the **Pianola** and originally called the Aeolian Duo-Art Pianola, it was introduced during the autumn of 1913.

The Duo-Art was not so much a piano as a reproducing mechanism, which was available to be installed in a number of Aeolian's range of instruments and in three distinct forms. Cheapest was the foot-operated **upright** instrument, which was pedalled like an ordinary Pianola and offered a rather basic performance from the special reproducing music rolls. Then came the all electric uprights and, third, the **grand** or concert instruments. In 1924, this last variety came with the Aeolian grand at $1,850, the

Steck at $2,085–$3,000, and the **Steinway**, with a choice of three models at prices from $3,875 to $4,675.

Unlike the rival and contemporary **Ampico**, every Duo-Art installation tended to be an individual or hand-built model, and minor varieties are numerous, especially in Britain where a further category of Duo-Art was extremely popular. This was the "pedal-electric" model, which could be foot-operated like a Pianola or run by electricity.

Early Duo-Art actions used graded pneumatic motors, the largest being used at the bass and the smallest at the treble. Soon, though, the economics of this procedure necessitated that all the pneumatic motors be of one optimum size.

The Duo-Art reproducing system is an extension of the Aeolian Themodist system invented by James William Crooks of Boston, Massachusetts, in 1900. Throughout its production life, the Duo-Art system remained largely unchanged, but in July of 1931, as a result of the Great Depression, Aeolian was forced to merge with its rival, the **American Piano Company**, makers of the Ampico reproducing piano. Subsequently, certain features became common to both systems, in particular the placing of the player mechanism and music roll in a special drawer under the **keybed** instead of the entire action being placed above the **keyboard**. Duo-Art production ceased in America sometime around 1935, but in London, where the Aeolian Company Limited operated as a separate entity, developments continued until several years later; nevertheless, by 1936 all but custom-order production had stopped.

The last stage of Duo-Art development was carried out in London during the mid-1930s by Aeolian's London inventor, Gordon Iles. Iles devoted considerable research into developing what he called "isolated instantaneous theme" (IST) which, in his opinion, would mark the absolute perfection of the reproducing system. The tracker-bar over which the music roll passed had two very closely spaced rows of openings, each connected to a separate valve stack. While the mechanism would also play ordinary Duo-Art rolls, when specially-cut rolls were used, the performance was dramatically enhanced. Two Steinway grand pianos were experimentally fitted with the IST action in 1939: one was destroyed during air raids early in World War II and the second has disap-

peared. The present author possesses part of an Iles twin-cut tracker bar.

Arthur W.J.G. Ord-Hume

Bibliography

Bowers, Q. David. *Encyclopedia of Automatic Musical Instruments.* Vestal, New York: Vestal Press, 1972.

Ord-Hume, Arthur W.J.G. *Pianola—History & Development* . . . . London: Allen & Unwin, 1984.

DUOCLAVE PIANOS

This name usually refers to pianos with a second **keyboard** opposite the first. This type of *vis-à-vis* piano seems to have been introduced in 1800 by **Matthias Müller** with the *Ditanaklasis*: two small **upright pianos** joined back-to-back. **Sébastien Erard** introduced his *piano secrétaire* in 1812, to which a second and opposite keyboard could be added. That very year Erard presented a variant: this piano consisted of a cylindrical column with two opposite keyboards. In 1821 the same firm **patented** a duoclave **square piano**.

Other builders worked along the same ideas: Jean-Baptiste Charreye (1825), E. Dodd (1840), François Van der Cruysse (1850). James Pirsson of New York built two opposed **grand pianos** enclosed in an oblong **case** in 1850.

See also Unusual Pianos.

F.J. de Hen

Bibliography

Harding, Rosamond E.M. *The Piano-Forte: Its History Traced to the Great Exhibition of 1851.* Cambridge: Cambridge University Press, 1933. Reprints. New York: Da Capo Press, 1973; Old Woking, Surrey: Gresham, 1978.

DUPLEX SCALING

Duplex scaling design permits a section of the **string** to vibrate in sympathy with the section struck by the **hammer**. This string section is generally between the treble **bridge** and the **aliquot**, a metal ridge just before the **hitch pin**. The aliquot may in some designs be moved to tune the duplex scale. Theodore **Steinway** first used the duplex scale in 1872. According to company literature, it "imparts more color to the fundamental tone by the addition of harmonic partial tones."

See illustration under Aliquot Scaling.

Philip Jamison, III

EBONIES

The ebonies are the black **keys** of a piano, called variously sharps or accidentals, which were once made of well-seasoned pine or other suitable woods and covered with strips of ebony (a hard, jet-black tropical wood of the genus *Diospyros*). Today piano manufacturers use black plastic to cover the accidentals in order to match the white plastic-capped naturals.

See also Ivories.

Peggy Flanagan Baird

EDWARDS, WILLIAM HENRY (FL. 1803–1805)

William Edwards was an obscure but significant maker of **square pianos** in early nineteenth-century London. Just three of his instruments are known to survive. They all display features that Edwards adapted from the clavichord structure: the elimination of the **case** bottom, which is then open for resonance to the **soundboard**, and a stand with holes in its tray. One of these pianos, a five-and-one-half-octave square, is publicly exhibited at The Georgian House in Edinburgh.

Martha Novak Clinkscale

Bibliography

Clinkscale, Martha Novak. *Makers of the Piano: 1700–1820*. Oxford: Oxford University Press, 1992.

Harding, Rosamond E.M. *The Piano-Forte: Its History Traced to the Great Exhibition of 1851*. Cambridge: Cambridge University Press, 1933.

Reprints. New York: Da Capo Press, 1973; Old Woking, Surrey: Gresham Books, 1978.

EHRBAR KLAVIERFABRIK

The famous Ehrbar piano company was founded in Vienna in 1855 by Friedrich Ehrbar (1827–1905). Born in Hanover, Ehrbar was an orphan who was apprenticed to a local organ builder. In 1848 he went to Vienna, where he worked with the piano builder Eduard Seuffert. After Seuffert's death in 1855, Ehrbar acquired ownership of the business. Ehrbar was a skilled and innovative builder who was among the first in Vienna to employ cast-iron **frames** in his instruments. His pianos won numerous medals and first prizes—Vienna (1845, 1873); London (1862, 1902, 1906); Paris (1867, 1878, 1900). In 1877 Ehrbar constructed his own concert hall, the Saal Ehrbar, which was particularly praised for its excellent acoustics. In a letter to Eduard Hanslick, **Franz Liszt** described the **tone** of Ehrbar's **grand pianos** as "soft, lovely yet very powerful and strong." Ehrbar grand pianos provided serious competition for **Bösendorfer** in the late nineteenth century. Ehrbar grand piano no. 10,000, built with an elaborate art **case**, was presented to Austrian Archduke Otto in 1890. After Ehrbar's death on 25 February 1905, the business was continued by his son Friedrich. In 1912 a new factory was constructed. **Serial numbers** and corresponding dates of manufacture for Ehrbar pianos constructed after 1880 can be found in *Pierce's Piano Atlas*.

Edward E. Swenson

Bibliography

Dolge, Alfred. *Pianos and Their Makers*. Covina, Cal.: Covina Publishing Co., 1911. Reprint. New York: Dover, 1972.

Ehrbar, Friedrich. *Ehrbar Co. Catalogue*. Vienna, c. 1912.

Pierce, Bob. *Pierce Piano Atlas*. Long Beach, Cal.: Pierce Publishing, 1985.

ELECTRONIC PIANOS

Electronic piano is the generic term for a keyboard instrument that incorporates features of the conventional piano but in which the **tone** is generated, amplified, and/or modified by electronic circuitry. Since the earliest experiments in electrifying a conventional (acoustic) piano in the 1920s, electronic pianos have grown in sophistication and popularity. They have been used widely as substitutes for conventional pianos and as unique instruments in their own right, for performance, recording, and educational applications. For classification and for historical reasons, it is useful to divide this subject into two broad categories according to the method of tone generation. (1) *Electric*, or more specifically, *electroacoustic* pianos produce tone physically from a **hammer** striking a vibratory body; the tone is then subject to electronic amplification and other possible processing. (2) *Electronic* pianos contain no mechanical vibratory bodies. Instead, purely electronic signals are generated using oscillators, or more recently, digital **samplers**. In common usage, the terms *electric piano* and *electronic piano* have been applied and interchanged indiscriminately.

Both electric and electronic pianos require a sound-reinforcement system in order to be heard. This includes an amplifier and a loudspeaker, and may include a variety of sound-processing devices. These may be separate components outside the instrument, connected by cables, or they may be built into the cabinet of the instrument itself. In either case, it is the loudspeaker that converts electrical energy into sound waves, becoming, in effect, the audible musical instrument—the counterpart of the **string/soundboard** complex on a conventional piano.

Electric Pianos

Electric pianos were developed earlier than electronic pianos and will be examined first. Conventional pianos are often electronically amplified by using a microphone to balance with other amplified instruments or to permit sound processing. However, to be classified as an *electric piano*, the instrument must include built-in electronic circuitry. The principal vibratory body of an electric piano may be strings, metal reeds, tone bars, rods, or other devices designed as part of or in proximity to a transducer. The function of a transducer is to convert physical energy (vibrations) into electrical energy (voltage). The need for acoustic diffusion of sound is eliminated since the instrument will be heard through a loudspeaker and electric pianos generally have no soundboard.

This type of transducer is commonly referred to as a *pickup*. Historically, there have been three basic subdivisions of electric pianos based on the type of pickup: (1) electromag-

netic, (2) electrostatic, and (3) piezoelectic. Electromagnetic pickups consist of a permanent magnet coiled with a fine wire. The magnetic field around the magnet is intersected by the coil of wire; the pickup is placed so that the string passes through the magnetic field. When the string vibrates, the magnetic field is periodically altered in shape; small electrical pulses are generated at the same frequency. Early electric pianos that utilized electromagnetic pickups included the Neo-**Bechstein** Flügel and the Radiopiano, both of German design in the early 1930s. An electrostatic pickup consists of a rectangular bar or plate that functions as one of the electrodes of a variable capacitor; the other plate is the string itself. Vibrations cause the capacitance between the string and the plate to vary at the same frequency, generating voltage. The earliest electric piano to use this type of pickup was B.F. Meissner's Electronic Piano built in the United States in the early 1930s. Piezo-electric crystal pickups were first utilized in conventional pianos for amplification and have been used in almost all electric pianos built since the 1970s. In a piezoelectric pickup, the vibrating string causes compression of a crystal which, in turn, generates electrical voltage. This method is used in electric **uprights** and **grands** made by **Aeolian**, Helpinstill, **Kawai**, and **Yamaha**.

One of the earliest attempts to electrify the piano occurred in Atlantic City in the mid-1920s. The sound of a **Chickering player** piano in a shop window in Atlantic City was amplified by using a microphone and was transmitted to passersby. Also in the 1920s, the *Radiano*, a contact pickup, was designed for higher fidelity in broadcast reproduction of piano sounds. Occupying a position midway between the conventional piano and an electric piano was Simon Cooper's Creatone (1930). The Creatone used electrical circuits to prolong the tones of a conventional piano but required no loudspeakers.

In the early 1930s, instruments were designed and built in both Europe and America that retained some of the features of a conventional piano but utilized electronic pickups and were heard through a loudspeaker. At least three of the pioneers, Walter Nernst and Oskar Vierling of Berlin, and Benjamin Franklin Meissner of New Jersey, made significant contributions. Nernst and Vierling designed and built the Neo-Bechstein Flügel. Meissner developed an electric piano that became a prototype for a number of instruments built in the U.S. during the 1930s and 1940s.

Adapting the conventional piano to an electric piano brought about significant changes in construction. The Neo-Bechstein retained strings as the basic vibratory body, but amplification made it possible to use shorter and thinner strings. Double-stringing was necessary only in part of the middle register and triple-stringing was eliminated altogether. Groups of five strings converged toward an electromagnetic pickup. Since electronic amplification also made the soundboard unnecessary, the result was a somewhat lighter framework and hammer action. In turn, the light hammer created new problems for the performer accustomed to a conventional **action**. These problems were addressed by providing hammers of the usual weight that struck, not the strings themselves, but a **rail**; the impact against the rail drove a small hammer, approximately one-twentieth the weight of a normal one, into the string itself.

The Neo-Bechstein raised interesting musical possibilities. As a result of reduced amplitude its tone was extraordinarily pure, sometimes compared to that of the clavichord. Damping was reduced, since no energy was dissipated through the soundboard. Conversely, sustaining power was greatly increased—up to sixty seconds in the case of bass strings! A volume **pedal** along with such sustaining power opened organlike expressive possibilities. Curiously, the Neo-Bechstein and other electric pianos of the era had speaker cabinets with a built-in phonograph and radio.

B.F. Meissner, already established as a pioneer in radio and electronic phonographs, played one of the most important roles in the development of electric pianos from the 1930s through the 1960s. During the 1930s, in his Millburn, New Jersey, laboratory, he experimented with electrifying various musical instruments—harmonica to timpani. A keen interest in the piano was encouraged by his brother Otto Meissner, then a significant music-educator who envisioned a teaching piano that was aesthetically acceptable, yet portable and inexpensive.

Meissner experimented with numerous types of vibratory bodies—among them reeds, tuning forks, rods, and metal bars. Finding most of them unable to produce the complex harmonic structure needed to create an acceptable piano tone, he eventually returned to a conventional piano with the soundboard removed. He then experimented with a variety of electrostatic pickups on each of the eighty-eight string groups. His first manufactured instrument, the Electronic Piano, was patented in the early 1930s, and for two decades thereafter he licensed a large segment of the electric-piano industry in the United States. His patents were used in the **Minipiano** by Hardman, Peck, and Company, the Electone by **Krakauer** Brothers, the Dynatone by the Ansley Radio Corporation, and several others.

All of these instruments were essentially conventional pianos with electrostatic pickups instead of soundboards. While they found warm success in both the professional and home markets, there were problems—primarily a muddiness of sound from the low damping rate. According to Meissner himself, the "effect was such as is heard on conventional pianos when too much sustaining pedal is used." In addition, the piano was no more portable and no cheaper than the conventional piano. It had no advantages in tuning stability.

Addressing these problems, Meissner developed an entirely new type of electric piano by 1954 that became the prototype for the **Wurlitzer** Electric Piano. The new piano used thin steel reeds $1/4$ inch across as a vibratory body. The reeds were struck by hammers using a greatly simplified, but serviceable action. He solved the waveform problems previously encountered with reeds by having the hammer strike each reed at the node of its third **partial**. The pickup was positioned so that it negated the second partial. This left only the fundamental to be translated by the pickup. The pickups themselves, along with special auxiliary circuitry, were designed to generate a fundamental with a series of odd and even harmonics. Made of machined brass, the pickups were placed near the ends of reeds. Each pickup was the same thickness as a reed (.032 inches) and was adjusted to overlap the end of its reed by one-half of its thickness. As a result of this design, when the reed moved symmetrically, the pickup would produce an asymmetrical waveform with many harmonics and a rich, complex sound. The pickup acted as the fixed part of a variable capacitor, while the vibrating reed acted as the moving plate. The changes in capacity due to reed vibration caused a high-frequency oscillator to produce a frequency-modulated signal that was then demodulated into sound by an

FM detector. This output was further modified by audio filters and tone formers designed to approximate the characteristics of the piano soundboard.

Meissner viewed his piano of 1954 as a first step in a new class of electronic musical instruments. It satisfied many of the criteria his brother had envisioned. Abandoning traditional cabinetry altogether, it was much smaller, lighter, and cheaper than any of its predecessors. The basic model, cabinet containing **keys**, action, reed-pickup assembly, and FM preamplifier, weighed a total of seventy-five pounds. It could stay in tune for decades and, using headsets, practiced in silence. Thus it became a standard instrument for networked systems designed for class piano-instruction in music schools during the 1960s and 1970s. The Wurlitzer EP200, designed in the early 1960s for home use, was also widely used by pop and rock performers because of its rich, unique sound.

Another leading figure in the development of the electric piano in the United States is Harold Rhodes. A successful teacher, Rhodes had established a national chain of music schools by age twenty. With the outbreak of World War II, he enlisted in the Air Corps. Asked to teach piano to patients in the base hospital, he realized the need for a cheap but serviceable keyboard instrument. With nothing else available, he designed and built the AirCorps Piano out of spare parts salvaged from disabled planes. Tone was produced by bare wooden hammers striking lengths of hydraulic tubing that had been straightened and cut into xylophone lengths. The ensuing program of instruction was such a success that thousands of the instruments were eventually built and Rhodes was decorated for his role in the humanitarian project.

After the war, Rhodes attempted to replicate his teaching success in civilian life. He designed a new three-octave instrument, the Pre-Piano, using tone generators very similar to those of the AirCorps Piano. These were about $3/8$ inch in diameter, ranging from one to eight inches long. This instrument used an electrostatic pickup, had an amplifier and a six-inch speaker built into the console. The Pre-Piano failed, according to Rhodes, because the manufacturer he chose did not produce a mechanically sound product.

Rhodes then designed and toured with a seventy-two-note keyboard using a similar tone-generating system in a cabinet much like that of a **baby grand**. On this tour, he contacted and formed a partnership with Leo Fender, the inventor of Fender guitars and amplifiers. After a number of years of working together, they joined CBS. In the ensuing years the Fender Rhodes electric piano, which became an industry standard, was developed.

The Fender Rhodes piano was built in four models. Stage 73 and Stage 88 consist of keyboard, tone-generation system and pickups and require external amplification and speakers. The "73" and "88" refer to the number of keys on the keyboard. Suitcase 73 and Suitcase 88 incorporate their own stereo amplifier and speaker as well as a stereo vibrato unit. The operation of the Fender Rhodes is surprisingly simple. The actual vibratory body is a modified tuning fork with legs of unequal length. The key activates a hammer through a cam system—as the key is depressed, the **damper** is directly lifted from the metal bar, referred to as the *tine*, which is then struck by the hammer. Timbre can be altered significantly by adjusting the position of the pickup and/or the **strike point**. The bell-like sound of the Fender Rhodes has been effectively incorporated into jazz, pop, and rock performances by leading artists worldwide.

Other instruments that fall under the heading "electric piano" are the Hohner Pianet and Clavinet, each with a unique method of tone generation. The Pianet uses a sticky pad resting on a metal reed at the end of each key. When the key is depressed, the pad pulls the reed until its elastic resistance overcomes the sticking force. The reed then springs back and vibrates freely; a pickup located near the key transforms the vibrations into electrical signals. In the Clavinet, a string is located directly under each key, which, when played, impinges the string on a small metal anvil, causing the string to vibrate. The vibration is picked up by a series of pickups under the strings, then filtered and amplified. The Pianet is known for a warm and mellow sound while the Clavinet has a bright, percussive quality. Both have been used by leading pop musicians.

The Pianet, Clavinet, Wurlitzer, and Rhodes electric pianos remained in wide use throughout the 1960s and 1970s as substitutes for conventional pianos, for a variety of reasons including cost, portability, and tuning stability, and as legitimate musical instruments in their own right, with a unique sound, technique, and repertoire. With the emergence of solid-state electronics and reliable piezoelectric pickups in the 1970s, electric **grands** and **uprights** that once again used strings as the principal vibratory body began to supersede the earlier electric pianos as substitutes for acoustic pianos requiring amplification. Of particular interest are the American pianos developed by Helpinstil, already famous for highly successful acoustic piano pickups. From Japan, the Yamaha CP70 and CP80 electric baby-grand pianos, as well as those made by Kawai, are significant and in wide use. Various new **cross-stringing** and double-stringing techniques have been developed to permit strings that are as long as possible. To make the instruments portable, they generally divide into two parts, one containing the keyboard and action, the other containing the strings, **frame**, and electronics.

Also contributing to the demise of Rhodes and Wurlitzer electric pianos in the later 1970s was the development of extraordinarily high quality electronic pianos and sophisticated **synthesizers** that could adequately replicate the electric piano among hundreds of other onboard voices.

Electronic Pianos

This category of instruments consists of pianolike instruments whose sound is generated entirely by electronic components—oscillators, digital sample playback systems, and/or hybrids of both. Unlike the electric piano, electronic pianos contain no mechanical vibratory bodies. It is again useful to maintain distinctions according to the specific method of tone generation.

While early attempts date from the 1950s, the oscillator-type electronic piano was first successfully developed in the 1970s. It is, in essence, a dedicated or preprogrammed synthesizer designed to simulate the features of the conventional piano along with its electric relatives, such as the Rhodes, Clavinet, and sometimes harpsichord and vibraphone. The electronic piano may have one to ten preset voices. It may have sixty-one to eighty-eight keys, which are velocity-sensitive and may be weighted so that they resemble the feel of a piano action. Sustaining pedals (and sometimes other types of pedals) are almost always included.

An oscillator is an electronic device that, like the vibratory body/pickup complex of electroacoustic instruments, produces regular fluctuations in an electrical current. A single oscillator can generate only a single frequency, hence in early electronic **keyboards**, there were oscillators for every **pitch**. There were considerable problems with the tuning stability of early oscillators, however. A twelve-oscillator top-octave system was designed to correct this problem. In this system the oscillators were tuned to the highest twelve pitches on the instrument, which were then halved successively, using complex circuitry to create the pitches of each lower octave. **Tuning** was improved, since each oscillator would remain in tune with itself.

During the 1970s, the invention of solid-state electronics and microprocessor-assisted circuitry allowed a fully polyphonic instrument to incorporate only a single oscillator. These pianos used subtractive synthesis—a process of regulating and filtering fixed waveforms to create different timbres. A problem created by this system was that all signals derived from a single oscillator are in phase with each other, resulting in a sound that is too "pure." Beats between notes of a chord are perfectly regular in contrast to the more complex phase relations of a conventional or electric piano. This resulted in the need for additional sound processing such as doubling, chorusing, and flanging to sound "realistic." Sound-processing devices can be separate components or built into the electronic piano.

Notable first-generation electronic pianos were the RMI Electra Piano and instruments by ARP (later purchased by Rhodes), Crumar, and Kustom (a division of **Baldwin**). These instruments used the twelve-oscillator top-octave system. Later models introduced by Yamaha and Crumar rely on a single high-frequency oscillator running around two megahertz, from which all pitches in the chromatic spectrum can be derived. They include the Yamaha CP20, CP25, CP30, and CP35, along with the Crumar Roadrunner.

With rapid advancements in synthesizer and computer technology occurring in the early 1980s, more sophisticated and precise methods of tone generation were developed for synthesizers; these were immediately applied to electronic pianos. Microprocessors were built into almost all electronic keyboards from this time forward, performing a variety of functions. At this point in history, the term *digital piano* generally replaces *electronic piano* as the more common and accurate usage.

Notable is Yamaha's proprietary FM (Frequency Modulation) system, which was initially developed by John Chowning and the Artificial Intelligence Laboratory at Stanford University. An extremely accurate method of tone generation, FM is the basis for the widely used DX series of synthesizers. Unlike the tone generation method in earlier electronic pianos using subtractive synthesis, FM is a process of additive synthesis that attempts to recreate the random harmonic structure of conventional and electric instruments. FM technology is the tone-generating system for the Yamaha PF and Clavinova series digital pianos, which are manufactured in several models. Features associated with these instruments include on-board speakers; sound processing; equalization; ten or more voices; sustain and soft pedals; and 76–88 weighted, velocity-sensitive keys. Modern digital pianos also include **MIDI**, which allows the instrument to share information with other MIDI devices— e.g., synthesizers, sequencers, computers.

Engineers at **Roland** developed another sophisticated method of tone generation known as *Structured Adaptive (SA) Synthesis* for extremely accurate reproduction of conventional and electric piano sounds. According to Roland, SA attempts to digitally recreate harmonic characteristics and timbral variations across a wide range of pitches and velocities. Roland HP, RD, and MKS series instruments utilize this method of tone generation and incorporate all or most of the features described in Yamaha digital pianos. Interestingly, Roland and Harold Rhodes, in collaboration, have developed a new Rhodes instrument, the MK-80 introduced in 1990. The MK-80 incorporates SA synthesis. Other significant manufacturers of digital pianos include **Casio**, Kawai, **Korg**, and Technics.

The latest method of tone generation to be applied to electronic pianos is digital sampling. Sampling consists of recording an actual piano's sound and storing it as digitized data, i.e., a stream of binary numbers in computer memory. The sample is then recalled and played back from a keyboard controller. In order to maintain timbral variety and integrity, samples are recorded in many registers of the piano and with many variations in key velocity—a process

known as multi-sampling. In this respect, and subject to other variables, many experts believe that sampling provides the most "realistic" electronic piano sounds. There is considerable debate over whether this is true or whether a process such as SA synthesis actually results in higher quality sounds.

Sampling involves extraordinarily large amounts of computer memory and was hence initially limited to expensive instruments such as New England Digital's **Synclavier**. The **Kurzweil** 250, another landmark instrument, employs sophisticated digital sampling to recreate not only piano, but a full range of other instruments with realism. These samplers provide the full programmability associated with a synthesizer. In the late 1980s, Korg, Kurzweil, and **Ensoniq** all marketed digital pianos using sample playback devices for tone generation but without the ability to create and manipulate new samples extensively. Low cost made these instruments widely available and other manufacturers followed rapidly with similar products. "Hybrid" instruments that combine digital samples stored in ROM with digital synthesis for tone generation have been successfully developed by several manufacturers. Generally classified as synthesizers, these instruments function as high quality digital pianos, among their other applications. Among them are the Kurzweil K1000 series and the Yamaha SY77.

The Yamaha **Disklavier**, arriving in the late 1980s, represents the completion of a full cycle from conventional to electric to electronic and back. The Disklavier is a conventional full grand or upright piano that incorporates full MIDI implementation. Its on-board computer can accurately record, playback, and manipulate all keyboard and pedal actions. Performance data, thus recorded, can be stored on computer disks. Using MIDI, performances can be transmitted to and from any other MIDI instruments.

Samuel S. Holland

Bibliography

Bacon, Tony, ed. *Rock Hardware: The Instruments, Equipment and Technology of Rock*. New York: Harmony Books, 1981.

Carden, Joy. *A Piano Teacher's Guide to Electronic Keyboards*. Hal Leonard Publishing, 1988.

Contemporary Keyboard (1975–) [continued as *Keyboard*].

Darter, Tom, ed. *The Art of Electronic Music: The Instruments, Designers, and Musicians Behind the Artistic and Popular Explosion of Electronic Music.* New York: Quill/A Keyboard Book, 1984.

Meissner, B.F. "The Application of Electronics to the Piano." *Proceedings of the Radio Club of America* xi (1934): 3.

————"The Electronic Piano." *Proceedings of the Music Teachers National Association* xxxii (1937):259.

Rhea, T.L. *The Evolution of Electronic Musical Instruments in the United States.* PhD diss. George Peabody College, Nashville, Tenn. 1972.

Vierling, O. *Das elektroakustische Klavier.* Diss., Technische Hochschule, Berlin, 1936.

ENGLAND, PIANO INDUSTRY IN

Music historian **Charles Burney** states in Rees's *Cyclopedia* that the first piano in England was made by an English monk residing in Rome, a Father Wood, whose **Cristofori**-styled instrument was brought to England by Samuel Crisp around 1752. The first advertisement in England for commercially available pianos was published in Thomas Mortimer's *Universal Directory* in 1763. Five years later, **Johann Christian Bach** gave one of the first public performances of solo piano pieces in London on a Zumpe **square piano** he had purchased for 50 pounds.

Johannes Christoph Zumpe was among a group of Saxon refugees of the Seven Years' War known as the **"twelve apostles,"** who were important contributors to the burgeoning piano industry. Zumpe had worked in Germany with **Gottfried Silbermann** (whose pianos were modeled after Cristofori's) and briefly apprenticed with the Swiss-born London harpsichord maker Burkhardt Tschudi (**Burkat Shudi**) before establishing his own shop in 1761. His clavichord-shaped **"square"** pianos with the English single **action** (which lacked an **escapement**) became the model of the early English piano makers. Zumpe returned to Saxony in 1784 and George D. Schoene advertised as "Successors to Zumpe."

Some other important eighteenth-century figures were **John Geib** of the firm **Longman and Broderip** (the "hopper" escapement), **Christopher Ganer**, Boyer & Buntebart, **Johannes Pohlmann**, Thomas Culliford, **Robert and William Stodart**, **Americus Backers**, Jacob Kirkman, and **John Broadwood**.

John Broadwood married Shudi's daughter in 1769 and took over the shop in 1771. The firm of John Broadwood & Sons still thrives and, as the longest-surviving manufacturer of pianos in the world, it is a microcosm of the English piano industry. Its founder was responsible for many of the innovations that are part of the modern piano.

The earliest extant Broadwood piano is dated 1774 and is after Zumpe's pattern. Broadwood later moved the wrest plank (**pinblock**) from the right to the back, straightened the **keys**, used an improved English double action with an escapement, and replaced knee levers with foot **pedals**.

By 1777 Broadwood had collaborated with Robert Stodart and Americus Backers to make the English **grand piano**. The improved English action featured regulating screws to adjust for wear. Broadwood also had scientific research done on the **stringing** and introduced a divided **bridge** that improved the bass.

By 1784 interest in the harpsichord had diminished to the point where Broadwood produced 133 pianos but only 38 harpsichords, the last Broadwood harpsichord being made in 1793. The firm became Broadwood & Son in 1795 and John Broadwood & Sons in 1807; by this time, with a high degree of specialization and a large number of workmen, the firm produced over 400 pianos per annum compared to fewer than 40 each by its numerous competitors in England and on the Continent. Broadwood was the first to make use of steam power. Increased production brought the price of a square down to about 20 pounds.

In 1820 metal bars were added to the grand and a metal string **plate** to the square. By 1842, 2,500 pianos were being produced annually and Broadwood & Sons was one of the twelve largest employers in London. 1851 was the high-water mark for the firm. However, slowness in adopting the cast-iron **frame** and **overstringing** caused it to lose its preeminence in a highly competitive market, which it has never regained.

In 1866 the last Broadwood square was made. The **cottage upright piano**, first produced by an Englishman named **Robert Wornum**, had made the square obsolete. Broadwood & Sons then took up the production of cottage uprights.

In 1902 the new century was ushered in with a new factory having new machinery and new methods. Cuthbert Heath, "the father of British insurance," married a Broadwood and as chairman introduced modern economic practices as well.

During the war years of 1914–1918, piano manufacturing was curtailed to produce aircraft for the war effort. (The early biplanes really were held together by piano **wire**.) The radio, the gramophone, and the depression caused many piano manufacturers to collapse. Though Broadwood survived, it was only with difficulty. The firm briefly diversified into gramophones, as it earlier had into **player pianos**.

Today Broadwood is conscious of its rich place in musical history. In 1978, the 250th anniversary of the company was marked with a concert performed on five Broadwood pianos made between 1787 and 1978 from the company's extensive collection. Broadwood is entering the 1990s confidently, with a new range of uprights and grands.

The other early giant in the English piano industry is **Muzio Clementi**: composer, pedagogue, piano manufacturer, music publisher, and promoter of the piano. He invested heavily in the firm of Longman and Broderip. The litany of name changes in the firm to the present day is representative of the bankruptcies, fires, mergers, splits, and acquisitions prevalent throughout the industry. For various reasons the firm's name changed to Longman, Clementi & Co.; Clementi, Banger, Hyde, Collard & Davis (or simply Clementi & Co.); Clementi, Banger, Collard, Davis & Collard; Clementi, Collard, Davis & Collard; and Clementi, Collard & Collard; after Clementi's death it became **Collard & Collard**. By 1850 it was second only to Broadwood in production. In 1929 it was taken over by **Chappell**. Chappell pianos are now made by Kemble, which has a full history of acquisitions since its founding in 1911.

Clementi's contributions to the exportation of English pianos are still manifest. Of lasting innovations to the design of the modern piano, the most significant is the use of paired strings of one length of wire sharing the same **hitch pin**, **patented** in 1827 by the firm's foreman, James Stewart.

Up until about 1850, the world of piano design was very much occupied with the quest for a small **upright** instrument. English contributions were important. Early designs had been strung from the **keyboard** up, but in 1800 **John Isaac Hawkins** extended the strings to the floor. In 1802 Thomas **Loud** patented

diagonal cross-stringing and in 1807 **William Southwell**, after experiments with an upright square, designed a **"cabinet piano"** with a **"sticker" action**. Hawkins experimented with a tapered "celeste" (practice) strip, controlled by the middle pedal. Robert Wornum made a cottage upright, with the **dampers** activated by the **jacks**, in 1811. In 1842 he designed the tape-check (**bridle strap**) action, which is the modern upright action, except for having over-dampers. This is the "bird-cage" action still made by Herrburger Brooks, though commonly thought obsolete. English, and particularly Wornum's, contributions to the modern upright were inestimable. They were copied by **Pleyel** and later by the Germans and often are mistakenly attributed to the French. By 1851, 80 to 90 percent of pianos made in England were uprights.

Further efforts in England regarding the upright have been toward smaller, lighter, and cheaper instruments, with a counter effort toward quality, stability, and durability. More care to the aesthetics of **case** design is exhibited than is usually found in their Continental, American, or Asiatic counterparts.

In 1850 Great Britain was by far the world's largest manufacturer of pianos. Almost all of the many English contributions to the development of the modern piano were made by this time. By 1870 the United States made nearly as many pianos as England, and France and Germany weren't far behind. **Erard** and **Bechstein** even had factories in London. Attachment to tradition and patent laws caused English firms to eschew new piano technology such as the cast-iron frame, **cross-stringing**, **agraffes**, larger **hammers**, and heavier strings. In addition, manufacturing methods became obsolete, remaining largely labor-intensive. Production increased to over 75,000 pianos a year by World War I, but this was a dwindling share of an increasing market.

Old established firms collapsed or experienced reduced sales. The old practice of making everything in-house produced an expensive product, and the failure to embrace new improvements produced a product not suited to new tastes.

Keyboards, actions, and other parts became available on credit from American, French, and German firms. This enabled some new firms to begin production of pianos, such as Bentley, Hopkinson, Rogers, Marshall & Rose, and

Chappell. Eventually the old firms that survived adopted new techniques and technology.

During World War I many firms turned to the production of aircraft. This increased their awareness of modern industrial practices. There was an economic boom during and after the war, but their new dependence on imported parts made the industry unable to take advantage of it. Around this time a domestic industry producing actions and other parts became more established, helped by the McKenna Duties of 33 and $1/3$ percent on imported musical instruments.

Between the wars, piano production fell worldwide due to new forms of passive entertainment, the automobile, and the depression. Production in England went from over 90,000 pianos in 1927 to about 30,000 in 1932. Introduction of miniature pianos (called **spinets** in the United States) increased production to 55,000 per annum by 1935, but many of these new pianos were of a poor quality.

World War II was also devastating to the piano industry, but new plastics, glues, and construction processes developed during the war were pioneered by Alfred Knight Limited (which still manufactures pianos), and were adopted throughout the industry. Production reached 19,000 pianos by 1960.

After the war an extremely high purchase tax caused, for a time, almost all pianos manufactured in England to be exported. This expanded the foreign market, but England still suffers a trade deficit in pianos. The latest figures available from the Central Statistical Office in London show the 1988 production to be worth 15 million pounds. Imports were 1,761 pianos worth 11.6 million pounds and exports were 1,573 pianos worth 6.7 million pounds. This would indicate that cheaper pianos are being exported and more expensive ones are being imported. Figures from the Pianoforte Manufacturers and Distributors Association Limited differ from these greatly. They show imports to have been 11,266 pianos and exports 2,559 pianos in 1988; and imports 9,401, exports 3,874 in 1989.

The *British Music Yearbook* of 1990 lists twenty-nine manufacturers of pianos, actions, or keyboards. This is only a fraction of the number that once existed, and even this number is inflated by inclusion of brand names owned by larger companies and by listings of foreign companies in England. Even the Kemble

Piano Group–which includes J.B. Cramer & Company, **John Brinsmead**, Rogers Ennglut, B. Squire, **Kirkman** (bought in 1896 by Collard & Collard), Collard & Collard, Temple Pianoforte Company, **Schmidt-Flohr**, and Chappell Piano Company–is now **Yamaha**-Kemble Music.

Herrburger Brooks is the largest manufacturer of piano actions in Europe and also makes keyboards. Its history dates from 1810. Branches in Paris and London joined to become Herrburger Brooks in 1920 and moved completely to England in 1953. In 1965 it was taken over by **Kimball** International Inc. (formerly Jasper Corporation), which has invested heavily in modernization, over a million and one-half pounds in the last decade.

Another large manufacturer worth mentioning is the Bentley Piano Company Limited. Founded in 1906, it has roots in Grover & Grover, founded in 1830, and has recently revived the Grover & Grover brand name. It acquired other companies in the 1980s, including Rogers, Hopkinson, Gerh, Steinberg, and Zender. The firm also manufactures and markets Lipp pianos by arrangement with Messrs. Lipp in Germany. It has expanded its foreign market aggressively since World War II and exports a third of its 1,500 pianos per annum production worldwide.

The Industrial Revolution and the piano industry in England run parallel courses. They both began about the middle of the eighteenth century. England led the world in innovations, production techniques, and volume of production until around the middle of the nineteenth century. A period of decline was accelerated by World War I, the depression, and World War II, while today England holds a modest but stable part of the world market.

Daniel E. Taylor

Bibliography

Bentley Piano Co. Ltd., The. Literature. Woodchester, Stroud, Gloucestershire, England, 1990.

British Music Yearbook. London: Rhinegold Publishing Ltd., 1990.

Broadwood & Sons. Literature. Stony Stratford, Milton Keynes, England.

Colt, C. F. *The Early Piano.* London: Stainer & Bell, 1981.

Gill, Dominic. *The Book of the Piano.* Ithaca, N.Y.: Cornell University Press, 1981.

Good, Edwin M. *Giraffes, Black Dragons, and Other Pianos*. Stanford, Cal.: Stanford University Press, 1982.

Grover, David S. *The Piano: Its Story from Zither to Grand*. New York: Charles Scribner's Sons, 1978.

Harrison, Sidney. *Grand Piano*. London: Faber and Faber, 1976.

Herrburger Brooks. Literature. Long Eaton, Nottingham, England.

Herzog, Hans Kurt. *European Piano Atlas*. Frankfurt am Main: Das Musikinstrument, 1978.

Hollis, Helen Rice. *The Piano*. New York: Hippocrene Books, 1984.

Pierce, Bob. *Pierce Piano Atlas*. Long Beach, Cal.: Pierce Publishing, 1985.

Sadie, Stanley, ed. *The Piano*. London: W.W. Norton & Co., 1988.

Sumner, W. L. *The Piano-Forte*. London: Macdonald and Jane's, 1971.

Wier, Albert E. *The Piano: Its History, Makers, Players and Music*. London: Longmans, Green and Co., 1941.

ENGLISH ACTION

The principle of the modified early **Cristofori** action (**Stossmechanik**) was improved with the addition of an **escapement** by piano makers in England and eventually was referred to as English **action**. This action can also be combined with the German action (Anglo-German Action), in which case the head of the **hammer**, pivoted or hinged to a fixed **rail**, points towards the **keyboard**.
See also Actions; *Stossmechanik*.

Donatella Degiampietro and
Giuliana Montanari

Bibliography

Dolge, Alfred. *Pianos and Their Makers*. Covina, Cal.: Covina Publishing Co., 1911. Reprint. New York: Dover, 1972.

Harding, Rosamond E.M. *The Piano-Forte: Its History Traced to the Great Exhibition of 1851*. Cambridge: Cambridge University Press, 1933. Reprints. New York: Da Capo Press, 1973; Old Woking, Surrey: Gresham Books, 1978.

Hirt, Franz Josef. *Stringed Keyboard Instruments 1440–1880*. Translated by M. Boehme-Brown. Boston, Mass.: Boston Book and Art Shop, 1968. Also, *Meisterwerke des Klavierbaus—Stringed Keyboard Instruments*. Dietikon-Zürich: Urs Graf (distributed in the USA by Da Capo Press), 1981.

Marcuse, Sybil. *Musical Instruments: A Comprehensive Dictionary*. New York: Norton, 1975.

New Grove Dictionary of Musical Instruments. Edited by Stanley Sadie. London: Macmillan Press; Washington D.C.: Grove's Dictionaries, 1984.

The Piano. (New Grove Musical Instruments Series.) New York: Norton, 1988.

ENGLISH DOUBLE ACTION

See Actions.

ENGLISH SINGLE ACTION

See Actions.

ENHARMONIC PIANO

The enharmonic piano, also called quarter-tone piano, is a piano having more than twelve intervals to the octave. Simple modulation from A-sharp to B-flat, C to B-sharp, and so on, was the subject of much experimentation around the end of the nineteenth century, and G. A. Behrens-Senegaldens of Berlin **patented** a quarter-tone piano in 1892, the same year that he published his theory of quarter-tone music.

August Förster made an enharmonic **grand piano** for the Moravian pianist Alois Hába (1893–1973) in the 1920s. This was a pair of superimposed instruments with one **keyboard** having six rows of **keys**—three white and three black—to produce quarter-tones. Hába, a quarter-tone protagonist, claimed to be able to sing the five divisions of each semitone, 60 to the octave (72 and 84 divisions have featured in experimental harmoniums and organs). **Grotrian-Steinweg** also made a "double grand," this with black, white, and brown keys, and 20 notes to the octave.

Moritz Stoehr of New York built a quarter-tone piano in 1924, as did the Russian Ivan Alexandrovich Vyschnegradsky in the late 1920s in Paris. In 1930, Hans Barth made a piano along this principle and performed his own piano concerto upon it. Their high cost, complexity, and weight made these instruments uneconomical to produce, and the 1929–1930 recession killed off further development. The concept of quarter-tone music is sustained today thanks to the capabilities of **electronic** musical instruments.

Arthur W.J.G. Ord-Hume

Bibliography

Ehrlich, Cyril. *The Piano: A History*. London: J.M. Dent & Sons, Ltd., 1976.

Grove, Sir George. *Dictionary of Music & Musicians*. 1st ed. London: Macmillan, 1879.

Harding, Rosamond E.M. *The Piano-Forte: Its History Traced to the Great Exhibition of 1851.* Cambridge: Cambridge University Press, 1933. Reprints. New York: Da Capo Press, 1973; Old Woking, Surrey: Gresham Books, 1978.

Oxford Companion to Music, Oxford: Oxford University Press, 1970.

ERARD, SÉBASTIEN (ET FRÈRES)

The firm of Erard was founded by Sébastien Erard (1752–1831), who was born in Strasbourg. As a young man he moved to Paris, where he began making harpsichords. Early in his career he secured noble and royal clients, thereby ensuring that he need be concerned only with instruments of the highest quality. At about the time of the French Revolution he opened a branch in England.

Erard's early work seems to have been remarkable for its quality rather than for technical innovations. In the early years of the nineteenth century he became interested in improving the **grand piano**. Erard's early grands generally followed the English model, although he made a few Viennese-action instruments. His first invention to achieve widespread use was the provision of separate flanges for the **hammers** of **English-action** pianos. While this innovation did not affect the playing quality of the **instrument**—indeed, the practice of hinging a dozen or more hammers with a continuous **wire** remained common well into the late nineteenth century—it did make it much more convenient to adjust the positions of the hammers.

His next invention of importance was the **agraffe**. This is usually explained as a means of preventing the **strings** from being driven upwards by hard blows of the hammers. However, **Viennese pianos** of the mid-1840s were normally made without either agraffes or *capo tasto* bars. This is true even of instruments by the best makers, in which no problems of strings lifting are to be observed, even during violent passages in pieces by **Franz Liszt**. Perhaps a more important reason for the invention of the agraffe was the inherent weakness of the wrest plank (**pinblock**) in English-style pianos. To allow an action of reasonable design to function properly, these pianos have wrest planks thinner than those of harpsichords. The agraffe makes it possible to provide more reinforcement to the wrest plank. The Viennese action allows the use of much heavier wrest planks, and thus the agraffe offers little advantage there.

At about the same time that he introduced the agraffe (1808), Erard also brought out his first repetition action. The simple action used by Erard and his French contemporaries for **square pianos** lacked a true **escapement**, but this had the advantage that a note could be repeated without letting the **key** return completely to its original height. The escapement action in grands lacked this convenience. Erard's *mécanisme à l'étrier* of 1808 combined the merits of both actions at the expense of a considerable increase in complexity. In 1821 Erard introduced a new repetition action that solved the same problem in a mechanically different manner. This second action is the basis of all modern grand piano actions. The importance of this invention is generally misunderstood. One frequently finds in modern secondary sources the explanation that this device combined the lightness of the Viennese action with the power of the English action, and that it had the sensitivity that the English action so notoriously lacked. There seems to be no support for this in period sources or in the instruments themselves. Erard grands were noted until at least the middle of the nineteenth century for having exceptionally heavy actions. For example, Wilhelm von Lenz, writing of his experiences of the 1840s, remarks that **Chopin's** (English-action) **Pleyel** was lighter in **touch** and easier to play than von Lenz's Erard. If English actions were really so insensitive, it is curious that Chopin, a player noted for his fine dynamic shadings, should have used them happily. Indeed, theoretically the Erard action should be slightly less sensitive than an English action because of the increased complexity of the linkage between key and hammer.

Erard's was an ingenious solution to problems of action design that became acute after 1850. As piano hammers grew heavier, the touch grew heavier. Easing the leverage ratios to give a deeper touch made the resistance less but increased the difficulty of rapid repetition. The Erard action not only eased the repetition difficulty; the peculiarities of the design made it possible to counterweight the keys to further lighten the touch. Also, the Erard action was a technological sales gimmick at a time when new inventions were very much in the public mind.

Whatever the merits of their actions, Erard pianos were typically extremely well made and well finished. By the standards of their time, their **tone** was exceptionally powerful, clear, and well suited to concert use. As Sébastien Erard sank into old age and death (1831), his nephew Pierre (1796–1855) took over the management of the firm. Pierre was very effective at ensuring that people of social and musical renown used Erard pianos. This sometimes involved giving or loaning pianos free of charge, but the firm was large and wealthy enough to absorb the expense. With Erards in the possession of Queen Victoria, Felix Mendelssohn, Franz Liszt, and Sigismond Thalberg, it seemed obvious to many affluent and/or musical people that Erard pianos were the best available.

In 1838, the Erard Company **patented** its "harmonic bar." This combination of a continuous agraffe with a bar provided both rigid support for the treble strings and structural reinforcement for the wrest plank. It also was probably the inspiration for the *capo tasto* bar that is so common today. Indeed, the Erard firm abandoned its original design for the *capo tasto* sometime in the 1860s.

While Sébastien and Pierre Erard made important contributions to the design of the modern piano, it should be emphasized that the excellence of their instruments was due to the skill and taste with which the various elements of their designs were combined to make instruments of exceptional musical quality. Also, it should be mentioned that much of the evolution of their design involved features such as **soundboard** design, hammer size and composition, **frame**, **scale**, and **strike points**, that do not lend themselves to concise, simple descriptions.

By the middle of the nineteenth century, the Erard craftsmen had arrived at a basic type of instrument that was to characterize their work into the early 1920s. They experimented continuously with details of design, some of them musically significant. Their grands were parallel-strung with a relatively light metal frame composed of separate pieces. The actions were a modification of their original 1821 design and had underdampers, and the checks were in front of the hammers. The tone of these pianos is characterized by clarity and a very marked change in tone color from soft to loud. In the late 1870s or earlier, the largest **concert grands** by Erard began to be provided with a range of 90 notes, GGG–c^5. These enlarged concert pianos were arguably the most sophisticated concert pianos ever designed; they combined the clarity and range of color of some early nineteenth-century designs with an enormous dynamic range and considerable power and sonority.

In the late nineteenth century Erard was threatened by German competition. The American-inspired German designs were better suited to large-scale production and required less hand work. Wages in France were low, but in England they rose, and this was probably behind the decision to close the Erard factory in London in 1890. Erard opened a new concert hall in London shortly thereafter, and continued to sell pianos in England. More serious than a purely commercial threat, the new German pianos presented a new aesthetic with considerable appeal to late-nineteenth-century tastes. Their tone was fatter and more velvety than the Erard ideal. This involved some sacrifice of clarity and variety of tone color, but it also made these pianos more forgiving of clumsy left hands and pounding right ones. Erard was the piano of Gabriel Fauré and Maurice Ravel, and Claude Debussy was certainly well-acquainted with them; but German pianos gained prestige from German musicians and music schools, and pianists trained on German instruments were often disdainful of French ones, particularly Erards. In 1901 Erard introduced its own **overstrung** pianos, and sometime between 1923 and 1928 the old models were discontinued.

The history of Erard after 1914 is one of decline. As with most piano companies, the effects of two world wars and the Great Depression were very bad for both profits and quality. After World War II the Erard was no longer an artist's instrument. German and American pianos became the standard of excellence in France. When the French market was opened to foreign competition, Erard failed. In 1971 the **Schimmel** Company of Braunschweig acquired rights to the Erard name, and French production ceased.

See also Actions.

Edmund Michael Frederick

Bibliography

Dossier Erard. Introduction by Anik Derriès. Geneva: Minkoff, 1980.

Good, Edwin M. *Giraffes, Black Dragons, and Other Pianos.* Stanford, Cal.: Stanford University Press, 1982.

Harding, Rosamond E.M. *The Piano-Forte: Its History Traced to the Great Exhibition of 1851.* Cambridge: Cambridge University Press, 1933.

Reprints. New York: Da Capo Press, 1973; Old Woking, Surrey: Gresham Books, 1978.

Hipkins, Alfred. *A Description and History of the Piano-Forte and of the Older Keyboard Stringed Instruments.* London: Novello, 1896. Reprint. New York: AMS Press, 1977.

Hirt, Franz Josef. *Stringed Keyboard Instruments.* Boston, Mass.: Boston Book and Art Shop, 1968. (Original German edition published by Urs Graf-verlag of Olten, Switzerland, 1955.)

ESCAPEMENT

Escapement can be described as a non-blocking **action** system, consisting of all those parts of a piano-action mechanism that enable the **hammer** to be lifted towards the **strings**, yet allowing the hammer to be disengaged right before striking the strings. This action permits the hammer to fall back, even if the **key** is still depressed, without blocking the vibration of the strings. The escapement mechanism allows for the fast repetition of a note. **Bartolomeo Cristofori** invented such a device as early as the beginning of the eighteenth century. **Sébastien Erard** later developed a repetition action in which the improved escapement allowed rapid repetition of a key.

See also Actions; Erard, Sébastien [et frères].

Donatella Degiampietro and Giuliana Montanari

Bibliography

Dolge, Alfred. *Pianos and Their Makers.* Covina, Cal.: Covina Publishing Co., 1911. Reprint. New York: Dover, 1972.

Harding, Rosamond E.M. *The Piano-Forte: Its History Traced to the Great Exhibition of 1851.* Cambridge: Cambridge University Press, 1933. Reprints. New York: Da Capo Press, 1973; Old Woking, Surrey: Gresham Books, 1978.

Hirt, Franz Josef. *Stringed Keyboard Instruments 1440–1880.* Translated by M. Boehme-Brown. Boston, Mass.: Boston Book and Art Shop, 1968. Also, *Meisterwerke des Klavierbaus— Stringed Keyboard Instruments.* Dietikon-Zürich: Urs Graf (distributed in the USA by Da Capo Press), 1981.

Marcuse, Sybil. *Musical Instruments: A Comprehensive Dictionary.* New York: Norton, 1975.

New Grove Dictionary of Musical Instruments. Edited by Stanley Sadie. London: Macmillan Press; Washington D.C.: Grove's Dictionaries, 1984.

The Piano. (New Grove Musical Instruments Series.) New York: Norton, 1988.

EUPHONICON

The Euphonicon is a type of **harp-piano** (or, more accurately, harp-shaped **upright piano**, since the **strings** are struck, not plucked) invented by John Steward (English **Patent** No. 9023, 1841) and manufactured by F. Beale and Company, 201 Regent Street, London.

It is bichord and vertically strung and has: (1) a complete iron **frame** in which the harp-shaped upper part of the section supporting the bass strings is open to view; (2) a complicated provision of **soundboards** and resonators attempting visually to simulate the curved shoulders of cello, viola, and violin; (3) unusual stringing and **tuning** arrangements; (4) an early example of a "drop-action." The mechanism consists of a tape-check, overdamper upright **action**, mounted beneath the level of the **keyboard**. This action is divided into two sections: in the bass area the **hammers** strike near the bottom of their strings; from the region of d^1 upwards hammers strike near the top of their strings. Overdamping on no. 131 finishes at g^2 sharp. The soft **pedal** shifts the complete action (on rollers) to the right.

Public collections with examples include the Victoria and Albert Museum, London; the Metropolitan Museum of Art, New York; and the Reid Collection, University of Edinburgh (no. 131, dated 1843). The sound of the Edinburgh instrument is mellow, rather like that of a **cabinet piano**.

Kenneth Mobbs

Bibliography

Harding, Rosamond E.M. *The Piano-Forte: Its History Traced to the Great Exhibition of 1851.* Cambridge: Cambridge University Press, 1933. Reprints. New York: Da Capo Press, 1973; Old Woking, Surrey: Gresham Books, 1978. 244–45, 257–59, 272.

Libin, Laurence. "The Metropolitan Museum of Art." *The Harpsichord and Fortepiano Magazine* Vol. 4, No. 7 (April 1989): 178–84.

Patents for Inventions. *Abridgments of specifications relating to music and musical instruments.* London, 1871, facs. pub. Tony Bingham, London, 1984: 136–37.

Victoria and Albert Museum (ed. Howard Schott). *Catalogue of Musical Instruments.* Vol. 1. London: Her Majesty's Stationery Office, 2nd ed., 1985: 122–23.

EUTERPE PIANO COMPANY

The Euterpe Piano Company has a long and involved history. Until recently, there were three brand names of piano (Feurich, Euterpe, and W. Hoffmann) produced at the factory in Langlau, a small town in the German Franconia area.

Julius Gustav Feurich (1821–1900) learned the art of piano construction in the first half of the nineteenth century in Paris at the renowned company of **Pleyel**. After his return to Germany in 1851 he founded the Feurich firm in Leipzig. He was one of the first to bring the craft of **upright piano** construction from France to Germany and to begin producing these instruments. To secure his position as an upright-piano producer he made a contract with Julius **Blüthner**, the owner of the other well-known piano company in Leipzig, that for a number of years he would build only upright pianos and Blüthner would only construct **grands**. However, in 1855 both companies began to produce both types of keyboard instruments. Feurich grew steadily and by 1911 a large new factory of 5,000 square meters was constructed in Leipzig-Leutzsch. In its prime—a short time before World War I—the number of employees rose to 360, who produced 1,000 uprights and 600 grands annually. In the 1920s and 1930s production declined.

Carl Müller (1900–1968), who was a representative of Feurich during those years, bought the ailing piano company Euterpe, of Berlin, which had been founded in 1875. A short while later he bought another failing Berlin firm, the W. Hoffmann Company. This latter company was first registered in 1904 and was founded by Wilhelmine Sophia Friederike Hoffmann. During World War II many companies were exiled to Silesia, and Müller's piano companies were moved to Coburg. After the war Müller returned to Berlin, where he produced both brands, Euterpe and W. Hoffmann.

During the 1930s Feurich was one of the most recognized makes in Germany. Worldwide, there were between fifty and sixty concert halls where a Feurich **concert grand** was the house instrument. During World War II the parent factory in Leipzig was destroyed. The factory in Leipzig-Leutzsch escaped the bombs of the war, but because of the lack of living space the building was converted into residential quarters, although two floors became working space for the relaunching of piano production.

Throughout its history the company has been led by several generations of the Feurich family: Hermann Heinrich (1854–1925), son of founder Julius; Erich and Julius Adolf (1885–1973), sons of Hermann; Julius Hermann (b.1924), great-grandson of the founder, who began to rebuild the firm after World War II.

In 1949–1950 Julius Feurich contacted Müller and assisted him in constructing a new factory in Langlau on the former site of a munitions factory, the present location of Euterpe Piano Company. With a staff of seven people the factory produced uprights and repaired furniture and other items made of wood.

In 1958 Feurich, along with other older companies, was nationalized by the socialist government of East Germany and was combined with the Euterpe and Hoffmann brands into one company, the Euterpe Piano Company. Although all three firms shared a common factory and a common management they were still considered independent as GmbHs. After gradually increasing production in the 1950s and 1960s, the three companies reached their highest production level in 1979, when 276 employees produced 2,500 upright pianos and 250 grands.

In April 1991 the youngest Feurich family member, Julius Matthias Feurich (b.1954), became responsible for the sales division of the Euterpe Piano Company. At that time 150 employees produced some 1,400 uprights and 150 grands per year. The production of uprights was divided into 70 percent with the W. Hoffmann label and 30 percent with the Feurich name; in the production of grands, 30 percent were Feurich and 65 percent were W. Hoffmann, with the remainder made under the Euterpe name. The Euterpe factory building in Langlau covers an area of 11,000 square meters built on an area of 42,000 square meters. Since the reunification of Germany, Feurich has petitioned to regain the old factory in Leipzig-Leutzsch. The most recent development in the firm's history is that in July 1991 the C. **Bechstein** Pianofortefabrik GmbH of Berlin (recently renamed Bechstein Gruppe) bought a majority of the shares of Euterpe GmbH. Production of the Euterpe brand ceased and now only the brands Feurich and W. Hoffmann are produced.

The Euterpe Piano Company produced an extensive line of models. It had five upright models, from 112 cm (3'8") to 125 cm (4'1"), and two grands, 173 cm (5'8") and 197 cm (6'5"), which were available in various case designs: Baroque, Rococo, Sheraton, and Modern. The W. Hoffmann models and the Feurich models were produced in the same sizes and designs. The **concert grand**, built by Feurich for Euterpe, was produced in only one model, 227 cm (7'5"). Feurich was the most respected brand of the three makes and had the highest quality, with more of its parts made by hand than the other two. Its combination of high quality and variety of lines among the three brands made the Euterpe Piano Company one of the largest piano firms in terms of production.

Carsten Dürer

EVERETT PIANO COMPANY

The Everett Piano Company was a manufacturer that became popular in the Midwest. Founded in 1883 by the John Church Company, a musical instrument dealer of Cincinnati, Everett first produced **upright** and **grand pianos**, later adding **player pianos** to their list of products. The firm remained quite small and after several decades it fell behind the rest of the industry in sales growth.

In 1926, Everett was acquired by the owners of the **Cable-Nelson Company**, who took the Everett Company name and moved production of Everett pianos while still also continuing Cable-Nelson pianos at South Haven, Michigan. During the following years, the production of uprights and players at South Haven declined rapidly as in the rest of the industry and Everett made the transition to production of **spinets**, **consoles**, and studio upright pianos by the middle 1930s. Production of a small number of Everett grand pianos continued. Piano manufacturing was interrupted when Everett produced wooden-glider parts during World War II.

After the war, the firm prospered as sales of Everett and Cable-Nelson pianos continued to grow. Everett studio uprights were especially popular for school use. To meet growing demands, the South Haven factory was enlarged and modernized by the installation of new types of efficient equipment.

In 1962, with its plans to enter the piano industry, the Hammond Organ Company acquired Everett. When after eight years (1970) the new owners did not find piano manufacturing as profitable as expected, Hammond sold Everett to the United Industrial Syndicate, a group of investors. Three years later

Everett was sold again, this time to **Yamaha** International Corporation. Yamaha took further steps in modernization and began to manufacture Yamaha as well as Everett vertical pianos in South Haven. Piano making continued here and finally ended in 1986. Since then, due to the limited Yamaha piano-production capacity in the United States, Everett studio uprights and consoles have been manufactured for Yamaha in the **Baldwin** factory at Trumann, Arkansas.

Jack Greenfield

Bibliography

Dolge, Alfred. *Men Who Made Piano History*, Covina, Cal.: Covina Publishing Company, 1913. New York: Vestal Press, 1980.

"Everett Marks 100th With Townwide Celebration." *The Music Trades* (September 1983): 38.

"Yamaha's First Century." *The Music Trades*. (August 1987): 72.

EXHIBITIONS AND WORLD'S FAIRS

During the nineteenth and early twentieth centuries, international exhibitions and world's fairs gave piano manufacturers opportunities to compete for prizes and recognition. Three fairs—those of 1851, 1867, and 1873—were especially important, in part because they acknowledged the accomplishments of piano manufacturers in the United States.

Trade fairs have been held for thousands of years, and a few of the most important—like those of Leipzig and Frankfurt—have grown during the past hundred years from vegetable markets into enormous exhibits of space-age technology. Pianofortes of various kinds were occasionally exhibited and sold at fairs as early as the 1780s, but it was during the nineteenth century that international expositions influenced the piano as a commercially viable musical instrument. The principal expositions took place in London (1851, 1862), New York City (1853–1854), Paris (1855, 1867, 1878, 1889, 1900), Vienna (1873), Philadelphia (1876), Chicago (1893), St. Louis, Missouri (1904), and San Francisco (1915). The most important of these, however—at least insofar as the piano was concerned—were the Great Exhibition presented in London in 1851, the Exposition Universelle presented in Paris in 1867, and the Welt-Ausstellung presented in Vienna in 1873. Subsequent fairs of comparable size and general importance—including those held in Paris (1937), New York (1939–1940), Brussels (1958), Montreal (1967), and Osaka (1970)—exerted little influence on piano technology.

The first of the great "piano" fairs, presented in London in 1851, was known formally as the "Great Exhibition of the Works of Industry of All Nations." Housed in the magnificent Crystal Palace (destroyed by bombing during World War II), the Exhibition was the first trade fair to award prizes for pianos manufactured on at least two continents: Europe and North America. The commercial and scientific orientation of the Exhibition created some curious situations. Complete pianos, for example, were considered "Philosophical Instruments" (as were surgical gear, microscopes, and cameras); piano **wire**, on the other hand, was "hardware." Most of the pianos at the Exhibition were handsomely constructed standard **square**, **upright**, or smaller **grand pianos**. A few were novelties; one instrumant, for instance, was housed in a papier-mâché box. Several kinds of prizes were offered, among them Council Medals and Prize Medals (the latter less distinguished) as well as certificates of Honourable Mention. The only Council Medal for pianos, awarded for "peculiar mechanical **actions** applied to pianofortes and harps," was won by **Erard** of Paris. Several firms received Prize Medals, though; among them were Addison of London (for a "transposing pianoforte"), Breitkopf & Härtel of Leipzig, and **Chickering** of Boston. Already American pianos were challenging European instruments; Chickering's was the only American piano to win a medal, but two other builders—Meyer of Philadelphia, and Gilbert and Company of Boston—were acknowledged in the official catalog, the latter for a "pianoforte with Aeolian attachment."

American instruments won a number of prizes at the New York Exhibition of 1853–1854, but the firm of **Steinway & Sons** (established in March 1853) was then too new to compete. By 1855, however, Steinway took a Gold Medal at the second "Crystal Palace" New York Exhibition of 1855. Twelve years later Steinway won a Gold Medal (the highest honor any piano manufacturer received) at the Paris Exposition of 1867. Chickering also won a Gold Medal in Paris, as did **Broadwood** of London and **Streicher** & Sons of Vienna. Silver Medals were awarded to several dozen lesser competitors, including **Mason & Hamlin** of Boston and New York. European firms that won Silver Medals included **Bechstein** of Berlin and **Bösendorfer** of Vienna. A special award went to M. Schäffer of Erard's firm: he was made a Knight of the Legion of Honor for his contributions to French culture and commerce. (Controversy raged for months among manufacturers about the superiority of medals versus knighthoods.) More significant historically, though, were the words of praise lavished on American piano manufacturers as a class. The official report issued by America's Commissioners to the Exposition, for example, stated that "in no branch of industry did the United States win more distinction . . . than in the manufacture of pianofortes. The splendid specimens exhibited by the two firms [of] Messrs. Steinway & Sons, of New York, and Messrs. Chickering, of Boston, created a profound sensation not only with artists and professional musicians, but also with the musical public at large." Even François-Joseph Fétis—a member of the 1867 Paris jury that awarded Gold Medals to Steinway and Chickering, and a critic noted for his discernment—expressed few reservations. Also notable was the general absence at Paris of eccentric or merely amusing pianos; jury members and visitors alike seem to have been more interested in quality of construction than novelty of invention. A "cycloid" piano exhibited by Lindeman & Sons, a New York firm, was one of several curiosities, but even the American commissioners reported that it "attracted some attention by its peculiarity of form, but received no recompense from the jury." Improved grand pianos had also begun to replace earlier models as prize-winners. Edwin Good has called the Steinway grands first built in 1864 and exhibited three years later in Paris "our first modern" concert instruments.

By 1873 American manufacturing methods had captured the imaginations of German firms (though not of the French or British). As a consequence, German and Austrian firms swept the boards at the 1873 Vienna Exhibition; the instruments were European, but the designs and mass-production techniques American. Attempts at the 1878 Paris Exposition to denounce American designs and methods proved futile; by the beginning of the twentieth century, most of the pianos made and sold around the world were American in origin or style.

Pianos displayed at the 1876 Centennial Exhibition at Philadelphia also testified to American progress, and few European manufacturers bothered to compete.

Pianos of various kinds continued to win medals at early twentieth-century world's fairs, but technical improvements ceased to attract spectators. Experiments like the **Jankó** keyboard were incomprehensible to the general public, and manufacturing developments like Dolge's **hammer**-covering machine were marketed successfully without world's fair publicity. Instead, electric gadgets and devices like the phonograph and **reproducing pianos** became the rage; these were eventually forgotten under a deluge of new discoveries and inventions. Consequently, international exhibitions after 1915 changed piano history little, if at all.

Michael Saffle

Bibliography

Allwood, John. *The Great Exhibitions.* London: Studio Vista, 1977.

Closson, Ernest. *La facture des instruments de musique en Belgique.* Brussels: [Presses des établissements degrace à Hov], 1935.

Good, Edwin M. *Giraffes, Black Dragons, and Other Pianos: A Technological History from Cristofori to the Modern Concert Grand.* Stanford, Cal.: Stanford University Press, 1982.

Mactaggart, Peter, and Ann Mactaggart, eds. *Musical Instruments in the 1851 Exhibition.* Welwyn, England: Mac & Me, 1986.

Paul, Oscar. *Geschichte des Claviers vom Ursprunge bis zu den modernsten Formen des Instruments.* Leipzig: A.H. Payne, 1868.

Reports of the United States Commissioners to the Paris Universal Exposition, 1867. 5 Vols. Edited by William P. Blake. Washington D.C.: Government Printing Office, 1870.

Rindlisbacher, Otto. *Das Klavier in der Schweiz: Klavichord — Spinett — Cembalo — Pianoforte.* Bern and Munich: Francke, 1972.

Schelle, E. "Musikalische Instrumente." *Officieller Ausstellungs-Bericht.* Vol.15. Vienna: 1873.

Spillane, Daniel. *History of the American Pianoforte: Its Technical Development, and the Trade.* New York: D. Spillane, 1890. Reprint. New York: Da Capo Press, 1969.

EXPRESSION PIANO

An expression piano is an automatic or self-playing piano in which a degree of pianistic interpretation or expression is achieved automatically by means of specially made perforated-paper music rolls, which can control the operating vacuum pressure as well as the operation of the sustaining and soft **pedals** of the piano. Although sometimes referred to as semi-**reproducing pianos**, this is not strictly accurate.

From the early years of this century, makers of self-playing pianos attempted a variety of means by the use of which the illusion of a hand-played performance might be produced. As early as 1895, mechanical **piano players** and **player pianos** had been equipped with a rudimentary means by which the treble notes could be played louder than those in the bass, and vice versa. This, although crude, was the start of a quest for not so much automation of the piano and its music, as for replication of the real performer. The goal of the reproducing piano was still some years away as inventors experimented with the now-universally accepted pneumatic actions.

When in 1900 James William Crooks of the **Aeolian Company** invented the Themodist expression system, whereby individual notes could be made to sound out over or within an accompaniment, this idea was taken up by virtually every other major maker of piano players and player pianos. It was given a variety of names such as Accenter, Solotheme, Automelle, Solodant, and others.

It was then found that by varying the vacuum tension of the air between the separate halves of the valve chest or stack (see Player Piano for explanation) and combining this with a Themodist-type accenter, and applying the same technique to both halves of the **keyboard**, a much more realistic performance could be produced.

The pianos that used this type of artificially enhanced music-roll performance were almost always electrically driven (the operating vacuum was produced by a suction bellows worked by a motor) and were called "expression pianos," and they were mainly produced in Germany and America as instruments for use in public places such as cafes, diners, and soda fountains. Musical capabilities were often enhanced by the incorporation of percussion instruments and, occasionally, organ pipes.

The era of the expression piano did not cease with the later perfection of the reproducing piano, and instruments offering up to seven or more degrees of artificial expression were made right up into the 1930s. Cheaper than the reproducing instruments, they were ideally suited to playing popular music in places of public use.

See Player Piano; Reproducing Piano.

Arthur W.J.G. Ord-Hume

Bibliography

Bowers, Q.David. *Encyclopedia of Automatic Musical Instruments.* Vestal, New York: Vestal Press, 1972.

Ord-Hume, Arthur W.J.G. *Pianola—History & Development. . . .* London: Allen & Unwin, 1984.

EXTEMPORARY RECORDING

Creating a repeatable copy of an extempory keyboard performance has been a challenge to musical inventors for centuries. The term commonly used for such a process before the age of electronics is "melography," this from the name of the instrument designed by Leonard Euler, the Swiss mathematician. The Reverend J. Creed, an English clergyman, proposed a machine "to write down extempore voluntaries as fast as any master shall be able to play them upon an Organ, Harpsichord, etc." News of the device was not published until 1747, after Creed's death. Euler's Melograph was built by Hohlfeld in Berlin in about 1752 and consisted of two revolving cylinders with a band of paper passing over them. Note positions and duration were marked onto the paper by the use of pencils connected to the piano **action**. Hohlfeld's instrument was preserved in the Academy of Arts & Sciences in Berlin until the building was destroyed by fire.

Johann Friedrich Unger of Einbeck challenged Euler, claiming to have invented a similar machine in 1745. There were many other attempts at making similar devices (including the "Melographic piano" presented to the French Institute in 1827 by one M. Carreyre), but among those who worked to a greater or lesser extent must be mentioned **Jean-Henri Pape**, who worked in Paris with **Pleyel** and was accorded no fewer than 137 inventions, including the first use of **cross-stringing** in Paris (1839). His machine appeared in 1824 and although it improved on those that had come before it, it still left unsolved problems of varying rhythms and tempo.

In 1836, another Parisian named Eisenmenger was granted a **patent** for a melographic apparatus that was the first to incorporate a means for measuring off the bars. This received a British patent, number 7058 of 1836, in the name of Miles Berry. By the late 1880s, inventors in America and Europe were seeking what many by then considered to be a chimera, but in 1881 Jules Carpentier exhibited at the Paris Exhibition a "repeating Melograph" attached to a small harmonium. Its inventor stated that it was to write down ordinary music played extemporaneously on the instrument *dans le langage* [sic] *de Jacquard.* The system operated by punching holes in paper electro-mechanically to produce a "note-sheet," which could then be played back using another apparatus.

The refinement of the process came with the expansion of moves towards producing music mechanically, first through the small reed-playing organette and then through the **piano player** and **player piano**. In these it was obviously of importance to find a means of producing a replayable "recording" using paper perforated in such a way that a musical performance could be re-created.

Practical melography did indeed come with the music-roll industry, which connected a piano to a punching machine so that a master music roll could be produced from a live keyboard performance. The ultimate came with the encoding not just of the notes but the nuances of expression, achieved with the **reproducing piano**, which gave birth to performances by name artists on reproducing-piano music-rolls.

Arthur W.J.G. Ord-Hume

Bibliography

Grove, Sir George. *Dictionary of Music & Musicians.* 1st ed. London: Macmillan, 1879.

Harding, Rosamond E.M. *The Piano-Forte: Its History Traced to the Great Exhibition of 1851.* Cambridge: Cambridge University Press, 1933. Reprints. New York: Da Capo Press, 1973; Old Woking, Surrey: Gresham Books, 1978.

Ord-Hume, Arthur W.J.G. *Pianola.* London: Allen & Unwin, 1984.

———. *Pianola—History & Development. . . .* London: Allen & Unwin, 1984.

———. *The Mechanics of Mechanical Music.* London: Ord-Hume, 1973.

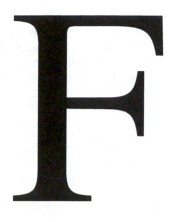

FALCONE PIANO COMPANY

This piano manufacturing company was incorporated in January 1984, by Santi Falcone, a piano technician and owner of a chain of seven retail piano stores. Falcone sought to make a **grand piano** of high quality that would compete with the finest European and American makes and which, at the same time, would be affordable.

In 1978 Falcone began to experiment with this idea at his workshop in Woburn, Massachusetts, and he sold New England Piano and Organ, Inc., his chain of retail stores, in order to make time and money available for the new project. He attracted a number of investors and technicians well known to Boston's long tradition of piano making. His first instrument was a six-foot grand piano finished in 1982; it was followed the next year by a nine-foot **concert grand**. He displayed these early models at his one remaining store in Woburn. At first his fledgling company made about two pianos a month and he employed eleven technicians. In 1985 the company bought and renovated an old shoe-factory in Haverhill, Massachusetts, to use as its factory. It opened in February 1986, and by the summer of that year a showroom/concert hall was in progress for the top floor of the building. In that same year the company opened another showroom in Boston. By 1987 Falcone had forty workers and was turning out four or five pianos a month. The company added dealerships in Detroit and other American cities, and by 1989 had increased its size to sixty employees producing about ten to twelve pianos a month.

Falcone Company specialized in grand pianos, building only three sizes—a nine-foot model, a seven-foot-four-inch size, and a six-foot-one-inch size. The firm did not build a **baby grand** because it believed that the smaller size would compromise the sound. Much of the work was done by hand, 500–600 hours per piano: the pinning, the felting, and the positioning of **capstans** were examples of such hand work. The **finish** might be black ebony or one of the natural wood grains, such as walnut, oak, or rosewood; the **rims** were of laminated maple held together with Franklin glue; the **lyres** were of poplar. **Soundboards** were made of Adirondack white spruce, a soft wood particularly suited to extremes of weather change. Falcone **patented** a "soundboard calibrator," which is a special soundboard-tuning device that alters the **tone** color of the piano. The **action** parts, made by **Renner**, were assembled by hand at the Falcone factory. The company bought its **strings** from West Germany and had a policy of using no plastic parts. Their steel **frames**, made according to Falcone's own wooden patterns, were cast at the Graniteville Foundry in Westford, Massachusetts.

By 1991 the Falcone Company had been sold and renamed the **Mason & Hamlin** Companies. This company, in addition to making the Falcone grand, also makes the Mason & Hamlin A (a five-foot-eight-inch grand piano), the BB (a seven-foot grand piano), and a fifty-inch vertical piano.

Falcone pianos have found favor with a number of well-known pianists, both jazz and classical; Virginia Eskin, Richard Goode, Leonard Shure, Ran Blake, and others have commented on the Falcone's good sound quality at every dynamic level, on the richness and evenness of sound throughout the entire range, and on the high quality of craftsmanship.

Camilla Cai

Bibliography

Ferguson, Laura. "Creating the Perfect, Affordable Piano." *North Shore Weekender* of the Essex County Newspapers (16 May 1985): D1 and D8.

Rhodes, Lucien. "Piano Man." *Inc.* 9 (January 1987): 52–56.

"Widely Acclaimed Pianos Symbolize Old Massachusetts City's Resurgence." *The New York Times* (22 March 1987): sect. I, p. 44.

FALLBOARD

Also referred to as the "dustboard" or "**nameboard**," the fallboard is a board of one or more pieces designed to cover the piano **keys**.

See also Case; Nameboard.

Philip Jamison, III

FELT

Woolen felt has always been important in piano construction, particularly in the **action**. A typical **grand** action may contain twenty-five different kinds of felt; this doesn't include felt strips used under the **strings**, in the **pedal** action, and elsewhere. Felt is used as cushioning to prevent knocks, as **bushings** to stop squeaks (see **Bushings**), as a dampener of vibrations, and also as a producer of vibrations. To date, no man-made material has successfully replaced it.

See also Damper; Hammer.

Philip Jamison, III

FERRINI, GIOVANNI (FL.1699–1758)

The Florentine harpsichord and pianoforte builder Giovanni Ferrini began his career as a student/apprentice of **Bartolomeo Cristofori**. The generous patronage of Queen Maria Barbara of Spain and the tremendous admiration of Don Carlo Broschi, the famous Italian *castrato* singer, attest to the excellence of Ferrini's work. However, little is known of his life besides the fact that he was active as a builder/restorer of harpsichords and pianofortes from the year 1699 to the time of his death in 1758.

After Cristofori's death in 1732 (*stile fiorentino* 1731, based on the liturgical calendar), Ferrini stayed on as conservator of the musical instrument collection for the Grand Duke Ferdinando de' Medici at Florence. However, later in the same year Ferrini left the service of the Duke, and the position was filled by Pietro Mazzetti.

There are two signed instruments by Ferrini still in existence. One is a *cembalo traverso* built c. 1732 with eight-foot and four-foot stops and a **keyboard** range of four octaves (C-c³). It is privately owned by Don Umberto Pineschi of Pistoia, Italy. The other is a 1746 **combination** harpsichord-pianoforte with a (Cristofori design) hammer-action upper manual and a two-register lower manual with the traditional plectrum mechanism. In 1984 it was purchased, and is privately owned, by Professor Luigi Ferdinando

Tagliavini of Milan. This unusual instrument is a fine example of Ferrini's brilliant engineering talent. It clearly illustrates his magnificent skill as a craftsman. The instrument is modelled after prototypes created by Cristofori. Ferrini's 1746 harpsichord-pianoforte has two keyboards of fifty-seven keys each: GG-e³ (lacking GG#), which are similar in structural design to an eighteenth-century double manual Italian harpsichord. However, Ferrini's combined harpsichord-pianoforte has several distinct new features: (1) the upper manual is a pianoforte and the lower a traditional harpsichord — each keyboard has its own complete, independent **action** system; (2) the instrument's lower keyboard has (from one to three) ballasted **lead** weights on each **key** lever; (3) it has a moveable lower keyboard that may easily be coupled to the upper register (pianoforte); and (4) the instrument's general overall **scale design** was slightly shorter than Cristofori's pianofortes. Furthermore, according to Alfons Huber, since both the **jacks** and **hammers** pluck and strike the same (pairs of unison) **strings**, Ferrini's harpsichord-pianoforte was probably strung with both brass and iron strings (the uppermost octave f² to f³ was strung with iron). The instrument has recently been restored (1988–1989) by Arnaldo Boldrini and Renato Carnevali in their workshop "Mastro del legno" in Bologna.

Another instrument, a harpsichord attributed to Ferrini, built in 1699, is presently located at the Württembergisches Museum in Stuttgart. It has a four-and-a-half-octave range, from GG-c³, with two eight-foot stops. However, its authenticity is not certain.

According to the inscription located on the **nameboard** of a 1666 Girolamo Zenti harpsichord, which is located in the Metropolitan Museum of Art, New York, Ferrini restored and altered the instrument in 1755. The instrument's keyboard range was expanded by increasing the number of keys in both the bass and treble.

It is not known exactly how many instruments Ferrini built during his lifetime. However, in addition to the above-mentioned instruments, a Ferrini pianoforte was built at Florence in the year 1730 and was purchased by Queen Maria Barbara (Elisabetta Farnese) of Spain. Since the Queen owned a total of five pianofortes that were constructed in Florence, it is highly probable that Ferrini built at least two of them. After the death of the queen in

1758, the 1730 Ferrini pianoforte was bequeathed to the renowned *castrato* singer, Don Carlo Broschi, known as Farinelli. Farinelli, who owned a great number of keyboard instruments, favored the 1730 Ferrini pianoforte above all others in his collection. In fact, the great singer was so inspired by the **tone** of the pianoforte that he composed several elegant keyboard compositions exclusively for the instrument. Furthermore, he so loved the instrument that he wrote on the nameboard in gold letters, *Rafael d'Urbino, Correggio, Titian, Guido,* etc., after the great Italian painters.

Ferrini was an exceptionally gifted builder of fine harpsichords and pianofortes. He proved to be as daring, skillful, and adventurous a craftsman as his teacher, Cristofori.

Ron Surace

Bibliography

Boalch, Donald H. *Makers of the Harpsichord and Clavichord 1440–1840.* Oxford: Clarendon Press, 1974.

Burney, Charles. *The Present State of Music in France and Italy.* London, 1771.

Casella, Alfredo. *Il pianoforte.* 2nd ed. Milan: Tumminelli & Co., 1954.

Fabbri, Mario. *L'alba del pianoforte: Verità storica sulla nascita del primo cembalo a martelletti.* Brescia: V Festival Pianistico Internazionale "Arturo Benedetti Michelangeli," 1968.

Huber, Alfons. "Were the Early Italian and Portuguese Pianofortes Strung Entirely With Brass?" *Das Musikinstrument* 37 (January 1988): 235–38.

Kinsky, George. *Musikhistorisches Museum von Wilhelm Heyer in Cöln: Katalog.* Vol.I: *Besaitete Tasteninstrumente, Orgeln und orgelartige Instrumente, Friktionsinstrumente.* Leipzig: Breitkopf & Härtel, 1910.

Kirkpatrick, Ralph. *Domenico Scarlatti.* Princeton, New Jersey: Princeton University Press, 1953.

Montanari, Giuliana. "Bartolomeo Cristofori." *Early Music* 19 (August 1991): 383–96.

Ponsicchi, Cesare. *Il pianoforte, sua origine e sviluppo.* Firenze: Presso G.G. Guidi Editore di Musica, 1876.

Russell, Raymond. *The Harpsichord and Clavichord: An Introductory Study.* London: Faber & Faber Limited, 1959. Reprint. New York: 1973.

Sacchi, Giovenale. *Vita del Cavaliere Don Carlo Broschi.* Milano, 1784.

Tagliavini, Luigi Ferdinando. *Catalogue of Luigi Tagliavini (1989).* Fribourg: UNI Institut de Musicologie (Photocopy).

———. "Giovanni Ferrini and His Harpsichord 'a Penne e a Martelletti'." *Early Music* 19 (August 1991): 399–408.

Interviews with Stewart Pollens concerning Giovanni Ferrini, 21 August 1988 and 20 March 1989 at the Metropolitan Museum of Art, New York.

FINGERING

In the early 1700s, keyboard playing made a departure from the archaic reliance on 2–3 and 3–4 pairings and came to involve all of the fingers including the thumb. Since then, fingering has been the aspect of pianism most subject to variation. Depending on the hand of the individual player, the particular instrument and its **action**, the **acoustics**, and — outside of solo performance — the ensemble, choices of fingering for a given passage can contrast radically. The musical effect desired by the composer also influences the selection of fingering. For instance, at the climax of the last movement *sempre più forte* passage in **Beethoven's** "Waldstein" Sonata, Op. 53, pianist Claudio Arrau used the thumb in a bizarre way to make the *sforzandi:* (see fig. below).

Alicia de Larrocha tells of changing a well-mastered fingering on the spur of the moment in concert to project better over the orchestra. Famous pedagogues have generally avoided imposing fingering except when a particular problem has remained unsolved by the student.

Beethoven, "Waldstein" Sonata Op. 53.

Notwithstanding this attitude of flexibility, virtually all pianists recognize the virtue of observing conventions established in the first half of the nineteenth century by Carl Czerny and others for fingering scales, arpeggios, and broken chords, and for connecting double-notes and octaves. Regular ascending scale fingering is 12312341 (RH) and 54321321 (LH). Irregular fingering is more complex, but works on a simple principle: as a black **key** leads to a white key, the thumb crosses onto the white key (this applies to the RH ascending and LH descending); as a white key leads to a black key, the thumb on the white key is crossed by 3 or 4 (as needed) going to the black key (this applies to the RH descending and LH ascending). For example, the fingering for E-flat Major is: 21234123 (RH up, LH down); and 32143213 (RH down, LH up). It is customary to use 2 in the RH when starting a scale with a black key, and to use 2 in the LH when arriving on a black note tonic at the scale's peak. As a special exercise, regular fingering is sometimes applied to all scales. Chromatic scales in German fingering use 3 on black keys; French fingering allows use of 2 and 4 for increased speed. Regular fingering for arpeggios is 1231 (RH up) and 5321 (LH up) or 5421 (LH up) when a minor third occurs between the first two notes. Irregular fingering for arpeggios follows the rubric for irregular scale fingering. In four-note chords bounded by an octave, the inner fingering varies with inversion from 2–3 to 2–4: if the interval inside the octave is a third or smaller, the former is used; if a fourth or greater, the latter. *Legato* double-notes and octaves are made by connecting the outer notes (the inner notes may be detached) and using crossings such as 4 or 3 over 5, or 5 under 4. Shifts also facilitate the connection of octaves.

Sliding from black key to white key, a practice associated with **Chopin**, is another method of connecting octaves:

Double Thirds.

Of the many issues that concern fingering, some of the more basic are: matching strong fingers with strong notes; changing fingers on rapid repeated notes; using as much of the hand as possible to avoid overly frequent crossings; pairing fingers of comparable length in double-third successions;

Chopin - Prelude Op.28, No.20 (bar 2)

Sliding

reinforcing a heavy accent, such as a bass note, by striking with two or three fingers on the same key at once (pianists with tiny hands even use the fist); retaining a consistent fingering pattern throughout a passage to aid memory. Comparing fingering in different editions of the same work, such as the Artur Schnabel and Heinrich Schenker editions of the Beethoven

Legato Octaves

sonatas, opens a door to understanding the process of finding an effective fingering.

Curt Cacioppo

FINISH

Finish is the exterior layers of coatings that protect the piano wood from climate changes and provide an attractive appearance to the piano **case.**

See also Case.

Kent Webb

FLÜGEL

Flügel is the usual German name for **grand piano**. It means "wing," which describes the shape of the **case** and the **frame.**

See Grand Piano; *Hammerflügel/Hammerklavier.*

Camilla Cai

FORTE PEDAL

The forte pedal is another term for the right pedal, which raises all of the **dampers** from the **strings**; also called the damper pedal.

See Pedals and Stops.

Edwin M. Good

FORTEPIANO

Fortepiano is as appropriate a name for the piano as pianoforte, and **Viennese piano** labels as late as the 1870s sometimes use the word "fortepiano." When various types of early piano were revived in this century, the need was felt for a term to distinguish the early pianos, particularly the Viennese-style instruments of the late eighteenth century, from the standard modern piano. The modern term "fortepiano" does not have precise limits; a Viennese **grand piano** of 1790 (or a modern copy of one) is clearly a fortepiano. An English grand piano of the same date may or may not be called a fortepiano. A Viennese grand piano of 1840 will probably be called a fortepiano; an **Erard** grand piano of 1850 will probably not.

Edmund Michael Frederick

FOURNEAUX, NAPOLEON (B.1830)

Napoleon Fourneaux was born in Paris in 1830. The Fourneaux family was closely involved in the making of musical instruments, and his father, Napoleon Fourneaux, Sr. (1808–1846)

contributed several inventions to the development of free-reed instruments and the harmonium. In 1863, Napoleon Fourneaux devised a mechanical **piano player** called the Pianista. This was the first known pneumatic piano player and it comprised a cabinet somewhat larger in size than a piano. It was placed in front of an ordinary instrument so that a row of wooden fingers at the back of the Pianista aligned with the **keyboard keys**. The playing action comprised a pinned barrel turned by a handle. Foot-treadled bellows provided wind (as in a harmonium) to operate pressure pneumatics, which in turn depressed the wooden fingers. The instrument was demonstrated at the Philadelphia Exhibition of 1876.

See also Player Piano.

Arthur W.J.G. Ord-Hume

Bibliography

Harding, Rosamond E.M. *The Piano-Forte: Its History Traced to the Great Exhibition of 1851.* Cambridge: Cambridge University Press, 1933. Reprints. New York: Da Capo Press, 1973; Old Woking, Surrey: Gresham Books, 1978.

Ord-Hume, Arthur W.J.G. *Pianola—History & Development.* . . . London: Allen & Unwin, 1984.

———. *Player Piano — History of the Mechanical Piano.* London: Allen & Unwin, 1970.

Sachs, Curt. *Real-Lexicon der Musikinstrumente.* Berlin, 1913.

FRAME

The component in the internal structure of the piano responsible for sustaining the drawing force of the **strings** is the frame. Until the nineteenth century, the frame was traditionally a wooden structure with timbers running lengthwise through the body of the piano. Cross-braces were dovetailed at right angles to these timbers and a wooden wrest plank (**pinblock**) and string-**plate** were then bolted to this internal structure. Iron was eventually added to strengthen the frame as the strain of the strings was exacerbated by ever-rising **pitch** and the addition of higher octaves. Composite frames utilizing metallic **braces** were accepted before the complete cast-iron frame and fell into two main categories: composite iron resistance frame (metallic bars) for resisting the strain of the strings, and compensation frames (compensating tubes) for combatting atmospheric changes.

Composite Iron Resistance Frames

Iron first entered the piano as a major component around 1800. In 1799, Englishman Joseph Smith patented a metal frame (English **Patent No. 2345**) based on the inner frame of the harpsichord while **John Isaac Hawkins** added metal braces to his **portable grand** pianoforte of 1800. Rosamond Harding concedes that these experiments had no direct bearing on the development of the metal frame and that **John S. Broadwood** was the first to successfully add metallic bracing bars of any significance to the interior of the piano. In 1808, Broadwood's English shop used three tension bars and increased that number to five in 1821. **Samuel Hervé**, a Broadwood employee, applied the first metal **hitch pin** plate to a **square piano** in the same year (1821) and Broadwood combined this plate and his tension bars for his patent of 1827 (English Patent No. 5485).

The French were eager to adapt the metallic braces to their own instruments and in 1825 Pierre **Erard** obtained an English patent (No. 5065) for a method of fixing iron bars to the wooden braces of the pianoforte. In the same year, the **Pleyel** house applied an iron frame and copper string-plate to one of their instruments.

The Austrians and Germans experimented with metal braces, but were slower to incorporate iron into their instruments. **Matthias Müller** of Vienna obtained a patent in 1829 for an iron frame and wrest-pin block with a suspension bar of iron, and Jacob Becker of Frankenthal obtained a patent in 1839 for square and grand iron frames. Johann Baptist **Streicher** reputedly used iron bars in his pianos as early as 1835. Acceptance of iron into the piano, however, was stagnated by the belief that iron was deleterious to the tone of the instrument. Also, the interlocking wooden structure of Viennese frames made the need for metal braces less urgent.

Conrad Graf, one of the most esteemed Viennese piano builders of the early nineteenth century, remained faithful to wooden framing throughout his career. Deborah Wythe, in her article on the pianos of Graf (*Early Music*, Nov. 1984, p. 454), claims that Graf's durable frame design and construction are unique. Frame components consist of three lengthwise and one or two crosswise beams, **belly rail**, and case-wall beams. The interlocking parts are constructed of five-ply oak and spruce and the entire framework is laminated to add to the instrument's durability.

Compensation Frames

In 1820, **James Thom and William Allen** (both employed by **Stodart**) patented a frame that prevented fluctuations in the pitch of the strings due to changes in temperature and humidity. The frame consisted of parallel tubes that were fixed in the frame above strings of similar metal beneath (i.e., brass above brass, steel above steel, etc.). The expansion or contraction of the strings would then be felt simultaneously by the complementary expansion or contraction of the frame.

Pierre Erard followed in 1822 with a patent (French Patent No. 2170) that appeared to be almost an exact copy of the Thom and Allen frame. Francis Melville applied two tubular bars to a square piano in his patent of 1825 (English Patent No. 5085) and Thomas **Loud**, Jr. of Philadelphia patented his metallic tubes in 1837. Daniel Spillane states that Loud's compensating tubes were adopted in New York in 1838.

The compensation frame was seen as a breakthrough by nineteenth-century contemporaries, but was short-lived in the light of a more pressing problem, that of sustaining heavier strings at a higher tension. Compensation frames became the secondary counterpart to composite iron resistance frames, as it was the challenge of builders to invent a frame that could withstand the inward pressure of the strings as well as maintain **tuning**.

Cast-iron Frame

The most significant improvement applied to the piano was that of the cast-iron frame. E. M. Good explains that because of cast-iron's high carbon content, it is imbued with high compressive strength (resistance to forces pushing in on the material), which allows it to withstand the enormous inward pressure of the strings.

Alpheus Babcock of Boston first patented a complete cast-iron ring frame for the square pianoforte on 17 December 1825. He later obtained a patent in Philadelphia (1830) for an almost identical frame that included three struts (instead of the single treble strut of 1825) and a new scheme of **cross-stringing**. Although Babcock's 1825 patent describes the frame as capable of resistance and compensation, most authorities agree that its main usefulness was that of resistance.

In 1826, **Jean-Henri Pape** of Paris patented a frame containing a cast-iron hitch pin block and **bridge** (French Patent No. 4918). Three years later, Pape's countryman Guillaume Petzold patented a cast-iron frame (French Patent No. 4089). Aside from Wheatley Kirk's English patent (No. 7094) for the first complete iron frame for an **upright piano**, American ingenuity dominated further experiments in the perfection of the complete cast-iron frame.

It was **Jonas Chickering** of Boston who made the most significant improvements in the cast-iron frame following Babcock's patent of 1825. His patented frame of 1840 for square pianos (U.S. Patent No. 1802) cast wrest plank and upper bridge, string-plate, and **damper** socket in one single piece, thereby eliminating any excess noise caused by loosening wooden parts. It is interesting to note, however, that most Chickering squares from the early 1840s contain cast-iron string-plates; the complete cast-iron frame was not commonplace until around 1850. In addition to his patent for square pianos, Chickering secured a patent fitting the **grand** with a full cast-iron frame in 1843 (U.S. Patent No. 3238).

The cast-iron frame was brought to modern standards in the latter half of the nineteenth century by **Steinway & Sons**. They dramatically improved the tone of instruments with single-cast frames by successfully cross-stringing their squares as early as 1853 and later applying that same principle to grands. The improvements made by Steinway & Sons, and especially by Theodore Steinway, attracted much attention in the London Exhibition of 1862 and in the *Exposition universelle* (1867) in Paris. Cynthia Hoover, in her article on Steinway pianos (*AMIS*, Vol. 7, 1981, p. 60), surmised that over two-thirds of the pianos at the Vienna Exhibition of 1873 were imitations of the American cast-iron frame and Steinway's **overstrung** system.

By 1875, Theodore Steinway claimed to have invented a plate that could withstand up to 70,000 pounds, more than twice the maximum weight in 1862. Steinway's Centennial grand, exhibited in the Philadelphia Centennial Exposition of 1876, contained a cupola iron frame patented in 1872 and 1875 that further increased the strength of the metal frame.

The cast-iron frame that was modified and improved by Steinway was the result of experiments and ideas seeded in the early nineteenth

century. The need for increased resistance to the drawing force of the strings stimulated the first use of metal in the framework of the piano. Temperature and humidity fluctuations motivated the use of compensation frames that stabilized tuning. In the midst of these innovations, it was not long before the full cast-iron frame was accepted by contemporary builders and became an essential element in the framework of the piano.

Mary Ellen Haupert

Bibliography

Good, Edwin Marshall. *Giraffes, Black Dragons, and Other Pianos: A Technological History from Cristofori to the Modern Concert Grand.* Stanford, Cal.: Stanford University Press, 1982.

Harding, Rosamond E.M. *The Piano-Forte: Its History Traced to the Great Exhibition of 1851.* Cambridge: Cambridge University Press, 1933. Reprints. New York: Da Capo Press, 1973; Old Woking, Surrey: Gresham Books, 1978.

Haupert, Mary Ellen. "The Square Pianos of Jonas Chickering." Ph.D. dissertation, Washington University in St. Louis, 1989.

Hipkins, A. J. *A Description and History of the Pianoforte.* London: Novello, 1896.

Hoover, Cynthia Adams. "The Steinways and Their Pianos in the Nineteenth Century." *American Musical Instrument Society Journal* 7 (1981): 47–89.

The New Grove Dictionary of Music and Musicians. Edited by Stanley Sadie. S.V. "The Piano-Forte," by Philip Belt. Vol. XIV: 682–714. Washington D.C.: Grove's Dictionary of Music, Inc., 1980, Vol. XIV: 682–714.

Smith, Fanny Morris. *A Noble Art; Three Lectures on the Evolution and Construction of the Piano.* New York: Devinne Press, 1892.

Spillane, Daniel. *History of the American Pianoforte: Its Technical Development, and the Trade.* New York: D. Spillane, 1890. Reprint. New York: Da Capo Press, 1969.

Wier, Albert E. *The Piano: Its History, Makers, Players and Music.* New York: Longmans Green, 1940.

Wythe, Deborah. "The Pianos of Conrad Graf." *Early Music* 12 (1984): 447–60.

FRANCE, PIANO INDUSTRY IN

The important advances made by French piano makers during the first half of the nineteenth century coincided with the establishment of

Paris as the world's center of pianistic activity. **Frédéric Chopin, Franz Liszt,** Sigismond Thalberg, and Frédéric Kalkbrenner were the friends of the leading manufacturers, **Sébastien Erard** and Camille **Pleyel,** and the latter founded concert halls that competed with ones owned by the inventor **Jean-Henri Pape** and the pianist-composer-piano-maker Henri Herz. This brilliant period of invention and interaction peaked around 1855, when Erard was the leading piano maker in the world. Thereafter, piano manufacture in France declined, yielding supremacy to German and American competitors by 1900.

The beginnings of the piano industry in France are obscure. Although projects for *clavecins à maillets* (harpsichords with **hammers**) were submitted to the Académie royale des sciences by an inventor named Jean Marius in 1716, there is no evidence that his instruments ever got beyond the planning stage. Most pianos heard in Paris prior to 1770 were English imports. The most popular of these were by the London maker **Johann Christoph Zumpe,** whose single **action** served as the model for the first French pianos.

The earliest French pianos include two made in Paris in 1770, one by Johann Mercken, the other by one Virbès (or Devirbès). Other early documented instruments are **Pascal (Joseph) Taskin's** first piano (1768) and Sébastien Erard's first **square piano** (1777) and first **grand** (1796).

The leading firms of the nineteenth century included Erard (founded c. 1780), Pleyel (1807), Pape (1815), Herz (with Klepfer 1825, independently 1851), Roller et Blanchet (1827), Boisselot (1828), Kriegelstein (1831), Bord (1843), and **Gaveau** (1847). All of the above except Boisselot (of Marseille) were located in Paris, where by 1847 there were 180 reported piano makers.

The most important French innovation was Sébastien Erard's repetition grand action with double **escapement,** which he allowed to be **patented** in 1821 by his nephew Pierre, who ran the London branch of the business. Other significant French achievements included the elder Erard's invention of the **agraffe** (1808), Camille Pleyel's cast-iron frame (1825), Pape's patents for **felt**-covered hammers (1826) and **cross-stringing** (1828), Pierre Erard's invention of the harmonic bar (1838), Antoine Bord's invention of the *capo tasto* (1843) and the spiral hopper-spring (1846), Boisselot's incor-

poration of a *sostenuto* pedal (1844), Herz's now-universally adopted modification of Erard's double escapement grand action (1850), and Napoléon Fourneaux's invention of the pneumatic **player piano** (1863). Of less importance were Erard's **transposing** piano (1812), Pape's eight-octave piano (1844), and such eccentric inventions as Pape's circular piano (1834) and the Pfeiffer et Petzoldt triangular piano (1806).

The early square pianos were soon supplanted in popularity by **upright pianos** made in a variety of sizes. The first upright in France seems to have been the "Harmomelo" by Pfeiffer (1806), with a Viennese action and **pedals** for harp and bassoon effects. Pleyel made inexpensive *pianinos* (1815) based on the **cottage pianos** of the London maker **Robert Wornum.** Other small French uprights included Pape's **overstrung** *pianinos* (1828), Kriegelstein's high-quality "Mignone Pianino" (1842), and Bord's inexpensive and sturdy "pianettes" (1857). These small instruments took second place, however, to high-quality uprights and grands. During the 1840s and 1850s the top five makers of those instruments—Erard, Pleyel, Pape, Kriegelstein, and Herz—held their own against growing international competition, and in the early 1860s French pianos accounted for about 40 percent of the world's production.

An exceptional success in the late nineteenth century was the French firm of Herrburger-Schwander, which became the world's leading maker of actions, exporting these in large numbers even to England and Germany. In 1913 this firm made approximately 100,000 actions for upright and grand pianos.

Ehrlich believes that the best period for French manufacturers was between 1848 and 1857, when production increased dramatically and exports flourished, especially to Belgium, the United States, Italy, and Latin America. Subsequently, the major French firms rested on their laurels, became insular, and resisted the new technology and business acumen being developed in Germany and the United States.

Criticism and rejection of French pianos by foreign musicians followed. By 1900 French manufacturers withdrew from competition in the world's markets and contented themselves with making thin-toned instruments for the home market. By 1920 exports decreased to only 4,000 pianos per year, compared with British exports of 9,000, and German exports of

80,000. By 1930 France produced fewer than 10 percent of the world's pianos.

The firms of Erard and Gaveau merged in 1960, and in the following year joined with Pleyel. Finally, in 1971 the conglomerate was acquired by **Schimmel**, the top-selling German company that now produces the three French-named pianos in small numbers and according to its own standards.

The piano industry in France is today reduced to two manufacturers, Klein (1871) and Rameau (1971). In 1980 these firms together made only about 4,500 pianos. France currently imports some 30,000 upright and grand pianos, mostly from Japan and Germany.

Charles Timbrell

Bibliography

Barli, Olivier. *La Facture française du piano de 1849 à nos jours*. Paris: La Flûte de Pan, 1983.

Closson, Ernest. *Histoire du piano*. Brussels: Editions universitaires, 1944. (New edition translated as *History of the Piano* by Delano Ames and edited and revised by Robin Golding. New York: St. Martin's Press, 1974.)

Dolge, Alfred. *Pianos and Their Makers*. Covina, Cal.: Covina Publishing Co., 1911. Reprint. New York: Dover, 1972.

Ehrlich, Cyril. *The Piano: A History*. London: J.M. Dent & Sons, Ltd., 1976.

Harding, Rosamond E.M. *The Piano-Forte: Its History Traced to the Great Exhibition of 1851*. Cambridge: Cambridge University Press, 1933. Reprints. New York: Da Capo Press, 1973; Old Woking, Surrey: Gresham Books, 1978.

————, et al., eds. *The Piano* (The New Grove Musical Instrument Series). New York: W. W. Norton, 1988.

Loesser, Arthur. *Men, Women and Pianos*. New York: Simon and Schuster, 1954.

Pierce, Bob. *Pierce Piano Atlas*. Long Beach, Cal.: Bob Pierce, 1977.

Pierre, Constant. *Les facteurs d' instruments de musique*. Paris: E. Sagot, 1893. Reprint. Geneva: Minkoff, 1971.

Pistone, Danièle. *La Musique en France de la Révolution à 1900*. Paris: Honoré Champion, 1979.

————, ed. *Revue Internationale de Musique Française* 15 (November 1984), issue devoted to *Le Piano Français au XXe Siècle*.

Place, Adélaïde de. *Le Piano-forte à Paris entre 1760 et 1822*. Paris: Aux Amateurs de Livres, 1986.

FREDERICK THE GREAT (1712–1786)

Apart from his historical significance as a political and military leader, Frederick II, King of Prussia, exerted considerable influence on the arts and music of eighteenth-century Germany. An accomplished performer on the transverse flute, Frederick also produced several compositions, especially instrumental works such as concertos that feature the flute. Although his particular love of the flute led to a long and close relationship with Johann Joachim Quantz he was also able to attract a number of other leading musicians to Berlin, including **Carl Philipp Emanuel Bach** as the court's principal harpsichordist.

Probably during the 1740s, Frederick II purchased one of the first pianos made in Germany, which was constructed by a noted builder of keyboard instruments from Freiberg (Saxony), **Gottfried Silbermann**. The new invention apparently pleased the monarch to such a degree that he ordered several more, as many as fifteen altogether, according to Johann Nikolaus Forkel. Forkel also gives the most complete account of **Johann Sebastian Bach**'s famous visit to the Prussian court in 1747 in which, immediately upon his arrival, he was led to each of the new Silbermann pianos to try them out. Having heard of the abilities that "the old Bach" possessed regarding counterpoint, Frederick II requested that the composer extemporize on a theme that he, the king, had written. Bach later used this theme as the basis for his *Musikalisches Opfer* (BWV 1079). Although there is no evidence as to whether Carl Philipp Emanuel Bach took any particular interest in the Silbermann pianos during his tenure in Berlin, his presence there makes him one of the first major composers to have regular access to a piano.

Darcy Kuronen

Bibliography

David, Hans T., and Arthur Mendel. *The Bach Reader*. New York: W. W. Norton and Co., Inc., 1966.

Helm, Ernest Eugene. *Music at the Court of Frederick the Great*. Norman: University of Oklahoma Press, 1960.

Pollens, Stewart. "Gottfried Silbermann's Pianos." *Organ Yearbook* 17 (1986): 103–21.

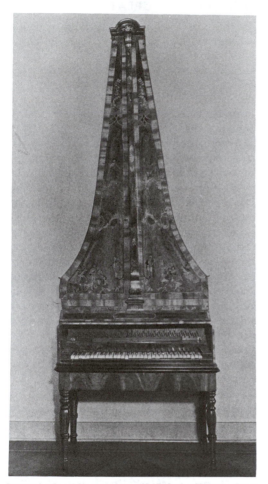

Pyramidenflügel [Pyramid grand] 1745—by Christian Ernst Friederici. Musée instrumental du Conservatoire Royal de Musique, No. 1631; Bruxelles.
(Courtesy of Da Capo Press [New York], agent for Franz Josef Hirt's Stringed Keyboard Instruments*)*

FRIEDERICI, CHRISTIAN ERNST (1709–1780)

Christian Ernst Friederici was the leading instrument maker of Saxony for several decades after the middle of the eighteenth century. He was the first prominent German builder of vertical pianos. He was born at Merane, Saxony, a town his parents had moved to from the Tyrol region of Austria. The family name, also spelled "Friderici," is the Italianized form of the German "Friederichs."

After his training in Freiburg as an apprentice to **Gottfried Silbermann**, Europe's leading instrument maker of the time, Friederici settled in Gera, Saxony, where he opened his own shop. His business grew well enough for him to have his younger brother, Christian Gottfried, (1714–1777), join him in 1744. After Silbermann's death in 1753, Friederici gained a reputation as Saxony's leading instrument maker. Although unsettled conditions during the Seven Years' War (1756–1763) caused some Saxony piano makers to migrate to England, the Friedericis remained and prospered in the post-war years.

Friederici's instruments of most interest to many scholars are the **upright pianos** he started to build in 1745. These were not the earliest uprights. An Italian upright built by **Domenico del Mela** is dated 1739. Friederici's uprights were called *Pyramidenflügel* ("pyramid grand") because of their shape. Surviving examples, now in European collections, include two dated 1745 and one dated 1750. The **strings** run diagonally upward, from **tuning pins** just above the **keyboard** terminating at **hitch pins** along the curved right side. The **actions** appear to be adaptations of the **Cristofori jack** action design simplified by omission of the intermediate lever. Tall jacks supported on the back ends of the **key** levers lift up against short lever arms or rounded blocks with cutouts to allow **escapement,** attached to the rear of the **hammer butts,** which pivot from a rail. **Dampers** are actuated through a series of levers and stickers.

During his time, Friederici's most popular instruments were his clavichords and **square pianos,** which were exported to other countries in Europe. Examples of square pianos by earlier builders that have been discovered more recently indicate that he did not invent the square piano, as stated in the past by some historians. Friederici also built pipe organs and harpsichords. In 1770 he advertised harpsichords with a type of action he invented that could produce a vibrato tone.

Among the prominent owners of Friederici instruments: **Carl Philipp Emanuel Bach** had two Friederici clavichords; **Mozart**'s family owned Friederici instruments (the two-manual harpsichord is mentioned in a letter from Leopold to Wolfgang on 13 November 1777); the family of the German poet Johann Wolfgang von Goethe also owned a Friederici harpsichord.

When Friederici died in 1780, his business was continued by Christian Gottlob Friederici

(1750–1805), the son of his brother, Christian Gottfried Friederici, who had died in 1777. Christian Gottlob had studied law at Leipzig University from 1769 to 1774 and then returned to Gera to work at instrument making with his uncle. Contemporary critics rated his instruments the equal of those of his uncle.

The Friederici business in Gera was carried on through two more generations by Christian Gottlob's son, Christian Ernst Wilhelm (1782–1872) and grandson, Ernst Ludwig (1806–1883).

Jack Greenfield

Bibliography

Boalch, Donald H. *Makers of the Harpsichord and Clavichord.* 1440–1840. London: George Ronald, 1956.

Harding, Rosamond E.M. *The Piano-Forte: Its History Traced to the Great Exhibition of 1851.* Cambridge: Cambridge University Press, 1933. Reprints. New York: Da Capo Press, 1973; Old Woking, Surrey: Gresham Books, 1978.

Pfeiffer, Walter. *The Piano Hammer.* Translated from the German by Jim Engelhardt. Frankfurt am Main: Verlag das Musikinstrument, 1978.

FUTURE OF THE PIANO

The late twentieth century is an era of paradigm shift—in society, politics, culture, and the arts. This is no less true in the musical instruments with which we choose to express ourselves. Yet, in the span of cultural time, the history of musical instruments has never remained static, nor is there any reason to expect it to remain so now. The dynamic interactions between artists, scientists, and engineers have continually expanded the limits of musical possibility through technology. At times, change has been driven by composers seeking new expressive horizons; at others the impetus has come from the scientist or engineer, who, in opening a new possibility, inspired new modes of composition. Though a large oversimplification, there is some truth in the view of the seventeenth century as an era dominated by the virtuoso singer, the eighteenth century by the virtuoso violinist, and the nineteenth century by the virtuoso pianist. Will history record the twentieth century as the era of the virtuoso conductor? Or the virtuoso electric guitarist? What, if any, instrument will be the voice of the twenty-first century?

This reference work traces the history of keyboard instruments in great detail from the intimate clavichord, through the noble harpsichord, to the pianoforte, and beyond. In a sense, this continuum illustrates the fact of change, the fact of instrumental evolution over the course of time. An instrument emerges, ascends as artists voice their timely and creative energies through it, and ultimately takes its place as an historical entity with a literature, a performance practice, a unique expressive modality, and a pedagogy all its own.

Evidence of many kinds suggests that the piano has now reached a late stage of its evolutionary history and that, while it may remain vital, it will never again hold center stage as it did in the nineteenth century. While remarkable and subtle refinements in the piano's construction have been made—including the double **escapement** and the improved metallurgy that permit higher **string** tension—the piano has remained essentially unchanged since the mid-nineteenth century. Major works for solo piano since the time of Bartók are extraordinarily rare when compared with the output of nineteenth-century composers. Once at the center of almost every major composer's output, the piano, if used at all, is now more supportive or peripheral. Composers of the mid-and late-twentieth century have written music for piano most typically in combination with other instruments for textural and rhythmic emphasis. From John Cage's **prepared piano** music onward, many composers have explored nontraditional techniques, but it seems as if now even this tonal palette is exhausted.

Data provided by the American Music Conference and the International Piano Manufacturers' Association indicates that conventional piano sales fell by approximately one-third between 1980 and 1989. During this same time, **electronic** keyboards proliferated with ever-decreasing costs, and ever-increasing sophistication. In 1985, ten times more electronic keyboards were sold than conventional pianos. In 1986, seventeen times more electronic keyboards were sold, and in 1987, over thirty times more were sold. It should be noted that these figures compare all electronic keyboards to all pianos. Therefore, sales of very low-cost instruments are compared with much more expensive ones.

What conclusions and inferences may be drawn from these simple observations, particularly with regard to artistic merit, are clearly open to serious debate. But, it seems clear that electronic keyboard instruments—digital pianos, **synthesizers**, samplers, and their relatives—are going to occupy an ever-increasing market share worldwide. It seems equally clear that they are the center-stage instruments of the emerging paradigm. Electronic keyboards are the original instruments of a vibrant literature that is being born all around, but not frequently within, the musical establishment. The role of the piano may now very well be compared to that of the harpsichord in the mid-eighteenth century—the elder statesman, the voice of a glorious past era.

These negative points notwithstanding, there is a brighter side for the future of the piano. Demand, though slowly falling, does persist. **Yamaha**, the world's largest piano manufacturer, produces and sells some 185,000 pianos per year. In a highly automated, robotic factory, **Kawai** makes over 80,000 pianos per year. Relatively small, elite **Steinway** and **Bösendorfer** respectively build some 6,000 and 800 handcrafted pianos per year. Other signs of the piano's health in the United States are the survival of the **Baldwin** piano company, the successful restart of **Mason and Hamlin**, and the highly regarded new **Falcone** piano.

There are other indicators of a continued life for the piano. While the artist of world-class individuality seems as rare as ever, international competitions set ever-higher standards of technical perfection in the reinterpretation of the classics. The audience for recorded, and subsequently live, piano music has grown through improved recording technique, marketing, and the eclectic idioms of jazz, New Age, and other contemporary styles. The piano occupies a vital and central role in the popular music culture—from musical theater to rock. Piano **pedagogy** has begun to emerge as a legitimate academic discipline, a subset within music education with its own unique tradition, research base, and promise for the future.

In imagining the musical paradigms of the twenty-first century and assessing the role of the piano, a comparison may be made to that of the eighteenth century. In that era, the contemporary keyboard player was skilled in several instruments—at least clavichord, harpsichord, organ—if not also violin and voice. This musician was involved not only in performance of solo and ensemble repertoire, but composition and improvisation in various styles of the time. In the new paradigm, the contemporary keyboardist will undoubtedly utilize computer, synthesizer, **MIDI**, and other emergent technologies, and because of its enormous past significance, the piano as well.

As in the eighteenth century, the musician will compose and improvise in the style of the day as well as participate in the continuing recreation of musical heritage.

Samuel S. Holland

GANER, CHRISTOPHER
(FL. C.1774–C. 1809)

Christopher Ganer was a London instrument maker, native of Leipzig, naturalized English in 1792, who specialized in **square pianos**.

He was particularly active from the late 1770s until approximately 1800, judging by the large number of squares surviving from that period, both under his name and under others (e.g., **Longman and Broderip**, c.1780, with ink signature "Chri^r. Ganer, No 47 Broad S^t. Soho, Lond^n." behind the **nameboard**, and Joseph Dale, c.1780, with "C. GANER LONDON" stamped on the **soundboard**). After about 1784 Ganer ceased to include the year on the nameboard.

The squares are of good quality, mostly 61-note, FF–f^3 (some early examples lack FF sharp), single **action**, overdamped, wrest pins (**tuning pins**) to the right, with three (later two) hand-stop levers. Around 1784 an additional model approximately six inches shorter than standard appeared. Several later instruments provided pedal-operated lid swell and **damper** lift, and some early ones appear to have had **pedals** added at a later date. One from around 1800 has wrest pins at the back and the later "mopstick" over-dampers, though still with 61 notes and single action, the whole being enclosed in a **case** with unusually bulbous sides. Few 68-note squares survive, which suggests a falling off of activity around 1800.

Around 1790 Ganer used an oval enamel plaque, styling himself a "GRAND & SMALL FORTE PIANNO [sic] MANUFACTURER," but any surviving **grand** must be very rare, if it exists at all. There is, however, an "organised piano" (minus the piano action) in Bristol City Museum, U.K.

Kenneth Mobbs

Bibliography

Boalch, Donald H. *Makers of the Harpsichord and Clavichord, 1440-1840*. 2nd ed. Oxford: Clarendon Press, 1974: 48.

The New Grove Dictionary of Musical Instruments. Edited by Stanley Sadie. S.V. "Ganer" by Margaret Cranmer. London: Macmillan; Washington D.C.: Grove's Dictionaries, 1984.

Harding, Rosamond E.M. *The Piano-Forte: Its History Traced to the Great Exhibition of 1851.* Cambridge: Cambridge University Press, 1933. Reprints. New York: Da Capo Press, 1973; Old Woking, Surrey: Gresham Books, 1978.

Kibby, Bill. *Piano Archives*. Lowestoft, U.K.

GAVEAU

Gaveau was a French campany, founded in Paris in 1847 by Joseph Gabriel Gaveau (1824–1903) to produce both pianos and harpsichords. Working first at the rue des Vinaigriers and later at the rue Servan, this firm gained an excellent reputation in the nineteenth century, especially for its small **upright pianos**. Joseph Gaveau worked to improve both the **tone** projection and **action** of his company's pianos so that by the last quarter of the century he was successful in producing and selling over 1,000 upright pianos a year.

By 1907 the firm had passed to Etienne Gaveau (1872–1943), the founder's son, who expanded the factory at Fontenay-sous-Bois and built Salle Gaveau, a concert hall that seats 1,100 people, at 45–47 rue la Boetié in Paris.

As was the family tradition, the brothers Marcel and Andre Gaveau eventually entered into their father's business; but they were soon faced with severe economic problems, especially during the decades of the two world wars. In an effort to compete with the rival **Pleyel** piano firm (founded 1807), also of Paris, the Gaveau family hired Arnold Dolmetsch to help design and produce small unfretted clavichords and spinets. Dolmetsch worked for Gaveau from 1911 to 1914, having previously worked for the **Chickering** & Sons piano company of Boston for seven years. When Dolmetsch returned home to England, the Gaveau firm soon returned to making only upright pianos.

In 1960, economics forced Gaveau to join with the **Erard** firm (founded c. 1780) to form a new piano company. Financial troubles continued. Finally, in 1971, the **Schimmel** Company of Germany (founded 1885) took over the French piano firms of Gaveau, Erard, and Pleyel. Today Gaveau pianos are imported to France from Germany.

Peggy Flanagan Baird

Bibliography

Adelmann, Marianne, ed. *Musical Europe*. New York: Paddington Press, Ltd., 1974: 149.

Belt, Philip R. et al. *Piano* (The New Grove Musical Instruments Series). New York: W. W. Norton and Company, 1988.

Good, Edwin M. *Giraffes, Black Dragons, and Other Pianos*. Stanford, Cal.: Stanford University Press, 1982; 216.

The New Grove Dictionary of Musical Instruments. Edited by Stanley Sadie. S.V. "Gaveau" by Margaret Cranmer. London: Macmillan; 1989: 28.

Sumner, William Leslie. *The Pianoforte*. New York: St. Martin's Press, 1966: 129.

GEIB, JOHN LAWRENCE (1744–1818)

John Lawrence Geib [Johann Lorenz Geib], the founder of a dynasty of **square-piano** builders, was originally an organ maker in Germany. About 1779 he emigrated to London, where he worked for the harpsichord workshops of **Burkat Shudi** and **Longman and Broderip**. In 1786 he **patented** his English double, or Geib grasshopper, **action** and subsequently opened his own shop. Geib left London in 1797 and moved to New York, where he began a new business, John Geib & Co., taking as partners his sons, twins John Jr. (1780–1821) and Adam (1780–1849), and George (1782–1842).

The firm underwent several changes of name after the senior John Geib's retirement in 1816. During the 1820s Adam and another brother, William (1793–1860), ran the business, and in 1829 Daniel Walker (d. 1870), Adam's son-in-law, became a partner in Geib & Walker, which continued until 1843. Adam's son William Howe Geib headed the firm until the 1860s.

No piano by the senior John Geib survives; however, many instruments that he built with his sons are exhibited in prominent American public collections, including the Smithsonian Institution, the Museum of Fine Arts, Boston, the Metropolitan Museum of Art, and the Colonial Williamsburg Foundation.

Early Geib pianos show the influence of their English heritage. Typically the instruments have a compass of five-and-one-half octaves, **ivory** naturals, **ebony** sharps, and one **damper pedal** mechanism. The **cases** are usually of mahogany and are decorated with inlays of lighter wood.

Martha Novak Clinkscale

Bibliography

Boalch, Donald H. *Makers of the Harpsichord and Clavichord, 1440-1840*. London: Oxford University Press, 1956, 2nd ed., 1974.

Clinkscale, Martha Novak. *Makers of the Piano: 1700–1820*. Oxford: Oxford University Press, 1992.

Gildersleeve, Alger C. *John Geib and His Seven Children*. New York: By the author, 1945.

Groce, Nancy Jane. "Musical Instrument Making in New York City during the Eighteenth and Nineteenth Centuries." Ph.D. dissertation, University of Michigan, 1982. Vol. 2, New York: Pendragon Press, 1991.

GERMAN ACTION

See Actions; *Prellmechanik.*

GERMANY, PIANO INDUSTRY IN

After the early developments of the pianoforte, which occurred in Vienna, England, and France, the last decade of the eighteenth century saw Germany entering the field and soon becoming one of the most important developers and producers of the piano.

The Rudolph **Ibach** Sohn firm, founded in 1794 in Barmen, was the first piano factory in Germany. Other companies followed: W. Ritmüller in 1795 at Göttingen, Ernst Rosenkranz at Dresden and — one of the most famous — that of Heinrich Steinweg, founded in 1835 at Seesen in the Harz Mountains. Most of these factories were family-owned and each had only a small staff (as late as 1907, most of them still had under twenty workers). The tradition of family-owned firms with only a few workmen continues to this day, with emphasis on quality rather than quantity. In the years between 1810 and 1860 many new piano firms were founded;

the Napoleonic wars interfered with production, but following the wars a number of firms were again established. At first these companies supplied only the local market, but with the beginning of industrialization in Germany, transportation and communication were improved and trading centers were developed; the earliest for the piano industry were those of Leipzig, Dresden, and Stuttgart; after 1870 these centers were followed by Berlin and Zeitz, where — with some exceptions like **Bechstein** (founded in 1853 in Berlin) — lower quality pianos were produced.

The industry flourished within Germany but played only a small part in the export trade. However, great changes in piano construction were occurring: in 1859, German-born Henry **Steinway** (Heinrich Steinweg), then active in the United States, **patented** the **overstrung** piano with crossed **strings** and the single-piece iron **frame**. These aspects of construction had a worldwide influence; **hammers** were no longer covered with **leather** but with **felt**, and strings were made of steel. No longer was it practical for the small German manufacturers to construct every part of a piano themselves. By the end of World War I in 1918, the production of the **plate**, the strings, and the **actions** was provided by supply industries. In 1924 there were sixteen factories (with a total of 2,300 employees) that built actions, and twenty-nine firms that supplied **keys**. The best-known companies (which still exist today) are Louis **Renner** in Stuttgart for actions and Hermann Kluge of Wuppertal for keys. Only a small number of piano firms held on to the tradition of building all the parts themselves. Piano firms would generally buy various parts from supply firms and then construct only the finished product. This resulted in the builders being dependent on the suppliers, a relationship that was further aggravated by the formation of associations within the supply industry, eventually resulting in a monopoly on the German market. The consequence was that the quality of the parts supplied became inferior, yet the piano industry had no influence in the production of these parts. The piano firms attempted to form similar associations (the first was the "Freie Vereinigung der Pianofortefabrikanten" in Berlin, followed in 1893 by the "Verein Deutscher Pianofortefabrikanten" in Leipzig, in 1916 by the "Convention der Pianofortefabrikanten," and at the end of the war by the "Verband Deutscher Pianofortefabrikanten"); but they were unsuccessful in their efforts because not all manufacturers joined the associations. Most companies continued to build their instruments by hand, as in former days, though there were a few whose production was combined with machines and who had a large work force, which resulted in increased output. The firm of Gebr. Zimmermann A.G. in Leipzig is an example of such collaboration; however, this is an exception.

Demands for war supplies in World War II drastically cut materials available for the piano industry. Most piano firms closed down or were converted to the manufacture of war materials. There were postwar problems also. Eminent companies like Zimmermann, **Blüthner**, Förster, and Rönisch were located in East Germany. The division of Germany damaged the image of eastern Germany's once superior quality of piano construction because the firms there were forced to use inferior building materials and had to fill a certain quota of instruments per year. These instruments were sold by Musima, the export agent for all types of musical instruments in East Germany. Piano production in West Germany also had its problems: in 1907 there had been 1,681 piano firms in all of Germany; after World War II, there were only fourteen remaining in West Germany. Many firms that had been founded in the eastern part of Germany came to postwar West Germany hoping to rebuild there (e.g., Thürmer and Feurich). At first there were no funds for machinery, so only a minimum number of instruments were built by a small staff; however, this supplied the limited market of the time. In 1954, a new association was formed (Fachverband Deutsche Klavierindustrie e.V.), which included among its members not only the piano producers but also the supply companies. From the 1950s production began to increase and by the early 1970s reached its highest level.

The importation of Asian pianos into Germany, and their lower selling prices, caused a decrease in the sales of German pianos, although many German firms increased their export quotas to counteract this market imbalance. Since the 1980s the market balance has improved and in 1990 West German piano companies produced 16,492 **uprights** and 4,064

grands. After the reunification of Germany in October 1990, many of the piano firms located in East Germany were returned to their original family operations (reprivatized). Now Blüthner, Leipziger Pianofortefabrik ("Rönisch" and "Hupfeld" brands) and the Eisenberger Pianofortefabrik ("Eisenberg," "Fuchs & Möhr," "Geyer," and "Klingmann" brands) have become privately owned corporations. A few companies of former East Germany had to close after reunification because they could not compete with the quality of western-made instruments. At present reunified Germany has twenty-two productive piano companies.

Carsten Dürer

Bibliography

Annual Report of the Fachverband Deutsche Klavierindustrie e.V.

Cieplik, Theobald. "Die Entwicklung der Deutschen Klavierindustrie bis zu ihrer heutigen Bedeutung als Exportindustrie." Dissertation, Giessen University, 1923.

Freytag, H. "Die Produktions- und Absatzbedingungen der Deutschen Klavierindustrie." Dissertation, Humboldt University, Berlin, 1949.

Instrumentenbau-Zeitschrift, 1990–1991.

Roos, Gerhard. "Die Entwicklung der Deutschen Klavierindustrie nach dem Weltkriege bis zur Aufhebung der Aussenhandelskontrolle im September 1923." Dissertation, Humboldt University, Berlin, 1924.

(Conversations with Anton Notker, marketing consultant, Neubeuern, Germany.)

GIRAFFE/PYRAMID PIANOS

Giraffe or pyramid pianos were **upright** forms of **grand pianos** with **hammer action** and vertical **strings**, built between the middle of the eighteenth century and the middle of the nineteenth century. The origins of these instruments reach back to the fifteenth-century *clavicytherium*, which was a vertical or upright harpsichord. One of the earliest *clavicytheriums* was built in 1480.

In the first half of the nineteenth century it was typical for grand pianos to have a length of nearly 2.5 meters and a width of 1.25 meters. The large **case** was needed because of the great tension of the strings. But soon efforts were made to produce the same full sound with an instrument of smaller dimensions. In 1739 the Italian **Domenico Del Mela** made his first upright hammer-action grand piano. The advantage of this upright version was that the sound was directed toward the audience. But with this advantage came a mechanical problem: the hammer action had to be modified because of the 90-degree angle between strings and **keyboard**. Upright pianos needed less room than conventional grands, an aspect that made them

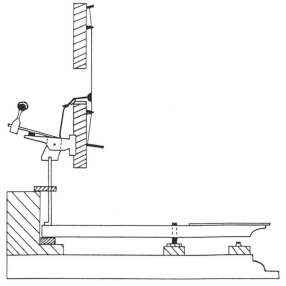

A simplified view of the action invented and built by Domenico Del Mela for his Upright Pianoforte (1739).
(Drawing by Carsten Dürer)

very popular as living space became more limited.

During the decade following Del Mela's upright version, the most important center for building these upright-grands was Vienna. In 1745 the famous German piano maker **Christian Ernst Friederici**, who was also known for his well-made **square pianos**, built the first pyramid piano with a symmetrical **soundboard**.

But development did not stop at this point. First, the pyramid shape was flattened; then in 1795 the Englishman **William Stodart** built an upright-grand piano in the "form of a bookcase" (so called in the **patent**) with a modified mechanism call "**English action**." Stodart placed the action behind the soundboard and thus the strings were struck from behind. The last two types to be constructed were the giraffe piano in the shape of a harp (similar to Del Mela's) and the lyra-piano (*Lyraflügel*), so called because the sides were formed like an ancient lyre.

In 1804 a rennaissance of upright instruments began with the first pyramid pianos by the Austrian makers Joseph Wachtl & Bleyer, and Franz Martin Seuffert. The German maker Christoph Ehrlich also became famous for his pyramids. The large number of surviving uprights testifies to his great activity. He was the first to build an upright with a rectangular shape. Other important makers of upright-grand pianos were Van der Hoef, the Swedish C.J. Nordquist, and the Swiss Andreas Flohr. The sound of these instruments could be modified by two to six **pedals**. Besides the *piano* and sustain-function, the pedals controlled effects like the bassoon-register. In the case of the Friederici instruments sound modifications were controlled by hand-stops.

The lyre piano was the last variation of the upright-grands. The first one was built by **Johann Christian Schleip** in the 1820s. All of the upright-grand pianos have the **pinblock** positioned directly above the keyboard, so the instruments are quite tall. About 1800, piano makers began to think of constructing instruments of smaller size. They located the pinblock at the top of the **frame**, so that the strings lay in a sloping position. With this innovation came a great increase in production of upright pianos, marking the transition to our modern upright pianos. This development put an end to the building of upright-grand pianos.

See also Upright Piano.

Carsten Dürer

Bibliography

Hirt, Franz Josef. *Meisterwerke des Klavierbaus — Stringed Keyboard Instruments*. Dietikon-Zürich: Urs Graf (distributed in the U.S.A. by Da Capo Press), 1981.

Junghanns, Herbert. *Der Piano- und Flügelbau*. Frankfurt am Main: Bochinsky/Das Musik-instrument, 1984.

van der Meer, John Henry. *Musikinstrumente: von der Antike bis zur Gegenwart*. München: Prestel, 1983.

New Grove Dictionary of Music and Musicians. Vol. 14. S.V. "Pianoforte." London: Macmillan Publishers, 1980.

Wohnhass, Theodor. "Zur Tätigkeit Christoph Ehrlichs als Klavierbauer in Bamberg." *Bericht des historischen Vereins* [Bamberg] Special Issue 104 (1968).

GIUSTINI, LODOVICO (1685–1743)

Lodovico Giustini was born in Pistoia (12 December 1685) and died there on 7 February 1743. He became known mainly through the fact that he composed a set of twelve sonatas specifically for the new "cembali con martelli," invented by **Bartolomeo Cristofori** and built by him or his pupils and former assistants. The sonatas were published in 1732 as Op.1 in nearby Florence, under the title *Sonate da cimbalo di piano e forte detto volgarmente di martelletti*. In Giustini's sonatas we find not only dynamic markings such as *piano* and *forte* but also *più piano* and *più forte,* not usual indications for a harpsichordist and playable properly only on a **fortepiano** (which during the eighteenth century was nearly always named "cembalo" or "cimbalo" in Italy) or a clavichord.

Interesting—and usually not properly noticed—is the fact that Giustini dedicated his sonatas to **Domenico Scarlatti**'s royal pupil Don Antonio Infante di Portogallo, who later became King of Portugal. This is one more reason to believe that Scarlatti had already introduced the new hammer-harpsichord of Cristofori at the court of Lisbon, where an eighteenth-century piano-building tradition can be traced today. The common statement, still to be found in music history books, that the very first sonatas for piano were written by Giustini and published as late as 1732, has to be revised, insofar as it was indeed Giustini who was the first to mention the new hammer-harpsichord in a printed edition; but Domenico Scarlatti used Cristofori's *cembalo con martelli* certainly earlier than Giustini. He was acquainted with them as early as 1703. And some of Scarlatti's sonatas were apparently written for the *cembalo che fà il piano e il forte,* which seems to have been the ideal instrument for some of them, the one he must have had in mind when composing them.

Eva Badura-Skoda

Bibliography

Badura-Skoda, Eva. "Domenico Scarlatti und das Hammerklavier." *Österreichische Musikzeitschrift* 40 (1985): 505f.

Caselli, Ala Botti. "Le 'Sonate da cimbalo di piano, e forte' di Lodovico Giustini." *Nuova Rivista Musicale Italiana* 12 (March 1978): 34–66.

Harding, Rosamond E.M. "The Earliest Pianoforte Music." *Music and Letters* 13 (1932): 194.

GRAF, CONRAD (1782–1851)

Conrad Graf was a piano builder in Vienna in the early nineteenth century whose luxury instruments were remarkable for their high quality and consistency of design. They were built in the standard Viennese style of the early nineteenth century and lack significant experimental features.

Jakob Schelkle trained Graf in piano making, and Graf eventually married Schelkle's widow. Graf opened his own workshop in Vienna in 1804 and by 1809 he had ten workers under him. He was admitted to the professional class of **keyboard** makers in 1822 and was honored in 1824 with a Royal Warrant recognizing his excellent abilities as a piano maker. He bought a building called *Mondscheinhaus* [Moonlight House] in 1826, remodeled it, and moved his growing factory there. The larger space was essential because he then had forty workers in his employ, and the shop had grown from a master-apprentice arrangement to a full-fledged factory where pianos were produced in separate stages. He held salons at his new home and factory to advertise his pianos, and in his day he was one of the most prestigious builders in the Austro-Hungarian Empire. The high point of Graf's career was the gold medal he won for his instruments at the Austrian Exhibition of Industrial Products (*Gewerbs-Produkten-Ausstellung*) in 1835. In 1842 he sold his factory and retired.

Graf was active as a builder for over thirty years (1804–1842) and produced approximately 3,000 pianos (the highest numbered extant piano is no. 2788). Over forty of these pianos survive (see Deborah Wythe for an inventory) and because of their sturdy, simple construction they have warped or cracked less than their contemporaries. Graf used fine woods and was particularly careful with matching grains and finishing the surfaces. These instruments were often highly ornate, with mother-of-pearl inlay and other elaborate decorative work. His three types of instruments can be distinguished by the design of their **cases.** The surviving pianos indicate that the earliest group (1812–1824) had a square tail and rounded corners. This group showed the greatest variety of design features. The second group (1824–1827), with angled tail and rounded corners, was of heavier construction and had an expanded range, from CC to g^4. The thicker **strings** of these pianos, which added increased tension, provided a bigger, more brilliant **tone.** The final group (1827–1835) had straight cheeks and an angled tail. Robert Winter has pointed out that these later pianos lose some of the earlier variety of tone color found in different ranges (pp. 281–82). Graf, in experimenting with a more limited number of **strike point** ratios, sought a bigger, more uniform tone throughout the range of the piano.

The length of Graf's pianos is consistent during his career, and the wooden **frame** design of his own making is largely responsible for the durability of his pianos. Six-and-a-half octaves was his normal range, and although he experimented with quadruple stringing, he generally used triple. He used both brass and steel strings and a variety of stringing patterns, adjusting the gauge of the string carefully to provide an effortless transition from brass to steel. He introduced English steel strings possibly as early as 1834 and also employed a new type of steel **bridge pin** that influenced the tone. An unusual feature in his pianos is the extra board above the strings, which muffled the individual sounds and allowed them to blend together more completely.

Graf did not experiment with new designs for the Viennese **action,** though he did make the parts slightly heavier. Instead he concentrated on fine craftsmanship that produced an action with a particularly responsive **touch.** His **dampers** are particularly known for their lack of extraneous noise and effective damping; **leather** wedge dampers stop the lower strings and wool cloth pads, the upper ones.

Graf's pianos sometimes had as many as six **pedals:** (1) a shift that moved the action for *due corde* and **una corda** effects; (2) a "bassoon," made by parchment that produced a buzzing tone; (3) and (4) a **moderator** that muffled the tone with one layer of cloth to produce *piano* and two layers for *pianissimo*; (5) the damper; and (6) a Turkish **janissary** that added bells, jangles, and a drum. Three pedals, however, was his usual number.

His most famous piano (undated and unnumbered but built after 1825) was owned by **Ludwig van Beethoven** and is now in the Beethoven House in Bonn. It had quadruple stringing in the treble and triple stringing in the bass, six-and-a-half octaves from CC to f⁴. Another well-known piano was the one built in 1839 and given to Clara Wieck on the occasion of her marriage to **Robert Schumann** in 1840. This piano, no. 2616, has the range CC to g⁴ and has the covering board over the strings. It is mostly triple strung with brass and steel strings and has four pedals. It is now housed at the Kunsthistorisches Museum (Vienna), but unfortunately has become unplayable.

Well-known artists, in addition to Beethoven and the Schumanns, have been associated with Graf's pianos. **Johannes Brahms** inherited the Schumann Graf; **Franz Liszt** and **Frédéric Chopin** concertized on Grafs. Today both Jörg Demus and Paul Badura-Skoda have made recordings using the Graf pianos (for a list of recordings, see Winter, pp. 174–75).

Graf was one of the best and most consistent builders of the **Viennese piano** in the first half of the nineteenth century. His instruments are known for their sweetness of tone, their singing quality, and their robust bass sound.

Camilla Cai

Bibliography

Good, Edwin M. *Giraffes, Black Dragons, and Other Pianos.* Stanford, Cal.: Stanford University Press, 1982.

Hirt, Franz Josef. *Meisterwerke des Klavierbaus.* Olten: Urs Graf-Verlag, 1955. Also as *Stringed Keyboard Instruments: 1440–1880.* Translated by M. Boehme-Brown. Boston: Boston Book and Art Shop, 1968. Also, Dietikon-Zürich: Urs Graf (distributed by Da Capo Press), 1981.

Luithlen, Victor. *Kunsthistorisches Museum: Katalog der Sammlung alter Musikinstrumente.* Part 1: *Saitenklaviere.* Vienna: Kunsthistorisches Museum, 1966, 43ff.

Newman, William S. "Beethoven's Pianos Versus his Piano Ideals." *Journal of the American Musicological Society* 23 (1970): 484–504.

Winter, Robert. "Performing Nineteenth-Century Music on Nineteenth-Century Instruments." *Early Music* 1 (1977–1978): 163–75.

———. "Striking it Rich: The Significance of Striking Points in the Evolution of the Romantic Piano." *Journal of Musicology* 6 (1988): 267–92.

Wythe, Deborah. "The Pianos of Conrad Graf." *Early Music* 12 (1984): 446–60.

GRAND PIANO

The grand piano is the most impressive looking and largest sounding of all the pianos today. It is distinguished from other pianos by its wing-shaped, harpsichord-like, horizontal **case**. This outer case is finished in a variety of natural wood veneers, but the most common **finish** is ebony black. This finish can conceal an inferior wood surface, thus it is less expensive to produce than a finish that highlights the grain. By tradition, such ebony black grand pianos are used for performances in major concert halls. The styling of the case depends on trends in furniture design and the taste of both the maker and consumer; it varies from extreme simplicity to ornately carved period pieces.

Today's grand piano comes in sizes from about five feet two inches to nine feet ten inches, but has been made both smaller (four and a half feet) and larger (up to twelve feet, usually by a customer's special order). The different sizes have been given their names based on where they are housed: the **concert grand** (nine feet or bigger) is the largest and is usually found in large or medium concert halls. The **living-room grand**, also called **parlor grand** or **boudoir grand**, can be six to seven feet and is found in small concert halls, private salons, or in homes with sufficient living-room space. The **baby grand** (from about five feet to five feet ten inches) is most common in smaller living rooms, conservatory practice rooms, and musicians' studios. Makers create additional names for advertising purposes and may have several models (with slightly varying sizes) in each category. The normal **pitch** range of the modern grand is AAA to c⁵ (seven and one-third octaves or 88 keys); the largest **Bösendorfer** descends to CCC.

The case consists of five elements: the **rim**, bracing, **keybed**, **soundboard**, and auxiliary parts. The rim is an outer structural support, and thus somewhat different in function from the protective outer case of the **upright**. The grand piano's heavy wooden bracing helps maintain the irregular shape of the rim. The keybed is a flat platform fixed horizontally to the bottom of the rim's open front, and the soundboard is a large wooden diaphragm with a slight upward **crown** in the center. It is usually made of quarter-sawn spruce averaging three-eighths inch in thickness. Wooden **braces** or **ribs** glued to the underside of the soundboard strengthen it, and the board is glued around its perimeter to the inside of the case.

The grand piano is covered by a hinged **lid** that, if raised at an angle and fastened with a top stick, serves as a reflecting surface for the sound. A key cover (**fallboard**) protects the **keys** and is hinged at each end to wooden blocks (cheek blocks). This combined assembly is easily removed so that the entire main **action** can be taken out for servicing, a design different from that of the upright. The **keyboard**'s natural keys are usually covered with white plastic while the accidentals are normally made of black plastic; the **ivory** and **ebony** surfaces found on older pianos are now rare.

The case rests on three substantial wooden legs; the two front legs attach to the keybed and the rear leg to a small platform under the narrow end (**tail**) of the piano. A **lyre** assembly attaches to the bottom side of the keybed and supports two or three **pedals**, usually three on American pianos. From right to left, the **damper pedal** (also called the **loud** or sustaining pedal) holds up all the dampers at once, and any key that is depressed will continue to sound after the key itself is released. All the other **strings** are also free to vibrate in sympathetic harmonics. The middle or *sostenuto* pedal holds up selected dampers—those belonging to keys already down when the pedal is first applied. Those selected strings continue to vibrate, independent of subsequent activity. This special-effects pedal is not usually found on European pianos. The soft or *una corda* pedal moves the keyboard and action to the right so that the **hammer** can contact only two of the three strings per note. This makes the sound softer,

and because the contact occurs on a part of the hammer where the **felt** is less compressed, it also changes the timbre.

The case encloses a single cast-iron or steel **frame** (**plate**) that is shaped like a wing or horizontal harp. This metal plate is bolted in position and supports between twenty and thirty tons of tension from the strings. Embedded into the far end of the plate are **hitch pins** for the strings. At the keyboard end of the piano, the strings are wound around **tuning pins** (wrest pins) that are forced into a **pinblock** (wrest plank) made of laminated hardwood, usually maple. The string's actual sounding length is marked at the tail of the piano by a **bridge** attached directly to the top side of the soundboard. This bridge may be divided into two parts, an S-shaped main bridge and separate bass bridge. At the other end of the piano (the keyboard end), the string's sounding length is marked by two different devices. In the treble range, an elevated portion of the plate, the *capo tasto* bar (*capo d'astro* bar), serves as the marker. For the remaining strings, **agraffes** or screws fastened to the plate delineate the sounding length. (The *capo tasto* bar and agraffes appear only occasionally on **upright pianos**.)

Throughout most of the range of the piano (treble, mid- and tenor range) strings are made of plain, drawn, steel music **wire**. These strings loop around the hitch pin and then return to the next tuning pin: thus, each single length of wire contains two sounding strings. A note on the keyboard is produced by two or three such strings sounding in unison; some large grands have four strings in the upper treble. In the bass register steel strings are wound with copper or occasionally iron so that the diameter and mass of the string can increase without losing flexibility. Each of these wound strings hooks around its own hitch pin. The bass strings cross over the others in a fan-shaped pattern at the tail of the piano. This **cross-stringing** (or overstringing) allows the strings greater length without increasing the case length and also brings them more nearly over the center of the soundboard. Some large grands use three finely wound strings per note at the top of this cross-strung bass; smaller grands use only two. On all grands the lowest eight to ten notes use one wound string per note.

The modern grand piano action (the keyboard and other moving parts that set the hammers in motion) is a modification of the action patented by **Sébastien Erard** in 1808. The action today uses the double-**escapement** or repetition principle, which allows a note to be replayed before the hammer or key has fully returned to its resting position. This device, exclusively found on grand pianos, permits particularly quick repetition of the same note. The hammer's upward striking motion further distinguishes a grand piano action from the upright action. This design, which uses gravity to aid the return of hammers and dampers to their resting position, makes the grand action simpler and more efficient than the upright action. Piano builders use a wide variety of wood types for the moving parts of the action, and some have experimented with plastic (teflon) parts. The hammers and dampers are covered with felts designed exclusively for use in pianos.

There is fairly general agreement that the sound quality of a good grand is preferable to that of a good upright piano. The soundboard, being exposed both below and above (if the lid is up), can freely transmit sounds that the upright, with its case-constricted soundboard, cannot. In addition, the grand's upward hammer stroke pushes the string up from the bridge, not down onto it as in the upright, and this upward motion reduces the percussive effect of the hammer. A difference in sound quality is particularly noticeable in the treble register, where the hammer strikes very close to the bridge. Finally, some makers believe that the design modification necessary to make small baby grands, those under five feet, compromises the full sound of the grand piano. Space considerations, however, often dictate the choice of a small baby grand or an upright piano.

In Germany the grand piano is generally called the *Flügel*, but *Hammerflügel* and *Hammerklavier* were also used in the early nineteenth century. *Hammerklavier* signifies a keyboard with hammers, as opposed to the *Kielklavier*, a keyboard with plectra; the term *Hammerflügel* signifies a wing-shaped instrument with hammers, as opposed to the **square piano** (*Tafelklavier*). The three terms have been used interchangeably. Beethoven's indication *für das Hammerklavier* on his Opp. 101 (1816) and 106 (1817–1818) sonatas tells us only that the pieces were to be played on an instrument with hammers, not on a plucked instrument.

The Italian name for grand piano is *piano (forte) a coda*, French is *piano à queue*, Spanish is *piano de cola*, and Portuguese is *piano de cauda*. The baby grand is *Stutzflügel* in German or *piano à queue mignon* in French.

The grand piano, by definition, includes all wing-shaped pianos beginning with **Bartolomeo Cristofori**'s first pianoforte, c.1698–1700. The term itself, however, was not in use until the late eighteenth century. In 1762 Charles Burney still called such wing-shaped instruments "pianofortes of large size" to distinguish them from other instruments using the hammer mechanism, according to Sibyl Marcuse (p. 329). The term "grand pianoforte" first appeared in a **Robert Stodart** patent (1777), according to Alfred Dolge. An advertisement in *The Observer*, 4 December 1791 mentions that the maker John C. Hancock had two types, the "grand and small pianoforte," i.e., a grand piano and either an upright or square piano, according to C. F. Colt.

The earliest grand pianos resembled harpsichords, particularly in the shape of the case, the thin legs, and the exterior finish with painting, ornamentation, and elaborate carvings. Extras on these early grands included candle holders and fancy music racks. Many used black ebony for the natural keys and light bone (or ivory) for the accidentals, but by the end of the eighteenth century the colors were reversed to the modern system. Hand stops, knee stops, or knee levers of the early grands were gradually replaced with foot pedals. Some grands had as many as six pedals, the most unusual ones operating instruments of the Turkish **Janissary** band (triangle, drum, bells, and cymbal).

Since the grand piano's inception, around 1700, every aspect of its construction has been altered. The earliest grands had wooden supporting frames, but as the range, string weight, and strings per note increased, the stress on these wooden frames grew dramatically. Struts, braces, hollow tubes, and string plates made of iron were added in the nineteenth century in order to compensate for the heightened pressure. Various designs of such partial or pieced-together metal frames were used throughout the nineteenth century, although **Jonas Chickering** patented a single cast-iron frame for the grand piano in 1843. A one-piece iron or steel frame became the norm for twentieth-century grand pianos. This design has been particularly effective in preventing the warping of wooden parts that are under extreme stress— a consideration especially important in the humid American climate.

The earliest grand pianos had ranges between four and five-and-a-half octaves, but today seven-and-one-third octaves is the usual size. The largest Bösendorfer grand, however, has eight octaves. As the range increased, the straight stringing of earlier pianos was replaced by the fanning out of the bass strings over the remaining strings. This allowed for longer bass strings but changed the resonance patterns of some overtones. The continuous bridge—used in early pianos in emulation of the harpsichord bridge—was replaced by a double bridge system with a separate bridge for the bass strings.

Strings had to be made thicker to withstand the increasing tension and added range. In the nineteenth century they were changed from iron to the stronger, stiffer cast or pulled steel, while the lower strings were changed from brass to a stronger type with copper wound over steel. Some of the earliest pianos had only two strings per pitch, each fastened to its own hitch pin, but this number was soon increased to three strings per pitch with a single **wire** looped around one hitch pin to divide into two separate strings.

Makers used many different designs for the grand-piano action: *Prellmechanik*, sometimes called German action (which evolved into the Viennese action in the nineteenth century), downstriking action, the **English action**, the Anglo-German action, the double-escapement action, and others. Numerous patents attest to the many experiments that purported to improve the action designs. Different **strike points** (where the hammer strikes the string) were also a constant source of experimentation, and important additions were brass agraffes and the *capo tasto* bar, both of which helped to hold the strings firmly in position as they were struck by the hammers. In general, heavier hammers became necessary to compensate for the stiffer strings. The early soft buff-**leather**, wool, or cloth coverings were replaced with harder **felt** ones. The damper material also changed from soft leather to felt. Not until the twentieth century did the double escapement action or repetition action finally become the norm for all grand pianos.

The grand piano has been the subject of continuous experimentation. Even today makers experiment with many elements: new **scale designs** and different striking ratios, and new techniques for seasoning wood and pulling steel strings. Though these changes today are not nearly as radical as earlier ones, the grand piano has never been fixed in time as a "perfect" or "completely developed" instrument.

Camilla Cai

Bibliography

Blackham, E. Donnell. "The Physics of the Piano." *Scientific American* 213 (December 1965): 88–99.

Colt, C. F., and Antony Miall. *The Early Piano* . London: Stainer & Bell, 1981.

Dolge, Alfred. *Pianos and Their Makers*. Covina, Cal: Covina Publishing Co., 1911. Reprint. New York: Dover Publications, 1972.

Fine, Larry. *The Piano Book*. Boston: Brookside Press, 1987.

Good, Edwin M. *Giraffes, Black Dragons, and Other Pianos*. Stanford, Cal.: Stanford University Press, 1982.

Harding, Rosamond E.M. *The Piano-Forte: Its History Traced to the Great Exhibition of 1851*. Cambridge: Cambridge University Press, 1933. Reprints. New York: Da Capo Press, 1973; Old Woking, Surrey: Gresham Books, 1978.

Hipkins, Alfred J. *A Description and History of the Pianoforte*. 3rd ed. London: Novello, 1929. Reprint. Detroit: Information Coordinators, 1975.

Hirt, Franz Josef. *Meisterwerke des Klavierbaus*. Olten: Urs Graf-Verlag, 1955. Also as *Stringed Keyboard Instruments: 1440-1880*. Trans., M. Boehme-Brown. Boston: Boston Book and Art Shop, 1968. Also, Dietikon-Zürich: Urs Graf (distributed by Da Capo Press), 1981.

Marcuse, Sibyl. *A Survey of Musical Instruments*. New York: Harper & Row, 1975.

White, William. *Theory and Practice of Piano Construction*. New York: Edward Lyman Bill, 1906. Reprint. New York: Dover Publications, 1975.

Winter, Robert. "Striking it Rich: The Significance of Striking Points in the Evolution of the Romantic Piano." *Journal of Musicology* 6 (1988): 267–92.

GROTRIAN-STEINWEG

Grotrian-Steinweg Pianofortefabrikanten is one of Germany's most distinguished piano manufacturing companies. In 1830 German-born

Georg Friedrich Karl Grotrian (1803–1860) moved to Moscow, where he began a successful career as a music dealer. In 1850 he returned to Wolfenbüttel, where he met Carl Friedrich Theodor Steinweg (1825–1889), who was later known in the United States as Theodore Steinway. Steinweg's father, Heinrich Engelhart Steinweg (1797–1871), had moved to America and had left his Wolfenbüttel-based piano company to Theodor. On Friedrich Grotrian's return to Wolfenbüttel in 1850 he became a partner in Steinweg's company. The new partners purchased a building in Braunschweig and forged a successful piano company. In 1865 Theodor Steinweg sold his shares and moved—like his father—to New York to take over the paternal company, **Steinway & Sons**. Grotrian's son Wilhelm (1843–1917) continued the tradition of fine craftsmanship; in turn, Wilhelm's sons Willi (1868–1931) and Kurt (1870–1929) joined the firm in 1895.

The company grew steadily and in 1913 it had 550 employees; by 1920 this number had increased to 1,000. At that time the production was 1,600 instruments a year. After some legal actions with the American Steinway, the family was allowed to use the hyphenated Grotrian-Steinweg name, a name that was already well-established in the piano industry. Following the deaths of Willi and Kurt, Kurt's sons, Erwin (b.1899) and Helmut (b.1900) Grotrian-Steinweg, became partners in 1928 and were able to steer the firm through the difficult years of the depression and wartime destruction to resume piano production again in 1948. The fifth generation of the family, Knut Grotrian-Steinweg (b.1935), the son of Helmut, entered the firm in 1961. His father and uncle saw to the building of an entirely new production facility in Braunschweig-Veltendorf and retired shortly after its dedication in 1974, leaving the firm in Knut's hands. Since 1956 the firm has sponsored the *Grotrian-Steinweg Klavierspielwettbewerbe* [Grotrian-Steinweg Piano Competition] to support youthful pianists.

Today the Grotrian-Steinweg Pianofortefabrikanten employs 130 people. In 1988–89 production reached a total of 1,467 pianos a year. The production includes four different types of **uprights**, ranging from 108 cm (42") to 132 cm (52"), and four **grands**, from 165 cm (5'4") to 277 cm (9'1"). All are available in various styles and most of the building is still done by hand. Nearly half of the firm's employees are piano builders; a special apprentice program sees to it that qualified successors will maintain the firm's high standards. The end of the family history of the Grotrian-Steinweg Company is not yet in sight, since the son of Knut Grotrian-Steinweg, Jobst (b. 1969), is a sixth-generation sharing partner in the company.

Carsten Dürer and
David Anderson

Bibliography

Rolle, Günter. "150 Jahre Grotrian-Steinweg." *Keyboards* (November 1985): 24–27.

GULBRANSEN INCORPORATED

According to **Alfred Dolge**, the Gulbransen-Dickinson Company was established in 1904 as part of Chicago's piano supply industry. The company specialized in player actions. Under the direction of Axel G. Gulbransen, a Swedish immigrant, the firm became a prominent manufacturer and aggressive advertiser of **player pianos**.

Pierce Piano Atlas indicates that the first instruments were produced in 1915 under two brand names: Gulbransen and Dickinson. Annual production exceeded 22,000 pianos by the mid-1920s. Unlike many players of lesser quality, the Gulbransen was capable of producing an expressive performance. Gulbransen-Dickinson's national advertising campaigns were among the most extensive and progressive in the industry. Full-page ads in such national magazines as *The Literary Digest* and *The Saturday Evening Post* stressed family values and invited consumers to "Try the Gulbransen Only Ten Minutes" and prove to themselves that the piano was "Easy to Play." Indeed, the firm's ambitious merchandising provided America with the Gulbransen-Baby trademark, symbol of "easy-to-play" technology: a happy toddler easily pushing the piano's bellows pedals (illustrated in Roell, *The Piano in America*). Axel G. Gulbransen developed the famous trademark (as esteemed in its day as RCA's famous dog, "Nipper") from an actual incident. The company even supplied its dealers with a papier-mâché baby to use as a window display. The slogan "All the fun without long practice" exemplified Gulbransen philosophy.

The company survived the collapse of the

player-piano market in the 1920s and the Great Depression in the 1930s in part because of the marketing initiative of Axel G. Gulbransen. In *The Music Trades* he admonished unprogressive dealers who still were not "selling the things a piano will do for the home [but were] merely selling so much wood, felt, strings, duco, and metal at a price." Apparently, however, Gulbransen ceased to be a family-run business and was on the edge of insolvency until bank-appointed S.E. Zack was made president in 1930. Under Zack, the company survived by making contract cabinets, clocks, and shipping crates until prosperity returned after World War II. In the 1930s the company also used the brand name Edward B. Healy Pianos; in the 1950s the firm owned the Bremen Piano Company in Franklin Park, Illinois. Zack took the company into electronic-organ manufacture, and he sold Gulbransen to the J.P. Seeburg Company (the venerable coin-piano and jukebox manufacturer) in 1963. The company discontinued piano manufacture in 1969.

By 1976, CBS Musical Instruments Division (which also had acquired **Steinway & Sons**) owned Gulbransen, concentrating on home-organ production from a factory in Hoopeston, Illinois. According to *The Purchaser's Guide to the Music Industries*, Gulbransen built the first transister organ, the first built-in Leslie speaker, the first automatic rhythm and authentic piano voice, the first automatic walking bass, the first electronic theater organ, and the first Musicomputer®. Mission Bay Investments of San Diego, California, owned Gulbransen In-corporated after 1985. Mission Bay Investments had pianos manufactured in Mexico and distributed them worldwide under the Gulbransen trade name. The firm, supporting an international network of dealers, manufactured **elec-tronic**-keyboard products that utilized software-based digital tone generation technology. Gulbransen Incorporated is presently (1991) headquartered in Earth City, Missouri, and makes "fine furniture home organs."

Craig H. Roell

Bibliography

"Chicago's Music Industry Is Huge." *Chicago Commerce* 24 (21 July 1928): 7–9, 29–30.

Dolge, Alfred. *Pianos and Their Makers*. Vol. 1. *A Comprehensive History of the Development of the Piano from the Monochord to the Concert Grand Player Piano*. Covina, Cal.: Covina Publishing Co., 1911. Reprint. New York: Dover, 1972.

Gulbransen, Axel G. "A. G. Gulbransen Issues Call to Arms." *The Music Trades* 78 (April 1930):3.

The Music Trades Corp. *Purchaser's Guide to the Music Industries*. Englewood, N.J.: Music Trades Corp., annually.

Pierce, Bob, comp. *Pierce Piano Atlas*. 9th ed. Long Beach, Calif.: Bob Pierce, Publisher. 1990.

Roehl, Harvey N. *Player Piano Treasury: The Scrapbook History of the Mechanical Piano in America as Told in Story, Pictures, Trade Journal Articles and Advertising*. Vestal, N.Y.: The Vestal Press, 1961; 2nd ed., 1973.

Roell, Craig H. *The Piano in America, 1890–1940*. Chapel Hill: University of North Carolina Press, 1989; trade paperback edition, 1991.

HAMMER

The hammer is the primary part that distinguishes the piano from all other stringed keyboard instruments. Its introduction (c.1698–1700) by **Bartolomeo Cristofori** into what was essentially a harpsichord created a new instrument, percussive in nature, with a wider range of expression than was possible with any of the keyboard instruments of the day. This opened the door to subsequent experimentation and advancement in design and construction in order to take advantage of the tonal production possibilities of the hammer, which in turn contributed to the development of new, more emotionally expressive forms of music.

The earliest piano hammer as used by Cristofori was a wooden block with a rectangular striking surface covered with soft **leather.** Since this type of hammer would tend to make contact with a large area of the **string** and mute out desirable harmonics, the next development was a round hammer, made of laminated strips of parchment in the shape of a circle, again covered with leather. The round striking surface of the new design possibly sounded better, but a new problem soon arose.

In order to take advantage of the wider range of expression made possible by the hammer action, piano designers kept increasing the overall size and string tension in their instruments to obtain more volume; the heavier instruments in turn required heavier hammers. In London, in about 1775, **John Joseph Merlin** developed a hammer made of several layers of leather covered with an outer layer of cloth.

Other manufacturers soon adopted and modified this design, layering different types of leather and skin over a wooden core, frequently with the hardest leather at the center and the softest, buckskin or deerskin, on the striking surface. Although leather had its drawbacks, in particular a tendency to become very hard and lose resiliency under regular use, this was the beginning of the design of our modern hammer. In *Pianos and Their Makers,* **Alfred Dolge** states: "The art in hammer making has ever been to obtain a solid, firm foundation, graduating in softness and elasticity toward the top surface, which latter has to be silky and elastic in order to produce a mild, soft tone for pianissimo playing, but with sufficient resistance back of it to permit the hard blow of fortissimo playing."

With the trend toward ever-heavier pianos in general, and the advent of the iron **frame** in particular, it became evident that leather was an inadequate material for hammer covering. Although several people were experimenting with different materials during the early nineteenth century, **Jean-Henri Pape**, a Parisian inventor and piano maker, is generally credited with producing the first **felt**-covered hammers (French **patent,** 1826). Used at first as the outer layer, felt soon took the place of leather for the underlayer as well, and by the middle of the nineteenth century, felt hammers were accepted as the industry standard.

Up to this point, hammers were made by hand, but again the ever-increasing string tension and the quest for more volume dictated development of a heavier hammer than could be made by manual methods. According to Dolge, a piano maker in Breslau named Wilke invented a hammer-covering machine as early as 1835. This development apparently made little or no impression on the European piano builders, since they continued to hand-make their hammers into the 1860s. In America, two hammer-making presses were patented in 1850, one by **Frederick Mathushek** and one by Rudolf Kreter. Each represented an advancement in design but both had the same drawback: the hammers could not be removed from the press until the glue had hardened, thus limiting the manufacturing potential. This problem was solved in 1863 by Benjamin Collins, who perfected a hammer press with a removable caul, a metal form used to force the hammer into its final shape; this allowed the machine to be used repeatedly. Although subsequent development has refined the machinery, methods, and materials somewhat, the same type of hammer press is still being used today.

The modern piano hammer is essentially a wooden form, to which is glued, under pressure, a tapered strip of felt. The wood, or molding, is cut from hardwood, glued together to form a long strip and then machined into the desired shape. The felt, made from a special blend of different types of wool fibers, is formed into large sheets, graduated in thickness from end to end. These sheets are sliced into individual strips, each of which will make an entire set of hammers. Sheets of hammer felt are graded according to density, expressed in pounds, with the heavier felt usually being used on the larger pianos. Therefore, a set of "16-pound hammers" are made of a strip from a sheet of felt that originally weighed 16 pounds.

The strip of felt, which in cross-section resembles a triangle with a flattened apex, is coated with glue and placed into the caul. The hardwood molding, held in place from above with its point down, is lowered to meet the apex of the felt, which is then forced up and around the wood. After the ends of the felt have reached the sides of the molding, the press is tightened further in order to compress and densify the hammers. This extra pressure is usually graduated, with the treble hammers hardened more than the bass.

After remaining under pressure for a specified period of time, the set is removed from the caul, sanded to the desired final shape and cut into individual hammers. The finishing process also involves shaping the tail end of grand hammers to match **back checks**, and drilling a hole for the hammershank, the wooden dowel on which the hammer will be mounted.

The quality of **tone** in a piano is determined primarily by the inherent characteristics of the strings and the hammers, and by the interaction between the two. The tonal nature of piano strings is determined by the scale of the instrument, the balancing of length, thickness, and tension among all the **wires** in order to achieve a uniform timbre and volume across all 88 notes. This scale is part of the original design and is rarely changed throughout the life of the instrument. The hammer, on the other hand, is a constantly changing factor in tone quality,

variable not only by the factory and technician, but also by the pianist in the course of playing, by wear and tear, weather conditions, and by the simple passage of time.

When a string is set in motion, it not only vibrates as a whole, but also divides into smaller vibrating segments that produce higher tones called harmonics or overtones. The timbre of any musical instrument is determined by the proportions of the fundamental tone and its harmonics. The generally accepted ideal in piano tone is approximately 50 percent fundamental, with diminishing amounts of higher overtones, up through the seventh **partial**; above the seventh, the overtones become increasingly dissonant and harsh. The hammer is positioned to strike the string at about one-eighth of its overall length because this largely eliminates these higher harmonics.

When the hammer strikes the string two important things occur: the hammer compresses and the string deflects upward. When the hammer reaches its maximum compression, it pushes itself back away from the string. If the hammer is too soft, with not enough resilience, it flattens out and remains on the string too long, robbing the string of energy and muting too many of the higher harmonics, resulting in a dull, soft tone. If the hammer is too hard, the string breaks up into smaller vibrating sections, emphasizing the dissonant higher harmonics. The effect is like a wooden ball bouncing on concrete, with a resulting harsh sound. The desirable consistency for a piano hammer is more like that of a tennis ball, in which the core is compressed and the outer covering is stretched. This combination results in a resilient hammer, which imparts the correct deflection to the string and pushes itself away quickly, leaving more of the energy of the blow in the string.

Other factors besides density can affect the sound a hammer produces. The shape of the end that strikes the string has a direct effect on the form of deflection in the string. Some piano makers, for example, insist that their hammers should be egg-shaped for optimum tone, while some other makers prefer a rounded form. The condition of the striking surface, or crown, is also extremely critical. As hammers are played they flatten out and eventually develop grooves where they strike the strings. The ideal striking surface is smooth and level, so that the hammer strikes all strings of a unison simultaneously.

The deeper the grooves are worn, the longer the hammer is in contact with the string, with a resultant loss of energy and tone quality. Also, as the crown becomes packed it gets harder, which results in a harsh, uneven tone. Humidity also plays a role in tone quality; aside from its effects on the body of the piano, excess humidity can cause the hammer felt to swell, resulting in a softer sound, whereas the effect is reversed under dry conditions, where the hammer becomes tightly packed, producing a sound often described as brittle and dry.

The tone quality of a piano can also be altered by the way it is played; as the force with which the hammer strikes the strings is varied by the pianist, so the harmonic response of the strings is altered. When the **action** of a **grand piano** is shifted sideways by the use of the **una corda** pedal, the string is struck by a different part of the hammer crown, and again a very different sound is achieved.

A further effect on tone quality emerges over time as the hammer wears. The grooves caused by the strings can be removed by reshaping the hammer with a sandpaper file, restoring shape and removing dead felt. As the striking surface approaches the core of the hammer, however, the felt gets harder and harder because of compression and because of the glue that fastens it to the molding. The resulting harsh tone necessitates replacing the hammers long before they have worn through.

The modern piano hammer, like the piano itself, is a nineteenth-century invention. Although both have benefited somewhat from the advent of twentieth-century materials and manufacturing techniques, the design is essentially still the same as it was one hundred years ago. Whether this means that the hammer has reached the apex of its evolution or not remains to be seen (some might say that hammers are not as good today as they were at certain times in the past); the hammer is, however, the primary reason a piano is able to sound a whisper or a roar at the whim of the pianist's **touch**, and as such, plays an important role in influencing the development of music for the piano.

Kerry Kean

Bibliography

Dolge, Alfred. *Pianos and Their Makers.* Covina, Cal.: Covina Publishing Co., 1911. Reprint. New York: Dover, 1972.

Fine, Larry. *The Piano Book: A Guide to Buying a New or Used Piano.* Jamaica Plain, Mass.: Brookside Press, 1987.

Good, Edwin M. *Giraffes, Black Dragons, and Other Pianos:* Stanford, Cal.: Stanford University Press, 1982.

Harding, Rosamond E.M. *The Piano-Forte: Its History Traced to the Great Exhibition of 1851.* Cambridge: Cambridge University Press, 1933. Reprints. New York: Da Capo Press, 1973; Old Woking, Surrey: Gresham Books, 1978.

McFerrin, W.V. *The Piano—Its Acoustics.* Boston: Tuners Supply Co., 1972.

Pfeiffer, Walter. *The Piano Hammer.* Translated by Jakob Engelhardt. Frankfurt (a.M.): Das Musikinstrument, 1978.

Piano Technicians' Conference. *Secrets of Piano Construction: Proceedings of the Piano Technicians' Conference, Chicago, 1916, 1917, 1918; New York, 1919.* (Previously published as *Piano Tone Building.* American Steel and Wire Co.) Vestal, N.Y.: Vestal Press, 1985.

White, William Braid. *Theory and Practice of Pianoforte Building.* New York: E. L. Bill Publisher, 1906. Reprint as *Theory and Practice of Piano Construction: With a Detailed Practical Method for Tuning.* New York: Dover, 1975.

Wier, Albert Ernest. *The Piano: Its History, Makers, Players and Music.* London: Longmans, Green and Co., 1940.

HAMMERFLÜGEL/HAMMERKLAVIER

These German names for the **grand piano** were used in the early nineteenth century. *Hammerflügel* means a wing-shaped instrument with **hammers**, while *Hammerklavier* means a **keyboard** with hammers and therefore includes both the **square** and the grand piano. **Ludwig van Beethoven**'s use of the expression *für das Hammerklavier* to describe Opp. 101 (1816) and 106 (1817–1818) would inform the performer that these pieces should not be played on the harpsichord.

See also Grand Piano; Flügel.

Camilla Cai

HANCOCK, JOHN CRANG (FL. C.1777–C.1794)

John Crang Hancock was a London builder of organs and pianos who took out a **patent** in 1790 (British Patent No. 1743) for "a new **grand piano** forte, with a spring key touch, German flute, and harp." The instrument described and depicted is a grand-shaped piano with a combined organ, although no examples of such instruments by Hancock are known to survive. The patent also illustrates Hancock's unusual piano **action**, the most important element of which is a wire spring pressing against the top of each **key** lever just behind the balance **rail**. The spring's tension can be adjusted to alter the **touch**, i.e., the finger weight needed to sound a note. Unlike the normal English grand action, the **hammers** in Hancock's action face toward the player and each **jack** escapes through a hole in the hammershank. On the basis of the reversed direction of the hammers, Harding has classified this arrangement as an Anglo-German action. The principles involved, however, are the same as those in other **English actions**, i.e., those of a *Stossmechanik*.

There are three surviving pianos that contain Hancock's action, each, with some variation, built in the shape of a bent-side spinet. All bear the name "Crang Hancock" and the address "Tavistock Street" on their **nameboards**. The instruments are dated 1777 (sold at auction at Sotheby's on 23 November 1988); 1779 (at the Finchcocks Collection in Goudhurst, Kent); and 1782 (at the Colt Collection in Bethersden, Kent). It is not clear whether these pianos were actually made by John Crang Hancock (with his first name omitted from the nameboard) or, perhaps, by the firm known as Crang and Hancock. This latter company was the result of a partnership formed in 1771 between John Crang (active c.1745-1792), an organ and harpsichord builder based in Wych Street, and one (or perhaps both) of two other instrument builders, John Hancock (active c.1770–1792) and James Hancock (active c.1770–c.1820). It has been suggested that John and James Hancock were brothers, and James was apparently either a brother-in-law or, according to the label on an extant organ, a nephew to John Crang. According to Boeringer, John Crang Hancock took over the "Crang and Hancock" business in 1792 when the two older partners died. His family relationship to John and James is not known and the occurrence of similar names and working addresses has created substantial confusion in standard reference works. In his 1791 patent John Crang Hancock's address is given as Wych Street, but an advertisement from 1791 shows him at Parliament Street.

At least two additional pianos survive that employ actions similar to Hancock's patent.

One is a short grand piano from 1789 by Davison and Redpath of London (at the Shrine to Music Museum in Vermillion, South Dakota). The other is an English grand piano or converted harpsichord, without its original nameboard (at the Colt Collection).

Darcy Kuronen

Bibliography

Boalch, Donald H. *Makers of the Harpsichord and Clavichord, 1440 to 1840.* 2nd ed. Oxford: Oxford University Press, 1974.

Boeringer, James. *Organa Britannica: Organs in Great Britain 1660–1860.* Vol. I. London and Toronto: Associated University Presses, 1983.

———. *Organa Britannica: Organs in Great Britain 1660–1860.* Vol. II. London and Toronto: Associated University Presses, 1986.

Colt, C.F. (with Miall, Antony). *The Early Piano.* London: Stainer and Bell, 1981.

———. "An Interesting Early Forte-piano." *English Harpsichord Magazine* 1, no. 7 (October 1976): 198–201.

Harding, Rosamond E.M. *The Piano-Forte: Its History Traced to the Great Exhibition of 1851.* Cambridge: Cambridge University Press, 1933. Reprints. New York: Da Capo Press, 1973; Old Woking, Surrey: Gresham Books, 1978.

Hirt, Franz Josef. *Meisterwerke des Klavierbaus.* Olten: Urs Graf-Verlag, 1955.

James, Philip. *Early Keyboard Instruments.* London: Holland Press, 1930.

Kuronen, Darcy. "An Unusual English Piano." *Early Keyboard Studies Newsletter* 3, no. 3 (June 1987): 1–3.

The New Grove Dictionary of Musical Instruments. Edited by Stanley Sadie. London: Macmillan, 1984.

Patents for Inventions. Abridgments of Specifications Relating to Music and Musical Instruments. A.D.1694–1866. 2nd ed. London, 1871 (facs., London: Tony Bingham, 1984).

HANGING ACTION

See Actions.

HARP-PIANO

In 1814 the enterprising German, Johann-Christian Dietz (1773 – 1849), introduced to Paris what would prove the most successful of many pianistic inventions **patented** by his family.

Claviharpe by Johann Christian Dietz, 1814. Musée instrumental du Conservatoire Royal de Musique, Cat.No.2513; Bruxelles. (Courtesy of Da Capo Press [New York], agent for Franz Josef Hirt's *Stringed Keyboard Instruments.)*

Called a *claviharpe* (harp-piano, or piano-harp), this curious but graceful instrument displays its **strings** in the form of a gilded harp resting just above the **keyboard** console. The **keys** when played, cause small **leather**-covered hooks to pluck the strings; the resultant sound strongly resembles that of a harp. The manufacture of the *claviharpe* was continued in Paris by Dietz's son, Chrétien (Johann-Christian) (1804–1888), and in Brussels by his grandson, Christian (fl.1880–1897), until nearly the end of the nineteenth century. Among the extant examples of the Dietz *claviharpe* are those at the Musik-instrumenten-Museum of the University of Leipzig, the Deutsches Museum in Munich, and in the Musée Instrumental du Conservatoire in Brussels. (See illustration.)

In an obvious attempt both to capitalize on

Dietz's success and to improve the resonance of the *claviharpe*, Dr. John Steward patented his **Euphonicon** in 1841. Steward was an enigmatic figure, active in Wolferhampton, Staffordshire, about the middle of the nineteenth century. His Euphonicon displays three sound boxes on the console top and just behind the strings. The "harp" itself has been narrowed but retains most of its height. F. Beale & Company manufactured Steward's Euphonicon in London from about 1842. Extant examples are owned by the Victoria and Albert Museum in London and the Metropolitan Museum of Art in New York. Curious and extremely ornate American examples of the harp-piano were made about 1860 by Henry Kroeger in New York, and Anthony Kuhn and Samuel Ridgeway in Baltimore.

See also Upright Piano.

Martha Novak Clinkscale

Bibliography

Clinkscale, Martha Novak. *Makers of the Piano: 1700–1820.* Oxford and London: Oxford University Press, 1992.

Dictionnaire des facteurs d'instruments de musique en Wallonie et à Bruxelles du 9e siècle à nos jours. Edited by Malou Haine and Nicolas Meeùs. S.V. "Dietz," by Haine, Malou. Liège and Brussels: Pierre Mardaga, 1886.

Libin, Laurence. *American Musical Instruments in The Metropolitan Museum of Art.* New York: The Metropolitan Museum of Art and W. W. Norton & Company, 1985.

———. "Keyboard Instruments." Reprinted from *The Metropolitan Museum of Art Bulletin* (Summer, 1989). New York: The Metropolitan Museum of Art, 1989.

HARPSICHORD TO PIANO, THE TRANSITION FROM

The **Cristofori** inventory of musical instruments of the Grand Duke of Tuscany in Florence in 1700 includes the first mention of a piano: "a newly invented harpsichord by Bartolomeo Cristofori which plays loudly and softly." The successors to **Jacob Kirkman** in London are reported to have produced their last harpsichord in 1809. Within this space of about 110 years the older keyboard instrument was gradually supplanted by the newer in a process still in the course of elucidation. This complex transition proceeded at different rates in various European musical centers.

A number of questions present themselves. When were pianos, locally made or imported, available in the various countries? How does eighteenth-century keyboard music reflect changes in musical taste and style, especially regarding dynamics (notably those within the phrase) and the isolated *sforzando* (nuances impractical on the harpsichord)? Why were these new demands not satisfied by late expressive devices on harpsichords, such as registration knee-levers, *peau de buffle* plectra, machine stops and **pedals**, and Venetian and lid swells? Was the first public use of the piano in a particular musical center just a novelty—without lasting effect—or a definitive change? As to domestic music-making, there is only indirect evidence: letters and diaries, literary references, depictions of music-making at home, advertisements, etc.

Much has been made at times of the wording of title pages of eighteenth-century published music. However, the use of various words for keyboard instruments and the order in which they are listed are unreliable criteria because marketing considerations undoubtedly played a part. Publishers did not wish to limit potential sales only to those who possessed a piano. Furthermore, music was performed in any case on the instrument at hand. The owner of a magnificent harpsichord or even a modest spinet would not have hesitated to compromise or even to disregard altogether inexecutable dynamic indications in the score. Present-day piety towards the urtext was not an eighteenth-century preoccupation. What is more, the conventional use of the words *harpsichord, clavecin,* and *cembalo* on the title pages of keyboard music for which it is utterly unsuited persisted long after harpsichords were no longer in use. It should not be forgotten that only in the autograph score of his very last piano concerto (K 595 in B-flat Major) did **Mozart** finally write *Piano forte* instead of *Cembalo*. No one would seriously contend that its predecessors were conceived for or, indeed, playable on the harpsichord. As late as 1846, **Liszt**'s *Tre sonetti di Petrarca*, transcriptions of his own song settings of three Petrarch poems (now part of the Italian volume of his *Années de pèlerinage*), were first published with a title page proclaiming them as *composti per clavicembalo*!

Turning first to the availability of pianos, we know that Cristofori continued to include some pianos in his production after making his first one before 1700. Following his death, his disciple **Giovanni Ferrini** continued this practice as well as building instruments with combined **jack** and **hammer action**. In 1739 **Domenico Del Mela** of Gagliano di Mugello, near Florence, built the oldest surviving **upright** piano. Tuscany was apparently the center of interest in the piano. It was there in 1732 that the first music specifically for the new instrument was published, **Lodovico Giustini**'s sonatas. But Italy as a whole seems to have long remained loyal to the harpsichord, so that piano making languished there until late in the century, when instruments of Viennese type began to be produced as well as imported.

In 1717, **Christoph Gottlieb Schröter** in Saxony commissioned the building of "a model of a new keyboard instrument with hammers," which he claimed to have invented, in ignorance of its anticipation by Cristofori. Marchese **Francesco Scipione Maffei**'s essay published in Venice in 1711 describing Cristofori's invention appeared in a German translation published in 1725 in Johann Mattheson's *Critica Musica*. **Gottfried Silbermann** of Freiberg, Saxony, finished two pianos on Cristofori's model by about 1736. **Johann Sebastian Bach** played one, praised its sound, but thought the treble weak and the action heavy. Bach was pleased, however, by Silbermann's improved models, which he played at the court of **Frederick the Great** in 1747, and even became a commercial agent for these instruments. In 1743 Gottfried Silbermann's nephew, Jean-Henri, returned to his native Strasbourg from a year in Freiberg and brought piano-making technology to Alsace. By 1755 Johann Andreas **Stein** of Augsburg began to make pianos and by 1773 had developed the improved "Viennese" **grand piano** action with an **escapement**.

Around 1760, a dozen Saxon piano builders, including **Johann Christoph Zumpe, Johannes Pohlmann,** Gabriel Buntebart, and **John Geib**—all of them refugees from the Seven Years' War that was devastating their native land—and **Americus Backers** from Holland, set up shop in London and began producing small **square pianos** with a simple action without an escapement. Americus Backers, with the help of **Robert Stodart** and his employer **John Broadwood**, developed the **English action** seen in a grand piano dated 1772. Stodart, now independent, **patented** his design for a grand piano in 1777.

English squares and grands now began to be widely exported to France and other European countries, as well as to the United States. The famous harpsichord workshops of **Shudi** & Broadwood and the **Kirkman** family began to produce square and grand pianos during the last quarter of the century, gradually shifting their production over entirely to the newer instrument. The last Shudi & Broadwood harpsichord was produced in 1793, sixteen years before the Kirkman workshop definitively abandoned manufacture of the older-style instrument.

The French Academy of Sciences received drawings of four different "hammer harpsichords" from **Jean Marius** as early as 1716, but this seems not to have led to actual manufacture. In 1758 Johann Andreas Stein of Augsburg visited Paris, stopping off twice en route at the Silbermann workshop in Strasbourg where pianos were being made. The following year "a harpsichord of new invention called *piano e forte*" was advertised in Paris but without specifying its maker or other details. The 1766 inventory of the estate of harpsichord maker François Etienne Blanchet included a "harpsichord with hammers," again with its maker unspecified, probably an imported instrument. In 1777 **Sébastien Erard** began making Zumpe-type square pianos in Paris. By 1784 **Pascal Taskin**, court harpsichord maker, was still importing square pianos from Shudi & Broadwood in London like the one **Muzio Clementi** had brought on tour to Paris three years before. Soon afterwards, Taskin himself was making grand pianos in Paris, but Erard, in spite of his longer experience with production of square pianos, only ventured to produce grand pianos on the English model in 1796.

Florentine pianos were in use by the 1730s at the Portuguese and Spanish royal courts and, no doubt, in the houses of the nobility as well. Lodovico Giustini's sonatas, previously mentioned, were dedicated to a royal Portuguese prince. A Belgian maker, Henrique Van Casteel, active in Lisbon from 1757 to 1767, built pianos there on the Cristofori model. Francisco Pérez Mirabal of Seville is known to have produced pianos around 1745 on similar lines. The 1758 inventory of the estate of Queen Maria Barbara of Spain, the patroness of **Domenico Scarlatti**, lists a number of Florentine pianos, including some that had been converted to harpsichords,

probably because local technicians could not repair and maintain the unfamiliar and complicated Cristofori-type action. Square pianos of English design were being built in Spain during the 1780s.

A few highlighted events will serve to illustrate the gradual supplanting of the harpsichord by the piano. The introduction of the piano in public concerts has been dated in a number of cities: Vienna, 1763; London, 1767; Paris and Dublin, 1768. However, keyboardists of the stature of Mozart and Clementi went on performing on harpsichords and clavichords as well as on pianos until the end of the 1780s at least. **Joseph Haydn** in 1790 still had to urge his close Viennese friend and patroness, Marianne von Genzinger, to replace her harpsichord with a piano by his preferred maker, **Johann Schantz**. Frederick the Great, for all his enthusiasm for Silbermann pianos, of which it is said that he owned fifteen, was still ordering five-and-a-half octave Shudi harpsichords from England during the 1760s and 1770s. Haydn procured a similar instrument in 1775 for his employer, Prince Esterhazy. (These large harpsichords were likely intended for orchestral and chamber music.) Leopold Mozart ordered a harpsichord from the workshop of the **Friederici** brothers (Christian Ernst and Christian Gottfried) in Gera, Saxony, as late as 1770. In 1791 Haydn conducted from the piano at the Salomon concerts in London, replacing the harpsichord used at the rehearsals. In 1793, the performance of the annual birthday ode for George III of England used a piano rather than a harpsichord for the first time. Finally, in 1799, the Paris Conservatoire replaced the prize for harpsichord with one for piano, and appointed its first professor of piano, the composer François Adrien Boieldieu.

As already noted, the wording of title pages can be misleading. A number of first mentions of the piano are nonetheless worthy of note. The first published music expressly designated for piano was Giustini's six sonatas, *da cimbalo di piano, e forte detto volgarmente di martelletti* (i.e., for harpsichord with piano and forte, popularly called with little hammers), issued in Florence in 1732. The German composer Johann Gottfried Eckard, who arrived in Paris with Stein of Augsburg and remained there, published in 1763 six sonatas *pour le clavecin* but with dynamic gradations that "render this work equally suitable for harpsichord, clavichord or the *Forte et Piano*," adding that if he had only had the harpsichord in mind, this would not have been necessary. In a second publication the following year, the two sonatas are described on the title page as *pour le clavecin ou le piano forte*. The first publication by a native French composer for *clavecin ou piano forte* came in 1768, six sonatas by Madame Victor Bayon-Louis. John Burton of London published ten sonatas "for the harpsichord, organ, or piano forte" in 1766, covering all bases. The conventional use of words like *clavier, clavecin,* and *cembalo* on published music in German-speaking countries renders it impossible to pinpoint the first mention of the piano on title pages.

The dynamic comparability, if not equivalence, of contemporary pianos and harpsichords is attested by **Carl Philipp Emanuel Bach's** double concerto of 1788 for them (H. 479, Wq. 47). This composer of the transition period is unique in having written music for clavichord, harpsichord, and piano distinctly labelled as such. When his younger brother, **Johann Christian**, elected to perform a "Solo on the Piano Forte" in London in 1768, it was not because he despised the tonally sumptuous English harpsichords of the period. He played on a small Zumpe square piano, a modest instrument by any standard, tonally weak and with a primitive action, far less refined than Cristofori's. The wish to present a novelty doubtless played a part, but more important by far were the new instrument's capacities, however limited, to allow the player to exercise dynamic control over the shaping of phrases and to balance the parts. In this respect, only the clavichord could equal the piano, but at a much lower volume level. Opening and closing the Venetian swell's shutters had far less effect on the sound of the harpsichord than the swell box did for the organ. Correctly manipulating the ingenious but complex system of six registration knee-levers on very late French harpsichords was a tour de force in itself and still did not provide the subtle gradations that were so easy to produce on the early piano. The soft leather *peau de buffle* plectra introduced in late eighteenth-century French harpsichords by Pascal Taskin and others afforded only very limited dynamic nuance. Instruments with both piano hammers and harpsichord jacks, either playable from the same **keyboard**, as in Giovanni Ferrini's and

John Joseph Merlin's inventions, or combining a harpsichord and a piano face-to-face (*vis-à-vis Flügel*) in one enormous case, such as Stein produced, were sports that never found general acceptance. Those who revelled in beauty and amplitude of sound for its own sake were less ready to accept the early piano as equivalent to the harpsichord. The writer, philosopher, historian, poet, dramatist, and general know-it-all Voltaire in 1774 dismissed the piano as a "tinsmith's instrument" and the composer Claude-Bégnine Balbastre, who later was to write much piano music, assured Taskin at about this time that "this bourgeois instrument will never dethrone the majestic harpsichord." We must not forget, however, that technical advances in piano building during the last quarter of the eighteenth century brought great improvements in tonal quality and volume as well as in the reliability and sensitivity of its action.

Howard Schott

Bibliography

Belt, Philip R., Maribel Meisel, et al. *The Piano.* London & New York: Macmillan Press and W.W. Norton, 1988.

Gustafson, Bruce, and David Fuller. *A Catalogue of French Harpsichord Music 1699–1780.* Oxford: Clarendon Press, 1990.

Loesser, Arthur. *Men, Women and Pianos: A Social History.* New York: Simon & Schuster, 1954.

Pascual, Beryl Kenyon de. "Francisco Pérez Mirabal's Harpsichords and the Early Spanish Piano." *Early Music* 15 (1987): 503–13.

Ripin, Edwin M. "Expressive Devices Applied to the Eighteenth-Century Harpsichord." *Organ Yearbook* 1:65–80.

Ripin, Edwin M., Howard Schott, et al. *Early Keyboard Instruments.* London & New York: Macmillan Press and W. W. Norton, 1989.

Schott, Howard. "From Harpsichord to Pianoforte: A Chronology and Commentary." *Early Music* 13 (1985): 28–38.

HAWKINS, JOHN ISAAC (1772–1855)

John Isaac Hawkins was born in Derbyshire, England, in 1772 and studied metallurgy and civil engineering. He thus followed in the footsteps of his father, Isaac Hawkins, who was born in Glossop, Derbyshire, around 1752 and was an engineer. John Isaac Hawkins went to America sometime before 1800 where he set up in business and, among other activities, produced pianofortes.

Between 1800 and 1845 he appears to have had a family residence at Bordentown, near Trenton in New Jersey (an early center for the American piano industry), but in 1799 he is referred to as a piano maker at 15 South Second Street in Philadelphia. Here he devoted himself to improving the then rather primitive American **upright piano**. All his inventions were **patented** both in America and in England (where they appear in the patent register under the name of his father). The first, in 1800, covered an extraordinary range of "improvements" including a high-speed repeating **action** by which, so long as a **key** was held down, the **hammer** would repeatedly strike the **string** with force. This he called his "Poiatorise stop." He also said that to avoid having the strings of an instrument (presumably not a piano) go out of tune as humidity varied, they could be made of "gut, silk or other strings" rendered waterproof.

Significantly, though, both he and **Matthias Müller** of Vienna reached a simultaneous but independent conclusion that the upright piano could be made shorter by dispensing with the stand or trestle and resting the instrument directly on the floor. His **"portable grand** pianoforte" of 1800 stood only 54.5 inches high.

There were other improvements: again to reduce the dimensions of the piano, the long bass strings could be replaced with **wire** strings or coiled metal. Furthermore, Hawkins used his knowledge of metals to introduce bracings to support the tension of the strings. This was not a full iron **frame** or **plate**, but a framework of individual steel members bolted inside the wooden frame.

His instruments were also sold in London; one instrument has been seen bearing John Isaac Hawkins's name with his father's address in Dalby Terrace, City Road.

In 1802, John Isaac Hawkins brought out the Claviol, a tall instrument like an upright piano that bowed its strings. In this he applied a method of string-tensioning that he claimed could also be used on pianos, the string being attached to a nut on a threaded rod that could be turned for **tuning**.

By 1812 Isaac Hawkins, Sr., was at 79 Great Titchfield Street, Mary-le-Bone; his last address was 26 Judd Place, New Road, London, around 1845, at which time he would have been around ninety-three years old. Throughout that time

he had interests in the coffee business as well as in stationery. John Isaac Hawkins, who also invented the self-propelling "ever-sharp" pencil, died in 1855.

Curiously, Daniel Spillane writes disparagingly of Hawkins's work and, presumably because Hawkins had no piano-making background, attacks his instruments as "worthless," an injustice that Edwin Good points out may have come from Spillane's bias toward the work of **Alpheus Babcock**.

Arthur W.J.G. Ord-Hume

Bibliography

Good, Edwin M. *Giraffes, Black Dragons, and Other Pianos: A Technological History from Cristofori to the Modern Concert Grand.* Stanford, Cal.: Stanford University Press, 1982.

Harding, Rosamond E.M. *The Piano-Forte: Its History Traced to the Great Exhibition of 1851.* Cambridge: Cambridge University Press, 1933. Reprints. New York: Da Capo Press, 1973; Old Woking, Surrey: Gresham Books, 1978.

"Hawkins' Claviole or Finger-Keyed Viol." *Music & Automata* (periodical): London. Volume 3, No. 11 (March 1988): 139–141.

Spillane, Daniel. *History of the American Pianoforte: Its Technical Development and the Trade.* New York: D. Spillane, 1890. Reprint. New York: Da Capo Press, 1969.

Wainwright, David. *Broadwood by Appointment, a History.* London: Quiller, 1982.

HAXBY, THOMAS (1729–1796)

Thomas Haxby, of York, was an organ, spinet, harpsichord, and piano maker, and a music publisher and seller. The early years of Haxby's life were primarily concerned with harpsichord and spinet building. It seems that he continued to develop the harpsichord at least up until 1770, in which year he **patented** a form of machine stop, and a harpsichord of 1777 still survives that incorporates it. Nevertheless, like many English instrument makers he must have been well aware of the need to move with the times, and his earliest surviving **square piano** dates from 1772. Thus, like the main English builders, e.g., **Shudi** and probably **Kirkman**, both types of instrument were made side by side in the workshops for a period of years. At least twenty square pianos survive dated between 1772 and 1794. David Haxby and John Malden (see bibliography) have been able to demonstrate that Thomas Haxby commanded a sizeable work force, and the sequence of numbers and dates on the surviving square pianos have shown that his workshops produced 375 in the period 1774–1792, though instruments also survive from 1793 and 1794. These instruments are invariably in the typical English style with crossbanded **cases** and well-made **keyboards** with **ivory** naturals and **ebony** sharps, though the compass of the instruments varies, some having as few as 59 **keys** with compass GG–f^3, while others have the more usual FF–f^3 with the full 61 keys. Many instruments have attractive **nameboards** with a range of decorative features highlighting the name of the maker, though these may have been made by a subcontractor.

Charles Mould

Bibliography

Boalch, Donald H. *Makers of the Harpsichord and Clavichord, 1440–1840*. 3rd Edition to be published by Oxford University Press; 2nd Edition, Oxford: Oxford University Press, 1974.

Haxby, David, and John Malden. "Thomas Haxby (1729–1796) Musical Instrument Maker." *York Historian*. Vol. 2, York: 1978.

HAYDN, JOSEPH (1732–1809)

Joseph Haydn was born in Rohrau/Lower Austria (31 March 1732) and died in Vienna (9 March 1809). Haydn's first acquaintance with the **forte-piano** might well have been during his apprenticeship years in Vienna around 1750. Recent research makes it obvious that pianos were already known in Vienna many decades earlier than hitherto believed, but under the name of *Flügel ohne Kiele* or *cembalo*, sometimes also *clavier*. In 1725 a *Flügel ohne Kiele* [harpsichord without quills] was advertised for sale in the *Wienerisches Diarium*. Hammer **actions**, built into harpsichord **cases**, probably already existed at the Imperial Court in Vienna by 1718 or 1720. The new harpsichord with **hammers**, invented by **Bartolomeo Cristofori**, was given the same name in Vienna that Cristofori himself had given it and thus was either called simply *cembalo*, or *cembalo che fà il piano e il forte*, or *cembalo con martelli*, etc. In German translation we find the term *flügel mit und ohne Kiele*, which eventually became the terms *Kielflügel* and **Hammerflügel**. The name *pianoforte* or **fortepiano** as a noun for the new kind of harpsichord was hardly known prior to 1760 in

Vienna; therefore its use in a document of 1763 found in the *Hofkammerarchiv* (a public concert on a "fortipiano" took place in the Burgtheater in 1763) is the real surprise in this document, not the fact that a piano was played publicly in 1763.

Presently, the question whether Joseph Haydn had a fortepiano at his disposal in Eisenstadt during the 1760s cannot be answered positively and thus it may be doubted, though some of Haydn's early clavier sonata movements probably sound best on old fortepianos. However, around 1770 it seems that Prince Esterházy acquired a **grand piano** for his new castle, Eszterháza. According to a contemporary report quoted by H. C. Robbins Landon, during a summer concert in 1773 "a musician [Haydn?] was heard on a piano-forte" in Eszterháza. This would explain far better the use of those more subtle dynamic signs that Haydn wrote in his great Sonata in C Minor, Hob XVI/20, composed in 1771, than any attempt to assign this work to a clavichord. While Haydn afterwards composed some sonatas that one could imagine were meant for a *Kielflügel* [harpsichord with quills], there can be practically no doubt that by the 1780s his keyboard works were intended to be played only on fortepiano instruments. In 1788 Haydn wrote to his publisher, Artaria: "In order to compose your 3 pianoforte Sonatas particularly well I had to buy a new fortepiano" (letter of 26 October 1788). This sentence means in all probability that his old fortepiano had to be replaced by a new one, because—perhaps—the old one may not have been built with the proper Viennese action (see **Anton, Walter**). In 1788 Haydn bought a fortepiano made by **Wenzel Schantz** and two years later he also recommended that his highly esteemed friend, Madame von Genzinger, buy a new fortepiano from Schantz and not from Anton Walter (see **Schantz , Johann**). There can be no doubt that Haydn's later sonatas are intended to be played on the fortepiano. On 20 June 1790 he wrote to Madame von Genzinger: "This Sonata was destined for Your Grace a year ago . . . . it is rather difficult but full of feeling. It's a pity however, that Your Grace has not one of Schantz's fortepianos, for Your Grace could then produce twice the effect." And in July 1790 he wrote to her: "I am simply delighted that my Prince intends to give Your Grace a new fortepiano, all the more so since I am in some measure responsible for it: I constantly implored Mademoiselle Nanette to persuade your husband to buy one for Your Grace . . . . A good fortepiano is absolutely necessary for Your Grace, and my Sonata will gain double its effect by it."

On Haydn's first visit to London, **John Broadwood** supplied him with a **concert grand**, and in Salomon's symphony concerts Haydn "conducted from the keyboard" using an instrument that was, according to one visitor, a "pianoforte," and to another a "harpsichord"— one more proof that even in England in the 1790s a pianoforte could still be called a harpsichord.

Eva Badura-Skoda

Bibliography

Badura-Skoda, Eva. "Prolegomena to a History of the Viennese Fortepiano." *Israel Studies in Musicology* 2 (1980): 77–99.

———. "Zur Frühgeschichte des Hammerklaviers." In *Florilegium Musicologicum, Festschrift für Hellmut Federhofer zum 75. Geburtstag.* Tutzing, 1988.

Landon, H. C. Robbins. *The Collected Correspondence and London Notebooks of Joseph Haydn.* London: Barrie & Rockliff, 1959.

———. "Haydn at Eszterháza, 1766–1790." In *Haydn: Chronicle and Works,* Vol. 2. London: Thames and Hudson, 1978: 343.

HAZELTON BROTHERS PIANO COMPANY

The Hazelton Brothers Piano Company was founded by Henry Hazelton (1816–?) in 1850. Hazelton, born in New York, was apprenticed for seven years to the firm of Dubois and Stodart where he learned every aspect of the art of piano making. In 1850 he joined with his brothers Frederick (fl. 1851–1880s) and John (fl. 1852–1890s) in founding the firm of Hazelton Brothers. Their pianos enjoyed an excellent reputation. They were among the most progressive builders in New York, adopting the full cast-iron **frame** and constantly working to improve their **stringing** scales, **case** and **action** design. After the retirement of the founders of the firm, control of the company was offered to a nephew, Samuel Hazelton, who had been trained by his uncles. The Hazelton name, purchased by **Kohler and Campbell** in 1957, died with the collapse of the Kohler Piano Company. **Serial numbers** with corresponding dates of manufacture for the years 1858–1957 can be found for Hazelton pianos in the *Pierce Piano Atlas*.

Edward E. Swenson

Bibliography

Dolge, Alfred. *Pianos and Their Makers.* Covina, Cal.: Covina Publishing Co., 1911. Reprint. New York: Dover, 1972.

Pierce, Bob. *Pierce Piano Atlas.* 8th Edition. Long Beach, Cal.: Bob Pierce, 1982.

Spillane, Daniel. *History of the American Pianoforte : Its technical Development and the Trade.* New York: D. Spillane, 1890. Reprint.New York: Da Capo Press, 1969.

HEBENSTREIT, PANTALÉON (1667–1750)

Pantaléon Hebenstreit was born in 1667 in Eisleben, Germany, near Halle. Nothing is known of his childhood years and in fact it may be that Pantaléon was not his baptized name. He lived in Leipzig as a university student, where he attempted to support himself by playing the violin and giving both dancing and clavier lessons. His debts mounted, however, and he was forced to move to a remote village near Merseburg, where he lived with a pastor's family and served as a tutor.

It was during this period (c. 1686–1690) that Hebenstreit first decided to make improvements on the hammered dulcimer, or *Hackbrett*, a popular instrument of the region. With the help of the pastor, he greatly enlarged the instrument and experimented with using both steel and gut strings. His fame spread quickly as a dancing master who could give energetic musical performances, and he was soon invited to play his new hammered dulcimer in Dresden, Leipzig, and Berlin.

Hebenstreit went to Paris in 1705 and performed for King Louis XIV, who christened this large dulcimer a "pantalon." According to Sarah E. Hanks, "the fact that the Sun King proposed naming the instrument after its inventor was a *double-entendre*. The term *pantalon* was a familiar designation in French and Italian comedy for a clown, and appropriately described the amusing jerks and leaps of the player's body, visible behind the large instrument."

Several references were made to enlarged dulcimers during Hebenstreit's lifetime, but there are many variations in spelling: Pantalon,

Pantaleon, Panthaleon, and Pantalone. There are also various descriptions of the instrument. Generally, the pantalon was of trapezoidal shape and was from four to over eight-feet wide. It had two **soundboards** and two or more **bridges** and soundholes. Some 200 or so **strings** were tuned by wrest pins in a range of up to five octaves.

The pantalon was an important predecessor of the **fortepiano**. **Keyboard** builders noted that the pantalonist used two hammers (covered on one end with hard **leather** and on the other end with padded cloth) to achieve a wider range of dynamics than was possible on the harpsichord or clavichord. It was also noted that when one set of pantalon strings was played upon, the other set (attached to the bottom, or "flip side" of the instrument) vibrated sympathetically. Piano makers later achieved this same musical effect for their instruments with a damper **pedal** or knee lever.

Hebenstreit hired **Gottfried Silbermann** of Freiberg to build pantalons for himself exclusively. But in 1727 Hebenstreit discovered that this well-known clavier builder had broken their business agreement and was selling pantalons to others. The matter was settled by a court order and Hebenstreit thereafter had the instruments built in Meissen by Johann Hähnel.

In 1729 Hebenstreit was appointed Director of Protestant Church Music in Dresden at the Catholic court of August the Strong. This unusual appointment provided the popular aging virtuoso with security and an adequate income for his remaining years. He died in 1750 at age eighty-three, leaving behind several capable students and ten suites for pantalon and orchestra. The Städtische Musikinstrumenten Sammlung of Munich has a pantalon that is believed to have been owned by Hebenstreit.

Peggy Flanagan Baird

Bibliography

Hanks, Sarah E. "Pantaléon's Pantalon: An 18th-Century Musical Fashion." In *The Musical Quarterly*. 55 (April 1969): 215–27.

Loesser, Arthur. *Men, Women and Pianos*: 24–29. New York: Simon and Schuster, 1954.

Marcuse, Sibyl. *Musical Instruments*: 395. New York: W. W. Norton and Co., 1975.

HEINTZMAN & COMPANY LIMITED

The longest-lived and best-known Canadian piano manufacturing firm, Heintzman & Company Limited pianos were characterized by superb craftsmanship as well as design improvements and innovations.

The firm was founded in the early 1860s (incorporated in 1866), in Toronto, by Theodore August Heintzman (1817–1899). Heintzman had arrived in New York from Berlin in 1850. He worked in various piano factories in that city, including Lighte and Newton, and in Buffalo before pre-Civil War unrest and an invitation from Canadian piano builder John Thomas prompted his move to Toronto in 1860.

Heintzman's improvements to the **agraffe bridge**, affecting the **tone** and **tuning** of the piano, his acoustic **rims**, which improved **upright piano** tone, and his duofulcrum method of mounting **keys** contributed to the growing reputation of the firm and secured a good export trade for the instrument. Heintzman pianos were owned by artists such as Caruso, Melba, and Tetrazzini.

Following Theodore's death Heintzman was managed by his sons, a trend that continued through much of the firm's existence. Retail outlets were opened and the export trade remained brisk through the early twentieth century. In addition to **grands** and uprights, **player pianos** were built until the 1920s. Nevertheless, even at its peak, production never exceeded 3,000 pianos per year, the firm eschewing mass sales in favor of its commitment to high quality.

In 1927 Heintzman acquired two of its main competitors, Gerhard Heintzman Company (founded by Theodore's nephew) and Nordheimer Piano and Music Company. The Heintzman firm survived the depression years by expanding its retail trade to include sheet music, phonographs and records, electronic organs, furniture, and large appliances. During World War II it relied upon defense contracts (building optical equipment such as bomb sight boxes).

In the 1950s, under the administration of a non-family member, Edward L. Baker, the peripheral retail lines were dropped and the firm concentrated again on manufacture and sales of pianos. Production rose, and retail outlets increased to fifteen across the country. In 1962 the production of uprights was moved to a new factory in Hanover, Ontario, while grands were still built in the Toronto area.

Following a steady decline in sales during the 1970s (largely due to U.S. and Asian competitors), an unsuccessful merger was effected in 1978 with the Sherlock-Manning Piano Company, the president and major shareholder of which was a great-grandson of Theodore Heintzman. The following year manufacture of uprights ceased and the subsequent year Heintzman Limited was sold to the Hanover furniture firm, Sklar Manufacturing Limited.

Sales increased following a period of revitalization during which the piano and its **case** were recrafted and improved, and new upright designs were introduced. The success was short-lived and in 1986 production ceased altogether. Late that year a retail enterprise, The Music Stand, purchased the intangible assets of the Heintzman firm from Sklar. To the present The Music Stand contracts various piano manufacturers in the United States to produce pianos with the Heintzman name.

Florence Hayes

Bibliography

Encyclopedia of Music in Canada. S.V. "Heinzman & Co. Ltd., by Helmut Kallman and Patricia Wardrop. Toronto: University of Toronto Press, 1981.

Gould, Malcolm. "Heintzman Pianos." *Canadian Music Trade* 7, 2 (April–May 1985): 18–19, 24–25.

Harbron, John D. "At Heintzman Hustle Replaces History." *Executive* (May 1961): 20–26.

Harper, Tim. "The Heintzman family: 110,000 Pianos Later." *Fugue* 2, 1 (September 1977): 22, 34–35.

HERVÉ, SAMUEL (FL. 1820s)

Samuel Hervé was an employee of the firm of **John Broadwood & Sons** who, in 1821, applied the first fixed metal **hitch-pin plate** to one of their **square pianos**. An early example of the plate is seen on the 68-note square no. 26910 (1822 or 1823) with "S. Hervé" signature (University of Bristol, U.K.). The plate, pierced by six holes, fills the right-hand area including the top right corner, where a decorative wooden fret is normally fitted. There is no strengthening arm across the action gap to the wrest plank (**pinblock**). All **strings** are attached to the plate, whose outline minimizes the over-length of strings between each of the two **bridges** and the plate (see illustration). In contrast, the plate on 73-note square no. 37524 (1829) is smaller, the bass bridge strings are not attached to it, and there is still a corner fret. It should be noted that not all late 1820 Broadwood squares have plates, e.g., no. 35944 (1828).

Kenneth Mobbs

Bibliography

Harding, Rosamond E.M. *The Piano-Forte: Its History Traced to the Great Exhibition of 1851*, 199–200, 396–397. Cambridge: Cambridge University Press, 1933. Reprints. New York: Da Capo Press, 1973; Old Woking, Surrey: Gresham Books, 1978.

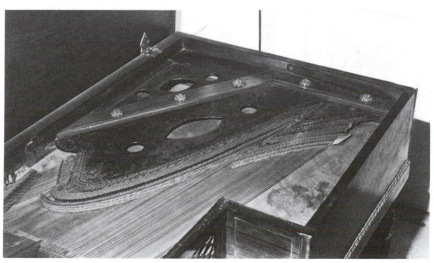

Square piano by John Broadwood & Sons, no. 26910 (1823).
View of hitch-pin plate. University of Bristol, England.

HITCH PIN

The hitch pin is a metal pin upon which the end of the piano **string** opposite the **tuning pin** terminates. In "modern" pianos (built after about 1850), these pins are driven into the cast-iron **plate**. In earlier pianos, the hitch pins are generally driven into wood.

See also Strings/Stringing.

Philip Jamison, III

HOFMANN, FERDINAND (C. 1756–1829)

Ferdinand Hofmann was an organ and piano builder in Vienna, where he became a citizen in 1784. He was chairman of the municipal organ and piano makers guild in 1808 and was granted the title "Kaiserlicher und Königlicher Hof Kammer Instrumentenmacher" [By appointment to the Royal and Imperial Court] in 1812. He is described as having had eight apprentices and to have produced one instrument each week. Hofmann's extant instruments are to be found both in private collections and in some of the major public collections around the world, including the Metropolitan Museum of Art in New York, the Germanisches National Museum in Nürnberg, the Kunsthistorisches Museum in Vienna, the Musikinstrumenten-Museum of the University of Leipzig, and the Gemeente Museum in The Hague. The instruments known to the author comprise one clavichord, three **square pianos**, and nineteen **grand pianos**. Of the latter, three are not verifiably by Hofmann.

The dates of these instruments range between about 1790 and 1825, with the greater number around 1800. Many of the instruments have original **string** gauge markings written on the front edge of their **soundboards** and some may well have even retained a number of original strings. The instruments vary in range: five octaves from FF to f³; FF to g³; FF to c⁴; and six octaves from FF to f⁴.

Like the pianos of many of his contemporaries in Vienna, the instruments of Hofmann are not dated. Nonetheless it is possible to arrange them in a rough chronological order. Different variables such as string lengths, **hammer**-head widths, **bridge** cross-sections, **bridge pin** thicknesses, and **keyboard** range all present a logical pattern that can be read as a chronological order. The string lengths of the grand pianos approximate Pythagorean **scaling** very closely in the upper half of each instrument, indicating great care and a conscious effort in the positioning of the nut and bridge. The later the probable date of the instrument, the shorter the scaling is and the heavier the string gauges are, thus maintaining a fairly constant tension from instrument to instrument. This pattern of balancing shorter scaling with heavier stringing is broken with the advent of the two much larger six-octave instruments of about 1812 and 1825, which are triple strung throughout and have much longer bass strings than the five-octave instruments, which are only double strung from c^2 downwards. The longer strings in the bass of the six-octave instruments and the fact that there are more strings, are both factors that contribute to an enormous increase in overall tension, which is matched by a new and much heavier construction of the **cases**, especially in the circa 1825 instrument.

The shortening of the scale in the earlier instruments cannot be accounted for in terms of a rise in **pitch**. The pitch of the oldest instrument would have to be more than two semitones lower than the youngest for this to be true. The changes in the choices of scaling and string gauges represent a shift in aesthetic taste away from the sound given by thinner, longer strings to the sound of thicker, shorter strings. There is, however, one instrument that Hofmann probably intended for use at Choir Pitch (Chor Ton) rather than Chamber Pitch (Kammer Ton). This instrument does not fit the general pattern unless it is assigned a pitch a semitone higher than the rest. The conclusion that tension was kept constant in the smaller instruments assumes a constant pitch. If the pitch did rise during the period in which these instruments were made, the tension would also have risen. But the case construction of the five- and five-and-a-half-octave instruments hardly changes. It is only the two later instruments that show a markedly higher string tension and commensurate case construction.

The weights of the hammers, the velocity of the hammer in relation to the speed of the player's finger, the bridge cross-section, and the sizes of the bridge and nut pins all increase in the later instruments, indicating an increasing demand for power, concomitant with the increasing thickness of the strings.

Whether the **key** covers are like those on a

modern piano, with white naturals and black sharps, or whether the colors are reversed does not appear to be any indication of the age of a particular instrument. The use of bone-covered naturals and **ebony**-topped sharps was reserved for instruments veneered in mahogany. Extant examples of such instruments all have veneered **lids**. Keyboards with ebony-covered naturals and bone-topped sharps were used for instruments with solid or veneered case sides and lids, using walnut, cherry, or yew as exterior wood. This latter category falls into three groups: the earliest have solid case sides, although the long side or **spine** is made of pine, veneered only on the inside with the same wood as that of the solid case sides. The lids of this group have solid lids made of framed panels. The middle-period instruments have veneered case sides and again, the spine is only veneered inside. The lids are solid and again, made of framed panels. The last group also has no veneer on the exterior of the spine, but not only are the other case sides veneered, but also the lids. Only the mahogony veneered instruments have veneer on the outside of the spine. The coupling of exterior wood type with the color disposition of the key coverings is abandoned in the later and larger instruments of six octaves. Both of these are veneered, including the exterior of the spine, with walnut. Both have bone-covered naturals and ebony-topped sharps. Until about 1812, then, the rule appears to be that mahogony instruments have white naturals, other woods use black. From about 1812 onwards, all instruments have white naturals. Apart from three dubious exceptions, the present author knows of no exceptions to these rules in German or Viennese piano manufacture.

Evidence from Hofmann pianos with their original lid **finishes** inside and out support the idea that the main lid was not opened for performance. It was either left closed or completely detached. The veneered lids have a superficial waxlike finish inside the main lid, in contrast to the high-quality finish inside the small lids and on the exterior of the instruments. Those lids that are panelled show plane marks on the unfinished insides of the main lid, while the small lids are finished inside to the same high standard as the outside case. All the lids are easily detachable. Many Hofmann instruments have retained their lid-sticks. These were probably used for technical servicing, for instance to facilitate the replacement of broken strings. There are contemporary instruments of other builders, including some by **Anton Walter**, that not only have very rough inside lids but also no lid- sticks at all.

The highly unusual brass hinges and hooks to be found on some of the earlier instruments of Hofmann are also present on a piano attributed to Johann Georg Holdrich, dated 1796, now in the Yale University Collection of Musical Instruments, New Haven. The Hofmann instruments with these same hooks and hinges have solid case sides and panelled lids. Such items as hooks and hinges must have been bought from an outside source. Other decorative items that appear to be unique to Hofmann are the gothic arcades on either side of the nameplate and in the **music desks**. But these are also found on instruments of **Joseph Brodmann** and Caspar Catholnik. The combined hammer rest and check, each one individually mounted on its respective key, is also used in some actions of **Johann Schantz**, Joseph Brodmann, and Sebastian Lengerer. It may not be coincidental in this context that Schantz and Hofmann were practically neighbors and that the last visit Hofmann made before his death was to his colleague Brodmann, who lived about twenty minutes away on foot.

Four extant Hofmann pianos have later soundboards. Two of these replacements must have occurred fairly early on in the lives of the instruments. In all four cases the original bridge was retained. The replacement of soundboards was not balked at early in the nineteenth century, even when it came to instruments of Walter. Two instruments by him, one in the Kunsthistorisches Museum in Vienna, Inv. Nr. 539, and one in the Germanisches National Museum in Nürnberg, MIR 1099, have later soundboards.

The gradual changes presented by the five- and five-and-a-half octave grand pianos of Hofmann indicate a change in aesthetic preference away from a less powerful, more sustained tone, richer in upper harmonics, towards a louder, fuller, and rounder sound. With the advent of the six-octave model, these changes are suddenly accelerated. The resulting increase in tension is matched by a new conception of case building with far stronger frame members and by a far heavier action. The instruments of Anton Walter, Johann Schantz, Johann Jakob

Könnicke, Nannette **Streicher**, and Johann Georg Gröber all show that Hofmann was not alone in making these changes, although not all of these other builders, especially Walter, were so predictable in their changes. The number of surviving instruments made by Hofmann, and the completeness of the data they provide, offer measurable and convincing evidence for the changes we imagine must have occurred in the Viennese piano-building tradition between the last years of **Mozart**'s life and the death of Schubert.

Michael Latcham

Bibliography

Colt, C.F., with Antony Miall. *The Early Piano.* London: Stainer & Bell, 1981.

Fontana, Eszter. "Der Klavierbau in Pest und Buda 1817–1872." *Studia Organologica* (Festschrift John Henry van der Meer). Band 6 (1987): 143–185.

Harding, Rosamond E.M. *The Piano-Forte: Its History Traced to the Great Exhibition of 1851.* Cambridge: Cambridge University Press, 1933. Reprints. New York: Da Capo Press, 1973; Old Woking, Surrey: Gresham Books, 1978.

Haupt, Helga. "Wiener Instrumentenbau von 1791 bis 1815." *Studien zur Musikwissenschaft, Beihefte der Denkmäler der Tonkunst in Österreich* 24 (1960): 120–84.

Huber, Alfons. "Mensuierung, Besaitung und Stimmtonhöhen bei Hammerklavieren des 18 Jahrhunderts (Teil I & II)." *Das Musikinstrument* (July–September 1986): 1–10.

———. "Dekelstützen und Schalldekel am Hammerklavieren." *Studia Organologica* (Festschrift John Henry van der Meer). Wissenschaftliche Beibande zum Anzieger des Germanischen Nationalmuseums. Herausgegeben Prof. Dr. Gerhard Bott. Band 6. (1987): 229–51.

Katalog Zu Den Sammlungen des Händel-Hauses in Halle (5. Teil). Halle an der Saale, 1966.

Kinsky, Georg. *Katalog des Muzikhistorischen Museums von Wilhelm Heyer.* Köln: Breitkopf und Härtel, 1910.

Luithlen, Victor. *Katalog der Sammlung Alter Musikinstrumenten - 1 Teil: Saitenklaviere.* Wien: Kunsthistorisches Museum, 1966.

Meisel, Maribel, and Philip R. Belt. "Germany and Austria, 1750–1800" and "The Viennese Piano from 1800." In *The Piano.* London: Macmillan, 1988.

Ottner, Helmut. *Der Wiener Instrumentenbau 1815–1833.* Tutzing: Schneider, 1977.

Stradner, Gerhard. *Musikinstrumente in Grazer Sammlungen.* Wien: Österreichischen Akademie der Wissenschaften, 1986.

Walter, Horst. "Haydns Klaviere." *Haydnstudien* Vol.2, Part 4 (1970): 256–88.

HOLLAND, PIANO INDUSTRY IN

See Low Countries, Piano Industry in.

HOME, THE PIANO IN THE

For nearly three hundred years the piano has provided the musical foundation for individuals all over the world. From the last half of the nineteenth century to the early decades of the twentieth century, the piano was a pervasive item, nearly indispensible, in the homes of the western world. The piano's social function in the home equalled its primary musical purpose.

When **Bartolomeo Cristofori** invented the piano (c. 1698-1700), little did he know how this instrument would affect the lives of millions of individuals throughout the world, generation after generation, and would continue to do so for nearly three hundred years. This combination of wood and **wire** touched the lives of countless numbers of musicians and lovers of music and became in itself the center of a worldwide industry.

In the last half of the eighteenth century, however, pianos were luxury items found only in the homes of the wealthy in Europe and America. By the early nineteenth century, piano builders flourished and began producing compact **upright** models that lower and middle-class families could also afford. Vienna alone had over one hundred builders in the early 1800s, and with mass production methods in England and later in America, the piano quickly became available to large numbers of people. By the 1850s and 1860s, a great number of comfortable middle-class families in Europe and America owned pianos.

Young ladies, who had leisure time and were expected to demonstrate grace and refinement—and what better way to do so than to be able to sing and play the piano?—made up the majority of performers in the home. They had a social duty to learn to perform on the piano, at least in a moderate way, and a significant amount of insubstantial music was written specifically for them. Their ability to play well demonstrated that they were dedicated, had good work ethics, and were culturally refined young women. Their musical talents added greatly to their romantic auras and seriously improved their prospects for marriage. Playing duets could also allow a young gentleman and a young lady the opportunity to sit close to one another and to cross hands occasionally—an opportunity not to be taken lightly in the nineteenth century.

On the other hand, a small number of non-professional musicians worked diligently to learn the fine points of playing the piano. For these students, the piano provided an opportunity to learn masterpieces by the great composers of the solo as well as the orchestral and chamber repertories.

Naturally, before these young people could learn to play well, they had to take lessons, which they did, usually in their own homes, with various degrees of frequency. Some took them daily, others weekly, and others in more rural areas, approximately once a month. They studied the latest *études* of Johann Baptist Cramer or Carl Czerny, or **Muzio Clementi's** *Gradus ad Parnassum;* but in all likelihood they spent most of their "practice time" playing and singing along with the tunes from the most recent musicals or operas they had seen or heard about. If they did not want to accompany themselves as they sang the tunes, they could always play the ubiquitous variations on the tunes of the day.

They also performed popular dance music (particularly the scandalous waltzes composed by Schubert and von Weber, as well as by numerous lesser composers), program compositions (storm scenes and sentimental death scenes were always "in"), and the omnipresent battle pieces. The latter were particularly popular with the young boys who could fill their heads full of military splendor as they participated without risk in the Battle of Waterloo or the Battle of Prague. The playing and singing of hymns at the piano was also of great importance, particularly in America.

Since playing the piano was not always a solitary affair, piano compositions often would include an *ad libitum* flute or violin part, so that others could join in the entertainment. Piano duets, family sing-alongs, and various chamber possibilities arose in the nineteenth century. The chief emphasis, however, remained one of entertainment, not of serious performance.

The quality of the piano playing in most homes can only be imagined. The majority of students who played for their own enjoyment probably did not know how to properly execute embellishments in classical compositions or understand the fine points of piano **technique**, and more often than not were playing on a piano that was not in the best of **tune** or condition.

Before the piano became standardized as it basically is today, various innovations and designs were explored. Some homes may have had **giraffe** pianos or pianos that also functioned as tables, cabinets, or beds; nevertheless, the majority of the pianos in the home were recognizably like today's instruments in appearance if not in actual sound.

The early twentieth century witnessed the rise and dominance of American piano-builders, both of concert instruments and those intended solely for the home. **Steinway**, **Baldwin**, **Kimball**, and hundreds of other companies had firmly established their markets and were producing thousands of pianos that the consumers rapidly purchased, bringing about a highpoint of piano ownership in the 1920s. (Nearly one in every two city-dwelling families owned pianos in America.) The automation of **player pianos** introduced the enjoyment of actively participating in creating music without the necessity of having any musical ability. All that was required was for the excited child to pump the pedals, or later turn the electric switch, and the glories of "Alexander's Ragtime Band" or "How Much is that Doggie in the Window?" poured forth. The trend of automatic pianos during the 1920s was so widespread in America that these entertainment devices actually outsold the traditional pianos of all types.

The depression years brought an end to the notion that nearly every home had to have a piano, and the piano market virtually collapsed. To find new buyers, smaller and cheaper models were produced (e.g., the **baby grand** and **spinet**), but the piano never again became as universal as it had been in the early years of the twentieth century. Even when Japan took over the leadership of producing pianos in the late sixties, a much smaller percentage of the population owned pianos than had sixty years previously.

As in the early days of the piano, the large **grands** of today are usually in the homes of professional musicians and the upper classes. The smaller grands are likely to be owned by the middle classes, and the uprights and spinets by the lower-middle classes. The piano continues to be a symbol of the educated class, and the market still has instruments available in price ranges for nearly any person who has the desire to learn to play the piano.

In this century, students have begun to play at earlier and earlier ages. Many take lessons because their families have inherited pianos and they want someone in the family to be able to play it. Many others learn because of the tradition of having musicians in the families. Whatever the reasons, hundreds of thousands of young students all over the world take lessons and practice compositions consisting of beginning method books, which take them step-by-step into the wonders of music, to the standard repertoire of **Bach** and **Beethoven.** Just as common, however, are pianists who are not immersed in the classics and who perform the latest movie hits or the Top 40, church hymns, or jazz tunes. In this age of pluralism, sheet music, anthologies, and scores of every type and description are available to students of music.

The outlook for the traditional piano in the home as we know it is not highly promising. The piano in the twenty-first century will likely diminish in importance as **synthesizers** and **electronic** keyboards of all types continue their popularity and become the dominant keyboard instruments. The piano will remain for the serious student of music, but its fate will likely be that of the clavichord and the harpsichord, as far as home ownership is concerned, in the not-too-distant future.

Ben Arnold

Bibliography

Carson, Gerald. "The Piano in the Parlor." *American Heritage* 17 (December 1965): 54–59.

Cooke, James Francis. "The Piano as a Home Investment." *The Etude* 47 (February 1929): 91.

Gaines, James R., ed. *The Lives of the Piano.* New York: Holt, Rinehart and Winston, 1981.

Gill, Dominic, ed. *The Book of the Piano.* Ithaca, New York: Cornell University Press, 1981.

Hildebrandt, Dieter. Translated by Harriet Goodman. *Pianoforte: A Social History of the Piano.* New York: Braziller, 1988.

Loesser, Arthur. *Men, Women and Pianos: A Social History.* Preface by Jacques Barzun. New York: Simon and Schuster, 1954.

Roell, Craig H. *The Piano in America 1890–1940.* Chapel Hill and London: The University of North Carolina Press, 1989.

Scott, Frank A. "A Survey of Home Music Study." *MTNA Proceedings* (1919): 171–77.

HUNGARY, PIANO INDUSTRY IN

One of the determining factors in the development of the piano industry in Hungary was its proximity to Vienna, one of the most important centers of piano building. Viennese piano makers produced large numbers of pianos, considerably surpassing the local needs. In addition, the work was divided among skilled craftsmen specializing in particular aspects of the instrument. For Hungarian builders this meant a perpetual challenge of craftsmanship and at the same time insurmountable competition. Beyond geographical proximity, political connections also played a role, in that almost all of the Hungarian piano makers had spent a period of time in Vienna during their learning years, and their work had followed the Viennese building practices. The major Hungarian centers of the piano industry were Buda and Pest (after 1872, Budapest) and there were important workshops in the cities of Pozsony, Kassa, Löcse, and Menhard (in Slovakian territories), and in Szeged, in southern Hungary.

In the first half of the nineteenth century, irrespective of whether there had been a guild of musical instrument makers in the town or not, piano makers worked according to classical guild traditions. They themselves purchased the necessary raw materials and parts for the piano (except the metal parts, **strings**, and **keyboard**, which had been brought from Vienna) and constructed the instruments themselves. The majority of the masters worked alone or with one or two assistants, and only in the larger workshops were there more than ten pianos made per year. The piano makers adjusted their plans to the requirements of the customers, making several kinds of models simultaneously. This practice made it impossible to increase productivity by means of a more efficient division of labor and thus reduce the cost of the instruments. The pianos made were sold in the workshop of the master or in the marketplace. Some of the larger workshops were active from as early as the first decades of the nineteenth century, among them that of the interior decorator and furniture-factory owner Sebastian

Vogel (1779–1837) in Pest, working with four assistants. In each of the Pest shops of Károly Drüner (fl.1813–1839), Jakab Lettner (fl.1810–1825), and Anton Matschinger (fl.1806–1824) there were four to six assistants who produced twenty to thirty instruments per year. About 1830 approximately three hundred pianos were made in Hungarian workshops. Except for the shipping charges and duty imposed on the imported Viennese pianos, the Hungarian and Viennese pianos were competitively priced and equal numbers of each were sold.

The 1830s–1840s was a period of Hungarian efforts for independence, with movements supporting national industry and culture. This resulted in a golden age for Hungarian piano makers. The number of self-employed masters increased, though their number was limited by the statutes of the guilds, and some of the workshops had eight to ten assistants. Thirty to forty pianos were made annually in the Pest workshops of Drüner, Vendel Peter (1795–1874), Vilmos Schwab (fl.1814–1856), and Ferenc Zobel (1793–1841), and by Károly Schmidt (1794–1872) in Pozsony. The craftsmen kept up with current developments in the piano industry and their products were acclaimed in the industrial expositions of Pest and Vienna (1835, 1839, 1845). Notable inventions were documented: according to contemporary press accounts, Károly Augustin had already begun his experiments with down-strike **actions** in 1822 and perfected it in 1824, the same year it was **patented** by **Matthias Müller** in Vienna; Schmidt made and patented a pressed **soundboard** and a "Clavi-Aelodicon" in 1826, and Schwab made and patented in 1839 a set of brass strings he called "Schlangensaiten" [snake strings] because they form a zigzag line.

The war of independence of 1848–1849 was a landmark in the history of the Hungarian piano industry. The old workshops working within the boundaries of guild practice did not survive the stagnation caused by the war, nor could they keep up with the economic changes of the country, including the dissolution of the guild system and the termination of the protective tariff. Among the firms that had been established in the first half of the nineteenth century only the two largest were able to increase their production to fifty or sixty instruments per year; these were Schmidt and Lajos Beregszászy (1817–1891). Up until the 1860s the piano dealers Peter and Gustav Chmel & Sohn (1844–1928) had imported mainly Viennese pianos, but after 1870 German pianos were also imported. Between 1870 and 1900, 1,500 to 1,900 instruments were sold in Hungary annually, but only 5 percent of this number were manufactured in Hungary. The most significant Hungarian builder was Beregszászy, whose workshop produced 1,500 pianos between 1846 and 1879. Among his inventions, the most interesting is the convex or "cello" soundboard (1873), which was also adopted by **Bösendorfer** in Vienna. The innovative six-tier keyboard invented in 1882 by **Paul Jankó** (1856–1919) in Tata caused a great stir in professional circles. Workshops of smaller capacity were János Fehér (fl. 1847–1874) with ten workers, Sándor Lédeczy (1846–1899) with eight to ten workers, Károly Végh B. (firm founded in 1884) with six workers who made fifty **uprights** and **grands** annually. Végh B. also had a patent for a **transposing** piano (1884). The "Harmonia" company founded in 1881 made 150 pianos yearly with thirteen workers, but it stopped manufacturing in 1889. The most significant workshop at the end of the nineteenth century was run by the furniture manufacturer Endre Thék (1842–1919).

In the first decades of the twentieth century the center of the piano industry was still the capital, Budapest, but the builders dealt mostly with trade and repairs rather than with production. The "Musica" company, founded in 1908, manufactured uprights and grands and also had a workshop for repairs; the firm employed 20–25 workers. In 1960 "Musica" ceased making grands and from this time on limited their production to 300–500 uprights annually. These instruments have been sold exclusively abroad under various names (Musica, Talisman, Ühlmann). The firm, after repeated changes of ownership, currently operates under the name of Lign-Art Limited and is now the only active piano-manufacturing company of Hungary.

Eszter Fontana

Bibliography

Fontana, Eszter. "Der Klavierbau in Pest und Buda 1817–1872." In *Studia Organologica, Festschrift für John Henry van der Meer*. Edited by Friedemann Hellwig. Tutzing: Hans Schneider, 1987:143–185.

Gát, Eszter. "Pest-budai zongorakészítök." In *Budapest várostörténeti monográfiák, 32. Tanulmányok Budapest Múltjából No.23*. Edited by Melinda Kaba and Emese Nagy. Budapest: Budapesti Történeti Múzeum, 1991: 147–259.

HUPFELD A.G., LUDWIG

Ludwig Hupfeld A.G. was the largest manufacturer of automatic musical instruments in the world. In 1872, J. M. Grob, A. O. Schulze, and A. V. Niemczik opened a business called J. M. Grob & Company in Eutritzsch, a suburb of Leipzig. During 1882 they began dealing in mechanical musical instruments. So great was the demand that the following year they began production of their own wares, taking out **patents** for improvements in 1884 that included the mandolin effect for **barrel pianos** and, in 1886, a player mechanism for pianos or organs. This was a mechanical system operated by a revolving perforated card disc.

Ludwig Hupfeld acquired the business in 1892, and the name changed to Hupfeld Musikwerke. Hupfeld soon launched the first of many **piano players**, and in 1899 the business was moved to a new factory. Rapid expansion demanded a much bigger plant, to which the business moved in 1911. This was at Bohlitz-Ehrenberg. Hupfeld produced the first European **expression piano** — the Phonoliszt — in 1904. This was developed from the Phonola 73-note **player piano**. A year later came the DEA, a full **reproducing piano** that was to rival the Welte-Mignon, the world's first reproducing piano. The firm subsequently produced a superlative range of **orchestrions** (Hupfeld called them "Orchestras"), which were really mechanical recital organs. The most notable achievement, though, was the creation of the *Phonoliszt-Violina* violin-player. The company acquired the Rönisch piano factory in Dresden (1917) and in the same year the A. H. Grunert piano factory in Erzgebirge. Later it bought up part of the **Aeolian Company's** German interests, including the Steck piano factory at Gotha (1920). In 1926, Hupfeld merged with Gebr. Zimmermann, and in 1946 (Leipzig now being in East Germany) it became VEB Deutsche Piano Union. Today the factory is a major producer of ordinary pianos. The last automatic instruments were made around 1930.

Arthur W.J.G. Ord-Hume

Bibliography

Bowers, Q. David. *Encyclopedia of Automatic Musical Instruments*. Vestal, New York: Vestal Press, 1972.

Grove's Dictionary of Music and Musicians. S.V. "Ibach," by Walter R. Creighton. 5th ed. Vol. 4: 435.

Hirt, Franz Josef. *Meisterwerke des Klavierbaus. Geschichte der Saitenklavier von 1440–1880.* Olten, 1955. Reprint. Frankfurt am Main: Verlag Das Musikinstrument, [1975]; 2nd ed. with Eng. trans. by M. Boehme-Brown, Zürich, 1981; 3rd ed. with Eng. trans. by M. Boehme-Brown, Boston, 1968.

"Ibach." *Das Musikinstrument.* 40 (April 1991): 22-24; and "Ibach remains Ibach": 126–27.

Neupert, Hanns. "Ibach." *Musik in Geschichte und Gegenwart* S.V. "Ibach," by Hanns Neupert. Vol. 6, p. 1033 ff.

ITALY, PIANO INDUSTRY IN

The piano industry in Italy achieved only a level of semicraftsmanship until the unification of the various states into a single kingdom (1860–1870). The production of pianos suffered from the excessive fragmentation of productive factories; in total, the manufacturers that we know of amount to about 230. Because the local product was limited to a few thousand instruments per year, the industry has constantly lagged behind the national demand; in addition, the Italian piano industry never had a true **concert grand piano** until the 1980s, when the newly established Fazioli firm qualified as one of the first on the international level.

From 1825 until the unification of Italy around 1870, every single state of the peninsula (*Regno di Napoli, Granducato di Toscana, Regno Lombardo-Veneto, Ducato di Parma, Regno di Piemonte e Sardegna*) developed its own piano industry, with the exception of the Vatican State, extending geographically as far north as Ferrara. However, the various regional industries were economically backwards and could not adopt a modern industrial mentality. The productive growth in this period was strongly inhibited by: (1) high customs taxes, even between Italian states; (2) not enough capital invested in the industry; (3) no partnerships among industrialists who, in general, were opposed by the government for political reasons; (4) a lack of factories producing accessories, such as metal **strings** and **pins, felt** for **actions, keys,** etc. To all of that add the snobbish love for imported products and strong preferences for lyric vocal music (something confirmed by the fact that, compared to the enormous number of opera houses in Italy, auditoriums for sym-

IBACH

The firm of Rudolf Ibach Sohn has long been recognized as one of the most distinguished of German piano manufacturers. It was founded nearly two hundred years ago when (Johannes) Adolph Ibach (1766–1848) opened his workshop in Beyenburg (now Barmen), near Düsseldorf, in 1794. Upon taking his elder son (Carl) Rudolf (1804–1863) as partner in 1834, Adolf revised the name of the firm to Adolph Ibach und Sohn. Rudolf's brothers, Richard (1813–1889) and (Gustav) Adolph, also joined the company, and after Adolph's death the firm continued under the name of Adolph Ibach Söhne, Orgelbauanstalt und Pianofortefabrik. In 1869 Richard and his nephew, P. A. Rudolf (1843–1892), split the organ and piano operations, with the former assuming command of the organ division. P.A. Rudolf Ibach and his descendants, as Rud. Ibach Sohn, broadened the business, bringing it into prominence as a factory of international repute. During World War II the Ibach factories at Barmen and Düsseldorf were severely damaged in bombing raids and the headquarters were consequently moved after 1945. Presently headed by Adolf Ibach (b. 1911), Rudolf Ibach Sohn are located in Schwelm, where they specialize in **grand** and **upright** models.

Martha Novak Clinkscale

Bibliography

Clinkscale, Martha Novak. *Makers of the Piano: 1700–1820.* Oxford: Oxford University Press, 1992.

phonic music or chamber music constructed in the course of the nineteenth century were almost nonexistent). There were varying trends and types of piano construction in each of the Italian states.

Kingdom of Napoli. Piano production began in the state of Naples shortly after Napoleonic rule. Ferdinand II (crowned in 1830) stimulated industrial growth in the Neapolitan provinces. During that period many foreign entrepreneurs were attracted to the region because it offered safe political conditions, protective taxes, good return on investment, and a promising consumer market. Promotion of musical instrument production, in particular, was given an impetus when *Reale Istituto d'incoraggiamento delle scienze naturali* [Royal Institute for the Encouragement of Natural Sciences] was formed to help stimulate the market. In Naples, piano builder Carlo De Meglio (fl. 1825–1854) was the first to produce pianos on a large scale. He had already been an award winner in the Industrial Expositions of 1825 and 1828. De Meglio patented his own action in 1840, making his family the best known among piano builders in Naples during the nineteenth century. Another early piano maker in the area was Y. Fischer (fl. 1825), followed by Muller & Reisig Bros. (fl. 1850–1854), who were the first to introduce the double **escapement** action in that state, for which they received a **patent** in 1850 and Giovanni Maurer (fl. 1850–1881), who in 1850 introduced a one-piece metal **frame**.

Other builders in this region include Helzel (father, Giorgio, and son, Egidio) (fl. 1832–1872), Federico Bros. (fl. 1854–1882), Vincenzo Mach (fl. 1854–c. 1872), Paolo Bretschneider (fl. 1854), Giacomo Schmid (fl. 1854–1881), Raffaele Muti (fl. 1854), Giovanni Stanzieri (fl. 1840s–1866), Giacomo Ferdinando Sievers (1810–1878), Federico Cappi (fl. 1888), Luigi D'Avenia (fl. 1878–1900), Enrico and Federico Del Gais (fl. 1881), Antonio Fummo (fl. 1861–1873), Giuliano (fl. 1876), Raffaele Madonna (fl. 1870), Guiseppe Marciano (fl. 1881), Aniello Napoletani (fl. 1881), Angelo Negri (fl. 1881), Luigi Nunneri (c. 1860–c. 1906), Tommaso Sciarillo (fl. 1881), Scognamiglio & Figli (fl. 1881–1888), Stefanelli (fl. c. 1880–1890), Antonio D'Ambrosio (fl. 1884–1892), and Giuseppe & Luigi Di Diego (fl. c. 1870–1877).

All of these artisans made use of every type of action available at the time — **Pleyel, Erard,** Boisselot, **Broadwood,** Viennese — often introducing their own personal innovations. Sievers, a manufacturer from Riga who relocated to Naples in 1830, became particularly renowned as the author of the only serious treatise on the construction of the piano in Italy from the nineteenth century until the present. In that work he illustrates two actions of his own invention and several methods of **tuning.** We must note that until 1880 the majority of Neapolitan manufacturers rejected equal temperament, preferring instead to use circular tunings even more unequal than the Vallotti temperament.

The number of workers employed by musical instrument builders in the kingdom of Napoli, excluding Sicily, in 1860 was around 1,500—piano being the major instrument produced. In that year industrial production was still protected from high customs taxes (as high as 10 to 12 percent). However, after the proclamation of the Kingdom of Italy (*Regno d'Italia*) customs taxes were drastically reduced to 3.5 percent, the lowest in Europe, a rate already in use in the Piedmont region. The result was that while in 1860 there were 42 piano factories in Napoli, by 1877 the number was reduced to 13, and only seven of those were active. Many workers found themselves suddenly unemployed and forced into delinquency. Of the 30 workers employed by Sievers in 1860, only 12 remained by 1877, of which two were in prison and one just released. At his death in 1878, Sievers left his factory to his employees, but things went from bad to worse, and they were soon forced to shut down. After a few years, Pasquale Curci (1855–1937), who for some time had tried to run the Sievers factory and who is known as the founder of the famous *Casa editrice musicale,* obtained the exclusive rights to sell the pianos of Erard and Pleyel in southern Italy, thus marking the end of this branch of industry in Naples. Piano builders in Sicily at this time were represented by Adolfo Braun (fl. 1873) in Messina, L. Lifonti (fl. 1878–1882) and Francesco Stancampiano (fl. 1861–1876) both in Palermo, and Luciano Strano and his successors (est. 1886) in Catania.

Grand Duchy of Tuscany. With the end of the Medici dynasty in 1737, Tuscany passed to a branch of the House of Hapsburg, becoming a district of the government of Vienna. Pianos were imported from Austria where they met immediate favor among the Tuscans, not only because they were among the very first but, unlike the pianos made locally, because they were polished to an extremely high luster. This preference for the Austrian pianos diverted attention from the prominent workshops of **Bartolomeo Cristofori** (1655–1732) and **Giovanni Ferrini** (fl. 1699–1758), leaving the impression that there was no true Tuscan school but just a few isolated artisans. The first pianos to be manufactured on a semi-industrial scale in Tuscany were produced by the House of Lucherini, directed by a German technician, using German labels on his instruments and also using the Viennese action. Around 1830–1831, the brothers Antonio and Michelangelo Ducci (fl. c. 1830–1847) built instruments almost identical to those of Karl Andreas **Stein**, with whom Michelangelo had served as apprentice. In 1841, the two brothers invented a hydraulic veneering machine, imitating the high polish used on the Viennese instruments so popular with the Florentines. Among the piano makers operating in Florence before 1850, Berlians was one of the first to introduce into Italy the double escapement of Sébastien Erard. The Ducci Brothers also produced pianos at that time, but were primarily known for their pipe organs. The Ducci firm introduced new types of actions — Pleyel, Elké, Bord — and eventually manufactured up to 40 pianos per month, but by 1876 all activities of the Ducci firm had ceased.

In 1875 Florence saw the rise of another factory, that of Brizzi & Niccolai (1875–c. 1918), which was soon destined to become one of the major piano firms on a national level. Other Florentine builders included Bindi (fl. 1800s), Saltini (fl. 1844), Zanetti (fl. 1800s), Alessandro Fattori (fl. 1800s), Sisto Petassi (fl. 1800s), Luigi Pini (fl. 1861), the firm of Pennetti & Fattori (fl. 1891), G. and C. Ceccherini (fl. 1900), Gustavo Volpi & Co. (fl. 1888–1892), and Reali Brothers (fl. 1861–c. 1875). Among the other Tuscan cities, around the 1860s Livorno was the chief site of piano manufacturing. Livorno builders around this time included Giuseppe Braccini, Giovacchino Casotti, Ferdinando Marini, Frediani, and Malenchini.

Kingdom of Lombardy—Venice and the Duchy of Parma. In Milan the piano industry officially got underway with Giuseppe Cattaneo (fl. 1834–c. 1844), who received a gold medal from the *Regio Istituto di scienze* in 1834 and may have been the first in Italy to have received financial backing from a local businessman to make it possible for him to transform his shop into a small modern factory. After his death, his pupil Ambrogio Riva (fl. 1845–1855) took over the business in partnership with Michele Voetter (fl. 1845–1851). By 1845–47 they were producing at least one pianoforte per week and 300 in the course of the first six years of their partnership. During the same time two other pupils of Cattaneo, Angelo Colombo (fl. 1851–1916) and Luigi Stucchi (fl. 1845–1871), traveled to France to improve their craft, the first with Boisselot, the second with Erard. When they returned to Italy, each was able to open an establishment similar to Riva's. In the following years other builders emerged, among whom Stefano Abate (fl. 1851–1853) should be mentioned, but the leadership of the Milanese piano industry was decisively taken over by Colombo. From 1855 to 1857 he was able to double the number of employees (up to 40), placing on the market about 150 pianos in two years. Price lists indicate that the pianos made with French actions cost twice as much as the ones made with Viennese actions. Colombo experimented tirelessly, treating **soundboards** of his pianos with a special violin varnish invented by his associate Camploy. Colombo also experimented with various types of frames reinforced with metal. The *Gazzetta musicale di Milano* (1871, pp. 326–27) also confirmed that prior to 1859 he was manufacturing pianos with **cross-stringing**, and incorrectly attributed the invention to him. Colombo, along with the other Milanese manufacturers, sold his instruments bearing the family name, not labels contrived of foreign names, as was the custom in other parts of the country. Other Milanese builders included: Giovanni Battista Angelini (fl. 1881), Michele Cessata (fl. 1800s), Giosuè Daverio (fl. 1894–1898), Rodolfo Grimm (fl. 1870–1881), Angelo Norcini (fl. 1888–1894), Palumbo (fl. 1861), Pirovano & Buffarini (fl. 1881), Emilio Ratti (fl. 1881), Ricordi & Finzi (fl. 1882), Antonio Stadler (fl. 1881), Tedeschi & Raffael (fl. 1898), Giuseppe Turconi (fl. 1884–1885), Vago (fl. 1851), and Domenico Vigo (fl. 1871–1885).

Centers near Milan included Vercelli, with the following builders: Giuseppe Giacchetti (fl. 1869–1881), Giuseppe Stangalini & Figlio (fl. 1884–1894), and Angelo Stangalini (fl. 1898);

Como — Giuseppe Gorli & Figlio (fl. 1868–1934; marks: "Gorli" and "Blutman"); Brescia — Luigi Bassolini (fl. 1889); Novara — Ottina & Pellandi (fl. 1898–1916), Vosgien (fl. 1876–1881), Pomella (fl. 1900s), Borgatta (fl. 1900s), Genestrone (fl. 1900s), and Faccenda & Violini (fl. 1900s).

Among other northern cities, some of them belonging to states then still under the rule of Austria, Parma was the site of the Berzioli brothers' factory, founded in 1836. In Bologna, Vito Dondi (fl. 1888) was active, while in Trento, the Bozzetta name was known. In Modena, the firms of Martinelli (fl. 1800s), Angelo Battaglini (fl. 1880), Silvio Dallari (fl. 1897), and Celso and Gaetano Stanguellini (fl. 1886–1888) should be mentioned. In Trieste, Enrico Bremitz (fl. 1874–1915), A. Cafol (fl. 1875–1885), and Giovanni Haichele (fl. c. 1800–1850) were active. In Piacenza, Adamo Cavana (fl. 1888) and Ranza (fl. 1887) produced instruments.

The Berziolis, along with the abbot Gregorio Trentin (1768–1854) in Padua, are credited with introducing the piano industry into northern Italy. Padua was already known as a pioneering area and by the 1830s the Nicolò Lachin firm had become established there. Twenty years later the celebrated pianist Sigismond Thalberg publicly expressed positive views regarding Lachin's instruments, which in large part were equipped with the Pleyel action. The number of employees in his establishment had to be tripled to fill the sudden demand. Another distinguished Venetian firm, founded in Rovigo in 1852 by Vincenzo Maltarello (1831–1907), expanded rapidly in early 1859 when he transferred it to Vicenza, producing "Maltarello" and "Zwikau-Pfeifer" pianos. At the 1867 Paris Exposition the pianos by this firm were judged the best among those made with Italian construction. By 1871 Maltarello employed 100 people and the production, not counting the parts furnished to other manufacturers, amounted to 150 per year, some exported to Dalmatia, Egypt, and Turkey. The Maltarello company is also credited as the first in Italy to have used felt-covered **hammers**. The firm ceased operations in 1938, with a total production of almost 13,000 instruments, some labeled with foreign names. Several other relatively early builders were active in the Venice area. In Belluno, Giovanni De Lucia (fl. 1871) and Tommaso Gregori (fl. 1871); in Treviso, Pio Marconi (fl. 1884); and in Venice itself, Antonio Aloysio (fl. 1873), Antonio Mariacher (fl. 1884), and Antonio Salvi (fl. 1877).

Kingdom of Piedmont and Sardinia. During the first half of the nineteenth century there were only a few sporadic artisans in this region, all active c. 1838. Among them were Carlo Panizza (Alessandria), Domenico Gregori (Nice), Luigi Alovisio and Francesco Weiss (Turin). As late as 1850 Turin could only rely on two small factories that produced **square pianos** at a semi-professional level. Even though this city was the last to develop a piano industry, in the course of a mere 20 years it transformed itself into one of the major producers of Italian **upright** pianos. This transformation paved the way for Giacinto Aymonino (marks: "Aymonino" and "Stechinge"), who founded his own factory around 1850, bringing qualified technicians from Paris. In a short time Aymonino was making his own actions and in 1873 was able to produce about 150 pianos per year, some of those exported to Latin America. Aymonino's successor was M. Levi, who still flourished in 1918.

In 1850–1852 the Turin establishments of the Berra Brothers (Giovanni and Cesare), making "Baer Berlin" and "I.C.B.," Felice Chiappo, and Carlo Roeseler (mark: "Roeseler") followed. The last mentioned was particularly fortunate, given that by 1878 his 70 employees were producing at least 450–500 pianos per year. The factory of the three Marchisio Brothers was established in 1862: two of them, Antonino (1817–1875) and Giuseppe Enrico (1831–1903), were also distinguished pianists (Antonino was considered the founder of the so-called *scuola piemontese di pianoforte*): furthermore, Giuseppe Enrico invented a frame reinforced with iron, which he called *"staticofone."* This renowned firm eventually employed over 100 people, with an output of 250–300 pianos per year; in 1875 two of the brothers died, and all operations terminated. The year 1862 saw the birth of another Turin firm, that of Giuseppe Mola (mark: "Mola"), which in 1900 was considered the largest in Italy, with 100 employees and an output of some 500–1,000 instruments per year. Another Turin builder, Carlo Perotti (fl. c. 1870–1916; marks: "Perotti" and "P. Charles"), was known to have used felt-covered hammers about the same time that Maltarello introduced them into Italy. Perotti's factory, founded around 1870 with 40 to 50 workers, soon became an important hallmark for Italian manufacturers. According to the estimates of the time, around 800 to 900 pianos per year were produced in Turin in 1880 and 1,600 in 1898. This production filled the demands of the Piedmont market and also that of nearby Liguria. The best-known, and perhaps the only active factory in Genoa at the time, was that founded by Giuseppe Francesco Pittaluga (1795–1865) in 1848. Its output was meager, producing *in toto* only 550 pianos from the time of its founding until 1953 when it ceased operation.

After the unification of Italy (*L'Unità d'Italia*), with the abolishment of local taxes and the rapid growth of the railway system, the quality of life greatly improved in Italy, especially for the middle class. This opened the possibility for the piano industry to assume national dimensions. Among the primary builders were Aymonino (Turin), Brizzi & Niccolai (Florence), Maltarello (Vicenza), followed by Angelo Colombo and Francesco Sala (both from Milan), Roeseler, Mola, Perotti, and Federico Colombo (all from Turin). Others were Carlo Amelotti, Bernando Bellotti, and Giovanni Gillone, all from Alessandria, active c. 1884. Around the same time, Locatelli and Angelo Rossi were active in Vicenza, and Severi worked in Genoa (fl. c. 1920; "Lehmann"). Piano builders in Rome included Paolo Alessandroni (fl. 1855–1873), Giovanni De Santis (fl. 1884–1894), and Garrati & Co. (fl. 1894).

Turin was a center of great activity around the turn of the century, with the houses of Francesco Allasia (fl. 1891–1899), Bertello (fl. 1900s), Michele Blando (fl. 1884), Giuseppe Bollarini (fl. 1884), Brossa (fl. 1880–1885), Vittorio Collino (fl. 1880–1927; "Barra"), Carlo Deponti (fl. 1884–1916; "von Bruche"), Giuseppe Fusella (fl. 1884–1899), Giuseppe Govino & Figlio (fl. 1893–1900; "Schwander"), Michele Miretti (fl. 1886–c. 1920; "Muchard" and "Webster"), Molinatto (fl. 1900s), Pastore (fl. 1900s), Giovanni Piatino (fl. 1910–1935; "Piatino," "Steinbach," "Herrmann," and "Zeider Breslau"), Vittorio Felice Quartero (fl. 1916; "Oskar" and "Killar"), Francesco Romani (fl. 1911), R. Savi (fl. c. 1905), Scarampi (fl. 1900s), and Benedetto Vigone (fl. 1884–1896).

The Neapolitan piano industry was in a phase of decline, even though the old De Meglio house as still producing quality **grand pianos**. However, these last instruments were steadily losing ground to the more popular uprights; almost every Italian manufacturer, especially in Piedmont, was busy copying the uprights of Bord, Elké, and Pleyel. Even though there were many Italian manufacturers of actions (Maltarello, Perotti, Berra, Mola), a builder of component parts was still missing in Italy in 1883 (i.e., strings, pins, felt, keys, etc.). To stimulate growth in this regard a heavy tax was levied on the importation of such parts, a tax four times as much as it cost to import a piano already assembled. After 1870 France had to rapidly give way to the new and powerful German piano industry. Of the total number of pianos imported into Italy in 1875, 750 were from France, 493 from Austria, and only 35 from Germany. Conversely, by 1910 the total number of imports indicated only 162 from France and 3,877 from Germany, with 292 from Austria.

The significant difference between the German and Italian piano industries was that the Italian industry could not raise its standard of quality, nor did its members enter the international market in any major way. Up to 1970, Italy's exportation amounted to no more than a few hundred pianos per year. These two factors made even stronger the tendency of the Italian manufacturers to sign their products with anonymous German names like the "F.E. Anton," "Kapman," and "Liszt" produced by Antonio Fea of Turin, and the "Roslau" and "Falkenstein Berlin" produced by the other Turin Feas, Giovanni and Achille, which proved detrimental to their credibility and inevitably to the quality of their product.

The twentieth century was characterized mostly by the production of modest studio instruments, a period in which the Anelli house distinguished itself for the superior quality of its uprights. Even though this firm had been founded in 1836 by Antonio Anelli (1795–1883), it became successful only in 1896, the year in which Pietro Anelli (1863–1939), son of Gualtiero (1841–1880), chose Cremona as a permanent location. Among his patents was one that met with particular success: that of 1912 which allowed the **regulation** of the amount of **keyboard** resistance. This innovation was given the approval of the Königliche Hochschule für Musik of Berlin, then the largest German music conservatory. In 1918 the Anelli Factory in Cremona was able to produce five pianos per day and in 1923 they had 300 employees. The instruments signed with the mark "Anelli" in 1961 amounted to a total of 21,000. Today the mark is used by the Farfisa firm in Ancona, which also produces pianos under the names of "Furstein," "Hermann," and "Hubschen." A still larger factory, the F.I.P. (Fabbrica Italiana Pianoforti), was founded in Turin in 1917 in order to consolidate all the small companies of the city. Very soon its 800 workers were able to produce 3,000 pianos per year. The F.I.P. also edited the well-known magazine *Il pianoforte* and organized seasons of piano recitals. Unfortunately, the factory lost its sponsors and had to close in 1929. As for grand pianos, a very reliable company, that of Schulze & Pollmann of Bolzano, was founded in 1928.

Around 1930 the Italian output of pianos amounted to some 6000 per year, produced by a total of more than 100 manufacturers, half of them operating in the Turin area. Known piano houses in the Turin area include: A.P.I. (fl. 1928; mark: "Kerschen Berlin"), Arduino (fl. 1920–c. 1940; "Euphonos"), Arosio (fl. 1920–c. 1940; "Kelinod"), Baldi (fl. 1920–c. 1940; "Forstner"), Baloire (fl. 1900s), Barra & Collino (fl. 1928; "Hugel & C."), Bassino (fl. 1920–c. 1940; "Kleiner"), Biancotto (fl. c. 1930; "Weisschen"), Calipso (fl. 1920–c. 1940; "Schumacher"), Capitani & Toffarello (fl. 1920–c. 1940; "A. Hauptmann"), Cavana (fl. 1935–1950; "Inap"), Conti (fl. 1920–c. 1940), Costa (fl. 1920–c. 1940; "Meger," "Kuster," and "Zeipzig"), Cugnone (fl. 1920–c. 1940; "S.C. Schubert"), Della Rovere & Macario (fl. 1928; "Bruckner" and "Steinert"), Giuseppe Del Mastro & Co. (fl. c. 1911), Forneris Bros. (fl. 1911; "Gebruder" and "Bacher"), Guerra (fl. 1920–c. 1940; "Krieg"), Lacchio (fl. 1920–c. 1940; "Care" and "Schuman Berlin"), Mazza & Perrone (fl. 1920–c. 1940; "Rudenbach & Sohn Hoff"), Merula (fl. 1920–c. 1940; "Rosenthal" and "Merual"), Migliano & Borella (fl. 1916; "Oscar Killard"), Morandi (fl. 1920–c. 1940; "Franz" and "Mundstein"), Olivotto (fl. 1920–c. 1940; "Rosenthal" and "Weiss"), Vincenzo Restagno (fl. 1920–1938), Rigatti (fl. 1920–c. 1940; "Kirkmayer" and "Wulner"), Francesco Rivoreda and his nephew (fl. 1920–c. 1940; "Rothenbach" and "Enfois"), and Zaccagnini (fl. 1928; "Sidmayer," "Brokner," "Bekstain," and "Walter").

Piano firms operating in Milan at this time (1920–c. 1940) were Avanti, Cervo (mark:

"Kirtsch"), Gorlini ("Richet"), Griffini ("G. Rudolf"), and Zari Bros. ("Homer" and "Mueller"). Centers near Milan included Novara, with the firm of Pedro Pombia (c. 1900–1928), whose firm was succeeded by the Oldani Bros. (1924–1934). Oldani made the "Optimus" under the Pombia name while establishing a facility under their own name (fl. 1929–1963), making the "Naumann." Other active building centers and manufacturers: in Salerno, Arturo Fabio ("Faber"); in Magenta, Antognazza ("Mullnir"); in Trieste, F. L. Magrina & Figlio, and Società Operaia Triestina; in Venice, Sanzin (fl. 1920–c. 1940; "E. Schurzerg" and "Scheller").

The industry was affected adversely, as were other national piano industries, by the economic crisis of the Depression of the early 1930s and by the increasing popularity of the radio in homes. In addition, Italian piano manufacturers had been supplying the market with inferior products, using exotic names, a practice that had already caused a formal protest on the part of the association of German piano builders in 1924. Finally, in June 1933, a new law was put into effect by the Fascist government, solicited by Pietro Anelli, that compelled builders to sign every single instrument with the mark of the manufacturer and the city in which it was made.

The period following World War II was characterized by a progressive growth in imports. Among the suppliers were not only a recovered West Germany but also some European countries behind the Iron Curtain, particularly East Germany and Czechoslovakia. Around 1962 Japan entered the field, followed some 15 years later by South Korea, two nations that together appropriated to themselves a large portion of the Italian market (from a .3 percent in 1962 up to 54.8 percent in 1988). According to the latest figures, their products have accounted for some 75 percent of Italian imports of grand pianos, a market traditionally dominated by Germany. In regard to Italian production, exportation (even though modest) has steadily increased. In the first nine months of 1989 it had reached the historic number of about 1,100 instruments, of which 43 percent were sent to France. The role model for commercial production at the present time developed at the Farfisa (Ancona) accordion factory, which around 1960 started to make pianos (3,600 uprights in 1978). In addition, also active were Schulze & Pollmann of

Bolzano, founded in 1928, Antonio Cuconato of Turin (fl. 1960s to present; "Furstenbach," "Schonclang," and "Zenway"), Clement (closed in 1991, but around 1983–87 their 25 employees were producing 600 instruments per year), Bachmann (3,000 per year in 1985), Steinbach (200 per year in 1991), Alfonsi in Rome, Romeo Tolin in Venice, Polverini Co. in Marcerata (marks: "Offenbach–Blutmayer" and "Steimach"), Nazzari Co. in Cremona, Egidio Galvan in Trento, and Lucio Maurutto in Turin ("Steinert"). A few of the smaller firms, however, are simply applying their own name to imported or assembled pianos.

As for grand pianos, Cesare Augusto Tallone (c. 1896–1982), after 20 years of experimentation succeeded in producing his *pianoforte dal suono italiano*, presented at the Milan Conservatory in 1967; Tallone, who was also the personal tuner of Arturo Benedetti Michelangeli, left *in toto* no more than 300 instruments of all kinds, each of them a prototype. In addition, a particular place must be reserved for Paolo Fazioli, a Roman engineer who in 1981 at Pordenone, in Veneto, founded a factory specifically for grand pianos. By 1991 he had produced a total of 400 instruments, of which 33 percent were exported to Germany and 100 were sold in Italy. Fazioli's present production amounts to 60 pianos per year, of which 90 percent are sent abroad. His models F278 (9 feet) and F308 (10 feet) are considered on a par with the best-known current international names. The F308, presented with much success at Carnegie Hall in New York in 1987, is the longest concert grand on the market at the present time. In more than one-and-a-half centuries of activity it seems that the Italian piano industry has finally been able to produce a concert instrument with its own individual personality and worldwide marketability.

Patrizio Barbieri
Translated by Anna Palmieri

Bibliography

Atti del R. Istituto d'Incoraggiamento alle scienze . . . di Napoli. Reports by Luigi Palmieri in the 3rd series, 5 (1885) and 6 (1887).

Barbieri, Patrizio. "Persistenza dei temperamenti inequabili nell'Ottocento italiano." *L'organo* 20 (1982): 57–124.

Colturato, Annarita. "L'industria dei pianoforti a Torino nell' Ottocento." *Miscellanea di studi,* edited by Alberto Basso. Torino: Centro Studi Piemontesi 3 (1991): 43–61

Confalonieri, Giulio. "Storia di Tallone e del suo pianoforte che parla italiano." *Epoca* 17/834 (18 September 1966): 95.

La Casa Musicale G. Ceccherini & Co. successori Ducci 1831–1981 . . . . Firenze: Giuntina, 1981.

De Rensis, Raffaello. *Cento anni di casa Anelli. Organi e pianoforti 1836–1936.* Cremona: Cremona Nuova, 1936.

Esposizione Industriale italiana del 1881 in Milano. Relazione dei giurati . . . Sezione XXVI, Classe 54a: Istrumenti musicali e loro parti. Milano: 1881.

Gazzetta Musicale di Milano. (Ricordi, 1842–1902).

Gazzetta Musicale di Napoli. 1–3 (1852–1854).

Piano Time. (Monthly magazine), Rome: 1983–1991.

Ponsicchi, Cesare. *Il pianoforte, sua origine e sviluppo . . . .* Firenze: Guidi, 1876.

Relazione illustrata della Esposizione Compionaria fatta per cura della Società Promotrice dell'Industria Nazionale. Torino: Doyen, 1871.

Ruta, Michele. *Storia critica delle condizioni della musica in Italia e del Conservatorio di San Pietro a Majella de Napoli.* Napoli: De Angelis, 1877.

Schmidl, Carlo. *Dizionario Universale dei Musicisti.* Milano: Sonzogno, 1937–38.

Sievers, Giacomo Ferdinando. *Il pianoforte . . . .* Napoli: Ghio, 1868.

Statistica del Commercio con l'estero. Italian State yearly publication, 1851–1990).

Strumenti e musica. (Monthly magazine), Ancona: 1967–1991.

IVORIES

The ivories are the white **keys** of the piano (also called naturals), which were once made of wood covered with three thin strips of elephant ivory. Because of strict laws enacted to protect the world's elephants, piano manufacturers now substitute a white glossy plastic, or ivorine, for the natural ivory.

Early pianos, especially those made in Germany, sometimes had **ebony**-covered natural keys and ivory-capped accidentals. Other builders used brown-stained boxwood for the natural keys. By the middle of the nineteenth century, piano makers **patented** cheap substitutes for ivory key covers. These included mother-of-pearl, white oxen-bone, enamel, porcelain, and glass. *See also* Ebonies.

Peggy Flanagan Baird

JACK

The jack (sometimes called the **"escapement"** or "hopper") is the part of the piano **action** that, when lifted by the **key**, propels the **hammer** to the **string**. The jack, as originally designed by **Cristofori**, allowed the hammer to rebound from the string immediately after striking it regardless of how quickly the pianist released the key. The principle of the jack remains unchanged today.

Philip Jamison, III

JANISSARY STOP

The janissary stop was found briefly in the early nineteenth century on European pianos, especially **giraffes**; the stop, operated by a **pedal**, rang a bell and caused a mallet to strike the **soundboard**. The purpose was to imitate the jingling and drum sounds in "Janissary" (Turkish) military bands, enormously popular in the late eighteenth century.

See Pedals and Stops.

Edwin M. Good

JANKÓ, PAUL VON (1856–1919)

Paul von Jankó was a Hungarian engineer and inventor; his place in this encyclopedia is assured by his invention of a radically redesigned **keyboard**.

A student of engineering and music in Vienna (piano with Hans Schmitt, composition with Anton Bruckner) and of mathematics (with Hermann von Helmholtz) and piano in Berlin (with Heinrich Ehrlich), Jankó was also inter-

ested in temperament. He wrote an important article on temperaments of more than twelve tones, showing the possibilities of pure **tunings** with scales of 41, 53, 347, 400, 506, 559, and 612 tones (see Bibliography). From 1892 he was employed in Constantinople in the Turkish government tobacco bureau, becoming section chief in 1904.

He also had time to pursue pianism. His keyboard was invented in 1882 and apparently evoked some interest from the always gracious **Franz Liszt**. Jankó explained the invention in a pamphlet in 1886 and exhibited it during his own concert tours; the first piano maker to produce exemplars was Kurka in Vienna. In about 1891 the New York firm of **Decker Brothers** began to put the keyboard into some of its **uprights** (most surviving Jankós are in Decker pianos), and Emil K. Winkler opened the Paul de Jankó Conservatory on East 17th Street, New York City, having written articles about the keyboard in the *Musical Courier* in that year. **Alfred Dolge** was enthusiastic about Jankó's invention in his book, a *Jankó-Verein* was organized in Vienna in 1905, and instruction in the keyboard was introduced in 1906 in the Scharwenka Conservatory in Berlin. A few pianists joined the Jankó ranks: Willy Rehberg, Karl Wendling, and some others.

The purpose of the keyboard was threefold: (1) to simplify **fingering**; (2) to extend the pianist's reach; (3) to fit the hand more comfortably. Jankó followed the lead—knowingly or not—of William A. B. Lunn [Arthur Wallbridge], who in 1843 devised a "sequential keyboard" with two parallel rows of **keys**, each in whole tones. Jankó's system involved the same: a lower row with whole tones from C, an upper row from $C^{\#}$, the keys of the two rows being staggered. He added two more touch pieces to each key, arranging them on risers like bleachers, so that the keyboard looks like six banked rows of keys. The player can use any of the three touch pieces to sound the note.

All major scales have the same fingering, as do all minor ones. The same intervals in any key have exactly the same pattern of reach. The octave spans six key-widths instead of the usual seven, and anyone who can easily reach an octave on a standard keyboard can easily reach a tenth on the Jankó. The alternative-touch pieces allow fingers, with their inconveniently differing lengths, to fit the keys more comfortably. Large arpeggios are easily managed, and thick, widely spaced chords can readily be encompassed.

The failure of Jankó's invention is inexplicable to those who suppose that civilization and technology operate on the basis of reason. It was a very intelligent, rational solution to the problems of the ordinary keyboard, but like most utopian solutions, it ignored human factors, including musical ones. It failed in part, certainly, merely because it was different. Every pianist would have had to completely relearn playing **technique**, and every piano would have had to be rebuilt or scrapped. Even Paul Perzina's reversible keyboard, made in Schwerin, Germany (1910), with which one could flip back and forth between conventional and Jankó keyboards, did not ease acceptance. The **touch** was very stiff from the outset, and efforts of such fine makers as **Blüthner** to lighten it did not provide sufficient relief. A very light but tough plastic key material might now serve better. Perhaps most important, with the Jankó some pianistic moves that are difficult on the conventional keyboard are made easy. Part of the musical texture of difficult piano music lies in surmounting those difficulties, exhibiting virtuoso daring. Removing the tension of that heroism alters the musical quality of a work.

It is reported that some experiments with modified Jankó keyboards in **synthesizers** are taking place, but details remain obscure.
See also Keyboards.

Edwin M. Good

Bibliography

Ehrlich, Cyril. *The Piano: A History.* 2nd ed. Oxford: Oxford University Press, 1990.

Good, Edwin M. *Giraffes, Black Dragons, and Other Pianos: A Technological History from Cristofori to the Modern Concert Grand.* Stanford, Cal.: Stanford University Press, 1982.

Jankó, Paul von. *Eine neue Klaviatur* [A new keyboard]. Vienna, 1886.

Jankó, Paul von. "Über mehr als 12-stufige gleichschwebende Temperaturen" [On equal temperaments with more than 12 tones]. *Beiträge zur Akustik und Musikwissenschaften* 3 (1901): 6–12.

Loesser, Arthur. *Men, Women and Pianos: A Social History.* New York: Simon & Schuster, 1954.

JAPAN, PIANO INDUSTRY IN

The history of the piano industry in Japan is a documentation of traditional values at work. Perseverance, intensive labor, and a keen eye for opportunity have catapulted the business in less than one century from a simple cottage industry, producing imitations of German and American models, to the world's largest manufacturer. The early, rapid progress of all companies involved in building Japan's enormous industry is remarkable, especially considering its development after approximately 250 years of isolation from the West. At a time when Western music heard in Japan consisted of Christian hymns and military marches, Torakichi Nishikawa, Torakusu **Yamaha** (1851–1916), and other intrepid pioneers manufactured and sold organs and pianos in an undeveloped, and largely ignored, market. By 1991, more than 250 companies had been registered with the government as independent piano builders, with about fifteen actively conducting business today.

Although the Meiji government officially opened its doors to the West in 1868, Western music existed in Japan from the early 1800s. Few records concerning early piano imports remain today. Generally, it is believed that Europeans and Americans who moved to Japan during the latter half of the nineteenth century brought their pianos with them. A German-made **square piano** was the first piano imported to Japan in 1823; a square piano was shown at the Paris Exhibition in Tokyo in 1878; and Luther Whiting Mason (1828–1896), who helped Shûji Izawa (1851–1917) establish the first school of Western music in Japan, imported ten **Knabe** square pianos from Boston in 1880 for classroom use.

Torakichi Nishikawa, Takurô Fukushima (1886–1957), Yoshimi Ono, and several other instrument builders apprenticed with Europeans, but lacked the craftsmanship and materials to create their own pianos and organs until the latter 1800s. Five years after the Tokyo Music School welcomed its first class of twenty-two students, Torakichi Nishikawa built the first domestic organ in 1885 at the Nishikawa Piano and Organ Manufacturing Company in Yokohama under the tutelage of the German technician J.G. Doering. Two years later, Nishikawa began to build **upright pianos**. Torakusu Yamaha, founder of Nippon Gakki/Yamaha Corporation, built his first reed organ in 1887, his first upright piano in 1900, and his first **grand piano** in 1902. By 1904, when

Yamaha's reed organs and pianos won an Honorary Grand Prize at the St. Louis World Exposition, the company was expanding rapidly with orders from the Ministry of Education, the Ministry of Agriculture and Commerce, and the Imperial Household Agency.

Western music was still relatively unknown to anyone but the Meiji government bureaucrats, who supported it as a means for studying Western culture, and the wealthy bourgeoisie, who considered it an enjoyable novelty. It did not begin to reach the general populace until 1900, when Rentarô Taki (1879–1903) wrote *Futatsu no piano shôhin* [Two Short Works for Piano], the first piano composition by a Japanese. Music journalism fostered an interest in Western-style music with the publication of *Ongaku no tomo* [Friends of Music] in 1901. Phonograph records were imported in 1897, and in 1909 they were manufactured domestically and distributed in Kawasaki. Yamaha's prize-winning pianos and organs were displayed at public exhibitions of industrial goods, and gradually in the early part of the twentieth century, the public was beginning to accept Western music as its own.

A classic story of the struggle to introduce new products against all odds is that of Torakusu Yamaha, the founder and first president of Nippon Gakki Company, Limited/Yamaha Corporation. A shift from feudalism to modernism forced men like Yamaha, a member of the warrior class, to reconsider his career as a *samurai*. In an age that demanded new ideas and massive restructuring, Yamaha apprenticed with an expert British watchmaker in Nagasaki at age twenty. Fueled with hope but with very little money, he had planned to found his own watchmaking company after several years of study, but shifted his focus to medical-equipment repair and moved to Osaka to seek new opportunities. In 1884, he was sent to Hamamatsu where he repaired foreign-made surgical equipment at the Hamamatsu Hospital.

Hamamatsu in the Meiji Era (1868–1912) was provincial compared to the more cosmopolitan, commercial centers of Tokyo, Osaka, or Nagasaki. Railway systems, machinery, and electrical equipment in the rural town of 17,000 people were nearly nonexistent, man-drawn rickshaws were the primary means of transport, and few residents had any knowledge of the West. In 1887, when a **Mason & Hamlin** reed

organ needed repair, Yamaha was summoned to rebuild the elementary school's expensive treasure. Sixty-three days later when Yamaha and his assistant, Kisaburô Kawai (1857–1916), were finished, Yamaha had gathered enough technical information to build his first organ from such incongruous materials as cow bones, *shamisen* plectrums, and black weather-stripping paper.

Word of Yamaha's bold experiment reached Shûji Izawa, Japan's first Western-music educator and president of Tokyo Music School, who invited him to study the fundamentals of Western music in a one-month intensive course at the school. When Yamaha returned to Hamamatsu in 1889 in the midst of a depression, he founded Yamaha Organ Manufacturing Company Limited with 100 employees and ¥30,000 capital. Railway service was extended to Hamamatsu the same year, transforming it into a new commercial center, and the company profited from the region's rapid growth. In 1889, the factory produced 250 organs, and 78 Yamaha reed organs were exported in 1892. In September and October 1897, Yamaha invested an additional ¥100,000 to incorporate under the name Nippon Gakki Company, Limited, and became the company's first president. By 1907, seven years after Yamaha built his first piano, 170 pianos were manufactured at the factory. Production had increased threefold by 1911, with a total of 501 pianos constructed, and in 1933, Nippon Gakki was controlling approximately 85 percent of the industry's total market share.

Several entrepreneurs were quick to recognize the opportunities in instrument building as Japanese interest in Western music grew. Prior to World War II, Nishikawa Piano and Organ Company (established 1885), Matsumoto Musical Instrument Company (established 1892), Ono-Horugel Piano Company (established 1933), Otsuka Piano Company, Mitsuba Musical Instrument Company (presently Tôyô Piano Company/Apollo Pianos, established 1934; Tôyô founded 1948), Tokyo Instrument Laboratory (Fukushima Pianos, established 1918), Hirota Piano Company (Wagner Pianos, established 1923), Schwester Piano Company (established 1929), and **Kawai** Instrument Manufacturing Company (established 1927) were competing successfully with Nippon Gakki.

Nishikawa, active from 1885 to 1916, constructed custom-made pianos and stencils according to their customers' specifications. Shinkichi Matsumoto, Japan's first piano technician and president of Matsumoto Musical Instrument Company, founded in 1892, produced a small quantity of excellent pianos and organs. Fluent in English and Dutch and trained in Europe and the United States, he passed his skills on to his heirs, who branched out to form three separate companies: S. Matsumoto (Shinkichi), H. Matsumoto (Shinkichi's son Hiroshi), and Matsumoto and Sons (wife of Shinkichi's sixth son). Employees of Fukushima, Hirota, Triflich, Rubenstein, S. G. Lea, S. Chew, Moutrie, Buchholz, and Schwester Pianos worked in their homes on straw mats to produce exclusive, custom-made pianos with specifications based on German and American brands.

Regardless of their efforts, a piano was an extravagant purchase for the average Japanese family until the mid-1950s. The least expensive Yamaha upright built before World War II cost ¥500, a Nishikawa upright model was ¥650, and a custom-made upright by Fukushima Pianos was ¥800. A domestic grand piano was ¥1,000, roughly equivalent to the price of a single family house. Tuning, at ¥5, was more than six times the daily wages of a skilled carpenter.

Good pianos equal or superior in quality to Nippon Gakki were made by smaller Japanese companies, but only a few could compete with Nippon Gakki's prices, marketing system, and distribution. Schwester and Matsumoto relied on a complex distribution system using expert piano technicians to recommend their products to wealthy buyers, but their size and stature restricted their business to the metropolitan Tokyo area.

When Koichi Kawai (1885–1955) established the Kawai Instrument Laboratory in 1927, Kawai pianos became Yamaha's primary competitor. Famous for his clever inventions and for mastering intricate details, Kawai was employed at Nippon Gakki from age eleven, invented the company's piano **action** at age fourteen, and was the company's manager of piano construction for twenty years. Under the patronage of the president—Chiyomaru Amano (1865–1936), Kawai was sent in 1921 on a study tour of piano factories in the United States, United Kingdom, France, Germany, and Italy, where he gathered information on the various techniques of piano construction. During a massive strike at Nippon Gakki in 1926, which paralyzed the company for several months, Kawai suddenly resigned to establish his own company. At age forty-two, Kawai with six employees began to assemble piano parts on straw mats at his small factory. Their first piano was a **spinet** model with sixty-one **keys**. With its compact size and inexpensive price of ¥350, it was extremely popular with middle-class families. In 1928, grand pianos were manufactured, and by 1935, Kawai Instrument Manufacturing Company, Inc. was producing seventy-five uprights and ten grand pianos per month.

As Japan's militarism escalated from the mid-1930s, materials became scarce, and factories, both large and small, suffered. From 1937, Kawai began to manufacture helmets, gliders, and other military items until 1940, when his company became the subsidiary of Nakajima Airplane Factory. From 1940 to 1944, the factory supplied airplanes and tanks for the military. At Nippon Gakki's peak in production and quality in 1937, company president Kaichi Kawakami (1885–1964) restructured his factory for the production of airplane propellers and tanks. Trying to protect his primary business interests to the end, Kawakami bargained with the Japanese government to continue building a small number of pianos if the factory filled its military quota. They continued to manufacture pianos until 1944 when all production of musical instruments was prohibited by government decree. Smaller builders barely survived by manufacturing torpedo shells and kitchen utensils. At the end of the war, factories and almost all the instruments in them had been destroyed or used as parts for military hardware. Not a single upright piano was left in the Nippon Gakki and Kawai factories.

Wartime damage was extensive, and all companies faced enormous difficulties as they restructured the industry. Tremendous costs and difficulties in obtaining the proper materials forced many smaller companies out of business, and the large number of piano manufacturers in the prewar years dwindled to a few dozen in the postwar. Unable to assemble the more complicated instruments, Nippon Gakki made harmonicas and xylophones for export to the United States in October 1945. In January 1946, they produced organs, and pianos followed in April 1947. Kawai Instrument Manufacturing Company resumed organ and piano production in 1948.

New strategies for industrial development were necessary in the postwar years. Nippon Gakki and Kawai placed a high priority on innovations in piano production, qualitative improvement of products, research and development, and the promotion of music activities through music schools and festivals. Koichi Kawai forged ahead with new inventions, and by 1955 his company had amassed twenty-seven **patents**. From 1952 to 1961, Kawai's profits increased 176 times, and in 1973 the factory was producing 5,000 pianos per month, rivalling Nippon Gakki in quantity and quality. Automated kiln drying-rooms that assured quality control and reduced the processing time were instituted in 1956 at Nippon Gakki's Tenryu Plant, and conveyor belt systems were adopted for quality control. Piano production, barely in the 24,000-unit range in 1960, was boosted to the 100,000-unit level by 1966.

Today both Yamaha and Kawai **concert grands** are promoted by some of the world's leading pianists. The Yamaha Concert Grand "CF" and the Conservatory Grand "C3" pianos, manufactured from 1967 after several unsuccessful attempts in the early 1950s, and Kawai's "EX" concert grand are widely praised for their excellent quality.

Companies with less capital and prestige established their reputations on excellent products suited to the domestic market. The Nichibei Musical Instrument Manufacturing Company (presently Atlas Piano Company), founded in 1955 by Tadashirô Yorikane (b. 1926), developed a new type of light, automatic piano action in conjunction with Brother Corporation, famous for sewing machines, typewriters, and computer printers. Tôyô Piano Company (established in 1934 as Mitsuba Musical Instrument Manufacturing Company), manufacturer of Apollo Pianos, resumed production in 1948 and patented a special **damper pedal** for practice in Japan's cramped living spaces. Their custom-designed pianos can be built from paulownia wood and lucite. Tokai Piano Company, founded in 1947 by former Kawai employees, distributed their small spinets and **baby grand pianos** from 1978 through joint ventures with U.S. and European firms. Schwester Pianos, established in 1929, built a small number of exclusive, high-quality pianos modeled after

the **Bösendorfer** and **Steinway** D-type grands.

The development in 1959 of an all-transistor *Electone* electronic organ, first in a successful series of Yamaha **electronic** instruments, was a milestone for Japan's music industry. Acoustic pianos were affordable and popular with Japan's new middle-class, but future successes depended upon new technology that captured the consumer's imagination. In 1978, Nippon Gakki introduced the world's first digital keyboard, model number CS-70M, based on an FM digital-synthesis tone-generation formula developed by Stanford University professor John Chowning (b. 1934). This was followed by an impressive selection of digital instruments, ranging from portable keyboards, electric pianos, and **synthesizers** to the *Clavinova*, which has placed Yamaha as the world's leader in electronic-instrument production. Kawai, **Roland**, and other makers followed closely behind to produce instruments equivalent in quality and price.

A significant event in the industry's history came in 1982 when Nippon Gakki developed the *Disklavier*, an acoustic piano with attached computer. Optical sensors behind each key measure the duration and intensity of the notes and the use of foot **pedals**. These signals are translated into **MIDI**, the musical computer language, and are accurately recorded onto three-and-a-half-inch computer disks. Recordings can be edited, overdubbed, transposed, and even transcribed. A **player piano** for the technological age, the *Disklavier* records and reproduces music electronically with the **touch** and **tone** of an acoustic piano. Although it originally was meant for professional studio and classroom use, it is popular as an alternative entertainment device for hotels, restaurants, and private homes.

Today, the Yamaha Corporation (company's name changed in 1987 from Nippon Gakki) alone produces more than 14,000 pianos per month. Excluding the *Clavinova*, this accounts for 17.7 percent of the company's total sales, with approximately 54.6 percent intended for the domestic market. The United States is Yamaha's largest piano importer to date, but the projected total demand for 1992 in South Korea may exceed the Japanese market. Sales of the *Disklavier* grand-piano model in the United States is almost equal to the number of sales in Japan; Japanese consumers prefer the smaller, upright version complete with *karaoke* disks to practice their favorite popular songs. Yamaha, like Kawai and other competitors, enhances business with comprehensive, after-service systems, academies to train piano technicians, and a worldwide network of more than 11,000 music schools.

Judith Ann Herd

Bibliography

Hiyama Rikurô. *Gakki gyôkai* [*The Musical Instrument Industry*]. Tokyo: Kyoiku-sha, 1977.

_____. *Yôkin piano no monogatari* [*The Story of the Piano: A Western String Instrument*]. Tokyo: Geijutsu Gendai-sha, 1988.

Iguchi Motonari. *Waga piano, waga jinsei: Ongaku kaisô* [*Our pianos, Our Lives: Musical Memoirs*]. Tokyo: Geijutsu Gendai-sha, 1979.

Imaizumi Kyoaki, ed. *Gakki no jiten: Piano*, [*Encyclopedia of Instruments: Piano*]. Rev. ed. Tokyo: Tokyo Ongaku-sha, 1990.

Kinebuchi Naotomo. *Piano chishiki arakaruto* [*Piano Knowledge A la Carte*]. Rev. ed. Tokyo: Musicanova/Ongaku no Tomo-sha, 1991.

Neff, Robert. "Yamaha's *Coup d'etat* is Only Half the Battle." *International Business Week* (9 March 1992): 26.

100: A Century of Excellence 1887–1987 Yamaha. Hamamatsu: Yamaha Corporation, 1987.

Piano no kôza, 8 vols. [*Lectures on the Piano*]. Tokyo: Ongaku no Tomo-sha, 1984.

Shirasuna Shôichi. "Nihon ni okeru piano." *Ongaku dai-jiten*. 6 vols. ["The Development of the Piano Industry in Japan." In *Encyclopedia Musica*], Vol. 4, 1989. Tokyo: Heibon-sha, 1983.

Specter, Michael. "The Diskette at the Keyboard." *International Herald Tribune*, (11 July 1990).

Tôyama Kazuyuki. *Piano ni yosete* [*The Piano Industry in Japan*]. Tokyo: Ongaku no Tomo-sha, 1989.

Ueno Akira. "Nihon no piano kyoku." *Piano ongaku jiten*. 2 vols. [*Sakuhin-shû*] [*Encyclopedia of Piano Music, Compositions*]. Tokyo: Zen Ongaku Shuppan-sha, 1982: 260–271.

JEFFERSON, THOMAS (1743–1826)

Music was Thomas Jefferson's favorite recreation—at home or in attendance at public musical events. He was an accomplished violinist. While he did not play a keyboard instrument, he had a deep interest in the piano. During his lifetime he owned, rented, or bought as gifts for his wife, daughters, and granddaughters who did play, at least five pianos and four other keyboard instruments. Several details are known about these instruments.

In 1771, soon after the first appearance of a piano in the British colonies, Jefferson requested his agent in London to buy one as a gift for Martha Wayles Skelton, Jefferson's bride in 1772. Jefferson's account books show the piano at Monticello was sold to a neighbor in 1779.

While serving in the Congress in Philadelphia from December 1782 to May 1784, Jefferson rented a harpsichord for his daughter Martha (Patsy), who had accompanied him there.

After arriving with Martha in Paris in August 1784 to assist John Adams and Benjamin Franklin in treaty negotiations, Jefferson rented a piano for Martha. Although Jefferson preferred the piano, while he was in Paris he ordered a harpsichord for Martha from **Kirkman** of London. It was delivered to Jefferson in Paris in November 1787 and it was sent to Monticello when the Jeffersons returned to the United States two years later.

While serving as secretary of state in Philadelphia beginning in 1789, Jefferson had a spinet sent to him from Monticello for use by Maria (Polly), a younger daughter who had accompanied him there. Jefferson's papers do not show when or how he had acquired this instrument.

In 1798, now serving as vice president, Jefferson bought a Kirkman harpsichord for Maria, at her request, although he had a stronger preference for the piano. In 1800, he bought a new type of **upright piano** built by **John Isaac Hawkins** of Philadelphia. While a significant advance in design, it was unsatisfactory as a musical instrument. Jefferson sent it back from Monticello after two years.

The only existing piano Jefferson may have owned is a small **Astor & Company** instrument built in London about 1799–1815 and now on display in Monticello. This piano may have been given to him by John Jacob Astor, while Jefferson was president in the **White House**. The last piano Jefferson bought was a gift to his granddaughter Virginia Randolph Trist in 1825. It was built by Currier and Gilbert of Boston. The Trists kept this piano for fifteen years before disposing of it.

Jefferson became a skillful technician in caring for the instruments his family owned. Jefferson's documents contain records of his purchases of tools, parts, and other supplies for this work. The Monticello music collection contains his keyboard **tuning** instruction book and his tuning pattern in fifths and octaves that he wrote out. His writings show that he had as much knowledge of keyboard instruments as most contemporary technicians.

Jack Greenfield

Bibliography

Cripe, Helen. *Thomas Jefferson and Music.* Charlottesville: University Press of Virginia, 1974.

Kirk, Elise K. *Music At The White House.* Urbana: University of Illinois Press, 1986.

Spillane, Daniel. *History of the American Pianoforte: Its Technical Development and the Trade.* New York: D. Spillane, 1890. Reprint. New York: Da Capo Press, 1969.

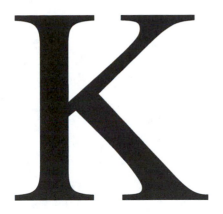

KAWAI

Kawai is a leading Japanese piano manufacturer with headquarters in Hamamatsu. The firm was established in 1927 as the Kawai Musical Instrument Research Laboratory. Koichi Kawai (1885–1955), the founder, had been an employee of **Yamaha** (1851–1916) since 1897. He worked with Torakusu Yamaha in building Yamaha's first piano. In 1929 the firm was renamed the Kawai Musical Instrument Manufacturing Company. During the early years Kawai produced **upright pianos**, **grand pianos**, and reed organs. Kawai was the first Japanese piano manufacturer to design and build piano **actions** rather than importing them.

In 1955 Koichi Kawai died and his son Shigeru Kawai (b. 1922) was appointed president. In the years that followed, the company adopted modern manufacturing procedures, enabling it to produce large numbers of instruments efficiently. Through the use of these methods, as well as through an extensive sales network, Kawai has become the second-largest piano manufacturer in the world (surpassed only by Yamaha). In 1955 Kawai operated one manufacturing plant; today there are fourteen factories, including the first Kawai facility in the United States, opened in 1989 in Lincolnton, North Carolina. The company produces over 100,000 pianos a year.

In 1963 the Kawai America Corporation was formed to begin importing and selling pianos and electronic organs in the United States. Since that time sales in the United States and other countries throughout the world have been very successful.

Kawai has diversified into other musical areas, including the production of **synthesizers** (1982) and the acquisition of TEISCO Electronics, a maker of sound-reinforcement equipment (1966), and the Lowrey Organ Company (1988).

In 1989 Hirotaka Kawai, grandson of the founder and son of the second president, became the third president of the firm. Currently the company produces pianos (uprights and grands), synthesizers, digital pianos, and drum machines under its own name. Kawai also manufactures piano parts for Hellas and Dong-A, as well as pianos for Iback and, beginning in 1991, the Boston line of pianos for **Steinway**. Kawai is a distributor of Nihon IBM office equipment and a producer of athletic equipment and furniture.

Several models of Kawai pianos are recognized for their high quality. Kawai pianos have been designated official instruments of the Arthur Rubinstein International Piano Master Competition and the Chopin International Piano Competition.

See also Japan, Piano Industry in.

Herbert Wise

Bibliography

Data from Kawai America Corporation.

"Kawai at 60." *Music Trades Magazine* 135 (May 1987): 74–76+.

KEYBED

The keybed is a wooden structural part of the piano that runs the length of the **keyboard** side of the instrument. This keybed serves as a support for the piano's **action**, keyboard, and **keyframe**. It is usually built of spruce.

Peggy Flanagan Baird

KEYBLOCK

The keyblock is a removable wooden piece that is placed at both sides of the piano **keyboard** to hold the **action** in place. The two keyblocks are stained to match the casework and are sometimes decorative as well as functional. Keyblocks are sometimes called cheekblocks.

Peggy Flanagan Baird

KEYBOARD COVER

A keyboard cover is one of the moving parts of a piano's cabinetwork; it is used to enclose and protect the **keys** when the piano is not in use. It

The "Technicon" by James Brotherhood (late nineteenth century). View of the arm exerciser. National Museum of American History (Smithsonian), Division of Musical History, cat. no. 66. 144.

is often called a fallboard. The piano maker's name is usually stenciled on the underside of the keyboard cover and is not visible until the cover is raised.

See also Nameboard.

Peggy Flanagan Baird

KEYBOARD PRACTICE AND EXERCISE AIDS

Changing styles in piano construction, repertoire, and technique throughout the nineteenth and early twentieth centuries brought about numerous inventions and **patents** for practice, hand guidance, and abstract exercise devices. Many became more or less well known under generic nomenclature, such as practice clavier, digitorium, dactylion, hand gymnasium, and legato monitor. Most went no further than the patent office, but several were marketed with varying success under exotic trade names, such as "Chiroplast," "Technicon," "Tekniklavier," and "Gyastik."

Practically all categories of Western instruments have received attention relating to simulator practice devices, usually directed toward reducing sound to avoid disturbing uninterested parties. Brasswind players have long had the advantage of their various mutes or the mouthpiece practiced separately, and sound-dampening practice bags with armholes suspended on a metal frame were once offered for clarinets and other woodwinds. Percussionists have commonly used snare drum practice pads, and entire drum-set practice-pad rigs have been devised incorporating the usual height and angle adjustability of the various components. Mute violins and cellos were once popular, which included the necessary extremities, stringing, and tuning elements but with the resonating

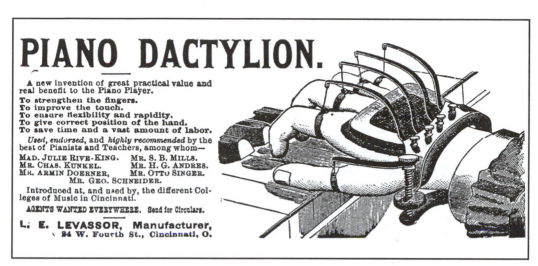

An advertisement of the "Piano Dactylion."

box greatly reduced or missing altogether. However, it was the piano that enticed musicians and inventors to design simulator practice devices and exercise or hand-guidance apparati ranging from bizarre contraptions to seemingly useful machinery.

Many of those that would now seem quite reasonable were simply attempts to make the piano neighbor-friendly by muting it to a degree well beyond that of the soft **pedal**. Patents in this area pertain to the **upright** instrument. Most utilize a middle pedal to lift, lower, or swivel a batten containing a strip of **felt** in front of the **strings** where the **hammers** strike. The principle was similar to late-eighteenth-century instruments with a hand stop or those of the early nineteenth century having one or more pedals that would shift a batten of buff **leather** tabs or other material in between the hammers and strings as an expressive device. (See **Moderator**.) The center muting pedal is currently available on numerous uprights manufactured in various Asian and American factories. They essentially reinvent patented mechanisms such as that by George Shearer of Oneonta, New York, who in 1893 received U.S. Patent No. 503,880 for a Piano Practice Pedal.

Not surprisingly, the rise of keyboard practice and exercise gadgetry parallels most other areas of mechanical engineering during the Industrial Revolution, with sporadic attempts still appearing at the Patent Office. However, all of this was foreshadowed by an interesting eighteenth-century hand-guidance example. In *L'Art de Toucher le Clavecin,* 1716, François Couperin (1688–1733) states:

> If a pupil holds one wrist too high in playing, the only remedy that I have found is to get someone to hold a small flexible stick which is passed over the faulty wrist, and at the same time under the other wrist. If the defect is the opposite, the reverse must be done. But this stick must not absolutely hinder the freedom of the player. Little by little this fault will correct itself; and this invention has been of great service to me.

The earliest patented and relatively successful attempt at devising and marketing a hand-guidance rig was the invention of Johann Bernhard Logier (1777–1846), a German composer, flutist, conductor, and music teacher who emigrated to England in 1791. By 1810 he was a resident of Dublin and becoming known for conducting group piano-instruction on multiple instruments. In 1814 Logier obtained

British Patent No. 3806 for an "Apparatus for Facilitating the Acquirement of Proper Execution on the Pianoforte." This is the earliest known attempt at a hand-guidance device attached to the piano, and it surely spawned what was to become an ever-continuing maze of inventions for guiding, exercising, and stretching the pianist's anatomy.

The Logier invention was marketed as the "Royal Patent Chiroplast" or "Hand Director." It consisted of two main elements. One was a "gamut board" containing the great staff, showing the diatonic notes pertinent to the average **keyboard** compass of the time and a chromatic version printed on the reverse. The gamut board was positioned over the keyboard with the various notes lined up over their respective **keys** for visual ready reference. The second or mechanical element was a "position frame" with two parallel mahogany rails attached to the instrument in front of the keyboard to restrict extreme vertical motion of the wrists and forearm. A few inches behind the wooden rails was a parallel brass rod or "bracing bar" containing two sliding brass hand-guides, "each having five compartments lined with leather to admit the thumb and four fingers of each hand." The guides were free "to slide upon the bracing bar, and have each a screw, by which they are fixed over such keys as may be required." The hand guides also included a brass wire, or "wrist guide," with "a regulator" to prevent the wrists from being inclined outwards. Logier's mechanical approach to playing posture combined with gamut-board information and group instruction probably represents the earliest effort to minimize teacher workload while maximizing income and time-slot efficiency, excepting, of course, the initial outlay to purchase and maintain multiple pianos, often ten or more.

The Logier teaching method created a controversy amongst professionals in the field, with both sides occasionally publishing articles and pamphlets pro and con. Over a half-dozen had appeared by 1818. Publicity from both sides, in effect, served to move it ahead, and by 1818 over two dozen Logier "Academies" and a "Chiroplast Club" had been organized in the United Kingdom. Logier's home office in Dublin was known as "Chiroplast Hall." With the exception of France, a certain amount of Logier-Method activity spread to other parts of Europe, with isolated examples appearing in the United States and as far east as India. It made special headway in Germany, where Logier was invited to Berlin in 1821 by the Prussian Government and there continued teaching until 1826. Support from the artistic community in opposition to Logier's critics included Louis Spohr, Samuel Webbe, and in particular, Frédéric Kalkbrenner, who eventually devised his own simplified form of the Chiroplast ("guide-mains"). The Kalkbrenner version was said to be still available in England as late as the 1870s. The Chiroplast was, of course, warmly endorsed by **Muzio Clementi**, since his company was the manufacturer and enjoyed brisk sales for a number of years. Although real interest in the Logier Method waned in less than a decade, numerous editions of his "First Companion to the royal patent Chiroplast . . . ." were published by the author (Dublin), Clementi & Company (London), J. Green (London), Spear and Ditson (Boston), and was still available in the 1840s.

1849 seems to be the earliest example of an American patent for any type of pianist's hand guidance or exercising invention; U.S. Patent No. 6,558 was issued to Ernest Von Heeringen of Pickensville, Alabama, for a "Piano Attachment," or as he also called it, a "Nolime-tangere" (touch me not). It essentially reinvents aspects of the Chiroplast (minus the gamut board) by attaching three adjustable rails to the instrument, two in front of the keyboard and a third farther back near the top of the **nameboard.** The lower of the two rails in front is for the student to avoid by keeping the wrists and arms in a "graceful position" over it. "Touch me not" certainly applies to this item, which was designed with vertical pins to prick the wrists, thus "producing pain" and serving to "sufficiently admonish the pupil" for allowing the wrists to sag. The other front rail is of polished metal and fitted with two cushioned "pieces" on which the wrists are to be strapped and supposedly slide freely, maintaining the hands at a right angle to the keys with all of the motion being "from the shoulders." The uppermost rail farther back over the keys has hanging from it two or four sets of five loops or rings attached to springs or elastic for obtaining finger strength and "independence." It supposedly offers an abstract exercise element, but the patent is not clear whether or not the spring units would allow lateral motion.

Whether knowingly or not, Von Heeringen's

hanging spring-loop exerciser is a version of the Herz Dactylion, patented in 1836 by the German pianist, composer, and teacher, Henri (Heinrich) Herz. It suspends two quintets of spring-retraction finger rings from a wooden frame that can be attached to a piano (or table) with the ring-exerciser units positioned over the keyboard. An example of it is preserved at the Musée instrumental de Bruxelles, object No. 1675.

Another American idea for an arm-hand guide attached (screwed) to the piano was patented in 1885, No. 326,444, by Charles F. Meyering of Rochester, New York. It consists of one keyboard-length roller bar, adjustable in height and from front to rear, upon which the wrists are to be supported as necessary. One of the patent's three claims includes a paper having a Logier-like gamut of notes covering the entire surface of the roller. The student may rotate it to search for rudiments as needed.

Hand-guidance rigs attached to the piano, usually an upright or **square** grand, are quite numerous in the U.S. Patent files. Many include some sort of sliding wrist-supports or "carriages," plus statements regarding proper right-angle arm position or posture philosophy in general. Some make no claim regarding novel invention, purpose, or necessity but instead claim only a novel way of attaching the rig to or neatly folding under a piano or organ, and in a few cases, free-standing in front of or just beneath the keyboard (or writing desk). One such invention in 1893 by Rebecca Kirk of Stratford, Ontario (U.S. Patent No. 492,889), specified an adjustable keyboard-width frame on its own legs that would fit neatly under the keyboard and be pulled out when needed. It contained a sort of track for two rolling arm-rest carriages, each incorporating a large recessed roller allowing front to rear motion. Rather than necessarily promoting specific technique, the main purpose was to reduce fatigue at the keyboard or writing desk.

Many of the patents for hand-guidance rigs attached to the piano included metal spring or elastic elements for relatively abstract finger exercises positioned on the keyboard itself. Ideas for free-standing and portable abstract exercising units began to appear near the mid-point of the nineteenth century. A common feature was a splaying device for increasing the span between fingers by forcing adjacent digits over a

(usually padded) wedge fixture. This aspect was possibly the most logical and helpful part of such devices if not pushed to the extreme.

It was certainly a safer means of achieving some degree of added flexibility without eventually resorting to "digital tenotomy" (or ring-finger operation), a procedure attributed to (or at least described by) Dr. William S. Forbes, in which the tendonous bands are severed between the fourth and fifth fingers. This relatively dangerous practice was being increasingly encouraged during the last quarter of the century, and numerous articles debating the risks and benefits appeared in scientific, medical, and music journals on both sides of the Atlantic. The controversy lingered on into the twentieth century, and a pro-side personality would occasionally exhibit a talented student who had undergone the operation and supposedly showed marked improvement.

Several devices were patented to address only the matter of increasing finger span or height, usually requiring the participant to force adjacent fingers over sized wedges or adjustable two-part wedge elements. One adjustable idea was "An Apparatus for Stretching the Hand and Strengthening Fingers and Wrists" by Richard Pitcher of London, England, in 1915, British Patent No. 3870, followed in 1916 with U.S. Patent No. 1,174,278. An 1899 example, the "Hand Extender" designed by Frederick Crane of Massachusetts, U.S. Patent No. 623,235, involved only passive exercises. A threaded rod adjusted the distance between two finger slings attached to it (one containing a nut with the corresponding thread count), in which any pair of fingers (not necessarily adjacent) could be forced apart for extended periods. Apparently the device did a little better than only achieving patent protection. Several early-twentieth-century advertisements in *Etude* indicated that the "Pianist's Hand Extender" was available for $2.

Free-standing portable and user-wearing exercise gadgetry was patented in many varying forms and given exotic and confusing nomenclature, some of it perhaps originally intended to be commercially distinctive but later becoming rather generic as competition expanded. Those machines patented or sold as "digitoriums" were, as the name implies, concerned mostly with finger and wrist development. They tended to be a simple box device having five spring keys, usually with adjustable tension, and with some other exercising or splaying element.

A relatively early and somewhat successfully marketed example is "Marks' Digitorium" patented in 1871 (U.S. Patent No. 117,791) by Myer Marks of London, England. An earlier version had received British Patent No. 3076 in 1866. It is merely a wooden box having five exercising keys (fixed tension in the earlier version), a pull-out adjustable wrist support, and four splaying wedges, one each on the top, back, and sides. Examples of it are at the Royal College of Music, London, and in at least one private collection.

A more elaborate form of digitorium could perhaps be classed under the heading of hand-gymnasia, in which several varying exercise stations are mounted on a board for use at a table. An early example is the "Chirogymnaste," patented in 1840 by a Parisian piano dealer, Casimir Martin. It included nine small exercise devices directed at finger span and dexterity. Two different models of it are preserved at the Musée instrumental du Conservatoire de Bruxelles. Of those that received patents, the one that actually went into reasonable production and sales was the "Technicon" or "Pianist's Hand Gymnasium," patented in the U.S. (No. 327,918) and six other countries in 1885 by James Brotherhood, a Canadian Railway official then living in Stratford, Ontario.

It was offered in two basic styles: "Teacher's and Student's," which essentially meant larger and smaller. The Teacher's Technicon involved four exercise stations mounted on the board. Front and center was a quintet of adjustable tension spring keys made of oak with short celluloid key tops. The adjustment was simply the location of the sliding fulcrum blocks underneath. Mounted over that unit was a vertical padded A-frame for stretching finger span. The exercising stations at the sides of the board were directed at arm and wrist development. That, to the user's right, consisted of a lever device above which was a steel rod containing a sliding iron cylinder weight. A set screw locked it into position for desired weight level. The arm, palm up or down, with the elbow resting on an optical cushion, lifted the device to exercise all the muscles affected in either position. To the user's left was a similar device in the form of a rocker-arm with spring tension that required a pull-down motion.

The Brotherhood Technicon was regularly advertised in various East Coast and European music journals around the turn of this century and sold by dealers such as J. Howard Foote in New York. An example of it is preserved at the National Museum of American History, Division of Musical History, object No. 66.144. (See illustration.)

Like most any abstract exercising or practice gadget to hit the market, the Technicon received pro and con coverage in the music journals. Criticism would lead one to believe that Brotherhood was just another contraption inventor. In fact, he was a fairly serious music-educator who published numerous articles on physiology and music, some of which were papers read before meetings of the Music Teachers' National Association in 1885, 1888, and 1889. Criticism in some cases accused Brotherhood of using MTNA as a forum to increase Technicon sales.

A J. Howard Foote catalogue of 1899 boasts the Technicon as "Recommended by the Greatest Living Pianists, and especially so by the late Abbe Liszt." Two endorsement letters are offered, beginning with "What the Abbe List [sic] wrote":

Weimar, October 14, 1885

Mr. J. Brotherhood

Dear Sir: Unfortunately I am too old now to derive benefit from your invention. I recommend, however, the "Technicon" to younger, energetic natures of whom there will be no scarcity.

Cordially yours, F. Liszt

One can easily interpret **Liszt's** clever comments as having made no commitment at all. This is followed by a 265-word letter to Brotherhood from William Sherwood, which is also curiously vague. Only in the final sentence does he allude to the Technicon by closing with "... which piano players will have to thank you and your modest invention for in a superlative degree as soon as they are able to know its value." The majority of famous-name endorsements for methods and technical equipment came from parties who achieved their status without ever using the methods or items involved.

Some free-standing exercise machine ideas were patented to offer passive exercise or finger therapy. Norace A. Nathan of Philadelphia received U.S. Patent No. 18,857 for his "flexomanus." The device has five finger-rings suspended alternately high and low from a rod that looks like an automobile crank-shaft. Crank handles at either side rotate the shaft with one hand while the other places the fingers in the rings to receive the rapid motion generated by the machine. It includes two integral clamps to secure it to a table or piano. A similar device secured French Patent No. 74,037 for August Vincent of Paris in 1866. Had it gone into production, a catchy trade-name would surely have been necessary to replace "Invention pour des perfectionnements apportés aux machines à délier les doigts." Instead of inserting the fingers into rings, as on Nathan's Flexomanus, they were to be placed directly and constantly on five pianolike keys with a padded rod supporting the wrist. The hand crank and a system of cams rapidly move the keys in any of a number of sequences that could be preset.

Numerous exercising and guidance rigs were designed and patented to be worn by the user. In the guidance-support category, U.S. Patent No. 627,646 was issued to District of Columbia resident Hugo Kuerschner for a "Hand Support for Piano Students" in 1899. This consisted of a strap worn over the neck and shoulders and terminating at each end in an arm-supporting loop attached with a swivel arrangement not unlike fishing-tackle connections. The overall length was adjustable but no mention is made of any elastic elements. One wonders how the inventor achieved his claim of "sufficient freedom" to reach all parts of the keyboard. Turn-of-the-century advertisements indicate that "Kuerschner's Hand Support for Beginners on the Piano" was available for fifty cents.

Another category of user-worn gadgetry involved various wrist and finger weights in the form of a cuff, bracelet, and finger ring(s). An early French patent (No. 30509) was granted in 1857 to François-Jules Monestier for "Un appareil dit: Agili-Main." It consists of a weighted bracelet and five weighted finger-rings that could be worn at either the first or second phalanx. Various weighted cuff and digital attachments (including gloves minus finger tips) were patented on both sides of the Atlantic.

A number of patented hand and arm-worn gadgets look very much like either medieval torture devices or orthopedic equipment. They were sometimes called dactylions and took any form from simple elastic exercising bands surrounding several or all fingers to complicated

frames with prepositioned, spring-loaded finger loops that exercised digits and supposedly controlled finger spacing. An example of the simplistic would be the "Un sort de dactylion dit: Veloce-Mano," French Patent No. 71075, awarded to Martine Emilie Louise Marie Faivre of Paris, 1866. It is nothing more than three elastic bands, each folded over in a figure-eight and joining two adjacent fingers for spreading and lifting exercise away from the keyboard. An example of the complex would be the "Manual Gymnasium for Musicians," U.S. Patent No. 494,197, granted to Joseph Hall of Kirmington, England, in 1893 with a British patent application still pending from the year before. It involves a bracelet for each wrist containing five finger rings worn at the medial phalanges. The rings are attached to elastic or narrow-gauge coiled metal springs that maintain tension and front to rear position by means of a strap leading back to the arm just above the elbow. The strap and spring arrangement is reversible to favor exercising either flexor or extensor muscles.

One American example actually went into limited production. One of the illustrations accompanying this article shows L. E. Levassor's Piano Dactylion as advertised in a March 1888 issue of *Kunkel's Musical Review*, St. Louis. It is quite similar to a "Finger-Exercising Device for Pianists," minus thumb (sp)ring, for which Alfons G. Gardner of New Orleans received U.S. Patent No. 272,951 in 1883. Both essentially develop an 1856 French patent, No. 28737, granted to William Prangley of Salisbury, England, which included only one spring-loop for exercising the fourth or ring finger. Most hand-worn dactylions were meant for use while at the keyboard.

One other miscellaneous user-worn gadget idea deserves mention for sheer novelty, if nothing else. In 1882, Steven Emory of Newton, Massachusetts, received U.S. Patent No. 253,857 for his "Legato Monitor for Piano Forte Players." This is not strictly a legato monitor in what pianistically came to be understood as the truest meaning of the term (discussed below). Emory's idea was an excess motion detector in the form of a bracelet(s) worn on one or both wrists. Mounted on the bracelet is a strip of spring metal in the form of a letter U turned on its side. The lower leg of the U has fixed to its end, vertically, a small bell. The upper end contains a down-pointing rod that terminates in a ball shape. This is the (external) clapper positioned quite close to the bell's rim. A wire and screw-eye adjustment mechanism farther back in the U-frame maintains a specific distance between bell and clapper. Undue motion in the execution of practically any keyboard exercise would set off the bell to warn the player of poor form. Or, it supposedly can be adjusted to sound "only when the accented notes are to be played." Instead of sustaining such torture aurally, the device is designed also to be used without the bell so the student can receive the warning taps directly on the wrist.

Elastic offered various possibilities to the inventor attempting to sell low-cost and portable exercise gadgetry to pianists and violinists. In 1894 Julia Strong of Brooklyn, New York, received U.S. Patent No. 530,669 for her "Exercising Machine." The patent includes seven claims for a simple strip of elastic terminating at one end in an arm or hand loop, with a foot loop at the other end. Forearm exercise seems to have been its main purpose. Strong did put it on the market on her own under the trade name "Gyastik." An advertisement in an 1898 *Etude* offers it for one dollar with two elastic strips, one "heavy" and one "light." A second dollar would buy the deluxe model with a clamp-on stand for attachment to a table or a door frame. Similar, and advertised by Theodore Presser in *Etude* during the 1890s, was the "Bidwell Pocket Hand Exerciser" for pianists and violinists. It was essentially the same thing but with an improved(?) stirrup-like foot loop and other finger-ring-terminated strips of elastic (rubber) hanging along the main one. It sold for $2 and apparently afforded more varied opportunities for exercise than the Gyastik.

Many free-standing exercisers submitted for patent protection took the form of a simple keyboard in a box having only five (or an octave) of keys. They usually featured some form of tension or key-dip adjustability. Several patents in this category illustrate devices that are complete in themselves but infer that the range could be extended to full keyboard compass. This, in effect, gets into a category of silent practice keyboards, some designed to fold in half for better portability. Such a folding keyboard manufactured by Wilhelm Gertz of Hamburg is preserved in the Smithsonian Division of Musical History, Cat. No. 299,842.

Those of limited compass sometimes retained the name Digitorium, such as U.S. Patent No. 307,863 issued to Adolph Lothhammer of Sacramento, California, in 1884, or the "Piano-Touch Instructor," U.S. Patent No. 643,028 by Alois Allmuth of New York City, 1900. Those claiming or intended to have full compass received obvious names such as "Exercising Keyboard" and "Dummy Piano." Most of the devices in all these categories were conceived by minor figures in the inventor or music world, but at least one well-known music-educator personality submitted an idea to the Patent Office. The eminent Boston-area pianist and teacher at the New England Conservatory, Carlyle Petersilia, received U.S. Patent No. 329,592 in 1885 for a "Mute Piano." The patent drawings show a simple silent keyboard **action** having a combination lead-weight and down-pressure spring return. Any adjustability would apparently require rebending or replacing springs individually, although the inventor does suggest a method for disengaging the springs when the device is not in use.

Some instrument patents in the silent or toneless keyboard category claim their usefulness as a legato monitor. The concept of playing legato (in the linear sense) at the keyboard and the use of mechanical ways to achieve it is rather limited to the fourth quarter of the nineteenth century and lingered on into the twentieth, especially in America. Legato can be interpreted to mean various things depending on any number of factors. However, late-nineteenth-century piano pedagogues increasingly tended to consider it to mean the progression from one note to another, perfectly timed so that the former ends exactly when the succeeding begins, or, overlaps it for a split second. For some parties it was a concept to be employed with mechanical efficiency, regardless of repertoire.

It is easily a debatable concept, but many attempts and patents were made to devise toneless keyboard instruments with audible metallic click sounds on the down-stroke and more often on both up and down strokes of each key. The click(s) of the key(s) depressed coinciding exactly with the click(s) of the key(s) released, in theory, indicated a properly executed legato, so-called, when those motions, well-rehearsed, were applied to the piano (a well-**regulated** piano, one should add). The concept was relatively prevalent at the time, and it most likely owes its development, in part, to the elaborate physiology-oriented teaching method of Mr. and Mrs. Almon K. Virgil. Their teaching instruments included the "technic table" and, in particular, the **Virgil Practice Clavier**. It was the most successful of all to incorporate the click principle in preference to musical pitches. (See Virgil Practice Clavier.)

The Virgils' operations and methods were extensive and well known during their nearly fifty years in business, and they eventually encountered mild attempts at competition. Lyon & Healy, Chicago, for example, devoted page 386 of its 482-page 1925 catalog to advertising its "Folding Valise Practice Keyboards." Four- and seven-octave models are offered. Both have "down and up clicks standard," and the copy includes a paragraph explaining the purpose(s) of the clicks.

The legato monitor practice-keyboard ideas submitted to the Patent Office sometimes carried matters to extremes. Louis Illmer, Jr., of Washington, D.C., submitted an eighteen-claim application, which in 1898 received U.S. Patent No. 610,448 for a "Mute Clavier." Virgil's commercial use of the term "clavier" was already beginning to reassociate its generic meaning to include toneless practice-keyboards in general. Illmer's legato monitor idea involved a mechanism for a key not released in time to be trapped in the down-stroke position when the following key was depressed, or, if released too soon, to sound a warning bell. Many of the inventor's eighteen claims concern only minor mechanism details, in addition to an integral music rack.

Patent applications were also submitted for methods to install a monitor click mechanism into the piano itself. This concerned upright instruments in which the action above the keys would be shifted upward and out-of-play, and the keys would then operate any of the various legato monitor elements ranging from simple to absurdly complex. Various patents in this relatively small category claim that such a mechanism can be installed into existing pianos. While technically possible, all the patent drawings show mechanisms which, from a bottom-line cost point of view, would only have been commercially practical if installed as original action parts at the factory.

A simple example would be one for which Edmund Pfeifer of Austin, Texas, received U.S. Patent No. 878,421 in 1908. Although he called it a "Mute Attachment for Pianos," the strings do not sound when the device is engaged. The action is shifted upward and out-of-play and the key ends then yield an adequate noise on their up and down strokes for the so-called legato monitor or other silent practice as desired.

Some rather more complex versions of this idea were patented and, in fact, preceded the Pfeifer plan. In 1895 J. H. Salmon of Cambridge, Massachusetts, received U.S. Patent No. 547,810 for an "Exercising Attachment for Pianos." Like the Pfeifer design, a lever shifts the sticker and hammer action upward and out of contact with the keys. The click effect then involves an elaborate set of "rocker arm" striker elements and elevated swiveling click rails. A version of this elevated click rail mechanism is the main action feature of the "Tekniklavier," an improved form of the Virgil practice clavier developed by Amos C. Bergman for Mrs. A. M. Virgil shortly after 1900. The Salmon patent predates Bergman's first patent (1901) by six years and Bergman's application of such mechanism pertains only to a straight practice clavier not combined with a piano action.

Those patents calling for combination piano and practice clavier-legato monitor complexity would perhaps rate Francis W. Hale of Boston as chief designer of the absurd. Two U.S. patents he obtained in 1889, Nos. 396,155 and 396,156, utilize sophisticated weight-of-touch control, a complex mechanical means of disengaging the action, and an electrical click or "sounder" mechanism operated by open or closed circuits for "detecting by an electric signal errors in the relative time of striking the keys." His next patent, in 1892, No. 474,827, calls for a similar electrical mechanism to operate alerting "sounders" (clicks), bells, or a dial, and the key shifting and tension design has been updated with even more complexity, much of it to be installed just under the keyboard as well as within the **case**.

His fourth patent, No. 493,622 in 1893, returns to a more practical idea: a "Pianoforte Mute." The practice clavier-legato monitor concept is not involved, but instead he offers a clever means of installing a felt piano-muting strip. His essential claim is a design that swivels the unit into position between the hammer-heads and strings but when not in use is positioned not to be in a technician's way and need not be removed when tuning or regulating.

It is certainly accurate to say that most of the keyboard physiology inventions submitted to the world's patent offices never appeared as working objects. In nearly all cases patent models were not submitted, including those ideas that did go into limited production or even successful production. A survey of the would-be inventors involved would probably show that some were simply inventors per se, with no overriding interest in music necessarily. Aside from the better-known music educators involved, a certain number of the lesser or unknown parties appear to have had a basic interest in music, judging from a few recurring patent applications in this area. An early American example would be Ernest Von Heeringen, whose 1849 patent for a hand and arm guide, "Piano Attachment," is described above. Earlier that year he obtained U.S. Patent No. 6,328 for "Improvements in Musical Notation," in which he claimed a "new note nomenclature" including different terminology for intervals and a color system for sharps and flats.

Piano-inventing mania prompted the following, which appeared in a March 1884 issue of *Etude*:

> An English musician, W. Ritchie, has invented a hand warmer for piano-practice in cold weather. It consists of an oblong lamp or stove, which is adjusted to the front of the keyboard, near the middle octaves. It burns four small lights, and by burning the best kerosene oil, no fumes are caused in the rooms. The next thing we will hear (is) that principals of our female colleges will be investigating the invention. Who will now supplement this invention with a feather-bed piano stool?

Robert E. Sheldon

Bibliography

Gerig, Reginald R. *Famous Pianists and Their Technique.* Washington-New York: Robert B. Luce, Inc., 1974.

Huron, David B. *Physiology and Music in the Late Industrial Revolution: A Catalogue of Sources.* Monograph, Department of Music, Conrad Grebel College, University of Waterloo, 1981.

Loesser, Arthur. *Men, Women and Pianos: A Social History.* New York: Simon & Schuster, 1954.

Logier, Johann Bernhard. *An Explanation and Description of the Royal Patent Chiroplast or Hand-Director.* London: Clementi & Co., 1816.

Nahm, Dorothea A. "The Virgil Clavier and Keyboard Pedagogy Method." Dissertation, The Catholic University of America, 1983.

The New Grove Dictionary of Music and Musicians. S.V. "Logier, Johann Bernard," by David Charlton. Vol. 11, Pp. 132–33, 1980.

Raspé, Paul. "Pianos, virtuoses et instruments de torture à l'époque romantique." *Clés pour la Musique* No 31/32 (July–August 1971): 11–14.

KEYBOARDS

The keyboard of the piano was patterned on those of the clavichord, organ, and harpsichord as they were at the end of the seventeenth century. Usual terms used for keyboard are: French, *clavier*; Italian, *tastiera*; German, *Klaviatur* or *Tastatur*. Throughout the history of the piano the keyboard has remained basically the same, with the **keys** for accidentals shorter than and above those for naturals, normally contrasting in color, and located at the back of the keyboard. Like many Italian makers, **Bartolomeo Cristofori** used boxwood for naturals and rosewood (darker) or an **ebony** covering for accidentals. During the eighteenth century, English and French pianos on the whole had white material (**ivory**, etc.) for naturals and dark material (stained wood or ebony veneer) for accidentals, whereas most German and Austrian makers used the opposite, wood stained black for naturals and white (usually ivory) for accidentals. Around the beginning of the nineteenth century, the convention of white naturals and black accidentals became universal and has remained stable to the present. The type of piano, whether **grand**, **square**, or **upright**, makes no difference for the keyboard. Some experiments and variations in keyboard design will be noted below.

Range. From the outset each note had one key (some split-key designs will be described below). Cristofori's earliest known piano (1720, Metropolitan Museum of Art, New York), has a range of four octaves and a fourth (C–f^3), but that of 1726 in Leipzig has only four octaves (C–c^3). This reflects variations in range available in Italian harpsichords. One occasionally finds the short octave, borrowed from harpsichord design, in early eighteenth-century fortepianos.

In the second half of the eighteenth century most pianos had five octaves, ordinarily FF–f^3.

Some early squares went down only to GG (often omitting GG#), and a few instruments went up to g^3 or even to a^3.

In 1790 or 1791, at the urging of the pianist Jan Ladislav Dussek, **John Broadwood** in London began to make squares and grands with five octaves and a fifth, FF–c^4, a range that persisted until the 1830s. Experiments with six-octave ranges began in 1795 with Johann Jakob Könnicke in Vienna and Broadwood in 1796, and they became more common toward 1810. On the whole, English and French makers designed for a CC–c^4 range, whereas Germans and Austrians used FF–f^4. Around 1815, some makers began to extend the compass to six octaves and a fourth, CC–f^4, which became the upper standard for many years, though narrower ranges continued to be available.

These extensions of range, increasingly demanded by musicians and composers, must have influenced the introduction in the 1820s of iron into the **framing**, for the added **strings** imposed enormous additional tension on frames. In the 1830s further extensions to g^4 and a^4 were common, and **Sébastien Erard** attempted seven octaves (CC–c^5) in 1824. **Franz Liszt** played his Paris debut on a seven-octave Erard that year, but it was far from perfected, and even at age thirteen Liszt was hard on pianos, breaking strings and knocking the instrument out of tune. During the 1840s, the seven octaves AAA–a^4 began to be commonly used, becoming in the 1850s the usual range for grands and increasingly for uprights. The experimental mood of the nineteenth century may be gauged by the fact that **Jean-Henri Pape** of Paris made an eight-octave piano, which was played in public in the 1840s, and in 1845 he **patented** a piano of eight-and-a-half octaves but probably never built it.

Around 1880 an additional third to c^5 came to be standard for grands, though the seven-octave range remained available for another twenty-five years or so. In the twentieth century, extensions downward have been made, especially by **Bösendorfer** in Austria, which has made pianos with seven octaves and a fifth (FFF–c^5) and eight octaves (CCC–c^5). Only a few composers have written for the additional range, which modifies the keyboard only in that the keys below AAA are either painted black or covered by a wooden flap when the notes are not to be used, in order to prevent the pianist's inadvertently reaching too far for a bottom note.

Experimental and Unconventional Keyboards. Some experimental keyboards were not at all radical. A keyboard designed by Emil Olbrich, a Berlin pianist, only lowered the accidental keys, easing the pianist's reaching them.

Split Keys. This experiment, to be found in earlier harpsichords, is also found in a few pianos in the eighteenth century. In order to accommodate the instruments to both a "just" and a "mean-tone" temperament, the accidental keys were divided across the center, and the player used either the front half or the back half to play two different sets of strings. Thus one part of the C# key would play C#, the other D♭. A plan view of such a keyboard in a **Zumpe** square of 1766 is in Harding, Plate IX.

Transposing Keyboards. **Transposing** functions do not affect the design of the keyboard, as they work by moving the entire keyboard. A late-eighteenth-century transposing square by Johann Matthäus **Schmahl** allows transposition by pushing the keyboard in, thus moving the **hammers** under different strings, the strings being parallel to the keyboard. Later transposers, even into the twentieth century (Irving Berlin's Weser Brothers transposing upright is in the Smithsonian Institution), worked by moving the keyboard sideways. Another way of providing transposition was to build a moveable false keyboard above the real one, so that one could play in any key by correlating the false keyboard to the real one. Patents for such false keyboards were awarded to Edward Ryley in 1801 and to **Pleyel**, Wolff & Cie. in 1872.

Concave Keyboards. Several efforts were made to alter the straight line of the keyboard, with the thought that the arms and hands could move more naturally over a concave keyboard, an idea also to be found in organs. About 1824, Johann Georg Staufer and Max Haidinger in Vienna incorporated the idea in a few pianos. Similar ideas are found in the work of Wolfel in Paris in the middle of the nineteenth century, and in an 1881 German patent by Gustav Neuhaus. In 1907, **Ferdinand Clutsam** patented the same design in Germany, to be found in a few instruments. About 1908 Albert Schultz made a *Strahlenklaviatur*, where the keys converge toward each other, but the keyboard ends in a straight line. An anonymous, probably

American, square of the late nineteenth century with a concave keyboard is in the collection of the Schubert Club, St. Paul, Minnesota.

Microtonal Keyboards. Pianos designed to play microtones have usually used the standard keyboard, sometimes with more than one manual. Two- and three-manual pianos with strings tuned a quarter-tone apart were built by such makers as **Grotrian** and Förster in the 1920s under the influence of composers Alois Hába, Ivan Vishnegradsky, and others. The Mexican composer Julián Carrillo worked up his *metamorfoseadores*, a series of pianos with **tunings** from $^1/_3$ to $^1/_{16}$ tones, using progressively smaller ranges in order to employ the standard keyboard (the $^1/_{16}$-tone piano used 97 keys to span one octave). The **Carl Sauter** factory in Spaichingen, Germany, built a grand in 1947 and uprights in 1957–1958 to Carrillo's specifications.

Multi-manual Keyboards. In addition to those for microtonal tuning, other multi-manual keyboards have been attempted. Könnicke's 1795 experiment with a six-octave range used a six-manual keyboard with six sets of strings in order to allow playing in every key with "just" tuning. Jozef Wieniawski designed reversed keyboards, two superposed pianos with one conventional keyboard and one with the treble on the left and the bass on the right. Patented by the French firm of E. J. Mangeot in 1876, the design enabled the same **fingerings** for the same passages by both hands and no doubt eliminated cross-hand playing. From 1922 to 1932, **Emanuel Moór** produced two-manual pianos of his own design, with one set of strings, the upper manual playing an octave above the lower, with couplers permitting the simultaneous use of both.

The Jankó Keyboard. In 1882, **Paul von Jankó** developed a radically redesigned "sequential" keyboard that William A. B. Lunn, using the name Arthur Wallbridge, had invented in 1843. Lunn used two rows of keys in whole tones, the lower row from C#, the upper from C. An earlier "chromatic keyboard" (with only one manual) had been presented in 1791 at the Berlin Academy by Johann Rohleder, with "naturals" and "accidentals" alternating, the whole-tone scale from C as the "naturals," the whole-tone scale from C# as the "accidentals." Something similar was advocated in the 1870s by the Chroma-Verein des

Gleichstufigen Tonsystems. Jankó extended the idea by triplicating the touch-pieces, giving three places for the finger to play each note. The advantages included a greatly extended reach for the hand because an octave is only 13 centimeters instead of the standard 16½ centimeters, identical fingerings for every major and every minor scale, identical distances for the hand for each interval, and alternative fingerings involving moving from one pair of rows to others. Some experiments with adapting it to **synthesizer** keyboards are said to be currently under way.

Edwin M. Good

Bibliography

Harding, Rosamond E.M. *The Piano-Forte: Its History Traced to the Great Exhibition of 1851.* Cambridge: Cambridge University Press, 1933. Reprints. New York: Da Capo Press, 1973; Old Woking, Surrey: Gresham Books, 1978.

Marcuse, Sibyl. *A Survey of Musical Instruments:* 234–242. New York: W.W. Norton, 1975.

Ripin, Edwin M., et al. *The New Grove: Piano.* : 70–74. New York: W.W. Norton, 1988.

KEYFRAME

The keyframe is a part of the inner wooden structure of the piano upon which the **keys** and the **action** rest. The keyframe (called *Schlitte* in German) may slide in or out of the piano **case** for repair work on the **keyboard** or action.

Peggy Flanagan Baird

KEYS

The keys of a piano are weighted wooden levers, between fourteen and sixteen inches in length, that a player presses to produce sound. The playing end of a key is usually covered with **ivory**, **ebony**, or plastic, while the remainder of the key is of natural wood and hidden from view by the **fallboard**.

Peggy Flanagan Baird

KEYSLIP

The keyslip is a removable wooden strip that extends the full front width of the piano, just under the **keys**, and is intended to cover the **keyframe**. It is stained to match the piano's casework.

Peggy Flanagan Baird

KIMBALL PIANO AND ORGAN COMPANY

The American piano and organ building firm of Kimball was founded by William Wallace Kimball (b. Rumford, Maine, 22 March 1828; d. Chicago, 16 December 1904). Kimball had no particular interest in music, having instead spent time as a teacher, insurance salesman, and real estate agent before his entry into the field that was to be his life's work. The company was founded in 1857 when Kimball traded a parcel of land in Decorah, Iowa, for four Grovesteen and Truslow **square pianos** and set up a retail business in the corner of a jewelry store at 51 South Clark Street in Chicago, under the name of W. W. Kimball and Company. Kimball's ability as a promoter became obvious as the business prospered despite a depressed economic climate. In 1864 he took sales rooms in the prestigious Crosby Opera House at 63 Washington Street. Pianos offered for sale included J & C Fischer, **Chickering**, Hallet & Davis, F. C. Lighte, and Emerson pianos, as well as the commercial pianos introduced by Joseph P. Hale (fl. 1860–1890). All of these instruments were produced by east-coast makers. The reed organ was as popular as the piano and sold for considerably less, often being used by dealers as an introductory instrument leading to the later sale of a more expensive piano. Organs sold by Kimball included the Taylor & Farley, Smith American, and Shoninger makes. The business continued to prosper but its progress was cut short by the Chicago fire of 1871, in which all of Kimball's holdings were destroyed. Though the firm suffered losses in excess of $100,000, Kimball set up operations in his home, and by the end of the decade sales had been posted in excess of one million dollars.

Kimball felt increasingly limited by his dependence on eastern sources for his goods, since deliveries were not always timely nor supplies adequate. Accordingly, he made moves to produce instruments of his own, concentrating at first on reed organs. The first instruments had **actions** built by the J. G. Earhuff Company, with **cases** made by outside contractors and the completed organs assembled in the Kimball repair shops. In 1880 production began of instruments built entirely by Kimball. In 1882 a 96,000-square-foot factory was built for the manufacture of reed organs, and the company was soon producing 15,000 instruments annually, making Kimball the world's largest organmaker. It was also in 1882 that the firm was incorporated, with Kimball, his brother-in-law Albert Cone (d. 1900), and Edwin S. Conway as principals.

For the reasons noted above, Kimball soon felt the need to produce his own pianos. In addition, it was felt that he could produce instruments of as good or better quality at a lower price than the east-coast makers. In 1887 a five-story building adjoining the organ factory was begun, and in 1888 piano production was commenced, five hundred instruments being produced the first year. The first pianos were less than satisfactory, and innovations instituted by a technician named Guricke, an ex-employee of **Steinway**, and Peter Tapper, who had been trained in the **Bechstein** factory, brought about significant improvements in quality. These improvements doubtless were instrumental in enabling Kimball to receive high honors at the World's Columbian Exposition held in Chicago from May to November, 1893. There was considerable antagonism between the east-coast makers and those of Chicago, and several leading eastern makers, including Steinway, declined to exhibit on the grounds that favoritism would be shown to local firms. Much of the dispute was caused by differences in philosophy. Whereas the older makers tended to depend on name and reputation to sell pianos, Kimball's success hinged on aggressive sales techniques and a thorough monitoring of the cost of each item and process that went into an instrument. This resulted in lower prices, which further exacerbated the dispute. In addition to numerous sales rooms, Kimball kept thirty-five to forty salesmen on the road to seek business in the most remote areas.

In 1890 a pipe-organ department was added under the supervision of Frederic W. Hedgeland, who had been trained in his family's organ-works in England. Kimball's first entry into the pipe-organ field was a novel "portable" instrument, hardly larger than an upright piano. The largest model had two manuals and pedals. Free reeds were utilized for the pedal stops. In the first half of the twentieth century, Kimball produced several notable organs in the Chicago area, undertook the rebuilding of the Mormon

Tabernacle organ at Salt Lake City (1901), and constructed a large instrument for the Municipal Auditorium at Pretoria, South Africa. Pipe-organ manufacture ceased in 1942 with a total of 7,326 having been built. Reed-organ production, once a mainstay of the company, was halted in 1922 after 403,390 organs had been produced.

The company was also active in the field of automatic piano-playing devices, their first being the "Artist Mechanism" of 1901. A **push-up** device attachable to any piano, it was superseded in 1904 by a newly designed self-contained mechanism. In contrast to many other firms that employed mechanisms built by independent suppliers, Kimball built its own, although the **Welte** Licensee reproducing mechanism built by the Auto Pneumatic Action Company of New York was also used. In 1895 Kimball founded a subsidiary, the Whitney Piano and Supply Manufacturing Company, to build piano actions for the trade. The latter part of the plan was never carried out, the Whitney name instead being applied to a piano manufactured by Kimball for the medium-priced market. Another piano, the Hinze, was intended for the low-priced market. From 1915 to 1925 Kimball also manufactured a highly successful phonograph perfected by Albert A. Huseby, an employee since 1894.

Throughout its history the Kimball firm was aided in its growth by the utilization of family members, although Edwin S. Conway, an employee since 1876 and later vice-president, was unrelated. Kimball's brother-in-law Albert Cone eventually became treasurer. In 1883 Kimball's nephew, Wallace W. Lufkin, joined the firm, eventually becoming president, as did another nephew, Curtis N. Kimball (d. 1936). On his death he was succeeded by Lufkin, who died in 1945. In that year, W.W. Kimball, Jr., a great nephew of the founder and son of C. N. Kimball, became president. Despite adverse conditions occasioned by the depression, the firm succeeded, but due to an overly conservative outlook, Kimball was reluctant to build the popular small pianos, particularly the thirty-seven-inch **spinets**, which aided other firms in their recovery. During World War II Kimball produced aircraft parts for Boeing, Lockheed, and Douglas. After the war Kimball resumed production but was unable to regain an adequate share of the market. W. W. Kimball, Jr., then president,

made a number of unfortunate decisions that helped edge the company toward insolvency. Lufkin's heirs exerted pressure to retire their sizable stock holdings, and in 1948 Kimball borrowed heavily and in 1956 sold property to buy them out. At the same time, in spite of the dismal financial situation, a lavish new plant was built in Melrose Park, Illinois, a suburb of Chicago, at a cost of two million dollars. The new plant proved inefficient and inoperable, and this, coupled with labor problems and a lack of sales and marketing direction, brought the company to the brink of insolvency by 1958. In 1959 the company was acquired by the Jasper Corporation of Jasper, Indiana, a manufacturer of cabinets and office furniture, and in 1961 the firm was moved to Jasper. The Jasper firm, headed by Arnold Habig, had no previous experience in piano building and had to begin from the ground up. Initially quality was a problem, and three out of every five instruments were returned to the factory. With effort and experience quality was improved, and in 1966 Kimball acquired the prestigious Viennese firm of **Bösendorfer** (est. 1828), incorporating some of that firm's features and techniques in its own instruments. Realizing that the name Kimball had far more currency with the public at large than did Jasper, in the mid-seventies the name of the firm was changed to Kimball International.

About 1960 Kimball attempted to enter the electronic-organ market with instruments utilizing the photoelectric principle in which photoelectric cells "read" waveforms from revolving discs. The instruments proved impractical, and subsequent organs used tones generated by twelve oscillators subject to frequency division. In 1980 Kimball purchased certain elements of the C. G. Conn Corporation to form a new company named Conn Keyboards, Inc. In the same year Kimball acquired the **Krakauer** Piano Company (est. 1869) and operated it as a separate facility until its closure in 1985. In 1984 Kimball introduced a line of electronic organs using computerized technology and capable of greatly expanded tonal possibilities. Kimball also owns the British firm of Herrburger Brooks, suppliers of Schwander and Langer actions. The keyboard division of the firm became known as the Kimball Piano and Organ Company and, later, Kimball Keyboard Products.

Kimball currently produces **grands** in 4'5",

5'2", 6'7", and 9' sizes. The 9-foot model is made in the Bösendorfer factory in Vienna. Vertical styles include a 42-inch console and a 46-inch studio piano. Kimball no longer makes spinets. Through the Jasper-American Manufacturing Company, Kimball produces inexpensive console pianos under various names as well as **stencil pianos** for the trade in Kimball's plant in Reynosa, Mexico. Names under which pianos are manufactured include Kimball, Conn, Jasper-American, W. W. Kimball, Hinze, Harrison, DeVoe & Sons, Whittaker, Becker, La Petite, and others. Kimball International is a Fortune-500 company with diverse interests in furniture, cabinetry for the trade, electronics, and plastics.

James Howard Richards

Bibliography

Armstrong, Durrell. *Player Piano Co., Inc. 1976–1977 Catalog*. Wichita, Kansas: Player Piano Co., Inc., 1977.

Bowers, Q. David. *Encyclopedia of Automatic Musical Instruments*. Vestal, New York: The Vestal Press, 1972.

Bradley, Van Allen. *Music for the Millions*. Chicago: Henry Regnery Company, 1957.

"Conn Keyboards Inc. to Make Full Line." *The Music Trades* 128 (July 1980): 22,24.

Dolge, Alfred. *Pianos and Their Makers*. Covina, Cal.: Covina Publishing Company, 1911. Reprint. New York: Dover Publications, Inc., 1972.

Fine, Larry. *The Piano Book*. 2nd edition. Boston: Brookside Press, 1990.

"How Kimball Ticks Without Time Clocks." *The Music Trades* 127(September 1979): 86–94.

"Kimball's 125 Year Saga." *The Music Trades* 130(October 1982): 46–52, 54, 96.

"Kimball Vows to Lead Industry With New Organs, Olympic Promo." *The Music Trades* 132(July 1984): 104–05.

The New Grove Dictionary of Musical Instruments. Edited by Stanley Sadie. S. v. "Electronic Instruments," by Hugh Davies; "Kimball," by Barbara Owen. London: Macmillan; Washington D.C.: Grove's Dictionaries, 1984.

Ochse, Orpha. *The History of the Organ in the United States*. Bloomington, Indiana: Indiana University Press, 1975.

KIRKMAN (KIRCKMAN, KIRCHMANN), JACOB, AND FAMILY

The Kirkman family was an eminent London manufacturer of harpsichords and pianofortes. Jacob Kirchmann (1710–1792), an Alsatian of Swiss extraction, was born at Bischweiler near Strasbourg and trained as a cabinetmaker. He moved to London sometime around 1730, where his name was Anglicized to Kirckman, and apprenticed himself to Hermann Tabel, a Flemish harpsichord maker who had brought to London the tradition of the Ruckers family of Antwerp. Hermann Tabel worked from his house in Oxendon Street "over against the Black Horse in Piccadilly [*sic*]." Ultimately, Jacob Kirckman became Tabel's foreman. Another of Tabel's apprentices was **Burkat Shudi** (Burkardt Tschudi). Tabel's work would be forgotten now were it not for his two eminent apprentices. Only one of his harpsichords is known today.

On Hermann Tabel's death in 1738, the business fell to his second wife, Susanna Virgoe. A month later, Jacob Kirckman proposed to Susanna over breakfast and married her before midday, securing with his new wife the large stocks of seasoned timber and stock-in-trade. Jacob Kirckman carried on the business "at sign of the King's Arms in Broad Street, Carnaby Market," later renumbered 19 Broad Street, Soho. Their marriage was short lived: two years later Susanna died, leaving her husband to continue with an increasingly prosperous business.

Meanwhile, Shudi, eight years older than Jacob Kirckman, had left Tabel's business by 1723, when he built his first harpsichord. Kirckman and Shudi (who later founded the house of **Broadwood**) were to become arch business rivals in the years that followed. When Shudi developed the "Venetian swell" for the harpsichord, Kirckman retaliated with the introduction of the so-called Nag's Head swell on his instruments. At peak, Kirckman was making forty harpsichords a year. The last was turned out in 1809, by which time pianofortes were the mainstay of the business. Kirckman's instruments were more expensive than Shudi's, since Shudi indulged in price- (and quality-) cutting to boost his sales.

With no male descendants, Jacob Kirckman took into partnership Abraham Kirchmann (1737–1794) of Bischweiler, son of his half-brother. Extant Jacob Kirckman **square pianos** date back to around 1770 ("Jacob Kirckman," 62 notes, GG to g^3, minus GG sharp) and 1775 ("Jacob and Abraham Kirckman," 59 notes, GG to f^3). Jacob Kirckman died in June 1792, leaving a fortune claimed to be worth £200,000. Abraham worked with his own son Joseph (the

Elder) from 1789 up to his death at the age of fifty-seven.

An interesting example of an early Joseph Kirckman square piano, dated 1797, has its 68 key-levers (on a single **keyframe**) compressed in the space of the normal 61. Two **grand pianos**, in period and outward dimensions very similar, one from 1798 (private ownership, formerly in the Haags Gemeentemuseum, N.L.), the other undated (Mobbs Keyboard Collection, Bristol, U.K.), have nevertheless important differences, suggesting experimentation in progress: (1) although both have c^2 at 28.2 cms, the Bristol example has shorter vibrating lengths in the top octave; (2) the ratio of sounding length to **hammer** striking distance averages 9.1 (Bristol) as against 10.4 (The Hague); (3) the grain of the Bristol **soundboard** runs parallel to the **spine**, the 1798 example is diagonal. A particularly long grand (257.2 cms) of 1806 also has diagonal soundboard grain and in addition features a baffle or dust-cover of parchment stretched on a wooden **frame**, masking all but the top octave of the 73-note compass.

By 1803 Kirckman was "Maker to Her Majesty" (soon after 1806 the "c" was dropped from the family name [Kirkman]), and by 1816 Royal patronage was extended to that of the Prince Regent. A **patent** (no. 4068 English) was obtained by the company in 1816 for "applying an octave stop to pianofortes." An instrument with this feature is in the Colt Clavier Collection, Bethersden, U.K.

Joseph Kirkman & Son [Joseph the Younger] of Soho Square and Dean Street exhibited at the Great Exhibition of 1851, showing four instruments: (1) a seven-octave, full grand pianoforte, "with repetition **action**"; (2) the "Fonda" semi-grand pianoforte; (3) a trichord oblique piccolo **upright** with metal bracing bars; and (4) a working miniature bichord grand (38 inches long and 27 inches wide). Interestingly, the repetition action (of the seven-octave grand) was favored by a contributor to *The Crystal Palace and Its Contents* over that of **Erard**. A Fonda grand (no. 8682, c.1856) with "Kirkman's Repetition Touch" reveals nothing more than what **Broadwood** had used in the 1840s: i.e., the addition to each **jack** of an angled metal loop so arranged that the back of the hammer **butt** nudges it as the **key** is released, thus helping the jack to return.

At the peak of its piano production, the Kirkman business was one of the top three producers in London: in 1870 the business made 1,000 instruments. Ten years later the total was 900, and in 1890 no fewer than 1,300 were turned out. Joseph Kirkman's son, Joseph the Younger (c.1790–1877), continued the business until his own death at the age of eighty-seven. It was Joseph the Younger who introduced the regular manufacture of the pianoforte to the business.

The final Joseph Kirkman, born in 1822, lived until 1896. There then being no male descendant, the only relative, a daughter, sold the business to **Collard** at cost, on the understanding that Collard would maintain its standing. Collard did so until that business in turn was taken over by **Chappell** forty years later.

Arthur W.J.G. Ord-Hume and Kenneth Mobbs

Bibliography

Boalch, Donald H. *Makers of the Harpsichord & Clavichord, 1440–1840.* Oxford: Clarendon Press, 2nd ed., 1974.

Colt, C.F., and Antony Miall. *The Early Piano.* London: Stainer and Bell, 1981.

The Crystal Palace and Its Contents, an Illustrated Cyclopaedia of the Great Exhibition of 1851. London: W.M. Clark, 1852.

Ehrlich, Cyril. *The Piano: A History.* London: Dent, 1976.

Galpin Society. *Made for Music.* Exhibition Catalogue (no. 188), 1986.

Gleich, Clemens von. *A Checklist of Pianos.* Musical Instrument Collection, Haags Gemeentemuseum, 1986.

Grove Dictionary of Music & Musicians. 1st ed. Edited by Sir George Grove, 1879.

Grover, David S. *The Piano: Its Story from Zither to Grand.* London: Hale, 1976.

Harding, Rosamond E.M. *The Piano-Forte: Its History Traced to the Great Exhibition of 1851.* Cambridge: Cambridge University Press, 1933. Reprints. New York: Da Capo Press, 1973; Old Woking, Surrey: Gresham Books, 1978.

Mactaggart, Peter, and Ann Mactaggart, ed. *Musical Instruments in the 1851 Exhibition.* Welwyn: Mac & Me Ltd., 1986.

The New Grove Dictionary of Musical Instruments. Edited by Stanley Sadie. London: Macmillan Press; Washington D.C.: Grove's Dictionaries, 1984.

Patents for Inventions. *Abridgements of specifications relating to music and musical instruments.*

London 1871, facs. pub. Tony Bingham, London, 1984.

Wainwright, David. *Broadwood by Appointment: A History*. London: Quiller Press, 1982.

KLAVIER

Current usage of the term *Klavier* in German-speaking countries refers to the piano and often distinguishes the **upright** [*Pianino*] from the **grand** [*Flügel*]. *Klavier* (or *Clavier*) comes from the Latin *clavis* [key], *claves* being **keys** that are assigned specific **pitches**. The term originally referred to the organ but was maintained for the **keyboard** applied to **strings**. In the mid-nineteenth century, *Klavier* might describe the organ, **spinet**, harpsichord, or pianoforte. Confusion arising from this ambiguity led to arguments as to whether **J.S. Bach**'s *Das Wohltemperierte Klavier* should be performed on the harpsichord or clavichord. **Carl Philipp Emanuel Bach** used *Klavier* in its modern sense: "When one speaks of the *Klavier* one thinks above all of the pianoforte" (1753: *Versuch über die wahre Art das Klavier zu spielen*).

Keith T. Johns

Bibliography

Closson, Ernst. *History of the Piano*. London: Paul Elek, 1947.

Ernst, Friedrich. *Der Flügel Joh. Seb. Bachs*. Frankfurt: C.F. Peters, 1955.

Wolters, Klaus. *Das Klavier*. Bern: Hallwag, 1975.

KNABE & COMPANY

The distinguished American piano-maker Knabe & Company was founded at Baltimore in 1839 by Valentine Wilhelm (William) Knabe (3 June 1803–21 May 1864). Born in Kreuzburg, Prussia, Knabe was apprenticed to a cabinet and piano maker in Meiningen. In 1833 he came to Baltimore, where he worked for the piano maker and inventor Henry Hartye. In 1839 Knabe formed a partnership with Henry Gaehle, manufacturing pianos under the name Knabe & Gaehle. Knabe bought Gaehle's interest in 1854 and continued making pianos with his sons Ernest (1837–1894) and William II (1841–1889). Later his son-in-law Charles Keidel was added to the partnership. By 1860 the Knabe Company had established itself as one of the finest piano makers in the country.

Before the outbreak of the Civil War, Knabe pianos dominated the Southern market, owing in part to the growing antipathy for articles manufactured in the North. The Civil War destroyed the market, and the stress and worry during the war years led ultimately to the death of the founder in 1864. His two sons continued the family business and built up a flourishing trade after the Civil War. William ran the factory while Ernest redesigned **grand** and **upright stringing scales** and assumed the responsibility for restoring finances. The post–Civil War period was one of considerable growth and prosperity for the Knabe company. In 1870 approximately 500 pianos were manufactured, but by 1890 annual production had quadrupled to 2,000 instruments. Salesrooms were established in New York and Washington, while new factories, equipped with the most modern machinery, were built in order to keep up with growing demand. Knabe pianos were greatly admired during this period, winning numerous prizes. At the Centennial Exhibition in Philadelphia (1876), a Knabe **concert grand** was particularly admired. In 1879 the Japanese government imported Knabe pianos for use in the public schools. Many famous artists, including Hans von Bülow, Saint-Saëns, Busoni, and Arthur Rubinstein were among the artists enlisted by the Knabe company, which also sponsored Tchaikovsky's appearance as guest conductor to open Carnegie Hall in New York in 1891. After the early death of the founder's two sons, the company was run by William's grandsons, Ernest (1869–?) and William III (1872–1939).

In 1908 the Knabe Company was one of the first piano makers, together with **Chickering** and **Mason & Hamlin**, to become absorbed by the **American Piano Company**, founded by George C. Foster and W.B. Armstrong. Although Ernest J. Knabe, Jr., was elected president and William Knabe III vice-president, the two brothers withdrew from the conglomerate in 1909 and organized the short-lived Knabe Brothers Company (1909–1914) in Norwood, Ohio.

The popularity of Knabe pianos continued to grow after the takeover by the American Piano Company; in 1916, annual production grew to 3,000 instruments. The Knabe was selected as the official piano of the Metropolitan Opera in 1926. After the bankruptcy and subsequent reorganization of the American Piano Company, Knabe became part of the **Aeolian American Corporation** in 1932. The Knabe Company ceased manufacture after the bankruptcy of the Aeolian American Corporation in 1985.

Edward E. Swenson

Bibliography

Baltimore Clipper & Baltimore Daily Gazette (14 November 1864).

Dolge, Alfred. *Pianos and Their Makers.* Vols. I & II. Covina, Cal.: Covina Publishing Co., 1911.

Martens, Frederick H. "Knabe, Valentine Wilhelm Ludwig." *Dictionary of American Biography*, vol. 10.

Spillane, Daniel. *History of the American Piano-forte: Its Technical Development and the Trade.* New York: D. Spillane, 1890. Reprint. New York: Da Capo Press, 1969.

KNUCKLE

The knuckle is the portion of the **grand hammer** shank that is lifted by the **jack**, causing the hammer to strike the **string**. It is usually made of **felt** covered with buckskin.

See also Actions.

Philip Jamison, III

KOHLER & CAMPBELL, INC.

In 1896 Charles Kohler (1868–1913) and John Calvin Campbell (1864–1904) formed a partnership in New York City. Within the next fourteen years their firm produced over 120,000 pianos and became one of the world's leading manufacturers of **upright, grand**, and **player pianos**, and automatic **reproducing** actions. By 1916 Kohler & Campbell Industries (as the parent corporation was called) had become one of the most powerful holding companies in the trade, controlling almost two dozen brand names. Annual production and sales ranked among the highest in the entire business.

Kohler, who according to **Alfred Dolge** had a "remarkable talent as a factory organizer and businessman," and Campbell, whom Dolge called a "mechanical genius" who scientifically studied piano construction, began making Kohler & Campbell pianos in a loft on West 14th St., New York City (an area then called "Piano Row"). By 1900 consumer demand for their instruments required expanding to a six-story building at 50th Street and Eleventh Avenue, eventually occupying over one million feet of floor space. After Campbell's death in 1904, Kohler continued as sole owner, organiz-

ing the firm into a big business with enormous output and pioneering in the manufacture of pneumatic and electric player actions.

When he died in 1913, Kohler left eleven successful subsidiaries. His Republic Player Roll Corp. manufactured perforated rolls. Almost every major piano manufacturer bought player actions from Kohler's ancillary Auto-Pneumatic Action Co. and Standard Pneumatic Action Co., which together produced more than 50,000 actions annually. Significantly, the celebrated Welte-Mignon reproducing-piano mechanism was manufactured under license by Auto-Pneumatic Action Co. after World War I. Among the distinguished piano firms Kohler & Campbell Industries acquired and continued to produce were Behr Brothers, **Hazelton Brothers**, Francis Bacon Piano Co. (which owned the historic John Jacob **Astor** trademark), Milton Piano Co., Davenport-Treacy, A.M. McPhail, and Waldorf piano companies.

Julius A. White, Kohler's son-in-law, consolidated much of the corporation's operations when he assumed directorship some time after he joined the firm in 1921. During the 1920s Kohler & Campbell Industries acquired Behning Piano Co., Bjur Brothers, Brambach Piano Co., Gordon & Sons, Stulz & Bauer, and Kroeger Piano Co. Eventually, the firm controlled more than fifty brand names. After World War II, Kohler & Campbell moved into a larger, more modern factory in the Bronx. In 1954 the entire manufacturing facility was moved to Granite Falls, North Carolina; production focused on the Kohler & Campbell brand name. Still controlled by descendants of founder Charles Kohler, the corporation underwent major expansions and factory modernizations in 1961–63, 1968–69, 1974, 1976, and 1980. But the 1980s proved difficult for many time-honored piano companies. In 1985 the family elected to suspend manufacturing while negotiating an ownership change. *The Purchaser's Guide to the Music Industries* has no listing for Kohler & Campbell as a piano manufacturer after 1984.

Craig H. Roell

Bibliography

Dolge, Alfred. *Pianos and Their Makers.* Vol. 1. *A Comprehensive History of the Development of the Piano from the Monochord to the Concert Grand Player Piano.* Covina, Cal.: Covina Publishing Co., 1911. Reprint. New York: Dover, 1972.

The Music Trades Corp. *The Purchaser's Guide to the Music Industries*. Englewood, N.J.: Music Trades Corp., annually.

Ord-Hume, Arthur W.J.G. *Player Piano: The History of the Mechanical Piano and How to Repair It*. London: George Allen & Unwin, 1970.

Pierce, Bob, comp. *Pierce Piano Atlas*. Long Beach, Cal.: Bob Pierce, Publisher, 9th ed., 1990.

Roehl, Harvey N. *Player Piano Treasury: The Scrapbook History of the Mechanical Piano in America as Told in Story, Pictures, Trade Journal Articles and Advertising*. Vestal N.Y.: The Vestal Press, 1961; 2d ed., 1973.

Roell, Craig H. *The Piano in America, 1890-1940*. Chapel Hill: University of North Carolina Press, 1989; trade paperback edition, 1991.

KOREA, PIANO INDUSTRY IN

Korea's piano-manufacturing history has had a rather short span of about thirty-five years. Nevertheless, since its inception the Korean piano industry has made unceasing efforts to improve its craftsmanship. Today the industry has rightly earned recognition for manufacturing pianos of high quality, and Korean piano products have made great inroads in domestic and foreign markets worldwide.

Korea's piano industry apparently began in the mid-1950s with the founding of Chung Eum Co. (founder: Se Joon Kim) in 1955. Another firm, Soodo Piano Manufacturing Co. (founder: Joong Kyu Park), established in the late 1950s, was also an active participant. These two early **upright piano** firms were short-lived yet noted piano makers during the very early stages of the industry. The two firms were closed in 1971; however, by this time the other prominent Korean piano manufacturers, **Young Chang** and Samick, were already underway in achieving significant progress in commercial production.

The first major phase of commercial production of pianos began in 1956 when Young Chang was founded (founder: chairman Jai-Sup Kim) and began assembling imported components parts into upright pianos. At that time the components were imported from various nations, i.e., England, Germany, United States, and Japan. In 1967, Young Chang signed an agreement with the Japanese piano maker **Yamaha** to acquire technical assistance; this association lasted until 1975. In 1968 Young Chang began manufacturing upright pianos and in 1971 began exporting them. Young Chang's production of **grand pianos** began in 1978 and digitals in 1990. Since the founding of the firm, Young Chang's continuous efforts to expand and improve its production facilities have resulted in completion of the first Inchon factory in 1976, a foundry for piano **plates** in 1977, and the expansion of the first plant in 1979, along with the addition of a second Inchon plant in 1987. The Inchon plants are equipped with modern automation and technological devices and are exclusively used for piano production. In 1990 Young Chang produced 107,238 uprights, 6,939 grands, and 1,340 digital pianos, and exported 23,635 uprights, 5,717 grands, and 594 digital pianos. For export some of their pianos are labeled "Weber," a brand name secured by Young Chang in 1986 from the American piano-maker **Wurlitzer**.

With the founding of Samick (by chairman Hyo Ick Lee) in 1958 the industry swung into full production. In 1960 Samick began building its own upright pianos with the brand name "Horugel." In the early 1970s the brand name "Samick" was added and in 1973 the firm began using the "Samick" label exclusively. In 1964 Samick shipped ten pianos to Hong Kong and thus became the first piano exporter in Korea. In 1970 Samick manufactured the first grand in Korea and in 1987 produced the first Korean digital piano, thus marking the beginning of two more significant phases of the industry. Since its founding, Samick has worked consistently on the expansion and improvement of its production facilities, beginning with the two Seoul factories completed in 1963 and 1965, respectively. In 1971, with the completion of the Pupyong plant in Inchon, Samick moved its guitar production division to the Pupyong location; piano production facilities followed in 1973. More factories were built or expanded in the following years: an upright-piano plant in 1980, a grand-piano plant in 1983, a wood-processing plant in 1983, and a digital-piano plant in 1987, all of them provided with modern automation systems and hi-tech equipment. In 1990 Samick manufactured 107,326 uprights, 7,583 grands, and 7,959 digital pianos and exported 23,296 uprights, 6,149 grands, and 3,350 digital pianos.

Handok pianos are manufactured by the Handok (Korean-German) Piano Mfg. Co. Ltd. Handok (president: Woon-Kwang Paek), founded in 1972, began by building piano components: **actions** and **hammer** heads. In 1974 Handok established a joint-venture enterprise with Saito Action Mfg. Co. Ltd., Hamamatsu, Japan, and manufactured actions exclusively for export. In 1976 Handok acquired an agreement for technical cooperation from German piano-maker **Schimmel** and began building upright pianos of the German Schimmel models; the agreement with Schimmel expired in 1986. To date, 1991, Handok has produced only upright pianos, and Handok pianos have been sold only on the export market. Up to 1989 Handok produced about 2,000 pianos per year. Since 1990 Handok has been in the process of moving into a new plant and its production figures are temporarily down to only about 1,000 pianos per year.

Daewoo (president: Soon Hoon Bae) entered the piano industry in 1977 by its affiliation with Korean piano-maker, Saujin. Founded in 1972, Saujin had been producing guitars and in 1976 began building upright pianos. In 1979 Daewoo moved into the newly completed Yoju plant, which had been under construction since 1977. In 1983 the production of grand pianos began and a new brand name, "Royale," came into use along with "Saujin." In 1983 Daewoo ceased production of guitars completely and started concentrating solely on piano production. The company began making digital pianos in 1989. In 1990 Daewoo produced 13,452 uprights, 2,364 grands, and 2,120 digitals, and exported 9,050 uprights, 2,688 grands, and 391 digitals. Daewoo has been exporting pianos since 1983; "Sojin" (not Saujin), "Royale," and "Daewoo" are the brand names carried in the foreign markets. The label "Daewoo" has been in use since 1990.

The rapid growth of the Korean piano industry since its infancy is remarkable. For the twenty years of 1971–1990 the *Monthly Statistics of Korea* (vols. 14–33, 1972–1991), published by Korea's National Statistical Office, shows an increase of figures from a total production of 5,722 pianos in 1971 to a production figure of 243,100 in 1990. The rapid growth of the industry coincided with the country's enormous economic development during this period. As their financial capacity grew richer more Koreans bought pianos for pleasure and/or for the musical education of their children. Moreover, from the early 1980s professional musicians and music schools began buying more Korean-made pianos, especially grands. By this time the grand

pianos had greatly improved in their **tone** qualities and playing mechanisms. The Korea Musical Instrument Industry Association roughly estimated (Association's *Newsletter* no.81, 15 May 1991) that the distribution of pianos in Korea in 1985 was approximately one per seventy persons, but by the end of 1990 it had reached approximately one per thirty-seven persons, thus nearly doubling the distribution rate.

The Korean piano manufacturers, Young Chang, Samick, Handok, and Daewoo, are continuously striving to construct pianos of superior quality and have earned their current reputation as successful piano makers. Their products have been awarded numerous prizes for their reputable qualities both within and outside of Korea and have earned great success both in domestic and international markets. They have won popularity in homes, schools, musical communities, and elsewhere. Korean-made pianos are exported to more than seventy nations on all continents. Both uprights and grands are built in many sizes and designs, similar to those found in the traditional models of the Western hemisphere. Full-sized **concert grands** are built by Young Chang and Samick, the two leading piano manufacturers of Korea. The digitals built as uprights or grands are made in diverse models and perform many different functions. To satisfy the fast-growing demands for digital pianos in the recent trade markets, both domestic and foreign, Korean piano makers are now intensifying their research on the development of digital pianos. And the piano industry is anticipating further expansion of the trade markets; as the middle-class population of Korea grows larger, the domestic market is expected to consume many more pianos; furthermore, the Korean piano makers are now meeting a new and enormous challenge to promote and advance their product in the vast yet unknown markets of Eastern Europe.

Seunghyun Choi

Bibliography

Korea Musical Instrument Industry Association. *Newsletter*. no.81 (15 May 1991).

Korean Musical Instrument Industry Association. *Annual Statistical Report*. July 1991.

National Bureau of Statistics, Economic Planning Board, Republic of Korea. *Korea Statistical Yearbook*. Vols. 19–37 (1972–1990).

National Statistical Office, Republic of Korea. *Monthly Statistics of Korea*. Vols. 12–33 (1970–1991).

KORG

Korg USA is the American division of Korg Inc. of Tokyo, Japan, a manufacturer of professional electronic musical instruments including the T1, T2, T3, and M1 music workstations, the DSM 1 sampling **synthesizer** module, and the **SG series sampling** grand, among many other sound-processing devices. Features of the *SG* digital piano include 88 full-size, weighted **keys**, whose response can be customized by the user, and twelve preset voices that include sampled acoustic and **electronic pianos**. ROM cards expand the sound library to include organ, vibraphone, and guitar. Other features include an onboard three-band equalizer, digital chorus, stereo speakers, and full **MIDI** implementation. The Korg P3 is a dedicated piano module with two sampled acoustic piano sounds and 16-voice polyphonicity designed for performance using an external **keyboard** or sequencer.

Samuel S. Holland

KRAKAUER

The Krakauer Piano Company was established by Simon Krakauer (b. Kissengen, Germany, 1816; d. 1905). Educated as a musician, he had a reputation as a noted teacher, conductor, and violinist. Emigrating to the United States in 1854, he began the manufacture of pianos in conjunction with his son David (1848–1900). David Krakauer was the practical member of the firm, having worked in the shops of A. H. Gale, Kind & Gruber, and Haines Brothers, as well as other New York makers. In 1869 at the age of twenty-one he began piano making in a small way, at the same time opening a retail store in the Bowery district of New York. He was joined earlier by his brother Julius, a talented pianist and violinist with the Theodore Thomas orchestra. In 1878 he was joined by his brother Daniel, at the same time leasing a small factory and opening warerooms on Union Square and changing the name to Krakauer Brothers.

The firm was incorporated in 1903, David Krakauer having died in 1900 and his father following in 1905. In 1900 I. E. Bretzfelder, son-in-law of Julius Krakauer, acquired an interest in the firm and became its president. By 1926 the firm had grown to include a seven-story factory

that covered an entire block on Cypress Street between 136th and 137th Streets in New York City. The family predilection for music of the highest artistic nature was reflected in the firm's pianos, and it was the company's ambition to produce instruments of the highest quality.

The company remained in family hands until 1977, when it was acquired by Howard Graves, an engineer with an ambition to build pianos. The plant was moved to the small Amish town of Berlin, Ohio, in order to take advantage of the low-cost but high-quality work force. The cost of starting a company, coupled with the financial recession prevailing at the time, proved prohibitive, and the company was sold to **Kimball**, Graves being retained as manager. The factory was operated separately from that of Kimball, and much higher standards were maintained. The company produced a handcrafted 41-inch **console** utilizing a Schwander **action**, with meticulous care given to the **case** and **finish**. Kimball closed the plant in 1985, citing adverse market conditions. The Krakauer name is still owned by Kimball.

James Howard Richards

Bibliography

Dolge, Alfred. *Pianos and Their Makers*. Covina, Cal.: Covina Publishing Company, 1911. Reprint. New York: Dover Publications, Inc., 1972.

Fine, Larry. *The Piano Book*. 2nd edition. Boston: Brookside Press, 1990.

Presto Buyers' Guide to Pianos, Player Pianos and Reproducing Pianos and their Manufacturers, 1926. Reprint. Seattle, Washington: Frank Adams, n. d.

The Purchaser's Guide to the Music Industries 1984. S.V. "Krakauer." New York: The Music Trades Corporation, 1984.

Spillane, Daniel. *History of the American Pianoforte*. New York: D. Spillane, 1890. Reprint. New York: Da Capo Press, 1969.

KRANICH & BACH

This American company of piano makers was established by Helmuth Kranich (b. Gross-Breitenbach, Germany, 22 August 1833; d. New York, 1902) and Jacques Bach (b. Lorentzen, Alsace, 22 June 1833; d. New York, 1894). Kranich came from a musical family; his father, an organist of some note, placed him as an apprentice to a piano maker at an early age. He came to New York in 1851 at the age of eighteen, finding work with the piano-making firms of Bacon and Raven, Schomacker, and finally, **Steinway & Sons,** where he worked in the area of tone **regulating** for some five years. Jacques Bach, trained as a cabinet-maker, came to the United States at the age of twenty, finding work at the New York piano factory of Stodart and Morris in 1853. In April 1864 the two immigrants joined fifteen other aspiring piano makers to form the New York Pianoforte Company. Conceived as a cooperative venture, the firm did not succeed, and in 1866 six of the members withdrew under the leadership of Helmuth Kranich and Jacques Bach to form the firm of Kranich, Bach & Company. In 1890 the firm was incorporated, with Frederick and Alvin Kranich, sons of Helmuth, and Louis P. Bach, son of Jacques, serving as directors and officers. On the death of Helmuth Kranich, his son Frederick became president, Jacques Bach Schlosser, vice-president, Helmuth Kranich, Jr., secretary, and Louis P. Bach, treasurer. By 1916 the company's capital stock was valued at $400,000.

The original Kranich & Bach piano was a high-quality instrument incorporating a number of improvements originated by its makers. The company also built a small **grand piano** of notable quality called the "Grandette." During the ascendency of the **player piano,** Kranich & Bach designed and built player actions specifically for use in their pianos, as well as utilizing the **Welte** Mignon Licensee mechanism. In 1926 the company had factories and warerooms at 235–243 E. 23d St., New York City, as well as warerooms at Michigan and Jackson Boulevards in Chicago.

In later years the firm was acquired by the **Aeolian** Corporation, and pianos under the Kranich & Bach name were made until at least 1981. Kranich & Bach pianos were also made by the Canadian firm of Mason & Risch, itself for a time controlled by Aeolian. In 1985 Aeolian was disbanded and the names it controlled dispersed. The name Kranich & Bach is currently controlled by **Baldwin,** and two small grands, the C141 (4' 7") and the C156 (5' 1"), are built bearing the Kranich & Bach name by the South Korean piano-manufacturer Samick.

James Howard Richards

Bibliography

Armstrong, Durrell. *Player Piano Co. Inc. 1976–1977 Catalog.* Wichita, Kansas: 1977.

Dolge, Alfred. *Pianos and Their Makers.* 2 vols. Covina, Cal.: Covina Publishing Company, 1911; vol. 2 repr. as *Men Who Have Made Piano History.* Vestal, N. Y.: The Vestal Press, 1980.

Graham, Susan. "1991 NAMM Show." *Piano Technicians Journal* 34 (March 1991): 12–17.

Music Product Directory. Acoustic piano ed. 6 (Spring/Summer 1991): 42.

Pierce, Bob. *Pierce Piano Atlas.* 9th ed. Long Beach, Cal.: Bob Pierce, 1990.

Presto Buyers' Guide to Pianos, Player-Pianos and Reproducing Pianos and their Manufacturers, 1926. Reprint. Seattle, Washington: Frank Adams, n. d.

Roell, Craig H. *The Piano in America.* Chapel Hill: The University of North Carolina Press, 1989.

Spillane, Daniel. *The History of the American Pianoforte.* New York: D. Spillane, 1890. Reprint. New York: Da Capo Press, 1969.

KURZWEIL

Kurzweil Music Systems, originally of Waltham, Massachusetts, is an American manufacturer of digital pianos, **keyboards,** and tone generators that are based on digital **sampling.** Ray Kurzweil, the company's founder, gained prominence through design and application of artificial intelligence in a computer reader for the blind. Kurzweil went on to apply related techniques to digital-sound sampling and processing. His first commercial musical instrument was the K250, marketed in the mid-1980s—a high-end (up to $20,000) professional keyboard workstation that incorporates a sampler integrated with **synthesizer** controls and a multitrack digital sequence recorder. Among many outstanding features of the K250 was a group of piano samples that became an industry standard for quality. In attempts to broaden markets through more affordable and accessible products, Kurzweil designed a series of digital pianos using this signature sound and the K1000 and K1200 series keyboards during the later 1980s. Financial difficulties led to the buyout of Kurzweil Music Systems by Young Chang America in 1990.

Kurzweil digital pianos are available in various product lines. The *Ensemble Grande* series, built in a contemporary **case,** features 24-note polyphonicity and a weighted, 88-note, velocity-sensitive keyboard (except for the entry-level EGP-K, which has 76 keys). There are 100 preset sounds categorized as pianos, strings, choirs, vibes, basses, brass, woodwinds, organs, synths, and drums. Based on K250 sampled sounds, these voices can be layered, assigned to various programmable splits, or can be used as a 16-channel multitimbral tone generator. *Ensemble Grande* series instruments incorporate two to six onboard speakers with appropriate amplification, standard **pedal** controllers, and full **MIDI** implementation.

Another product line, built in traditionally styled wood cabinets, includes the G5-41 Modern Grand, the C5-46 Console, and the M5-32 Spinet. Offering many of the same general features of the *Ensemble Grande* series, these instruments are built with nineteen preset sounds, which can be layered into thirty-six preset layers or combined into six preset splits. In addition, this series incorporates built-in reverb and effect units.

Though not classified as a digital piano, the Kurzweil K1200 series is a significant professional sample playback/synthesizer. The K1200 is based on a 24-voice, 16-channel multitimbral module (similar to that of the digital pianos), which incorporates more voices and permits much of the flexibility and programmability associated with a synthesizer. The K1200 is available in both 88-key and 76-key models, as well as in a rackmount module. New to the Kurzweil product line in 1991 is the K2000, a powerful synthesizer based on Variable Architecture Synthesis Technology (VAST). VAST has been hailed as a major advancement in tone generation.

Samuel S. Holland

LAYING TOUCH

Laying touch is the term commonly used to describe the act of **key** leveling and key **dip** adjustment. Laying touch can also describe the total adjustments of **aftertouch**, **let-off**, and **drop** in relation to key leveling and dip.

See also Regulation; Touchweight.

Kent Webb

LEADS

In order to balance the piano **action** and to provide a specified **touch** weight, lead weights are inserted into holes drilled in the sides of piano **keys** and are secured in place by compression. In some instances the weights may be attached with screws to the top of the key. In **grand piano** actions the leads are almost invariably installed between the balance **rail** and the front of the key, while in vertical actions it may be necessary to install the lead between the balance rail and the back of the key. In no case should leads be installed on both sides of the balance rail.

Another type of key lead, temporarily attached to the back of the keys during **regulation** of grand piano actions, is used to simulate the weight of the action stack while it is removed from the **frame** for key leveling.

Danny L. Boone

LEATHER

Leather—the prepared skin of an animal—was used in historical pianoforte building for various purposes. Of most importance was its use to cover **hammer** heads, hammer beaks (German

action), **dampers**, and **back checks**. The skins of sheep or lamb, goat or kid, calf, chamois, roe deer or stag were prepared in various ways depending on the intended use. The first step in preparation was to remove the remains of flesh, fat, wool, or hair by soaking the skins in a solution containing chalk or ash. For the actual tanning process, three types of tannery were in use.

For *bark tanning* the hides were put into an extraction of the bark or wood of oak, spruce, chestnut, or mimosa. Bark-tanned leather is of brown color, is quite even in texture, and becomes more fluffy through a final preparation with oil or fat.

The tanning agent for *Alum tanning* is a liquor of alum, salt, wheat-bran, and egg yolk mixed with water. Because of the light color of this leather, the production is called "White tannery." In contact with metals, corrosion may be caused by residues of salt.

In *oil tanning*, the tanning material is train oil of whale, seal, or cod. The leather is very soft and fluffy and does not cause rusting, so it was widely used for block dampers. Oil-tanned deer leather was in use in **Viennese action** pianos for hammer heads until around 1930. Hammer leather of good quality should be strong as well as fluffy, so that it can be manipulated in order to achieve the desired **tone** quality.

See Hammers.

Alfons Huber

Bibliography

Fischhof, Joseph. *Versuch einer Geschichte des Clavierbaues.* Wien: Wallishausser, 1853.

Harding, Rosamond E.M. *The Piano-Forte: Its History Traced to the Great Exhibition of 1851.* Cambridge: Cambridge University Press, 1933. Reprints. New York: Da Capo Press, 1973; Old Woking, Surrey: Gresham Books, 1978.

Latz, Karl, and Andrew D. Hypher. "Leather in Organ Building." *International Society of Organ Builders* (Lauffen/Nekar: Rensch) (24 April 1984): 5–12.

Prechtl, Johann Joseph. "Leder." In *Technologische Enzyklopaedie* Vol. 9. Stuttgart: Cotta, 1833.

Welcker von Gontershausen, Hans. *Der Flügel oder die Beschaffenheit des Pianos in allen Formen.* Frankfurt/Main, 1856.

LESAGE PIANOS LIMITED

The family-run firm, Lesage Pianos Limited, was one of Canada's longest surviving piano companies, manufacturing instruments of elegant design for nearly 100 years in the province of Quebec.

Damase Lesage (d. 1923) established the company in Ste-Thérèse-de-Blainville, near Montreal, following his purchase of the assets of the Canadian Piano Company, owned by the Foisy family. A retired farmer and railway employee with no knowledge of the piano business, Lesage went into partnership with Procule Piché in 1892. The name Lesage & Piché was used until 1904, when Damase's son Adélard joined the business and it became Lesage & fils.

During the 1900s Lesage produced about 500 pianos per year. Some of these were under the names of successful Quebec retailers, C.W. Lindsay and Willis Piano Ltd. The latter firm, turning its attention to manufacture, purchased the majority of Lesage shares about 1900. The partnership was not satisfactory to the Lesage family and in 1911 Adélard sold the remaining shares to Willis and started the new firm, A. Lesage (joined later by his sons, Jacques-Paul, Jules, and Gérard).

Production increased and the factory was enlarged in 1916 and again in 1926. Lesage acquired three major piano-manufacturing firms: the Craig Piano Co. of Montreal in 1930, Bell Piano and Organ of Guelph, Ontario, in 1934, and Weber Co. of Kingston, Ontario, in 1939. It specialized in the manufacture of **upright pianos** under the Lesage name as well as the brand names Bell, Mendelssohn, Schumann, and Belmont. Some **grand pianos** were produced during the 1930s and 1940s and an **electronic piano** during the 1970s.

In 1942 the business adopted the name Lesage Pianos Limited/Pianos Lesage Ltée. The firm employed 50 to 60 people, and by 1950 it had produced some 30,000 pianos. Following that, production seems to have averaged between 1,500 and 2,000 each year. Lesage pianos were known for their excellent sound, variety of design, and durability. For a time the pianos were exported to the United States, Europe, South America, and Asia. By 1970 distribution was limited to within Canada.

Lesage was one of three remaining Canadian piano manufacturers when it was purchased in 1986 by the Toronto firm PSC Management, owned by Grant Clark. It had existed under family ownership and administration for 85 years. Despite plans to expand and improve marketing, the firm was closed in 1987.

See also Canada, Piano Industry in.

Florence Hayes

Bibliography

L'Ecuyer, Christian. "Le village de Ste-Thérèse de Blainville, Québec, et la Compagnie des Pianos Lesage Ltée." [The village of Ste-Therese-de-Blainville, Quebec, and the company Lesage Pianos Limited.] Carleton University, Institute of Canadian Studies, 1980 (unpublished paper for the Masters Degree in Canadian Studies).

LET-OFF

The term let-off describes the point at which the piano **hammer** is no longer directly propelled by the **wippen** and **jack**. Manufacturers usually specify that the hammer travel under its own inertia the final $1/8''$ to $1/16''$ of hammer travel. Let-off prevents the hammer from blocking against the vibrating **string**.

See also Regulation.

Kent Webb

LID

The lid (or top) is the wooden top of the **case**, which when closed protects the interior of the instrument. It can be raised and propped to stay open with the **lid prop**; in this position the sound of the instrument can radiate more freely. Certain period instruments had elaborate paintings on the underside of the lid.

R. P.

LID PROP

A holdover from harpsichord design, the lid prop, or propstick, supports the **lid** of the piano, directing the sound toward the audience.

Philip Jamison, III

LISZT, FRANZ (1811–1886)

Celebrated as a composer, pedagogue, and pianist par excellence, Franz Liszt was also interested in piano technology. During his long life he was intimately associated with several of Europe's and America's most important piano-makers, published testimonials on behalf of a variety of pianos, and experimented with unusual instruments. Most of his compositions for piano reflect his fondness for instruments of large scope, rich sound, and considerable flexibility.

Although born in rural Austro-Hungary, Liszt spent much of his youth in Paris, where he developed a close personal and professional relationship with the Erard family, famous during the early nineteenth century for manufacturing excellent seven-octave pianos equipped with **double-escapement action**. During the late 1820s and 1830s Liszt performed regularly, although by no means exclusively, in the Erard showrooms; he also took Erard instruments with him on several tours, testified to the high quality of Erard pianos, and even published one or two early piano pieces with **Sébastien Erard**'s approval and financial support. The brilliant runs, trills, and repeated-note passages characteristic of Liszt's early virtuoso studies, paraphrases, and transcriptions may have been conceived with the sound of Erard instruments in mind. During his "transcendental" European tours of 1838–1847, however, Liszt performed on and provided testimonials for many other pianos. In Vienna, for example, he played regularly on **Graf** and **Streicher** instruments; in southern France, Portugal, and Spain he used Boisselot pianos; and in Germany he tried instruments manufactured by a dozen different firms, including Breitkopf & Härtel of Leipzig.

Liszt's interest in particular pianos often combined admiration with expediency. In a letter addressed to Pierre Erard on 22 April 1850, Liszt confessed that he considered it his duty "not to hinder the soaring of local and national [piano] industries." Consequently, he tried out many different kinds of pianos, especially during the 1840s, and his letters of praise for several of them were published and republished in newspapers and magazines around the world. Later in life Liszt grew less willing to provide testimonials on request, although he did not hesitate to express his admiration for **Bösendorfer** instruments; he also wrote several testimonials for **Steinway** and **Chickering** pianos. Visitors to the Altenburg (Liszt's home in Weimar during the 1850s) and to his apartments in Budapest during the 1870s and 1880s encountered pianos bearing the names of Erard, **Bechstein**, Boisselot, Streicher, Bösendorfer, and even **Broadwood**—the last an instrument previously owned by **Beethoven** during the last years of his life.

Liszt was not an expert in piano engineering, but he was interested in technological innovations and always ready to put them to the test. He employed dumb keyboards as practice instruments during long voyages; he tried out pianos with bass **pedals** and encouraged their

improvement; he wrote passages of music for the "armonipiano" (an instrument equipped with a pedal that produced tremolo effects); and he owned a **combination** piano-harmonium that belongs today to the Kunsthistorisches Museum, Vienna. In his later years Liszt apparently came to prefer **overstrung** to straight-strung pianos and, although fond of delicate effects both in his compositions and in performance, he often preferred to practice on instruments with unusually heavy actions.

In certain respects Liszt's compositions for piano may be thought to reflect his experiences with different kinds of pianos. In his earliest original works he wrote music of limited scope and light texture—evidence, perhaps, of his experience with the "pre-Erard" instruments. His later works, especially those composed after the early 1860s, are much thinner in texture—again, perhaps, because the rich, even sound of metal-framed, overstrung instruments gave such music sufficient body and beauty of tone to satisfy him. In other respects, Liszt's spectacular piano writing—full of scales, arpeggios, octave passages of various kinds, cross-hands passages, thumb melodies, and other showy devices—made the best possible use of whatever instruments were available to him. In his most taxing works, however, he often provided "ossia" variants to simplify (if the performer so chooses) extraordinary difficulties; in many of his early works he even provided six-octave "ossie" for contemporary musicians unable (or unwilling) to make use of seven-octave instruments.

Michael Saffle

Bibliography

Gábry, György. "Das Klavier Beethovens und Liszts." [The Piano that belonged to Beethoven and Liszt]. *Studia Musicologica* 8 (1966): 379–90.

Keeling, Geraldine. "The Liszt Pianos—Some Aspects of Preference and Technology." *New Hungarian Quarterly* 27/104 (Winter 1986): 220–32.

———. "Liszt's Pianos: Années de Pèlerinage." *Liszt Society Journal* [Great Britain] 10 (1985): 12–20.

Pohl, Richard. "Letter from Thüringia (Liszt's Piano-Harmonium)." *Journal of the American Liszt Society* 18 (1985): 47–51.

Saffle, Michael. *Franz Liszt: A Guide to Research* [esp. Chapter XX on Lisztian pedagogy, performance practices, and instruments]. New York: Garland, 1991.

LIVING-ROOM GRAND

A living-room grand is a six- or seven-foot **grand piano** commonly found in an average-sized living room or small concert hall.

See Grand Piano.

Camilla Cai

LONGMAN AND BRODERIP

Longman and Broderip was an important English firm of music publishers/retailers and instrument makers/retailers in existence under the above names from 1776 to 1798, at no. 26, Cheapside, London, and also (from 1782 or 1783) at 13, Hay Market.

It is likely that the construction of the firm's keyboard instruments was subcontracted out: names on the back of **nameboards** of surviving pianos include "Chris.ʳ Ganer" (no number, c.1780); "Culliford" (number not known, after 1786); and "Mr. Rolfe" (no.2093, c.1790). No.358 has a signature "Loud 1796."

Many **square pianos** with the firm's nameboard survive. A very early example (GG to f³, 59 notes, unnumbered) has the name and address inked on an elongated oval boxwood insert. The 60-note square no. 12 (c.1778, Smithsonian Institution) lacks the bottom FF-sharp, as was often the case at this time. Normally, squares up to 1794 are 61 notes in compass, FF to f³, with three hand stops, two of which separately control treble and bass damping, the third operating a buff stop that brings up a layer of **leather** to touch very close to the ends of the **strings**. Occasionally, as in the "Ganer" example above, or in another (c.1790, no number), there is provision for a pedal-operated lid swell, raising a lid flap to the right of the instrument.

In 1786 **John Geib**, an employee of the firm, took out a **patent** (English, no.1571) for what became known as the "English double **action**." Longman and Broderip obtained the rights, thus their squares with this **escapement** action were the most sophisticated available in the British Isles in the eighteenth century. However, the styling "By Royal Patent," seen on the oval enamel plaques being used at this time, did not necessarily guarantee the patent action (e.g., no.2762, c.1790, still with "single action"). The baffle, or dust cover, was usually made of spruce, covered with green silk; underneath it instructions on adjusting the action were attached,

worded in English and French. At least two versions of these labels exist, the earlier recommending a "set-off" distance of 0.25 inches (adjusted by the fingers), the later one 0.125 inches (adjusted by small pliers).

The so-called buff stop in the 1786 Geib Patent was a means of producing an *una corda* effect in square pianos, which could also be used as an aid in **tuning**. A bar, attached to the end of the **belly** board and fitted with small squares of leather, was raised by a knob to the right of the **keyboard** treble cheek, the leathers damping single adjacent strings of adjacent notes (e.g., in square no.1018, c.1786).

In 1794 **William Southwell** took out a patent (English, no.2017) for additional **keys**, which "act in another compartment of the instrument under the **soundboard**." The firm used this patent; thus, 68-note instruments, FF to c⁴, were styled "New Patent" even though the old "single action" was sometimes still fitted to this larger square. Squares may also have the so-called Irish **dampers** (also described in the patent), which screw into buttons at the far end of the keys and so make the removal of the keyboard a slow operation.

There seem to have been very few **grand pianos** produced by Longman and Broderip; an important example, however, is that which **Haydn** took back with him to Vienna in 1795 after his second London visit. An illustration of a similar instrument—possibly the very same— is in *Haydn: A Documentary Study* by H.C. Robbins Landon (London: Thames and Hudson, 1981, p.116).

In 1798 the firm of Longman and Broderip was declared bankrupt. **Muzio Clementi** invested in the bankrupt firm and continued producing similar models in partnership with John Longman under the title "Longman and Clementi." The new name of "Muzio Clementi & Co." about 1802 eventually evolved through partnership changes into "**Collard & Collard**" about 1832.

Kenneth Mobbs

Bibliography

Boalch, Donald H. *Makers of the Harpsichord and Clavichord, 1440–1840.* Oxford: Clarendon Press, 2nd ed., 1974.

Cobbe, Alec. *A Century of Keyboard Instruments, 1760–1860,* Pp. 27–28. Yattendon, Berks., U.K.: Alec Cobbe, 1983.

Harding, Rosamond E.M. *The Piano-Forte: Its History Traced to the Great Exhibition of 1851.* Cambridge: Cambridge University Press, 1933. Reprints. New York: Da Capo Press, 1973; Old Woking, Surrey: Gresham Books, 1978.

Kibby, Bill. *Piano Archives.* Lowestoft, U.K.

Landon, H.C. Robbins. *Haydn: A Documentary Study.* London: Thames and Hudson, 1981.

New Grove Dictionary of Musical Instruments. S.V. "Longman and Broderip," by Peter Williams. London: Macmillan, 1984.

Patents for Inventions. *Abridgments of specifications relating to music and musical instruments.* London, 1871; facs. pub. Tony Bingham, London, 1984: 18–19, 28–29.

Smithsonian Institution, U.S.A. *A Check-list of Keyboard Instruments.* Washington, D.C.: Smithsonian Institution, 2nd ed., 1975: 20.

Victoria and Albert Museum (Howard Schott, ed.). *Catalogue of Musical Instruments.* Vol.1. London: Her Majesty's Stationery Office, 2nd ed., 1985: 105.

LOUD AND COMPANY

Thomas Loud, Sr. (1770–1833), was a London piano maker who is credited with the invention of "overstringing." The son of a Maidstone clergyman, he was born in 1770 and by the early 1800s was in business in Hoxton, Shoreditch, East London. He was granted British **Patent** No.2591 on 9 March 1802 for an **upright piano** six-feet-three-inches high. This patent included reference to the possibility of making a more portable piano by "oblique **stringing**," with the bass strings running from top left to bottom right, thus allowing the bass strings their full length in a piano a mere five-feet, two-inches high. As David Wainwright points out, although the rationality of this seems to have been slow to dawn on the piano makers, this was the first attempt at making the upright smaller, shorter, and more portable.

Thomas Loud, Jr. (1792–1866), followed his father in the business but by 1811 had moved to America, setting up in business at Prune and Fifth streets in Philadelphia. He was joined later by his brothers Philologus, John, and Joseph, moving first to 361 High Street, later known as Market Street. The history of the Loud family has been somewhat confusing because of the fact that Thomas Loud, Sr., also moved to America, settling in New York in 1816, where he maintained a piano shop through the 1820s. He introduced the "piccolo" or **cottage piano** to America as early as 1830; he died in New York in 1833.

The Philadelphia Thomas Loud (Jr.) played an important part in the development of the piano in America. He continued to improve the instrument but above all will be remembered as a pioneer of piano production in America; in 1824 he was the most extensive manufacturer in the country and made 680 instruments. On 15 May 1827 he was granted an American patent for a **down-strike action** for **square** or **grand pianos** and later devised "compensating tubes" to stiffen the **frame** and allow heavier stringing.

His piano business, then at 306 Chestnut Street, Philadelphia, continued as "Loud Brothers" for a few years until a reverse in fortunes caused the business to close. Thomas C. Loud (b.1812), Thomas Loud's son, revived the business at 305 South 10th Street about 1838 but the name disappeared after about 1854.

Arthur W.J.G. Ord-Hume

Bibliography

Dolge, Alfred. *Pianos and Their Makers.* Covina, Cal.: Covina Publishing Co., 1911. Reprint. New York: Dover, 1972.

Good, Edwin Marshall. *Giraffes, Black Dragons, and Other Pianos: A Technological History from Cristofori to the Modern Concert Grand.* Stanford, Cal: Stanford University Press, 1982.

Harding, Rosamond E.M. *The Piano-Forte: Its History Traced to the Great Exhibition of 1851.* Cambridge: Cambridge University Press, 1933. Reprints. New York: Da Capo Press, 1973; Old Woking, Surrey: Gresham Books, 1978.

Libin, Laurence. *American Musical Instruments in the Metropolitan Museum of Art.* New York: Metropolitan Museum of Art, 1985.

Spillane, Daniel. *History of the American Pianoforte.* New York: D. Spillane, 1890. Reprint. New York: Da Capo Press, 1969.

Wainwright, David. *Broadwood by Appointment, a History.* London: Quiller, 1982.

LOUD PEDAL

The loud pedal is another term for the **damper** or **forte pedal**, the right pedal, which raises all the dampers from the **strings**. It does not actually make the sound louder but sustains it, giving an illusion of greater volume.

See Pedals and Stops.

Edwin M. Good

LOW COUNTRIES, PIANO INDUSTRY IN THE

Belgium. If harpsichord making had a great impact on the production of Belgian instruments, then it must be said that the piano had lesser influence and attraction. The reason for this is a historical phenomenon; the advent of the piano in the Low Countries coincided with harsh and deep economic regressions that resulted in a cultural depression. It is sometimes claimed that **Pascal Taskin** (1723–1793) made the first piano in Paris. Should this be so, then the instrument, even if made by a Belgian maker, belongs undeniably to the French patrimony, for it was in France that Pascal Taskin made his career. As this piano has not survived, however, there is some doubt as to whether it actually did exist. It is also interesting to point out that the center of keyboard-instrument making shifted from the northern part of Belgium (for harpsichords) towards the center and the southern part of the country for the piano.

Not until the last quarter of the eighteenth century was there to be a Brussels instrument maker, Henri-Joseph Van Casteel (1722–1790). He was succeeded by Jean-Baptiste Winands (1750–1811). Matthias Bremers (1741–1803), also established in Brussels, tried to obtain protective measures against instruments imported from abroad. He was joined by Jean-Baptiste Ermel (1719–1801) from Mons. This latter builder was famous for his organ-ized pianos (that is to say, a **combination** of an organ and a piano in one and the same instrument).

One of Ermel's sons, Symphorien (1761–1842), established himself in Ghent, where he constructed the first pianos. Other Belgian makers in the early years of piano making include Jacques Ermel (1763–after 1834), Louis-Joseph Fétis (1758–1833), Toussaint-Joseph Dumoulin (c.1770–1839), and Charles Lemaître (1752–after 1809). **Jean-Joseph Merlin** (1735–1804), who emigrated to London, is said to have made a combination of harpsichord and a piano that could write out music played upon it. According to Paul Raspé, only one instrument survived (presently in the Deutsches Museum in Munich).

During the first half of the nineteenth century many foreign makers established themselves in Brussels. This resulted in an increase in the inventiveness of the Belgian makers: more than forty **patents** were granted in less than twenty-five years (e.g., the altopiano, the piccolo piano, the piano with a **keyboard** that can be lifted, etc.). In general the instruments made were of very good quality, but not outstanding.

Also, it was quite typical for Belgian piano manufacturers to refrain from constructing concert pianos; instead they concentrated on those instruments intended for domestic use (mainly **square** and **upright pianos**).

An important firm was established in Brussels by Lambert Hoeberechts (1772–1847) and Jean Groetaers (1764–1832). Both makers had learned the trade in London. Their atelier in Brussels exported numerous square pianos to Holland as a result of their appointment as court furnisher to William I of Holland. The instruments made by Groetaers show exceptional craftmanship.

Other less important piano makers of the first half of the nineteenth century are: François-Joseph Lavry (1788–1852), Charles Kadel (1773–after 1833), Jacques-François Vogelsangs (1797–1868), Charles Ross (1790–1849), and a few makers of German origin (Wilhelm Stadeler [fl.1835–1847], Christian Horstmann [fl.1835–1847], François-Joseph Teichmann).

In Liège, piano making seems to have been restricted to local consumption. This is true also for smaller towns in the northern part of Belgium such as Antwerp, Ghent, and even Geraardsbergen (e.g., Charles Anneessens [1835–1903] et alia). Until about 1850 the piano makers worked with just a few men; however, from 1850 onwards they expanded their businesses and employed fifty or more workers. The better-known makers were Berden & Cie, Félix Jastrzebski (1805–after 1865), Jacques-Noël Günther (1822–1868), the firm Dopere, and the firm Hanlet (founded in Verviers by Alexandre-Joseph Hanlet in 1866, later transferred to Brussels).

World War I dealt a terrible blow to Belgian piano production. During the war it was impossible to find the required wood. After the war, cheap German brands flooded the market due to the devaluated mark. The 1930s brought the economic crisis that was soon followed by World War II. The result was that most firms ceased instrument production. Most of the old firms that remained in business were content with representing foreign brands, particularly German and Japanese ones, as well as with restoring and repairing old and/or ancient instruments (e.g., Knud Kaufmann, Brussels; Chris Maene, Ruiselede).

There has been no specific inventiveness in Belgium, as far as the piano is concerned. Hermann Lichtenthal (fl.1828–1851) established himself in Brussels in 1828. He invented among other things the *piano-viole,* a piano with "prolonged notes." However, this instrument really did not deserve to be called a piano. Instead of the **strings** being struck with **felt hammers**, they were rubbed by an endless bow string. Other inventions of Lichtenthal's did indeed relate to the piano proper and were chiefly intended to modify the intensity of the sound.

Towards the end of the nineteenth century, the Brussels pianist Joseph Wieniawski (1837–1912) commissioned the Mangeot Bros. of Nancy to build a double piano with the keyboards inverted. This instrument did not meet with any success, nor did the one developed by Pierre Hans, with two superimposed keyboards at a half-tone interval, inspired by the **Paul von Jankó** (1856–1919) keyboard (1917). Georges Cloetens (1870–1949), a pupil of Arthur De Greef, invented the *luthéal.* This is a piano with a modified tone color produced by a comb resting with its teeth upon the piano strings. The *luthéal* was used by Maurice Ravel in the first version of *Tzigane.*

Finally, mention should be made of Gérard Dykhof, who, around 1948, tried to build a piano with narrow **keys** so as to make piano playing easier for ladies with small hands.

Holland. Here, as in Belgium, the manufacturing of pianos occupied a fairly modest part of the country's economy. Just as in Belgium, it took quite some time after the French rule before the financial situation was sound again.

The earliest source quoting pianofortes is mentioned in 1758, but one has to wait until 1779 before Meincke Meyer (a former partner of the London-based **Johann Zumpe** [1726–1791]) settled in Amsterdam, together with his brother Pieter, as makers of the pianoforte.

Numerous builders appeared around 1800. Those in Amsterdam included Meincke & Pieter Meyer (c. 1779–c.1820), Andreas van der Haar (1758–1826), Cornelis van der Does (1769–1827), Joannes van Raay (1775–1845), Johannes van Diepen (1790–1844), Johannes Duwar (1791–1865), and Johannes Kupers (1793–1869). Others were established in The Hague: Pieter Fabritius (1769–1828), Frans Schrimpf (1795–1853), Johan Baptist Traut (1809–1875), and Joannes Cuypers (1809–1881); and in smaller places such as Middelburg (Frederik van de Weele, 1752–1840); Leeuwarden (Johann Schulze, 1804–1863); Groningen (Henricus de

Wit, 1811–1877); Deventer (Carel Naber, 1797–1861; or Breda (Cornelis van Oeckelen, 1798–1865; Petrus de Ruyter, 1810–1892). In Rotterdam, Jan Paling (1796–1879) and Franciscus Coenen (1802–1875) were active, whereas in Utrecht, Marius Broedelet's name (1806–1864) should be mentioned.

It is rare to find a Dutch **grand piano**. The reason is that Dutch piano makers seemed to have made square pianos almost exclusively, apart from a few **giraffe** pianos.

A contrast between Belgian and Dutch piano makers should be noted: both countries employed foreign, mainly German craftsmen, but Belgium seems to have been oriented mainly to French and/or German piano **actions**. Holland, on the contrary, favored **English actions**. Both countries produced square pianos with several stops (handstop as well as knee-lever): **damper** or forte-piano, *una corda* stop, lute stop **(leather strip against the strings),** *dolce* (felt strip against the strings), bassoon (thin tube of parchment against the strings). Triangle and drum were also generally added.

F.J. de Hen

Bibliography

Closson, Ernest. *La Facture des Instruments de Musique en Belgique.* Huy : Degrace, 1935.

Gleich, Clemens von. *Literatuur betreffende de vroege piano in de muziekbibliotheek van het Haags Gemeentemuseum.* s'Gravenhage: Haags Gemeentemuseum.

———."De pianobouwers Meincke en Pieter Meyer te Amsterdam." In *Museum Memo,* s'Gravenhage: Haags Gemeentemuseum, 1973.

———. *Pianofortes uit de Lage Landen* [Pianofortes from the Low Countries]. Buren: Haags Gemeentemuseum, 1980.

———. private communication, 1990.

Godfroid, Stéphane. *Muziekinstrumentenbouw te Geraardsbergen van de 15e eeuw tot heden.* Geraardsbergen: Stedelijke Culturele Raad, 1986.

Hen, Ferdinand Joseph de. *Music in Belgium.* Brussels: Ministry of Foreign Affairs, External Trade and Cooperation in Development, N° 186, 1979.

Mahillon, Victor-Charles. *Catalogue descriptif et analytique du Musée Instrumental du Conservatoire Royal de Musique de Bruxelles.* Gand: A.Hoste,1893–1922.

Wangermée,Robert, and Philippe Mercier. *La Musique en Wallonie et à Bruxelles.* Brussels: La Renaissance du Livre, 1980.

LYRAFLÜGEL

Lyraflügel [lyre piano] is the German term for an **upright pyramid** piano, named for the resemblance of the upper **case** front to a large lyre. The Berlin maker **Johann Christian Schleip** was probably the first and certainly the best-known manufacturer of pianos of this design.

See also Giraffe/Pyramid Pianos.

Martha Novak Clinkscale

LYRE

The lyre is a removable unit of wooden posts and a **pedal box** supported by metal rods and braces, which is attached to the bottom of the **grand** piano case and holds the **pedals.** Although this complex may not always be shaped like the classical Greek stringed instrument, it is still called a lyre by tradition. Simple lyres with carved fretwork were first added to pianos by 1806. During the first half of the nineteenth century, elaborate lyres became important decorative features of grand pianos and reflected the fashionable furniture of the period. Today, the lyre is quite simple in design and is usually made of two turned posts stained to match the casework.

Peggy Flanagan Baird

LYRE BOX

(*See* Pedal Box)

McTAMMANY, JOHN (1845–1915)

The latter half of the nineteenth century saw a great flurry of activity in the development of automatically played musical instruments. John McTammany was an inventor and musical instrument maker who made significant contributions to self-playing instrument technology. In 1868 he produced the first fully pneumatic player mechanism for reed organs utilizing a perforated-paper roll, an improvement over the earlier "Pianista" of **Napoléon Fourneaux**. The Pianista was a large mechanism that employed a combination of power pneumatics and a pinned barrel that read from perforated cardboard cards. McTammany's improvements on his earlier device culminated in a **patent** of 1876, which placed the completely pneumatic mechanism inside the **case** of the instrument and provided for it to be driven by treadles, in contrast to Fourneaux's invention, which was housed in a separate case and acted on the **keys** of the piano from the exterior while a crank was turned.

McTammany took out numerous further patents involving self-playing instruments, particularly as applied to the reed organ, and established the McTammany Organette Company at Worcester, Massachusetts, to produce instruments utilizing his improvements. These instruments were seldom sold under the manufacturer's name, appearing instead as the Mechanical Organette, Mechanical Orguinette, Automatic Melodista, National American Organette, New Musical Orguinette, and others, as well as under his own name. McTammany at one time had two factories at Worcester, but he was apparently employed by the Munroe Organ Reed Company during the latter 1880s or possibly until 1892, when Munroe was taken over by the **Aeolian** Organ and Music Company. McTammany's abilities as an inventor were not matched by his abilities as a businessman, and his business ventures were unsuccessful. Lacking the funds to renew his patents, he was unable to profit from them and was forced to watch helplessly as others benefitted from his inventions.

There is some disagreement as to the complete validity of his claims, as numerous other inventors, notably Merritt Gally, were active in the field at the same time. However, it seems likely that McTammany's work with pneumatically-operated player mechanisms was directly influential in the later development of the **player** and **reproducing pianos**. Toward the end of his life McTammany wrote two books in an attempt to justify his claims as the inventor of the player mechanism. *The History of the Player* appeared about 1913 and *The Technical History of the Player* in 1915, but the industry that had been built largely on his work had passed him by, and he died penniless.

See also Player Piano.

James Howard Richards

Bibliography

Bowers, Q. David. *Encyclopedia of Automatic Musical Instruments*. Vestal, N.Y.: The Vestal Press, 1972.

Bowers, Q. David, and Arthur A. Reblitz. *Treasures of Mechanical Music*. Vestal, N.Y.: The Vestal Press, 1981.

Dolge, Alfred. *Pianos and Their Makers* . Covina, Cal.: Covina Publishing Company, 1911. Reprint. N.Y.: Dover Publications, Inc., 1972.

McTammany, John. *The Technical History of the Player*. Introduction by William Geppert. New York: The Musical Courier Company, 1915. Reprint. Vestal, New York: The Vestal Press, n.d.

The New Grove Dictionary of Musical Instruments. Edited by Stanley Sadie. S. v. "McTammany, John" by Barbara Owen.

Ord-Hume, Arthur W. J. G. *Collecting Musical Boxes and How to Repair Them*. New York: Crown Publishers, Inc., 1967.

———. *Player Piano: The History of the Mechanical Piano and How to Repair It*. New York: A. S. Barnes and Company, 1979.

MAFFEI, FRANCESCO SCIPIONE (1675–1755)

Born in Verona, Republic of Venice, Francesco Scipione Maffei was a dramatist, archaeologist, and journalist. In 1710 he was one of the founders of *Giornale de' Letterati d'Italia* [Journal of Italian Men of Letters], an influential literary journal in which he disseminated his ideas about reforming Italian drama. Maffei was a prolific writer of librettos, plays, translations, history, and occasional verse.

In 1709, while visiting Prince Ferdinand De' Medici in Florence to seek his patronage for the new journal, Maffei interviewed **Bartolomeo Cristofori**, a Paduan harpsichord maker who was employed from about 1693 by Prince Ferdinand. He closely examined four of Cristofori's new **fortepianos**, and gathered opinions from musicians who had played or heard the instruments. Maffei, impressed with the new instruments, wrote in volume five (1711) of his new journal an article on Cristofori and the new *gravecembalo col piano, e forte* (harpsichord with soft and loud). It appeared with a crude drawing of Cristofori's piano **action**. This article, the first published reference to the invention of the piano, was translated into German and later published in Hamburg in *Critica musica* (1725).

Danny L. Boone

Bibliography

Good, Edwin M. *Giraffes, Black Dragons, and Other Pianos.* Stanford, Cal.: Stanford University Press, 1982.

Greenfield, Jack. "A Contemporary Journalist's Report on Cristofori and His Work." *Piano Technicians Journal* 28 (August 1985): 25–27.

———. "Cristofori's Initial Piano Design."*Piano Technicians Journal* 28 (September 1985): 22–24.

———. "Cristofori's Soundboard Design." *Piano Technicians Journal* 28 (October 1985): 21–23.

The New Encyclopedia Britannica. Vol. 7, 15th edition. Chicago: The University of Chicago.

Wainwright, David. *The Piano Makers.* London: Hutchinson & Co., 1975.

MARIUS, JEAN (FL. 1700–D. 1720)

Jean Marius was the first French instrument maker who offered plans for **hammer actions** for harpsichords designed to allow control of loudness by finger-touch. Besides this and other work on musical instruments, the records of the Paris Academy of Sciences show that Marius also applied his talents to nonmusical mechanical and scientific activities. Included among his inventions submitted for approval was a series of folding tents and umbrellas. His assistance to Joseph Sauveur in acoustical experiments was acknowledged in 1713. Marius also helped René A.F. de Réaumur in the development of the design of water pumps.

During his time, Marius was best known for his invention of the *clavecin brisé*, a portable harpsichord designed for travel. It was made up of three hinged sections that folded together to form a compact box. At least five Marius folding harpsichords are still in existence. Dates on these instruments in European collections fall within the period 1700–1715.

By 1716, when Marius introduced his proposal for harpsichords with hammers, **Bartolomeo Cristofori** in Florence had already designed and built hammer harpsichords for at least sixteen years. The possibility that news of Cristofori's work had been carried by Italian musicians or other travelers to France cannot be ruled out. Cristofori listed a French folding harpsichord, probably built by Marius, in a 1716 inventory of Medici instruments, evidence of the passage of information on new musical instruments in the opposite direction, from France to Italy.

Marius submitted four different designs in 1716, each labeled *clavecin à maillets*. The Academy's approval he received was the equivalent of **patent** protection for twenty years. Drawings and descriptions were first published in *Machines et inventions approuvées par l'Académie Royale des Sciences*, Vol. 3, 1735. The wording indicates that the descriptions may have been written by the editor or some other person. It is not certain whether the published drawings are accurate copies of drawings or models prepared by Marius. Important details of the drawings are as follows:

1. A four-key trichord-strung action model: the **keys** are simple levers. The hammers are thin wooden squares positioned upward to strike the **strings** on the thin edge like clavichord tangents.

2. A two-key trichord-strung action model: thin wooden squares used as hammers are mounted on the front end

of separate strips of wood pivoted on a **rail**. The hammers are impelled by depression of separate key levers. Different arrangements are shown, both for upstriking the strings from below or downstriking from above.

3. A simplified sketch of a trichord-strung vertical harpsichord and the action details for a single note: the plectrum has been replaced with a wooden peg wrapped with cloth.

4. A simplified sketch of a bichord-strung harpsichord with two keyboards and action details of a pair of keys for a single note: the striking end of one key holds a standard quilled harpsichord **jack**, the other holds a small block that serves as a hammer. The hammer and jack can be moved separately or coupled to move together.

There is no evidence that an instrument with any of the hammer actions designed by Marius was ever built, either by him or anyone else. While other builders copied his portable harpsichord, his plans for hammer harpsichords were ignored and forgotten later in the eighteenth century. The *Encyclopédie Méthodique*, published in 1785, omitted any mention of Marius in an article on early piano builders. Later, after his work was rediscovered by French music historians, his hammer action designs were recognized as the earliest forms of the piano action to appear in France and he was honored at the Paris Exposition of 1855.

See also Actions.

Jack Greenfield

Bibliography

Cohen, Albert. "Jean Marius' *Clavecin brisé* and *Clavecin à maillets* Revisited: The 'Dossier Marius' at the Paris Academy of Sciences." *Journal of the American Musical Instrument Society* 13 (1987): 23–38.

Good, Edwin M. *Giraffes, Black Dragons, and Other Pianos*. Stanford, Cal.: Stanford University Press, 1982.

Harding, Rosamond E.M. *The Piano-Forte: Its History Traced to the Great Exhibition of 1851*. Cambridge: Cambridge University Press, 1933. Reprints. New York: Da Capo Press, 1973; Old Woking, Surrey: Gresham Books, 1978.

Marcuse, Sybil. *A Survey of Musical Instruments*. London: David and Charles, 1975.

Rimbault, Edward B. *The Pianoforte*. London: Robert Cocks, 1860.

Russell, Raymond. *The Harpsichord and Clavichord*. New York: W. W. Norton, 1973 (revision of Faber and Faber 1959 edition).

MASON & HAMLIN

The name Mason & Hamlin is an old and illustrious one, its origin firmly entrenched in the history of music in the United States. A firm of organ and piano makers, it was established in Boston in 1854 by Henry L. Mason (1831–1890) and Emmons Hamlin (1821–1885). Hamlin had discovered a method of voicing free reeds while working as superintendent of **tuning** at the reed-organ firm of George A. Prince. Henry Mason's father, Lowell Mason (1792–1872), composer and founder of public-school music in the United States, suggested to his son that he go into business with Hamlin to produce reed-organs and, with music publisher Oliver Ditson, he supplied the funds to establish the new company. Mason & Hamlin's activities in the reed-organ field made it world famous, and in 1883 the manufacture of pianos began.

The Mason & Hamlin piano was from its inception an instrument of superior quality, and several features were peculiar to its design. One was a **stringing** system that did away with the **tuning pins** and **pinblock**, employing instead a flange cast into the metal **plate** and supplied with machine screws to adjust string tension. Intended to provide improved tuning stability, the system was nonetheless discarded in 1905, probably because of its cost. A more permanent feature was the tension resonator, the invention of Mason & Hamlin employee Richard W. Gertz. This device consists of several adjustable steel arms disposed radially from a central connecting point beneath the piano, their outer ends firmly fastened in the grand **rim**. Expansion of the rim was prevented, thus preserving the **crown** of the **soundboard**.

From the early part of the century until the late 1920s, Mason & Hamlin was **Steinway's** most serious competitor for the concert stage, a high-quality instrument advertised as "the costliest piano in the world." However, Mason & Hamlin lacked the stability afforded by continuity of ownership and family association enjoyed by Steinway. In 1911 the company became a part of the **Cable-Nelson Company** and in 1924 was absorbed by the **American Piano Company**. From 1930 to 1932 it was a part of the **Aeolian Company**, and in the merger of

Aeolian and American in 1932, became part of the Aeolian American Corporation. Probably because of these changes in ownership, Mason & Hamlin never quite regained its former position of prestige. In 1959, control of Aeolian American was acquired by Winter & Company, and a long period of decline set in. In 1982 Aeolian closed its Rochester, New York, plant where Mason & Hamlin and other Aeolian **grands** had been produced, and in 1983 Aeolian was purchased by Peter Perez, ex-president of Steinway. Aeolian encountered increasing quality and cash-flow problems, and in 1985 the firm went out of business. Mason & Hamlin's patterns, scales, equipment, and works-in-progress were acquired by **Sohmer** & Company, one of the few manufacturers in the United States considered capable of doing the name justice. In June 1989 Sohmer was in turn acquired by the **Falcone Piano Company** of Haverhill, Massachusetts, a small maker of high-grade pianos. In 1990 the Mason & Hamlin was made in a 50-inch vertical and two grands: Model A (5'8") and Model BB (7'). Other models are projected.

See also United States, Piano Industry in.

James Howard Richards

Bibliography

"Aeolian Closes East Rochester Division." *The Music Trades* 130 (August 1982): 20, 22.

DeMars, Dawn. Falcone Piano Company, Haverhill, Massachusetts. Telephone interview, 23 March 1990.

Dolge, Alfred. *Pianos and Their Makers*. Covina, Cal: Covina Publishing Company, 1911. Reprint. New York: Dover Publications, Inc., 1972.

"Ex-Steinway Head Perez Buys Aeolian." *The Music Trades* 131 (March 1983): 18, 21.

Fine, Larry. *The Piano Book*. Boston: Brookside Press, 1987.

Gellerman, Robert F. *The American Reed Organ*. Vestal, N.Y.: The Vestal Press, 1973.

The New Grove Dictionary of Musical Instruments. Edited by Stanley Sadie. S. v. "Mason & Hamlin," by Margaret Cranmer and Barbara Owen.

Roell, Craig H. *The Piano in America, 1890–1940*. Chapel Hill: The University of North Carolina Press, 1989.

Spillane, Daniel. *History of the American Pianoforte*. New York: D. Spillane, 1890. Reprint. New York: Da Capo Press, 1969.

"W. G. Heller 1889–1974." *The Music Trades* 122 (October 1974): 60–63, 105.

MASTER PIANO TECHNICIANS

Master Piano Technicians of America (MPT) is a social and professional association of piano-tuner technicians, formed loosely along the lines of the **Piano Technicians Guild**, its larger, sister organization. First registered as a non-profit organization in 1977, MPT was originally conceived by its founders as an alternative to PTG, which they considered at that time to be too centrally controlled and unresponsive to individual members. From the original five members, MPT has grown to a total of over 185 members, comprising seven chapters and representing thirty-five states (as of December 1991).

Master Piano Technicians of America holds an annual convention at various locations in the eastern United States, offering technical workshops and classes, as well as social functions. A newsletter is published four times a year, with technical articles and industry and organization news. Although these services and its overall structure are based on those of the Piano Technicians Guild, MPT leaders say there are important differences between the two groups. Although MPT is a national organization, the leadership exerts little control over the membership, preferring instead to grant individual chapters wide autonomy in holding meetings, accepting new members, and conducting local business. MPT has only one class of membership, the Master Piano Technician, as opposed to PTG, where ranking of members has been debated and changed numerous times over the years. Membership requirements and standards of technical ability are left largely to the discretion of the local chapters. This again differs from PTG, which has established standardized tests for both tuning and technical skill levels.

Although MPT was begun as an alternative to an established organization, a number of technicians hold membership in both groups. While not as well known as PTG, MPT has established itself as a separate viable organization, serving a tradition of diversity within the piano-service profession.

Kerry Kean

MATHUSHEK, FREDERICK (1814–1891)

Born in Mannheim, Frederick Mathushek emigrated to New York in 1849 after learning the craft of piano making in Germany, Austria, and in Paris at the workshop of **Jean-Henri Pape**. He demonstrated inventiveness early in his career, producing an ingenious octagonal piano (*Tafelklavier*) while still in Germany. In New York he was immediately employed by the Dunham firm and by 1850 had devised a **scale** for **overstrung square pianos** and a **hammer**-covering machine. In 1852 he set up on his own, working after 1857 with Spencer B. Driggs, who had notions of revolutionizing piano construction. In 1866 he moved to New Haven, where he established the Mathushek Piano Co. There he developed a small square model, dubbed "Colibri," with a linear **bridge** and an equalizing scale, of extraordinary tonal richness. His attempts at building square pianos with a downstriking **action** in the manner of Pape, however, were unsuccessful. In 1871 he returned to New York and established Mathushek & Son together with his grandson. In 1879 Mathushek **patented** an "equilibre" system to maintain soundboard **crown**, which proved effective but excessively costly. Mathushek's other contribution to the field of piano making was his duplex **soundboard**, patented in 1891, which combined two cross-banded boards glued together and thickest in the center to better withstand the pressure of the **strings**.

Howard Schott

Bibliography

Dolge, Alfred. *Pianos and Their Makers*. Covina, Cal.: Covina Publishing Company, 1911. Reprint. New York: Dover Publications, 1972: 84, 100, 108–09, 321–25.

Good, Edwin M. *Giraffes, Black Dragons and Other Pianos: A Technological History from Cristofori to the Modern Concert Grand*. Stanford, Cal.: Stanford University Press, 1982: 171–72, 178, 194–95.

Spillane, Daniel. *History of the American Pianoforte: Its Technical Development and the Trade*. New York: D. Spillane, 1890. Reprint. New York: Da Capo Press, 1969: 226–27.

MÉCANIQUE À DOUBLE ÉCHAPPEMENT

See Actions; Erard.

MERLIN, JOHN JOSEPH (1735–1803)

John (Jean) Joseph Merlin was a Walloon inventor and instrument maker who settled in London while a young man. He was born on 6 September 1735 and was baptized that same day at the Church of Saint-Pierre-outre-Meuse in the village of Huy, near Liège, Belgium. He was the third child of Maximilien Joseph Merlin, an adventurous blacksmith, and Marie-Anne Levasseur, the daughter of a master locksmith and craftsman. In 1739, at age four, John Joseph was enrolled in the blacksmith's guild, but it is not known if he ever practiced this trade.

Recent research by Pierre Bauwens of Huy, reveals that Merlin's early childhood was a difficult one. The family suffered financial difficulties and moved often from one residence to another within Huy. Merlin's mother died when he was eight and his stepmother died just three years later. (It is believed that Merlin's father married a third time, because a half-brother, Charles, of Strasbourg, is mentioned in his will.)

When he was nineteen, Merlin went abroad and first lived some six years in Paris, developing his mechanical and scientific interests at the Paris Academy of Sciences. In 1760, he moved to London as a technical advisor to the Spanish Ambassador, Conde de Fuentes (d. 1771), a man sent by his government to gain information about a newly invented marine timekeeper. Merlin stayed with the Spanish Count about three years before obtaining a wide variety of jobs involving mechanical instruments.

For a time, Merlin worked as a harpsichord and piano tuner. It was perhaps in this capacity that he met Dr. **Charles Burney**, the great musicologist, and his daughter, Fanny (later Frances D'Arblay), a novelist who wrote of Merlin often in her *Diary* (1768–1788). Dr. Burney commissioned several keyboard instruments from Merlin, including a pianoforte in 1777 with an extended **keyboard** range for the expressed purpose of performing the duets he had composed that year. (Dr. Burney's *Sonatas* were the first duets ever published for two players at one keyboard.)

Throughout his career, Merlin experimented with unusual clavier designs. In 1774, he **patented** (English Patent No. 1081) a "compound [combination] harpsichord." This hybrid instrument included a piano **action** having a set of sixty **hammers** covered with several layers of leather and cloth. It also had a mechanism controlled by a **pedal**, which caused each hammer to strike either one, two, or three strings at a time. The Deutsches Museum in Munich has a combination harpsichord-piano made by

Merlin in 1780. This instrument combines a downstriking piano action with a single manual harpsichord having three registers at sixteen-foot, eight-foot, and four-foot pitch. In fact, this is the only known English harpsichord with its original sixteen-foot register. The instrument is fitted with buff leather plectra. It has the added feature of a notating machine, a Merlin invention consisting of a long strip of paper set in motion by clockwork with a row of pencils activated by the **jacks** to notate the music being performed.

The Colt Clavier Collection includes a Merlin claviorganum of 1784. With a five-octave keyboard and **tuning pins** on the right, this combination organ and piano appears like any other mahogany and satinwood **square piano** of the period. (The organ pipes were built and signed by Robert and William Gray, 31 January 1784.) The claviorganum's **damper** mechanism, which is controlled by a handstop, is based on an earlier mopstick principle and is cleverly designed so that it can be easily removed in one unit for repair work. A handstop pulls the action forward a few centimeters so that the buff leather hammers will strike only one of the two strings for each **key**. Another handstop disengages the piano action so that the double-duty instrument may be played as an organ.

The Conservatoire Royal de Musique in Brussels owns the only known **upright piano** by Merlin (date effaced). This Sheraton-style instrument is best described as a square piano whose action and **soundboard** have been set at a steep angle behind the keyboard. The back of the piano has been fitted with a Venetian swell that is controlled by a knee-lever. The instrument is bichord throughout and the dampers and hammers are guided by loops of **wire**.

Evidently Merlin's fame as a keyboard inventor spread to America. In 1783, **Thomas Jefferson** requested that the Philadelphia lawyer and amateur musican, Francis Hopkinson, assist him in buying a double harpsichord with Merlin's fortepiano stop for his daughter, Patsy. Hopkinson wrote to his former theory teacher Robert Bremner in London about this purchase. In a letter dated 31 March 1789, Hopkinson reported to Jefferson that Bremner had advised against buying a Merlin combination instrument, as "the one Instrument injures other so that neither of them is good. . . ." Hopkinson then added the stinging observation that Mer-lin instruments were frequently available in second-hand shops for half price. This must have been a painful disgrace to the ingenious Merlin.

The year 1786 seems to be the last-known date for any of Merlin's keyboard instruments. Around that same time, this creative man opened Merlin's Mechanical Museum on Princess Street, Hanover Square. Here he charged a fee for people to view and perhaps purchase his practical gadgets as well as his mechanical inventions and curious entertainment machines. He also planned to build Merlin's Necromancic Cave, which was to include a Magic Room and a Temple of Music. But, this fantastic entertainment center was never erected. Merlin was in declining health for several years and died on 4 May 1803. It was reported in *The Gentleman's Magazine* that he was buried in Paddington, London. His will directed that the "curious and valuable Museum, the making of which has closely employed me for thirty years" should be sold.

Merlin's work as a keyboard builder is immortalized in a painting by his friend Thomas Gainsborough, which now hangs in Buckingham Palace, London. Gainsborough has generously painted Merlin's nameplate on the square piano in the portrait of Johann Christian Fischer, the oboe player who was Gainsborough's son-in-law. In 1983, The Iveagh Bequest of Kenwood House, London, purchased a portrait of John Joseph Merlin by Gainsborough, after it had been identified by Lindsay Stainton of the British Museum. Painted about 1781, it shows Merlin wearing a scarlet jacket trimmed in gold and holding one of his latest inventions, a beam for a gold-coin scale.

In the summer of 1985, the Greater London Council sponsored an exhibit, "John Joseph Merlin: The Ingenious Mechanick" at The Iveagh Bequest, Kenwood House. A number of Merlin's mechanical devices and inventions as well as some of his musical instruments were a part of this special exhibit (John Jacob, Curator). Included were a Dutch oven with a spring jack to rotate meat, a personal weighing machine, a pocket-sized scale for weighing gold coins, a self-propelled wheelchair for invalids, and even some rollerskates.

Peggy Flanagan Baird

Bibliography

Bauwens, Pierre. "Jean Joseph Merlin, ne a Huy, inventeur genial a Londres (1735–1803)." In *Annales du Cercle Hutois des Sciences et Beaux-Arts.* Tome XIII. Huy: Ville de Huy, 1988: 9–26.

Boalch, Donald Howard, and Peter Williams. "John Joseph Merlin." In *The New Grove Dictionary of Musical Instruments,* Vol. 2: 644. Edited by Stanley Sadie. London: Macmillan Press Limited, 1989.

Boyd, Julian P., ed. *The Papers of Thomas Jefferson* Vol. 6: 359 and Vol. 7: 57. Princeton: Princeton University Press, 1952.

Colt, C. F., with Anthony Miall. *The Early Piano,* 32–34. London: Stainer and Bell, 1981.

French, Anne. "John Joseph Merlin." In *John Joseph Merlin: The Ingenious Mechanick.* pp. 11–47. London: Greater London Council, The Iveagh Bequest, Kenwood, 1985.

Harding, Rosamond E.M. *The Piano-Forte: Its History Traced to the Great Exhibition of 1851.* Cambridge: Cambridge University Press, 1933: 48, 70, 180. Reprints. New York: Da Capo Press, 1973; Old Woking, Surrey: Gresham Books, 1978.

Thibault, G. (Mme. De Chambure), Jean Jenkins, Josiane Bran-Ricci. *Eighteenth Century Musical Instruments: France and Britain:* 196. London: Victoria and Albert Museum, 1973.

MIDI

MIDI is the acronym for Musical Instrument Digital Interface. This is a computer protocol that enables **synthesizers**, sequencers, computers, digital rhythm programmers, and other MIDI devices to be interconnected and to communicate through a common interface. The MIDI Specification 1.0 was standardized by an international consortium of synthesizer designers and manufacturers in 1983. Since that time, its widespread acceptance has made it possible for instruments of different manufacturers to communicate various types of musical data easily. MIDI data includes note-on and note-off commands (specific information about notes played and released), **key** velocity (normally interpreted as volume and/or timbre), patch changes (changes among preset voices), and various controller data such as sustain, modulation, and/or pitch bend. MIDI data is transmitted over a network of sixteen parallel channels that are assigned and allocated by the musician according to specific needs.

In its simplest application, MIDI permits a musician to play two or more instruments from a single **keyboard** controller in order to layer **tone** colors. In more comprehensive applications, MIDI provides the means for a multitrack computer-based composing system by connecting multiple instruments to a digital-sequence recorder. MIDI data, once recorded in a digital sequence, can be played back and edited with the same facility a word processor allows for written text. It can also be converted directly into conventional musical notation and printed. The practical and commercial ramifications of MIDI swept the music industry almost overnight. More profound creative and pedagogical applications of MIDI continue to be explored in the first years of the 1990s. Many experts claim that the significance of MIDI can only be compared to the invention of musical notation or the development of sound recording, in the sense that the fundamental relationship between musical creator, the creative act, the musical product, and the listener are profoundly changed.

Samuel S. Holland

Bibliography

Anderton, Craig. *MIDI for Musicians.* New York: Amsco Publications, 1986.

Casabona, Helen, and Dave Frederick. *Using MIDI.* Van Nuys, Cal.: Alfred Publishing Co. Inc., 1988.

Contemporary Keyboard (1975–)

Darter, Tom, ed. *Synthesizers and Computers.* Milwaukee, Wis.: Hal Leonard Publishing Corp., 1985.

Rona, Jeff. *MIDI—The In's, Out's & Thru's.* Milwaukee, Wis.: Hal Leonard Publishing Corp., 1986.

MIRRAPIANO

The MirrApiano came into being during World War II when American piano factories faced closure for lack of materials. Patented in 1943 by its inventor, Louis Bromberg (1893–1972), the MirrApiano was produced by numerous piano companies, including **Aeolian**, Jannsen, Winter, and Weser. The process involved modernizing the **cases** of large pre-existing **upright pianos**, a procedure known as "restyling."

After rebuilding the interior, the bottom board was recessed into the piano, the piano lowered to the floor, and new arms, legs, front

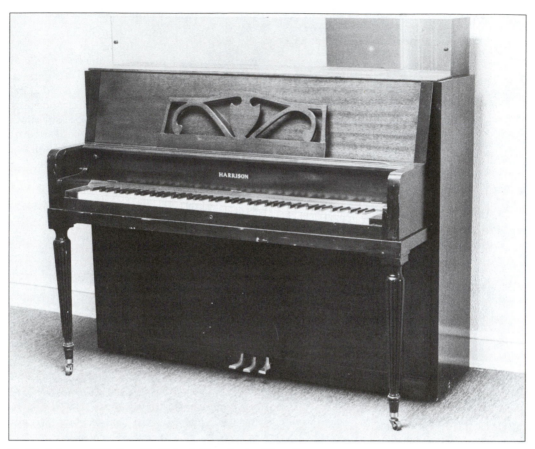

The MirrApiano c. 1950. Owned by Richards Piano Service, Waco, Texas.

panel, and **music desk** were provided. The massive upper portion of the case was removed and the ends of the case cut off slightly above the hammer line. The exposed top and ends of the **pinblock** were veneered, a new upper shelf was placed above the **hammers**, and a mirror, whence the process got its name, covered the **tuning pins**. The mirror reflected the upper shelf, giving the illusion of a piano approximately eight inches shorter, or about the height of a modern studio piano. The case was refinished and new keytops installed. Restyling was done at company headquarters at 19 Flatbush Avenue, Brooklyn, N. Y., and after the war, franchises were sold to qualified shops throughout the United States. MirrApianos were promoted on the basis of the tonal superiority inherent in their large **soundboards** and long bass strings, as well as the excellent **action** response due to full-size **key** and action compo-nents. Smaller franchise holders were difficult to police, and these, along with some unfranchised shops, sometimes used a cheapened version of the process to dispose of pianos of poor quality. Such pianos were sometimes disparagingly called "cut-downs." MirrApianos were produced by franchise holders until the late 1950s and early 1960s, when demand gradually ceased.

James Howard Richards

Bibliography

Bromberg, Robert. Letter to James H. Richards, 23 June 1986.

"The MirrApiano." *The Purchaser's Guide to the Music Industries.* New York: *The Music Trades*, 1956.

Richards, James H. "The MirrApiano." Paper presented at the Meeting of the Southwest Chapter of the American Musicological Society, University of North Texas, 12 April 1986.

MODERATOR

Moderator was the term used for a register operated by a **pedal** or a knee lever, which inserted a strip or tongue of cloth between the **hammer** and the **strings**, thus muting the sound. The **tone** was affected at the moment of the hammer blow by the amount of cloth interposed under the strings but also by the thickness, the hardness, and the layers of the material. The device was almost exclusively used on **Viennese pianos** during the eighteenth and nineteenth centuries.

See also Pedals and Stops.

Donatella Degiampietro and
Giuliana Montanari

Bibliography

Harding, Rosamond E.M. *The Piano-Forte: Its History Traced to the Great Exhibition of 1851.* Cambridge: Cambridge University Press, 1933. Reprints. New York: Da Capo Press, 1973; Old Woking, Surrey: Gresham Books, 1978.

Hirt, Franz Josef. *Stringed Keyboard Instruments 1440–1880.* Translated by M. Boehme-Brown. Boston, Mass.: Boston Book and Art Shop, 1968. Also, *Meisterwerke des Klavierbaus – Stringed Keyboard Instruments.* Dietikon-Zürich: Urs Graf (distributed in the USA by Da Capo Press), 1981.

Marcuse, Sybil. *Musical Instruments: A Comprehensive Dictionary.* New York: Norton, 1975.

The Piano. (New Grove Musical Instruments Series.) New York: Norton, 1988.

MONTAL, CLAUDE
(1800–1865)

Born in La Palisse (Allier) on 28 July 1800, Claude Montal was an influential Parisian piano technician and maker from the 1830s until his death on 7 or 8 March 1865. His accomplishments, which included the authorship of a well-known treatise on piano **tuning** and repair and the development of the *sostenuto* **pedal**, were all the more remarkable in that he was blind.

Soon after Montal lost his sight because of typhoid fever at age six, he was able nevertheless to demonstrate his innate intelligence and mechanical ability by making a primitive violin and, a few years later, by helping his father, a saddler. In 1816 he entered a school for the blind in Paris, where he learned to read Braille and to play the oboe, violin, and piano. Montal and a fellow student taught themselves to tune the school's pianos. Later, they completely disassembled and rebuilt an old piano and, with the help of a cabinetmaker and a tinsmith, restored the organ in the school's chapel. After leaving the school in 1830, Montal supported himself as a tuner and teacher of tuning. In 1834, upon learning that a student of his was about to publish a treatise disclosing Montal's methods, within twenty-four hours he dictated, had printed, and copyrighted a brief treatise of his own. A version in German was published the next year, followed in 1836 by an expanded French version, *L'art d'accorder soi-même son piano.* This popular treatise was reissued in several new editions during succeeding decades.

In 1835 Montal began to manufacture pianos. Starting modestly with a single workman making small **upright pianos**, the firm by 1839 employed a dozen workers building **square** and **grand pianos** in addition to the mainstay of the business, uprights. The firm, which remained relatively small (about one-tenth the size of large manufacturers such as **Erard** and **Pleyel**), making about 100 instruments a year, seems to have been well regarded. It was regularly awarded prize medals at trade expositions, and in 1851 Montal himself was made Chevalier of the Legion of Honor. After his death, the firm stayed in business for several decades, but with a diminished reputation, under the successor Tessereau and later under Donasson.

In the early 1840s Montal adapted Sébastien Erard's double escapement **action** for use in square and upright pianos. In 1844, he was one of the first, perhaps *the* first, to devise a *sostenuto* pedal (called *pédale à son prolongé*), by which notes whose **keys** are held down when the **pedal** is pushed remain undamped after the keys are released, until the pedal is released. (The date 1862 that some sources give for this invention by Montal is probably the date of an improved version.) Other Montal innovations, ultimately regarded as less useful, included a jalousie-swell pedal, a transposing mechanism, and a *pédale d'expression* that controlled the hammer-stroke distance.

John Koster

Bibliography

Barli, Olivier, *La facture française du piano de 1849 à nos jours.* Paris: La Flûte de Pan, 1983.

Dufau, P.A. [Pierre Armand], Paul Emile Benaimé, and M. Tahan. *Claude Montal, facteur de pianos (aveugle); sa vie et ses travaux.* Paris: Didot Frères, Fils et Cⁱᵉ, 1857.

Haine, Malou. *Les facteurs d'instruments de musique à Paris au XIXe Siècle*. Faculté de Philosophie et Lettres XCIV. Brussels: Editions de l'Université de Bruxelles, 1985.

Harding, Rosamond E.M. *The Piano-Forte: Its History Traced to the Great Exhibition of 1851*. Cambridge: Cambridge University Press, 1933. Reprints. New York: Da Capo Press, 1973; Old Woking, Surrey: Gresham Books, 1978.

Mactaggert, Peter, and Ann Mactaggert, eds. *Musical Instruments in the 1851 Exhibition*. Welwyn, England: Mac & Me, 1986.

Montal, C. *L'art d'accorder soi-même son piano*. Paris: J. Meissonier, 1836.

Pierre, Constant. *Les facteurs d'instruments de musique, les luthiers et la facture instrumentale: précis historique*. Paris: Ed. Sagot, 1893.

MOOG, ROBERT ARTHUR (B. 1934)

Robert A. Moog is best known as the inventor of one of the first voltage-controlled modular **synthesizers** and other electronic musical instruments. He has written and lectured internationally on electronic music. Moog received the B.S. in physics from Queens College, New York City, the M.S. in electrical engineering from Columbia University, and a PhD. in engineering physics from Cornell University (1965). From the early 1950s, Moog designed and built theremins, using the income to finance his education. From 1965 on, his principal concern was designing and building synthesizers. His firm merged with MuSonics in 1971 to form Moog Music, Inc. In 1973, this company became a subsidiary of Norlin Industries in Buffalo, New York.

Moog designed his first modular synthesizer using voltage control in collaboration with composer Herbert Deutch (b. 1932). Other significant artists who have worked with Moog include John Cage (1912–1992), Walter Carlos (b. 1939), Keith Emerson (b. 1948), Gordon Mumma (b. 1935), and Vladimir Ussachevsky (b. 1911).

In the early 1970s, Moog's name more than any other became associated with commercial synthesizers. This was due in part to the success of Walter Carlos's "Switched-On Bach" album released early in 1969, the largest-selling classical record of all time. Carlos used Moog synthesizers exclusively. At the same time, Moog's synthesizers, particularly the *MiniMoog* (in production from 1971 to 1981), were gaining worldwide distribution.

Since that time, Moog has remained active in electro-musical research and in the development of new instruments. His primary focus has been on developing more sophisticated controllers and ways of applying control signals to enhance electronic sounds. In 1977, he left Norlin and founded a new company, Big Briar, in Leicester, North Carolina, which manufactures **keyboards** and pressure-sensitive plates for precise control of analog and digital synthesizers. From 1986 through 1989, Moog was vice president of New Product Research for **Kurzweil** Music Systems in Waltham, Massachusetts. Currently he is research professor at the University of North Carolina, Asheville.

See also Electronic Piano.

Samuel S. Holland

Bibliography

Contemporary Keyboard (1975–).

Crombie, D. "The Moog Story." *Sound International*, 6 (1978): 66.

Darter, T., ed. *The Art of Electronic Music: The Instruments, Designers, and Music Behind the Artistic and Popular Explosion of Electronic Music*. New York: Quill/A Keyboard Book, 1984.

Lee, J. "Interview: Robert Moog." *Polyphony* (January–February 1982).

Rhea, T. "The Moog Synthesizer." *Contemporary Keyboard* vii/3 (1981): 58.

MOÓR, EMANUEL (1863–1931)

Emanuel Moór was a Hungarian composer, pianist, and inventor. A prolific composer of works in all genres, large and small, Moór was an active soloist in Europe and America and the accompanist of such luminaries as Lilli Lehmann.

During the 1920s he invented his Double Keyboard Pianoforte (also called "Duplex Coupler Pianoforte"), in which two **keyboards** are attached to one **action** and one set of **strings**, the upper manual playing an octave higher than the lower. The upper **key** is exactly above the lower, and a tracker mechanism transmits the motion to the **hammer** an octave higher. The keyboards can be coupled together, enabling the player to play octaves with one finger, thick chords with an easy reach, and to make such virtuoso gestures as chromatic glissandi. Promoted by Moór's second wife, the pianist Winifred Christie-Moór (1882–1965), the invention required adding to an already advanced piano technique a quite new one. The coupling stiffened the **touch** and rendered certain note combinations impossible, in addition to inviting the player to double notes in stylistically doubtful places. About sixty-four instruments, including **Steinways, Bechsteins,** and **Bösendorfers,** were fitted with the keyboard (The Metropolitan Museum of Art, New York, owns one). An Emanuel Moór Double Keyboard Piano Trust in England gives fellowships and promotes the instrument.

See also Keyboards.

Edwin M. Good

Bibliography

Moór, Emanuel. "The Duplex-Coupler Pianoforte." *Journal of the Royal Society of the Arts* 70 (1921–22): 363.

Shead, Herbert A. *The History of the Emanuel Moór Double Keyboard Piano.* Old Woking: 1978.

MOZART, (JOHANN CHRYSOSTOM) WOLFGANG AMADEUS (1756–1791)

Wolfgang Amadeus Mozart, Austrian composer and pianist, was born in Salzburg (27 January 1756) and died in Vienna (5 December 1791). He was the son of Leopold Mozart (1719–1787), who was violinist and composer in the court of the Prince-Archbishop of Salzburg. Mozart, along with **Joseph Haydn,** twenty-four years his senior, brought the Viennese Classical style to its height, a style that was enlarged upon and expanded by **Ludwig van Beethoven** into the early years of the nineteenth century.

Mozart's extraordinary gift for music was discovered at an early age while his father was teaching his older sister Maria Anna (Nannerl) (1751–1829) at the harpsichord. Leopold began teaching his son and noted in the music notebook prepared for Nannerl that Wolfgang had learned some of the pieces at the age of four. Leopold also recorded Wolfgang's earliest compositions, an Andante and an Allegro, K. 1a and 1b (NMA, IX:27,1—p. 87), in the notebook with the inscription *Des Wolfgangerl Compositiones in den ersten 3 Monaten nach seines 5ten Jahre.* In January 1762, both Wolfgang and Nannerl were presented to the Elector of Bavaria in Munich, where they performed upon the harpsichord. On 18 September of the same year, the Mozart family set out for Vienna, passing through Linz and Passau where they played before the local nobility. Except for a brief excursion to Pressburg (Bratislava), they remained in Vienna until the end of the year, with the children appearing on several occasions before the Empress Maria Theresa and her court at Schönbrunn during this period.

Upon their return to Salzburg, 5 January 1763, Leopold began planning a more ambitious tour, which would take them to Paris, London, and The Hague. This tour lasted from 9 June 1763 to 29/30 November 1766, during which time Leopold published Wolfgang's first four *opera* containing sonatas for keyboard with the accompaniment of the violin:

Op. 1. 2 Sonatas, K. 6 & 7: Paris, 1764
Op. 2. 2 Sonatas, K. 8 & 9: Paris, 1764
Op. 3. 6 Sonatas, K. 10–15: London, 1765
Op. 4. 6 Sonatas, K. 26–31: The Hague, 1766.

The period during which the young Wolfgang began his musical studies, and on through his early adulthood, was one of continuous experimentation in the construction and evolution of keyboard instruments. At the beginning of this period the harpsichord was the prevalent instrument, with the clavichord as a favorite instrument for the more intimate ambience of the home. By the 1780s, the **fortepiano** had challenged the harpsichord's position. The nomenclature applied to keyboard instruments during this transitory period is often disconcerting and inexact (See E. Badura-Skoda, "Prolegomena to a History of the Viennese Fortepiano"). In addition to the organ—during their travels, Leopold would have Wolfgang test the local organs—there were basically three types of keyboard instruments available to the young Mozart: the harpsichord, the clavichord, and the fortepiano.

The keyboard instruments in the Mozart home.

In a letter dated 9 October 1777 (Bauer-Deutsch, No. 346, 18–22), Leopold cautions his son, prior to his impending visit to the famous organ-builder and maker of keyboard instruments, Johann Andreas **Stein** of Augsburg, not to mention the instruments from Gera in the Mozart household, as Stein might be jealous of the work of **Christian Ernst Friederici** of Gera. If that should not be possible, then Wolfgang should inform Stein of the manner in which the instruments were obtained. The instruments formerly belonged to Count Leopold Pranck, (1728–1793), who was forced to leave Salzburg because of his epilepsy. Although the date of the transaction between Count Pranck and

Leopold is unknown, it evidently occurred while Wolfgang was quite young. It is most significant that Leopold used the plural "von unsern Instrumenten von Gera," for elsewhere he referred to only one of these instruments as being by (Christian Ernst) Friederici of Gera. A description of this instrument appeared in the listing advertising the auction of Leopold's estate in the *Salzburger Intelligenzblatt*, 15 September 1787:

> . . . as also *fourthly* a harpsichord by the celebrated *Friderizi* of *Gera* with two manuals of ebony and ivory throughout five entire octaves, with moreover a special cornet and lute stop (Dokumente, NMA X:34, p. 262).

No further mention of this instrument exists, and therefore its fate remains unknown.

This may have been the instrument to which Leopold referred in his correspondence with his landlord, Lorenz Hagenauer. Leopold wrote from Vienna, 10 November 1762, "Er [Wolferl] lasst [sic] fragen: wie das Clavier lebt?—dessen er sich gar oft erinnert; denn hier haben wir noch kein solches gefunden." (Bauer-Deutsch, No. 41, 35–37). In a letter dated 8 December 1763, Paris, Leopold wrote to Hagenauer that they were staying in the hotel of Count van Eyck, where the Countess had provided them with her harpsichord, and like their own, it had two manuals (Bauer-Deutsch, No. 73, 39–44). Leopold specifically referred to the Friederici instrument in a letter dated 13 November 1777 to his son in Mannheim about his correspondence with Leopold Heinrich Pfeil of Frankfurt concerning a possible appointment there. Herr Pfeil suggested the possibility of a private concert, for which he could supply the instruments from his own collection:

> . . . and he said that you would find at his house a collection of instruments which would mean for you an embarrassment of choice. He mentioned that in addition to his large Friderici [sic] harpsichord [*Flügel*] with two manuals like our own, he had a perfectly new and very large *fortepiano* in mahogany, which he described at length and with the greatest enthusiasm. Further, he has a clavichord also in mahogany, which he would not sell for 200 gulden, as he says that this instrument simply has not got its equal; that the descant sounds like a violin being played softly, and the bass notes like trombones. In addition, he has a number of fortepianos, as he deals in these, all by Friderici (Bauer-Deutsch No. 369, 79–88).

(Eva Badura-Skoda has recently discovered evidence that the Friederici instrument in the Mozart household was not a normal harpsichord but a two manual compound (**combination**) instrument, which may explain why the young Mozart had the possibility from the very beginning to play an instrument *che fà il piano e il forte*.)

In the correspondence of the Mozart family, three different clavichords are mentioned. The first of these is an *artiges clavierl* [charming little clavichord] that Leopold purchased from the Augsburg organ maker Johann Andreas Stein in the summer of 1763 for practice purposes while traveling (Bauer-Deutsch No. 63, Letter from Leopold Mozart to Lorenz Hagenauer, 76–78). This instrument may have been drawn into service during the subsequent travels to Vienna, Italy, and Munich. Wolfgang mentions it again in October 1778 on his return from Paris, where he had suffered the tragic loss of his mother. He wrote to his father from Nancy on 3 October 1778:

> I should also like to have beside my writing desk the *clavierl* [little clavichord] which [Dominico] Fischietti and [Jakob] Rust had, as it suits me better than Stein's small one (Bauer-Deutsch, No. 494, 55–59).

The clavichord that replaced the Stein instrument had recently come into the hands of Leopold Mozart. The former owners, Fischietti and Rust, had each served as second Kappelmeister to the Court in Salzburg: Fischietti from September 1772 to 1775 and Rust from 1777 to 1778. The request by Wolfgang that this instrument be placed beside his writing desk indicates that he very probably used it extensively during the process of composition. In his reply to Wolfgang's request, Leopold reassured him, in a letter dated 23 November 1778, that "the clavichord [*clavicordin*] has been under your writing table for a very long time" (Bauer-Deutsch No. 506, 108).

In a letter from Constanze (Mozart) Nissen to Gaspare Spontini (April 1828), she describes the clavichord, then in the possession of Wolfgang's sister, Maria Anna (Nannerl) von Berchtold zu Sonnenburg, as having only five octaves (Bauer-Deutsch No. 1425). In the inventory of Nannerl's estate taken on 25 January 1830, two keyboard instruments are listed: "1 Wiener Fortepiano" and "1 Klavikor." Nannerl's fortepiano was built by organ and instrument maker Johann Schmid (c. 1757–1804) in Salzburg. The clavichord, described by Leopold as a *grosses Clavicord* in the letter dated 21 February 1785 (Bauer-Deutsch No. 848, 44), was presented to Nannerl by her father following her wedding. Vincent Novello provided a description of this clavichord when he and his wife, accompanied by Mozart's young son, Franz Xaver (1791–1844), visited Nannerl on 25 July 1829. After describing the state of Nannerl's health—she was bedridden, partially paralyzed, and had been blind since 1825—Vincent noted in his diary:

> In the middle of the room stood the instrument on which she had played duets with her brother. It was a kind of Clavichord, with black keys for the naturals and white ones for the sharps like on old English cathedral organs.

> The range was from contra-*F* to *f*³ and had evidently been constructed before the additional keys were invented. The tone was soft and some of the bass notes, especially those of the lowest octave from *c to C* were of good quality; at the time it was no doubt considered an excellent instrument. You may be sure that I touched the keys (which had been pressed by Mozart's fingers) with great interest. Mozart's son also played a few chords upon it with evident pleasure. The key he chose was that of C minor, and what he did, though short, was quite sufficient to show the accomplished musician (Mary Cowden Clarke. *The Life and Labours of Vincent Novello*, p. 26ff).

Mozart on Tour

No documentary evidence exists as to whether there was a fortepiano in Salzburg during Mozart's childhood. It is not until Mozart's visit to the workshop of Johann Andreas Stein in Augsburg during October 1777 that he demonstrated any enthusiasm for the instrument, or rather for the recent improvements in the **escapement** of the Stein fortepiano. During their various tours, the Mozart family most certainly came into contact with fortepianos, for the earliest recorded recital in Vienna on the instrument was 1763. There was ample opportunity in London during the tour of 1764–65 to become acquainted with not only the newer experiments in harpsichord building but also with the fortepiano, which was in its early stages of development.

In a letter detailing expenses to Lorenz Hagenauer of a concert given 5 June 1764 in London, Leopold Mozart listed among other things: "Each keyboard instrument [Clavier], of which I had to have two on account of the concerto for two keyboard instruments [2 Clavecins], costs half a guinea" (Bauer-Deutsch No. 89, 52–53). After Leopold's illness in August, when the Mozart family was forced to retire to Chelsea for two months during his recovery, he felt the need to improve his financial situation. The children were to appear in a series of concerts culminating in the benefit concert given 13 May 1765 at the Hickford's Great Room in Brewer Street. The notice in the *Public Advertiser* (13 May 1765) gave the following details:

> For the Benefit of Miss MOZART of thirteen, and Master MOZART of Eight Years of Age, Prodigies of Nature.

> HICKFORD's Great Room in Brewer Street, this day, May 13, will be a CONCERT of VOCAL and INSTRUMENTAL MUSIC.

> With all the OVERTURES of the little Boy's own composition.

> The Vocal Part by Sig. Cremonimi; Concerto on the Violin, Mr. Barthelomon; Solo on the Violoncello, Sig. Cirii; Concerto on the Harpsichord by the little Composer and his Sister, each single and both together, &c.

> Tickets at 5s each, to be had of Mr. Mozart, at Mr. Williamson's, in Thrift-Street, Soho (Dokumente, NMA X:34, p. 44).

In a later announcement, the *Public Advertiser* (9 July 1765) stated: "The Two Children will play also together with four Hands upon the same Harpsichord, and put upon it a Handkerchief, without seeing the keys" (Dokumente. NMA X:34, p. 45). Wolfgang's music for two harpsichords or for four hands on one harpsichord from this early period has not survived, with the single exception of the Sonata in C Major, K. 19d, which appeared in two unauthorized editions about 1789, Roullede in Paris and H. Andrews and R. Birchall in London. The frequent collision of the hands between the two performers suggests it was written for a two-manual instrument. A description of such an instrument appeared in the *Europaeischen Zeitung*, Salzburg, 6 August 1765. It has been suggested that this notice was written by Leopold Mozart.

> *London, 5 July 1765.* The very famous clavier maker Burkard Thudy [*sic*] of this city, Swiss by birth, had the honour of making for the King of Prussia a wing-shaped instrument [*Flügel*] with two manuals which was

very much admired by all who saw it. It has been regarded as particularly noteworthy that Mr. Thudy connected all the stops to a pedal, so that they can be drawn by treading, one after another, and the decrease and increase of tone may be varied at will, which crescendo and decrescendo has been long wished for by clavier players. Mr. Thudy has moreover conceived the good notion of having his extraordinary instrument played for the first time by the most extraordinary clavier player in this world, namely by the very celebrated master of music Wolfg. Mozart, aged nine, the admirable son of the Salzburg Kapellmeister, Herr Mozart. It was quite enchanting to hear the fourteen-year-old sister of this little virtuoso playing the most difficult sonatas on the harpsichord [Flügel] with the most astonishing dexterity and her brother accompanying her extempore on another harpsichord. Both perform wonders (Dokumente NMA X:34, p. 47).

This instrument is now preserved in the Kunstgewerbe Museum, Wroclaw.

The increasing and decreasing of **tone** referred to was made possible through a crescendo device that appeared in the English two-manual harpsichords by the instrument makers **Burkat Shudi** and **Jacob Kirkman** in the early 1760s. A **pedal** stop was added that overrode the manually operated stops. When depressed, it disengaged the 8-foot register of the upper manual and, at the same time, engaged the lute stop. The coupling of the 4-foot and 8-foot on the lower manual was simultaneously replaced by the 8-foot alone. This pedal stop could be disengaged to resume the normal hand-stop operation. By 1766, Shudi had developed another crescendo device, the Venetian swell, which he **patented** in 1769. The swell consisted of a device that enabled the performer to raise and lower the lid of the harpsichord and, at the same time, include a series of louvres, or shutters, that covered the **soundboard** and could be opened at will. Through the combination of these various devices an effective crescendo could be produced. The Mozarts left London at the end of July 1765, before some of the later developments were perfected.

On their first Italian tour, a portrait of Wolfgang sitting before a harpsichord was painted by the artist Saverio dalla Rosa on 6–7 January 1770 for Pietro Lugiati, the Mozarts' host in Verona. The inscription on the harpsichord reads "Ioannis Celestini veneti MDLXXXIII." In this portrait, Wolfgang is looking away from the keyboard toward the painter. Before him is an open manuscript, perhaps of one of Wolfgang's compositions for keyboard, which dalla Rosa painted in detail. This is the only source for this *Molto allegro* , published for the first time in the *Neue Mozart Ausgabe* (K. 72a—IX:27, 2, p. 169).

The earliest account of Mozart performing on the fortepiano was written by Christian Friedrich Daniel Schubart in the *Deutsche Chronik*, 27 April 1775. Mozart was in Munich for the premiere of his opera buffa *La finta giardiniera* (K. 196). The competition between Wolfgang and Ignaz von Beecke, music director to Prince Kraft Ernst von Oettingen-Wallerstein, described in this account, took place during the winter of 1774–75 in the residence of Franz Albert on Kaufinger Strasse.

Just think, brother, what a delight that was! In Munich last winter I heard two of the greatest clavier players, Herr *Mozart* and Captain *von Beecke*; my host, Herr Albert, who is enthusiastic about all that is great and beautiful, has an excellent fortepiano in his house. It was there that I heard these two giants in contest on the clavier. Mozart's playing had great weight, and he read at sight everything that was put before him. But no more than that; Beecke surpasses him by a long way. Winged agility, grace, melting sweetness and a quite peculiar, self-informed taste are clubs which nobody is likely to wrest from this Hercules (Dokumente, NMA X:34, p. 138).

Mozart's earliest preserved sonatas for the solo keyboard [K. 279–284] were written during the early months of 1775 in Munich. It would be interesting to know more about the fortepiano of Herr Albert in respect to these works. Mozart's letters contain nothing about this event.

In September 1777, Wolfgang, accompanied by his mother, set out on a tour that would take them to Munich, Augsburg, Mannheim, and Paris. After his mother's death on 3 July 1778 in Paris, Wolfgang was to make the journey home alone. Mozart armed himself for whatever occasion might arise with music of various genres that he had composed between 1773 and 1777. Among the compositions involving keyboards were the four Concertos—D Major, B-flat Major, C Major, and E-flat Major (K. 175, 238, 246, 271); the Concerto for Three Klaviers (K. 242); the Divertimento in B-flat Major for Keyboard, Violin, and Violoncello (K. 254); the six Sonatas (K. 279–284); and the *Fischer* Variations (K. 179). In Munich on 2 October 1777, Mozart humorously wrote his father that on the next day they were to have a "kleine schlackakademie . . . auf den elenden Clavier Nota bene. auweh! auweh! auweh." Four days later he described the occasion, which took place on the fourth of October, in which he played his three concertos in C Major, B-flat Major, and E-flat Major, followed by the Divertimento, before demonstrating his abilities as a violin soloist in the Divertimento in B-flat Major, K. 287. In some writings it has been assumed that the wretched clavier that Mozart played on this occasion was a fortepiano, but his letters are vague about the type of keyboard instrument he used.

In his letter of 17 October 1777 from Augsburg, Mozart told of his visit to Johann Andreas Stein. Stein is credited with the development of an individual escapement for the *Prellmechanik* in constructing his fortepianos, which would soon be adopted by other makers, including Johann Schmid of Salzburg. Several days later, Mozart wrote his much-quoted letter to his father praising the advancements of the Stein fortepiano:

> This time I shall begin at once with Stein's pianofortes. Before I had seen any of his make, Späth's claviers had always been my favorites. But now I much prefer Stein's, for they damp ever so much better than the Regensburg instruments. When I strike hard, I can keep my finger on the note or raise it, but the sound ceases the moment I have produced it. In whatever way I touch the keys, the tone is always even. It never jars, it is never stronger or weaker or entirely absent; in a word, it is always even. It is true that he does not sell a pianoforte of this kind for less than three hundred gulden, but the trouble and the labor which Stein puts into making of it cannot be paid for. His instruments have this special advantage over others in that they are made with escape action. Only one maker in a hundred bothers about this. But without an escapement it is impossible to avoid jangling and vibration after the note is struck. When you touch the keys, the hammers fall back again the moment after they have struck the strings, whether you hold down the keys or release them. He told me himself that when he has finished making one of these claviers, he sits down to it and tries all kinds of passages, runs and jumps, and he shaves and works away until it can do anything. For he labors solely in the interest of music and not for his own profit; otherwise he would soon finish his work. He often says: "if I were not myself such a passionate lover of music and had not myself some slight skill on the clavier, I should certainly long ago have lost patience with my work. But I do like an instrument which never lets the player down and which is durable." And his claviers certainly do last. He guarantees that the sounding-board will never break or split. When he has finished making one for a clavier, he places it in the open air, exposing it to rain, snow, the heat of the sun and all the devils in order that it may crack. Then he inserts wedges and glues them in to make the instrument very strong and firm. He is delighted when it cracks, for he can then be sure that nothing more can happen to it. Indeed he often cuts into it himself and then glues it together again and strengthens it in this way. He has finished making three pianofortes of this kind. Today I played on one again (Bauer-Deutsch, No. 352, 2–34).

From this letter, it can be ascertained that Mozart previously had experience with various models of fortepianos, and of these he had preferred those by Franz Jakob **Späth**, builder of organs and claviers in Regensburg. But the superiority of the *Prellmechanik* escapement as perfected by Stein, which avoids the stuttering and blocking common to other instruments, brought about Mozart's enthusiastic endorsement. He was especially pleased when he tried out the Sonata in D Major, K. 284, which "sounds exquisite on Stein's pianoforte. The device, too, which you work with your knee is better on his than on other instruments. I have only to touch it and it works; and when you shift your knee the slightest bit, you do not hear the least reverberation" (Bauer-Deutsch, No. 352, 49–53).

On 22 October 1777, Mozart presented a program in the concert hall of Count Fugger at Augsburg. Among the works included were the Concerto for Three Klaviers, K. 242 (assisted by Johann Michael Demmler, organist at the Augsburg Cathedral, and Johann Andreas Stein), the Sonata in D Major, K. 284, and the Concerto in B-flat Major, K. 238. A review from the *Augsburgische Staats- und Gelehrten Zeitung* of 28 October 1777 gives the following account:

> . . . the rendering on the pianoforte so neat, so clean, so full of expression, and yet at the same time extraordinarily rapid, so that one hardly knew what to give attention to first, and all the hearers were enraptured. One found here mastery in thought, mastery in performance, mastery in the instruments, all at the same time. One thing always gave

relief to another, so that the numerous assembly was displeased with nothing but the fact that pleasure was not prolonged further. The patriotically minded has the special satisfaction . . . to hear a virtuoso who may place himself side by side with the great masters of our nation, and yet is at least half our own—and to hear instruments which according to the judgment of strangers by far surpass all others of the kind. And Stein also belongs to us: he himself plays, and has a taste for the more refined music (Dokumente, NMA X; 34, p. 150).

While a certain degree of ambiguity may hover over which keyboard instrument may have been intended for his works composed prior to October 1777, it is most certain that his compositions for keyboard after that date were intended for the fortepiano. Among the first of these to be written during the fall of 1777 in Mannheim were the Sonatas in C Major and D Major, K. 309 and K. 311, followed by the Sonata in A minor, K. 310, composed about the time of his mother's death in Paris during the summer of 1778. All three of these works demonstrate not only the new compositional techniques that Mozart had acquired during his stay in Mannheim, but also an awareness of the new capabilities of the fortepiano as perfected by Stein.

Vienna (1781–1791)

In the inventory taken on 9 December 1791 of Mozart's estate, the only keyboard instrument listed was "1 Forte-piano with pedal." However, in the *Wiener Zeitung* of 21 March 1795, the following advertisement appeared:

Forte Piano and Clavichord for sale

A large Forte piano and a Clavichord of the late Mozart's are for sale each day. Prospective purchasers are invited to inquire at the sign of the Black Elephant in the Rothe Thurmgasse, where the coffee-house is, on the first floor, right hand side, before 1 o'clock p.m (Dokumente, NMA X:34, p. 414).

There is some uncertainty as to the fate of these instruments between the years 1793 and 1810, when Constanze presented the two instruments in question to her sons. Karl Thomas Mozart (1784–1858), who was living in Milan, received the fortepiano built by **Anton Walter** and upon Karl's death it was bequeathed to the Mozarteum in Salzburg. The clavichord went to the younger son, Franz Xaver (Wolfgang Amadeus, *fils*), who returned it to his mother in 1829. Upon her death in 1841, it again became the property of Franz Xaver and, following his death in 1844, was also bequeathed to the Mozarteum in Salzburg. Both instruments are on display at the Mozart Geburtshaus in Salzburg.

When Constanze received the clavichord from her son in 1829, she entered the following comment in her diary:

11 August 1829—My dear clavier: upon which Mozart had played so often and had composed *Zauberflöte*, *La clemenza di Tito*, the *Requiem* and *Eine Freimaurer Cantate*: to receive it; how very happy I am about it, I can barely describe it. Mozart had so loved this clavier, and for that reason I love it doubly (Bauer-Deutsch, No. 1438).

In her will, this instrument is listed as a clavichord (Bauer-Deutsch, No. 1471).

It is too often overlooked that the clavichord played an important role in Mozart's life, even after his enthusiastic endorsement of the fortepiano. The latter became his public instrument, while the former was used in the more private surroundings of the home, and, if Constanze is to be believed, as the instrument upon which he tried out his masterpieces in the process of composing them.

In his correspondence with his father during the Mannheim-Paris tour of 1777–78 and the early years in Vienna (c. 1781–84), Mozart often gave a description of his latest improvisations on the clavichord. In Augsburg, prior to his visit with Stein, Mozart met with the Arch-Magistrate von Langenmantel where he improvised and read at sight some pieces by Johann Friedrich Edelmann on a "good" clavichord by Stein. Several days after Mozart wrote his enthusiastic letter concerning the Stein fortepiano, he rehearsed some symphonies and concertos with the orchestra at the Church of the Holy Cross. Afterwards, they brought out a small clavichord upon which Mozart played one of his sonatas (from K. 279–284) and the *Fischer* Variations (K. 179). Then Mozart improvised a fugue. On his return trip from Salzburg to Vienna, Mozart arrived in Linz on the morning of 30 October 1783, "just in time to accompany the 'Agnus Dei' on the organ. . . . We spent the whole day there and I played both on the organ and on a clavichord" (Bauer-Deutsch, No. 766, 7–11).

After his success with *Idomeneo* in Munich in the early part of 1781, Mozart was summoned by the archbishop of Salzburg to join his entourage in Vienna. Once in Vienna, Mozart became an almost daily visitor to Countess Wilhelmine Thun, who owned a Stein fortepiano. Mozart was invited by Joseph Starzer to perform for the annual benefit concert for widows of musicians, to be given by the Wiener Ton-Künstlersozietät on 3 April 1781. At first the archbishop refused permission, and Mozart complained in a letter to his father, stating:

> I am not only sorry for the following reason. I would not have played a concerto, but (as the Emperor sits in the proscenium box) I would have extemporized and played a fugue and then the variations on "Je suis Lindor" on Countess Thun's beautiful Stein pianoforte, which she would have lent me. Whenever I have played this program in public, I have always won the greatest applause (Bauer-Deutsch, No. 585, 83–87).

It so happens that Mozart was finally given permission to perform for this occasion, but he did not give the details of which pieces were played or if he had the Countess Thun's fortepiano at his disposal. She did provide her fortepiano for another occasion, the contest between Mozart and **Clementi** before Emperor Joseph at the Hofburg on 24 December 1781. From Mozart's report to his father, he was able to extemporize and play some sonatas by Giovanni Paisiello, but when the two were to improvise on a theme and develop it at two pianos, Mozart played the inferior instrument out of deference to the visiting composer. Unfortunately, the instrument was out of tune and three keys were stuck. In the process of composing *Die Entführung aus dem Serail,* Mozart often brought his latest efforts to the Countess, both to try out on her pianoforte and to keep her abreast of his progress.

After his dismissal from the archbishop's court, Mozart obtained lodgings with Frau Cäcilie Weber, his future mother-in-law. In a letter dated 27 June 1781 he mentioned that he had in the house two *Flügel,* "one for galanterie playing," and the other was "strung with the low octave throughout, like the one we had in London, and consequently sounds like an organ. So on this one I improvised and played fugues" (Bauer-Deutsch No. 608, 23–26).

Upon settling permanently in Vienna, Mozart soon became established as an extraordinarily gifted pianist. He gave a concert on 23 November 1781 with his pupil Josepha Auernhammer at her father's house, in which they played the Concerto in E-flat Major for Two Pianos, K. 365, with the added orchestration of two clarinets, two trumpets, and tympani. For this occasion, Mozart wrote his Sonata in D Major for two pianos, K. 448. The following year he appeared in concert playing his Concertos in C Major, E-flat Major, and D Major (K. 246, 271, and 175). For the last mentioned he composed a new finale, the Konzert Rondo in D Major, K. 382. During the winter of 1782/83, he wrote a Konzert Rondo in A Major, K. 386, and the three Concertos in A Major, F Major, and C Major (K. 414, 413, and 415).

Sometime between 1782 and 1785, Mozart purchased his fortepiano built by Anton Walter. The assumed date most often given is about 1783, but the earliest description of it appears in a letter of Leopold Mozart to his daughter dated 12 March 1785:

> Since my arrival your brother's fortepiano has been taken at least a dozen times to the theater or to some other house. He has had a large fortepiano pedal made, which stands under the instrument and is about two feet longer and extremely heavy. It is taken to the Mehlgrube every Friday and has also been taken to Count Zichy's and to Prince Kaunitz's (Bauer-Deutsch, No. 850, 40–45).

Ulrich Rück describes the instrument, which is preserved in the Mozart Geburtshaus in Salzburg, as having five octaves. There are two knee levers to work the **dampers**; the right knee lever raises only those of the treble. A **moderator** operated by a knob is placed in the middle of the **case** above the keyboard (Ulrich Rück: "Mozarts Hammerflügel erbaute Anton Walter, Wien"). The pedal board that Mozart had built especially for the instrument no longer exists.

Mozart may have already procured this piano before he took his bride to his parental home in Salzburg in 1783. If so, then the Piano Sonatas, K. 330–332, written presumably in Salzburg (according to the latest studies in paper types and handwriting), and the Sonata in B-flat Major, K. 333, written on his return to Linz, were composed with this instrument in mind. All four of these sonatas were published the following year by Artaria and Torricella.

In the *Jahrbuch der Tonkunst von Wien und Prag* of 1796, fortepianos by various makers were compared. The Walter fortepianos were recommended for their full, bell-like **tone**, a precise response, and a strong, resonant bass. For pianists fond of a powerful sound and a rich tone, and who could attempt the most ticklish runs and fast octaves, the Walter fortepiano would be ideal. These were exactly the qualities Mozart desired in performing his twelve great concertos written between 1784 and 1786.

In recent years, the concertos for fortepiano, in particular, have drawn the attention of those interested in "historically informed" performances. Between 1983 and 1989, Malcolm Bilson recorded the twenty-three original concertos on an instrument modeled on Mozart's fortepiano preserved in the Geburtshaus, built in 1977 by Philip Belt of New Haven, Connecticut. John Eliot Gardiner conducts The English Baroque Soloists on authentic instruments. For the double and triple piano concertos, they are assisted by Robert Levin and Melvyn Tan on instruments modeled on those of Walter. These performances are based upon the *Neue Mozart Ausgabe* in consultation with the original autographs. They have generated rethinking in terms of Mozart's notation regarding the performance of articulations, appoggiaturas, dynamics, basso continuo, and the balance between the solo instrument and orchestra. One of the consequences of this renewed interest, especially in anticipation of the bicentennial commemoration of Mozart's death in 1991, was a symposium on Mozart's fortepiano concertos, sponsored by the University of Michigan from 16 to 19 November 1989. This MozartFest brought many important scholars under the directorship of Neal Zaslaw into contact with leading fortepianists. Ten concertos were performed by different artists, with Roger Norrington conducting the Ars Musica Baroque Orchestra. The interest generated by this symposium could not fail to have an impact on the various conferences projected for the Mozart Year (1991), in which "historically informed" performances were a key issue.

The publication of the individual concertos in "study score" format (i.e., larger than the pocket-size miniature score), based on the *Neue Mozart Ausgabe*, is in progress by Bärenreiter. For this edition, the errata listed in the *Kritische Berichte* have been emended except for the concertos, whose autographs resurfaced only in 1977, and are now housed at the Biblioteka Jagiellonska in Kraków, Poland. They had been sent to Silesia for safekeeping in 1941 and disappeared at the end of World War II. For the concertos in question, the errata based on the re-study of the autographs are given as an appendix in the respective issue.

In addition to the concertos, Malcolm Bilson has recorded the sonatas for fortepiano and violin with Sergiu Luca (issued by Nonesuch), and is presently recording the complete piano sonatas (issued by Hungaroton). The piano trios have been recorded on period instruments by the London Fortepiano Trio (issued by Hyperion).

Recent books on eighteenth-century performance practices, such as Sandra Rosenblum's *Performance Practices in Classic Piano Music*, published by Indiana University Press, are more cognizant of the importance of understanding the original instruments even for a "historically informed" performance on modern instruments. This recently acquired knowledge, with the near completion of the *Neue Mozart Ausgabe* and the greater accessibility of facsimile editions, is changing our concepts of the performance of Mozart works, not only in regard to authentic instruments but also in its application to how the music can be "authentically" produced on modern instruments.

W. Richard Shindle

Bibliography

Badura-Skoda, Eva. "Prolegomena to a History of the Viennese Fortepiano." *Israel Studies in Musicology* 2 (1980): 77–99.

Badura-Skoda, Eva, and Paul Badura-Skoda. *Interpreting Mozart on the Keyboard*. London: Barrie & Rockliff, 1961; New York: St. Martin's Press, 1962.

Bauer, Wilhelm A., and Otto Erich Deutsch. *Mozart. Briefe und Aufzeichnungen. Gesamtausgabe*. 1–4, Basel-London-New York: Bärenreiter Kassel, 1962–1963.

Bilson, Malcolm. "The Mozart Piano Concertos Rediscovered." *Mozart Jahrbuch 1986*; 58–61.

Broder, Nathan. "Mozart and the Clavier." *Musical Quarterly* 27 (October 1941): 422–32.

Clarke, M. Cowden. *The Life and Labours of Vincent Novello*. London, 1864.

Deutsch, Otto Erich. *Mozart: Die Dokumente seiner Lebens*. [*Neue Mozart Ausgabe. Serie X/32*] Kassel, 1961.

Kinsksy, Georg. "Mozart-Instrumente." *Acta Musicologica* 12 (1940): 1–21.

Rück, Ulrich. "Mozarts Hammerflügel erbaute Anton Walter, Wien." *Mozart Jahrbuch 1955*, 246–62.

Russell, John F. "Mozart and the PianoForte: A Prelude to the Study of His Concertos." *Music Review* 1 (August 1940): 226–44.

Schönfeld, Johann Ferdinand von. *Jahrbuch der Tonkunst von Wien und Prag 1796.* Im Schönfeldischen Verlag (Wien und Prag) 1796.

Willner, Channan. "Michigan MozartFest and Mozart's Fortepiano Concertos." *Musical Times* 131 (June 1990): 330–33.

MUIR, WOOD AND COMPANY (1798–1818)

The leading firm of piano makers in Scotland during the early nineteenth century was Muir, Wood and Company. In 1798, following the failure of his brother's music retailing businesses, John Muir formed a new firm in partnership with Andrew Wood. The roles of the partners were contrasting but complementary: Muir, one of the capital's most prosperous merchants, provided the finance, retailing experience, and commercial acumen; Wood, a skilled craftsman apprenticed under a local maker of keyboard instruments, James Logan, directed manufacturing, **tuning**, and repairing activities.

The firm's shop occupied various sites in Edinburgh's New Town, notably in Leith Street. The partners also established a modest outlet in London. In 1804, George Small became a partner; he ran the extensive retailing side of the business. Trading continued until Muir's death in 1818.

A sizable work force was employed at the Calton Hill factory. In addition to pianos, the company made organs (church, chamber, and barrel), harps, violins, cellos, tambourines, triangles, drums, and serpents. In 1799 the firm's prestige was enhanced by the award of a royal warrant as "Musical Instrument Makers to his Majesty."

Muir, Wood and Company produced some 2,200 **square pianos**; there is no evidence that the firm made **grands**. All extant instruments have a $5\frac{1}{2}$-octave compass (FF–c^4), and most adopted the **Broadwood** system of **stringing**, with **tuning pins** placed along the back of the case. After about 1803, a damper-lift **pedal** mechanism was fitted as standard. Changes in furniture design generally followed contemporary London fashions. French **frames** were retained until about 1809, and square-fronted, six-legged models were standard after about 1814. However, in the interim, cases with unusual, sharply-rounded front corners and four turned legs became the norm: this contrasts with mainstream London design. Although economies were made concerning technical details, notably in the preference for the English single **action** and brass under-**dampers** until about 1814, innovative experiments were occasionally apparent. Some early examples were fitted with compensating tuning springs (Litherland's **patent**, no.2430); a later instrument was adorned with three **soundboard** bridges.

See also Scotland, Piano Industry in.

John Cranmer

MÜLLER, MATTHIAS (1769/70–1844)

Matthias Müller was one of the most ingenious Viennese piano builders of his time. Although he was born in Germany he became a citizen of Vienna in 1796. His instruments reflected the many developments and innovative concepts of the day. In 1797 he constructed a "piano in the form of a lying harp," but his best-known invention was the *"Ditanaklasis* ("Dittanaclasis" or "Ditaleloclange") (1800), one of the first **upright pianos** (with **frame** to the floor). During this same time Müller built a violin-piano, the "Xaenorphica," which was a keyboard instrument tuned like a harp, with the **strings** activated by violin bows. Müller **patented** a downstrike **action** in 1823, and in 1827 he patented his invention of the "Gabel-Harmon-Pianoforte," in which certain **bridge pins** were replaced with tuning forks that were tuned to the note of their particular strings, thus purportedly giving the **tone** a fuller and bell-like quality.

See also Hawkins, John Isaac.

Alfons Huber

Bibliography

Beschreibung der Erfindungen und Verbesserungen, für welche in den k.k. Österreichischen Staaten Patente erteilt wurden. Edited by k.k. allgemeine Hofkammer. Vol. 1 and Vol. 2. Wien: Hof- und Staatsdruckerei, 1841.

Harding, Rosamond E.M. *The Piano-Forte: Its History Traced to the Great Exhibition of 1851.* Cambridge: Cambridge University Press, 1933. Reprints. New York: Da Capo Press, 1973; Old Woking, Surrey: Gresham Books, 1978.

Haupt, Helga. "Wiener Instrumentenbauer von 1791–1815." In *Studien zur Musikwissenschaft.* Edited by Erich Schenk. Vol. 24. Wien-Graz-Köln: Böhlau, 1960.

MUSIC DESK

The music desk is that part of the case of a piano designed to hold printed music upright for performance. Depending on the style of the instrument, a piano's music desk or music rest (British term) may range from plain, solid, and stationary to fancy, carved, and hinged. Some decorative models even include metal grillwork (which may develop an annoying rattle).

Early pianos had music desks that allowed the performer to enjoy a variety of adjustments, both to the angle of the desk and to the height and placement of the unit. Adjustable platforms for holding candlesticks were also an early feature of the music desk.

Peggy Flanagan Baird

MUSIC FOR THE PIANO

Since the middle of the eighteenth century, the piano has played an overwhelmingly important role in the development and dissemination of Western music, while compositions for that instrument have grown into a body of literature of enormous size. Piano music may be divided into five principal chronological categories: (1) early, c. 1750–1780; (2) Classical, c. 1770–1828; (3) Romantic, c. 1810–1848; (4) post-Romantic and Impressionist, c. 1848–1918; and (5) modern, beginning c. 1900. Other kinds of piano music can be placed into a sixth category: i.e., jazz, rag, and popular piano styles.

Early. Although **Bartolomeo Cristofori's** three surviving pianos date from the 1720s, the first idiomatic compositions for piano were probably completed after 1750. (The "piano" sonatas published by **Lodovico Giustini** in 1732 are considered by many musicologists to have been a mere publicity stunt.) **C.P.E. Bach**, for example, mentions the piano in his *Versuch über die wahre Art das Clavier zu spielen* ("Essay on the True Art of Playing Keyboard Instruments"; 1753), and Johann Gottfried Eckard's Sonatas, Opp. 1–2, which call for piano, were composed during 1763–64. The comparative unimportance of Giustini's and Eckard's pieces does not mean, however, that the piano existed unrecognized and unplayed for almost half a century. **Domenico Scarlatti**, Georg Friedrich Handel, and **Johann Sebastian Bach** were acquainted with pianos manufactured by several different firms, although they wrote no music specifically designed for those instruments. It should

also be remembered that much of the music composed for harpsichords, clavichords, and other early keyboard instruments since the late sixteenth century can be and has been performed on the modern piano. Pieces by Renaissance composers, among them selections from collections like *Parthenia* (1612–13) and the *Fitzwilliam Virginal Book* (c. 1609–19) sometimes appear on recital programs today, while movements from the clavecin compositions of François Couperin and Jean-Philip Rameau have become staples of certain pianists' repertories. No less a virtuoso than the late Vladimir Horowitz, for instance, helped during the 1950s and 1960s to popularize as piano music some of the 555 keyboard sonatas composed by Domenico Scarlatti. (**Liszt** attempted the same task during the 1840s, with somewhat less success.) Unfortunately for modern audiences, the harpsichord works of Handel are much less well known. Finally, the importance of the keyboard works of J.S. Bach to the evolution of piano performing technique and literature can scarcely be exaggerated. **Beethoven, Chopin, Schumann, Liszt,** and **Brahms** were deeply influenced by Bach's brand of keyboard writing as well as by his overall musical genius. Bach's sets of clavier pieces—among them six Partitas, six French Suites, and six English Suites, as well as occasional works like the Italian Concerto and especially the two volumes of preludes and fugues known as the "Well-Tempered Clavier" (1722, 1744)—began during the nineteenth century to appear frequently on recital programs and continue to appear today, even after several twentieth-century revivals of "authentic" Baroque performance practices.

The most important pre-Classical composer of genuine piano music, however, was probably Carl Philipp Emanuel Bach, son of J.S. Bach and himself an artist of considerable distinction. C.P.E. Bach appears to have abandoned the clavichord in favor of the piano sometime after the 1740s; he published six piano sonatas as his Op. 1 in 1768 and he included works specifically designed for the piano in his "Kenner und Liebhaber" ["Experts and Enthusiasts"] series between 1779 and 1787. His "Abschied von meinem Silbermannischen Claviere, in einem Rondo" ["Departure from my Silbermann Piano, written in the form of a Rondo"; 1781] exploits the ability of Cristofori's invention to enhance "empfindsamer" ("sensitive") effects:

sudden contrasts in dynamics as well as texture, and prolonged single notes and chords.

Classical. **Johann Christian Bach**, another of J.S. Bach's children and (at least for a time) the most outwardly successful of them, may be thought to have launched Classical piano music in 1763, with the completion of his so-called London concerto. J.C. Bach's keyboard compositional style featured glittering passage work and sweet, often extremely simple harmonic progressions—effects characteristic of the "Galant" (or "noble") style and very different from the sudden mood and key shifts of C.P.E. Bach's piano works. Despite his accomplishments in symphonic music, J.C. Bach is perhaps best remembered for his influence on the compositions of **Wolfgang Amadeus Mozart**. Mozart first copied J.C. Bach when he began work on his first (unfinished) Sinfonias (K. 19). Later, Mozart arranged as concertos three of J.C. Bach's Op. 6 piano sonatas (originally published in 1766). The imprint of J.C. Bach's concerto style may be felt in almost every Mozart piano-concerto movement, especially in the more straightforward, lyrical passages.

Borrowing from all three Bachs as well as from **Joseph Haydn** and other eighteenth-century figures, Mozart completed a considerable body of piano music: twenty-three piano concertos and several concerto fragments perhaps deserve pride of place, followed by sonatas, sets of variations, chamber works of many kinds, and works for two pianos and piano four-hands. "Galant" gestures appear throughout Mozart's piano compositions, but so do *Sturm und Drang* ["Storm and Stress"] figures: the first-movement development of his C-minor piano concerto (K. 491), for example, reaches its climax when the principal theme, played by a single flute, is supported by piano arpeggios in the unusual key of F-sharp minor. At other moments Mozart strikes "empfindsamerisch" (or "sensitive") poses: the Rondo in A minor (K. 511) is unusually contemplative, while the Fantasy in C Minor (K. 475) anticipates the turbulence of many Romantic keyboard rhapsodies and ballades. Less often associated with piano literature, Haydn nevertheless wrote a great deal of it; sixty-two piano sonatas (including lost and fragmentary works) as well as variation sets and fantasies comprise only part of his keyboard output, which also includes almost thirty piano trios and several piano concertos.

Less idiomatic than Mozart's pieces in their keyboard writing, less accessible perhaps in their quirky good-humor and surprising shifts of dynamics and key, Haydn's piano sonatas are today finding a place for themselves in the repertories of important European and American performers.

Beethoven studied with Haydn, and his early piano music reflects that tutelage. Yet Beethoven's mature piano works—like his symphonies and string quartets—could have been written by no one else. A meticulous craftsman as well as an improviser of enormous skill and a capable chamber musician, Beethoven composed thirty-seven complete and fragmentary sonatas for piano between 1783 and 1822. The thirty-two sonatas published during his lifetime, together with the so-called Diabelli Variations (Op. 120) and several other variation sets, comprise one of the cornerstones of piano literature. Beethoven also published five piano concertos, a "triple" concerto for piano, violin, and cello with orchestra (Op. 56), a fantasy for piano, chorus, and orchestra (the so-called Choral Fantasy, Op. 80), and—almost equally important—three sets of Bagatelles (Opp. 33, 119, and 126) that anticipate the Romantic taste for character pieces, works of charming if often enigmatic significance. Also a master of piano-chamber composition, Beethoven wrote piano trios, sonatas for violin and cello with piano support, and a variety of shorter pieces. Best-known today for what musicologists often refer to as his "middle-period" works —among these, the tremendously energetic "Appassionata" Sonata (Op. 57)—Beethoven is also remembered by young performers struggling with "Für Elise" (WoO 59), perhaps the nineteenth century's most famous bagatelle, as well as by those artists capable of grappling with the technical and interpretive difficulties of the composer's last five sonatas (Opp. 101, 106, and 109–111).

A younger contemporary of Beethoven, Franz Peter Schubert devoted himself to piano composition with considerable success. Much of Schubert's best piano writing is found in the accompaniments to the hundreds of songs he completed before his death at the age of thirty-one. Among his most impressive works for solo piano are more than a dozen sonatas; among them the last five sonatas and the so-called Duo Sonata (D. 812), for piano four hands, hold pride of place. A master of Biedermeier intimacy and sentimentality, always willing to compose for as well as perform at domestic functions, Schubert wrote volumes of keyboard "Ländler" and waltzes, as well as character pieces like the Op. 90 Impromptus. Later orchestrated by Liszt, Schubert's "Wanderer" fantasy-sonata of 1822 (D. 760) was one of the first large-scale nineteenth-century keyboard works to employ thematic transformation as a unifying device in all four of its movements. But Schubert's anticipations of Romanticism in keyboard music were scarcely unique. A number of lesser composers—among them the Czech Jan Vaclav Voŕišek and the Irishman John Field—contributed a great deal to the perfection of the Romantic character piece. Compositions with titles like "Eclogue," "Nocturne," or "Impromptu"—later, "Ballade" or "Apparition"—figured in the catalogs of virtually every composer at work with piano music between 1815 and 1848.

Romantic. The opening decades of the nineteenth century witnessed several styles of piano composition. The works of Schubert, Field, Voŕišek, and even Beethoven were in certain senses Romantic (or at least pre-Romantic). In other senses they were Classical: Schubert's sonatas, for example, were modelled to a considerable extent on well-established sonata-allegro traditions, and the sonatas of other composers—among them Jan Ladislav Dusík (or Dussek) and **Muzio Clementi**—belong almost entirely to the Classical literature. Only in the works of composers like Chopin, Mendelssohn, Schumann, and Liszt did Romanticism achieve fruition in its own right. Chopin, often considered "first-born" of the Romantic piano composers, wrote his first keyboard works as a boy living in Poland. After settling in Paris, he completed two piano concertos before turning almost exclusively to the creation of piano sonatas and character pieces renowned for their variety and exquisite polish: fantasies, polonaises, mazurkas, waltzes, preludes, impromptus, and nocturnes. Chopin's ingenious, elegant, and effective (if not always entirely idiomatic) keyboard figurations made him one of the most important and influential artists of his day. No less influential, at least during the mid-nineteenth century, was Mendelssohn, a successful pianist and musical organizer as well as a prolific, well-rounded composer. Mendelssohn is still widely acclaimed for his

several books of "Lieder ohne Worte" ["Songs without Words"], collections of character pieces varied in terms of their extra-musical associations as well as their demands upon performing abilities. But Mendelssohn also published three piano sonatas, two piano concertos, and six preludes and fugues for piano (Op. 35), as well as the work many authorities consider his masterpiece: the Variations sérieuses (Op. 54).

Widely educated, a student of law, and the most perceptive music critic of his day, Schumann may have turned full-time to composition because he seriously injured one of his hands preparing for a concert pianist's career. Many of Schumann's most important piano works were completed before the mid-1840s; among these were the suites of character pieces known as Papillons (Op. 2) and Carnaval (Op. 9)—albums of brief, brilliant musical "impressions" of people and places, which became part of the concert repertory almost as soon as they were published, thanks in large part to the sensitive performances they received from the hands of **Clara Wieck Schumann**, wife of Robert and herself a composer of keyboard works. Robert Schumann was deeply influenced by Bach's music and made use of Baroque figurations throughout his life; his *Album for the Young* (Op. 68), a pedagogical anthology that anticipated similar compilations by other nineteenth-century composers and, even later, those by Béla Bartók, includes several "Bachian" works. After the mid-1840s Schumann became less interested in solo piano music, but he continued to produce masterpieces in other forms, among them the A-minor Concerto for Piano and Orchestra (Op. 54).

Several of the most flamboyant Romantic composers wrote little or no piano music; among these figures were Hector Berlioz, who virtually ignored the piano, and Richard Wagner, who abandoned the instrument after trying his hand at a few student works. Equally flamboyant, however, was Franz Liszt, unquestionably the Romantic musician most closely associated in the minds of many music lovers with the piano and piano composition. A student of Carl Czerny, himself a prolific keyboard composer and transcriber, Liszt mastered in childhood such pre-Romantic performing vehicles as the Concerto in B minor of Johann Nepomuk Hummel and the Konzertstück for piano and orchestra by Carl Maria von Weber, then went on during the 1830s to reinvent piano writing in his early operatic paraphrases and such formidable original works as the second version of what became the *Etudes d'un exécution transcendante* ["Studies of Transcendental Difficulty"] (1838). After touring Europe for a decade as a virtuoso performer, Liszt abandoned public performing in favor of composing and orchestral conducting as Kapellmeister to the Weimar court. It was in that small town that he completed or drafted the final version of the "Transcendental Studies" (1852) as well as two piano concertos, the Totentanz for piano and orchestra, the Grosses Konzert-Solo, and the remarkable Sonata in B minor, which looks back to Beethoven and Schubert even as it anticipates certain developments in late-nineteenth- and early-twentieth-century musical style.

Post-Romantic and Impressionist. Chopin, Mendelssohn, and Schumann were dead by 1856, but Liszt lived another thirty years—long enough for him and some of his younger contemporaries to develop what may be called post-Romantic music. Some of Liszt's late piano pieces, especially those composed during the 1870s and 1880s, might also be called Impressionistic. *"Le jeux d'eau à la Villa d'Este"* ["The Fountains of the Villa d'Este"] from the third book of pieces known as *Années de pèlerinage* ["Years of Pilgrimage"] (1883), for example, anticipates, and is echoed in, similar pieces written much later by Claude Debussy and Maurice Ravel. And Liszt's gloomy late character pieces, full of augmented triads and unresolved dissonances, must have had an impact on the development of Alexander Scriabin's and even Igor Stravinsky's musical styles. The most important post-Romantic composer was not Liszt, however, but Johannes Brahms. Influenced as a young man by both the ideas and music of Schumann, Brahms published three Schumannesque sonatas and the four Ballades (Op. 10) before temporarily abandoning solo-piano music in favor of vocal and orchestral works. Later he became deeply involved with the music of eighteenth-century composers; the impact of the Baroque style appears not only in works like the Variations on a Theme by Handel (Op. 24), but in the contrapuntal writing found in many of his late rhapsodies and intermezzos. Brahms was also a composer and performer of virtuoso keyboard music; his two piano concertos and brilliant chamber pieces

(among works in the latter category, the powerful quintet for piano and strings [Op. 34] is a particular favorite with pianists) display his preference for warm, rich, yet powerful instrumental sounds.

The rise of nationalism throughout Europe found expression in the piano compositions of many post-Romantic artists: Antonin Dvořàk (Czech), Edvard Grieg (Norwegian), and Modest Mussorgsky (Russian) were only a few of them. The finest Slavic composer of his generation, Mussorgsky wrote several attractive piano pieces and songs with piano accompaniment, as well as the collection of interlinked compositions known in English as Pictures at an Exhibition (1874) and more familiar in the famous orchestral arrangement by Ravel. Grieg was a master of the piano miniature, although he also published sonatas, piano-chamber works, and a suite entitled "From Holberg's Time" (1884), one of the first nineteenth-century works written in deliberate parody of Baroque music. Dvořàk produced dances and other short keyboard pieces as well as a number of substantial chamber compositions with piano. Other post-Romantic nationalists of the late nineteenth and early twentieth centuries were the American composers Louis Moreau Gottschalk, whose charming Latin rhythms and energetic keyboard writing have recently become popular again; and Edward MacDowell, a pupil of Liszt, whose etudes, character pieces, and Concerto in D minor have been studied by generations of New World piano pupils. But the most overtly nationalist of all American composers was Charles Ives. More interested in symphonic and vocal music than music for solo piano, Ives nevertheless produced one of the early twentieth century's keyboard masterpieces: the Sonata No. 2 subtitled *Concord, Mass.: 1840–60* (composed 1910–1915). Ives also wrote several violin and piano sonatas, as well as miscellaneous character pieces—a few of them with such utterly American titles as "Some South-Paw Pitching!"

The most representative composer of Impressionist piano music was Debussy, the most important French musician of his generation. Although he wrote no concertos or compositions for piano with large chamber ensembles, Debussy earned a reputation as one of history's most accomplished keyboard stylists with two books of Préludes (published in 1910 and 1913), two books of Etudes (published in 1916), and suites like "The Children's Corner" (published in 1903). Although the etudes and suite movements bear inventive titles, the Préludes are titleless—at least at the beginning of each piece. The caption placed at the end of each prelude thus serves the function not of explaining the music in advance, but of clarifying the performer's impression of its inspiration or significance. Like Debussy, Maurice Ravel wrote Impressionist works of brilliance and harmonic subtlety; Ravel's *Jeux d'eau* (1901) carries Liszt's late style to extraordinary lengths, while pieces like *Le tombeau de Couperin* (composed 1914–17) conjure up the spirit of "antique" music also captured by the "Doctor Gradus ad Parnassum" movement of Debussy's "Children's Corner." Among other turn-of-the-century figures, Erik Satie is remembered for piano pieces crammed with ingenious chord progressions and capped by eccentric titles like "Three Pieces in the Form of a Pear."

Modern. Piano music began to decline in importance even before World War I, although it has remained extremely popular—especially with concert audiences—up to the present day. Although composers like Scriabin used the piano for harmonic and formal experiments, other progressive figures all but ignored it in favor of unusual instrumental or vocal combinations. Arnold Schoenberg, for example, produced only a handful of piano pieces—although it must be admitted that some of them were among the earliest atonal compositions—while Alban Berg composed almost exclusively for wind and string instruments and for voice. Igor Stravinsky wrote almost nothing for piano besides a single sonata (1924), a sonata for two pianos (1945), and the Piano-Rag-Music pieces (1919) occasionally performed today. Even Paul Hindemith employed the piano almost exclusively as a chamber instrument; his only mature solo-piano composition was the *Klaviermusik* collection (composed 1925–27). Béla Bartók thus remains the most important piano composer of the twentieth century. Born in an outlying province of Hungary, Bartók was trained in Budapest as a concert performer before turning primarily to composition and to research into ethnomusicological problems. His numerous solo-piano works—among them the Op. 38 Bagatelles, a muscular sonata (Op. 80), and a graceful sonatina (Op. 55), as well as the 156 pedagogical pieces

published during the 1920s and 1930s under the collective title *Mikrokosmos*—made Bartók the most representative piano composer of the inter-war years. Sergei Prokofiev's brilliant sonatas are also an important part of the piano repertoire of these years. Sergei Rachmaninoff, who wrote significant inter-war keyboard works like the Rhapsody on a Theme of Paganini (1934) for piano and orchestra, is more often associated with the splendid concertos and preludes he completed before World War I began.

Since 1945 or thereabouts the piano has become even more of an anachronism, at least in the eyes of avant-garde composers and performers. It continues to be used, alone and in ensembles, but it either serves harmonically to consolidate comparatively conventional works, or is treated in revolutionary and often hilarious ways. Pianos thus have been beaten on, kicked, subjected to mechanical "preparation" of various kinds, electronically amplified, torn to pieces, and even "fed and watered" (the last by composers of so-called Paper Music). No postwar piano piece has captured the imagination of concert audiences as have Krysztof Penderecki's Threnody for the Victims of Hiroshima (1960) for string orchestra, or the outlandish and entertaining chamber combinations of pseudo-popular composers like George Crumb.

Jazz, Rag, and Popular Styles. By 1865, when the American Civil War came to an end, the piano was already the most widely-studied and performed-upon musical instrument in the United States. It was only in the 1890s, however, that the style known as ragtime was invented—a style remarkably well-suited to the piano. Scott Joplin, the most famous of ragtime composers, published several dozen solo pieces and a ragtime "tutor" in addition to the "Maple Leaf Rag" (1899) that made the genre famous. James P. Johnson also wrote rags; his "Carolina Shout" (published in 1925) exemplifies ragtime harmonies at their most sophisticated. Associated at first with jazz, ragtime was actually a species of piano character-piece that combined military march with syncopated cakewalk; jazz, on the other hand, was a way of handling musical materials of virtually every kind, from the simplest blues pattern to the most complex of Debussy's chord progressions. Consequently, jazz pianists and piano composers have manifested a host of musical predilections. Edward

Kennedy "Duke" Ellington, for example, wrote and performed rags and popular songs as well as film scores and stage works; in his performances, as in the performances of so many jazz masters, inspiration and improvisation cannot be separated from composition. Ellington was a comparatively "conservative" figure in jazz history; Thelonius Monk, on the other hand, experimented with jazz styles from bop to the freeform music of John Coltrane and his contemporaries. Other jazz pianist-composers like Dave Brubeck have concentrated on perfecting piano-chamber jazz, while the Modern Jazz Quartet has often used the piano in pieces reminiscent of Bach and other Baroque composers. Only George Gershwin wrote successfully both for Classical and for jazz performers; his "Rhapsody in Blue" (1924) is a symphonic poem for piano and orchestra, albeit with jazz overtones, while his popular songs are "real" jazz with piano accompaniment. It is unfortunate for pianists that the jazz songs of Gershwin and his contemporaries were among the last popular compositions to make regular use of their instrument. Since the 1950s, and especially since the 1960s, the electric guitar has replaced the piano as an accompanying instrument, and the popular piano character-piece has virtually disappeared from existence.

See also "Chamber Music and Accompanying."

Michael Saffle

Bibliography

Abraham, Gerald. *Chopin's Musical Style.* London: Oxford University Press, 1960.

Brown, A. Peter. *Joseph Haydn's Keyboard Music: Sources and Style.* Bloomington, Ind.: Indiana University Press, 1986.

Chissell, Joan. *Schumann Piano Music.* Seattle, Wash.: University of Washington Press, 1972.

Dale, Kathleen. *Nineteenth-Century Piano Music: A Handbook for Pianists.* London: Oxford University Press, 1954.

Gillespie, John. *Five Centuries of Keyboard Music.* Belmont, Cal.: Wadsworth, 1965.

Hinson, Maurice. *Guide to the Pianists' Repertory.* 2nd. ed. Bloomington, Ind.: Indiana University Press, 1987.

———. *The Pianists' Guide to Transcriptions, Arrangements, and Paraphrases.* Bloomington: Indiana University Press, 1990.

Keller, Hermann. *Die Klavierwerke Bachs: Eine Beitrag zu ihrer Geschichte, Form, Deutung und Wiedergabe* ["The Clavier Works of Bach: A Contribution to our Understanding of their History, Form, Significance, and Influence"]. Leipzig: C. F. Peters, 1950.

Newman, William S. *History of the Sonata Idea.* 3 vols., especially *The Sonata Since Beethoven.* 3rd ed. New York: W. W. Norton, 1983.

Parks, Richard S. *The Music of Claude Debussy.* New Haven, Conn.: Yale University Press, 1989.

Radcliffe, Philip. *Schubert Piano Sonatas.* Seattle, Wash.: University of Washington Press, 1971.

Tovey, Donald Francis. *A Companion to Beethoven's Piano Sonatas.* New York: AMS Press, 1976.

Walker, Alan, ed. *Franz Liszt: The Man and His Music.* London: Barrie and Jenkins, 1970; esp. pp. 79–167.

Wolff, Konrad. *Masters of the Keyboard: Individual Style Elements in the Piano Music of Bach, Haydn, Mozart, Beethoven, and Schubert.* Bloomington, Ind.: Indiana University Press, 1983.

Yeomans, David. *Bartók for Piano.* Bloomington, Ind.: Indiana University Press, 1988.

MUSICIANS AND PIANO MANUFACTURERS

Pianists and Piano Manufacturers. Professional pianists are always the ones most interested in any changes or innovations in the construction of the piano. Their feedback and involvement in these activities seems to have been important to manufacturers, especially from the mid-eighteenth to the end of the nineteenth century, in the period of the most intense development of playing mechanism and **frame** construction. Some companies were started by pianists like Henri Herz and **Muzio Clementi**, who used their personal expertise to improve details in the mechanism and their reknown to market the new versions. During the nineteenth century, competition focused on differences between the English and the German (Viennese) construction. Companies looked for pianists who would champion and use exclusively their pianos on tours, thus popularizing them and increasing sales. Very often, letters from famous artists were publicized, in which the artists praised particular qualities of their favorite pianos. This relationship changed at the end of the nineteenth century, soon after the construction of the **grand piano** reached its final stage and after the major piano companies were firmly established. Today, although the names of the artists playing a particular name-brand certainly influence the potential buyer, a rising pianist is often the one waiting to be accepted as a company's exclusive artist, and is subsequently referred to, for example, as a **Bösendorfer**, **Steinway**, or **Yamaha** artist.

One of the early contributors was the Bohemian pianist Jan Ladislav Dussek, who convinced **Broadwood** to expand the **keyboard** range in 1790 or 1791. A six-octave keyboard had already been introduced in 1777, when such a piano was made by special order for the English music historian Dr. **Charles Burney** to accommodate two ladies in hoopskirts playing four-hand music. Dussek was also mainly responsible for the development of **Erard's** single **escapement action** (1795, improved 1816). The double escapement **action** was presented by Erard at the Paris Exposition in 1823, after consultation with and approval from Ignaz Moscheles, a famous German pianist of Bohemian origin. It was improved and simplified by Henri Herz in 1841. This model, with some changes in materials, format, and added weight to the leverage, became the basis of today's grand piano action.

Some of the most prominent pianistic schools of the nineteenth century have grown out of and relied upon the specific **touch** and sound of a playing mechanism. Thus the school of Muzio Clementi preferred the English pianoforte with its heavier but richer touch, whereas that of Johann Nepomuk Hummel preferred the lighter Viennese mechanism. Moscheles used Clementi's pianos, which had "more supple mechanism for . . . repeating notes, skips and full chords." Describing a concert played in London in 1822 by John Baptist Cramer, German-born English pianist, Moscheles observed that the strong metal **plates** used by Broadwood gave a heaviness to the touch, adapting it well to Cramer's legato, but resulted in fullness and vocal resonance of the sound. In 1823 Moscheles played a historic concert in Vienna using both a **Graf** piano and **Ludwig van Beethoven's** Broadwood to demonstrate the differences between the two systems. French instruments were also known for their resistance, and the similarity in touch between the French and the English pianos was apparently so obvious that **Frédéric Chopin** called Broadwood "a London Pleyel." **Robert Schumann** described his wife **Clara's** playing as "Hussar-like," probably as the result of struggling with French pianos, which her father Friedrich Wieck called "tough

bones." In 1839 Clara wrote to Robert from Paris, complaining about the stiffness of the Erard she had to play, mentioning that the **Pleyel** was just a touch lighter. Tobias Matthay, English pianist and teacher, tried an Erard at the end of the nineteenth century, and still found it very heavy. It seems to have been impossible to play it by striking the **keys** from a distance because the surface resistance was very strong. The full weight of its action was left against the player, since the weight was not balanced by leaden weights inserted in the fronts of the keys. The development of the Erard mechanism was especially influenced by pianists Carl Czerny, Frédéric Kalkbrenner, and Hummel.

It was not uncommon for pianists to modify the mechanism according to their particular needs. Kalkbrenner placed a piece of cork under the treble **damper** rail, so that the upper two octaves of German (Viennese) pianos would almost not be damped. More recently, Vladimir Horowitz experimented with removing the "fringe" red tape at the back of the **strings**, while Glenn Gould's famous Steinway 318 had such a fine hair-trigger **regulation** that the **hammers** would often rebound and strike the string a second time. Famous French pianist Alfred Cortot often played forte passages under *una corda* **pedal**, achieving the characteristic sonorous but soft sound. Josef Hofmann, American pianist of Polish birth, owned two custom-built Steinway grands. Their keys were made slightly narrower, to relieve Hofmann's hand during chords and stretches (his hand barely reaching a tenth). He also had the *sostenuto* (middle) **pedal** removed from them, being afraid of inadvertently stepping on it. Hofmann experimented with piano action in his workshop, and in 1940 was awarded a **patent** for a frictionless movement of levers. This refinement offered more subtle control of mechanical movements, thereby expanding the range of available dynamic nuances.

In choosing their pianos, pianists often had problems of other than artistic nature. For a time, 1923–1933, the American Steinway company refused Artur Schnabel its pianos in the United States unless he gave up playing **Bechstein** in Europe. Schnabel, though, had praise for Bechstein pianos, emphasizing their neutral sound and, consequently, their capability of imitating more instruments and timbres than Steinway. To avoid such risk, Ignace Jan

Paderewski, Polish pianist and president, played Erard pianos in Europe but Steinway pianos in the United States. Paderewski made statements about the "fine sonority" he could draw from an Erard, describing it as the world's finest until Steinway came along. His contemporaries, though, mentioned Erard's "harpsichord-like" sound. Hans von Bülow, a prominent **Liszt** student, used Bechstein pianos a great deal, and wrote letters to the Bechstein company, explaining his precise needs from an instrument, thus influencing their design. However, he seems to have liked **Chickering** pianos the best, and because of this fondness he increased the amount of his practicing (of which he was not fond).

Composers and Piano Manufacturers. Two opposing views exist today on the causality and priority between composers and manufacturers. One, represented by writers such as Gerald R. Hayes, states that the instruments were developed first and the music for them followed. The other view, as expressed by writers like Sir Donald Tovey, Cyril Ehrlich, and Edward J. Dent, is that only second-rate composers are stimulated by mechanical inventions, implying that composers' innovative and progressive thinking spurred technical improvements. Backing up the latter hypothesis is Tovey's observation in the preface to the Associated Board edition of Beethoven's sonatas that "the compass of the piano hampered Beethoven in all his works for it." Still, it was on Beethoven's advice that the **Streicher** company abandoned the softness, giving-in, and roll of Viennese instruments, and put more resistance and elasticity into the pianos, so that virtuosi acquired more power over sustaining quality and projection of the sound. According to Johann Friedrich Reichardt in *Wiener Reisebriefen* [Letters from a Journey to Vienna], the instrument won a greater and more versatile character, "pleasing not only those who were after easy-shining, brilliant play." It is also a fact that some of the most orchestral-quality piano pieces, such as Schumann's Fantasy and Franz Liszt's Sonata, were written before the modern piano. The majority of Liszt's music had been composed during the era of the flat-strung Erard models—Steinway's **overstrung** pianos appearing only in the 1870s.

Robert Andres

Bibliography

Backus, John. *The Acoustical Foundations of Music.* New York: Norton, 1970.

Cooke, James Francis. *Great Pianists on Piano Playing.* Philadelphia: T. Presser, 1913.

Ehrlich, Cyril. *The Piano: A History.* London: Dent, 1976.

Gerig, Reginald R. *Famous Pianists and Their Technique.* Washington: Luce, 1974.

Good, Edwin M. *Giraffes, Black Dragons, and Other Pianos.* Stanford, Cal.: Stanford University Press, 1982.

Harding, Rosamond E.M. *The Piano-Forte: Its History Traced to the Great Exhibition of 1851.* Cambridge: Cambridge University Press, 1933. Reprints. New York: Da Capo Press, 1973; Old Woking, Surrey: Gresham Books, 1978.

Husarik, Stephen. "Josef Hofmann, the Composer and Pianist, with an Analysis of the Available Reproductions of His Performances." Ph.D. diss., University of Iowa, 1983. Ann Arbor: University Microfilms no. 83–27, 390, 1983.

Lenz, Wilhelm von. *The Great Piano Virtuosos of Our Time.* New York: G. Schirmer, 1899.

Loesser, Arthur. *Men, Women and Pianos.* New York: Simon & Schuster, 1954.

Paul, Oscar. *Geschichte des Klaviers.* Leipzig, 1868.

Rimbault, Edward F. *The Pianoforte: Its Origin, Progress, and Construction.* London: Cocks, 1860.

N

NAMEBOARD

The nameboard is the part of the piano's **case**, just above the **keyboard**, that bears the manufacturer's name (and often the location of the factory) in gold script. Modern pianos have the maker's name stenciled directly on the wood. Earlier pianos have very elaborate nameboards with *etiquettes,* or labels, inlaid into decorative satinwood or sycamore. Colorful flower paintings were popular on nameboards from about 1796 to 1807.

A nameboard is usually the under side of a piano's **fallboard,** or **keyboard cover.**

Peggy Flanagan Baird

NATIONAL PIANO FOUNDATION

The National Piano Foundation (NPF) is the educational arm of the Piano Manufacturers Association International (PMAI), one of the oldest trade associations in the United States. Founded as the National Piano Manufacturers Association (NPMA) in 1896, the association concentrates on manufacturing issues and collects piano shipment data.

The decision to establish a piano foundation was the result of a study from the Harvard School of Business that was commissioned by the piano manufacturers. Completed in September 1961, the Harvard Report recommended that a piano research foundation be formed to coordinate research, stimulate new developments and coordinate their implementation, and to build piano sales. After reviewing the Harvard Report, the piano manufacturers formed the National Piano Foundation in 1962 with

the stated purpose of encouraging and assisting piano teachers to promote the participation in and enjoyment of music through keyboard instruction, to raise professional standards, and to teach broader musicianship through the use of innovative methods and materials.

Dr. Robert Pace from Columbia University was retained as Educational Director of NPF to implement seminars, musicianship pedagogy sessions, musicianship festivals, ensemble festivals, and preschool programs throughout the United States. When Pace resigned in June 1977 to become director of the International Piano Teaching Foundation, Dr. Robert Steinbauer was appointed chairman of NPF's Education Advisory Board, which included representatives from related music associations. From 1977 to 1985, this board instituted a series of programs that included group instruction, but also expanded the programs directed toward the collegiate and private studio teachers.

The piano manufacturers changed the direction of both PMAI and NPF in 1985. In addition to inviting overseas piano companies to become members, the NPF mission was revised by a long-range planning committee: to educate the general public about the value, benefit, and enjoyment of playing the piano; to contribute to the professional well-being of the teaching community; to support the music-study success of piano users; and to promote the productive interaction and cooperation of all segments of the music industry.

In an attempt to reach the consumer more directly, NPF began producing videos, brochures, posters, and pamphlets that encouraged Americans to actively participate in music by playing the piano. It also began promoting research investigating the benefits of piano study, exploring demographic trends in the U.S., and polling Americans through the Gallup Poll to determine their past and current piano-playing behavior and their attitudes toward playing.

Although the National Piano Foundation is young as foundations go, its purpose has not wavered from 1962 to the present. Consistently, NPF has supported participation in music through the piano. It has continually encouraged teachers to strive for the highest standards and has encouraged them to improve their methodologies. It also has aggressively promoted networking with other piano-related associations. Through its programs and materials, the NPF articulates to the general public that playing the piano is an enrichment opportunity available to everyone and that there are distinct benefits from active participation in music.

Brenda Dillon

NOSE

The nose is that portion of the **plate** (usually near the center) supported by bolts ("nose bolts") onto which are screwed nuts. The nose bolts are screwed to the cross beams (also called "posts" or "struts"), which run beneath the **soundboard** (behind in **uprights**). A similar support is sometimes used near the center of the "belly **rail**" or "cross block" in **grands**. This is a wood section at the front end of the soundboard, just behind the **action**. Braced with either a wedge or a flange cast as part of the plate, the belly rail is prevented from bending.

See also Frame.

Philip Jamison, III

NUNNS, ROBERT AND WILLIAM (FL. 1824–1858) AND (FL. 1824–1840)

Robert and William Nunns emigrated from London to New York around 1821. After working at the piano makers Kearsing & Sons, they founded their own firm, R. & W. Nunns, in 1823. They were alert to innovations in piano technology, adopting Charles Sackmeister's **scaling** with heavier **stringing** in 1827. In 1830 they received an award for "the best **square** pianoforte, with the grand or French **action**," while competitors continued using the older English mechanism. In 1833 another Englishman, John Clark (fl. 1833–1850), joined the firm, renamed Nunns, Clark & Co. Their instruments were exhibited at London's Great Exposition in 1851 and, to great acclaim, at New York's Crystal Palace Exhibition in 1853. William Nunns withdrew in 1839 and the firm was thereafter styled Nunns & Clark. In 1850 they began using

Rudolph Kreter's machinery for covering "a whole set of **hammer**-heads at one operation" with graduated layers of **felt**. The firm ceased trading in 1860.

William's solo ventures in piano manufacture and sales, some in association with the John and Charles Fischer firm, included the development in 1847 of the "Melodicon," a piano with chromatic kettledrums. These efforts were ultimately less successful, however, and ended in his bankruptcy in 1853. William Steinway is said to have worked at William Nunns' establishment shortly before **Steinway & Sons** was founded in 1853.

Howard Schott

Bibliography

Dolge, Alfred. *Pianos and Their Makers.* Covina, Cal.: Covina Pub., 1911. Reprint. New York: Dover Pub., 1972: 174, 289, 308.

Good, Edwin M. *Giraffes, Black Dragons, and Other Pianos: A Technological History from Cristofori to the Modern Concert Grand.* Stanford, Cal.: Stanford University Press, 1982: 169–74, 178, 180, 192, 194.

Harding, Rosamond E.M. *The Piano-Forte: Its History Traced to the Great Exhibition of 1851.* Cambridge: Cambridge University Press, 1933. Reprints. New York: Da Capo Press, 1973; Old Woking, Surrey: Gresham Books, 1978: pp. 141–42, 147.

Loesser, Arthur. *Men, Women and Pianos: A Social History.* New York: Simon & Schuster, 1954: 476.

The New Grove Dictionary of Musical Instruments. Edited by Stanley Sadie. S.v. "Nunns & Clark," by Laurence Libin. London & New York: Macmillan Press, 1984.

Pauer, Ernst. *A Dictionary of Pianists and Composers for Pianoforte with an Appendix of Manufacturers of the Instrument.* London & New York: Novello, Ewer & Co., 1895: 149.

Spillane, Daniel. *History of the American Pianoforte: Its Technical Development, and the Trade.* New York: D. Spillane, 1890. Reprint. New York: Da. Capo Press, 1969:116–18, 150–51, 194–95.

ORCHESTRION, PIANO

A piano orchestrion is a self-acting or automatic piano to which are added other instruments such as percussion, accordion, or small pipe organ, generally all contained within the one cabinet.

It was the reputation of the orchestrion organ as an instrument of entertainment that inspired the piano makers to produce a smaller and more affordable instrument. An added advantage was that it could be maintained inexpensively by a piano tuner or **player-piano** technician.

The first piano orchestrions were developed from the **coin-operated**, **barrel**-operated mechanical pianos popular in bars and cafes. These were clockwork-driven; later, all were electrically powered, with music in the form of perforated paper rolls.

Piano orchestions were produced in large numbers in France, the Low Countries, and Germany and were the forerunners of the coin-operated instruments produced widely in America for use in bars. In this developed form, the core of the instrument was the **expression piano**, along with the addition of percussion and one or more ranks of organ pipes.

The piano orchestrion in the majority of public locations was superseded by the introduction of the jukebox.

Arthur W.J.G. Ord-Hume

Bibliography

Bowers, Q. David. *Encyclopedia of Automatic Musical Instruments*. Vestal, N.Y.: Vestal Press, 1972.

Ord-Hume, Arthur W.J.G. *Clockwork Music—An Illustrated History*. London: Allen & Unwin, 1973.

————. Arthur W.J.G. *Pianola—History & Development*. . . . London: Allen & Unwin, 1984.

ORPHICA

The orphica is a small portable piano invented in Vienna in the late eighteenth century by Carl Leopold Röllig (c. 1745–1804). It employs a Viennese-type **action** to strike metal **strings** running transversely to the player. The strings extend over a soundbox with **tuning pins** at the right to an open harp-shaped **frame** with **hitch pins** at the left.

Upon patenting the orphica, Röllig apparently made arrangements with Joseph Dohnal (1759–1829), a Viennese piano maker, to manufacture his new instrument. Surviving orphicas by Dohnal resemble, in most respects, the illustration in the frontispiece of a 1795 pamphlet by Röllig entitled *Orphica: Ein musikalisches Instrument*. Dohnal's instruments possess certain differences from the pamphlet's description, such as single stringing (rather than double) and varying compasses, but these were probably approved by Röllig. Despite efforts to prevent it, unauthorized copies of the orphica were produced, usually unsigned in an effort to avoid **patent** infringement. Orphicas continued to be made until about 1830, by which time the patent had long since expired.

In his 1795 pamphlet Röllig proposes several different ways to position the orphica for performance. It could be played in its own outer case (when provided with screw-on legs) or placed separately on a table. He also suggests that it could be held on the lap while seated or even played in a standing position with the aid of a strap over the shoulder. In addition to the model with piano action, Röllig mentions an orphica with single gut strings and a harpsichord action, but no surviving examples of this type are known.

The orphica was designed to appeal to amateur players, its name invoking an association with the classical lyre of Orpheus. Surviving instruments contain forty-nine notes at most and as few as twenty-five. The **scaling** of examples not by Dohnal often imply that they were tuned higher than 8' pitch. Röllig, however, described his creation as a "bass" instrument with a topnote of c^2. Because of the orphica's small size its action is necessarily miniaturized; the **keys** are substantially narrower than contemporary piano keys. All of these aspects, along with an occasional lack of provision for **dampers**, serve to limit performance to simple pieces.

Darcy Kuronen

Bibliography

Harding, Rosamond E.M. *The Piano-Forte: Its History Traced to the Great Exhibition of 1851.* Cambridge: Cambridge University Press, 1933. Reprints. New York: Da Capo Press, 1973; Old Woking, Surrey: Gresham Books, 1978.

Hirt, Franz Josef. *Meisterwerke des Klavierbaus.* Olten: Urs Graf-Verlag, 1955.

Koster, John. *Catalogue of Keyboard Instruments.* Boston: Museum of Fine Arts, forthcoming.

Marcuse, Sibyl. *Musical Instruments: A Comprehensive Dictionary.* 2nd ed., New York: Norton, 1975.

The New Grove Dictionary of Musical Instruments. Edited by Stanley Sadie. London: Macmillan, 1984.

van der Meer, John Henry. *Musikinstrumente: von der Antike bis zur Gegenwart.* Munich: Prestel, 1983.

Röllig, C. L. *Orphica: Ein musikalisches Instrument. Erfunden von C. L. Röllig.* Vienna, 1795.

OSBORNE, JOHN (1792–1835)

John Osborne (Osborn), American piano manufacturer trained by **Benjamin Crehore**, was one of the leading makers in the U.S. from 1815 to 1835. He began business for himself in 1815 in back of 3 Newbury Street in Boston. Osborne moved his shop in 1819 to 12 Orange Street and manufactured pianos there through 1821. Apprentices to him in the Orange Street shop included such notables as **Jonas Chickering**, Lemanuel and Timothy Gilbert, William Danforth, John Dwight, and Elijah Bullard. Osborne conducted business for a short while with James Stewart, terminating the partnership about 1822.

According to Cynthia A. Hoover, he remained in Boston until 1829, at which time he moved to Albany and began work with Meacham & Pond and later (1831–1833) with Peter King. In 1833 he moved to 184 Chambers Street in New York City and in the same year received a gold medal at the Mechanics Institute Annual Exhibition. Osborne's prospering business prompted the erection of a large factory in New York City on 3rd Avenue and 14th Street in 1834. Spillane's records find that Osborne committed suicide in 1835. The factory was later occupied by Stodart, Worcester & Dunham.

Mary Ellen Haupert

Bibliography

The New Grove Dictionary of Music and Musicians. Edited by Stanley Sadie. S.v. "Osborne," by Cynthia Adams Hoover. London: Macmillan, 1984 Washington D.C.: Grove's Dictionary of Music, Inc., 1980, Vol. XIV: 2.

Spillane, Daniel. *History of the American Pianoforte: Its Technical Development, and the Trade.* New York: Reprint. New York: Da Capo Press, 1969. Spillane, 1890.

OVERSTRUNG

This term refers to a type of construction in which the lower **strings** of pianos pass diagonally across higher strings on a separate plane. In **grand pianos** the bass strings (AAA to E on a modern **Steinway**) run above and across the tenor strings (F to b) to the central and most responsive part of the **soundboard**. The concomitant shifting of the **bridges** and other adjustments also enhance the vibration of the board, creating a more powerful sound in which the lowest bass notes are somewhat less clear than they are on straight-strung instruments.

Jean-Henri Pape (1789–1875) made the first overstrung **upright pianos** in 1828. Other European and American builders began to produce overstrung uprights and **squares** during the 1830s. However, it was the American Steinway firm that **patented** the combination of a cast-iron **frame** and overstringing for grand pianos in 1859, thus completing the basic technological innovations on which the modern piano is based. **Streicher, Pleyel,** and **Bösendorfer** adopted overstringing for grands by 1867, 1870, and 1873 respectively, but prejudice, especially on the part of English and French firms, slowed its eventual universal acceptance.

Although writers now use overstrung and cross-strung synonymously, the term cross-strung has also been used specifically to designate a method of stringing in which a double length of wire crosses over itself as it is looped around the **hitch pin** to return to another **tuning pin**.

Sandra P. Rosenblum

Bibliography

Ehrlich, Cyril. *The Piano: A History.* London: J.M. Dent & Sons, Ltd., 1976.

Good, Edwin M. *Giraffes, Black Dragons, and Other Pianos: A Technological History from* *Cristofori to the Modern Concert Grand.* Stanford, Cal.: Stanford University Press, 1982.

Hipkins, A. J. *A Description and History of the Pianoforte.* London: Novello, Ewer, 1896.

PAPE, JEAN-HENRI (JOHANN HEINRICH) (1789–1875)

The inventive French piano maker, Jean-Henri Pape, was born in Sarstedt, near Hanover, 1 July 1789 and died in Asnières, near Paris, 2 February 1875. Like so many instrument builders of his day, Pape came to Paris (1811) to work in the new piano factory of Ignace **Pleyel** (1757–1831). By 1815 he had established his own piano workshop. At that time there were less than thirty piano makers in all of France.

Pape quickly established an international reputation as a prolific and versatile piano inventor. During his career he took out some 137 **patents** in France, England, and Germany. He

became known for his early use of **felt** made of rabbit hair and lamb's wool to cover the **hammers** (1826, French patent), his use of **cross-stringing** (or **overstringing**, [1828, French patent]), and his use of **wire** made of tempered steel or German silver (1845, English patent). Another of his important designs was a down-striking grand **action**, which became known as the "French Action" across Europe and in America. Lesser-known designs included a device for turning worn hammer felt, a **tuning** gauge with a visual tension indicator, and a special saw for cutting thin veneers of **ivory** for covering the **keys** or even the entire piano **case**. He also designed and built **square pianos** with the **keyboard** in the middle (instead of to one end) and oversized **grand pianos** with eight octaves.

Pape's most famous invention is perhaps his tiny "piano-console" or **"pianino"** (1828, French patent), which employed cross-stringing in order to be compact. These **upright** instruments were seldom much more than three feet (92 centimeters) tall and were designed so that the bass **strings** crossed over the treble strings, allowing a longer speaking length. These small, inexpensive consoles, or pianinos, became very popular in both France and England by the middle of the nineteenth century.

Pape's clever inventions and profound influence on other builders of his generation were never matched by financial success. Although

Square piano by Jean-Henri Pape (1840). Germanisches Nationalmuseum, Klavierhistorische Sammlung Neupert, MINe211, Nürnberg.(Courtesy of Da Capo Press [New York], agent for Franz Josef Hirt's Stringed Keyboard Instrument.)

he had once employed some 300 men in his firm, and had even had a shop in London for over ten years, he died a poor man. Towards the end of his career, he spent great amounts of time and money building oval, round, and hexagonal pianos, but these odd shapes were not popular with the buying public.

The Pape firm became one of the three most famous French piano workshops of the first half of the nineteenth century, along with the Pleyel and **Erard** firms. Luigi Cherubini used one of Pape's 1817 square pianos when he composed. The pianist-composer Ignaz Moscheles also purchased one of Pape's pianos, as did opera composers François Boïeldieu and Daniel Auber. The German piano maker, Wilhelm Carl **Bechstein**, came to Paris in 1852 to work with Pape for one year before opening his own firm in Berlin the following year. A **console piano** with an Empire-style mahogany case and a 78-note keyboard was offered for sale at the auction house of Sotheby Parke Bernet, Inc. in New York in 1981.

Peggy Flanagan Baird

Bibliography

The New Grove Dictionary of Musical Instruments, Edited by Stanley Sadie. S.v. "Jean Henri Pape," by Margaret Cranmer. London: Macmillan Press Ltd., 1989. Vol. 3: 16–17.

Ehrlich, Cyril. *The Piano*. Rev. ed.,Oxford: Clarendon Press, 1990: 27, 30, 73.

Gill, Dominic, ed. *The Book of the Piano*. Ithaca, N.Y.: Cornell University Press, 1981: 242, 249.

Good, Edwin M. *Giraffes, Black Dragons, and Other Pianos*. Stanford, Cal.: Stanford University Press, 1982: 119–120, 148–149, 180.

Harding, Rosamond E.M. *The Piano-Forte: Its History Traced to the Great Exhibition of 1851*. Cambridge: Cambridge University Press, 1933: 101, 165–167. Reprints. New York: Da Capo Press, 1973; Old Woking, Surrey: Gresham Books, 1978.

Loesser, Arthur. *Men, Women and Pianos*. New York: Simon and Schuster, 1954. 339, 386, 407–409.

PARLOR GRAND

A parlor grand is a six- or seven-foot **grand piano** commonly found in a reasonably sized room of a home. It is an old fashioned term, the parlor being either the formal room of the middle class where guests were received or a smaller room off the great hall of an upper class home.

See Grand Piano.

Camilla Cai

PARTIALS

Partials are the individual sounds present in a musical note, due to the different modes of vibration of a **string** or air column. Their presence and relative strength is very important for the quality of the produced sound.

The several modes of vibration of a string all have their own frequencies, and the resulting tones are the partials of a sound. The lowest frequency (the one we hear) gives the fundamental partial, and the higher modes generate the overtones. Both the fundamental and the overtones are partials.

In theory, all the overtones are harmonics since the overtone frequencies are integer multiples of the fundamental frequency and the overtone wavelengths are integer fractions of the fundamental wavelength. In other words: the frequencies and wavelengths of overtones are aliquot-parts of the fundamental frequency and wavelength. The arithmetic relation between fundamental and i-th overtone is therefore:

$$f_i = if_1 \text{ and, } \lambda_i = \lambda_{1/i}$$

Since our division of the octave is based upon a logarithmical interpretation of the frequency, the higher we go, the smaller the musical interval between two subsequent partials becomes, while the frequency interval increases.

In acoustical sound generation, the overtone frequencies are usually not integer multiples of the fundamental frequency, but approach these multiples closely. For metal-stringed instruments, such as the piano, this deviation is to a great extent due to the material properties of the string and the forces acting on it. For the piano the actual frequency of the partials moves upwards. Technical restrictions make this stretching unavoidable, and the tuner will have to resolve the inharmonicity using "stretched scaling."

Fourier-analysis of musical sounds has shown that the presence and relative strength of different partials is very determinative for its color. As

Table
PARTIALS 1 - 25

Number i	Distance in cents from the 1st partial $c=1200/\log_{10}(2)\log_{10}(i)$	Note	Interval in cents $c=1200/\log_{10}(2)\log_{10}(i+1/i)$	Interval
1		C		
2	1200	c	1200	
3	1901.955	g	701.955	octave
4	2400	c^1	498.045	pure fifth
5	2786.31371	e^1	386.31371	pure fourth
6	3101.955	g^1	315.64129	natural major third
7	3368.82591		266.87091	natural minor third
8	3600	c^2	231.17409	
9	3803.91	d^2	203.91	major whole tone
10	3986.31371	e^2	182.40371	minor whole tone
11	4151.31794		165.00423	
12	4301.955	g^2	150.63706	
13	4440.52766		138.57266	
14	4568.8259		128.29824	
15	4688.26871	b^2	119.44281	
16	4800	c^3	111.73129	diatonic semitone
17	4904.95541		104.95541	
18	5003.91	d^3	98.95469	
19	5097.51302		93.60301	
20	5186.31371	e^3	88.8007	
21	5270.78091		84.46719	
22	5351.31794		80.53703	
23	5428.27435		76.9546	
24	5501.955	g^3	73.68065	
25	5572.62743	gis^3	70.67243	chromatic semitone

such, partials play an important role in musical and psycho-acoustical appreciation.

See Acoustics; Tuning.

Peter G.C. van Poucke

Bibliography

Askill, John. *Physics of Musical Sounds*. New York: D. Van Nostrand Company, 1979.

Rossing, Thomas D. *The Science of Sound*. Reading: Addison-Wesley, 1982.

White, Harvey E., and Donald H. White. *Physics and Music. The Science of Musical Sound*. Philadelphia: Saunders College, 1980.

PATENTS

Although the piano has, from its very beginnings, attracted intense inventive activity, patents seem to have played a surprisingly minor role in its commercial development. In particular, the first half of the nineteenth century saw the perfection of most essential elements of the modern piano: the iron **frame**, the repeating **double escapement action** for **grands**, the tape **check** action for **uprights**, the **agraffe**. Nonetheless, no single maker or small group of makers came to dominate the market during this period. In and around London alone the number of known piano makers grew, in approximate figures, from a dozen in 1775 to twenty-five in 1800, fifty in 1825, and nearly two hundred in 1850. Thus, at no time did patents exert the influence that they would in such industries as sound recording, where control of a few basic patents enabled Edison and Columbia to dominate the market for cylinders in the United States during the late nineteenth and early twentieth centuries and enabled Columbia and Victor to do likewise with respect to disc records until after World War II.

Diverse legal, technical, and social factors combined to minimize the effects of piano patents. Perhaps most important, the instrument's fundamental development came before adequate legal machinery existed to protect it. When **Cristofori** built his *Gravecembalo col piano e forte* in c.1698–1700, organized patent systems as we know them were just beginning to evolve. While the English Statute of Monopolies of 1624 had laid the foundations for modern Anglo-American patent law, English patents were not required to include so basic a feature as specifications until the reign of Queen Anne (1702–1714). In England and elsewhere, patents might be granted to reward innovation, but they might just as easily be granted as a sign of royal favor or as a means of raising revenue. By the time patent systems matured sufficiently to cope with a complex, rapidly evolving development like the piano, what we would call the fundamental invention had been old art for decades—indeed, such key elements as the escapement action had been present from the first in Cristofori's instruments. Thus, the only properly patentable inventions would fall in the class of improvements.

By the very nature of the piano and its market, no maker was likely to achieve market dominance solely on the strength of an improvement patent. The instrument's complexity gave rise to a multitude of alternative approaches, many equally valid, to every problem it raised. Moreover, the piano is a purely mechanical device, and a skilled craftsman could easily examine and analyze even the most innovative improvements with an eye to further development. In addition, a builder's shortcomings in one area might offset his advantages in another, as where a builder with great genius for designing actions had a poor grasp of **scale design**. Only relatively late in the nineteenth century did manufacturing technology develop to the point that the action expert could make a business of supplying ready-built actions to other makers. The lack of mass production techniques also limited the number of instruments a particular maker, however innovative, could produce, and hence the degree to which one maker could dominate the market.

Compounding these mechanical factors were certain social idiosyncrasies of the piano market. Buyers, then as now, had differing tastes in the qualities of instruments, particularly **touch** and **tone**. To cite two illustrious examples, **Mozart** wrote enthusiastically of the **Stein** instrument, which had a light German action (**Prellmechanik**) and clear tone, while **Beethoven** preferred the more sonorous **Broadwood** with its heavier **English action**. Thus, any given innovation might appeal to some but by no means to all buyers, leaving room for builders following different approaches. Indeed, eighteenth-century builders often simultaneously constructed instruments with the so-called German action and with various adaptations of Cristofori's escapement action in the same shop to accommodate different buyers. Moreover, as piano ownership grew in social status, the generally high cost of instruments and small production available from even the most prolific firms guaranteed a ready market for makers who could produce inexpensive instruments, even if they embodied obsolete or inferior technology.

In addition to the varying tastes of buyers, builders themselves often proved resistant to change or prejudiced against certain construction techniques. Many old, established European makers, particularly in France and England, refused to adopt such advances as the full iron **frame** and overstringing long after they became standard practice among American and more innovative European firms. Although their technological backwardness doomed most of them to declining sales and, generally, to eventual commercial failure, they nonetheless tended to linger on over a long period; even if merely trading on their respected names, their continued existence ensured that patent holders would not immediately dominate the marketplace. Perhaps more important, even the innovative builders appear to have made little effort to patent their inventions or to pursue active programs of enforcement outside their home territories. Thus, after **Steinway** demonstrated conclusively the superiority of the one-piece metal frame with **overstringing**, numerous European makers began producing instruments modelled after the Steinway, which they promoted as embodying the "American system" or even the "Steinway system."

Despite their relatively limited impact on the piano's commercialization, however, patents do seem to have served their purpose of encouraging innovation. **Jean Marius** bears the distinction of having received the first patent for a piano design, his *Clavecin à maillets*, in 1716, although only a relative handful of such grants predate the turn of the nineteenth century. From that time forward, however, inventors increasingly sought patent protection as patent systems matured to accommodate the requirements of the Industrial Revolution. For example, only four patents on actions are known to have been granted prior to 1750, two more between 1751 and 1775, and another fourteen between 1776 and 1800. The next twenty-five years, however, saw the grant of twenty-six action patents, and the years 1826 to 1850 a full one-hundred- fifty. **Soundboards** were the subject of only seven patents in the eighteenth century, all in its last quarter; by contrast, the first quarter of the nineteenth century saw fifteen soundboard patents, and the next quarter approximately one hundred.

Of course, the sheer number of patents granted is somewhat misleading; the majority of these nineteenth-century patents, like patents of any other period, were for minor or even meaningless innovations, a tendency aggravated by the then-common practice of advertising patents as though they were certificates of merit. For example, **keyboard** layout, whose outlines were largely standardized by harpsichord makers long before the piano's conception, was a particularly fruitless area of inquiry, which nonetheless received repeated patented attempts at innovation. The **Moór** double keyboard, the subject of seven patents, is only one relatively recent (c. 1920) effort in this direction. Others would include designs for playing all major and minor keys with a single **fingering** by John Trotter (1811; two ranks of keys) and Allison and Company (1851; color coding); convex and concave designs by various makers; a wildly complex two-level design by Theophile Auguste Dreschke (1846), which comprised an interlocking pattern of geometric shapes; and assorted keyboards or keyboard devices intended to facilitate the playing by children. Other stillborn but patented inventions would include various devices for altering the instrument's sound, such as lute stops, bassoon stops, and the like.

Major advances, on the other hand, did not necessarily generate many patents. The agraffe, to take one conspicuous example, gave rise to only six patents, two English and four French, between its invention by **Sébastien Erard** in 1808 and the Great Exhibition of 1851. It provides a perfect illustration of the casual patenting practices common in its day, for Erard obtained no patents outside France, and in fact agraffes quickly passed into common use by myriad builders.

In general, every imaginable aspect of the piano has provided the subject matter for pat-

ents at one time or another. Those generating the most activity were its action and, belatedly, its soundboard. Among the many others that drew considerable attention were **dampers**, metal frames and **braces, pedals and stops**, transposing mechanisms, **player** mechanisms, and **stringing**, not to mention such associated subjects as cabinetmaking machinery, **hammer felts**, and the **wire** for strings. Thus, despite their minimal impact on the piano's commercial development, patents do provide the researcher with an invaluable source of information about the instrument's development over time.

David R. Hoehl

Bibliography

Gill, Dominic, ed. *The Book of the Piano*. Ithaca, N. Y.: Cornell University Press, 1981.

Harding, Rosamond E.M. *The Piano-Forte: Its History Traced to the Great Exhibition of 1851*. Cambridge: Cambridge University Press, 1933. Reprints. New York: Da Capo Press, 1973; Old Woking, Surrey: Gresham Books, 1978.

Hauhart, Robert C. "The Origin and Development of the British and American Patent and Copyright Laws." *Whittier Law Review*, 5(1983): 539–563.

Ramsey, George "*The* Historical Background of Patents." *Journal of the Patent Office Society*, 18 (1936): 6–21.

Rimbault, Edward F. *The Pianoforte, Its Origin, Progress, and Construction*. London: Robert Cocks and Co., 1860.

Ripin, Edwin M. et. al. *The Piano*. (New Grove Musical Instrument Series). New York: W.W. Norton & Co., 1988.

Shead, Herbert A. *The History of the Emanuel Moór Double Keyboard Piano*. Old Woking, Surrey: Unwin Brothers Limited, 1978.

PATERSON, MORTIMER AND COMPANY

The Scottish firm of Paterson, Mortimer and Company was formed in Edinburgh in 1819 and shortly thereafter acquired Andrew **Rochead**'s workshops. Much of the workforce was imported from London. The company produced **square pianos** and a few **cabinet pianos**; the former imitate contemporary **Broadwood** models, although none was fitted with a metal **hitch-pin plate**. Despite commercial success, growing animosities between the partners caused the dissolution of the company in 1826. Total output probably exceeded 1,000 instruments.

George Mortimer then joined with Robert Anderson. Although Mortimer, Anderson and Company produced some six-octave square pianos, they soon confined themselves as Scottish agents for a London firm, **Stodart** and Son. Robert Paterson, in conjunction with a local piano dealer, P.W. Roy, also continued to manufacture. However, following pressure from Broadwood, these activities were abandoned. By 1828, Paterson and Roy operated solely as dealers of London-made pianos. As Paterson and Company, business continued from shops in major Scottish cities into the 1960s.

John Cranmer

PEDAGOGY, SURVEY OF PIANO

Piano pedagogy is a broad topic, and its history includes a brief examination of the evolution of the piano, the evolution of musical interpretation and technique, and a survey of some famous pedagogues and treatises. Although pedagogy is defined as teaching children, modern piano pedagogy has evolved to encompass the adult student as well.

The history of piano pedagogy has been influenced largely by the development of the piano. In c.1698–1700, **Bartolomeo Cristofori** produced a new set of technical questions in keyboard playing with the development of what was known as the *gravecembalo col piano e forte*, now known as the pianoforte, or piano. This new instrument was capable of producing a variety of dynamic levels, owing largely to the fact that the **strings** were struck by **hammers** rather than plucked, and more revolutionary, different *colors* of sound could be produced; the pianist was able to control the **tone** quality through the approach to the **keys**, or **touch**. Later the piano evolved into a heavier, more sonorous instrument, and the **action** was refined until it was very responsive and quick. Composers and teachers had to address the growing capabilities of the instrument.

The matter of authenticity in performance style is an age-old question, and music publishers offer editions of compositions with widely varying instructions regarding tempos, pedaling, articulation, dynamics, embellishments, and occasionally, the notes or rhythm. In some instances, composers have been careless in notating their intentions. In other instances, certain performance practices were traditional; composers may have felt no need to notate their intentions clearly.

Although we have written accounts, method books, and treatises by and about the great pedagogues of the past, much is handed down in the form of oral, and even visual tradition. The subtleties that give a performer or teacher that successful "edge" are simply not possible to record on the printed page. Modern technology makes it possible to record accurately the work of contemporary performers and teachers in the form of audio, film, and video recordings, thus ensuring a careful passage of traditions to future generations.

The first National Keyboard Teachers Videoconference, presented by *Clavier* magazine and **Baldwin Piano and Organ Company**, was held on 29 January 1987 and broke a record for participatory training conferences in any field. With more than 8,000 teachers and pedagogy students at 127 locations across the country, KTV participants had the opportunity to get a good feel for the way their colleagues were thinking. Participants could see instantaneous results to polls conducted during the conference, and then had a chance to discuss the results.

In 1990, The National Conference on Piano Pedagogy appointed the Oral History Committee. Under the direction of Fernando Laires, the committee's function is to assess subjects, research, and preservation techniques of this tradition.

While the goal of piano pedagogy is to teach musical expressiveness, written accounts must deal almost exclusively with the technical means to achieve that end. The technique required for early keyboard instruments such as the harpsichord and clavichord focused primarily on finger attack and economy of movement, with the upper arm remaining still. The use of the arm muscles became a basic technical issue in the development of piano-playing skills, owing to the difference in the key depth and the ease of its downward movement compared to earlier instruments. The action was eventually changed to allow a deeper and heavier touch, such as with the instrument created in the late eighteenth century by **John Broadwood**. Greater varieties of tone quality and dynamic range were possible with this change, and composers in turn began to write compositions requiring greater physical strength, endurance, and variety of approach to the keyboard.

Initially, pedagogues did not alter their approach to the instrument in keeping with its developments, perpetuating what is known as the *finger school* of technique. Applying solely the finger touch to the newer, heavier keyboard action could possibly cause stiffness to the hand, wrist, and arm, and in extreme cases, could cause irreparable physical damage.

The nineteenth century saw an emergence of more complex, expressive, and virtuosic literature, requiring more explanations and exercises. This type of composition was partly in response to the public's demand for this type of literature, and partly in response to the growing capabilities of the still-evolving piano. Such developments as increased range, double escapement (affecting the speed of the action), and the modern **pedals** made new technical feats possible, thus influencing the course of piano pedagogy.

The second half of the nineteenth century was a time of growing interest in the use of weight and relaxation in playing the piano, as well as a quest by some to arrive at a technique that would be identical for all players. This scientific approach was a trend perpetuated by the so-called *anatomic-physiological school*, and was ardently argued against by some well-known pedagogues, such as Theodor Leschetizky. Leschetizky recommended a "no method" approach to piano teaching, insisting that every pianist's hand is different. Although Leschetizky's students have offered written accounts of his teachings, there is little insight offered about how he achieved his enormous success as a teacher; the written technical accounts offer the same information available in other exercise books of the day.

One of the first references in pedagogy history to the use of mechanical aids to teach position was by François Couperin, who discussed the use of a mirror as a practice aid.

The first of many mechanical gadgets (see **Keyboard Practice Aids**) from the nineteenth century designed to assure a quiet arm and hand and "Viennese" finger technique was the *Royal Chiroplast*, invented by Johann Bernhard Logier and patented in 1814. Logier wrote a method book, *The First Companion to the Royal Chiroplast*, and in 1822 was invited to Germany by the Prussian government to set up a

Chiroplast training school for teachers. One of the first references to class piano was with Logier's system using the Chiroplast. Groups of students, as many as thirty or forty, played special etudes at the same time.

Other mechanical devices invented in the nineteenth century were the Hand-guide, invented by Friedrich Kalkbrenner in 1830; the *Dactylion*, invented by Henri Herz, a pedagogue renowned for his technical development book, *Scales and Exercises*; the *Digitorium*, invented by Myer Marks; the *Technicon*, designed by James Brotherhood; and the *Tekniklavier*, invented by Almon Kinkaid Virgil.

Gymnastic exercises away from the piano, but without mechanical devices, were introduced in 1818 by August E. Mueller. In 1874, *Gymnastics for the Fingers and Wrist* by E. Ward Jackson was published, the first English collection of finger gymnastics.

Attention was directed toward the freedom of the fourth finger in the nineteenth century; **Robert Schumann** devised a contraption to strengthen his fourth finger, which (along with tendon inflammation) ultimately contributed to his disabling hand affliction. In the 1880s, musical and medical magazines presented discussions about an operation to cut the tendons between the fourth and fifth fingers.

How to teach the effective use of the pedal can be one of the most mysterious pedagogical techniques, partly because of limited instructions by composers. In addition, the pedals have different uses, from sustaining notes that the hand is unable to sustain to changing the color of a passage. In 1783, John Broadwood **patented** (English Patent No. 1379) the sustaining pedal; before that time, stops and then knee levers operated the dampers. The first printed pedal markings are found in the Opus 37 sonatas of **Muzio Clementi**. The first published instructions regarding the use of the **damper** and *una corda* pedals were offered in Louis Adam's *Méthode*, written in 1804. Early composers rarely notated pedal instructions. Carl Czerny adroitly pointed out that the *una corda* pedal's shifting action not only produces a quieter sound, but a different tone quality. He taught that dynamics should be achieved by touch, and that the *una corda* pedal should be used to enhance delicacy.

Method books and treatises throughout the centuries have addressed such issues as **finger-**

ing, finger position, hand weight, arm weight, pedaling, and position at the keyboard, all in an effort to teach about facility and tone production. In addition, these written pedagogical accounts offer insight into performance practices of different eras.

Some of the earliest pianoforte method books were *Guida di Musica* Op. 34, published in two parts in 1785 and 1794 by the Englishman James Hook; *Klavierschüle*, one of the most authoritative source books of interpretive and expressive details of the time, written for pianists and harpsichordists by Daniel Gottlob Türk and published in 1789 in Germany; and *Instructions on the Art of Playing the Piano-forte or Harpsichord* written by Jan Ladislav Dussek, published in 1796. *Die Wahre Art das Pianoforte zu Spielen* [*The True Art of Piano Playing*], written by Johan Peter Milchmyer and published in 1797 in Dresden, was the first method book addressed primarily to the pianist.

Versuch über die wahre Art das Clavier zu spielen [*Essay on the True Art of Playing Keyboard Instruments*], by **Carl Philipp Emanuel Bach**, was originally published in two parts, in 1753 and 1762. It is considered the most important method book of the late eighteenth and early nineteenth centuries. *Versuch* was used in the studios of **Joseph Haydn**, **Wolfgang Amadeus Mozart**, **Ludwig van Beethoven**, and Carl Czerny. It was republished several times, and a modern English translation was made available by William J. Mitchell in 1949. Part One offers some technical advice and insight into performance practices of the period. C.P.E. Bach describes the forearms slightly above the keyboard, rounded fingers, and relaxed muscles. Fingering is recommended that is useful in nineteenth- and twentieth-century music. Up until that time, pianists were instructed to allow thumbs to hang freely, keeping them out of the way of the other fingers. C.P.E. Bach taught that using the thumbs is "the key to all fingering." *Versuch* is one of the best sources of information concerning ornamentation. Muzio Clementi, Johann Baptist Cramer, and Johann Nepomuk Hummel built their work directly on information from *Versuch*.

Mozart is credited with defining the ideal Viennese piano-technique, and although he carried a non-legato style over from the harpsichord, he made specific comments about such details as fingering and how they should be different on the pianoforte. Mozart did very little teaching, but much has been learned about his ideas from the students that he did have and letters that he wrote to his family.

Clementi, who is considered to be the patriarch of nineteenth-century piano technique, introduced pianistically idiomatic compositional enhancements (and technical problems) into his work. In addition, Clementi's passage work is played legato, a departure from the previous custom of *leggiero*, or non-legato playing for passage work. Clementi's *Introduction to the Art of Playing the Pianoforte*, written around 1803, is one of the earliest piano methods. It contains details of music fundamentals, fingering directions, and a number of one-measure finger exercises. In addition, it is an excellent collection of fifty moderately easy pieces for piano, either original or transcribed. It is noteworthy because it is one of the first attempts to make use of already existing pieces by composers other than the compiler as materials for studies. *Gradus ad Parnassum*, also by Clementi, was published in sections between 1817 and 1826, and is one of the best-known technique books in the history of piano pedagogy. The original work contained one-hundred compositions. It contains some of the most important early compositions that use five-finger scale and broken and arpeggiated chord patterns. Clementi employs a repeated pattern throughout each exercise in an effort to achieve even tone, equal finger action, and strength and fluency of the fingers. Carl Tausig published his own version of twenty-nine selections from the set in the mid-1800s, which is the best-known version of the work.

Clementi's students who have had a major impact on the field of piano pedagogy included John Field, Cramer, and Hummel. Cramer published his *Etudes*, Opus 39, in 1803 and 1804, and Opus 40 in 1810. The *Etudes* influenced his teacher's commanding treatise, *Gradus ad Parnassum*. Beethoven found the work of Cramer and Clementi vital in his teaching. Field's pianistic style had a strong influence on the music of **Frédéric Chopin**.

Hummel was a pianist and teacher whose technique was greatly influenced by his teachers, Mozart and Clementi. He produced students who developed successful concert careers, and in 1828 published one of the most important treatises of the nineteenth century, *A Com-*

plete Theoretical and Practical Course of Instructions on the Art of Playing the Piano Forte, a three-volume work. The work consisted of more than 2,000 exercises to develop control and strength of the fingers. In his preface, Hummel recommended a full hour of instruction each day for at least six months, and preferably for a year, which was the custom at that time.

Beethoven significantly shaped the future of piano pedagogy through his compositions and his students, most notably Czerny. Beethoven advocated the use of the arm to back up finger strength, and influenced the development of the bigger and more durable instruments as his compositions, teaching, and playing called for bigger sounds than those available on the instruments of the day. He strove for freedom and "natural" playing in piano technique.

Czerny, Beethoven's most notable student, had an enormous impact on nineteenth-century piano pedagogy. Among his students were Theodor Leschetizky, Theodor Kullak, and **Franz Liszt**. Czerny believed in developing technique independently from the music. Czerny started the trend of developing technique first, then later using it to meet artistic expression needs. In addition, Czerny advocated constant repetition of a problem passage until it was worked into the hands. His exhaustive treatise on nineteenth-century piano playing, *Complete Theoretical and Practical Piano Forte School*, Opus 500 (published in 1839), gives a clear picture of Czerny's pedagogical ideas, and his method book, *Piano Forte School*, presents the finger school in detail, and, according to Adolph Kullak, "closes an epoch."

Chopin influenced the development of piano technique through the demands that he placed in his compositions. His nocturnes called for a singing legato. His etudes called for a very flexible hand to play the interval of a tenth or more in some cases. Revolutionary changes in pedaling and fingering can also be found in his works. His main objective with his students was a supple hand and wrist, and use of the arm to help support and strengthen the fingers.

Liszt, who studied with Antonio Salieri and Czerny, felt that the musician should listen first, then train his body and fingers to produce the sounds that his ears wanted. Each finger movement was incorporated into the whole arm movement. He recommended a higher seat than was previously common. The three editions of his *Etudes* demonstrate the metamorphosis of his thought as he moved from the style of Czerny in his first edition, to an increased level of virtuosic composition in the second edition, then back to a more poetic expression in the third edition. Liszt is the originator of the master class. During his years of teaching in Weimar, he devoted most of his time to the master class rather than to private lessons. The classes usually met three or four times a week for two or more hours at a time. Students were encouraged to play with original interpretation rather than to imitate, and to work on music only within the bounds of their maturity.

Ludwig Deppe is considered to be the first to develop a system contrary to the isolated finger technique of the old finger-school. He taught the importance of free movements and dropped weight of the arm in the production of better tone. He was also concerned with the increased endurance made possible through this increased flexibility. Deppe's student, Elisabeth Caland, who wrote accounts of his teachings after Deppe's death, wrote about what Deppe referred to as "controlled free fall" applied to exercises. This term describes allowing the hand and arm to fall from above the surface of the key, which demonstrates his concern with the use of larger movements in piano playing.

Rudolf Maria Breithaupt wrote an influential book discussing the use of arm weight, *Die Grundlagen der Klaviertechnik* [*The Foundation of Piano Technique—School of Weight-Touch*] in 1907. Many of his points are valid; however, an unclear writing style caused some ambiguities, therefore misinterpretation of his work.

Tobias Matthay, an Englishman who is considered one of the most successful teachers of his time, was especially helpful to students suffering from tension problems. He was a strong advocate of relaxation and the use of weight, but as with Breithaupt, was somewhat misunderstood because his writings are difficult to read. Matthay worked in later years to clarify the meanings of his early writings, explaining that by discussing relaxation, he did not wish to imply the absence of finger and hand exertion.

Isidor Philipp, Marguerite Long, and Alfred Cortot represent some of the best twentieth-century French piano teaching, and each produced influential pedagogical works: Cortot's *Rational Principles of Pianoforte Technique* (1928),

Philipp's *Complete School of Technic for the Pianoforte* (1928), and Long's *Le Piano* (1959).

It was not until the second half of the nineteenth century that Russian pianists began to be recognized. Adolph von Henselt, who had studied with Hummel, began teaching in St. Petersburg, where he was influential in the founding of the Russian school of pianism. Leschetizky also taught in Russia for several years. Some other famous Russian teachers include Anton Rubinstein; Vasily Safonov; Genrikh Gustovovich Neigauz [Heinrich Neuhaus], who wrote *The Art of Piano Playing* (1958); Josef and Rosina Lhévinne; and Dmitri Kabalevsky.

Several famous music schools were formed in America during the late nineteenth and early twentieth centuries: the Oberlin, Cincinnati, New England, and Peabody conservatories, Chicago Musical College, and the Institute of Musical Art, which later became part of what is now the Juilliard School. After World War I, many of the famous pedagogues from Europe such as Josef and Rosina Lhévinne, James Friskin, Ernest Hutcheson, Josef Hofmann, and Rudolf Serkin migrated to the United States and began teaching in these schools.

Otto Rudolf Ortmann, an American writer of piano technique, wrote *The Physiological Mechanics of Piano Technique* (1929), which is considered one of the most important source books about piano technique. Ortmann laid the foundation for the later development of technique through his extensive research and writings.

The latter part of the nineteenth century saw the beginnings of the specific study of the mind's role in piano playing. Understanding the relationships between piano playing and the central nervous system, development of motor skill, and learning theories have become central issues in twentieth-century piano pedagogy.

The 1930s was a time of enormous growth in the development of music education. The average-age beginner and the preschooler were influenced by a large interest in publishing methods for these age groups. The average-age beginner is seven or eight years old, about the age that a child develops certain technical skills and the ability to read fairly well. Most piano courses are designed for beginners in this age group.

Since the 1960s, piano methods have been classified by the approach to reading. Many modern methods, however, are eclectic, combining the best features of each approach.

The *middle-C approach* begins with the student reading melodic lines divided between the hands with both thumbs on middle C. Working exclusively in one key before moving to other keys creates a sense of security for the beginner, and permits the student to absorb small amounts of information. The middle-C approach is the most popular, and has been used in most method books since the 1930s. *Very First Piano Book,* written in 1925 by John M. Williams and Shaylor Turner, is one of the original works of the middle-C approach. Williams is considered the first composer of methods materials to instruct the student to begin with both thumbs on middle C and work outward. *Teaching Little Fingers to Play,* a middle-C approach book written in 1936 by John Thompson, is the primary book for the most popular piano method series in history.

The *multi-key approach* is geared toward teaching "functional" piano; the student learns to read patterns by playing in many different keys, or transposing. This approach allows the student to learn harmonization and improvisation more easily. In addition, its proponents feel that the method encourages technical freedom of the arm and shoulder because of playing in a variety of locations. The multi-key approach has its roots in group piano, with the *Oxford Piano Course,* written in 1928, a piano course designed for the public school classroom.

The *landmark* or *intervallic approach* encourages directional reading with attention to spatial relationships. *The Music Tree* series, written by Frances Clark and Louise Goss and published beginning in 1955, is one of the earliest series using the intervallic method.

The Beginner's Book for Older Pupils was published in 1929, written by the authors of the *Oxford Piano Course.* Most early method books for adults consisted largely of the same material as the children's books, with a format more appealing to adults. Some methods even had the same text material, with changes in the artwork and titles. The 1950s produced an increased interest by colleges and universities in group piano-instruction to music majors who played the piano as a second instrument. During this decade, the emergence of **electronic piano** laboratories created a greater need for group-instruction materials. These materials consisted largely of functional skills: transposition, sightreading, chord symbols, and adding accompaniments to melodies.

The 1970s produced the largest growth of new methods and materials for the older beginner. More materials were developed that can be used in the independent studio as easily as in a classroom setting. While these new materials continued to develop functional skills, more attention was paid to performance of compositions, with scales, chords, and other patterns presented in a format as a basis for understanding the compositions.

As early as the time of Couperin, advice was given that a child should begin to study the keyboard at age six or seven, as the hands are more easily molded at that age. Some modern methods suggest that, under proper guidance, the child should begin formal lessons by the age of three. Preschool music instruction falls into three categories: a general introduction to music that does not use the piano, a general introduction to music in which the piano is used for a variety of activities, and preparatory courses for piano performance. Most preschool music programs include the piano as part of an overall music enrichment experience, and have their beginnings in Europe and Asia. Only one of these methods, the Suzuki method, is designed as an actual piano performance method. In the 1930s, a great deal of attention was paid to early childhood development, and as a parallel, several preschool piano methods were developed. The 1970s saw another increase in preschool piano methods publishing, once again in tandem with a general interest in early childhood education.

Emile Jaques-Dalcroze created his system for teaching ear training and improvisation in 1892. A professor at the Geneva Conservatory of Music, Jaques-Dalcroze discovered that his students could not hear the chords that they were writing. He began an ear-training program for young children. "Eurhythmics," which means "good rhythms," has come to be associated with the Dalcroze method. The Dalcroze method involves teaching rhythm through movement, ear training, solfege, and interpreting through movement the elements of a musical example, improvised by the teacher at the piano. The method was designed to develop a strong sense of rhythm, musical memory, interpretation, and creativity.

Also popular was a method developed by Carl Orff. Orff avoided the use of the piano for teaching young children, but his methods are often included in piano preparation classes. Another method for training young children was produced by Zoltán Kodály. As in the Orff method, Kodály avoids using the piano to teach young children.

The Suzuki method, created by Shinchi Suzuki in Japan, is a unique preschool method in that it is an actual piano method; it is designed to teach piano performance. In addition, the Suzuki piano method is designed to teach one child at a time, rather than a group. The Suzuki method began with teaching young children the violin, and the principles were transferred to piano teaching by Suzuki, his sister-in-law, Shizuko Suzuki, and Haruko Kataoka. The *Suzuki Piano School* was published in Japan in 1970, and the first English edition was published in 1972. Observation and imitation is the foundation for the Suzuki approach to music education. Suzuki's philosophy is: just as very young children learn to speak their native language easily through listening and imitation, so should they learn the language of music. He goes on to point out that a child learns to listen and imitate first, then to read and write later. Suzuki refers to this approach as the "Mother Tongue Method." The Suzuki method of teaching piano is not offered in print for self-study by teachers. Teachers must attend workshops. These workshops are available through the Suzuki Association of the Americas, an organization that has been registering teacher-trainers since 1980.

Since the 1950s, electronic pianos have been used in teaching laboratories in college music programs. These keyboards usually allow the students to work independently with headphones. A central monitoring station generally allows the teacher to listen to and communicate with each student independently or with more than one student at a time. The new smaller electronic keyboard labs have made this arrangement a popular option for many private studios as well. **Synthesizers**, sequencers, **MIDI samplers**, and personal computers are offering wide pedagogical options for piano teachers for training, drilling, and evaluation in a variety of study areas: ear training, sight playing, technique, ensemble, style, improvisation, basic recording techniques, and practice routines.

Music teacher associations and conferences in the United States offer journals, meetings, student activities, and a wide variety of support and information pertinent to the modern piano teacher. Music Teachers National Association (MTNA), the oldest music-teachers' association in the United States, was founded in 1876. Other American teacher organizations are National Guild of Piano Teachers and Music Educators National Conference. The National Conference on Piano Pedagogy is a biennial meeting that assembles people from all over the world who are concerned about the field of piano-teacher training. Started in 1979, activities include demonstration teaching, conference committees with open-forum sessions, and the presentation of papers. A conference report is published at the close of each conference, and includes reviews of pedagogical materials in addition to papers and in-depth reports covering the conference.

Pedagogy instruction has always been a part of the curriculum for keyboard performance majors on the college level. In recent years, more attention has been given to the pedagogy degree, especially at the graduate level. Whether offered as one or two courses in a performance program or more in-depth as a major, piano pedagogy often includes the study of teaching literature and method materials, teaching strategies, learning theories, history, business practices, and technology, in addition to observation and student teaching. The National Association of Schools of Music has included the baccalaureate degree in pedagogy in its handbook since 1985, and the National Conference on Piano Pedagogy publishes a directory of piano pedagogy offerings in American colleges and universities.

Regardless of the methodology and materials adopted by a pedagogue, thorough training in piano teaching is of utmost importance. Performance practices, proper piano technique, and learning theories must be understood well enough to pass on to students, and technical dangers must be avoided. It is a mistake for someone who has only been trained to *play* the piano to assume enough knowledge to *teach*, as students will bring to the keyboard different capabilities and problems than those the teacher experienced in his or her own training.

See also Technic, Survey of Piano.

Helen Smith Tarchalski

Bibliography

Banowetz, Joseph. *The Pianist's Guide to Pedaling.* Bloomington, Indiana: Indiana University Press, 1985.

Fay, Amy. *Music-Study in Germany.* Mineola, New York: Dover Publications, Inc., 1965.

Ferguson, Howard. *Keyboard Interpretation from the 14th to the 19th Century.* New York: Oxford University Press, 1975.

Gerig, Reginald. *Famous Pianists & Their Technique.* Washington-New York: Robert B. Luce, 1974.

Hinson, Maurice. *The Piano Teacher's Source Book.* Melville, New York: Belwin-Mills, 1980.

Holland, Sam. *Teaching Toward Tommorrow: A Music Teacher's Primer for Using Electronic Keyboards, Computers, and MIDI in the Studio.* Cincinnati, Ohio: Debut Music Systems, 1993.

Kochevitsky, George. *The Art of Piano Playing.* Secaucus, New Jersey: Summy-Birchard Inc., 1967.

LeHuray, Peter. *Authenticity in Performance: Eighteenth-Century Case Studies.* New York: Press Syndicate of the University of Cambridge, 1990.

The National Conference on Piano Pedagogy Proceedings and Reference, 1988–1989 and 1990–1991. Princeton, New Jersey: The National Conference on Piano Pedagogy, 1989 and 1991.

The National Conference on Piano Pedagogy Proceedings and Reference, 1990–1991. Princeton, New Jersey: The National Conference on Piano Pedagogy, 1991.

Schultz, Arnold. *The Riddle of the Pianist' s Finger and Its Relationship to a Touch-scheme.* New York: Carl Fischer, 1949.

Uszler, Gordon, and Elyse Mach. *The Well-Tempered Keyboard Teacher.* Schirmer Books, 1991.

PEDAL BOX

The pedal box, or lyre box, is a rectangular wooden unit from which the **pedals** of a **grand piano** protrude. It also forms a supportive base for the decorative lyre. The pedal box is stained to match the **case** of the piano.

See Lyre.

Peggy Flanagan Baird

PEDALFLÜGEL/PEDALKLAVIER

Pedalflügel or *Pedalklavier* is the German term for pedal piano.

See also Pedal Piano.

R.P.

PEDAL PIANO

A pedal piano (Italian: *Pianoforte organistico*; Ger.: *Pedalflügel, Pedalklavier*; French: *Piano à pédalier*) can be either: (1) a separately stringed instrument with a **hammer action** and a pedal board, which is placed under a **grand piano** but can be removed; (2) a piano connected with a pedal board whose **pedals** strike (by rods and trackers) the same **strings** as those operated by the **keyboard**; or (3) a piano in which the pedal-operated hammers strike strings located underneath the **soundboard** of the keyboard-operated strings (a second soundboard is attached to the main corpus). In all cases the pedal piano sounds an octave lower and thus it is a "sixteen foot" instrument of usually a two-octave compass.

Pedal clavichords were already described around 1460 by Paulinus Paulirinus, by Sebastian Virdung (1511), and by others, and for centuries served mainly as practice instruments for organists. One of these *Pedalclavichords*, built by David Gerstenberg in 1760, is preserved today in the instrument collection of the University of Leipzig, Germany. Descriptions of pedal harpsichords can likewise be found prior to the eighteenth century. During the Baroque period, according to Edwin Ripin, separate pedal harpsichords were more common in France and Germany than in Italy; the Italian pedal instruments usually were pedal clavichords with only one set of strings. **Johann Sebastian Bach's** trio sonatas BWV 525–530 were written for a keyboard instrument with pedal.

No preserved pedal piano of the eighteenth century is known today—only various instruments built shortly after 1800. However, we know that **Mozart** owned a pedal fortepiano. In an invitation to a concert in March 1785 he announced that he would play a fantasy on an "especially large Forte piano Pedal." About the same time Mozart's father wrote in a letter to his daughter about her brother: "He has had a large fortepiano pedal made, which stands under the instrument and is about two feet longer and extremely heavy." Unlike the pedal clavichord used by organists, Mozart bought this instrument certainly not for organ practice purposes but with the intention to reinforce the sound of his **fortepiano** and to extend its range. The builder of it was probably the piano maker who had supplied him also with his **concert grand piano: Anton Walter**. After Mozart's death his pedal piano was lost, as were so many other instruments of the eighteenth century, while his fortepiano was given eventually to the

Mozarteum in Salzburg by Mozart's son and is exhibited today in Mozart's birth house.

While no pedal pianos of the eighteenth century are known today, a considerable number of pedal pianos of the nineteenth century are preserved. One from approximately 1815, built by **Joseph Brodmann** in Vienna, is presently exhibited in the instrument collection of the Kunsthistorisches Museum in Vienna; another one by Johann Schmid is owned by the Museum Carolineum in Salzburg. During the late nineteenth and the early twentieth centuries, a substantial number of pedal pianos were still being built, mainly in Germany and England. **Robert Schumann** wrote his Op.58 for such an instrument, and Charles Gounod also used one. Relatively few of these instruments survived World War II and are still in use today.

Eva Badura-Skoda

Bibliography

Adlung, Jakob. *Musica Mechanica Organoedi.* Berlin: Bärenreiter, Dokumenten-Serie, 1768, II p. 157f.

Badura-Skoda, Eva, and Paul Badura-Skoda. *Interpreting Mozart on the Keyboard.* London: Barrie & Rockliff, 1961; New York: St. Martin's Press, 1962 (pictures of pedal pianos on pp.7f. and 22f.).

Handschin, Jacques. "Das Pedalklavier." *Zeitschrift für Musikwissenschaft* 17 (1935): 418f.

van der Meer, John Henry. *Musikinstrumente von der Antike bis zur Gegenwart.* München: Prestel, 1983 (picture of pedal clavichord on p.167).

PEDALS AND STOPS

Pedals and stops are devices attached to the piano to change its **tone** in various ways. "Stop" is the more general term, derived from the nomenclature of the organ, and pedals are one kind of mechanism used for stops. Though the modern conventional (acoustic) piano has no stops other than pedals, they began to be used only seventy years or more after the piano's invention (c.1698–1700), and it was another twenty-five or more years before the use became general.

Mechanisms to operate stops have been of three basic kinds: (1) hand stops used in the eighteenth century were sometimes drawbars, sometimes laterally moving or revolving rods; (2) knee levers, operated by bringing the knee up against the bottom of the **case**, were used in

European pianos toward the end of the eighteenth century; (3) pedals, at first attached to the front legs of **grands**, and later mounted on **lyres** hung below the front of the case in grands and **squares**, and protruding through the lower part of the case in vertical pianos, began to be used in about 1770, by 1800 were the most common stop mechanism, and are now universal. All of these mechanisms operated trap-work of various kinds to bring the stops into play. Pedals are better than hand stops for the player needing both hands to play, and the principal advantage of pedals over knee levers (which some writers persist, oxymoronically, in calling "knee pedals") is that they can readily be operated by persons with various lengths of leg.

All stops have the purpose of changing the sound of the piano: (1) to prolong the sound (e.g., **damper** stops); (2) to shorten the sound (e.g., lute or harp stops); (3) to make the sound louder or softer (e.g., swells, "soft pedals"); (4) to add sounds (e.g., **Janissary stops, couplers**); (5) to modify the tone (e.g., bassoon stops, mutes, *una corda* stops). At certain times stops were a fad, the first half of the nineteenth century having seen works of the most fecund imagination. It would be nearly impossible to give an exhaustive account of stops actually used in pianos, and some of those mentioned below may never have been tried. Some instruments carried as many as eight pedals, though one stop was often worked by two different pedals. Terminology has varied so much that sometimes the same name was used in different places to refer to stops with quite different functions.

1. *Stops for prolonging the sound*. One of the problems of piano sound is its rapid decay. The lower the tension on a **string**, the more rapid is its decay. In the first 150 years of the piano's history, when framing was of wood or partially of metal, string tension was quite low. Even so, these instruments needed dampers to keep the sound of one note or chord from impinging cacophonously upon following ones. One of the earliest stops is a damper stop, which holds the dampers up from all or some of the strings. Some damper stops worked for bass strings only, and in some early pianos (frequently in **Broadwoods**) the damper pedal was split, so that the player might raise only bass dampers, only treble dampers, or all dampers. A similar

combination is sometimes seen with the knee levers of eighteenth-century **Viennese pianos**. Early squares often had hand stops for the dampers, pushing slats of wood under the damper levers. A special case of the damper stop is the *sostenuto* stop, **patented** by **Steinway** in 1874–75, the middle pedal of most modern grands, which works a rod that holds up dampers that are already off the string but not others, allowing selective sustaining only of those notes.

Other devices for prolonging sound have come to be lumped together as "*sostenente pianos*," all evanescent and unsatisfactory. Three types were known: bowing mechanisms, "Aeolian harp" mechanisms to keep strings sounding by columns of air, and mechanisms to cause repeated **hammer** blows. A number of experiments used the **keyboard** to bring strings into contact with a constantly circulating bow of horsehair or other material, which caused the strings to vibrate by friction. Strictly speaking, these were mostly not pianos, as hammers were usually replaced by the bowing mechanisms. We find them from the first years of the nineteenth century in England, the U.S., and Europe up to the ingenious device by Roeder of France (1847), in which rags or other soft material attached to a revolving cylinder flapped against the strings to keep them vibrating.

Another effort was to direct columns of air across already vibrating strings in order to keep them vibrating. This "Aeolian harp" effect, almost entirely useless, was first proposed in the 1790 "Animo-Corde" (not the last linguistic corruption among such devices) of Schnell and Tschenky. In some instruments, the wind current was combined with a bowing mechanism, and in some it followed a regular hammer blow. It is astonishing how long such things continued, and especially that so keen a mind as that of **Jean-Henri Pape** worked on such a device for more than ten years.

The repeating hammer stop (which Rosamond Harding mistakenly compared to the technique of *Bebung* on the clavichord, which has nothing to do with repeated finger strokes) engaged a revolving cylinder whose projecting teeth came into contact with the hammer and kept it flying back and forth to the string. Such stops are patented from 1800 (Isaac Hawkins, England, for his son, **John Isaac Hawkins** of Philadelphia) until 1844 (Charles Sautter, England). Both Jean-Henri Pape and the **Erard** company perpetrated experiments, and one French patentee in 1841, Madame Girard-Romagnac—one of the few women who obtained patents pertaining to the piano—claimed that the stop achieved what she called an "Italian tremendo."

2. *Stops for shortening the sound*. On the whole, the sound was shortened by bringing damping material against the string. We find "lute," "buff" (or *jeu de buffle*), "mute" (or *sourdine*, *sordino*), and "harp" used more or less interchangeably for this kind of stop, which had mostly died out by the end of the eighteenth century. But those terms are also to be found among stops that modify tone (see below). In some of the shortening stops, a rod covered with **leather** or cloth is lowered or raised to the whole length of strings. In others, a slide brings a piece of leather, wood, or cloth against the side of one of the strings, thus producing something like the *una corda* effect (which is actually a tone modifier). The latter type was sometimes used to assist in **tuning**.

Another such device is the "pizzicato pedal" patented by **Robert Wornum** in 1826. Though Harding describes this as a variant of the lute stop, Wornum's patent suggests that the stop kept the damper on bass strings when the **key** was struck.

3. *Stops to change dynamics*. One might think that the nature of the piano, where the player's fingers are the means for changing dynamics, would obviate the need for such devices. Perhaps early pianists and makers had not grasped the principle, and we find stops designed both to soften sound and to make it louder.

The former, apart from softening devices like mute stops (which actually modify tone and will be touched on below), was done mainly by shifting the hammer closer to the string, thus shortening its blow and lessening the speed with which it strikes the string. That device somewhat softens the tone, and it has become the standard left ("soft") pedal on modern **uprights**. It was sometimes called the "piano" stop, sometimes, confusingly, *Jeu céleste*. A variant in modern uprights is a middle pedal that slides into a slot at the bottom of its opening, which operates the hammer shift and is intended to allow practicing without troubling the neighbors. The *una corda* stop and various

mutes and **moderators**, though they have the effect of making the sound softer, are principally stops to change timbre and are discussed below.

We meet two devices to make the sound louder in the eighteenth century. The "Venetian swell," directly derived from an English harpsichord device, was like Venetian blinds above the strings, the louvers of which were rotated open and shut by the stop. In the harpsichord, as in swell boxes in organs, this allowed more or less sound to escape and thus gave the illusion of dynamic change. The other device, confined to square pianos, was jocularly known as the "nag's head swell," from the shape of its lever. The stop opened and closed the small flap on the lid to the player's right, when the top of the piano was closed. As pianists increasingly realized that their art lay in their fingers and not in their feet, such stops lost currency and by the beginning of the nineteenth century were hardly to be found.

4. *Stops to add sound*. Some of the musical fads of the early nineteenth century involved the use of stops that would add piano sounds beyond those caused by the keys struck, or that would produce sounds other than piano sounds by means other than hammer blows upon strings.

The former type is exemplified by the addition of couplers, as in the organ, by which additional strings were activated, especially at the octave. We find octave couplers as early as 1793, but a number of experiments with them in the nineteenth century began with no less a maker than Erard Frères in 1812, continuing with Johann Baptist **Streicher** in 1824, and tapering off over the next twenty-five years or so with lesser inventors in England, France, Canada, and the United States. The matter was revived in the 1920s by **Emanuel Moór**, whose two-manual piano included a coupler to allow the lower manual to add the upper, which sounded an octave higher. All of these coupler mechanisms, whether sounding the octave above or below the note struck, added weight to the **touch**, and that very undesirable factor proved the coupler's undoing.

The most unusual stop that adds sound to that of the piano is no doubt the Janissary music stop. Derived from the late-eighteenth-century craze for Turkish military band music, with its drums, bells, Jingling Johnnies, and other struck and jangled metallic objects (the name "Janissary" comes from an elite Turkish corps), the Janissary stop used one or more pedals to produce drum and bell sounds. By about 1830, the stop had disappeared from new pianos.

The only other way to add sounds to those of the piano was through pianos combined with various other instruments, which could be brought into play by stops that allowed the piano keys to work them. Various types of **combination pianos** are to be found. Perhaps the earliest is the patent submitted in 1716 by **Jean Marius** to the Paris Academie Royale, which contained both piano and harpsichord actions that the player could use at will. Johann Andreas **Stein** of Augsburg invented such a combination in 1769, calling it, in the polylingual fashion of the day, Polytoni-Clavichordium. Other combinations are piano-organs (again Stein and others in England, France, and Germany), piano-harmoniums (Alexandre of Paris and others), and combinations with wind instruments (Hancock of London), and even with musical glasses (Day of England, 1816)—worked not by wetted fingers but by hammers. In each case, the additional instrument was played from the piano keyboard, and in some cases the two instruments could be played simultaneously.

5. *Stops to modify the tone of the piano.* The difference between this category of stops and the others is that here we discuss mechanisms that change the tone quality of the sound the piano makes by its ordinary means. Some of these stops work by affecting the string, some by changing the blow to the string, some by temporarily altering some other sounding part. This category does not include such innovations as the "prepared piano" of John Cage and others, which is not technically a "stop" because it cannot be applied and removed at will during the playing.

Perhaps the best known way of affecting the string was the bassoon stop of the early nineteenth century, in which a rod to which a piece of parchment was loosely attached was brought into contact with the string before the hammer blow. The parchment buzzed against the vibrating string, which reminded some listeners of a bassoon. The stop usually occupied the lowest two octaves or so, and it was mostly abandoned by about 1830. Another, sometimes named the "harmonic swell" and sometimes not named,

allowed sympathetic vibration of non-vibrating lengths of the string, almost always between the **bridge** and the **hitch pins**, or, in F. W. **Collard's** English patent of 1821, between two **soundboard** bridges. A rod or slat with damping material, lying on the strings, was raised by a pedal, and the resulting soft sound added a vague shimmer to the sound. One sometimes finds this device worked by the left pedal on **Alpheus Babcock** squares, and it depended on the absence of other damping material on the non-vibrating parts of the string. The principle of this sympathetic vibration is the one used by Theodore Steinway's "**duplex scale,**" still designed into Steinways and other contemporary pianos. A "harmonic sounds" stop, found in North America and Europe in 1820–1850, lowered a bar to the string at a node point, so that the string would continue to vibrate at the rate of a **partial.**

Several types of stop worked by modifying the way the hammer struck the string. The most familiar is the one still found on grands, miscalled *una corda*, as the hammer strikes two of three strings instead of one. Technically it should probably be called the "keyboard shift" stop, because the pedal moves the entire keyboard and **action** to the right (some early examples moved left) so that the hammer misses one string of the three. In early versions, the keyboard shift could move far enough so that the hammer struck only one of three strings. This stop softens the sound somewhat, but more exactly it makes the timbre thinner, as can be heard more clearly on early pianos with a true *una corda* stop. The tone of a single string is noticeably different from that of two or three.

A different effect of both softening and varying tone quality is in various mute and moderator stops (called by a number of names in the late eighteenth and nineteenth centuries). Here the tone was changed by interposing material between the hammer and the string, sometimes cloth, sometimes leather. The muting effect could be varied by the thickness of the material. Some moderator stops used a strip of wool cloth that was thicker at one side, and the farther down the player depressed the pedal the thicker material the hammer struck (sometimes called the "pianissimo" stop). In many German and Austrian pianos in the late eighteenth century this stop was worked by a draw bar that protruded toward the player through the **nameboard.** The moderator was the standard function of the left pedal on American squares throughout the nineteenth century, using tongues of leather between hammer and strings. It has been revived in some contemporary uprights, often as a "practice mute" worked by a middle, third pedal. A variant, which worked much the same way, was the eighteenth-century harpsichord or cembalo stop. Leather or cloth strips brought between hammers and strings were tipped with whalebone or **ivory**, and the hammer blow caused that hard surface to strike the string in an imitation of the harpsichord. In the twentieth century the **Pleyel** company devised a harpsichord stop that interposed brass strips wound around **felt** between strings and hammers.

Perhaps the oddest modification of tone was the "Dolce Compana" (another linguistic mutilation), patented in 1849 by James A. Gray in the U.S. and W. P. Parker in England. A rack with heavy weights at one end was attached to the soundboard bridge, and moving a pedal caused the weights to push the bridge—and through it the soundboard—up and down to provide a cumbersome sort of vibrato. No record exists of damage thus inflicted, but many instruments must have objected to this punishment.

Several modern experiments in modifying the tone have been asked for by composers. Sheets of paper wound among the strings are a modern sort of "bassoon" stop, and a "luthéal" stop by George Cloetens provides imitations of **cimbalom**, harpsichord, and lute by bringing metal bolts or felt to the strings.

A stop that does not exactly fit any of the five classifications above is the wooden rod 14 and $3/4$ inches long that Charles Ives calls for in his "Concord Sonata." This rod, laid across the upper keys, is occasionally struck by the pianist to sound all the notes simultaneously, thus producing tone clusters surpassing even those Henry Cowell demanded from the player's forearm.

Edwin M. Good

Bibliography

Ehrlich, Cyril. *The Piano: A History.* Rev. ed. Oxford: Clarendon Press, 1990.

Good, Edwin M. *Giraffes, Black Dragons, and Other Pianos: A Technological History from Cristofori to the Modern Concert Grand.* Stanford, Cal.: Stanford University Press, 1982.

Harding, Rosamond E.M. *The Piano-Forte: Its History Traced to the Great Exhibition of 1851.* Cambridge: Cambridge University Press, 1933. Reprints. New York: Da Capo Press, 1973; Old Woking, Surrey: Gresham, 1978.

Marcuse, Sibyl. *Musical Instruments: A Comprehensive Dictionary.* Corr. ed. New York: W. W. Norton & Company, Inc., 1975.

Ripin, Edwin M., et al. *The Piano* (New Grove Musical Instrument Series). New York and London: W. W. Norton & Company, 1988.

PERFORMANCE PRACTICES—STYLISTIC CONSIDERATIONS (1700–1990)

Performance Practice denotes the study of information relevant to the performance and perception of music in various historical contexts. Such information may be found in manuscript and printed scores, mechanical or electrical recording devices, music and dance treatises, books and letters, media accounts and visual documentation of concert settings, instrument designs and temperaments, etc.

A temporal art, live music can only manifest itself in ever-varied performances, yet it "remains unchanged behind this relativity" (Rosen). The relationship between the absolute and the relative aspects of music constitutes the basic concern of performance practice. Depending on the resolution of this relationship, two orientations have evolved. The first asserts the inherent value of the past, seen as a repository of the composer's intentions, and hence the source of presumably immutable truths about proper musical performance. By contrast, the second orientation affirms the all-important contribution of the present, seen not necessarily as a corrupting factor but rather as a recreative one without whose impulse music would ossify into a lifeless repetition of the past.

The three major topics of performance practice—notation, perception, and instruments—will be treated from the often conflicting perspectives of the two orientations, and exemplified by findings of recent research.

Implicit versus Explicit Notation. The notation of piano music evolved from lesser to greater explicitness, as typified by the notation of the improvisational aspects of music which, in the eighteenth century, still afforded the performer a considerable degree of creative input. This age of the performer-as-composer was manifested not only in "preluding" (improvising to set the mood and the tonality) and extemporizing (improvising variations on a theme), but also in requiring the performer to prepare or extemporize cadenzas and *Eingänge* (lead-ins), to embellish and ornament slow movements and rondo reprises, and to realize continuo. Without the performer's creative input, some of **Haydn's**, **Mozart's**, and **Beethoven's** solo, chamber, and orchestral pieces remain unfinished works. For posterity, the problem is how and when to improvise.

The "how" of improvisation is facilitated by authentic models. Their recurring features intimate a composer's improvisational style—the relationship between its constant and variable aspects. Pianist Robert D. Levin opts for re-creating the spirit of the past without resorting to its letter (in order to re-create the element of surprise inherent in performances of the Classical era when composers rarely published cadenzas, embellishments, and continuo realizations in the scores of concertos).

The "when" of improvisation is determined by context. A fermata on a tonic $^6/_4$ chord implies a cadenza; on a dominant seventh chord, an *Eingang;* but what of the possibility that some fermatas denote an explicit rather than an implicit meaning (prolongation rather than improvisation)?

Controversy also surrounds embellishment and ornamentation. The context that implies their need is the "something missing" that Mozart's sister Nannerl spotted in a bare melodic outline of the Concerto in D Major, K. 451, second movement. Mozart supplied the deficiency by mailing a lavishly embellished version of the same. If used as a model of explicitness versus implicitness, this example could lead to the recognition of "something missing" in similar spots, such as in Mozart's Concerto in C Major, K. 503 II: 35–42, shown in one of many possible embellished versions in Example 1. (The fingering given for the broken thirds was in common use in the eighteenth century, and it produces an effect that is musically superior to that of modern fingerings.)

To be stylistically proper, the density of embellishments must suit that of their environment (the very principle that enabled Mozart's sister to spot the "something missing"). When observed, this principle tolerates even the most lavish embellishments (such as occur in the Minuet of Mozart's Concerto in E-flat Major, K. 271, as well as in the Variations K. 264, 354, 455, 573, and 613). To ensure proper embellishment of such controversial spots as Mozart's Concerto in A Major, K. 488 II: 80–82, 86–87, 90–91, one must first create a proper environment by embellishing the recapitulation (II:53–68). Without such preliminary contextual embellishment, even the most reserved elaboration of the controversial spots will seem excessive. A model for embellishing the recapitulation may be found in the explicitly notated slow movement of Mozart's Piano Sonata in F Major, K. 332 as printed in the original editions of Artaria and Schott (as opposed to the implicit notation of the composer's autograph manuscript).

Whereas the spirit of improvisation was manifested in ever-changing forms during the age of the composer-as-performer and performer-as-composer, its letter gained supremacy with the advent of Beethoven's "Emperor" Concerto of 1809. In this work, the composer has curtailed the performer's improvisational input through the explicit notation of not only the cadenzas and the embellishments, but also through the spelling out of the soloist's continuo activity during the orchestral tuttis. The explicit continuo notation in the "Emperor" is in sharp contrast to the implicit notation of continuo in the Classical symphonic repertoire, where the keyboard player's activity is notated explicitly only in exceptional cases, such as the eleven measures of arpeggiated obbligato accompaniment in high register at the end of Haydn's Symphony in B-Flat Major, No. 98.

Notational Conventions versus Face Value Interpretation. The Baroque convention of notating triplet rhythms as dotted figures (J. S. Bach: Partita No. 1, *Corrente*) was adopted by Mozart (Concerto in B-flat Major, K. 450 I: 56), Franz Schubert (Klavierstück in E-flat Minor, D. 946 No. 1, second episode—see *Wiener Urtext,* preface by Paul Badura-Skoda), **Frédéric Chopin** (Prelude Op. 28, No. 9, autograph manuscript), **Robert Schumann** (Romanze Op. 32, No. 3, and Phantasiestück Op. 111, No. 2, Peters Edition, Adolf Ruthardt editor), Aram Ilich

Example 1. Mozart: Piano Concerto in C Major. K. 503. II:35–42.

Khachaturyan (Trio in G-Minor for Clarinet, Violin and Piano, last movement), etc. In uncorrupted sources, vertical alignment should indicate rhythmic execution. Ambiguity arises because of the composer's occasional misalignment, or the engraver's unawareness of this notational convention. Given the occasional persistence of Baroque notational conventions in the nineteenth and twentieth centuries, it is possible that Schumann might have intended that the dotted rhythms of his Kinderszenen Op. 15, No. 1 be played in continuous triplets (see the alignment in the composer's autograph manuscripts). Similarly, Sergei Prokofiev's time signature $^4/_4$ equals $^{12}/_8$ in his Piano Sonata in A Minor Op. 28 might imply the same performance practice as J. S. Bach's time signature *alla breve* equals $^{12}/_8$ in his Prelude in D Major from *Das Wohtemperierte Klavier*, vol. II.

The concept of pulse as opposed to meter has far-reaching consequences for performance. In much of J. S. Bach's music, the "C" time signature implies two pulses per measure (as opposed to its later meaning of four beats per measure). In this sense, the Fugue in C Minor from Bach's *Das Wohltemperierte Klavier*, vol. I, should be felt as having two (not four) pulses per measure (in the same sense that the Prelude in C Major from the same volume contains only two pulses per measure). Awareness of the distinction between pulse and beat affects not only the phrasing, but also the tempo. For example, the above-mentioned fugue will most likely be played faster when felt in two pulses per measure. Most important, awareness of the half-measure units clarifies the work's structure, since the motivic, rhythmic, and harmonic units consistently coincide with the half-measure concept of the piece.

In Beethoven's Sonata in E Major Op. 109, the basic triple pulse established at the beginning of the last movement's Variation No. 6 should be retained throughout the remainder of the piece regardless of the notated changes in time signature (from $^3/_4$ to $^9/_8$ and back to $^3/_4$). Perhaps unaware of this notational convention, or possibly in spite of it, Arthur Schnabel insists (in his edition of this sonata that one must retain the face value of the eighth-note rather than the time value of the opening pulse. This theory results in a rhythmic conversion within the same piece that is unknown in the Classical

era: the transition from $^3/_4$ to $^9/_8$ proposed by Schnabel entails the switch from a beat equaling a quarter-note to one equaling a dotted quarter-note, where the time value of the dotted quarter is longer by one eighth-note than the previous beat. Curiously, when faced with the changes in time signature of the variation movement of Beethoven's Sonata in C Minor Op. 111, Schnabel admits that his theory cannot be applied there because his conversion ratio between variations would yield an unplayable tempo.

Notation versus Perception. Neither *Urtext* editions nor the mere use of period instruments can reveal the inner life of music as perceived by the composer. To regain that perception, a working knowledge of compositional techniques is required. Most composers unify single and multi-movement works by deriving their motives from the opening measures (Arnold Schoenberg's twelve-tone row is a modern adaptation of this timeless principle). For example, all movements of Beethoven's "Waldstein" Sonata in C Major Op. 53 begin with a single pitch in low register followed by at least two repeated notes in higher register. Known as the *il filo* principle (the thread that unites single movements and larger works into an organic unity), these relationships can best be discovered by retracing the music from the end to its beginning. This yields the musical "genes" out of which whole compositions blossom forth as though improvised. However, the "genes" often elude the eye, as in Mozart's Fantasia in C Minor, K. 475. To reveal the voice leading of its opening, the notes must be redistributed between the two hands, and rebeamed as in Example 2, where Mozart's implicit notation is substituted with its explicit meaning.

Example 2. Mozart: Fantasie in C Minor, K. 475, mm. 1–4.

The true voice leading of this opening is very difficult to guess from the implicit notation, yet even its explicit version poses one of the most difficult problems of **touch** differentiation in keyboard literature. The complexity of the voice leading is a result of the composer's orchestral concept, and this is equally difficult to realize on both period and modern instruments. Nevertheless, it is the performer's duty to examine the author's compositional style in order to discover these sometimes elusive motivic "threads" and to attempt to approximate their orchestral effect on the piano or fortepiano.

Original versus Modern Instruments. If authenticity in performance means "to approximate the composer's intentions as an act of truth and fidelity" (Newman), then the realization of this ideal requires at times "to strip away the accretions and the traditions of the past (including those accepted by the composer himself)" (Rosen). Some effects intended by the composer can only be achieved on modern instruments. For example, the *subito fortissimo* climax in Felix Mendelssohn's Rondo Capriccioso (Henle *Urtext*) requires that the left hand play an octave on the downbeat of m. 227; yet this octave was unavailable on Mendelssohn's own **fortepiano**, and has become available only on the later fortepianos and the modern pianos. Another example is **Franz Liszt**'s Sonata in B Minor, which seems to end on a short note in low register. It has been suggested, however, that Liszt may have intended an orchestral effect—the prolongation of the B-major $^6/_4$ tonic that would thus end the piece in high rather than in low register. This orchestral effect became possible on the piano only later, with the adoption of the improved **Steinway** *sostenuto* mechanism of 1876. There are but few pieces in piano literature that do require the instrument for which they were written (for example, Béla Bartók's Rhapsody Op. 1, for piano and orchestra, written for the seven-and-a-half-octave range of modern **Bösendorfers** that is unavailable on modern Steinways).

Yet composers did not encourage dogmatic attitudes towards the ranges and the sounds of various instruments. The autograph of Beethoven's "Emperor" Concerto contains two versions of the keyboard part that accommodate the ranges of fortepianos popular in his day. This cavalier attitude towards the medium of performance is evident in the widespread use of the generic term *cembalo* that designates an infinite variety of ranges and sounds of both harpsichords and fortepianos from 1700 to well into the first half of the nineteenth century. For example, Beethoven still uses this term on twelve occasions in the full-score autograph of the "Emperor" Concerto (1809), where it designates any fortepiano of any range or sound available at the time of the performance. Beethoven did entertain the idea of recomposing his earlier keyboard works in order to eliminate the compromises made to accommodate the limited range of the early fortepianos; unfortunately, he "never quite realized that new edition" (Newman). Even **Brahms**'s love for **Streicher** pianos did not prevent him from using a host of other pianos during his concert tours, including two Steinways and one **Knabe**. A noteworthy ideal of the great pianists of the Golden Age of Piano Playing (the Romantic tradition) has always been to transcend the sound of the piano per se: "when he [Liszt] played, the instrument did not sound like a piano . . . it was an unspeakable sound, which I, now after twenty-seven years, still hear clearly" (Leyetchkiss).

Though "authentic" instruments have become "a kind of religion" (Towe), "the spurious notion that interpretations on period instruments are intrinsically more novel or persuasive than those on modern instruments needs to be abandoned" (Winter). Unfortunately, many present-day pianists are ignorant of certain **pedal** effects that prompted Anton Rubinstein to declare that "the pedal is the soul of the piano." Understandably, present-day fortepianists wage campaigns aimed at exposing the alleged limitations of the modern piano. Such limitations are, however, not inherent in the construction of the modern **grand**. Contrary to popular opinion, it is indeed possible to produce on the modern piano any gradual or sudden *diminuendo* effect on a single note or chord. For example, the *forte-piano* (*fp*) effect on the first chord of Beethoven's "Pathétique" Sonata in C Minor Op. 13 can be achieved as follows: first, the right (**damper**) pedal is depressed prior to attacking the first chord; then the first chord is played as loudly as is needed to approximate the sound of a full orchestra. While the pedal is held fully depressed, the fingers are completely released. As soon as *diminuendo* is desired, the depressed pedal is gradually released until the dampers begin to touch the **strings**—thus gradually eliminating the rich overtones while reducing the dynamic level. The rate of *diminuendo* is determined by the speed with which the damper pedal is released. When the leftover vibration in the strings is reduced to the desired *piano* effect, the pedal is released no farther, and the performer proceeds to play the *piano* chords in the normal manner. Due to the modern grand's greater contrast between *forte* and *piano*, the implied effect of a full orchestral *diminuendo* is more successfully approximated on the modern grand than on the fortepiano. More important, this case demonstrates that a knowledgeable performer using the modern grand does not accept passively the rate of sound decay of the instrument, but actively manipulates it. Due to the rich overtones of the modern grand, it is even possible to approximate a *crescendo* effect on a single chord by gradually depressing the pedal after the chord is struck. Nevertheless, "you have to pay for everything that you gain with a corresponding loss" (Towe), and some effects easily attainable on the fortepiano are next to impossible on the modern grand.

By challenging performers on modern instruments, the historical performance movement has inspired effects that were considered to be impossible on the modern grand. For example, by insisting that "the soloist in a Mozart piano concerto must be involved in the sound of the *tuttis*," Nikolaus Harnoncourt has challenged modern pianists to discover the technical and musical means that would enable them to perform continuo "so that it didn't sound like Rachmaninoff, and so that the piano is still there in the tuttis" (Towe). Recent reviews that exalt the sound of the modern grand functioning in the dual role of *continuo* and *solo* instrument prove not only the little explored possibilities of modern instruments but demonstrate also the fructifying effect of the historical performance challenge.

Live versus Recorded Performances. "Music recorded by machines hardens into something stationary," i.e., deprived of the very life of music —its "variability"; "if mechanical music were to flood the world to the detriment of live music," then it would "develop into a calamity equivalent to the seven Egyptian plagues" (Bartók). It is a sign of the times that, thirty years after Bartók's plea that recordings be used only for pedagogic or scientific purposes, Glenn Gould saluted the "time-transcending luxuries of recording" (i.e., splicing) while predicting the disappearance of public concerts in the twenty-first century. Ideally, mechanical or electrical recording devices "offer the possibility for the composer to pass on to the world . . . minute nuances which cannot be expressed notationally" (Bartók). By converting recorded performances into scores that translate the relative durations of notes into proportionally longer or shorter bars (i.e., time equals space), László Somfai has pioneered a method of translating the aural experience into a visual one. His studies of Bartók's own performances of "Evening in Transylvania" (from *Ten Easy Piano Pieces*) has shown that the four recordings (including two on piano rolls) and the two distinct editions of this piece yield six variants with individual traits. Nevertheless, certain basic characteristics of Bartók's *parlando rubato* style remain relatively constant over a period of several decades. But the attempt to single out one "ideal" performance is a futile effort for, as Bartók put it, "it would not be advisable to listen to these compositions perpetually like that [i.e., played by the composer] . . . because it would cover the composition with boredom . . . . The best imaginable phonography, therefore, will never be able to act as a substitute for completely live music. . . . Mechanical music is a manufacturing industry; live music is an individual handicraft."

Conclusion. Recent studies have shown that the cultural environment of bygone ages was less concerned with sharply defined concepts and practices than our own. In previous cultures, the concepts of consistency and standardization as we apply them today were the exception rather than the rule. This explains the great variety of approaches to notation, instrument building, and performance that have flourished concomitantly in the past. If the historical performance movement will resist the temptation to reduce performance practice and instrument building to a set of externally applied rules and regulations, it can bring about a renaissance of our own musical life. Perhaps the most pressing challenge facing today's historical performance movement is to find the ways and means of resurrecting a perception of musical practice that was paramount in the consciousness of bygone ages: the perception of the spiritual aspect of music-making. In an age in which tendencies towards consumerism threaten to reduce music to a commodity aimed at providing sensual entertainment, the performance- practice movement may play an important role in regaining the perception of the "inner nature of music" (Steiner).

Tibor Szász

Bibliography

Brown, Howard Mayer, and Stanley Sadie, eds. *Performance Practice: Music After 1600* (New Grove Handbooks in Musicology). New York: Norton & Co., 1990.

Bartók, Béla. "Mechanical Music." In *Béla Bartók Essays.* Edited by Benjamin Suchoff. London: Faber and Faber, 1976: 289–98

Gould, Glenn. "The Prospects of Recording." In *The Glenn Gould Reader,* edited by Tim Page. New York: Alfred A. Knopf, 1984: 331–53.

Leyetchkiss, Vladimir. "My Memories of Franz Liszt by Alexander Ilitch Siloti: Translated, with an Introduction, Commentary and Notes by Vladimir Leyetchkiss." *Journal of the American Liszt Society* 15 (June 1984): 5–38.

Newman, William S. *Beethoven on Beethoven: Playing His Piano Music His Way.* New York: Norton & Co., 1988: 29, 62, 260.

Rosen, Charles. "Should Music Be Played 'Wrong'?" *High Fidelity/Musical America* 21 no. 5 (May 1971): 54–58.

Somfai, László. "Über Bartók's Rubato-Stil: Vergleichende Studie der zwei Aufnamen 'Abend am Lande' des Komponisten." *Documenta Bartókiana* 12 (1970): 205–32.

Steiner, Rudolf. *The Inner Nature of Music and the Experience of Tone.* Spring Valley, N.Y.: The Anthroposophic Press, 1983.

Szász, Tibor. "Liszt's Symbols for the Divine and Diabolical: Their Revelation of a Program in the B-minor Sonata." *Journal of the American Liszt Society* 15 (June 1984): 39–95.

———. "Figured Bass in Beethoven's 'Emperor' Concerto: Basso Continuo or Orchestral Cues?" *Early Keyboard Journal* 6–7 (1988–89): 5–71.

Towe, Teri Noel. "Nikolaus Harnoncourt: The Dynamic Conductor Won't Be Locked into the Early-Music Stereotype." *Ovation* (Detroit Edition) 6 no. 4 (May 1985): 8–12.

Winter, Robert. "Performing Beethoven's Early Piano Concertos." *Early Music* 16 no. 2 (May 1988): 214–30.

PERIODICALS

Considering the pervasiveness of the pianoforte in the concert life of the past two hundred years, and the fascination that the instrument has maintained among composers, it is curious to find what a small place it has made in the journal literature. Of more than 5,000 musical periodicals listed in the most recent inventory (Fellinger 1980) only seventy-five titles include the word "piano" or any of its translations. (A few more began publishing after 1980.) Furthermore, many of those journals had the briefest of lives, and several others require the piano to share space with other keyboard instruments.

Bartolomeo Cristofori's invention did receive early notice in periodicals of the time; indeed the first musical periodical of them all—*Critica musica,* edited by Johann Mattheson (Hamburg, 1722/23–1725)—printed a translation of **Scipione Maffei's** premier account. This had first appeared in the *Giornale de' letterati d'Italia* in 1711, as "Nuova inventione d'un Gravecembalo col piano e forte. . . ." Although made known in Italy and Germany while the inventor was still building his instruments, the pianoforte did not gain quick acceptance. It was mid-century before the musical values of the instrument were established (assisted by the approval of **Johann Sebastian Bach, Carl Philipp Emanuel Bach,** and Johann Joachim Quantz) and a distinct repertoire began to be composed. Finally in the 1760s there were public concerts, and piano building began to be a significant industry.

Yet in the eighteenth century there was sparse writing about the new musical voice. After the appearance of the Maffei article the next study in a periodical seems to have been by Niels Brelin in the 1739 yearbook of the Swedish Research Academy. This piece, suggesting improvements to the piano mechanism, was translated into German and published in the second volume of Friedrich Wilhelm Marpurg's journal *Historisch-kristische Beyträge zur Aufnahme der Musik* (Berlin, 1754/55–1760/78). Brelin wrote some further essays, in the 1757 and 1760 yearbooks, but they remained in Swedish only.

Anyone who cares to scan the contents of the principal eighteenth-century musical periodicals may find the task less forbidding than it sounds, since one fine scholar, Johann Forkel, has compiled a good journal-by-journal summary (Forkel 1792). Aside from the items already cited above, nothing further that deals specifically with the pianoforte, its music, or its performers is to be found in Forkel's inventory.

Although journal writing about the pianoforte did not emerge in quantity during the instrument's first century, compositions for it did appear in periodicals. *Piano-Forte Magazine*

(London, 1797–1802) was the earliest serial publication entirely devoted to the presentation of piano music. Works by Ignace-Joseph **Pleyel, Joseph Haydn**, Thomas Arne, **Wolfgang Amadeus Mozart**, and **Muzio Clementi** were among the hundreds of pieces printed in the sixteen volumes of this title. A French magazine came to light at about the same time: *Journal d'Apollon pour le forte piano* (Hamburg, 1798–1804). Despite its German place of issue, it carried primarily music by French composers such as Nicolas-Marie Dalayrac, André-Ernest-Modeste Grétry, Jean-Pierre Solié, and Etienne-Nicolas Méhul.

The Musical Journal for the Piano-Forte (Baltimore, 1799/1800–1803/1804), edited by Benjamin Carr, was the first item of this genre to appear in the United States. Compositions by Carr and James Hewitt were printed, but most of the works were from the well-known Europeans. Germany's initial *Zeitschrift* containing piano music was the *Auswahl der besten Compositionen für das Clavier oder Pianoforte von den berühmtesten Componisten* (Hamburg and Hannover, 1800); it survived only one year, printing pieces by Pleyel, Haydn, Mozart, Paisiello, Clementi, and some lesser figures. This type of periodical—comprised of music only, without articles—was ubiquitous into the early nineteenth century. Imogen Fellinger describes more than 250 of them, some thirty-five of which are devoted to piano compositions, while most of the others include piano accompaniments for vocal works (Fellinger, 1986).

Le pianiste, journal spécial, analytique et instructif (Paris, 1833–1835) stands first chonologically among journals about the piano—as distinct from journals that carried music to be played on it. Its first number, issued in November 1833, was edited by Charles Chaulieu, a pianist who had won the Paris Conservatory prize in performance. During its two years of publication, *Le pianiste* carried biographies of noted pianists such as Clementi, Johann Baptist Cramer, and Johann Nepomuk Hummel; descriptive notes on various individual piano compositions (by **Chopin**, Czerny, etc.); lists of newly published piano works; reviews of concerts; and letters from readers. There was also a serially published course in basic music theory.

A number of early periodicals dealt with the construction and maintenance of the pianoforte. The first of these were the *Zeitung für den Pianofortebau* (Leipzig, 1843; one volume only) and the *Zeitung für Orgel, Clavier- und Flügelbau*, which was also concerned with the organ and with string instruments (Weimar, 1844/47–1853/55). Another category was the trade journal, e.g., *Piano, Organ and Music Trades Journal*, originally the *Pianoforte Dealers' Guide* (London, 1882–1901), and the *Piano, Organ and Musical Instrument Workers' Official Journal* (USA, 1899–1911). Trade journals served the interests of an industry that grew to vast proportions during the century: by 1898 Britain alone was publishing (according to a contemporary report) some 40,000 pieces of music in 8,000,000 copies annually; and production of **parlor** pianos in Britain was around 75,000 a year (Coover 1990). In other countries there was a comparable flowering of the industry: in 1910 Germany made 120,000 pianos, and the United States produced 370,000 instruments. Although world production declined thereafter, it began to revive in the 1970s, especially in America and Japan.

Concerns of those industry-centered periodicals were legalities, **patents**, performing rights, suppliers, new instruments, and new music available. Although the piano is not found in all those journal titles, the centrality of the instrument gave it an important place in them. In at least one case the title changed from a general one to a more specific one that identified its primary content: *Music Trade Journal* (New York, 1879) was renamed several times, becoming in 1956 the *Piano and Organ Review*—though it took yet another general title two years later as the *Musical Merchandise Review*.

These were the dominant formats of the nineteenth century. Another type of periodical was aimed at piano teachers, such as the *Pädagogische Erfahrungen beim Klavierunterrichte*, issued monthly from the Conservatorium von Xaver Scharwenka (Berlin, 1882–1884). What we do not find in the nineteenth century is any successor to *Le pianiste*, a journal of discussion and review concerned with the music of the piano and its interpreters.

In the early twentieth century most of the new piano periodicals held to the established molds: there were journals for piano builders and technicians, e.g., *Tuner's Magazine* (Cincinnati, 1913–1916); for merchants, e.g., *Standard Player Monthly* (concerned with the **player piano**, New York, 1916–1929) and *Pianos-Province: organe de la Fédération des marchands de* *pianos de France* (Nantes, 1913–1914); and for teachers, e.g., *Pianist Pedagogue* (Chicago, 1926, which became *American Musician* before expiring a year later) and *Piano Teacher* (1958–1965; incorporated into *Clavier* [see below]). The brief lives of these publications were typical of the music periodical press until very recent times. A new category also appeared: the scholarly journal of reflection and research. Two came from Italy, and each assumed a wider scope after a few issues. *L'arte pianistica nella vita e nella cultura musicale* (Naples, 1914–1926) became *La vita musicale* (1926–1928); and *Il pianoforte: revista mensile della F.I.P. (Fabbrica Italiana Pianoforti)* (Turin, 1920–1927) was transformed into the major musicological journal *La rassegna musicale*, later the *Quaderni della Rassegna musicale*, running until 1972. During its lifespan as *Il pianoforte*, the journal included historical essays and discussions by such prominent scholars as Victor Mikhailovich Belaiev, Alfredo Bonaccorsi, Michel-Dimitri Calvocoressi, Andrea Della Corte, Guido Gatti, and Guido Pannain. It carried news reports from major cities of the world, reviews of new music and books, and selective lists of articles from other periodicals. Reflecting the tendency that led to its change of title, even the early issues of *Il pianoforte* dealt with general musical topics as well as material relating to the piano.

Not until after World War II did a comparable periodical appear in English. The *Piano Quarterly* (New York, 1952/53–1972; Melville, N. Y., 1972–1974; Wilmington, Vermont, 1975–) has proved durable and useful as a medium for discussion and research. It includes documented historical and analytical studies as well as book reviews, new music reviews, interviews, and conference reports. In mid-1990 it remained the only scholarly journal in English completely devoted to the piano, its music, and its personalities. *Das Klavierspiel* (Hamburg, 1959–1966), continuing as *Das Klavier: Zeitschrift für alle Fragen der Tasteninstrumente* (Wiesbaden, 1966–) is another specimen of the more scholarly journal. Germany also brought forth the useful *Piano Jahrbuch* (Recklinghausen, 1980–), a yearly gathering of concert news, interviews, book reviews, directory information, current contents of many periodicals, plus solid essays and bibliographies. A postwar technical publication was *Euro Piano* (Frankfurt, 1961–), a trade magazine for piano makers, **technicians**, and tuners.

Contemporary Keyboard (Saratoga, Cal., 1975–), with a continuation as *Keyboard* (Cupertino, Cal., 1981–) offers material on popular and classical topics, delivered in a light style. Recent issues have emphasized **electronic** aspects.

The present scene (1990) displays a rather meager inventory of piano periodicals. In *Music Index* only a few titles, all American, are covered regularly: *Clavier* (Northfield, Ill., 1962–), *Keyboard Classics* (Paramus, N.J., 1981; consisting of "how-to" articles and several actual compositions), *Keyboard, Piano Quarterly*, and *Piano Technicians Journal* (Seattle, Wash, 1942– [presently Kansas City, Mo.] began as *Piano Technician* in Delavan, Wis.). Probably the most popular is *Clavier*, a bimonthly publication about teaching, pianists, and concert life, without scholarly aspirations. As the title suggests, *Piano Technicians Journal* concentrates on the instrument itself; however, it has a wide vision that makes it useful to anyone seeking historical information (recent issues have had articles on Cristofori, on **Beethoven's** piano builder, and on early French piano designs).

Other current U.S. publications of interest are *Piano Guild Notes* (Austin, Tex., 1945–), from the National Guild of Piano Teachers, aimed at teachers and younger students; *On Key* (Mountainside, N.J., 1982–), presenting articles, workshops, and games for six-to-fourteen-year-old children; and *Keys* (Northfield, Ill., 1986–).

Recent additions from other countries include *Piano Time* (Rome, 1983–), which began as a journal about the piano, then branched into opera and concert life; it has essays, interviews, reviews, a calendar, and some actual musical works. *Piano Journal* (London, 1980–) offers material on pianists and teaching, with reviews and news of its sponsoring body, the European Piano Teachers Association. Other recent journals are *Keyboard Player* (London, 1982–) and *Key Vive* (Middle Cover, New South Wales, 1973–), issued by the Australian Society for Keyboard Music.

Guy A. Marco

Bibliography

Coover, James. "Victorian Periodicals for the Music Trade." *Notes* (Music Library Association) 46–3 (March 1990): 609–21.

Ehrlich, Cyril. *The Piano: A History*. London: Dent, 1976.

Fellinger, Imogen (1969). "Zeitschriften." In *Musik in Geschichte und Gegenwart*, Vol.14, columns 1041–1188.

———. (1980). "Periodicals." *New Grove Dictionary of Music and Musicians*, Vol.14, pp. 407–535.

———. (1986). *Periodica musicalia (1789–1830)*. Regensburg: Gustav Bosse, 1986.

Forkel, Johann Nikolaus. *Allgemeine Litteratur der Musik oder Anleitung zur Kenntniss musikalischer Bücher*. Leipzig: Schwickert, 1792. Reprint. Hildesheim: Georg Olms, 1962.

Mendel, Hermann. "Zeitschriften." *Musikalisches Conversations-Lexikon*. . . . (Leipzig: List & Francke, 1870–1879), Vol.11, pp. 443–62.

Palmieri, Robert. *Piano Information Guide: An Aid to Research*. New York: Garland, 1989.

Robinson, Doris. *Music and Dance Periodicals*. Voorheesville, N.Y.: Peri Press, 1989.

PFEIFFER, CARL A.

Joseph Anton Pfeiffer (1828–1881) founded his piano-building firm in 1862 in Stuttgart. With a work force of fourteen he was able by 1872 to finish his thousandth instrument. Three of his seven children were also piano builders: Otto Pfeiffer (1859–1899) was co-owner of the firm between 1888 and 1896; Julius Friedrich Pfeiffer (1865–1917) founded a large and well-known piano store in Yalta, earning the title of "Imperial Russian Court Supplier." Carl Conrad Anton Pfeiffer (1861–1927), the third son, after experience with firms in London and New York, returned to Stuttgart, where after 1912 he was sole proprietor of the firm that to this day remains "Carl A. Pfeiffer."

The firm expanded greatly, and Carl Anton Pfeiffer became known for the quality of his instruments. He was a pioneer in establishing the collection of historic keyboard instruments at the German Museum, Munich, as well as the founder of the collection of musical instruments of the Württembergisches Landesmuseum in Stuttgart. He created a copy of a **Gottfried Silbermann** instrument used by **Carl Phillipp Emanuel Bach**, supposedly from the estate of **Johann Sebastian Bach**, other exemplars of which are to be found in the Bachhaus in Eisenach and the Württembergisches Landesmuseum in Stuttgart.

After the death of Carl A. Pfeiffer, his son Walter (1886–1960) took over the firm. Walter was particularly interested in the scientific exploration of mechanical problems of piano building. His publications are among the most important in the field and include *Flügel oder Klavier?* (1940), *Vom Hammer* (1948), and *Über Dämpfer, Federn und Spielart* (1952).

The Pfeiffer concern was destroyed in 1943, but by 1953, when Helmut Pfeiffer (1921–1991) took over the leadership, it had recovered its stature. Helmut continued to develop the firm, with its crowning achievement being the development of its Model 191, which has been highly acclaimed.

The firm is now under the leadership of Helmut's son, Dr. Georg Pfeiffer. While Pfeiffer pianos were originally sold almost exclusively in Baden-Württemberg, since 1964 they have been available on the world market.

David Anderson

Bibliography

Rolle, Günter. "125 Jahre Pfeiffer Klaviere (1)." *Keyboards* (June 1987): 28–29.

Stöhr, Gerd. "Geschäfts-und Personal-Nachrichten: Helmut Karl Pfeiffer." *Das Musikinstrument* 40 (June 1991): 4.

PIANINO

The term *pianino* originally referred to a low **upright piano** with **strings** that extended to the floor. Characterized by vertical stringing, it was brought out originally in 1815 by **Pleyel** et Cⁱᵉ, Paris, in imitation of the **cottage piano** invented by **Robert Wornum**, London, 1811.

Pianino is also a term often used in Europe to refer to any upright piano.

Martha Novak Clinkscale

PIANO/PIANOFORTE

Piano, or pianoforte, is a struck chordophone activated by a **keyboard**. The name stems from the inventor, **Bartolomeo Cristofori**, who between 1698 and 1700 made an instrument he called *gravecembalo col piano e forte*, "harpsichord with soft and loud." *Piano e forte* was soon shortened to *pianoforte* or *fortepiano*. Terminology fluctuated during the eighteenth century. "Pianoforte" and "fortepiano" became "piano" in English, Spanish, and French, though Italian retained *pianoforte*. German *Hammerklavier*, "hammer keyboard," was shortened to the ambiguous *Klavier*, "keyboard." Russian and Polish retain *fortepiano*.

The piano's distinctive characteristic is its

mode of activating the **strings**: depressing the **key** causes a **jack** to throw a **hammer** to the string. Because the hammer flies free, it strikes the string with speed commensurate with the weight and speed of the player's striking the key, and the sound's loudness is therefore exactly proportionate to the attack. The free flight causes the hammer to bounce away from the string, which can vibrate freely to prolong the sound. Thus Cristofori's proud boast, *piano e forte*: a soft **touch** on the key produces *piano* and a hard blow produces *forte*. The organ or harpsichord player's touch has no effect on the volume of sound produced. Cristofori's Florentine patron, Prince Ferdinand de' Medici, wanted an expressive harpsichord. The principle that striking a string harder or faster produces more volume was already known from such instruments as the clavichord and the hammer dulcimer. But the clavichord could play only within a range from soft to exceedingly soft, and the dulcimer was an instrument of low social standing.

Jean Marius in Paris and **Christoph Gottlieb Schröter** in Dresden independently invented such hammer instruments (Marius called his *clavecin à maillets*, "hammer harpsichord"), but nothing followed from them. A 1711 article by **Scipione Maffei** about Cristofori's instrument, translated in a Hamburg magazine in 1725, led the Dresden organ builder **Gottfried Silbermann** to attempt his own version, which ultimately led to the purchase of Silbermann's instruments by **Frederick the Great**, king of Prussia and, through Silbermann's apprentices, to wider distribution. Cristofori's and Silbermann's pianos had the wing shape of the harpsichord (Germans called it the *Flügel*), but before long we begin to find clavichord-shaped pianos, ultimately called "**square**." The earliest known survivor is dated 1742. As early as the late 1730s come vertical pianos from **Domenico Del Mela** in Italy and **Christian Ernst Friederici** in Germany. The concept was probably derived from the clavicytherium, an upright harpsichord. German types were sometimes called "pyramid" pianos because of a symmetrical shape, requiring longer bass strings to be strung obliquely in the case.

Cristofori and his followers designed **actions** with the hammers mounted on a **rail** above the keys, usually with their heads away from the keyboard. Some early makers, including Marius and Schröter, attempted down-striking actions in imitation of the dulcimer's hand-held hammers. In Germany, possibly under Schröter's influence, action types were found with hammers mounted in forks on the keys, heads pointing toward the keyboard, and activated by a tail on the hammer bumping against a rail at the back of the key (***Prellmechanik***, "bumping action"). Late in the century, the *Prellmechanik* was transformed into the "Viennese action," perhaps by Johann Andreas **Stein** of Augsburg, by slicing the rail into segments corresponding to the keys and springing them, thus providing a check action. The Viennese action, responsively light and subtle, was that known by **C.P.E. Bach**, **Haydn**, **Mozart**, **Beethoven**, and most German composers of the nineteenth century.

A different direction was taken in England and France. Some of Silbermann's former pupils came to England, displaced, according to legend, by the Seven Years' War (1756–1763). They made many small squares for use in the home and even in concert. Some **grand pianos** were also made in England. English makers developed the Silbermann-Cristofori action type, especially with the "English grand action" patented by **Robert Stodart** in 1777, which the London firm of **John Broadwood & Sons** still used in a heavier version in its grands 120 years later, and the "grasshopper action" patented by **John Geib** in 1786, staple in squares for nearly fifty years. French makers generally followed the English lead in design. English pianos were reputed to have bigger **tone** than the German and Austrian ones.

By the end of the eighteenth century, the piano had virtually displaced the harpsichord as the principal concert keyboard instrument in Europe, propelled by such works as Mozart's concertos, **Clementi**'s idiomatic sonatas, and Beethoven's early works. Still light in tone and ordinarily only five octaves in range, though some $5^1/_2$-octave pianos were available, the piano would see its fortunes—and its size—grow as the nineteenth century brought new social and economic forces to bear.

Two related social and economic needs propelled the design and manufacture of pianos in the first decades of the nineteenth century. One was the rise of a moneyed middle-class that aspired to cultural goods previously available only to the aristocracy, the clergy, and the wealthy. Enabled by the Industrial Revolution to pay for musical instruments and admission to concerts, this new middle-class provided a ready market for pianos designed for the home and also significantly broadened the audience for musical performances. Concert halls that would seat great numbers began to be built. The Odeon in Munich, seating 3,000, was built in 1828, and others followed. The availability of professional musical performances to which anyone possessing money to buy a ticket could be admitted soon made instrumental music as popular as opera and choral music. The manufacture of good pianos for the middle-class home, whether grands, **uprights,** or squares, allowed the training of amateur players, who could try to duplicate what they heard in concerts and encourage their children (mostly, in the nineteenth century, daughters) to learn to play. Thus the heightened economic power of the middle class in the late eighteenth and early nineteenth centuries accompanied the development by piano makers of good instruments, both inexpensive and costly, for the home, especially squares and large vertical pianos (the German "**giraffe,**" the English "**cabinet** grand," grand pianos turned vertically on their heads), and, as the 1820s went on, small uprights, such as those designed by **Jean-Henri Pape,** and known in Europe commonly as *pianinos*. The new economic strength also encouraged the design of the highest grade of pianos for use by professional pianists in the new or newly refurbished concert rooms.

The rise of the professional concertizer was a response to the foregoing social factor. If enough people bought tickets to concerts to support the artist, the independent "concert pianist" (violinist, singer, etc.) became occupationally possible. This phenomenon spanned the Romantic period, and was assisted by Romantic views of genius and individual imagination. Its nearly incredible apogee in the world of the piano was **Franz Liszt.** Performers demanded instruments that could withstand powerful muscles and stay in tune, that could be moved without being damaged, that could be heard over the growing orchestras and throughout the growing concert halls of Europe. The little 5-octave fortepianos of Mozart's day were not enough for the Odeon or the Salle Erard.

Beginning as early as 1796, makers were extending ranges from the $5^1/_2$ -octaves, a transitional standard that would remain available into the 1830s, to six octaves (in Germany and Austria mostly FF–f^4, in England mostly CC–c^4). By 1815, a few makers such as **Conrad Graf** and probably Nanette **Streicher** in Vienna made $5^1/_2$ -octave pianos (CC–f^4). In 1824, **Sébastien Erard** made a 7-octave grand (CC–c^5) which Liszt played (and knocked badly out of tune) at his Paris debut that year at the age of thirteen. The 7-octave range did not come more generally into use for another twenty-five years or so, but through the 1820s and 1830s makers were often making pianos with $6^1/_2$ octaves or more, CC–f^4, g^4, and a^4.

The added ranges put enormous strains on the framing of the instruments. Some makers responded with more powerful wooden **frames,** such as Graf's laminated braces along with heavier string-**plates.** Others began to use metal to withstand the tension and to compensate for atmospheric changes that affect **tuning.** The first compensation frame was a tubular one patented in England in 1820 by **James Thom** and **William Allen.** John Broadwood & Sons in London used iron string-plates in squares in 1821 and iron tension bars in grands in 1822, adding metal string-plates to grands in 1827. **Jonas Chickering** in Boston used iron string-plates in squares in 1823 or 1824, and French makers Erard and **Pleyel** were doing the same in the mid-1820s. In 1825, **Alpheus Babcock** of Boston **patented** a full metal frame for squares, which held the string tension from all sides. For some time, most makers continued to use only a metal string-plate, though they added tension bars to the framing of grands. In 1840, Chickering began putting full metal frames into grands, perhaps under Alpheus Babcock's influence (he then worked for Chickering), and in 1843 received the U.S. patent.

Another innovation in the use of metal was the invention in 1808 by Sébastien Erard of the **agraffe,** a brass stud screwed into the **pinblock,** with holes through which the strings ran from the pinblock to the **bridge.** This **downbearing** on the strings at the **tuning pin** end helped to stabilize tuning. In 1838, his nephew Pierre turned the treble agraffes into a harmonic bar, which worked the same way, and Antoine Bord of Paris invented the *capo tasto* bar for the same purpose in 1840.

Three other aspects of the piano received

important attention during the first decades of the nineteenth century. Perhaps most important was the action. The two Classic types of action, the "Viennese" and the "English," continued basically unchanged throughout the nineteenth century, except that hammers became larger and the action heavier in order to sound louder. Broadwood in London was still using the English grand action, derived from Cristofori, in 1900, and Austrian makers continued to offer grands with the Viennese action until 1910 or so. In 1821, Sébastien Erard patented a double-escapement "repetition" action, which was intended to combine the strength of the English type, with rail-mounted hammers, and the quick responsiveness of the key-mounted Viennese hammers. A simplification in about 1840 by Henri Herz of Paris proved in time to be definitive, and the Herz-Erard type of action is still standard in acoustic pianos. Other makers quickly set about making "repetition" actions of their own. Jean-Georges Kriegelstein of Paris made one that was modified in the 1860s by Julius **Blüthner** of Leipzig. Pleyel in Paris continued to use the English action but would later devise several different types. Chickering in Boston used an action invented by Edwin Brown.

Another effort in the early nineteenth century was to find ways to modify piano tone by means of various mechanisms. There had previously been damper stops, which prolonged tone by keeping the **dampers** raised off the strings; lute stops, which shortened tone by a light pressure against the strings; mute stops, which introduced **leather** or cloth between the hammers and the strings to alter the tone-quality; and stops that moved the hammers sideways, so that they struck only one or two strings instead of the two or three. By the beginning of the nineteenth century, hand-stops and knee-levers had been almost entirely displaced by **pedals** as the means of activating the stops. One sometimes sees six to eight pedals on grands and large vertical pianos of 1800–1825 or so. Apart from the continuing necessity of damper and *una corda* stops, the most popular were **Janissary**-music devices, which produced an imitation of drum and bell sounds; **moderators**, where a strip of cloth or leather, often graded in thickness, was moved between strings and hammers; and bassoon stops, where a rod with a piece of parchment loosely attached came into contact with the bass strings and

produced a buzzing tone that reminded listeners of bassoons. Other, seldom successful, tone-prolonging devices included bowing mechanisms, usually in ring shapes, ways to repeat the hammer blows as long as the key was held down (an imitation of the *Bebung* technique on the clavichord), and methods for blowing air on the strings, in imitation of the Aeolian harp. Octave couplers were fitted by such fine makers as Erard, Pleyel, and Johann Baptist Streicher.

The capability of the piano could be extended by mechanisms of transposition, most of which worked by bodily shifting the keyboard and action sideways, causing hammers to strike other strings. Another extension of the instrument was the double piano, all the way from **Matthias Müller**'s little upright *Ditanaklasis*, which used two keyboards and actions on opposite sides of the **case**, to large double pianos with two complete grands inside a single case, such as those devised by James Pirsson of New York in 1850 and by Pleyel later. Experiments with more than one manual were not as successful as with the harpsichord, but they were attempted as early as 1794, when Johann Jakob Könnicke in Vienna made an instrument with six manuals, so that the piano could be played in every key with just tuning.

The proliferation of stops during the first half of the nineteenth century gave testimony to the spirit of experiment and even daring of that Romantic time. Like much experiment in other fields, it produced its share of bizarre and musically useless devices, and it was accompanied by new shapes, making the piano round, hexagonal, or oval; or by multiple functions, making the piano appear almost anything else— a dressing table, a headboard, a sewing table. Jean-Henri Pape even mounted the **soundboard** over a tympani-like copper bowl resonator.

The experiments also produced inventions of lasting importance, in addition to the repetition action, the full iron frame, the agraffe, and the *capo tasto* bar. In devising very small vertical pianos, Pape in 1828 devised **cross-stringing**, running longer bass strings above the plane of shorter strings, thus allowing the longest possible strings in the short case. The idea was occasionally applied to squares in the 1830s, and by the early 1850s it was quite common. Pape also contributed the successful use of **felt** as a hammer-covering, which ultimately supplanted the previously nearly universal deer leather.

None of these inventions was immediately and universally adopted. Lesser efforts declined and disappeared only as time passed, and the second half of the nineteenth century does not exhibit the same bewildering diversity of design. Indeed, the second half of the nineteenth century saw the definitive standardization of the piano, though enough diversity remained to keep the instrument from stagnation.

The demise (or suspension) of the square required the entire half-century. By 1860, the square was nearly obsolete in Europe. The American trade kept the square alive for another forty years, though signs of its decline were to be observed. **Steinway & Sons** made its last square in 1889 and led the way in displacing the square by the upright as the instrument of choice for the American home. In 1904, urged by the editor of the *Music Trades Review*, the association of piano manufacturers meeting at Atlantic City, N.J., gathered all the squares they could find, piled them into a fifty-foot pyramid, and burned them.

The place of the square was taken by large uprights, sometimes five feet high, the size of which allowed enough string length for good tone and enough soundboard expanse for good resonance. These instruments occupied considerably less floor space than their square counterparts, important when city-dwellers were more and more living in apartments rather than in houses. The actions were many—none as effective as horizontal actions—the most successful being descendants of the tape-check action often associated with **Robert Wornum** (who patented it in 1842), but which had a predecessor invented in 1832 by Herman Lichtenthal (who flourished 1828–1851 in Brussels and, after 1851, in St. Petersburg).

The success of Steinway & Sons and Chickering & Sons at the Paris Exposition in 1867 showed the way in which concert instruments would go, though Steinway's entry had its signal innovation of cross-stringing with the single-piece iron frame, where Chickering's was straight-strung. Cross-stringing was taken up by many makers, especially in Germany, Austria, and North America, and by 1910 or so it had become all but universal. Ranges were either seven octaves (AAA–a⁴) or seven octaves and a third (AAA–c⁵) during the rest of the nineteenth century. The Herz-Erard double-escapement action dominated the grands, though several other effective actions were used by individual makers, such as **Blüthner**, Broadwood, Streicher, **Bösendorfer**, and other German and Austrian makers. This period sees the beginning of companies that specialized in action making, e.g., Isermann in Hamburg, Herrburger-Schwander in Paris, T. & H. Brooks in London (the two combined into Herrburger-Brooks in London in 1920). As such companies succeeded in expanding their sales, the actions available became more and more standardized.

A few innovations are to be found in this time. Blüthner patented his **aliquot** stringing system, which placed a fourth, sympathetically vibrating string above those of the upper three octaves, in 1873. C. F. Theodore Steinway made several important improvements, such as the laminated case, lighter than most others; the **Duplex scale**, which made non-speaking string lengths between agraffes and tuning pins proportional to the speaking lengths; the "cupola" frame, which allowed freer resonance and a single bridge for all of the strings. Albert Steinway patented the *sostenuto* pedal, an idea that had been tried earlier in Paris by Blanchet et Roller, Alexandre-François Debain, and Claude Montal. Throughout the last half of the nineteenth century Moritz Pöhlmann of Nürnberg worked to improve the tensile strength of steel **wire**.

By 1900, the modern piano was in all essentials in place, though other types could still be purchased. It was available in various sizes of grands and uprights (squares were almost gone, though the **Mathushek** company unsuccessfully resurrected them briefly in the 1930s), its range was definitively AAA–c⁵, its action was predominantly the double-escapement type in grands and the tape-check type in uprights. Grands had two pedals in Europe (*una corda* and dampers), three in North America (*una corda*, dampers, and *sostenuto*). Iron frames were universal, as was cross-stringing.

The twentieth century has seen little of design change. No new action designs have gained currency, and the only important change in resonation is the development of electronic amplification instead of acoustic. In the last thirty years or so, some pianos, conventional in other respects, have had electronic pickups in the bridge, which carry the string vibrations electronically to loudspeakers, in the place of wooden soundboards. Other types of **electronic** keyboard instruments do not have strings at all, and are therefore not strictly pianos.

Major changes have come in sizes and shapes,

in materials, and in manufacturing methods. The sizes of grands available have diminished. The **concert grand** remains about nine feet long, though the Bösendorfer Imperial with 8-octave range is six inches longer (and **Challen & Son**, the English company, celebrated King George V's silver jubilee with a grand eleven feet, eight inches long). Companies have made several smaller sizes of grands down to tiny ones, barely four feet long (and deserving the name of **baby** but not of grand). Likewise, the tendency of the vertical pianos has been downward. Uprights in the late nineteenth and early twentieth centuries often stood five feet and more high. The upright has reverted to the sizes of the *pianinos* in which French makers excelled in the 1830s and 1840s. Three standard sizes have become the norm: the **"studio,"** about three feet, nine inches; the **"console,"** about three feet, six inches; and the **"spinet,"** about three feet. The earlier larger ones exceeded these small sizes in the quality of tone they could get, both because their longer strings gave a richer mix of **partials**, and because soundboard surfaces were larger. But the smaller sizes allow lower prices. In many spinets, the keyboard is situated so high relative to the top of the frame that the only practicable action design is a "hanging" action, in which the hammer heads rest below the level of the keys. That action design is not new, being familiar from German and Austrian "giraffes" from the early nineteenth century.

Most important materials are unchanged. Spruce remains the material of choice for soundboards, felt for hammer coverings, steel for strings, and various woods for action parts. Steel now has higher tensile strength than it once did, and pianists rarely have the experience of breaking a string. In American pianos, the use of **ivory** for natural key coverings has been stopped by act of Congress, and perfectly acceptable plastic substitutes have been found. Some European companies continue to use ivory from legitimate sources. The military demands of World War II led to a number of advances in materials, the most important of which for pianos have been resin glues, which solve most of the problems the older glues caused, plastic coatings of various kinds (such as the shiny polyurethane **finish** on many modern pianos), and high-impact, high-strength plastics, which can be found in unconventional cases for both grands and uprights.

The watchword of twentieth-century manufacturing is automation. A great many processes of production are now done by machine, from kiln-drying wood to stringing, key-cutting, and testing of actions. The development of specialized-parts companies was well under-way in the nineteenth century, and it has continued, though major piano manufacturers have often bought action companies. There may be no American or European firm that now carries out every step from curing wood to final regulation under its own roofs, though the **Yamaha** company in Japan claims to do so. The high-specialty function of frame-casting is contracted to foundries, though Yamaha is again an instance where a proprietary vacuum casting method, developed in Yamaha's motorcycle division, has proven its worth for piano frames.

Perhaps the main new design in the twentieth century was the automatic piano, the **player piano** or the **piano player**. Using various technologies, but most importantly the punched-paper technique originated in Jacquard weaving, companies in the earlier part of the century made an enormous impact on the piano industry, so that by the 1920s more than half of piano production was of player pianos. The mechanisms were pneumatic, using air pressure either motorized or from foot pedals operated by the player. The depression of the 1930s vastly diminished both player production and piano production in general, and it also saw the introduction of the radio and the spread of motion pictures, which displaced personal music-making as a means of amusement. Piano production nearly stopped during World War II, as military products were demanded from piano factories, and the industry was slow to recover after the war.

Most rapid was the Japanese recovery, and by 1970 Japanese production led the world. It continues to do so today. But in the years since World War II, the hegemony of the piano as *the* keyboard instrument has been successfully threatened by electronic keyboards that imitate pianos and by keyboard-driven **synthesizers**. The popular magazine *Keyboard* (originally *Contemporary Keyboard*) now contains a great deal more advertising for and articles about synthesizers and other electronic keyboards than about acoustic pianos. It also, to be sure, contains a great deal more about popular music-making than about "classical" music. Two interesting instances of partial throwbacks in this electronicization of the keyboard industry may be noted. The typical electronic piano or synthesizer keyboard, mounted on legs or a stand, looks more like a square piano than like any other kind. And computer and electronic technology has informed the most recent developments in player-piano technology, especially with Yamaha's Disklavier, a computer-driven device installed in a standard, acoustic piano that plays back by a system of electronic switches, which cause the keys to move. So one can have both a conventional piano and the latest electronic wizardry at the same time!

How long will the combination last? Many devotees of the piano prefer not to think about it, but many expect that normal changes in cultures and societies will make the piano in its turn obsolete, an interesting artifact of a bygone day.

Edwin M. Good

Bibliography

Dolge, Alfred. *Pianos and Their Makers.* Covina, Cal.: Covina Publishing, 1911. Reprint. New York: Dover, 1972.

———. *Men Who Have Made Piano History.* Repr. of Vol. 2 of *Pianos and Their Makers*, Covina, Cal., 1913. Covina Publishing, Reprint. Vestal, N.Y.: The Vestal Press, 1980.

Ehrlich, Cyril. *The Piano: A History.* Rev. ed. Oxford: Clarendon Press, 1990.

Gill, Dominic, ed. *The Book of the Piano.* Ithaca: Cornell University Press, 1981.

Good, Edwin M. *Giraffes, Black Dragons, and Other Pianos: A Technological History from Cristofori to the Modern Concert Grand.* Stanford, Cal.: Stanford University Press, 1982.

Grover, David S. *The Piano: Its Story from Zither to Grand.* New York: Charles Scribner's Sons, 1978.

Harding, Rosamond E.M. *The Piano-Forte: Its History Traced to the Great Exhibition of 1851.* Cambridge: Cambridge University Press, 1933. Reprints. New York: Da Capo Press, 1973; Old Woking, Surrey: Gresham Books, 1978.

Hildebrandt, Dieter. *Pianoforte: A Social History of the Piano.* Translated by Harriet Goodman. New York: George Braziller, 1988.

Hirt, Franz Josef. *Meisterwerke des Klavierbaus: Stringed Keyboard Instruments.* Dietikon-Zürich, Switzerland: Urs Graf-Verlag, 1981.

Hollis, Helen Rice. *The Piano: A Pictorial Account of its Ancestry and Development.* New York: Hippocrene Books, 1975.

Junghanns, Herbert. *Der Piano- und Flügelbau.* 6th ed., rev. and enl. by H. R. Herzog. Frankfurt am Main: Das Musikinstrument, 1984.

Kent, Earle L., ed. *Musical Acoustics: Piano and Wind Instruments.* Benchmark Papers in Acoustics, no. 9. Stroudsburg, Penn.: Dowden, Hutchinson & Ross, 1977.

Loesser, Arthur. *Men, Women and Pianos: A Social History.* New York: Simon & Schuster, 1954.

Ripin, Edwin M., et al. *The Piano* (New Grove Musical Instruments series). New York and London: W. W. Norton & Company, 1988.

Wolfenden, Samuel. *A Treatise on the Art of Pianoforte Construction.* Rev. ed. Repr. of London and Woking, 1916, ed. with Supplement, 1927. Old Woking, England: Unwin Brothers, 1977.

PIANO À BUFFET

Piano à buffet is an obsolete French term meaning **upright**. Present usage favors the term *Piano droit*.

Martha Novak Clinkscale

PIANO À PÉDALIER/PIANO AVEC PÉDALIER

Piano à pédalier or *Piano avec pédalier* is the French term for **pedal piano**.

R.P.

PIANO À QUEUE

Piano à queue is the French name for **grand piano**.

Camilla Cai

PIANO À QUEUE MIGNON

Piano à queue mignon is the French name for **baby grand** piano.
See Grand Piano.

Camilla Cai

PIANO CARRÉ

Piano carré is the French phrase meaning **square piano**.

R.P.

PIANO DE CAUDA

Piano de cauda is the Portuguese name for **grand piano**.

Camilla Cai

PIANO DE COLA

Piano de cola is the Spanish name for **grand piano**.

Camilla Cai

PIANO DE MEDIA COLA

Piano de media cola is the Spanish term for **baby grand** piano. Another Spanish term for baby grand is *Piano cuarto de cola*.

See also Grand Piano.

R.P.

PIANO DE MESA

Piano de mesa is the Spanish term for **square piano**. Another Spanish term for square piano is *Piano cuadrado*.

R.P.

PIANO DROIT

Piano droit is the French term for an **upright piano** with oblique **stringing** in which the bass strings begin at the upper left corner and extend to the lower right corner near the floor. This practice was first mentioned by **Thomas Loud** in his London **patent** of 1802 but had been used much earlier by **Christian Ernst Friederici** in his 1745 pyramid piano.

The term *piano droit* has been used rather imprecisely to indicate any upright piano.

Martha Novak Clinkscale

PIANOFORTE A CODA

Pianoforte a coda is the Italian name for **grand piano**.

Camilla Cai

PIANOFORTE A MEZZA CODA

Pianoforte a mezza coda is the Italian term for **baby grand piano**.

See also Grand Piano.

R.P.

PIANOFORTE A TAVOLA

Pianoforte a tavola is the Italian phrase for **square piano**.

R.P.

PIANOFORTE VERTICALE

Pianoforte verticale is the Italian phrase meaning **upright piano**.

Martha Novak Clinkscale

PIANOLA

Pianola is the registered trade-name of the **piano players** and, later, **player pianos** made by the **Aeolian Company**. Aeolian's first player was called the Aeriol, but after the invention of the Pianola **push-up piano player** by Edwin Scott Votey in 1897, this name was adopted for all subsequent player developments by the company. While many other player piano manufacturers capitalized on variations of the name, especially names ending in "ola," the word "pianola" became accepted as a popular, if incorrect, generic name for a player piano of any make.

See also Player piano.

Arthur W.J.G. Ord-Hume

Bibliography

Ord-Hume, Arthur W.J.G. *Player Piano—History of The Mechanical Piano*. London: Allen & Unwin, 1970.

PIANO MÉCANIQUE

The *Piano mécanique* was a mechanically operated automatic piano that could be played just by turning a handle. Invented by French harmonium maker **Alexandre-François Debain** and **patented** in 1846, it was developed from the *Antiphonel*, an early form of keytop player that rested on top of the **keyboard** of a piano, harpsichord, harmonium, or organ. The upper surface was flat and provided with a mechanical **keyframe** through which protruded small steel levers; these controlled a series of trackers, which in turn operated a row of **felt**-tipped wooden plungers, one above each piano **key**.

The musical program was a series of studded wooden boards, called *planchettes*, varying in length from about ten inches to two feet, each representing part of the piece of music. The length of music that could be played was limited only by practical constraints on how many boards could be used.

To play the *Antiphonel*, the studded board was laid down on the keyframe so that a toothed rack along one edge engaged with a drive cog. Turning the handle propelled the *planchette* across the keyframe levers, the projections pushing the levers down, thus playing the piano keys. Each *planchette* was numbered and the playing sequence marked on the upper surface.

It required only simple skills to ensure that the next *planchette* was pushed into place behind the one being played.

The success of the *Antiphonel* inspired Debain to develop the system further and the result was the *Piano mécanique*, which had the *Antiphonel* mechanism built in. Two versions were produced: one was a keyboardless self-playing instrument and the other, more popular one, had a keyboard for manual playing as well. This had two distinct hammer actions, one for the keyboard and one for the *Antiphonel* mechanism.

Unlike the **barrel piano** with the program limitations of its barrel, Debain's instrument could play as much music as the owner might wish.

Arthur W.J.G. Ord-Hume

Bibliography

Ord-Hume, Arthur W.J.G. *Pianola — History & Development* . . . . London: Allen & Unwin, 1984.

PIANO PLAYER

A piano player is a separate mechanism, normally pneumatically operated and playing perforated paper music-rolls or piano-rolls, which, when placed in conjunction with an ordinary piano, enables it to be played automatically.

The piano player, also called a cabinet player or, in popular terms, a **push-up piano player**, was the forerunner of the **player piano** and was generally built in the form of a detached cabinet containing the pneumatic mechanism. A row of **felt**-covered wooden fingers at the back rested upon the **keyboard** of the piano in order to play it. The greater majority of these instruments were suction-operated, foot-operated exhaust bellows being provided for the performer to pedal. In Europe, towards the end of the nineteenth century, some mechanical piano players were made that played perforated cardboard disks, rolls of heavy waxed paper, or zig zag, folded music books.

A variation is the keytop player, which is a much smaller and simpler mechanism mounted on top of the keyboard. While **Alexandre Debain**'s *Antiphonel* was a mechanical keytop player from as early as 1842, electrically pumped pneumatic-action keytop players enjoyed some small popularity in America during the 1940–1960 period. These were not serious attempts at replicating a piano performance but were more

for playing pop and dance-music rolls. *See also* Push-up Piano Player.

Arthur W.J.G. Ord-Hume

Bibliography

Bowers, Q. David. *Encyclopedia of Automatic Musical Instruments*. Vestal, N. Y.: Vestal Press, 1972.

McTammany, John. *The Technical History of the Player*. New York: Musical Courier Co., 1915.

Ord-Hume, Arthur W.J.G. *Piano — History & Development* . . . . London: Allen & Unwin, 1984.

Roehl, Harvey. *Player Piano Treasury*. New York: Vestal Press, 1961 and 1973.

PIANO TECHNICIANS GUILD

The Piano Technicians Guild (PTG) is an organization of more than 3,800 tuners, technicians, and other piano-service specialists throughout the United States and Canada. PTG is governed by a council of delegates from its 168 chapters. Its activities include an annual convention and technical institute, which each July features more than 200 hours of classroom instruction in various aspects of piano technology. Chapter, state, and regional organizations also sponsor educational seminars and conferences throughout the United States and Canada.

Attempts to organize piano tuners and technicians began in Chicago during the Columbian Exposition of 1893 with the founding of the National Tuners Association. This organization was short-lived, as was a similar group founded in New York during 1904.

On 9 January 1910, however, a group of four technicians, Julian Elliott Diez, Albert Endress, Basil Britain Wilson, and William Braid White, formed an organization known as the American Guild of Piano Tuners (AGPT). Its first meeting was in June of that year and attracted 50 technicians from around the United States. It continued to grow, reaching a membership of nearly 2,000, and was instrumental in the establishment of A=440 as standard **pitch**.

According to White, that organization, which had changed its name to the National Association of Piano Tuners (NAPT) in the 1920s, began to disintegrate during the depression. In 1941, seceding members formed yet another organization, the American Society of Piano Technicians (ASPT). Both NAPT and ASPT continued to operate until 1957, when a committee of representatives from both organizations worked out details of a merger. The new organization became the Piano Technicians Guild, with Erroll P. Crowl and John Travis as co-presidents and Allan Pollard as its first executive secretary. The merger was confirmed 10 July 1958, during the new organization's first convention in Washington, D.C.

The earliest technical publication for piano tuners was issued by Sumner L. Bales as *The Tuner's Magazine* in January 1913. This monthly magazine soon became the official AGPT publication. Both NAPT and ASPT continued to publish technical journals until the merger, when they were combined into *The Piano Technicians Journal*. The *Journal* is now published monthly from PTG's home office in Kansas City, Missouri, and features articles on **tuning**, repair, refinishing, and **restoration** of pianos.

All PTG members are required to subscribe to a code of professional ethics and rules of business conduct. PTG has two classes of membership: registered tuner-technicians, also known as craftsman members, and associate members.

Registered tuner-technicians, the organization's franchised members, have completed a series of three examinations. A written examination covers general piano knowledge. A technical examination using **action** models covers repair and **regulation** procedures. A tuning examination compares the applicant's tuning with a computerized recording of an examination committee's tuning of the same instrument.

Associate members may be students of piano technology, non-tuning technicians, piano retailers, or suppliers of products or services to technicians.

Through its Piano Technicians Guild Foundation, continuing-education scholarships to piano teachers and grants for technical research are provided. The Foundation also works to preserve resource materials in piano technology and publishes new works on the subject.

The Guild also works closely with other technicians' organizations around the world. It is a founding member of the International Association of Piano Builders and Technicians (IAPBT). It serves as an information clearinghouse for members of IAPBT, which includes technicians' organizations in Japan, Korea, Taiwan, and Australia, as well as individual members in other countries.

Through its educational and organizational activities, PTG and its predecessors have a long history of increasing technical standards in the piano-service profession, keeping the piano user's needs and best interests uppermost.

Larry Goldsmith

Bibliography

Bales, Sumner L. "Raison D'Etre." *Tuner's Magazine* (January 1913): 3.

Hoskins, Leslie J. "For the Record." *Piano Technicians Journal* 1 (January 1958): 2.

White, William Braid. "What Are We Doing?" *Tuner's Magazine* (February 1913): 8.

——. "Sidelight On History." *Piano Trades Magazine* (July 1957). Reprinted in *Piano Technicians Journal* 1 (January 1958): 21–22.

PIANO VERTICAL

Piano vertical is the French term for **upright piano**; it is also a term that refers to other types of uprights, such as *pianino*, **Jean-Henri Pape**'s piano-console or **console**, and the *piano droit*. This model was made especially popular in France during the middle of the nineteenth century by **Pleyel** et Cie .

Martha Novak Clinkscale

PIANO VERTICALE

Piano verticale is the Spanish term for **upright piano**.

R.P.

PIN

See **Tuning Pin**.

PINBLOCK

More formally known as the *wrest plank*, the pinblock is the part of a piano into which the **tuning pins** (wrest pins) are embedded. The pinblock stretches across the front of a **grand piano**, along the top of a vertical piano. The pinblock, which is typically about 55 inches long, $1^1/_2$ inches thick, and of varying width, is

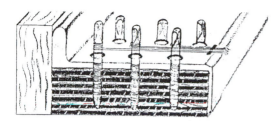

Cross section of a grand piano pinblock showing laminations and tuning pins.

Frequencies of the tonal scale of a piano (from the lowest A [AAA] 27.500 Hertz, to the highest C [c⁵] 4186 Hertz).

normally covered by the **case** and **plate** and is therefore not visible to the casual observer.

Although panels of solid hardwood (such as maple) have been used for pinblocks, it has long been nearly standard practice for piano manufacturers and rebuilders to use blocks made of several layers of hardwood glued together in such a way that the laminations are oriented with varying grain directions. Modern pinblocks may have from three to dozens of laminations, usually consisting of maple or beech.

A good pinblock is essential to the proper performance of a piano. The block must at once grip the tuning pins with sufficient firmness that the piano can stay well in tune, while still leaving the pins free enough that they can be readily manipulated by the tuner. The block must also be carefully fitted to the case and **frame** of the piano, in order to withstand with stability the many tons of tension that the **strings** impart. (See illustration.)

Steven R. Manley

PINBLOCK RESTORER

A liquid preparation intended to enable old, failing **pinblocks** to regain their ability to grip their **tuning pins** adequately. Treating a piano with pinblock restorer is an inexpensive procedure that can add some years to the life of an old block. However, applying such preparations to a pinblock effectively spoils it as a candidate for subsequent restringing with larger tuning pins. Piano technicians are generally reluctant to resort to the use of pinblock-restoring liquids.

Steven R. Manley

PITCH

Pitch is an aurally perceived frequency resulting from the speed of sound waves in the air when emitted by musical instruments, voice, and other noise sources. These sound waves must originate from a vibratory source such as a piano **string** or the moving diaphram/cone of an electronic speaker, etc. Sound waves vary in frequency with changes in the vibrating source. These differences then become evident as changes in pitch.

Pitch is particularly important in musical instruments, since relative unity of the instruments played together is dependent to a large degree on the **tuning**. A=440 today has been established as the accepted pitch standard for manufacturers of musical instruments. This insures that instruments when played together can be tuned to common frequencies. A=440 corresponds to the A in the fourth octave (A49) on a piano **keyboard**. That note, when played, emits sound waves that vibrate 440 cycles per second (cps). Another term for cycles per second is Hertz. Sound travels at approximately 1,100 feet per second, though this varies in relation to ambient temperature.

Lower pitches produce slower and longer sound waves. For example, A37, one octave lower than A=440, is comprised of soundwaves that vibrate at 220 cps. Each successive octave vibrates at half the frequency of the octave above. A standard piano **scale** with notes from A1 to C88 has a range of frequencies from 27.5 cps to 4,186 cps (see the chart for frequencies of notes on a piano).

Most of today's instruments are designed to a scale called "equal temperament." This means that each successive note-to-note interval is based on a mathematical constant. The difference in any half step in equal temperament is defined as 100 cents of pitch deviation. Therefore, F# is 100 cents higher in pitch than F.

To calculate the pitch, or frequency, of each half step, the frequency of a given note is multiplied by 1.059463. For example, the frequency of A49 (440cps) times the constant 1.059463 gives a frequency of 466.16, which is the frequency for A#50. If we need to calculate a one-cent difference instead of a half step, we use the constant 1.0005779. We would then see that A49 (440 cps) times 1.0005779 equals 440.25 cps. It is apparent through successive multiplying that 1,200 cents would equal one octave. The calculating of cents of pitch deviation is critical in the manufacturing of musical instruments, test instruments, and tuning devices that must provide extreme tolerances in pitch detection.

Kent Webb

PLATE

A structure, usually made of cast iron, to which the **strings** are attached. This unyielding structure, in conjunction with the wooden **frame**, sustains the high tension exerted by the strings.

R.P.

Bibliography

Mason, Merle H. *Piano Parts and Their Functions.* Seattle, Wash.: Piano Technicians Guild, 1977.

PLAYER PIANO

A player piano is a pianoforte that performs music by means of a self-playing mechanism, normally pneumatic, using a program in the form of a perforated paper music-roll or pianoroll.

The term "player piano" became the correct generic term for a pneumatically operated, paper-roll-playing piano that is set into automatic music-playing by the operation of foot treadles and controlled by a number of finger levers or buttons. In Britain, however, the extreme popularity of **Aeolian** and its **Pianola** led to the use of the word pianola as becoming almost a generic term: it actually appears in many dictionaries up to this day.

The player piano was the developed form of a whole series of pioneering piano-playing systems, some of the earliest being mechanical and a few being electrically operated. The player piano became a practical proposition with the joint development of perforated paper music and the pneumatic action, the invention of which had already produced the first generation of pneumatic piano-playing machines. These were the **piano players**, which were also known as **push-up** or cabinet players and were

in the form of a separate device placed in front of an ordinary piano so that special wooden fingers could physically depress the **keyboard** keys.

After the mechanical players of **Alexandre-François Debain**, with his *Antiphonel* and *piano mécanique* and **Napoléon Fourneaux**, with his barrel-operated *Pneumatic Pianista* organtype piano playing machine, many inventors applied themselves to designing self-acting pianos. **Ludwig Hupfeld** was among the more prolific and better-known of the European makers, his player using thin, perforated cardboard music-rolls to move the levers of an all-mechanical action.

The player piano was a radical improvement on all that went before it. Instead of needing a large and separate cabinet with which to play the piano, here was a system that made all earlier mechanical systems obsolete. The player piano is thus a self-contained instrument, meaning that the player mechanism is contained wholly within the body of the piano itself.

Pneumatic action, fundamental to the player piano, had been developed and refined first through the small, portable, automatic reed-instrument called the organette, of which many hundreds of different types were made (mainly in Germany and later in England and America) during the 1880s. From the organette was developed the player reed organ, and in this development the technique of designing small and sensitive pneumatic mechanisms became understood.

While most organettes operated on the same pneumatic principle as the harmonium, namely that normal or atmospheric air was compressed, using force bellows, in order to produce sounds from the musical elements (in the case of the organette, free reeds), the power of air at pressure below that of the atmosphere was found to be more easily controllable and offered a greater range of attainable pneumatic effects. For this reason, player mechanisms for pianos concentrated on the use of "negative pressure" created by suction bellows for their operation.

Although Robert W. Pain built a 39-note player piano for Needham & Sons in 1880, following it up with a 65-note electrically-operated one in 1888, and although Wilcox & White of Meriden, Connecticut, successfully combined a piano and reed organ with a roll-playing inner player as early as 1892, the first piano to have a practical pneumatic player mechanism built into it—the so-called inner player—was patented by Theodore P. Brown of Worcester, Massachusetts, in 1897.

Leading up to this, considerable experimental work had been taking place, not just in America but also in Germany, namely in the workshops of Hupfeld and Edwin **Welte**. While Hupfeld produced a practical player piano almost at the same time as Edwin S. Votey in America, it is generally accepted that the first practical production player pianos emanated from the United States.

It was the work of two men, Votey and Melville Clark, working separately in the United States, that led to the design and production of the player piano as we know it today. Votey produced the first Pianola **piano player**, the mechanism of which was later adapted to form that company's first inner player, in 1896. Melville Clark built his first "inner-player" player piano in 1901 and was, incidentally, the first person to fit a player mechanism to a **grand piano**: that was in 1904.

Pneumatic action as applied to the player piano made use of a perforated paper music roll. This paper roll formed a sliding valve for a separate pneumatic striking action for every note of the piano: where there was a hole in the paper indicating a note to be sounded, the pneumatic action would at once strike the required string. This principle is generally known as the "paper-as-a-valve" system. Various pneumatic mechanisms could be incorporated in the circuit between the music roll and the piano **hammer** to regulate or otherwise vary the force applied to the hammer, and, in its developed form, this became, first of all, the **expression piano** and, subsequently, the **reproducing piano**.

To begin with, the compass of the piano keyboard that could be played by the player system was somewhat abbreviated. In the beginning of the piano player, instruments that played on 58 of the keyboard's notes were common. Other models were produced that worked on 61, 65, 70, 73, 82, and 88 notes. The lack of standardization was a major problem to the manufacturers of music rolls.

In 1910, at a convention of player manufacturers held at Buffalo, New York, it was agreed to standardize on 65 and 88 notes for all except player reed organs (58 notes and 112 notes) and pipe organs (which in any case required more

tracks of perforations to operate stops and shades).

The manufacture of player pianos became one of the major industries of the western world. The number of manufacturers throughout the United States is almost impossible to assess accurately: many companies were insignificant or short-lived in their contribution to the 2.5 million instruments sold between 1900 and 1930. In London alone, a 1922 trade directory listed no fewer than fifty-two makers.

The success of Aeolian's Pianola, referred to earlier, inspired many makers to attempt to capitalize on sound-alike names, the suffix "ola" being seen as an important selling gimmick. Names like Triumphola, Odeola, Monola, and so on, were rife, while even the controls were given fanciful names such as Phrasiola, Tempola, Automelle, and Transposa.

Sheer commercialism of this type did little for the true value of the instrument, for there is little doubt that the player piano popularized a great deal of music that might otherwise never have been widely known. As an instrument of musical education, it was widely acclaimed by educators as well as by those famous pianists of the time who were handsomely paid to write testimonials.

The peak of the player piano's vogue was in the mid-1920s. Every piano retailer, from the up-market, aristocratic outlets such as London's Harrods store through to the smallest out-of-town shop sold players and their rolls. Indeed the music-roll business was a lucrative one and many lending libraries were established where, for a small sum of money, a number of rolls could be borrowed for a set time.

All was to change with the Wall Street crash in October 1929, and in the year that followed, player sales dwindled virtually to nothing. The market was also influenced by the rising popularity of the radio set, and with less disposable income available to the listening public, the radio and phonograph administered the final blow to the player piano. From a radio audience estimated at sixteen million in 1925, by 1932 more than sixty million Americans were listening to radio.

During the early 1930s there was a concerted attempt to revive the player-piano market, especially in London where piano makers were suffering deprivation. In spite of several late contenders in the way of new models (including what was arguably the smallest player piano in the world, produced by Barratt & Robinson of London), the industry was dead long before the outbreak of World War II in September 1939.

In the immediate post-war years, several fresh attempts at revival were made, notably in the United States, where a new form of piano player was devised. This "keytop" player was a small and separate mechanism that reverted to the early Debain *Antiphonel* principle in that it rested on top of the keys of the piano. Several keytop players were made up until the mid-1950s, but none made any significant impact on the market. Basic player pianos are still produced in America, but rather than being intended as serious musical interpreters, they are generally only intended as recreational instruments for playing popular song rolls to accompany singing.

Arthur W.J.G. Ord-Hume

Bibliography

Dolge, Alfred. *Men Who Made Piano History*, [original title, *Pianos and Their Makers*. Vol 2, *Development of the Piano Industry in America Since the Centennial Exhibition at Philadelphia* 1876] Covina, Cal.: Covina Publishing Co., 1913. Reprint. Vestal, N.Y.: Vestal Press, 1980.

Ord-Hume, Arthur W.J.G. *Pianola—History & Development*. . . . London.: Allen & Unwin, 1984.

Roehl, Harvey. *Player Piano Treasury*. New York: Vestal Press, 1961 and 1973.

PLEYEL, IGNACE-JOSEPH (ET Cᶦᵉ)

Ignace-Joseph Pleyel was born in Ruppersthal, Austria, on 18 June 1757 and died in Paris on 14 November 1831. He was active as a composer, music publisher, and founder of a leading piano firm. After study with **Joseph Haydn** in Eisenstadt (c. 1772–77), Pleyel was appointed Kapellmeister to Count Erdödy, composed on commission in Naples, and in 1789 became Kapellmeister at Strasbourg Cathedral. During the Revolution he conducted a series of concerts in London and, after moving back to the Strasbourg area, was arrested under suspicion of being pro-Austrian. After his release he moved to Paris in 1795 and flourished there both as music publisher and piano maker until his death.

Pleyel founded his piano firm in Paris in 1807, and it quickly rose to eminence. With the help of **Jean-Henri Pape** from 1811 to 1815, he introduced the *pianino*, a low, vertically strung **upright** based on the **cottage pianos** by the London maker **Robert Wornum**. In 1815 Pleyel took on as partner his eldest son Camille Pleyel (born Strasbourg, 18 December 1788; died Paris, 4 May 1855). As a performer who had studied with Johann Dussek and Daniel Steibelt, Camille's contributions were valuable because of his association with other artists, including Johann Baptist Cramer, Frédéric Kalkbrenner, and **Frédéric Chopin.** During a four-month stay in London at the beginning of his partnership, he was able to examine pianos, gain business expertise, and make contacts with **John Broadwood** and other makers. Camille assumed an important role in the Pleyel firm during the 1820s, when his friend Kalkbrenner, then the leading Parisian pianist, also became a partner and strong promoter.

The firm opened a concert hall, the Salle Pleyel, on 1 January 1830, with Kalkbrenner as the featured pianist. Chopin made his Paris debut in this hall in 1832 and also played his last Paris concert there in 1848. Chopin's advocacy of Pleyel's pianos is well known: "When I feel out of sorts, I play on an Erard piano where I easily find a ready-made tone. But when I feel in good form and strong enough to find my own individual sound, then I need a Pleyel piano" (Eigeldinger). One of Chopin's pupils, Emilie Gretsch, reported that the master considered it dangerous to practice too much on a piano with a ready-made **tone.** In her opinion Chopin's Pleyel, with its light, almost Viennese **touch,** was ideal for obtaining subtle nuances. According to Eigeldinger, Chopin's grand Pleyel 7267, made in 1839, had a single **escapement** action that was not uncommon in Pleyels of the time. Two other Pleyels are known to have been owned or used by Chopin: the *pianino* shipped to Majorca, and Pleyel 14810, which was in Chopin's possession from 1847 until his death. In 1839 Chopin dedicated the French and English editions of his Préludes Op. 28 to Camille Pleyel.

Pleyels were also the favored instruments of Kalkbrenner, Ferdinand Hiller, and in the twentieth century, Alfred Cortot. **Erards,** preferred by **Franz Liszt,** Henri Herz, and Sigismond Thalberg, sounded less delicate and were deemed better for large halls. Arthur Rubinstein observed in 1904 that the tone of Erards could be tinny compared to the warmer Pleyels and **Bechsteins.** The differing qualities are audible to some extent on modern recordings made on restored Pleyel and Erard pianos of the 1840s.

Generally less innovative than Erard or Pape, the firm of Pleyel is credited with at least three important advances: a method of tempering brass and steel **wires** (1810), the manufacture of *pianinos* (1815), and a **patent** for a cast-iron **frame** (1825).

In 1855 the firm passed to Camille's son-in-law, Auguste Wolff (1821–1887), and was known as "Pleyel, Wolff & Cie." It was under Wolff's direction that the company's production advanced dramatically. A comparison of serial numbers shows that by 1865 Pleyel had produced as many pianos as Erard (approximately 36,000 each), this despite the fact that Erard's firm was twenty-seven years older. By 1905 Pleyel had made more pianos (133,000) than Erard would make by 1959—even including the pianos that were produced in Erard's London factory before its closure in 1890.

In 1887 the firm passed to Wolff's son-in-law, Gustave Lyon (1857–1936), and was known as "Pleyel, Lyon etC^{ie}." Under Lyon's direction, new kinds of instruments were manufactured, including the chromatic harp (without pedals and with nearly twice the usual number of **strings**), chimes, timpani, the *Pleyela* (a reproducing **player piano**), a double **grand piano** (two facing grand pianos in one **case**), practice **keyboards**, two-manual harpsichords, and a specially designed harpsichord (1912) for Wanda Landowska.

Pleyel's firm achieved its peak annual production of approximately 3,000 pianos around 1910, when Erard was making only 1,900 pianos. By then French piano makers were no longer competitive in the world market, but Pleyel continued to dominate the market in France and in 1934 acquired the firm of Antoine Bord. In 1961, however, Pleyel was forced to merge with the already combined firms of Erard and Gaveau. Finally, in 1971 the conglomerate was acquired by the German maker **Schimmel**, which today produces a limited number of Pleyels each year according to its own standards.

See also France, Piano Industry in.

Charles Timbrell

Bibliography

Barli, Olivier. *La Facture française du piano de 1849 à nos jours*. Paris: La Flûte de Pan, 1983.

Closson, Ernest. *Histoire du piano*. Brussels: Editions universitaires, 1944. (New edition translated by Delano Ames and edited and revised by Robin Golding. New York: St. Martin's Press, 1974.)

Dolge, Alfred. *Pianos and Their Makers*. Covina, Cal.: Covina Publishing Co., 1911. Reprint New York: Dover, 1972.

Ehrlich, Cyril. *The Piano: A History*. London: J.M. Dent & Sons, Ltd., 1976.

Eigeldinger, Jean-Jacques. *Chopin vu par ses élèves*. Neuchâtel: Editions de la Baconniède, 1970. (New edition translated as *Chopin: Pianist and Teacher, as Seen by His Pupils* by Naomi Shohet and edited by Roy Howat. Cambridge: Cambridge University Press, 1986.)

Harding, Rosamond E.M. *The Piano-Forte: Its History Traced to the Great Exhibition of 1851*. Cambridge: Cambridge University Press, 1933. Reprints. New York: Da Capo Press, 1973; Old Woking, Surrey: Gresham Books, 1978.

Loesser, Arthur. *Men, Women and Pianos*. New York: Simon and Schuster, 1954.

Pierce, Bob. *Pierce Piano Atlas*. Long Beach, Cal.: Bob Pierce, 1977.

Pierre, Constant. *Les facteurs d'instruments de musique*. Paris: E. Sagot, 1893. Reprinted Geneva: Minkoff, 1971.

Place, Adélaide de. *Le Piano-forte à Paris entre 1760 et 1822*. Paris: Aux Amateurs de Livres, 1986.

POHLMANN, JOHANNES (FL.1767–1793)

Johannes Pohlmann was one of the earliest makers of pianofortes in London. One of the "**Twelve Apostles**," he and his compatriot, **Johann Christoph Zumpe**, left Saxony in 1760 to begin making the **square** pianoforte in London. Johannes Pohlmann set up his workshop at Compton Street, Soho, and later was at 113 Great Russell Street.

Zumpe's pianofortes quickly gained an early reputation, and the demand for instruments forced him to subcontract orders to his friend Pohlmann, who was thus able to capitalize on this success. Some of Pohlmann's instruments were more complicated than those of Zumpe and featured the addition of hand stops and a pedal swell. This business relationship between the two men was mutually beneficial, and indeed Pohlmann's pianofortes became almost as celebrated as those of Zumpe. Johannes Pohlmann continued in business until 1793, which appears to have been the year of his death.

There were two other significant businesses

with the name Pohlmann. One was the Victorian piano maker, Pohlmann & Sons in Halifax, Yorkshire. This firm began business in 1823 but claimed its origins back to the "Twelve Apostles," implying a family connection with Johannes Pohlmann. This cannot be established. Pohlmann & Sons ceased trading in 1881.

The second business with this name was that of Moritz Pöhlmann (1823–1902) in Nuremberg, Germany. A maker of piano **wire**, he devoted much skill and technology to producing a material for piano **strings** that became renowned throughout Europe around the middle of the last century. The modern piano wire industry owes its origins to Pöhlmann's research. It is unknown whether he was associated with Johannes Pohlmann.

Arthur W.J.G. Ord-Hume

Bibliography

Ehrlich, Cyril. *The Piano: A History*. London: Dent, 1976.

Grover, David S. *The Piano: Its Story from Zither to Grand*. London: Hale, 1976.

Harding, Rosamond E.M. *The Piano-Forte*. Cambridge: Cambridge University Press, 1933. Reprints. New York: Da Capo Press, 1973; Old Woking, Surrey: Gresham, 1978.

Wainwright, David. *Broadwood by Appointment, a History*. London: Quiller, 1982.

POLAND, PIANO INDUSTRY IN

The oldest extant Polish piano was built in 1774 by Jan Skórski in Sandomierz. During the first half of the nineteenth century there were piano workshops in Warsaw, Cracow, Kalisz, Vilna, Lvov, Poznań, Płock, Łęczyca and elsewhere. The central part of partitioned Polish lands, called Polish Kingdom, was the most active in developing craft and industry, mainly in Warsaw. Here, near the middle of the century, small workshops expanded gradually into manufacturing firms and factories. The largest and the most respected plant was that operated by Antoni Krall and Józef Seidler (1830–c.1897), the ex-employees (or perhaps apprentices) of Antoni Leszczyński (an apprentice of **Muzio Clementi**, active in Warsaw 1818–1830). By 1853 it was already a factory in the full meaning of that word, where fifty workers produced over one hundred pianos yearly.

In this period the Viennese influence was reduced to the use of the still-popular and inexpensive Viennese **action**. English models of **grand pianos** and the structural innovations connected with those models were generally used. The metal string **plate** was introduced to Poland in 1837 by Thomas Max (Warsaw, 1822–1864). During the same year, Poland was introduced to the *capo tasto* bar, as well. In the 1840s the half iron **frame** with four **braces** became popular. There were also some native improvements, original or inspired by foreign inventions. Some of those were the **hitch pin** block (several layers of wood glued together), **patented** in 1838 by Wojciech Kamieński (Warsaw, fl.c. 1835–1838), and the metal hitch-pin block covered with veneer, patented by Krall & Seidler in 1857. In 1847 Józef Budynowicz (Warsaw, fl.1840–c.1888) built the first piano with a solid cast-iron frame, for which he obtained a patent on 15 August of that year. Other Polish innovations include the piano with pedal **keyboard** built by Fryderyk Buchholtz (Warsaw, fl. 1815–1837) and the piano with shifted **transposing keyboard** produced by Krall & Seidler in 1836 and by Ferdinand Müller (Warsaw fl.c. 1856–1881) in 1858. In 1841 the French mechanic Philippe de Girard, who was active in the Polish textile industry, constructed a *tremolofon*, a kind of sustaining piano (French patent in 1841 by Mme. Girard-Romagnac, Philippe's sister; Polish patent in 1843), which was built by Kasper Zdrodowski (Warsaw, c.1837–1860). Among the performers on the *tremolofon* were Feliks Wilczek in Warsaw in 1842 and **Franz Liszt** in 1844 in Paris. In 1842 Girard patented a piano octave **coupler** in both Warsaw and Paris.

Just as in France, the construction of the **square piano** in Poland was succeeded comparatively soon by the building of **uprights**. As early as 1839, there is a note of the first patent for some improvement of the upright, obtained by Franciszek Wilczek (Warsaw, fl.c.1838–1841). Polish pianos were equal to those made in the leading world centers. Using identical technology they were, however, produced in much smaller numbers. Polish production did not exceed a few hundred pianos yearly during this time. It was, however, sufficient to satisfy local needs and the export to the Russian market. The quality of the instruments was highly rated at Polish and so-called all-Russian exhibitions. In 1843 Liszt wrote an official laudatory letter to Krall & Seidler after playing concerts on their grands.

In the period up to World War I among the several dozen plants then active, only a few major factories built a large number of instruments. They applied the concept of division of labor and had many auxiliary machines. The leading plants in Warsaw were those of Kerntopf & Son (1840–1939), Budynowicz, Feliks Julian Nowicki (1880–1941), Julian Małecki (1860–1939), Antoni Hofer (c. 1845–1880); in Kalisz: Teodor Betting (1887–1939, but after World War I in Leszno Wielkopolskie), Arnold Fibiger (c. 1840–1939, presently Calisia), Fibiger Brothers (Apollo, 1899–1939). Expansion of the factory system of production was accompanied in the Polish piano industry by plants specializing in the production of separate parts or units of the instruments. Some of those were: in Warsaw— Ignacy Bugaj (c. 1896–1941, actions, keyboards, **hammers**), Henry Artzt (c. 1896–1902, keyboards); in Kalisz– Konrad Eibl (c. 1902–1925, keyboards) and Rudolf Fibiger (1896–1939, cast-iron frames). Up to about 1900 Warsaw was still the main center, but at the beginning of the century Kalisz took the lead. In accordance with universal tendencies, the leading manufacturers began to use American construction designs with full iron frames and **crossstringing**, which were accepted in Europe after the Paris exhibition of 1867. Such a piano, made by Krall & Seidler, won a gold medal at the St. Petersburg exhibition in 1870. Kerntopf's plant introduced the American system in 1872 and simultaneously stopped using the Viennese action altogether.

Polish pianos of 1864–1914 were equal to the instruments of the leading European firms. Some examples of prizes awarded: Hofer, Vienna 1873 (medal of merit); A. Fibiger, Paris 1906 (gold medal, Grand Prix), London 1906 (Grand Prix), London 1907 (gold medal); Kerntopf & Son, Paris 1889 (gold medal, Grand Prix); Małecki & Szreder (Warsaw 1860–1869), Paris 1867 (silver medal); Małecki, Vienna 1873 (medal of merit), Paris 1878 and 1889 (silver medals); Krall & Seidler, Vienna 1873 (medal of progress), Philadelphia 1876 (gold medal), Paris 1878 (silver medal). Until World War I, total production increased to about 1,500–2,000 pianos a year.

In the years 1918–1939 the lack of political and economic stability in the newly organized state proved an obstacle. Signs of activity in the 1920s were checked by galloping inflation. Only between 1925 and 1930 was there a notable increase in production and the setting-up of new firms to manufacture pianos. After 1935 even the large firms failed to return to their former glory and achieved barely 10 percent of their production potential. Warsaw had only one big factory, that of Kerntopf & Son. The main piano industry was concentrated now in the west of Poland, with factories in Kalisz (Fibiger, Fibiger Brothers), Leszno Wlkp. (Betting), Poznań (Antoni Drygas, c. 1917–1939), Bydgoszcz (Brunon Sommerfeld 1905–1930, Otton Majewski c. 1932–1939, Wilhelm Jähne c. 1928–1930) and Rawicz (Artur Ecke, 1929–1939). The largest factories were Sommerfeld's (about 200 workers in 1929–1930) and A. Fibiger's. In the best year, 1929, Polish production reached some 2,500 pianos and employed about 700 workers.

During World War II and the Nazi occupation the Polish piano industry and its manpower were completely destroyed. Since 1947 there have been two active piano factories in Poland: Calisia in Kalisz (previously A. Fibiger's) and Legnica in Legnica (on the site of E. **Seiler's** former factory), with a piano-action factory in nearby Lubin. Calisia produces mainly uprights (over 123,400 instruments as of 1989); similarly Legnica's production—only uprights—reached 139,000 instruments as of 1989. The Polish piano industry produces instruments mainly for the local market, yet also sells part of the production to other countries.

Benjamin Vogel

Bibliography

Vogel, Benjamin. *Budownictwo fortepianów na ziemiach polskich do II wojnyświatowej.* [Piano making on Polish lands until World War II]. Warsaw: Warsaw University, 1988.

——. *Kolekcja Zabytkowych Fortepianów Filharmonii Pomorskiej.* [Old Pianos Collection of the Pomeranian Philharmonic] Bydgoszcz: Filharmonia Pomorska, 1987.

——. *Instrumenty muzyczne w kulturze Królestwa Polskiego.* [Musical Instruments in Culture of the Polish Kingdom] Cracow: Polish Music Publications, 1980.

PORTABLE GRAND PIANO

Portable grand pianoforte is the name of a small **upright**, barely 5 $^1/_2$ feet tall, designed by **John Isaac Hawkins** in Philadelphia about 1802. With a **keyboard** that folds into the **case**, and carrying handles on either side, it was apparently designed to be carried aboard ship.

See also Upright Piano.

Martha Novak Clinkscale

PORTUGAL, PIANO INDUSTRY IN

See Spain and Portugal, Piano Industry in

PRATT, READ & COMPANY

Pratt, Read & Company was for many years the only independent United States manufacturer of **keyboards** and **actions**. The name was widely known in this country and in Europe and commanded much respect. Initially the firm worked with ivory to produce ivory combs. In 1798 Phineas Pratt (1747–1813) invented a circular saw to cut teeth in **ivory** combs. The saw was put into operation in 1800 by Phineas and his son Abel (1775–1864). In 1808 one of Phineas's younger sons, Julius (1791–1869), joined them until 1818, when he left to begin his own business. In 1863 George Read & Company, Pratt Brothers, (Ulysses [1813–1881] and Alexis Pratt [1814–1872], grandsons of Phineas and nephews of Julius) of Deep River, and Julius Pratt of Meriden merged under the name Pratt, Read & Company, of Deep River, Connecticut. They were then cutting ivory veneers and had undertaken the manufacture of ivory keyboards.

One of their competitors was Comstock, Cheney & Company of Ivoryton, Connecticut until December 1936, when the two companies merged and became Pratt, Read & Company. The use of the plants in Deep River and Ivoryton continued until October 1938, when it was decided to centralize all operations in Ivoryton. When World War II began they returned to Deep River. Their business was declared nonessential to the war effort, so they turned to building Waco CG-4A gliders for the U.S. Army and training gliders for the U.S. Navy under the name of Gould Aeronautical Division. After the war they sold the Deep River plants and moved back to Ivoryton and the difficult task of reviving the production of keyboards and actions. Imports and **electronics** caused the downfall of their keyboard and action business and in 1986 the division was sold to the **Baldwin Piano Company**.

Edith M. DeForest

Bibliography

Conniff, Richard. "When the Music in Our Parlors Brought Death to Darkest Africa." *Audubon Magazine* 89 (July 1987): 76–93.

———. "The Towns that Ivory Built." *Yankee* 53 (November 1989): 66–152.

Kraus, Rev. Wm. H. *History of Middlesex County 1635–1885: With Biographical Sketches of Its Prominent Men.* ("Industries" pp.548–49) New York: J.B. Beers & Co., 1884.

Latham, Margaret, et al. *History of Pratt, Read & Company of Deep River.* Deep River, Conn.: Ivory Committee of the Deep River Historical Society, Inc., 1973.

Collections (Actions, Keyboard Veneer Cutting Machines, etc.) at Connecticut State Library Museum (Hartford, Conn.), Eli Whitney Museum (Hamden, Conn.), and Stone House (Deep River, Conn.).

PRELLMECHANIK

Prellmechanik refers to a German or Austrian type of piano **action** in which the **hammer** heads face towards the player, with the connecting shank located behind the head; each hammer is hinged from or held in a fork-like device called a *Kapsel* attached to the back of the **key** (see fig. 1). This arrangement contrasts with the **Cristofori, English,** and modern actions, in which the hammer heads face away from the player, and the hammers are hinged from a fixed **rail**. Because Vienna became the center for *Prellmechanik* design, it is known as "Viennese action." The most significant improvement to the design was the **escapement** added by Johann Andreas **Stein** in the 1770s. Pianos fitted with this type of action achieved unequalled lightness of **touch,** clarity of **tone,** and ease of articulation. Later versions of the *Prellmechanik* grew increasingly heavy, and the Viennese action lost out in prominence to the English-type action design after about 1850, although some manufacturers continued to build the Viennese type on into the twentieth century.

Whereas Cristofori's pianoforte had represented an attempt to create a harpsichord with expressive dynamics, early German **square pianos** evolved directly out of the clavichord. The simplest squares were in essence clavichords with a hammer attached either directly to the key or in a *Kapsel,* replacing the tangent. The hammer had a small "beak" on the end opposite from the head which, when the key was played, pressed up against a fixed rail (*Prelleiste*) or against the underside of the **hitch-pin** apron, thereby flipping the hammer towards the

Figure 1: Prellmechanik *without escapement (primitive German action). The hammer pivots in the fork or* Kapsel *connected directly to the key.*
(Courtesy Da Capo Press [New York], agent for Franz J. Hirt's Stringed Keyboard Instruments*)*

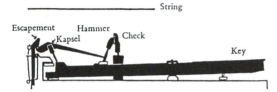

Figure 2: Prellmechanik *with escapement (developed German action). The beak on the hammer slips free of overhang on escapement level just before hammer strikes string. Check catches hammer on rebound.*
(Courtesy Da Capo Press [New York], agent for Franz J. Hirt's Stringed Keyboard Instruments*)*

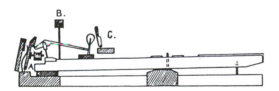

Figure 3: Prellmechanik *with adjustable escapement by Streicher 1829 (Viennese action). A - regulating screw, B - damper, C - check. Regulating screw adjusts position of escapement lever.*
(Courtesy Da Capo Press [New York], agent for Franz J. Hirt's Stringed Keyboard Instruments*)*

string (see fig. 1). The earliest extant German square (1742) is by Johann Söcher of Sonthofen (Bavaria), now in the Germanisches Nationalmuseum in Nürnberg.

The simple *Prellmechanik* had several drawbacks, the most severe of which was the blocking of the hammer against the string when the key was held down. The development of an escapement device to alleviate this is generally credited to Johann Andreas Stein of Augsburg; the earliest known surviving example is a **grand**

labelled 1773 (date somewhat uncertain) now located in the Musik Instrumenten Museum of the University of Leipzig. In the Stein type of action each key has its own individually hinged escapement lever, which is provided with a separate escapement return spring. The **leather-covered** hammer beak fits into a notch in the escapement lever, "escaping" from it just before the hammer head strikes the string, thus preventing the hammer from blocking. When the key is released, the beak slips down the upper face of the escapement lever back into the notch (see fig. 2).

In Stein's action design the hammer rests on a small post covered with soft thick cloth to absorb the shock upon return. The small, light hammer heads themselves are covered with a strip of leather over the striking surface. A "sled" or drawer slips under the **keyboard** to bring the action sufficiently close to the strings. Individual **dampers** are housed in a rack located above the strings. The typical compass of a Stein grand was five octaves (FF to f^3).

Anton Walter (1752–1826) introduced several departures from Stein's methods, including the use of longer and larger hammers, thus making the instrument louder. Other Walter developments included a moveable rail to adjust the escapement point, brass *Kapseln*, which allowed a freer hammer pivot than those by Stein (which were of wood), and, finally, a **back check** rail. This last improvement, in effect replacing the cloth-covered hammer rest-posts, prevented the hammer from restriking the string by catching it on its return. All these innovations were subsequently adopted at varying rates and with some modifications by following generations of builders, becoming permanent features of *Prellmechanik* design.

Like its English counterpart, the *Prellmechanik* grew larger and heavier during the first half of the nineteenth century, part of an overall trend that included heavier stringing and **case**, larger compass, and iron bracing. Both squares and grands were built in considerable numbers, as well as various types of **upright** ("giraffe," "pyramid," "lyre"). Among the most prominent Viennese builders during this period were **Johann Schantz**, **Conrad Graf**, Stein's son Matthäus Andreas Stein and Stein's daughter Nannette who, along with her husband, Johann Andreas **Streicher**, worked under the name "Nannette Streicher née Stein" (for a diagram of an action by Nannette Streicher see fig. 3).

Although later nineteenth-century composers such as **Brahms** still appreciated pianos fitted with the *Prellmechanik*, the advantages for which Viennese actions had originally been known—lightness and clarity—were lost or considerably diminished by increasing size and weight. For this reason, they suffered in competition with the English type of piano which, traditionally possessing a deeper, heavier action and fuller tone, better suited the taste of the public. **Bösendorfer**, the most prestigious Viennese builder of the later nineteenth century, discontinued the Viennese action as a standard model in 1909, although some were produced afterwards to special order.

Seth A. Carlin

Bibliography

Bilson, Malcolm. "The Viennese Fortepiano of the Late Eighteenth Century." *Early Music* 8, 2 (April 1980): 158–62.

Colt, C.F. *The Early Piano.* London: Stainer and Bell, 1981.

Ehrlich, Cyril. *The Piano: A History.* London: Dent, 1976.

Good, Edwin M. *Giraffes, Black Dragons, and Other Pianos: A Technological History from Cristofori to the Modern Concert Grand.* Stanford, Cal.: Stanford University Press, 1982.

Gough, Hugh. "The Classical Grand Pianoforte." *Proceedings of the Royal Musical Association* 77 (1952): 41–51.

Harding, Rosamond E.M. *The Piano-Forte: Its History Traced to the Great Exhibition of 1851.* Cambridge: Cambridge University Press, 1933. Reprints. New York: Da Capo Press, 1973; Old Woking, Surrey: Gresham Books, 1978.

Haupt, Helga. "Wiener Instrumentenbauer von 1751 bis 1815." [Viennese Instrument Builders from 1751 to 1815] *Studien zur Musikwissenschaft* 24 (1960): 120–84.

Hipkins, Alfred J. *A Description and History of the Pianoforte.* London, 1929. Reprint. Detroit: Information Coordinators, 1975.

Hirt, Franz Josef. *Stringed Keyboard Instruments, 1440–1880.* Translated by M. Boeme-Brown. Boston: Boston Book and Art Shop, 1968. Also, Dietikon-Zürich: Urs Graf (distributed by Da Capo Press), 1981.

James, Philip. *Early Keyboard Instruments, From Their Beginnings to the Year 1820.* London: Holland Press, 1960 (first published 1930).

Loesser, Arthur. *Men, Women and Pianos: A Social History.* New York: Simon and Schuster, 1954.

Lutge, Wilhelm. "Andreas und Nannette Streicher." *Der Bar (Jahrbuch von Breitkopf und Härtel)* 4 (1927): 53–69.

Rück, Ulrich. "Mozarts Hammerflügel erbaute Anton Walter Wien." [Mozart's Grand Fortepiano Built by Anton Walter of Vienna]. *Mozart-Jahrbuch des Zentralinstituts für Mozartforschung* 6 (1955): 246–62.

Schott, Howard. "From Harpsichord to Piano: A Chronology and Commentary." *Early Music* 13, 1 (February 1985): 28–38.

Sumner, William Leslie. *The Pianoforte.* London: Macdonald and Jane's, 1966.

PREPARED PIANO

Since its invention around 1700, the piano has undergone many changes, but none so vital as its extended sonority. Richness of sound and volume was stock-in-trade of nineteenth-century piano music. This goal having been accomplished—and noticeably exhausted—it was inevitable that a way would be found to modernize the sound of the piano once again.

While still preserving the piano's shape, form, and mechanics, a prepared piano—most practically a **grand piano**—is "prepared" for performance by the insertion of bolts, screws, pencil erasers, coins, clothespins, (and yes, there are other uses for a credit card) between appropriate **strings** anywhere along the entire range. The resulting effect produced by normal playing of the piano is unique. The instrument can produce drumlike sounds, as well as altered pitches or, more usual, nonpitches. Often accompanying this method of composing is the addition of instructions for the performer to pluck, muffle, strum, or in some other way treat the strings with the hands, fingers, or other objects, e.g., screwdriver, nails, mallets, marbles.

The seminal work involving a prepared piano dates back to 1940, with the premier of the ballet score, *Bacchanal*, choreographed by Syvilla Fort, with music written by John Cage. At that time, as a ballet accompanist and composer for a Seattle modern dance group, Cage created a work that was to initiate a change in approach to writing for, and performing on, the piano; this innovation would influence a host of subsequent composers to this day.

Richard Bunger, who was very much involved with the evolution of the prepared piano, has written an excellent manual on the subject (the most accessible volume in English). The manual touches on all aspects of the medium, including choice of materials for possible use in preparing a piano, preparation techniques, notation, and, most helpful, a student's guide to music for prepared piano that includes a listing of some thirty-four prepared piano works, graded in difficulty. Composers include, among others, Cage, Barney Childs, George Crumb, John Diercks, and Bunger.

Frederic Schoettler

Bibliography

Bunger, Richard. *The Well-Prepared Piano.* San Pedro: Litoral Arts Press, 1981.

The New Grove Dictionary of Music and Musicians. Sixth edition. Edited by Stanley Sadie. S.v. "Prepared piano." London: Macmillan, 1980.

PRESSURE BAR

In the **upright piano**, the pressure bar is a removable bar of metal with a shape like a solid U found in the middle and treble areas. It is placed round-side down between the **tuning pin** area and the top V-bar (a V-shaped **bridge** of iron usually cast as part of the **plate**) to hold the **strings** securely down on the V-bar, thus creating a definite end to the speaking length of the strings. The pressure bar also creates friction that is necessary for **tuning** stability.

Joel and Priscilla Rappaport

PURCHASING A PIANO

Acquiring a piano, like any other major purchase, involves initial assessment of the buyer's wants or needs followed and possibly modified by exploration of the market. The buyer's ultimate satisfaction will generally depend on the time and effort expended in this process.

Initial Considerations

Perhaps the most important of several points to consider at the outset is the buyer's motivation. Some common possibilities and their implications:

(1) A beginning student needs a practice instrument. The most practical choice is probably a good but fairly modest **upright**. Although it need not be especially expensive, it must provide room for growth and should be enjoyable to play. Even if free, a poor instrument is a false economy; it will hinder the student's progress and kill any joy in learning to play. Furthermore, whatever the claims of merchants, **electronic** instruments are no substitute, as a student who takes seriously to music will probably outgrow one within months.

(2) For personal enjoyment, the buyer wants to replace an electronic instrument or casually acquired piano. Here the buyer's own preferences and resources will be paramount.

(3) The buyer wants a piano for an accompanist or partner in chamber music. Obviously, any particular accompanist should be consulted and satisfied; if several potential players are contemplated, the piano should be requisite with the quality of the desired results. Thus, a good upright should satisfy casual players while more serious amateurs or professionals may prefer a small—or even large—**grand** (so long as enough space remains for several musicians to cluster around it). Again, a poor instrument will be a false economy under any circumstances.

(4) A non-musician wants a piano for others to play. Depending on the goal, be it providing an instrument for a institution or for social gatherings, the buyer may prefer anything from a **concert grand** to a **spinet** or even a **player piano**. Controlling factors will be the size of the space to be served, the sophistication of the intended users, and the buyer's willingness to maintain the instrument.

(5) A non-musician wants a piano as a decoration. Only in such circumstances will the piano's **case** take precedence over its musical qualities.

Available space, which may be an equally important factor, principally affects search flexibility. Residents of efficiency apartments will perforce limit their search to uprights, while residents of larger apartments may want to consider small grands and home owners even larger grands.

The buyer's budget also affects flexibility. A tight budget will require careful and probably protracted shopping, very likely ending in the purchase of a used instrument. With increasing budget, the buyer may consider new or larger used instruments and may avoid a lengthy search, although the wise buyer will nonetheless thoroughly explore the market, new and used. Note that the budget must include **tuning** and maintenance in addition to acquisition costs.

Desired tonal characteristics are a matter of taste. Piano **tone** can vary from rich, or even murky, to brilliant, or sometimes painfully bright; the current fashion in new instruments tends toward the latter extreme. In general, a sound somewhere in between will probably be best, although jazz and popular music often benefit from brightness, which is less appropriate for Classical and particularly Romantic music. Likewise, an instrument to accompany a church choir in a large auditorium should generally be brighter than a practice instrument for a small, sparsely furnished apartment.

Unless the piano will be strictly decorative, case styling is a secondary consideration. As the purpose of a piano is to make music, its sonic and mechanical qualities must be paramount; nonetheless, no one wants to live with an eyesore, and before beginning to search the buyer should consider what styles and finishes will blend harmoniously (or at least not clash) with the intended location. In general, a conservative styling and finish will probably be the best choice, both to allow for changes in the buyer's tastes and to ensure good resale value.

Finally, the buyer must consider how much "shopping" is acceptable: evaluating used pianos in the field takes considerable patience and perseverance, and those with little time or inclination to search should probably limit themselves to piano stores. If possible, however, the buyer should explore the used market carefully, as private parties and tuners usually charge less than stores for similar instruments, used or new.

The Search

The buyer who has realistically considered the foregoing factors can expect careful shopping to yield a fair approximation of the "ideal" instrument but should not expect a perfect match. Indeed, beyond the basics discussed above, preconceptions can be a hindrance. Good and bad instruments exist in nearly all categories and price ranges; moreover, the same instrument can be good for one player and poor for another. Thus, brand names and designs are at best initial indicators of quality (or the lack of it), and only the buyer's personal evaluation of each individual instrument can assure a satisfactory choice.

Nonetheless, a buyer of limited playing ability should get a more accomplished friend to demonstrate at least those instruments that come under serious consideration. While the decision to purchase must finally depend on the buyer's own judgment, a good consultant can reveal tonal and mechanical limitations that might be hidden to a less demanding player.

General Considerations

The beginning shopper should know common terms for piano sizes. Grands are best described in feet and inches from the **keyboard** edge of the case to the farthest reach of the back curve with the **lid** down, uprights in inches from the floor to the top of the case. Certain imprecise categories are often used instead, however. Indiscriminate use has rendered the term "**baby grand**" nearly meaningless, but it properly applies to instruments under about five and a half feet, while "concert grand" indicates approximately nine feet. Among many terms for intermediate sizes are "studio," "conservatory," and "**parlor**." Upright sizes are "full" (50 inches or more), "studio" (roughly 45 to 48 inches), "**console**" (usually about 42 inches), or "spinet" (under 40 inches).

Ideally, a grand should sound better than an upright because of its long **strings** open to the air in a horizontal orientation. On the other hand, a large (52-inch) upright may actually have better bass than a small grand by virtue of longer bass strings. Moreover, a poor grand can sound fully as wooden in the bass and glassy in the treble as any upright. Thus, the buyer must evaluate each instrument with closed eyes and open ears.

Among uprights, good **action** and pleasing tone are most likely in the full and studio sizes. Some consoles can also be perfectly satisfactory, particularly for casual players or beginning students. Spinets, however, compromise all musically important components to fit a small case: **frame**, string length and position, **soundboard**, and action are all markedly inferior to their counterparts in taller instruments taking no more floor space (although some inexpensive consoles share the spinet's unresponsive indirect action). Thus, the buyer should avoid spinets unless expense is absolutely determinative.

In grands, the leftmost, or *una corda*, **pedal** should shift the entire action laterally. It is not properly a "soft" pedal, but rather alters tone color by reducing the number of strings sounding each note. In lesser-quality and converted player grands, the left pedal may merely move the **hammers** toward the strings; this approach is nearly universal in uprights.

Many fine instruments, particularly uprights and European imports, omit the rarely used center, or "*sostenuto*," pedal. A good *sostenuto* pedal should catch only the **dampers** that are raised when it is depressed rather than lifting all the bass dampers simultaneously. Note that in even an excellent upright, the center pedal, if present, may duplicate the action of another pedal, or else control a "practice mute," a **felt** strip which the pedal presses against the strings (potentially useful for apartment dwellers, although inevitably harmful to the instrument's tone when engaged).

New Instruments

Buying a new instrument allows the buyer to be highly selective about all its aspects, as the availability of many comparable instruments compensates for the typically wide variation of **touch** and tone among instruments even of the same model. Of course, the best instrument to play may not be in the buyer's favorite case; here, if music-making is the goal, the instrument with better musical qualities will give the most long-term satisfaction.

The principal concerns about a new piano are action and tone. Harder to judge, life expectancy is also important. Every piano worth considering, be it grand or upright, will have an even, responsive action. The hallmark of responsiveness is ability to yield a full dynamic range with complete control between its extremes. It is not lightness of touch; while easy trills should be possible on all notes, an overlight action is difficult to control. Indeed, poor control is the most likely failing of an action, and the slightest sluggish, rubbery, or imprecise feeling should be grounds for instant rejection. Two other common failings affect dynamics: the same volume of sound may emerge no matter how the **keys** are depressed, or else dynamics may be effectively limited to *mezzoforte* or louder. Again, both should be regarded as fatal flaws.

While responsiveness concerns each key individually, evenness concerns the entire keyboard. An even action becomes progressively but moderately lighter from bass to treble in smooth, imperceptible increments. Unlike responsiveness, evenness is generally not problematic in new instruments except spinets and the most inexpensive consoles. Nonetheless, defects in evenness quickly become exasperating, and so should disqualify any instrument manifesting them.

A properly versatile instrument should be tonally balanced, with rich, warm bass and brilliant (but not piercing) treble. Balance, of course, is ultimately a matter of personal taste, but the wise buyer will sample a wide variety of good instruments to form that taste fully. In evaluating tone, the buyer should pay particular attention to the sound of bass chords, which will reveal an insufficiently resonant bass more readily than notes sounded singly. This failing is common in uprights and by no means unknown in grands; brittle, overbright treble is common in both. Either flaw justifies rejecting the instrument.

Factors influencing a piano's life expectancy include the quality of its construction and the maintenance that it receives. A well-maintained piano of intermediate or better quality can be expected to last a lifetime, while even the best maintenance may not suffice to preserve a very inexpensive instrument beyond a relatively small number of years. The buyer's best approach is probably to discuss any potential purchase with a good technician.

The buyer of a new piano should evaluate both the instrument and the dealer. A good dealer will provide a range of goods and services in conjunction with the sale, generally including free delivery, a bench, and a complimentary tuning after delivery (preferably two weeks to a month later, after the instrument has acclimated to its new environment). Many also allow repeat customers full purchase price in trade toward a larger instrument. The dealer may provide an extra store warranty and should at a minimum provide full service under the manufacturer's warranty.

Both dealers and tuners can provide invaluable advice and guidance. Although tuners are more likely to be objective, the best dealers also love pianos and are happy to discuss them with potential customers, explaining both their own wares and also general points of quality and design.

On the other hand, the business has a less admirable side. For instance, some dealers emphasize the superiority of German design and European traditions of craftsmanship embodied in certain inexpensive instruments, not mentioning that they actually are second-line Asian products sold under the Germanic-sounding names of defunct American builders. Others, motivated by the high profits on electronic instruments, package simple **electronic** keyboards with in-store lessons specifically designed to create a demand for more expensive keyboards.

To summarize, then, the buyer of a new piano will do best by examining numerous instruments for action, tone, and life expectancy, ultimately making the purchase from a knowledgeable and trustworthy dealer who specializes in acoustic instruments.

Used Instruments

Used pianos demand flexibility from the buyer. New models may exist in multiple copies, but each used instrument is unique. Thus, the buyer must be patient, willing to compromise, and able to assess an instrument's qualities unassisted. On the other hand, a fine used piano will almost certainly cost less than a comparable new one, may actually be a better instrument, and could be a better investment (although pianos have little or no "antique value" outside their musical qualities).

Although a used instrument's touch and tone are crucial, the buyer should consider them only after evaluating its current state of preservation. No matter how fine originally, a piano with a cracked frame is junk—and possibly unsafe. More common but scarcely less debilitating is tuning instability. A piano with loose pins cannot be tuned and has no musical value. Replacing a **pinblock** is justified only for grand pianos of the finest quality, e.g., **Steinway**, **Bechstein**, **Mason & Hamlin**, **Knabe**, or **Chickering**. Cracked **bridges** also impair tuning stability, although not as much; again, replacement of cracked bridges is possible but expensive.

Age and wear can also adversely affect a used instrument's action and case. Keys with lateral play may need new **bushings**; a generally loose action may need complete rebuilding. While neither operation is as serious as pinblock or bridge replacement, both are expensive and weigh against an instrument. Case refinishing is also prohibitively expensive for any but truly fine quality instruments. Damaged key tops, on the other hand, are relatively inexpensive to replace, although badly chipped or broken key tops may be symptomatic of poor treatment that will manifest itself in other ways.

Finally, the buyer should avoid certain used instruments whose inferior or obsolete designs pose serious maintenance problems. In particular, "**square** grands" and uprights with the so-called bird-cage action generally cannot be serviced. Indeed, parts may be difficult to obtain even for a Steinway built at or before the turn of the century.

Obviously, used pianos present great risks and potentially outstanding virtues. The buyer can greatly diminish the risks, however, by hiring a technician to examine any used instrument under serious consideration. The buyer should forego such advice only if sufficiently experienced to differentiate between a true bargain and a piece of junk priced to move.

Where and How to Search

Most piano stores stock both new instruments and used ones taken in trade; they tend to be the most expensive source. Private parties are the most economical source for used pianos, although they do not provide such advantages as warranties, free delivery, and complimentary tunings. A good compromise may be one of the many tuners who run side businesses selling used or even new pianos. Both private parties and tuner/dealers may be found through classified advertisements or bulletin boards in music schools.

Among possible search strategies, a good one is to begin with piano stores, learning as much as possible about a wide range of new and used instruments. If not satisfied with these choices, the buyer can then apply the knowledge so obtained to instruments for sale by private parties. In short, the buyer should exercise patience and persistence, virtues which will be amply repaid in years of playing enjoyment.

David R. Hoehl

Bibliography

Fine, Larry. *The Piano Book: Buying & Owning a New or Used Piano.* Second Edition. Boston: Brookside Press, 1990.

PUSH-UP PIANO PLAYER

A push-up piano player is the popular term for a **cabinet** player or **piano player**. While piano players come in several varieties, a push-up is always a separate playing cabinet by the use of which an ordinary piano can be played automatically.

See also Piano player.

Arthur W.J.G. Ord-Hume

Bibliography

Ord-Hume, Arthur W.J.G. *Pianola—History & Development.* . . . London: Allen & Unwin, 1984.

PYRAMID PIANO

See Giraffe/Pyramid Pianos

QUERFLÜGEL

Querflügel is the German term for "diagonal **grand**," a type of horizontal piano, built in England and Europe in the late eighteenth and early nineteenth centuries, derived from the bentside spinet style of harpsichord in which the **keyboard** is set at a sharp angle to the **spine**. The "**cocked-hat grand**" is a descendant.

Edwin M. Good

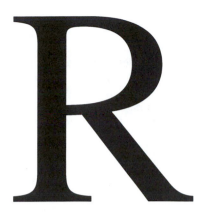

RAILS

There are numerous rails in a piano. The function of a rail is primarily to support a common body of parts or to support one element of the instrument. Merle Mason lists over thirty-eight rails in his excellent compilation of piano parts. Here are a few: **action** support rail—a bar across the lower framework of an **upright**; **damper** guide rail—a thin wooden bar positioned above and protruding beyond the forward edge of the **soundboard** into the action-housing; **hammer** rail—in an upright, the long cloth-covered bar on which hammer shanks lean when at rest; main action rail—a bar, generally of wooden construction, varying in thickness and running the entire length of the action, which provides a stable base for the moving parts of the action. The **keys** operate on three rails: the front rail (under the front end of the keys), the balance rail (on which the keys pivot), and the back rail (where the back end of the keys rest). Some additional rails are: hammer shank rail, damper lift rail, damper stop rail, damper guide rail, belly rail, key slip rail, and **music desk** rail.

R.P.

Bibliography

Mason, Merle H. *Piano Parts and Their Functions*, 93–96. Seattle, Wash.: Piano Technicians Guild, 1977.

REBUILDING

Rebuilding is the process by which a piano is improved through evaluation of its existing condition and a subsequent plan of repair procedures is formulated and performed to complete its restoration. While usually thought of as a total restoration, rebuilding can involve any number of repairs to restore the piano to various levels of performance and appearance. A rebuilding is normally divided into two main categories: refinishing and technical rebuilding. Refinishing involves refurbishing the piano **case** along with case parts such as the **lid** and **fallboard**, brass hardware, and bench. Other miscellaneous parts that are disassembled from the piano are also refinished to give the piano a consistent appearance.

The technical rebuild can include repairs to the **action** components and restringing with new **strings** and a new **pinblock**. Also addressed is the condition of the **soundboard** and **bridges**. These two main areas of work are then planned to insure the most efficient work flow in the rebuilding workshop.

Evaluation is the first step in the process. The technical aspects and **finish** condition are assessed for various repair needs, both individually and in relation to each other. Because of the dual nature of the piano—furniture and musical instrument—the intertwined relationship must be considered to make the restoration complete and cost effective. For example, a pinblock cannot be repaired without restringing the entire piano, and, if a **plate** is out for pinblock work, consideration should be given to plate refinishing while disassembled, even though this was not originally a high-priority item in the restoration, since the opportunity might not become available again for many years. These peripheral procedures, if overlooked, can diminish the benefit of the work that is completed.

With the above overview in mind, individual items are now evaluated to plan the restoration. These include:

finish	case assembly	bench
key bushings	wippens	action centers
bridle tapes	touchweight	action felt
back checks	hammers	dampers
regulation	damper guide rail	hammer butts
knuckles	treble bridge	bass bridge
downbearing	soundboard	ribs
strings	tuning pins	pinblock
relative pitch	voicing	pedals

There are many sub-assemblies within the items listed above that should be considered during a complete repair.

After the evaluation, parts are ordered that must be custom made for the individual piano. This would normally include bass strings that have copper or, in older pianos, iron windings; the pinblock, which must be custom cut for a proper fit to the plate; **hammers** that may have a unique set of bore coordinates; and bridges that are made from original samples. Some repair facilities have the necessary equipment to customize the above parts from stock selections. Other repair shops will send these parts to specialized supply houses for duplication. Many items used in repairs are standard parts that can be kept in the shop inventory to facilitate faster repairs. Some of these items include case **felts** and protective rubber buttons, casters, keytops, bridle tapes for vertical pianos, **damper** felts, **knuckles**, **tuning pins**, and treble music **wire** in the common sizes.

The finish work will proceed while the custom parts are manufactured or purchased. Numerous components in a piano must be refinished or cleaned before assembly. The downtime while awaiting technical parts provides an excellent window of shop time for aesthetic case refurbishing. Typically, the case and case parts such as the lid, fallboard, shelf and desk, etc., are stripped of the old finish so that a new stain and finish can be applied. The cast-iron plate is sanded to provide a suitable surface for rebronzing or relacquering in traditional gold tones. The soundboard is scraped or chemically stripped of the old finish in preparation for a new finish application.

The refinisher will encounter many conditions in the existing finish that will dictate the correct course of action. Typical defects or effects of age include bleached or faded finishes, orange peeling in the finish, flaking chips of old finish material, blistered veneer or finish, and checking finish.

Depending on the defects, the refinisher will determine if the existing finish can be improved. If the finish condition is too severely damaged, stripping and refinishing is the recommended procedure. After the components have been stripped, they will undergo successively finer grades of sanding to accept the various coatings that provide a finished appearance. Fillers, sealers, stains, and protective top coats will be applied after the prescribed sandings.

Refinishing a **grand** or vertical piano requires a sequence of steps that will provide the best possible results with an optimum use of shop time. The piano is disassembled into smaller components. Grand refinishing may include removal of the plate if pinblock work is needed for the technical restoration. Pinblocks are seldom replaced in vertical pianos since the procedures are more extensive and the lower resale value of a vertical in comparison to a grand usually does not justify the cost of replacement. These smaller case parts (sometimes called fly parts) and the case are stripped either chemically or by sanding. Hardware such as brass hinges and **pedals** will be cleaned and polished if the original parts are to be reused.

Minor repairs will often be necessary on pianos undergoing rebuilding. Case defects, such as dents in the finish and missing veneer, will be corrected. After finer grades of sandpaper have been used to prepare the surface, a stain is applied that will accentuate the grain of the wood used in the face veneer of the cabinet. Some pianos will have an opaque finish, usually white or black. These opaque finishes will not require a stain, since the grain is hidden by the pigments in the finish.

A wash coat is applied to the stained wood to raise the small fibers of the wood. These fibers are sanded to provide the smoothest surface possible. After sanding the wash coat, a filler is spread to fill the remaining open grain. The cabinet is sanded again to remove any excess filler. A sealer must be applied to seal in the filler and to prepare the wood for the finish coats.

Lacquer is the most common finish coat used today because of the fast drying time between coats and the durability of the finish. Other finishes are sometimes used depending upon the desired finished effect. These include polyester or polyurethane, varnish, and shellac. After the finish coats are applied, the finish is rubbed with steel wool or very fine sandpaper to achieve the desired sheen.

Simultaneously, the technical restoration is in process. This is usually broken down into the broad categories of action rebuilding and restringing. Soundboard replacement and pinblock replacement can be viewed as expanded procedures in restringing. Action rebuilding approaches the **touch** and **tone** capabilities of the piano in relation to the playing mechanism. The various components that comprise the action are scrutinized for weaknesses that will diminish the tone and touch of the piano. Hammers are commonly replaced with new. As a hammer is played, the felt that makes up the surface of the hammer can become compacted and distorted in shape. Older hammers can be reworked or reshaped if sufficient felt remains on the hammer surface. Shanks and flanges are also replaced if the **bushings** on which they pivot are worn beyond repair. **Wippens** are also replaced if springs are rusty or if the bushings are severely worn, though wear is usually not as advanced as in the hammer flanges.

Damper felt can become grooved, flattened, or crusty, thus necessitating replacement. The wooden damper heads are normally reused, as are the damper wires and damper flanges, though a very complete restoration will include replacement of these flanges.

After replacement of the action parts, the action is thoroughly regulated. This is the adjustment of the action parts to prescribed specifications to provide the best touch response and repetition.

The keytops are normally replaced with new ones, although older keytops made of real **ivory** can be bleached and polished to new condition. This is often desirable if the original ivory has not been chipped beyond repair. Key bushings are also replaced to prevent a loose, wobbly feel to the pianist. Balance-rail felt and front-rail felt is replaced with new and is sized with the proper cauls for optimum fit over the key pins.

The soundboard is either replaced or repaired as necessary. Repairs will include shimming or filling any cracks that may have appeared within the spruce planks. The soundboard should have a **crown** or upward bow in its surface to provide the best resonance. If the crown has flattened, the board can be replaced.

The plate is re-installed in the piano after finishing work is done. At this point bridge work and soundboard repairs have been completed and restringing can begin. In the past, the choice of string sizes was based on duplicating what was taken out of the piano during breakdown. Unfortunately, this perpetuated any **scaling** discrepancies that may have been built into the piano during manufacturing in previous decades, when the physics of piano design

was less understood. With research and the introduction of the computer, string scaling has become much more refined than in the earlier days of manufacturing. This technology has introduced the capability of taking the existing string lengths and design parameters of a given piano and developing an improved scale that is more balanced and more tunable than the original scale. This can produce a significant improvement to pianos that were manufactured in an earlier era by smaller firms that were undercapitalized and could not spend large sums on research and development.

The piano is reassembled after the stringing and subsequent **tunings**. It will undergo final **regulation** and voicing, along with final case assembly and hardware installation, before being inspected and released for shipment back to the owner.

The art of piano rebuilding has progressed, as has the art of piano building itself. With today's better understanding of piano technology, restoration of older instruments can be approached with the goal of improving the design of the original piano by utilizing the methods and data currently available. In many situations a restoration can be a viable alternative to purchasing a new instrument. Careful analysis of the existing condition and the potential of the prospective piano to be restored are the most crucial initial steps in determining the costs versus the benefits of a piano restoration.

Kent Webb

RECORDINGS

As popular as the piano was in the home and in public recitals around the turn of the twentieth-century, it appeared as a solo instrument in only a small fraction of the many recordings of that time. Most recordings featured vocal repertory and utilized the piano as an accompaniment only, because the piano registered poorly (compared to the voice) in the primitive acoustic recording process then in use. Gradual recording improvements were incorporated until 1925, when the acoustic process was replaced by the electrical process. Pianists typically had problems in making acoustic recordings, whether as accompanists or soloists. The relative placement of the recording horn to the piano was critical, otherwise fortissimo playing could suddenly "blast" and soft passages could totally vanish beneath the characteristic noisy surfaces. Even with ideal horn placement, the pianist was normally constrained to a narrow dynamic range (which interfered with freedom of musical expression). Speed control of the early acoustic recording lathes was often inconsistent, resulting in a noticeably wavering piano **tone**.

In addition to purely mechanical limitations, early piano recordings suffered from the poor conditions under which they were usually made. The studio was normally set up to accommodate vocalists, the recording horn being set up at the height of the average adult's mouth. A piano would therefore fail to register unless placed on a riser (instrumentalists and vocalists had to be quite close to the horn to be picked up). Normally an **upright piano** was set on a fairly high platform (about three or four feet above the floor) so that the back of the **soundboard** was close to and level with the recording horn. Other inhibiting factors were: the necessity to fit a performance (or section of a performance) onto a side no longer than four minutes, with the concomitant requirement to start and stop for each side; the lack of an audience to induce spur-of-the-moment inspiration; and the concern that any slip or artistic flaw would be preserved for posterity. Many pianists found making records under such conditions to be a repugnant and difficult task, some artists demanding perfection by repeating the same side over and over.

The versatile and accessible piano was the accompaniment of choice on early recordings for most of the few solo instrumentalists (especially violinists) and numerous vocalists in popular and art song. The piano was an economical orchestral-reduction substitute for operatic and oratorio arias. Accompaniment with either a piano or a small cluster of instruments was extremely difficult to record. Again, the problem was the difficulty of proper placement of the acoustic-recording horn in relation to the ensembles or the piano.

The earliest commercial recordings in the 1890s often presented local accompanists who were not famous or well-known enough to be even mentioned by name on the cylinder box or the etched label (particularly on Berliner discs). When mentioned, accompanists were sometimes ambiguously identified only by a sur-

name (e.g., "Mr. Guttinguer" on an early Pathé cylinder).

Cylinders

The first significant recordings of a famous pianist were noncommercial private two-minute wax cylinders (mentioned in letters but unfortunately lost or destroyed) recorded by the twelve-year-old prodigy pianist Josef Hofmann, made during a visit to Edison's laboratory in 1888. In 1889, **Johannes Brahms** was the first major composer known to have made a cylinder, recorded during a visit to Vienna by an agent of Edison. Although the fidelity of this important historical document (a fragment of his Hungarian Dance No. 1) was exceedingly poor (just discerning the melodic line is extremely difficult, even if the listener knows the piece), it still represents an example of the composer's performance. The announcement "Herr Brahms" is plainly audible on the cylinder (issued on LP by the International Piano Archive IPA 117).

Before mass production of cylinders was devised by means of a molding process, early cylinders (i.e., those before the turn of the century) had to be individually inscribed, which meant that mass production at that time was on a very limited scale. The process involved running a row of recording machines successively, thus necessitating that the performer repeat a composition incessantly over and over. This resulted in one copy of a specific catalog number usually being a different "take" or performance than another copy with the same catalog number. Pianists listed in Bettini catalogs who each made a dozen such semi–mass-produced cylinders around 1898 were Aimé Lachaume (playing pieces of **Beethoven**, **Chopin**, Godard, Debussy, **Liszt**, and the pianist's own works) and Joseph Pizzarello (playing Chopin, Godard, Grieg, Hoffman, Liszt, Moszkowski, Paderewski, **Schumann,** and the pianist's Gavotte). Due to both limited production and fragile construction, few of these Bettini cylinders are known to still exist even as copies.

Cylinders became more prevalent after methods were developed for mass production by means of the molding process (as distinct from the stamping process for discs). Edison cylinders, sometimes dubbed from so-called diamond discs and produced long after most competitors had abandoned cylinders for discs, frequently included pianists, but primarily in the role of accompanists. Except for a few classical favorites such as Chopin Mazurkas and Liszt's Liebestraum played by Walter Chapman, almost all of the repertory consisted of accompaniments and/or popular music, an important example being Zez Confrey playing "Kitten on the Keys." Some piano cylinders were also produced by other companies, such as Pathé (e.g., c.1905 pianist Lucien Lambert).

Discs

Few piano solo recordings were available at the turn of the century. An "Improved Gram-o-phone" catalog (the predecessor of Victor) listed only three, all recorded in 1900: "A Cork Dance," composed and played by Arthur Pryor (famous as a trombonist and bandleader rather than as a pianist); "Hello Ma Baby," an original fantasy by Frank P. Banta; and "Variations on the Mariner's Hymn," played by the composer Mr. C.H.H. Booth.

The earliest truly significant commercial solo piano records comprise about one hundred discs done by Gramophone & Typewriter Limited (commonly called G&T) recorded in major European cities from about 1900 to 1909. The repertory consisted almost exclusively of such nineteenth-century composers as Brahms, Chabrier, Chopin, Godard, Grieg, Liszt, Massenet, Mendelssohn, Rachmaninoff, Raff, Schubert, Schumann, Volkmann, and arrangements of J. Strauss and Wagner, except for a few isolated examples of eighteenth-century favorites (Handel and **Scarlatti**) originally for harpsichord.

Of particular importance on G & T were pianist-composers who recorded only their own compositions: Camille Saint-Saëns (considered the earliest-born major pianist to make commercial acoustic discs); Edvard Grieg; and Cécile Chaminade (famous for salon miniatures). The heavy predominance of nineteenth-century Romantic repertory reflected in these earliest solo-piano acoustics, with special emphasis on Chopin and Liszt along with a heavy smattering of assorted salon-type offerings, continued throughout the entire acoustic era. Many Chopin specialists emerged, such as the legendary eccentric Vladimir de Pachmann, whose antics of chatting while playing concerts brought him the nickname "the Chopinze."

Only a few world-renowned pianists made

solo Edison diamond discs, the most significant being the great composer-pianist Sergei Rachmaninoff, who in 1919 recorded Liszt's Hungarian Rhapsody No. 2 (three sides of Edison 82169–82170, incorporating an apparently improvised unpublished two-minute cadenza), Scarlatti-Tausig's Pastorale (filler of Edison 82170), **Mozart's** theme and variations from the Sonata in A Major, K. 331 (known for the Turkish Rondo, which Rachmaninoff later recorded for Victor in 1925), two Chopin waltzes, and the composer's own Polka de W.R., Barcarolle, Op. 10, and the renowned Prelude in C-sharp Minor, Op. 3. Rachmaninoff, soon thereafter lured over to record for Victor, continued to make numerous records documenting his art until shortly before his death.

Other well-known Edison keyboard artists were E. Robert Schmitz, heard in a 1914 disc of Chopin's Valse Posthume, and the great Moriz Rosenthal, heard in several 1929 experimental electric lateral-cut discs (issued on LP Mark 56, 723 and 725) of Chopin compositions, inscribed just before Edison ceased producing recordings. Particularly well-known as an accompanist, André Benoist also recorded a few solos for Edison around 1918–1920. However, Edison's catalog included mostly lesser-known pianists. The great inventor's personal, prolific staff-pianist/arranger, Ernest L. Stevens, claimed to have made over 600 records (including experimental discs) as soloist, accompanist, and ensemble pianist (trios, quartets, dance orchestras, etc.), many under pseudonyms.

Famous pianists who often recorded in Europe were heard in America on Victor, Columbia, and Brunswick discs from around 1910 to 1925. Victor's most prestigious artists were issued on the "Red Seal" label series. Pianists less celebrated at the time were relegated to the less prestigious (and less expensive) black, purple, and blue labels; these included Benno Moiseivitsch (who later advanced to red status), and "Master" Shura Cherkassky (b. 1911), "recorded at the age of eleven" (according to the labels). Although some of the repertory seems rather frivolous by today's standards (e.g., transcriptions of popular songs like "Listen to the Mocking Bird," "Silver Threads Among the Gold," "Carnival of Venice Variations," and a piano transcription of the sextette from *Lucia*, all played by Ferdinand Himmelreich), concert miniatures composed by Beethoven,

Moszkowski, Chaminade, Chopin, Gottschalk, Godard, Mendelssohn, Sinding, Liszt, Rachmaninoff, and Poldini were also issued. The first piano record of music by the then-contemporary composer Debussy ("En Bateau" played by Charles Gilbert Spross about 1911), was also relegated to a less prestigious series.

The piano concerto repertory was even more limited than solo piano in the acoustic era, the first piano concerto recording having been made by Wilhelm Backhaus of the Grieg Concerto in A Minor, Op. 16 by HMV about 1910. In the Victor catalog, the sparsely recorded concerto repertory was at first chiefly relegated to the non-red series and included just a few favorites (all in truncated form) such as the Adagio from the Grieg Concerto (Victor 70043) and Adagio from the Beethoven "Emperor" Concerto (Victor 55030), both played by Frank La Forge; the Grieg Concerto (Victor 55154–55155) and Saint-Saëns Concerto No. 2 in G Minor, Op. 22 (Victor 55160–55161), both played by a famous student of Liszt, Arthur De Greef. However, Rachmaninoff's first recording of a concerto, the famous Concerto No. 2 in C Minor, Op. 18, movements two and three only (Victor 8064–8066), recorded in 1924, did appear on the Red Seal series. Rachmaninoff's recording of this concerto was soon remade uncut as an electric in 1929. The composer's own authoritative performances of his other three concertos, as well as the Rhapsody on a Theme of Paganini, were also subsequently issued. Vassily Sapellnikoff, who had played the Tchaikovsky Concerto No. 1 in B-Flat Minor, Op. 23, under the composer, recorded it on an abbreviated late acoustic Vocalion.

After 1925, the rapidly expanding electrically recorded piano catalogs of Victor, Columbia, and other companies provided a relatively splendiferous choice of artists, genre (solo, chamber, and concerto), repertory (more than just a predominance of nineteenth-century Romantic miniatures), multiple versions, and multirecord sets. The record buyer no longer had to settle for a short, truncated movement of a lengthy work. Although the Victor Red Seal catalog tended to predominate in the U.S.A. (with some acoustic-period artists such as Rachmaninoff, Ignace Jan Paderewski, and Alfred Cortot for Victor, and Leopold Godowsky for both Columbia and Brunswick), some important lesser-known artists continued to be issued on the non-red labels, such as the recordings of pianist-composer Hans Barth, and of jazz pianists such as Hoagy Carmichael and Fats Waller. European labels such as HMV (which exchanged some releases with its American affiliate Victor), Parlophone and Odeon (some licensed to American Decca), Polydor (some licensed to Brunswick), Homocord, and others brought out important releases. Smaller companies such as Musicraft, Concert Hall, and Vox presented, especially toward the end of the 78-rpm era, innovative repertory, often by artists who later became world famous. The wellspring of electric 78s after 1925 became a virtual deluge of LPs after 1948—and compact discs after 1983—resulting in an exponential expansion of postwar pianists and piano records.

Reproducing Piano Rolls

Concurrent with acoustic recordings and early electric recordings, reproducing piano rolls provided an alternative means for capturing and playing back piano performances. The **reproducing piano**, not a mere mechanical device like a music box and distinctively different from a **player piano** or **Pianola**, was designed with the intent to play back the notes, rhythm, dynamics, and tonal characteristics captured in a pianist's performance. The pianist performed on a specially equipped piano that marked a master roll that later was punched and replicated for distribution (see **Reproducing Piano**).

Like modern recordings mastered on magnetic tape (but unlike a 78-rpm disc cut in one continuous take), reproducing piano rolls could be edited for wrong notes, uneven passage work, and other technical shortcomings on the part of a pianist. Furthermore, the tempo of a performance could be accelerated (or retarded) without alteration of **pitch** so that original performance tempos are suspect. Dynamics could also be unreliable. Several Josef Hofmann rolls, played back for transfer to long-playing disc, were advertised as directed and approved by the artist, who notated the score in order to guide dynamic-range manipulation by engineers tampering with the recording volume control (early 1950s LP Rondo Gold 1002).

Reproducing pianos utilizing recent scientific developments have been made in limited quantities in recent years. In the 1970s, an invention called the pianorecorder used computer digital technology to provide the means to transfer piano rolls onto magnetic tape cassettes. In the 1980s, a computer-driven record/playback system producing extremely realistic results was made available installed in **Bösendorfer** pianos.

The number of pianists and choice of repertory was much greater for reproducing rolls than for acoustic discs. Although some pianists made rolls for more than one company, some performances appeared on more than one brand of roll. According to Sitsky, some rolls listed in manufacturer catalogs are known only as listings and are not actually known to exist. Many of the same pianists who made acoustic and early electric recordings also made reproducing rolls.

Reproducing piano rolls were made by numerous composers. Carl Reinecke (1824–1910) was the earliest-born significant composer to make any type of recording (rolls only, not cylinders or discs). Most composers who made recording rolls tended to commit to rolls primarily their own works, both original piano compositions and transcriptions of orchestral and vocal works. The composer's rendition, even if reduced to a piano version, provided at least some valuable clues as to performance practice. A few composers, such as Sergei Rachmaninoff, and particularly Aaron Copland and Igor Stravinsky, made numerous analog recordings as pianist and conductor, solidly documenting their interpretive intents.

Reproducing rolls were not exclusively solo performances, since some famous pianists committed duets to rolls. Examples listed in catalogs include Alfredo Casella and Ottorino Respighi playing a transcription of "Fountains of Rome," and Harold Bauer and Ossip Gabrilowitsch playing the Arensky Waltz (originally for two pianos but arranged for one reproducing piano) from The Suite, Op. 15 (the original two-piano version was recorded as an electric disc Victor 8162).

Numerous rolls can be heard and studied from transfers onto commercial recordings. Although a few 78-rpm transfers were issued by American Decca, the first large sampling was a five-LP anthology (**Welte**-Mignon material recorded under adverse conditions just after World War II) by Columbia (ML4291–ML4295). Several record labels devoted exclusively to such transfers were Distinguished, Welte Treasury, and Klavier. Major classical labels that issued important roll releases included Argo, Oiseau-Lyre, Telefunken, and Everest. Quality of the roll-to-disc transfers varied considerably, depending on the quality of the instruments and the skill of the piano technicians even more than on the quality of tape, disc, or CD recording techniques. Comparisons can be made of some pianists who recorded the same work on disc and roll. One example is the magnificent pair of performances of the Schulz-Evler paraphrase of Strauss's Blue Danube Waltz played by Josef Lhévinne. The electric disc (Victor 6840) compares very favorably with the **Ampico** roll (issued on Argo DA 41) although it is a slightly different and longer version. Reproducing rolls and their recorded transfers, so readily available to students and scholars, should not be forgotten or summarily dismissed, since they are an important source of information to be weighed in the study of historic performance practice.

Performance Practice

Time constraints of acoustic 78-rpm sides posed a major limitation to early piano recordings. Because early acoustic records were one sided, works or movements longer than four minutes, if recorded at all, were often truncated. The few longer works, e.g., sonatas, normally appeared as one movement renditions, typically truncated. That repeats were seldom observed (except *da capo* repeats) would thus not provide a reliable clue as to whether repeats were observed in concert. Relatively few of the late acoustics (i.e., after about 1920) even devoted both sides of a double-sided disc to one composition; most were couplings of different works issued earlier as single-sided discs.

Truncations did not merely consist of omitting repetitious sections. Beethoven's 32 Variations in C Minor, recorded in 1925 by Rachmaninoff, utilized two sides but was still truncated, since six variations were omitted. The early acoustic recordings of Mendelssohn's Andante and Rondo Capriccioso, Op. 14 as recorded by Maria Roger-Miclos (Fonotipia 39256, c.1905), by Josef Hofmann (Columbia A 6078, c.1915), and by Alfred Cortot in an early 1920s recording (Victor 74810), all entirely omit the twenty-six-measure lyrical "andante" introduction. (Roger-Miclos also omits thirty measures just before the broken octave coda.) In comparison, Hofmann's 1913 Welte reproducing roll (3031) is uncut and includes even the andante opening. Tempos, especially if fast and scrambled, were as likely dictated by side time limits as by artistic conception. Most truncations were well-planned to sound as inconspicuous as possible, but the Louis Diémer disc of Chopin's Nocturne in D-flat Major, Op. 27, No. 2 (G & T 35544 c.1903) finishes before the piece finishes, with the last measures conspicuously missing! Record companies in the electric era were fortunately free to record more lengthy compositions that required two sides or even two or more records.

Conversely, presentation of a composition was on rare occasions expanded or markedly varied. Because Eugene Goosens's Casperle Theatre (The Punch and Judy Show, Op. 18, No. 6 from Kaleidoscope), a brief, sprightly, almost avant garde half-minute work, would not sufficiently fill a disc's side, the recording by Eugene d'Albert (Deutsche Grammophon B 27045 reissued on LP Veritas VM 110) repeats this miniature after the recording technicians (and perhaps the pianist?) provide some prominently audible applause and laughter. The recording by Harold Bauer of Brahms's Waltzes, Op. 39, Nos. 15 and 16 (Schirmer Records 2004 reissued on LP Veritas VM 108) repeats No. 15 to create the effect of an ABA structure.

Performances from the 78 era (pre-1948 electrics and especially pre-1925 acoustics) provide significant and reliable clues (compared with written accounts, such as letters or reviews) to the performance practices of the late nineteenth-century. Though the mature artists who performed on 78s did not totally replicate the approaches they had been taught or the performances they had heard in their formative years, they certainly reflected these influences in their own personal styles.

Early twentieth-century piano recordings frequently present aspects of style and execution that stand out as striking (sometimes even exaggerated or eccentric) to late-twentieth-century ears. These stylistic aspects include significant modifications and variants from the score: adding passage work, interpolating measures or cadenzas, rolling chords, exaggerating rubatos, changing tempos and rhythms, and introducing pronounced retards and accelerandos. Such original touches are today considered mannerisms and are generally perceived as old-fashioned.

Awesome, if not perfect, digital command

(even without the use of magnetic tape, which was developed around the end of the 78-rpm era and which could be spliced to artificially create a note-perfect recording in the LP era) was often demonstrated on these early piano records, although characteristics such as beauty, originality, spontaneity, nuance, and style were more highly valued than merely playing all the notes accurately.

Historical Reissues

Numerous long-playing and compact-disc reissues and first issues have been made of historical piano recordings. For example, RCA and its budget subsidiaries RCA Camden and RCA Victrola have provided a significant sampling of the vast Victor heritage. The most monumental single release by RCA was the complete known extant recorded performances by Sergei Rachmaninoff in five volumes (fifteen LPs issued about 1973), which included some test pressings issued for the first time. This has been recently reissued (1992) on ten CDs. Other commercial labels, particularly Veritas, Rococo, Pearl, Opal, and "Music and Arts," have made available significant historical materials, as have the non-profit releases bearing the labels of the International Piano Archives at Maryland (IPAM) (previously known as the International Piano Archive [IPA] and prior to that as the International Piano Library [IPL]). Source material other than early commercial cylinders and discs includes private recordings (concerts and even parties) and off-the-air dubbings of broadcasts (often lovingly saved for posterity by amateur home recordists in the 1930s and 1940s). All of these have resulted in extremely significant piano recordings being issued for the first time on LP and CD that were captured long before the LP era (pre-1948).

Examples of such important historical offerings include the private (and only known recording) cylinder by Brahms already mentioned and one by Isaac Albéniz (two improvisations recorded in 1903), both issued on IPA 109. Privately recorded concert performances have also seen the first light of day on LP and CD, such as Josef Hofmann's "Golden Jubilee" concert on 28 November 1937 to commemorate the fiftieth anniversary of his American debut (IPA 5001–5002), which featured romantic solo works and a grand performance of the Piano Concerto No. 4 in D Minor, Op. 70 by Anton Rubinstein (with whom Hofmann privately studied as a prodigy). Percy Grainger, on IPA 508, performed two versions of the Grieg Concerto in A Minor, Op. 16 (in 1945 and 1956), which included the commercial 1908 cadenza excerpt (G & T 5570) made only a few years after Grieg coached the young performer Grainger in its interpretation. Paderewski's Polish compatriot and student Sigusmund Stojowski (who also studied with Diémer) played Stojowski and Chopin on a recording obtained from a 1944 broadcast (IPA 115). Some commercially recorded discs not issued at the time for various reasons, such as poor sound or rejection by the artist, were eventually issued, including Josef Hofmann's 1935 RCA test pressings (LP Victrola VIC 1550). Reissues, if broadly defined, are not limited to LPs and CDs, since numerous early single-sided acoustic discs were frequently reissued later as double-sided acoustic offerings; some acoustics were even reissued as electric 78s.

Many long-playing issues of historical piano cylinders and 78s have unfortunately long since been deleted and are very difficult to obtain. Nonetheless, since the originals (such as the early piano G & Ts, some not even available in major archives) are exceedingly rare or even unique, LP (and currently CD) issues provide an opportunity and great service to pianists, musicologists, and others who wish to hear and study performance style and traditions of the past. In addition they insure the preservation and survival of these notable performances and interpretations.

In conclusion, pianists who recorded at the turn of the century rarely hesitated to infuse their playing with personal ideas and they interpolated liberties in the grand nineteenth-century romantic tradition. Succeeding generations of pianists gradually sought a new approach to displaying musicianship, by demonstrating how precisely an artist could adhere to the printed score. Ironically, many older scores used by recording artists were typically over-edited, with misleading indications when compared with the autograph or urtext scores of today. Currently, pyrotechnical display generally has to be executed with precision to be considered acceptable. Early piano recordings are a link with the past and came at a gradual transitional period that shifted from a freer individualistic style to a generally more uniform interpretation of standard repertory. The

expanded availability of and exposure to records, radio, and video formats has contributed significantly to homogenizing interpretative style while at the same time it enlightens present and future generations by giving them glimpses of older musical tastes and traditions.

Steven Permut

Bibliography

Basart, Ann P. *The Sound of the Fortepiano: A Discography of Recordings on Early Pianos.* Berkeley, time. Cal.: Fallen Leaf Press, 1985.

Capes, S.J. "Early Pianoforte Records." *British Institute of Recorded Sound Bulletin* No. 3 (Winter, 1956):13–19.

Crutchfield, Will. "Brahms by Those Who Knew Him." *Opus.* Vol 2, No. 5. (August 1986): 12–21, 60.

Dubal, David. *The Art of the Piano: Its Performers, Literature, and Recordings.* New York: Summit Books, 1989.

Holcman, Jan. "The Honor Roll of Recorded Chopin, 1906–1960." *Saturday Review.* 43 (27 February 1960): 44–45, 61–62.

———. "Liszt in the Records of his Pupils." *Saturday Review.* (23 December, 1961): 45–46, 57.

International Piano Archives at Maryland. Catalog of the Reproduction Piano Roll Collection. International Piano Archives at Maryland, College Park, Md.: University of Maryland, 1983.

Methuen-Campbell, James. *Catalogue of Recordings by Classical Pianists.* Vol. 1: *Pianists Born to 1872.* Chipping Norton, Oxfordshire: Disco Epsom, 1984.

———. *Chopin Playing: From the Composer to the Present Day.* New York: Taplinger Pub. Co., 1981.

———. "Early Soviet Pianists and Their Recordings." *Recorded Sound.* No. 83. (January, 1983):1–16.

Sitsky, Larry. *The Classical Reproducing Piano Roll: A Catalogue-Index.* 2 vols. New York: Greenwood Press, 1990.

Wodehouse, Artis Stiffey. "Early Recorded Pianists: A Bibliography." D.M.A. Thesis, Stanford University, 1977.

REGULATION

Regulation is the adjustment of the individual components of a piano **action** to maintain or improve the playability of the instrument. A piano is designed with certain criteria for lever mechanics and action geometry that optimizes the **touch** response for the pianist. To accu-

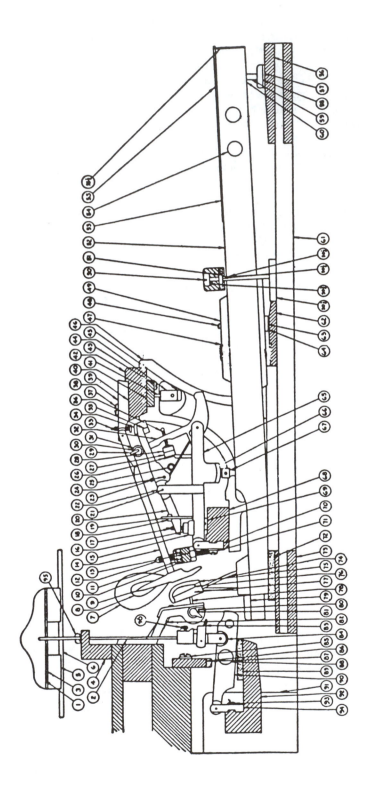

Section of Baldwin Grand Piano Action

1 Damper head
2 Damper wire
3 Damper head trim felt
4 Damper guide rail
5 Damper felt
6 String
7 Hammer outer felt
8 Hammer under felt
9 Hammer molding
10 Hammer rail
11 Hammer rail cloth
12 Hammer rail support prop
13 Hammer rail support regulating nut
14 Hammer shank
15 Repetition button felt
16 Repetition lever regulating button
17 Repetition lever regulating screw
18 Repetition hook felt
19 Repetition lever stop hook
20 Repetition lever
21 Bushing cloth and center pin
22 Support flange for repetition lever
23 Repetition spring regulating screw
24 Cord for repetition spring
25 Repetition spring
26 Jack stop spoon
27 Jack regulating button felt
28 Jack regulating button
29 Knuckle insert
30 Knuckle under cushion
31 Knuckle leather
32 Jack
33 Drop or repetition screw
34 Drop or repetition screw cloth
35 Jack cushion felt
36 Jack regulating screw
37 Hammer flange screw
38 Hammer flange
39 Hammer rail friction covering
40 Let-off rail
41 Let-off dowel wire
42 Hammer flange rail
43 Let-off rail screw
44 Let-off dowel
45 Let-off dowel cloth
46 Action bracket
47 Key button
48 Balance rail pin
49 Key button bushing (not shown)
50 Key strip
50 1/4 Key strip prop
50 1/2 Key strip prop fibre nut
50 3/4 Key strip prop brass nut
50 7/8 Key strip prop block
51 Key strip felt
52 Key
53 Ivory tail
54 Key leads
55 Ivory head
55 1/2 Celluloid front
56 Front rail
57 Front rail paper punching
58 Front rail cloth punching
59 Front rail pin
60 Key bushing (not shown)
61 Key frame
62 Balance rail
63 Balance rail cloth punching
64 Balance rail paper punching
65 Wippen
66 Capstan block cloth
67 Capstan screw
68 Wippen flange rail
69 Wippen rail screw
70 Wippen flange
71 Wippen flange screw
72 Key frame cloth
73 Back rail
74 Back check wire
75 Back check leather
76 Back check felt
77 Back check head
78 Sostenuto pull finger
79 Damper lever lifting felt
80 Bushing for sostenuto bracket
81 Sostenuto rod
82 Sostenuto rod bracket
83 Sostenuto lever lip
84 Damper lever wire flange
85 Damper stop rail screw
86 Damper stop rail
87 Damper lever stop rail felt
88 Lead weight for damper lever
89 Damper lever board felt
90 Damper lever
91 Damper lever board support block
92 Damper lever board
93 Damper lever flange screw
94 Damper lever flange
95 Damper guide rail bushing
96 Damper wire screw

rately accomplish regulation, a technician must perform the adjustments in a proper sequence. However, even the correct sequencing of the work does not eliminate repetition of certain steps. To better understand regulation, the transfer of motion in a piano action should be understood.

The following steps describe the **grand piano** action. However, the vertical action is similar in many ways and the same principles apply. Certain components are omitted in a vertical action and the force of gravity as applied to a grand action is simulated in a vertical action by springs.

Figures in parentheses refer to the illustration accompanying this article.

1. The **key** (52) is depressed by the finger.

2. The back of the key and **capstan** (67) push up on the **wippen** arm(65).

3. The wippen arm pushes the **jack** (32) and **repetition lever** (20) upward.

4. The jack and repetition lever push the **hammer** and shank (7,14) toward the **string**.

5. When the key is depressed to the halfway point, the **felt** on the back of the key (79) starts to pick up the **damper** assembly (90,1).

6. When the hammer is $1/16$" away from the string, the repetition lever and jack simultaneously contact the **drop** screw (33) and **let-off** button (44). From this point the hammer is moving toward the string on its own inertia. Without this **escapement** the hammer would block against the string and repetition would be greatly hindered.

7. The hammer hits the strings and rebounds, checking against the **back check** (77) at approximately $5/8$" from the strings while at the same time pushing down and depressing the repetition lever (20).

8. As the key is released, the spring of the repetition lever (25) raises the hammer assembly (7) to allow the jack (32) to return under the **knuckle**(31). The pianist can repeat the note as soon as the jack is back in position under the knuckle.

9. As the key is returned to its up (at-rest) position the damper assembly is allowed to fall down onto the string, thus stopping the vibration of the string.

The events described above should happen in the time it takes to play a staccato note. A good grand piano should be able to perform this sequence eight times per second with no difficulty at all.

There are numerous steps involved in regulating a piano. Most of the regulating process should be performed in a prescribed sequence. For fine regulating however, many procedures will be repeated until the touch response is fine tuned to performance specifications.

Before an action can be regulated the technician must be sure that all the action components are working properly; this requires a thorough check for broken or badly worn parts. Many assemblies in an action contain felt between contact points to eliminate noise. Sometimes this felt becomes too compressed to be regulated. Replacement of the felt is then necessary to assure a professional regulation.

The preliminary work includes checking the **keyframe** for warpage, cleaning the **keybed** of excessive dust and debris, hammer filing and shaping to remove excessive grooves caused by accumulated playing time, action center pin lubrication or **repinning** to attain the proper friction, and checking the tightness of action assembly screws for proper torque. At this point the action is ready for regulation.

Regulation is then accomplished with the following steps: Figures in parentheses refer to the illustration accompanying the article.

Bedding the keyframe (61). The keys must have a firm foundation to rest on but at the same time not have too much friction present to inhibit the sliding of the action that is necessary for **una corda** playing that is activated by the soft pedal. The adjustment of the keyframe to keybed relationship is adjusted by key-glides located on the underside of the keyframe. These allow the weight of the action to rest on polished metal contact points, thus keeping friction at a minimum.

Centering the hammers under the strings. All hammers must equally contact the unison strings when played. Hammers that are off center can produce an unclear tone in comparison to the rest of the piano.

Spacing the repetition levers. The transfer of motion in the action will lose efficiency if the repetition levers are not squared under the hammer shank and knuckle.

Squaring, leveling, and spacing keys. The keys should appear evenly spaced and level to help provide a consistent note-to-note touch. Key height can be referenced from the keybed or, with some manufacturers, the floor. Usually naturals (white keys) are leveled first, and sharps (black keys) are leveled a specified height above the white keys.

Setting the key dip. The natural keys on modern pianos should depress .400"± .025". The key **dip** is critical to pianists. If this depth is too shallow the pianist will feel that there is insufficient power in the touch. If the touch is too deep the repetition of notes will be slowed. This step is also called "laying the touch."

Aligning the jacks to the knuckle. The jack should rest so that the back side of the jack lines up with the wood molding of the knuckle. If the jack is set too far back it will hang up on the knuckle due to excessive friction and not allow a note to repeat as quickly as possible.

Adjusting the wippen repetition spring. The wippen arm tension is controlled by a repetition spring that assists the wippen arm in raising the hammershank to a point where the jack can position itself back under the knuckle quickly. This repetition feature is perhaps the innovation in piano action designs that heralded the modern grand action in use today.

Adjusting jack height. The jack top must rest slightly ($1/_{64}$") below the surface of the repetition lever to permit the jack to reposition itself under the knuckle.

Adjusting let-off. The jack heel or protrusion contacts the let-off button when the hammer is $1/_{16}$" away from the string. This prevents the hammer from blocking against the string. Let-off is set as close as possible so that the pianist can retain control of the hammer movement as long as possible. Momentum carries the hammer the final distance to the string.

Setting hammer blow. The hammers are set a prescribed distance from the string. This adjustment is made by adjusting the capstan screw at the back of the key. Normal blow distance for grands is $1^7/_8$". Vertical pianos range from $1^5/_8$" to $1^7/_8$" normally.

Checking aftertouch. **Aftertouch** is the amount of distance the key moves downward after the jack and wippen have ceased directly pushing the hammer to the string. If the hammer blow distance is set correctly and the key dip is correct, the aftertouch should be from .025 to .060". Absence of aftertouch will convey a feeling of inadequate power to the pianist.

Setting hammer drop. The drop screw is adjusted so that the wippen arm will not push the hammer to the string after the let-off point has been set. Without the drop screw the wippen arm would push the hammer against the string, causing a blocking that would initiate a cessation of the sustained note. Drop is normally set $1/_{16}$" below the let-off point. Vertical pianos do not have a drop screw since there is no repetition lever arm.

Back check adjustment. The back checks are adjusted so that on a firm blow the hammer is caught, or checked, a uniform distance from the string—usually $5/_8$". This allows the jack to slip back under the knuckle so that a repetitive note can be played without the key rising to its full at-rest position. The back checks are also adjusted for a proper angle in relation to the tail of the hammer. If the bevel of the back check is not set properly the hammer will not catch uniformly for notes played with different levels of touch from soft to hard. Severe irregularities in bevels will not allow checking at all. This results in a very bumpy feel for the pianist, with a possibility of bobbling notes.

Regulating dampers. The dampers are adjusted so that each damper picks up at the same time for the sustain **pedal** and for each key. Adjustment is usually made by positioning the damper wire a variable depth within the damper lever wire flange.

Regulating pedal trapwork. The *una corda*, or soft, pedal is adjusted so that when depressed the hammers will strike only two strings of the three-string unisons. This produces an effect of softer **tone** and enhanced harmonics. The *sostenuto* **pedal** assembly is adjusted, or in the absence of a *sostenuto*, the bass sustain is adjusted in a similar manner to the full sustain that was set during damper regulation. The *sostenuto* pedal allows the pianist to selectively choose individual dampers for tone prolongation.

After the regulation is completed the piano should conform to prescribed **touchweights** and repetition rates for that particular model. The hammers can then be voiced to suit the room acoustics or pianist's preferences. A piano that is properly regulated for its design will enable a pianist to perform with the full compass of nuances necessary for demanding music and artistic expression.

Kent Webb

RENNER, LOUIS GMBH & COMPANY

The Louis Renner firm was founded in Stuttgart, Germany, in 1882. Its headquarters and main factory are located in Stuttgart, with additional factories in Odenheim and Zeitz. Renner manufactures complete **grand** and **upright** piano **actions**, in addition to special piano parts, **hammers**, accessories, tools, and professional literature. They supply the primary piano-action components to the world's leading piano makers and piano technicians in approximately eighty countries. Combined employment in their three factories is approximately 350.

Renner piano actions are world renowned for their quality, as noted by one famous piano maker who said "the individual characteristic sound, the *touch*, of each **grand piano** is the product of cooperation between the maker of the action, the keyboard manufacturer, and the piano maker. A perfect action is the prerequisite for a fine *touch*."

Like many other major German companies, Renner began modestly but solidly. In thirty years, the number of employees reached one hundred. That was in 1911. At this time there was a change-over in the production process from belt drive to individual drive with hundreds of electric motors. By 1914, staff numbers had reached 175 and in the 1920s reached almost 400. The good reputation that the Renner action had acquired nationally and internationally prompted the expansion of the business, but all this came to an abrupt halt on 24 July 1944, when nearly all of Stuttgart was in flames following a bombing raid.

It speaks for the diligence, thoroughness, and energy of the owners, and for the extreme loyalty of the employees, that production was restored in 1948 with the same high quality as before. Output increased rapidly, aided by continual investment in state-of-the-art manufacturing equipment, and the company quickly regained its position at the top of a global market. Stuttgart was also the source of new developments. With the change in the living-space situation in postwar Germany there came the trend towards upright pianos. To cope with this trend, Renner developed a new action for uprights at the start of the 1960s that set new standards in **touch** and perfection. This action was to serve as a model for new developments in many countries.

The Odenheim factory was added in 1974. A third factory was established in 1991, following the reunification of Germany, and is located in Zeitz (near Leipzig). The parts department and additional factories have become important divisions of Louis Renner. The astonishing parts-catalog is highly valued in the trade.

The most important materials for the production of piano actions are woods (white beech, red beech, birch, oregon, mahogany, kotibe, and bubinga), **felt** (Renner uses seventy-five felt and cloth specifications), deerskin, and **wire** goods.

Lloyd W. Meyer

REPETITION ACTION

See Actions; Erard, Sébastien.

REPETITION LEVER

Before the nineteenth-century, **grand piano** mechanisms were such that the **key** had to rebound completely before another forte (loud) blow could be struck. This limited the expressive possibilities of the piano, especially in rapid musical passages of varying volume. In 1821, the French piano maker **Sébastien Erard** patented the repetition lever. Instead of relying on the **jack** only, this spring-loaded lever supported the **hammer** *away* from the jack, allowing the jack to reposition itself more efficiently. Thus, repetition was possible with the key in any position. The repetition lever is also called the "**balancier.**"

See also Actions; Erard, Sébastien.

Philip Jamison, III

REPINNING

Repinning is the term used for the replacement of a piano's center pins. Every hinged segment of the piano **action** pivots upon a metal pin. These may corrode or become loose and require replacement. Pins that fit too tightly slow the speed with which a note may be repeated. Pins that are too loose cause parts to move irregularly, thus producing excessive wear and unwanted noise.

Repinning also refers to the installation of **tuning pins** of a larger diameter in order to provide a tighter fit and prevent slipping.

Philip Jamison, III

REPRODUCING PIANO

The reproducing piano is a self-playing or automatic pneumatically operated piano that can, when using special reproducing piano rolls, reenact the **touch** and expression of the pianist who made that roll. A reproducing piano roll can be described as a recording of an actual pianist's interpretation that, when played back, will reenact that performer's original performance.

Developed from the ordinary **player piano**, the precursor of the reproducing piano was the **expression piano**, which actually remained in production as a cheap form of artistic interpretation instrument well into the 1920s.

The first successful reproducing piano was the **Welte**-Mignon invented by Karl Bockisch and Edwin Welte and produced in Freiburg, Germany in 1904. The Welte reproducing system, which produced the various shades of piano playing by the careful adjustment of the suction levels in the piano's expression mechanism, was **patented** and formed the basis of all the reproducing pianos that were made subsequently.

While many makers produced reproducing pianos, the four most successful ones that followed the Welte were the DEA, introduced in 1905, and the Triphonola of 1918, both made by the Ludwig **Hupfeld** firm of Leipzig, Germany. Then came the Philipps Ducanola produced in Frankfurt, Germany, in 1909. But by far the most common of the trademarks were Aeolian's **Duo-Art**, manufactured in the United States in mid-1913, followed by the **American Piano Corporation's Ampico**, first marketed in the same year.

Many famed artists of the time made reproducing piano rolls of their performances. All the makes operated in a different way, which meant that a roll cut for one make of reproducing piano, such as the **Welte**-Mignon, would not play on any other make of reproducing piano.

However, in order to extend their respective catalogues of rolls quickly, several of the makers, notably Welte, Aeolian, and Ampico, pooled their artists' recordings, licensing other makes to reprocess the rolls to suit their own reproducing systems.

The final stage of development in the reproducing piano was undertaken in England shortly before World War II and at a time when the demand for the reproducing piano had virtually disappeared. Working for the British arm of the Aeolian Company at Hayes, Middlesex, engineer and inventor Gordon Iles developed the IST (Isolated Instantaneous Theme) control, which was to confirm the Duo-Art as the most faithful piano-performance recording system. In this, refined pneumatic control overcame the difficulty of accenting one or more notes in, for example, a chord. Only two pianos were made: one was destroyed by enemy bombing during World War II and the second disappeared.

In recent years, some doubt has been cast on the absolute fidelity of the reproducing piano and its rolls. It has long been accepted that the reproducing piano must be in first-rate condition and proper adjustment to re-perform the roll properly, but a question remains as to how much additional work was done on the master roll between its cutting on the master recording piano and its ultimate issue. Besides the removal of wrong notes and the insertion of missing ones, roll editors were known to "adjust" playing dynamics and pedalling where they felt the original artist might be lacking. In certain cases this was permissible, but it can no longer be determined how much pianist and how much editor went into the making of each roll.

See also Expression Piano.

Arthur W.J.G. Ord-Hume

Bibliography

Bowers, Q. David. *Encyclopedia of Automatic Musical Instruments.* Vestal, N.Y.: Vestal Press, 1972.

Ord-Hume, Arthur W.J.G. *Pianola—History & Development.* . . . London: Allen & Unwin, 1984.

RESTORATION OF EARLY PIANOS

The difficulties involved with restoring antique pianos and returning them to playing condition are considerable. Very little is known about the special tools, building methods, and materials used by early builders, particularly during the first hundred and fifty years of piano history, when the wood-framed **fortepiano** reached an extraordinary state of perfection. Replacement materials, including **hammers**, **dampers**, **action** parts, and even suitable **strings** are usually not available. In the case of very early pianos, which do not incorporate cast-iron **frames** and often have hammers made of laminated **leather**, both the restorer of original instruments and the replica builder face considerable challenges in their pioneering attempts to duplicate the craftsmanship and the materials of the original builders.

The large number of early fortepianos that have survived, often with original strings, hammers, **keyboards**, and **case finish**es, is a tribute to both the excellent skill and high-quality materials used by period builders. After an interruption of over one hundred years in the building of fortepianos, it is not surprising that modern replica makers and restorers must struggle to recreate the mastery of builders who grew up in a flourishing tradition of competitive hand craftsmanship. The skill of famous builders such as the **Stein** family, **Anton Walter**, **Conrad Graf**, and the **Streichers** lives on in their instruments, but their methods were not adequately described in writing at the time. Famous makers obviously wanted to maintain their competitive edge and they jealously guarded their secret building procedures.

Working with antique pianos requires an enormous amount of thought and care. Every instrument presents its own unique problems and challenges. An antique instrument must not be approached as though it were inherently technically inferior to the modern piano. All attempts to "modernize" an antique piano using new **soundboards**, **pinblocks**, modern music **wire**, and oversize **felt** hammers and dampers in place of the original materials, must be assiduously avoided. An antique instrument is reduced in importance in direct proportion to the number of original parts that have been removed. One of the definitions of the noun "restoration" is "to put back into nearly or quite the original form." The task of the restorer who hopes to enhance the instruments in his care is to retain and preserve as much of the original instrument as possible.

Increasingly, the curators of museums and musical instrument collections are beginning to question whether the rare musical instruments in their trust should be restored or played at all. Clumsy restoration often diminishes the historical value of an instrument, and playing them inevitably results in deterioration and wear and tear on original parts. Our right to hear the sound of historic instruments often conflicts with the obligation museums have to preserve the instruments for the scholars, researchers, and replica builders of the future. Museums are full of instruments that have been greatly reduced in historical value through attempts to restore them and make them play.

Age is not the only consideration that determines if an instrument should receive special consideration. Any piano, particularly if it has special qualities such as an elaborate art case, limited production, manufacture by a famous maker, unusual technical features, and outstanding musical qualities, is potentially historically important. Instruments owned by famous musicians have particular importance. The **Broadwood, Erard**, and Graf fortepianos owned by **Beethoven**, the **Pleyel** owned by **Chopin**, Paderewski's **Steinway**, and Bartok's **Bechstein** are all obviously important instruments, as they provide valuable information about the nature of piano sound in different generations. Many pianos built in the last fifty years are potentially important. The piano restorer must treat such instruments with great caution in order to preserve the intrinsic value of the instruments as historical documents. A musical instrument can be regarded both as a work of art and as a significant historical artifact because of what it can tell us about the history of culture, science, and technology.

Several important considerations enter into the question of whether an instrument should or should not be restored and made playable. The age, condition, and rarity of the instrument are of foremost consideration. If the instrument is one-of-a-kind and still in original condition, every caution must be taken to preserve and conserve the original parts. The goals in restoring a rare antique have to include preserving the instrument in original condition, saving, documenting, and photographing anything that has to be removed, and protecting the instrument against further deterioration. Not every instrument can or should be made playable. In other circumstances the restoration may not result in 100 percent satisfactory playability. Above all, the original components of the instrument, to the extent that they are still present, must be preserved and documented.

The work of a responsible restorer is always accompanied by a written report, supported by photographs, drawings, measurements, and a detailed explanation of the procedures used in the restoration. Moreover, any alterations should, if possible, be rendered reversible by using water-soluble animal glues. It is also incumbent upon the restorer to offer suggestions for the continued preservation and maintenance of rare instruments.

The use of a skillfully made replica instrument instead of a restored original has numerous advantages. Replicas are usually less expensive and they can be transported and used in situations and environments that would be unsuitable for historical instruments.

The motivation for the current fortepiano revival is that we should be allowed to hear the music of **Mozart**, Beethoven, Schubert, and others on those instruments the composers originally intended. Although replica builders are rapidly improving in their attempts to recreate the skill of period makers, it is still questionable whether modern replicas or restored original instruments are really as good as the new instruments used by Classic and Romantic period composers.

Edward E. Swenson

Bibliography

Barnes, John. "Does Restoration Destroy Evidence?" *Early Music* 7 (1980): 153–159.

Hellwig, Friedemann. "Restoration and Conservation of Historical Musical Instruments." In *Making Musical Instruments*. Edited by Charles Ford. New York: Pantheon Books, 1979.

O'Brien, G.G. "Attitudes to Musical Instrument Conservation and Restoration." *Bulletin of the Fellowship of Makers and Researchers of Historical Instruments* 3 (1976): 15–18.

Plenderleith, H. J., and A.E.A. Werner. *The Conservation of Antiquities and Works of Art: Treatment, Repair and Restoration*. London: Oxford University Press, 1971.

Swenson, Edward E. "Restoring Antique Pianos, Part 1." *Piano Technicians Journal* 31 (January 1988): 23-28.

———. "Restoring Antique Pianos, Part 2: Documentation." *Piano Technicians Journal* 31 (March 1988): 24–29.

———. "Restoring Antique Pianos, Part 3: Cleaning and Conservation Techniques." *The Piano Technicians Journal* 31 (May 1988:) 24–29.

———. "Restoring Antique Pianos, Part 4: Making Looped Strings, Clamping and Woodworking Techniques." *The Piano Technicians Journal* 31 (August 1988): 37–40.

———. "Ein Glücksfall: Ein Fortepiano von Conrad Graf." *Concerto, Das Magazin für alle Musik*. (March 1988): 10–16.

RIBS

Ribs are structural components, normally made of spruce or other light woods, that are attached to the **soundboard** of a piano on the side opposite the **strings** and **bridges**. On a **grand piano** they can be seen underneath the piano. On a vertical piano they are found on the back.

Ribs are commonly designed and manufactured as thin square strips of varying lengths with tapered ends. They are glued to a soundboard at an angle of approximately ninety degrees to the spruce planks of a soundboard to strengthen the side-to-side gluing of the individual soundboard planks. This is necessary since the normal soundboard thickness is only $3/8$", which is insufficient glue surface to insure a long life for the soundboard.

Ribs also help to insure the **crown** of the soundboard. Piano soundboards have a crown, or convex curvature, toward the strings. Ribs are sometimes manufactured with a corresponding curvature to assist in maintaining the crown. Ribs that are not pre-crowned develop a crown through the clamping process.

In this process the floor of the rib press has a crown that matches the designed crown for a particular soundboard. The soundboard is laid onto the press with the ribs arranged in a prescribed pattern. After the glued ribs have dried in the clamp the soundboard assembly can be removed, with a pronounced crown as a stable characteristic.

See also Soundboard.

Kent Webb

RIM

The rim is the curved wooden casework of a **grand piano**, having a **spine**, **tail**, and **bentside**. In order to force wood into the familiar sinuous form of a grand piano, the builder must first laminate thin sheets of wood (veneers) into a long, flexible slab. Often the laminated rim consists of up to twenty-two layers of eastern rock maple glued together to a thickness of eight centimeters. The final veneer is usually a piece of mahogany and is the wood that will be **finish**ed to match the entire **case** of the piano.

The multi-laminated rim slab is attached to a cast-iron press (shaped like a grand piano) and is held in place by vises and clamps. Usually the rim remains clamped to the form overnight so that the glue can dry. It is next removed from the iron form (by at least four workers) and set aside to cure, or settle in place, for ten weeks. Some builders today use high-frequency electrical current to fuse the laminated wood in less than thirty minutes.

Peggy Flanagan Baird

ROCHEAD AND SON

Andrew Rochead worked as a musical instrument maker in Edinburgh, Scotland, between about 1793 and 1818. His prior training and professional life are unclear: he may have made spinets for a local dealer, Neil Stewart (fl.c. 1759–1805).

During the 1790s, Rochead worked from premises in the Old Town ("back of the weighhouse, Castlehill"). In 1804, he took his son, John, into partnership. As Rochead and Son, a shop was opened in the fashionable New Town, at no. 4 Greenside Place. The firm enjoyed considerable success; by 1808 the partners were appointed "Musical Instrument Makers to his Royal Highness the Prince of Wales." Manufacturing continued until 1818, when the partnership fell victim to a widespread economic slump.

Rochead probably produced over 1,000 pianos. These were mostly **squares**, although after 1813 six-octave **grands** were also advertised. The changing appearance of the firm's instruments imitates the leading London makers. However, in technical details, considerations of economy took precedence over those of modernity.

John Cranmer

ROLAND DIGITAL PIANOS

Roland is a Japanese manufacturer of a wide range of electronic musical instruments including digital pianos, portable **keyboards, synthesizers, samplers,** sequencers, and various signal-processing devices. With one of the most extensive and varied catalogs of any major electronic musical instrument maker, Roland's digital pianos are marketed under several product lines depending on the targeted consumer. The *HP* series is marketed in at least seven different models for the home consumer and educational markets. These keyboards, which incorporate onboard speakers, are built in a cabinet designed to be aesthetically appealing. The professional counterparts include the *RD* series and the *Rhodes MK* series (designed in conjunction with Harold Rhodes). Professional instruments, designed for the touring musician, are built in a more durable, portable housing. They usually require outboard amplification and speakers, but provide enhanced control over voices, signal processing, and memory.

Internally, both the consumer and professional series products utilize Roland's proprietary *Structured Adaptive Synthesis* as a basis for tone generation. This is a precise and subtle method of synthesizing (not sampling) acoustic and electronic sounds. Most of the keyboards feature eighty-eight weighted, velocity-sensitive **keys**. The **actions** in upper end models use a rotary oil damper construction that is designed to simulate the **touch** mechanism of a **concert grand piano**. Polyphonicity ranges from fourteen to sixteen voices and additional controls include brilliance, chorus, tremolo, reverb, and transposition. As usual with digital pianos, the Roland instruments include five to eight preset voices including acoustic piano, electronic piano, vibraphone, harpsichord, and clavichord. Professional instruments allow the musician to modify these presets and to store the customized voices in additional memory locations. All pianos incorporate a sustain **pedal**; some also incorporate a soft and/or *sostenuto* **pedal**. All feature full **MIDI** implementation.

See also Electronic Pianos.

Samuel S. Holland

ROLFE, WILLIAM AND SONS

The Rolfe name was associated with design innovation and self-acting pianofortes for almost a century, yet only a few examples of their work survive. The family firm of piano builders and inventors was active from around 1798 to 1889. William Rolfe (b. 1756) was a partner in the musical-instrument-making business of Culliford, Rolfe and Barrow at 112 Cheapside

(London) from around 1790 to 1797. When the partnership was dissolved in 1797, Culliford & Barrow became pianoforte and tambourine makers at Surrey Street in the Strand. William Rolfe continued at the Cheapside address as a music seller and publisher who also made pianos. In 1806 the name became "William Rolfe and Sons," and in 1813 supplementary premises were added at 28 London Wall. By the middle of the century, the business was flourishing, and in 1850 the firm moved to 61 Cheapside.

On 31 January 1797, in conjunction with Samuel Davis, William Rolfe was granted British **Patent** No. 2160 for improvements to harpsichords, **square**, and **grand pianos**. These improvements were to cater to the then increasing popularity of so-called Turkish-sounding music and included replacing the wooden **soundboard** with a "vibrating substance" of "vellum, parchment, silk, wool, hemp, flax, cotton, thread, or pasteboard, varnished, oiled, papered or otherwise rendered strong and durable." To this, membrane **pedals** and **hammers** could act to form an accompaniment, producing a "pleasing and powerful vibration swell throughout the whole instrument" (Harding, p.267). This was the earliest specification for "Turkish music" in relation to pianos, the drum mechanism being a modification of the English "single **action**," variations of which were later developed in Germany (*Prell-mechanik*). This modification is also sometimes termed the **Janissary** stop.

Square piano by William Rolfe and Sons, no. 5929 (c.1810). View of double music desk. Mobbs Keyboard Collection, Bristol, England.

Several examples of Rolfe instruments survive. Two 61-note square pianos (nos. 3117 and 3409) are in the Smithsonian Institution. A 68-note grand, c. 1798 (Bath Preservation Trust, U.K.) features a baffle (dust cover) over all except the top 19 notes, delicately painted with floral groups. A 68-note square piano, no. 4611, c. 1801 (Bath Preservation Trust) is an interesting transitional instrument, built on a framed stand, using the **John Geib** "hopper" double action, by then generally available, but still retaining the early form of whalebone-spring overdamping. Already, however, it has built on to the dust cover what was to become the Rolfe specialty: two separate music stands, one for the performer and one for the accompanist (pianist). (*See* illustration.) An extremely rare upright grand dated 1807 (Lisbon Conservatory, Portugal), with a compass of 68 notes, has the styling "Wm. Rolfe and Sons," showing that Rolfe's sons Nicholas and Thomas (?) had joined him by then, and for a time around 1820 piano **nameboards** were styled "Wm. Rolfe and Co." This first quarter of the century saw the production of elegant examples of craftsmanship. Squares from this period often have three drawers (the center one curved), deep ornamentation frets for supporting candlestick holders, and occasionally nameboards lavishly decorated with floral paintings, e.g., nos. 4811 (c. 1801) and 5397 (c. 1808); (Colt and Miall, *The Early Piano* has an illustration of another on p. 92). A printed paper label to the left of the action on no. 5829 (Mobbs Keyboard Collection, Bristol, U.K.) gives instructions in minor adjustments to the action but also appends the **stringing** gauges. The older name of "Wm. Rolfe and Sons" was revived about 1825 (e.g., square no. 8029 [c. 1830], Castle Museum, York, U.K., and **cottage piano** no. 1656 [c. 1835], Mobbs Keyboard Collection Bristol U.K.). In the latter the **music desk**, when not in use, is kept separately under the **keyboard.** At the Great Exhibition of 1851, William Rolfe showed a "two-unison common cottage piano confirming the advantages of the ordinary repetition and check or double actions; a piano in which stability, economy and excellence are the objects aimed at."

William Rolfe's son, Thomas Hall Rolfe, was closely associated with the development of the **barrel**-and-finger piano and was granted British Patent No. 5831 on 11 August 1829 for improvements to the action and design, one of which was a method of pinning barrels so that they played "piano" or "forte." These instruments were powered, when used for mechanical playing, by clockwork using the energy of a heavy weight that could be wound up to the top of the **case**. An improvement on the smaller barrel-only instruments of John **Longman**, Thomas Hall Rolfe's piano used two sets of hammers, one for manual playing and the other for mechanical playing, placed behind the soundboard and striking through a slit in the soundboard. The style was adopted later by organ- and piano-builder Theodore Charles Bates.

In 1860 Edward F. Rimbault was still able to write, "William Rolfe, the founder of a most respectable house, in being at the present day." Nevertheless, James, the son of Nicholas, became primarily a piano tuner and repairer rather than a builder. The final collapse of the firm came around 1889.

Kenneth Mobbs and
Arthur W.J.G. Ord-Hume

Bibliography

Boalch, Donald. *Makers of the Harpsichord & Clavichord, 1440–1840*. Oxford: Oxford University Press, 1974.

Ehrlich, Cyril. *The Piano: A History*. London: Dent, 1976.

Harding, Rosamond E.M. *The Piano-Forte. Its History Traced to the Great Exhibition of 1851*. Cambridge: Cambridge University Press, 1933. Reprints; New York: Da Capo Press, 1973. Old Woking, Surrey: Gresham Books, 1978.

RUSSIA AND THE COMMONWEALTH OF INDEPENDENT STATES (FORMERLY THE USSR), PIANO INDUSTRY IN

The piano industry in the former USSR is about seventy years old and has almost two centuries of prehistory. Its material foundation and technology, primarily borrowed from previous Russian piano producers, noticably changed under the political, social, and economic processes that began in Russia after the October Revolution of 1917. The principal impetus was to produce a great number of pianos, but without sufficient maintenance there were inevitable losses in quality. Technology developed only on the theoretical level. Iâkov Uchitel gives a detailed and documented survey of the piano industry in prerevolutionary Russia, as well as the organization of Soviet piano building and the development of its scientific-technical base.

Stringed keyboard instruments have been known in Russia since the end of the eighteenth-century, when harpsichords and clavichords were imported by Western builders. The great innovations of Peter the Great and of the Russian Enlightenment aroused interest in Western culture and in the spread of keyboard instruments on Russian ground. During the eighteenth-century, keyboard instruments made primarily by foreigners living in Russia were advertised and sold in Russia. Up to the beginning of the nineteenth-century many instrument builders worked in St. Petersburg. Among them were F.K. Bitsch, Iâ. Seidletz, D. Kolosov, I.A. Batov, Bär, J. Kessler, Kunst, Ludwig, Merkenberg, Ia. Pratsch, Zimmermann, Ellert, L. Kester, Schantz, A. Nechaev, and Carimatis. In Kiev, Gerstenberg, Bauer, Gerichswald, and Krestenberg were well-known names. In the nineteenth-century the cottage piano industry grew to such proportions that factory production was required.

In St. Petersburg the factory of Friedrich Diderichs (1779–1846) was founded in 1810. From 1878 it was known as "Brothers R. & A. Diderichs" and continued production until 1914. At first imitating the Viennese piano of the **Streicher** family, this firm eventually produced solid and beautiful instruments with cast-iron **frames**, straight and **cross-stringing**, **square** and **grand pianos**. In 1899, 600 pianos were produced by the Diderichs company.

The firm of Johann Friedrich Schröder (d. 1852) was founded in 1818 and closed in 1918. Compared with the Diderichs instruments, the Schröder pianos were of higher quality, largely because of the mechanization of production (applying cast-iron frames of whole-curve design and the system of "discant bell"). The Schröder firm supplied Russian and foreign customers. In 1913 it produced 1,200 instruments. The factory of Jacob Davidovich Becker (Bekker) (d. 1879), founded in 1841, produced high-quality instruments because of rigorous work procedures that included attention to detail, improved construction methods, and the utilization of innovations such as the *capo tasto* and the **Erard** repetition **action** (which Becker first introduced in Russia in 1865). The Becker firm averaged a production of 1,800 instruments a year at that time. The firm was nationalized in 1918. The piano factory of Franz

Adolf Mühlbach (founded in 1856 and closed in 1917) was a market leader in the 1880s. Mühlbach had concentrated on the production of miniature grands (**"mignon"**), which reportedly had a remarkably beautiful sound. In 1913 the firm produced 1,100 instruments. A small number of fine instruments were also built by the firms of Johann August Tischner (1774–1852) and Heinrich Hermann Lichtenthal (fl. 1828–1854). Tischner's company existed from around 1818 to 1852. Lichtenthal was the first to utilize cross-stringing and two **soundboards** in Russia. His firm began in 1840 and steadily declined from the time of his death in 1854 to the end of the nineteenth-century.

There were also other factories and workshops in St. Petersburg: H. Hentsch (1865), R. Ratke (in 1892; transferred from Derpth where his firm had been founded in 1867), the brothers W. & H. Mayer (1871), Smith & Wegener (1800), W.K. Reinhardt (1874), Hetze (1880), Leppenberg (1888), A.G. Gergens (1890), A. Rauser & A. Bitepage (1894), K. Rönish (1898), the brothers W. & I. Offenbacher (1900–1901), E. Ise (Hijs) (1903), A. Askolin (1878).

In Moscow there were about twenty firms that were well known. The principal ones were R. Besekirsky (c.1830), L. Stürzwage (1842), A. Eberg (1852), and Meybom (1865); other factories and assembly plants were A. Uslal, F.I. Detlaf & Co., A. Petrov, Hilweg, Meykov, Struiev, Sigunov, Grotrian & Lange, Wichmann, A. Kampe, F. Korezky, P. Karklin, Koch, G. Petrov, N.S. Rudko, E. Ivanovsky, A.K. Lezky, S.P. Nikovnov, and P. Jurgenson.

Pianos were also produced in Kiev—A. Strobl (1873), H.J. Mecklenburg (1876); in Kharkov—E.S. Kruschel, A. Horn, A.M. Berman (1890); in Odessa—A. Schen (1843), M. Rausch (1856); in Rostov-na-Donu—L. Adler (1880); in Saratov—M. Erichson; in Tiflis (Tbilisi)—A. Kopp (1888); in Riga—Tresselt (1871); in Revel (Tallinn)—Kreemann, Olbrei, J.H. Tust.

Before World War I Russia produced around 13,500 pianos per year. This productive base showed promise of development (especially in St. Petersburg), but after the war, two revolutions, the nationalization of industry, and the resultant economic dislocation, the piano industry in the Soviet Union came to a halt. The nation was devastated by famine, plunder, and economic disaster. In 1922, it was stated that conditions in the USSR were such that the production of musical instruments was utterly out of the question.

The former factory of Schröder (now referred to as the first USSR piano factory) was renamed after writer-politician Anatol Lunacharsky in 1922 and began the slow process of renewal by producing 100 pianos that year. From 1924 "Muspred" (founded in 1921) began to restore some of the factories, but not always for piano manufacturing. The former Becker factory resumed production in 1925, but mostly made balalaikas, accordions, guitars, and grammophones. Mühlbach (renamed "Krasniy Partisan") made only accordions.

In 1924, an amalgamation was formed consisting of the leading piano factories: Lunacharsky (formerly Diderichs), Offenbacher, Mühlbach, and Becker. The primary site was located on the Becker property. In 1927 this amalgamation was named "Krasniy Octiabr'" [Red October] and represented the largest piano-producing company in the USSR. Starting with an output of 173 instruments, it produced instrument number 350,000 in 1983. Action parts were made at the Lunacharsky plant, **felt** in the Moscow factory ("Piatiletie Octiabria"), and **tuning pins** and cloth in the Leningrad (now St. Petersburg) factory ("Krasniy Tkach"). Since 1932, the USSR has supplied its own wood for soundboards. Soundboards and **strings** were produced at the plant "Krasniy gvozdil' schik." Before World War II the Kuibyshev plant in Leningrad/St. Petersburg made cast-iron frames. Manufacturing of pianos in the USSR reached a peak in the 1930s: from 1924 to 1934, 19,731 **uprights** and grands were produced at "Krasniy Octiabr'." The enormous market demanded a greater output of instruments and for the sake of increased production, quality suffered. New factories arose in Kushelevka, Kiev (1933), Odessa (1933), Tbilisi (1931), and Borisov (c.1935). In the summer of 1941 other factories were formed in Sverdlovsk, Saratov, Ufa, Kuibyshev, Gor'ky, and other cities in the USSR, all of them assembling uprights for "Krasniy Octiabr'." In 1941 the USSR produced 10,104 pianos, most of them not of the best quality.

The solution to the problem of improving the quality of the instruments seemed to lie in forming research laboratories and preparing specialists. As early as 1928, laboratory examinations of Western piano manufacturing and the production of "Krasniy Octiabr'" were carefully compared. In 1930 a special college opened in Leningrad/St. Petersburg that dealt with this study. Finally, in 1931 research institutes in Moscow and Leningrad/St. Petersburg researched and put into practice the sciences dealing with piano making; specialists and factory workers studied and practiced the art of constructing quality uprights and grands. Research in technology, materials, and industry organization developed rapidly.

Again, the industry was curtailed because of World War II. The industry began new life at the end of 1943 when "Krasniy Octiabr'" made thirty-four pianos. By the end of 1949, the prewar level of production was again achieved, although at first there was a deficit of specialists, materials, and machinery. The technological division of "Krasniy Octiabr'" continued its forward movement with utilization of nitrocellulose varnishes, colored veneers of exotic woods, creation of new models of uprights, e.g., minipiano (whose designer S.M. Allon was also called the "father of Soviet grand pianos"). The industry flourished and factories in Rostov-na-Donu, Gor'ky, Kasan', Perm', Sverdlovsk, Kaluga, and Ivanovo built uprights and parts for grands made by "Krasniy Octiabr'."

Since 1949, grands (later also uprights) were built in Tallinn. The factory in Riga (on the base of the former Tresselt company) started active production in 1956. During the 1950s new factories were built in the suburbs of Moscow, making models named "Zaria" and "Lira." By 1966 there were fifty piano factories in the USSR. However, the market was insatiable and large united firms arose: "Kavkaz" (built by three factories in Rostov, Krasnodar, and Ordjonikidze), "Kama" (with parts built in Sarapul and assembled in Perm' and Ijevsk), "Akkord" (two factories in Kaluga), "Ural," and "Sibir'."

The construction of parts became specialized: the factory in Alatyr monopolized the production of strings up to 1970; the factory in Urasov and later the united firms called "Ural" produced cast-iron frames that previously had been made by as many as twenty factories. In 1971, fifteen factories were occupied with building metal parts, eight factories were making only actions, and four factories (instead of the former twenty seven) worked with the case. The number of small companies increased, and production again was geared towards quantity

rather than quality. Some examples of production growth: 1950—11,900 instruments; 1957—55,300; 1965—118,000; and 1968—172,310.

As for quality, laboratories in the factories of "Krasniy Octiabr'" and "Zaria," plus the new Research Institute (NIKTIMP, Moscow 1968), made their own designs, researched materials, tools, technology, etc. Innovations were put to use, e.g., high-oscillation-frequency electric contact device (which shortened the gluing time), a mechanism for pressure **tuning**, pneumatic automatons, presses. In Tashkent research was focused on the testing of wooden parts in varying climates, etc. As in other nations, piano production began to decline from 1970 to the 1980s and some of the firms began making other kinds of musical instruments.

As of 1990, there were about thirty factories in the USSR involved with the piano industry; some built parts and others actually constructed the instrument. The yearly output of the industry was approximately 120,000 pianos. The biggest producers are located in: Borisov—21,000; Chernigov—16,000; Sverdlovsk—9,200; Moscow—8,650; Leningrad/St. Petersburg—8,200; Kaluga—8,100; Moscow suburbs—6,600; Rostov-na-Donu—6,500. Piano production also continues in: Riga—5,000; Penza—4,200; Vladimir—3,250; Vyshniy Volochok—3,000; Kazan'—3,000; Krasnodar—2,500; Magnitogorsk—2,050; Alatyr—2,000; Tbilisi—2,000; Yartsevo—2,000; Krasnoiarsk—1,800; Odessa—1,500; Perm'—1,500.

The basic models assembled at most of the factories were designed by the Research Institute of NIKTIMP and utilize the technology of "Estonia" and "Krasniy Octiabr'." These basic models are: upright models 104, 110, and 120 (with various labels); the concert grands labelled "Estonia" and "Rossiya"; and the smaller grands labelled "Estonia-4," "Chaika," "Leningrad-2," and "Min'on." Export is minimal.

Sergei A. Ryiaarev

Bibliography

D'iaconov, N.A. *Roiali i pianino* (construirovanie i proizvodstvo). Moskva: "Lesnaia promyshlennost'," 1966.

D'iaconov, N.A., M.N. Fedorov, D.V. Popov, S.R. Kalinov, N.M. Uspenskii. *Materialy, primeniaemye v proizvodstve klavishnykh instrumentov*. Moskva-Leningrad, 1936.

Findeizen, Nik. *Ocherki po istoriĭ musiki v Rossiĭ s drevneishikh vremen do kontsa XVIII veka.* T.2, Moskva-Leningrad: Gosudarstvennoe izdatel'stvo, 1929.

"Issledovanie svoĭstv materĭalov dlĭa proĭzvodstva musikal'nykh instrumentov." NIKTIMP, Ministerstvo mestnoĭ promyshlennosti RSFSR, Moskva, 1981.

Katalog spetsĭal'nogo tekhicheskogo oborudovaniĭa dlĭa proĭzvodstva muzykal'nykh instrumentov. NIKTIMP, Ministerstvo mestnoĭ promyshlennosti RSFSR, Moskva, 1984.

Lelikov, V.E., and V.S. Bugrov. *Mekhanizirovannaĭa potochnaĭa linĭa dlĭa izgotovlenĭa futora pĭanino.* Ministerstvo mestnoĭ promyshlennosti RSFSR, Moskva, 1966.

"Metodicheskie materĭaly po metrologicheskomu obespechenĭu proĭzvodstva musykal'nykh instrumentov. Ministerstvo mestnoĭ RSFSR, Moskva, 1988.

"Novoe v proĭzvodstve musikal'nykh instrumentov." Ministerstvo mestnoĭ promyshlennosti RSFSR, NIKTIMP, CBNTI, Moskva, 1969, 1970, 1988.

"Osnovnye napravlenĭa razvitĭa musikal'noĭ promyshlennosti (Proĭzvodstvo klavĭshnykh instrumentov)." Ministerstvo mestnoĭ promyshlennosti RSFSR, Moskva, 1978.

Otĭugova, T., and A. Galembo, I. Gurkov. *Rozhdenie musikal'nykh instrumentov.* Leningrad: Muzyka, 1986.

Uchitel', Ĭa. *Sovetskoe fortepĭano.* Moskva-Leningrad: Muzyka, 1966.

Zimin, P. *Istorĭa fortepĭano i ego predshestvennikov.* Moskva: Muzyka, 1968.

SABEL

The Sabel Company, a Swiss piano manufacturing firm, was founded by Bonifaz Bieger (1820–1870), a German immigrant. Bieger started with a small piano workshop in Häggenswil and moved to Rorschach in 1856. After the founder's death in 1870 his three sons headed the company. The annual production of pianos grew steadily to almost 300 by 1919, when the firm was bought by Lorenz Sabel (d.1941), who had worked in the Bieger company since 1908. Under the new name of "Sabel," the production of pianos rose to 450 per year between 1920 and 1930. As with other companies, the depression and World War II brought a decline. In 1948 the firm was converted into a holding company, Sabel AG. The annual production again reached about 280 pianos from 1960 onward. The competitive market worldwide, however, forced the company to halt its production completely in 1991.

Since 1986 Sabel has harbored the Swiss piano building school, which had been moved there from Burger & Jacobi in Biel. Thus, Sabel AG is maintaining its traditional training of apprentices in a factory now geared toward repair and maintenance work. Aside from this limited engagement, Swiss piano manufacturing seems to have reached a moratorium.

See also Switzerland, Piano Industry in.

Werner Iten

Bibliography

Burkart, Josef. "Beim Klavierbauer." *Schweizerische Schreinerzeitung* 30 (26 July 1990): 691–97.

Europe Piano Atlas. Revised by H.K. Herzog, Frankfurt am Main: *Das Musikinstrument,* 4th ed., 1978.

Rindlisbacher, Otto. *Das Klavier in der Schweiz.* Bern and Munich: Francke Verlag, 1972.

Sabel Flügel- und Pianofabrik Rorschach 1842–1942 (centennial publication of the firm Sabel), 1942.

SAMPLER

A sampler is an instrument that digitally records sounds from a microphone or an audio line input and plays them back in a musically useful way. Along with **synthesizers**, samplers have provided the raw sonic materials for electronic musical instruments since the late 1970s, including drum machines, digital pianos, and various **keyboards**.

Historically there have been keyboard instruments that utilized actual analog tape loops of strings, voices, or other musical sounds. The *Mellotron* of the 1960s and 1970s was such an instrument. When a **key** was depressed, an appropriately pitched tape loop would play. This method had serious mechanical limitations, inconveniences, and reliability problems. The process of sampling, or digital recording, uses an entirely different and highly reliable principle. Instead of storing the sound wave itself, a sampler stores numbers (digits) that describe the sound wave. To do this, an incoming sound wave is measured or *sampled* at a regular time interval. As the waveform changes over time, the numbers are stored in computer memory. When a key on a sampler is depressed the process is reversed. The numbers in memory are used to reconstruct the original waveform. The quality of a sampler depends primarily on how fast it can record changes over time, the sampling frequency, and the amount of computer memory and processing capability the instrument has onboard. While actually functioning as sound recorders, rather than synthesizers, samplers often have controls similar to those found in analog synthesizers for processing sounds, such as filters and envelope generators.

Using a sampler, it is possible to produce extremely realistic replications of sounds that have complex changes over time, such as piano and voice. The envelopes of most analog and digital synthesizers do not provide sufficient detail to synthesize such sounds well. On the other hand, the actual process of creating musically useful samples can be extremely complex, requiring extensive high-quality recording and detailed editing using a computer.

Notable instruments that have incorporated sampling technology include New England Digital's *Synclavier*, first developed in the mid-1970s, and **Kurzweil's** *K250*. Because of the large amounts of computer memory required, these highly sophisticated instruments tended to be extraordinarily expensive. In the mid-1980s, Ensoniq introduced the first low cost keyboard instrument to use sampling technology—the *Mirage*. Since that time, all major manufacturers of electronic musical instruments—including **Yamaha, Roland, Korg**, and others—have introduced product lines that are based on sampler technology or hybrids of sampler and synthesizer technology.

See also Electronic Pianos.

Samuel S. Holland

Bibliography

DeFuria, Steve, and Joe Scacciaferro. *The Sampling Book*. Milwaukee, Wis.: Hal Leonard Publishing, 1990.

Additional information provided by Yamaha International, Roland Corp. US, Korg USA, and New England Digital.

SAUTER PIANOFORTEFABRIKEN, C.

One of the oldest piano manufacturing companies in Germany is that of C. Sauter, whose founding goes back to the year 1819 in Spaichingen, located at the base of the Schwäbisch Alb in southern Germany. The history of this company reflects one of the longest traditions of single-family ownership in piano building.

In the year 1813 Johann Grimm (1790–1845), a young joiner journeyman, left Spaichingen to visit the center of the musical world at that time, Vienna. Vienna was not only the center of music activities, but also home to a flourishing handcraft industry, so there were a great number of important instrument makers located there. Johann Grimm was fortunate to be taken into the workshop of Johann Andreas **Streicher**, one of the leading Viennese piano builders at this time. Six years later, after a solid education, Grimm returned to Spaichingen and opened his own workshop, where he shared his knowledge with his adopted son, Carl Sauter

(1820–1863). Sauter was very successful in building pianos and founded a substantial factory with a staff of ten to twelve journeymen. Since that time the firm has remained a family company.

The next family member to lead the firm was Johann Sauter (1846–1909), who travelled all over the world seeking new ideas regarding piano building, ideas that were then tested and worked out in his Spaichingen shop. A change in production methods took place under the leadership of Carl Sauter II (1876–1948). He systematized production and introduced modern methods of piano construction. Hans Sauter (1921–1968), the elder brother of present firm director Carl Sauter III, soon recognized the necessity not only to produce instruments efficiently, but also to sell them worldwide with an effective marketing policy. Thus the **upright pianos** of C. Sauter were well known in the international market by the time that Carl Sauter III took over the leadership. Under the present director a new type of **action** for upright pianos was developed. Not satisfied with the notable difference between the actions of uprights and **grands**, he developed the new "R^2-action" for series production, which purportedly reacts more like the action of a grand.

In 1984 a new factory was dedicated. The new building is one of the most modern for piano production in Germany and houses a large number of specialized machines to improve the building process. Nevertheless, many parts are still made by hand, as they traditionally have been. A few years ago Ulrich Sauter, Carl Sauter III's son, also joined the company, thus continuing the family tradition.

Carsten Dürer

SCALE

The word "scale" has several different meanings in piano building:

Strings: Diameter measurement and length of **strings**; additionally, copper to core **wire** ratio in bass strings.

Action: The **action** parts are mounted on action **rails** that must be interrupted occasionally by support feet. The action scale is the number of sections within the action, the number of action parts within those sections, and the spacing of those action parts.

Bass String Spinning: A marked stick or pegboard

used by the bass string spinner to show where on each bass string the copper begins and ends. Each spun string in a piano is unique when all factors—**hitch pin** to **bridge**, bridge to start of copper, copper end to **agraffe**, and agraffe to **tuning pin**—are taken into account.

Joel and Priscilla Rappaport

SCALE DESIGN

Scale design is the term used in the part of piano design that deals with the relationship between the **strings** and the rest of the piano. It is an integral design factor, in close correlation with the design of the **case**, **soundboard**, **bridge**, and **ribs**. A vibrating string sets up an overtone series that must be assessed according to sound quality and tunability, among other things. Different **wire** sizes for a given note emit varying overtone series. There are more than twenty sizes of plain wire (diameter measurement) from which to choose, and this is the job of the scale designer. Scale design involves not only decisions about when to change wire sizes, but also when to go from plain wire to wrapped strings, how many strings there shall be for each note, and the length of each string. Bass string design involves all the foregoing factors plus the proportion of copper to core wire in the string.

See also Soundboard.

Joel and Priscilla Rappaport

SCANDINAVIA, PIANO INDUSTRY IN

The piano industry in Denmark, Finland, Norway, and Sweden has demonstrated continued excellence, taking many prizes in world exhibitions and supplying piano industries throughout the world with knowledgeable and experienced craftsmen. At the World Exhibition in Vienna in 1873 it was noted that Sweden, Norway, and Denmark "combined an energetic striving and the practical advances won in America with understanding and taste," according to Paul and Schelle.

Denmark

It is generally agreed that Hornung and Möller was the most influential firm building pianos in Denmark during the nineteenth century. Conrad Christian Hornung (1 July 1801, Skelskör–11 June 1873, Copenhagen) studied outside Denmark but established the Hornung workshop and finished his first piano in Skelskör in 1827. The workshop was moved twice: in 1834 to Slagelse and in 1842 to Copenhagen, where cast-iron **frames** were introduced and Conrad became instrument maker to the Danish Court. In 1851 Hornung withdrew from leadership of the company and his co-worker of many years, Hans Peter Möller (1802–1859), took over, the firm becoming Hornung and Möller. After Möller's death his widow took over the firm under the control of their eldest son. In 1869 this son became head of the firm, this position later being shared with his brother. The firm's pianos won many prizes, including: 1867 World Exhibition in Paris, Bronze Medal; 1873 World Exhibition in Vienna, *Fortschrittsmedaille*, where the firm displayed an **upright** with overdamper **action**, and a cross-strung **concert grand** with **English action** and an appealing **tone** that was thought to be a little weak in the middle register (Paul, p. 635; Schelle, p. 49).

Andreas Marschall (15 November 1783, Ternau in Hungary–9 February 1842), like Hornung, received his training outside Denmark, notably from Beckmann in Kassel. Nevertheless, it was in 1810 that he came to Copenhagen, working for a year under Peter Christian Uldahl (1778–1820) before establishing his own firm in 1813. After his death the firm was led by his son, Hjorth, until 1847. The importance of this builder is magnified by the training he gave to some of the leading makers: Johan Gustaf Malmsjö (1815–1891) of Sweden, and Emanuel Schöne (d.1851) and Christopher Thomle (1794–1858) of Norway.Uldahl, Andreas Marschall's Danish teacher, was a student of Joseph Wachtl (fl.1801–1832) in Vienna, and founded his piano business in Copenhagen in 1809.

J.H. Ehlert must also be included in a consideration of leading Danish piano builders. He established his firm in Copenhagen in 1867 and won a *Verdienstmedaille* at the 1873 World Exhibition in Vienna with an overdamper **cross-strung** upright piano of average tone. Another respected Danish builder represented at the same exhibition was Carl Görgenden of Copenhagen.

In 1983 the Egtved Piano Builders School [Egtved Pianobyggerskole] was started in Vejle, Denmark. The school, attempting to revive the Danish piano-building tradition, has two main purposes: to educate students in piano building and **tuning**, and to develop a new Danish piano. The school has an annual production of some twenty premium studio uprights [model: EP 108] using a **Renner** action and Kluge **keyboard.**

Some other Danish makers include: Richter-Bechmann, established 1814; J.N. Gade, early nineteenth century in Copenhagen; Herm. N. Petersen and Son, founded 1849 in Copenhagen; Carl Alpers, mid-nineteenth century; Harald Hindsberg, founded 1853 in Copenhagen, who in 1878 took over Ludwig Wulff and Co. (founded in Copenhagen in 1853); J. Larsen and Son, established 1855 in Copenhagen; A.C. Sundahl, student of Hornung, founded around 1860 in Copenhagen; C. Landschultz, established 1865 in Copenhagen; A. Aversen and Co., founded around 1870; Emil Felumb, founded 1872 in Copenhagen; A.H. Giesler, established 1876 in Copenhagen; Wedell and Aberg, established 1881 in Copenhagen; Jensen and Sons, established 1893 in Copenhagen; Louis Zwicki, 1899–c. 1957 in Copenhagen; B. Jorgensen, founded 1913; A. Christensen, 1918–1960; Brothers Jørgensen, Copenhagen, 1948–1965; Knudsen and Son, Hillerød, 1949–1966.

Finland

Although the piano industry in Finland was not as intensive as in Sweden or Denmark, it is well represented in the nineteenth century by Westerlund (1875–c. 1960) of Helsinki and in the twentieth century by the Fazer and Hellas piano companies. At the end of March 1989 Hellas-Piano Company purchased the other Finnish piano manufacturer, Fazer Piano, and both Hellas and Fazer brands are manufactured by the Hellas-Piano Company.

The first Hellas factory was founded in 1901 in Hyvinkää, but was quickly moved to Helsinki. The founder, K.O. Rehnström, had served his apprenticeship with German builders working in St. Petersburg. The company produced a bread-and-butter model with a height of 130 cm., but between the two world wars they also built a small number of **grand pianos.** The Great Depression saw a change of hands, and Albin Fenander took over the firm in 1932. During these difficult years production fell to about six pianos per year and after World War II Hellas consisted of a few half-finished pianos and one craftsman. With some technical knowledge of pianos, having traded in second-hand

instruments, Olavi Waldemar Mertelius and Pekka Mäkelä bought the firm in 1949. Their intention to quickly finish the half-completed instruments and close the factory was overturned with the appearance of Eero Virtanen, the factory's last apprentice. Six pianos were built in 1950. In an attempt to circumvent the embargo on imported parts for their actions, the owners disguised themselves as tourists and attempted, not always successfully, to smuggle. In 1951 the workshop moved to Rajamäki but the retail store and management remained in Helsinki.

With the post-World War II boom, Eero Virtanen and Mäkelä developed new small, inexpensive models with tuning stability and employed new production technology to meet the growing demand. A new factory with a floor space of 11,000 square meters was completed in 1963 and although today some 60 percent of total output is exported, in 1968 their first export shipment included thirty-eight pianos. In 1977 Mertelius sold his share of the company to Mäkelä. In 1985 a new factory, headed by Juha Virtanen and employing some thirty craftsmen, opened in Hyvinkää to produce their "Hohner" line of pianos and the iron **frames.** The wooden parts are still produced at Rajamäki, where some 180 craftsmen are employed. Hellas produces approximately 8,000 pianos per year, 2,000 coming from the Hohner plant. Since the founding of the company over 100,000 pianos have been built. The Fazer Piano Company, established in 1950 in Helsingfors and now a part of Hellas-Piano, made uprights. Fazer uses an action called the "Langer B.p.J.," which introduces an important feature of the grand-piano action into an upright piano, namely its capacity for in-the-key repetition: it is not necessary to allow for a full return of the key before it can be struck again.

Sweden

Sweden occupies a central place in a consideration of the piano industry in Scandinavia, with the company of J.G. Malmsjö as a great Scandinavian maker. Johan Gustaf Malmsjö (born 14 January 1815 in Lund, South Sweden, died 13 September 1891 in Göteborg) was a student of Akström in Malmö and Marschall in Copenhagen, where he stayed for six years. He settled in Eckström in Malmö, where he built his first two table-pianos, and in December

1843 he founded his own firm in Göteborg. During the first thirty years he built almost exclusively **square** and upright pianos. He became maker to the Swedish Court. By 1877 the firm had completed 2,500 instruments. By 1893, when the firm celebrated its fiftieth anniversary, 5,600 instruments had been sold. By the end of the century, with an output of about 135 pianos per year, the company was the largest and most important in Sweden, being also its only maker of grands. After Malmsjö's death, his son-in-law, Vilhelm Seydel, was appointed director. The firm's pianos received many awards including: 1851, 1866, First Prizes at the Exhibition of Stockholm; 1860, 1871, Göteborg; 1862 World Exhibition in London, Medal; 1867 World Exhibition in Paris, Bronze Medal; 1872, 1880, Copenhagen; 1865, 1881, Malmö; 1862, Karlsbad (Sweden); 1873 World Exhibition in Vienna, *Fortschrittsmedaille*, where the firm displayed three pianos including a concert grand, all based on **Steinway**; 1876 World Exhibition in Philadelphia, total of nineteen First Prizes; 1891, special prize of honor in Göteborg. In 1966 the firm merged with Ostlind and Almquist, ceasing production in 1977. Ostlind and Almquist was established in 1888 in Arvika.

In the nineteenth century Ekström (Ekstrem) and Company, established 1836 in Malmö, enjoyed an excellent reputation for the production of fine pianos. The company was taken over by A.B. Nordiska in 1976. Billbergs Piano factory, established in 1868 in Göteborg, enjoyed success at the 1873 World Exhibition in Vienna, where it displayed two instruments: a concert grand with English action and a light and beautiful tone, although the descant register was thought to be too soft in comparison to the bass, and an upright with overdamper action and a light and even tone (Paul, p. 636; Schelle, p. 49).

Other Swedish makers include: Matthias Petter Kraft (born 14 July 1753 in Gälve, died 9 July 1807 in Stockholm), student of Peer Lundborg (fl. 1772–1796) (clavichord builder), firm founded in 1778 in Stockholm, became Court Instrument Maker in 1780; Peer Lindholm (1742–1813), who built clavichords and square pianos in Stockholm from 1780 (between 1803 and 1806 the instruments also carried the name of his son-in-law: "Peer Lindholm and Söderström"); George Christopher Rackwitz, builder of clavichords and pianos, Stockholm,

end of eighteenth, beginning of nineteenth century; Johan Söderberg, Stockholm, early nineteenth century; J.H. Daugh, Göteborg, early nineteenth century; Olof Granfeldt, Stockholm, early nineteenth century; J.G. Högvall, Göteborg, early nineteenth century; N.G. Hultenberg, Stockholm, early nineteenth century; Magnus Asell, Söderhamn, around 1821; Carl J. Nordquist, Stockholm, active 1823–1826; Anders Söderberg, Stockholm, 1832; Lindköping, mid-nineteenth century; D. Hansson, Lund, 1854; August Friedrich Hoffmann, Stockholm, who took over business from Söderberg in 1859; A.F. Sätherberg, Norrköping, who won a medal at the 1862 World Exhibition in London; J.P. Nyströms, Karlstad, 1865; L. Stavenow, Stockholm, who received an honorable mention for his pianos at the 1867 World Exhibition in Paris; Baumgardt, 1872–1966; A.G. Ralins Piano Factory, Amal, 1885; John Pettersson, Stockholm, 1889; Löfmark and Hoglund, Malmö, established 1899; C. Svahnquist, Stockholm, 1899; Wennberg, late nineteenth century; J. Löfmark, Göteborg, established 1903; Standard Piano Factory, Arvika, 1904; A.B. Svenska Piano Factory, Sundyberg, established 1917; Nordiska Piano Factory, Vetlanda, founded 1926 (pianos now manufactured in other countries).

Norway

The most notable piano building firm in Norway was established by the Hals Brothers (Brødrene Hals), Karl Marius Anton Johan (1822–1898), and Petter Martin Emil Nilson, (1823–1871) in Christiania (now Oslo) on 3 November 1847. Petter and Karl both trained as carpenters. When Petter died, Karl carried on the business alone at Wilberg, the family estate near Christiania. Karl's sons, Thor (b. 1852) and Sigurd (b. 1859), became partners, and Olav (1857–1883) worked in the technical division from 1880. In 1897 the firm employed around one hundred craftsmen, producing ten to twelve instruments per week. Their grand and upright pianos won many medals: 1862 World Exhibition in London; 1866, Stockholm; 1867, 1878, 1880, Paris; 1873, Drammen; 1874, 1880, Christiania; 1888, Melbourne. The company operated between 1847 and 1925.

The importance of Norway in piano building in the nineteenth and twentieth centuries is made evident in Peter Andreas Kjeldsberg's valuable study. Active builders were resident throughout the country. Julius Berg was known to be in operation in Christiania in the 1880s as a producer of upright pianos. Paul Christian Brantzeg (1821–1900) studied in Trondheim with Albrechtsen, the organ builder, and with various organ and piano builders in London and Paris, and with C.C. Hornung in Copenhagen. Brantzeg built upright pianos (c. 600 units), organs, and harmoniums in Christiania from 1850 to around 1900. Martin Bredesen was known in the 1880s as an upright builder in Christiana.

Otto Büchner (d. 1942) studied with Feurich in Leipzig and **Bechstein** in Berlin before taking over the Riisæs factory in Bergen in 1907. In 1917 the firm was sold to Emil Cappelen Pty. Ltd. of Oslo, but Büchner remained as technical director. Büchner produced uprights and employed thirty in 1920, producing around 250 instruments per year, the factory ceasing production in 1924. Emil Cappelen Pty. Ltd. bought Büchner and Thoresen's factories in 1917, building uprights in Christiania between 1917 and 1924. J.W. Cappelen employed about ten in Oslo between 1953 and 1959 and built around 500 units of two upright piano models using Renner actions.

J. Eilersen was known as an upright builder in Christiania between 1859 and 1861. Eng produced instruments in Strømmen, Vestfold, around 1860. Engelstrad worked in Tromøy ved Arendal around 1869. John Enger built uprights and grands in Christiania in the 1850s. One of Enger's grands with four **pedals** (forte, piano, triangle, drum) is in the Norwegian Folk Museum in Oslo. Gerhard Evensen (1861–1919) built uprights in Christiania between 1905 and 1910. Evensen's firm employed about twenty and in 1906–1907 he took out a **patent** for the development of a **soundboard** and iron-frame construction.

The Forende Pianofabrikker [Incorporated Piano Factory] was established as a subsidiary company to the Swedish firm, A/B Förende Piano- och Orgelfabriker. It was in production in Oslo between 1933 and 1959, building around 2,150 upright models using Schwander and Renner actions. In 1954 they employed eleven craftsmen. Anton Gjermstad (1843–1892) built uprights using Schwander actions between 1887 and 1892 in Ytterøya, Nord Trøndelag. Grøndahls Flygel- og Pianolager A/S [Grøndahl's

Grand and Upright Piano Company Pty. Ltd.] began as a textile company founded by Anders Grøndahl (1879–1947). Grøndahl's company built around 200 uprights per year between the 1940s and 1957. H. Hansen (d. 1854) was known in the 1840s as a square-piano builder.

Georg Daniel Schöne (1750–1807) built square pianos, clavichords, and various other instruments between 1788 and 1805 in Christiania. Schöne trained in London and with Christian Shean. Abraham Worm (d. 1816?) built **fortepianos**, grands, square pianos, clavichords, and harpsichords in Strømsø between 1792 and 1805. Lars Modom was known as a builder of grands and square pianos in Christiania between 1803 and 1820. G.C. Martinsen (d. 1828) was known as a builder in Bergen in 1827. Christopher Thomle (1794–1858) trained with Andreas Marschall in Copenhagen but built square pianos in Christiania between 1830 and 1838. C.F. Waarum (d. 1839) was known as a square-piano builder in Christiania in the 1830s. T.L. Tollachsen was known as a builder in Bergen between 1835 and 1859. Christian Stolz was known as an upright builder in Bergen between 1838 and the 1860s. Jens Hoff (1802?–1888) built square pianos in Laurvig. R.E. Sæther (possibly known as Sæther and Koch Piano Builders, and Sæther and Berg) built uprights in Christiania between 1844 and the 1880s. Støhrmann built uprights in Bergen between 1848 and the 1860s. Mads Jansen (1825–1871) employed two or three to build uprights in Trondheim between 1854 and 1871. R. Holther built uprights in Christiania between 1855 and the 1880s.

Jens Peder Smidt Aarestrup (1827–1893) trained in other countries but established his factory in Bergen to make uprights between 1857 and 1886. Henrik Severin Riisnæs (1858–1909) bought Aarestrup's factory in 1886, and in 1907 it was sold to Otto Büchner, who in turn sold it ten years later to Emil Cappelen Pty. Ltd. of Oslo.

Johannes Thoresen (1829–1886) studied with various piano builders in Germany and Switzerland before establishing his factory in 1863. After Thoresen's death, Petter Hansen (b. 1860) took over the factory, which went public in 1906 and was taken over by Emil Cappelen Pty. Ltd. in 1917. Thoresen's operated between 1863 and 1924, building grands and uprights in Christiania. By 1920 they had produced 4,030 units.

The Norsk Orgel- og Harmoniumfabrikk [Norwegian Organ and Harmonium Factory] was established in 1873 by Petter Berntzen in Vardal. In 1916 this factory moved to Gjøvik and in 1928 to Snertingdal. The firm built around 2,000 uprights, employing sixty craftsmen in 1960. Sundwall and Company ceased building uprights in Christiania in 1877. Emanuel Schöne (d. 1851) trained with Andreas Marschall in Copenhagen; his company built square pianos in Christiania in the 1880s. Holo Neupert (1844–1896) employed about six to build uprights in Christiania between 1881 and 1896.

Vestre Orgel-og Pianofabrikk built upright pianos between 1888 and 1982, using an imported action. Jacob Knudsen (1873–1928) established the A/S Flygel- Piano- Orgelfabrikk and built around 10,000 units in Bergen between 1896 and 1975. In 1928 Wilhelm, Jacob's brother, took over the firm and led it until 1946, when Christen Faye took over. Stanley Koch (1856–1935) built uprights in Oslo around 1920. The Oslo Pianofabrikk took over from Brødrene Hals, building uprights in Oslo between 1929 and 1930. F. Hellström Flygel- og Pianofabrikk [F. Hellström Grand and Upright Piano Factory] was established by Fritz Carl Bruno Hellström (1910–1985) in Oslo in 1946. Hellström's built around 6,000 units between 1946 and 1981, employing around thirty in 1965. Aage Svensen built uprights using Renner actions between 1956 and 1960 in Oslo.

Keith T. Johns

Bibliography

Dolge, Alfred. *Piano and Their Makers*. Covina, Cal.: Covina Publishing Company, 1911. New York: Dover, 1972.

Ehrlich, Cyril. *The Piano: A History*. London: Dent, 1976.

Hirt, Franz Josef. *Meisterwerke des Klavierbaus*. Olten, Switzerland: Graf, 1955; Dietikon-Zürich: Urs Graf, 1981.

Kjeldsberg, Peter Andreas. *Piano i Norge*. Oslo: Huitfeldt, 1985.

Pauer, E. *Dictionary of Pianists*. London: Novello, 1895.

Paul, Oscar. *Musikalische Instrumente: Amtlicher Bericht über die Wiener Weltausstellung im Jahre 1873*. Vol. 2. Braunschweig: Friedrich Vieweg, 1874.

Schelle, Ed. *Officieller Ausstellungs-Bericht heraus, durch die General-Direction der Weltausstellung 1873*. Wien: K.K. Hof- und Staats-Druckerei, 1873.

Brochures

"85 Years Hellas Pianos 'Made in Finland'." Hellas-Piano Company, reprint from *Das Musikinstrument*, 1986.

"Hellas-Piano Finland." Hellas-Piano Company.

"The Keys to Music." Fazer Piano Company.

SCARLATTI, DOMENICO (1685–1757)

Domenico Scarlatti was born in Napoli (26 October 1685) and died in Madrid (23 July 1757), where by then he was called Domingo Escarlatti. Domenico was by far the most gifted son of the famous composer Alessandro Scarlatti (1660–1725). His main teacher seems to have been his father. Domenico soon became known as an excellent keyboard player in his native town of Napoli. When he was almost sixteen he was appointed organist and composer of the Royal Chapel of Naples, of which his father was the *maestro di cappella*. In the autumn of 1702, Scarlatti father and son obtained a leave of absence for four months and visited the court of the Medici in Florence. We can take it for granted that Domenico not only met **Bartolomeo Cristofori** in Florence during these months but also concertized on Cristofori's new *cembalo che fà il piano e il forte*, which had existed by then for at least two to three years. In 1705 Domenico visited Florence again on his way to Venice, and at least once more on his way back to Rome (1709?), where he entered the service of the Polish Queen Maria Casimira in 1710.

From Florentine archive material we learned recently (Montanari) that Cardinal Pietro Ottoboni of Rome owned a *cembalo con martelli*, which he sent back from Rome to Florence in 1716, to have it repaired by Cristofori. Whether this *cembalo con martelli* was already in the possession of Cardinal Ottoboni in 1709 is hard to say. According to Handel's biographer John Mainwaring, Georg Friedrich Handel and Domenico Scarlatti played in Cardinal Ottoboni's house, and a contest in virtuosity was organized. It has been said that Handel was the winner at the organ and Scarlatti at the "cembalo" (harpsichord). It may well have been Cristofori's *cembalo con martelli*, because throughout the eighteenth century the single word *cembalo* was used generically for *cembalo con penne* as well as for *cembalo con martelli* and therefore could mean either instrument. (Even in the early nineteenth century in Italy, pianos officially belonged to the instrument family of *cembali* and were sometimes still named *cembali*.)

When Scarlatti accepted a position at the Royal Court in Lisbon in 1719, where he became the teacher of the Crown Prince Don Antonio, younger brother of King João V, and the King's daughter, Maria Barbara, he must have brought a pianoforte to Lisbon. Not without reason, Ludovico Giustini's *Sonate da cimbalo di piano e forte detto volgarmento di martelletti* are dedicated to *Don Antonio, Infante di Portogallo*. Princess Maria Barbara married the crown prince of Spain, and Scarlatti followed her to Seville and Madrid and remained in her service until his death. Maria Barbara eventually became Queen of Spain. We do not know the dates when she acquired the five pianos that are mentioned in her will, but it is quite clear that she did this under the influence and with the help of her music master Domenico Scarlatti. It may well be assumed that Domenico Scarlatti also owned privately at least one piano in the course of his life (built by Cristofori or by his pupil **Giovanni Ferrini** or by a Spanish instrument builder), but no traces of instruments once belonging to him have been found.

Eva Badura-Skoda

Bibliography

Badura-Skoda, Eva. "Domenico Scarlatti und das Hammerklavier." *Österreichische Musikzeitschrift* 40 (1985): 505f.

Kirkpatrick, Ralph. *Domenico Scarlatti*. 2 vols. München: Verlag Heinrich Ellermann, 1972.

Montanari, Giuliana. "Bartolomeo Cristofori." *Early Music* 19 (August 1991): 383–96.

SCHANTZ, JOHANN (C. 1762–1828)

Johann Schantz, born around 1762 in Kladrob, Bohemia, was the younger brother of **Wenzel Schantz** (1757–1790); he died 26 April 1828 in Vienna. We do not know where the two Schantz brothers spent their apprenticeship years. No document is known to verify a remark by Franz Hirt that the brothers learned their craft with Johann Andreas **Stein** in Augsburg, and Hirt admitted orally in later years that a reason for his statement was a misunderstanding of a much-quoted passage found in Schönfeld's yearbook of 1796 (which E.L. Gerber had more or less copied in his article on Schantz in his *Neue*

Tonkünstler-Lexikon of 1814) that the **fortepianos** of Schantz are built "similar to those of Stein."

Johann Schantz may have joined the workshop of his older brother relatively early. After his brother's death he applied for (in 1790) and received (in 1791) the title *Meister* and thus became a certified organ and piano builder. He also acquired the *Bürgerrecht* in 1791, approximately at the same time as **Anton Walter**. A sizeable number of **grand pianos** built and signed by Johann Schantz are extant.

His grand pianos are designed with divided **bridges**, the way Saxon and English piano builders used to construct them, and he also built *Tafelklaviere* "in the English style" (Schönfeld), which were praised for their beautiful and clear **tone** and their accurate and agreeable **action**. The design of the bridge is one of many construction details in which the instruments of Johann Schantz differ from those of Anton Walter on the one hand, and Nannette and Matthäus Stein, the children of Johann Andreas Stein, who had settled in Vienna in 1794, on the other. A *forte* chord played on a Schantz is as loud as on a Walter grand piano from the same period and certainly stronger than on a Stein *Flügel*. Also the tone color of the grand fortepianos by Schantz differs from that of pianos of the other Viennese builders. This also sets the instruments of Johann Schantz clearly apart from those of the members of the Stein family prior to 1800—reason enough to reject a remark by Schönfeld in his *Jahrbuch der Tonkunst von Wien und Prag 1796*, in which he wrongly claimed that the instruments of Schantz are nearly copies of those of Stein.

While Johann Schantz's grand pianos suited **Ludwig van Beethoven** better than those of Nannette Stein-Streicher—at least prior to 1809—Anton Walter's instruments from the 1790s were probably still stronger in the bass register than those of Schantz. But they certainly sounded less clear and distinct in the treble, which is especially beautiful on Schantz's pianos. Altogether, Walter's pianos may have been considered perhaps "more modern" around 1790 than those of Schantz, especially with regard to their darker tone color. Their sound could rightly be called "more romantic."

While **Wolfgang Amadeus Mozart** acquired an instrument from Anton Walter in 1782 or 1783 and Beethoven also wanted one from

Walter in 1803 (in later years he also owned one by Schantz), **Joseph Haydn** clearly preferred the instruments of the brothers Schantz to those of Walter. In a letter to his beloved Madame Genzinger dated 4 July 1790, he wrote:

> It is quite true that my friend, Herr Walter, is very celebrated . . . . I know Herr von Nikl's fortepiano [made by Anton Walter]: It's excellent, but too heavy for your Grace's hand, and one can't play everything on it with the necessary delicacy. Therefore I should like Your Grace to try one of Herr Schantz, his fortepianos are particularly light in touch and the mechanism very agreeable.

Eva Badura-Skoda

Bibliography

Badura-Skoda, Eva. "Prolegomena to a History of the Viennese Fortepiano." *Israel Studies in Musicology* 2 (1980): 77–99.

Haas, Robert. *Bach und Mozart in Wien.* Wien: Paul Kaltschmid Verlag, 1951.

Haupt, Helga. "Wiener Instrumentenbauer von 1791 bis 1815." In *Studien zur Musikwissenschaft, Beihefte der Denkmäler der Tonkunst in Österreich* Vol. 24 (1960): 170.

Hirt, Franz Josef. *Meisterwerke des Klavierbaus.* Olten, Switzerland: Urs Graf, 1955; Dietikon-Zürich: Urs Graf, 1981.

Landon, H.C. Robbins. *The Collected Correspondence and London Notebooks of Joseph Haydn.* London: Barrie & Rockliff, 1959: 79, 105–07.

Pohl, Carl Ferdinand. *Joseph Haydn.* Vol. 2 Leipzig: Breitkopf & Härtel, 1882: 157f.

Schönfeld, Johann Ferdinand von. *Jahrbuch der Tonkunst von Wien und Prag 1796.* Im Schönfeldischen Verlag (Wien and Prag) 1796, facs. reprint ed. by Otto Biba, München-Salzburg, 1976.

SCHANTZ, WENZEL (C. 1757–1790)

Wenzel or Wenzl Schantz was born around 1757 in Kladrob, Bohemia and died early in 1790 in castle Pardubitz, Bohemia. He was the older brother of **Johann Schantz** (1762–1828). We do not know where the two Schantz brothers spent their apprenticeship years. No document is known to verify a remark by Franz Hirt that the brothers learned their craft with Johann Andreas **Stein** in Augsburg, and Hirt admitted orally in later years that a reason for his statement was a misunderstanding of a much-quoted passage found in Schönfeld's yearbook of 1796 (which E.L. Gerber had more or less copied in his article on Schantz in his *Neue Tonkünstler-*

Lexikon of 1814) that the **fortepianos** of Schantz are built "similar to those of Stein."

There is not one instrument preserved today that can be attributed to Wenzel Schantz, though it is likely that he built excellent fortepianos in the 1780s in Vienna. However, he probably did not sign them in order to avoid problems with the authorities, since he had acquired neither the *Meisterrecht* nor the "dispense of foreign birth" nor the *Bürgerrecht,* all necessary procedures for legally opening a workshop. For all of these rights he would have had to pay a considerable amount of money in addition to passing an examination before the guild of organ and instrument builders (See Walter, Anton).

We may assume that the brothers Schantz had unofficially established for themselves a workshop in a suburb of Vienna and had achieved a good name by around 1785. In a letter to his publisher Artaria, **Joseph Haydn** wrote (26 October 1788) that he had to buy a new fortepiano, and he asked Artaria to pay Wenzel Schantz thirty-one gold ducats on his behalf. The address mentioned by Haydn (*Leimgrube im blauen Schiff Nr. 22*) is not registered in city documents, but the district shows that the brothers Schantz had their own workshop and probably also their home near that of **Anton Walter**, who lived in the same *Vorstadt* [suburb] of Vienna. Wenzel Schantz was married twice, first to a certain Katharina, who died 27 April 1785, and afterwards to Maria Anna, with whom he had two children; they did not survive infancy.

While **Mozart** acquired an instrument from Anton Walter in 1782 or 1783 and **Beethoven** also wanted one from Walter around 1800 (though in later years he also owned one by Johann Schantz), Haydn clearly preferred the instruments of the brothers Schantz. In a letter to his beloved Madame Genzinger dated 4 July 1790, he wrote:

> It is quite true that my friend, Herr Walter, is very celebrated . . . . I know Herr von Nikl's fortepiano [made by Anton Walter]: It's excellent, but too heavy for your Grace's hand, and one can't play everything on it with the necessary delicacy. Therefore I should like Your Grace to try one of Herr Schanz, his fortepianos are particularly light in touch and the mechanism very agreeable.

Eva Badura-Skoda

Bibliography

Badura-Skoda, Eva. "Prolegomena to a History of the Viennese Fortepiano." *Israel Studies in Musicology* 2 (1980): 77–99.

Haas, Robert. *Bach und Mozart in Wien.* Wien: Paul Kaltschmid Verlag, 1951.

Haupt, Helga. "Wiener Instrumentenbauer von 1791 bis 1815." In *Studien zur Musikwissenschaft, Beihefte der Denkmäler der Tonkunst in Österreich* Vol. 24 (1960): 170.

Hirt, Franz Josef. *Meisterwerke des Klavierbaus.* Olten: Urs Graf, 1955; Dietikon-Zürich: Urs Graf, 1981.

Landon, H.C. Robbins. *The Collected Correspondence and London Notebooks of Joseph Haydn.* London: Barrie & Rockliff, 1959: 79, 105–07.

Pohl, Carl Ferdinand. *Joseph Haydn.* Vol. 2. Leipzig: Breitkopf & Härtel, 1882: 157f.

Schönfeld, Johann Ferdinand von. *Jahrbuch der Tonkunst von Wien und Prag 1796.* Im Schönfeldischen Verlag (Wien and Prag) 1796, facs. reprint ed. by Otto Biba, München-Salzburg, 1976.

SCHIEDMAYER

The Schiedmayer family were distinguished builders of clavichords, harpsichords, and pianos in eighteenth-century Bavaria. Three sons of Balthasar Schiedmayer (1711–1781), a clavichord maker in Erlangen, continued as both clavichord and piano makers. Johann David Schiedmayer (1753–1805) was the most energetic and ultimately the most successful of the progeny and became instrument maker to the Court at Ansbach before moving his workshop to Nuremberg in 1797.

The modern branch of the firm was founded in 1809 in Stuttgart as Dieudonné & Schiedmayer by Johann David's son, Johann Lorenz Schiedmayer (1786–1860), and Carl Dieudonné (c. 1780–1825), who met as fellow workmen in Nannette **Streicher**'s Vienna workshop. Their eclectic output of **grands, squares,** and pyramids was of the highest quality and the variety of style unusual for the early years of the nineteenth century. At Dieudonné's death Schiedmayer changed the name of the factory to reflect his own dominance and that of his family. In 1845 he took as his partners his sons Adolf (1819–1890) and Herman (1820–1860) and renamed the company Schiedmayer & Söhne. Nine years later the younger sons of Johann Lorenz, Julius (1822–1878) and Paul (1829–1890), opened J. & P. Schiedmayer, a

harmonium factory. However, at their father's death they changed their business to that of piano building, renaming their firm the Schiedmayer Pianofortefabrik, which ultimately became a vital and predominant force in the German piano industry. In 1969, these two branches merged to create a giant manufacturer of grands and smaller pianos for the home. A Würzburg branch, Miller-Schiedmayer, was founded in 1874 by sons of Lorenz Schiedmayer's daughter; it continued until 1943.

The Schiedmayer factory in Stuttgart was bombed during World War II and several of the earliest pianos in the important family collection were destroyed. Nevertheless, interesting examples of early Schiedmayer pianos do survive, for the most part in the collections of the German National Museum in Nuremberg, the Deutsches Museum in Munich, and the University of Erlangen.

Martha Novak Clinkscale

Bibliography

Clinkscale, Martha Novak. *Makers of the Piano: 1700–1820.* Oxford: Oxford University Press, 1992.

Ehrlich, Cyril. *The Piano: A History.* 2nd ed. Oxford: Oxford University Press, 1990.

Rupprecht, Margarete. "Die Klavierbauerfamilie Schiedmayer: ein Beitrag zur Geschichte des Klavierbaues." Dissertation, Friedrich-Alexander-Universität zu Erlangen, 1954.

———. "Schiedmayer, Familie." *Die Musik in Geschichte und Gegenwart* 11: 1702–1704.

SCHIMMEL

The largest piano manufacturer in western Europe, Wilhelm Schimmel was founded in a small workshop on 2 May 1885, in the vicinity of Leipzig, by Wilhelm Schimmel, Sr. (1854–1946). The Schimmel piano had already earned a good reputation by 1891 when the first factory was built in Leipzig-Reudnitz, to be followed by a second, larger factory in Leipzig-Stötteritz in 1897. The relatively young firm was also named Court Builder for the Grand Duchy of Saxe-Weimar as well as for the king of Rumania.

Shortly before World War I the firm had completed its 10,000th piano, only to be hampered in its further development by the turbulence of the war and the subsequent economic upheavals of the 1920s. In 1927 the leadership of the firm was taken over by Arno Wilhelm Schimmel (1898–1961), and in 1929, in response to the collapse of the market, it joined the cooperative "Deutsche Piano Werke AG" and moved from Leipzig to Braunschweig. Arno Wilhelm Schimmel left the DPW in 1931, continuing his family's tradition of fine piano building as "Wilhelm Schimmel Pianofortefabrik GmbH" until the destruction of their facilities by bombing in 1944.

By 1948, after reconstruction, Schimmel pianos were again exhibited at the Hanover Trade Fair, and by 1960, 400 employees celebrated the completion of the firm's 50,000th piano. Schimmel became synonymous with modern design, particularly a plexiglass see-through **grand** for contemporary pop music.

Following the death in 1961 of Arno Wilhelm Schimmel, the third generation leadership of the firm was taken up by Nikolaus Schimmel (b. 1934), and by the 1960s yearly production exceeded 6,000 instruments (in 1975, 7,218), approximately 30 percent of all pianos built in the Federal Republic of Germany. From 1971 on, Schimmel and the Société Gaveau-Erard, Paris, produced pianos under the trademark "Les Grandes Marques Réunies," and after 1974, under the marks "Gaveau," "Erard," and "Pleyel." The range of grands and **uprights** built by Schimmel comprises a total of 264 versions.

See also Germany, Piano Industry in.

David Anderson

Bibliography

Joppig, Gunther. "Schimmel—Innovation in Piano Making." *Das Musikinstrument* 39 (September 1990): 68–73.

Rolle, Günter. "100 Jahre." *Keyboards* (July 1985): 39–42.

Schimmel, Nikolaus. *Schimmel.* Braunschweig: Aco-Druck, 1984.

SCHLEIP, JOHANN CHRISTIAN (FL. 1813-1848)

Johann Christian Schleip was a piano maker active in Berlin during the first half of the nineteenth century. He is said to have been from Tüngeda (near Gotha, Germany), although the exact year of his birth is not known. By 1813 there is evidence of him building pianos and in 1816 he moved to Berlin. It has been suggested that there he worked under an instrument maker named Sylig, but the evidence appears to rest solely on an inscription on the interior of an early Schleip instrument. Schleip is listed in Berlin directories until 1847 as a piano maker working at 72 Wallstrasse. Schleip himself died in 1848, but the firm bearing his name continued in operation for some time, listed at 21 Behrenstrasse from 1855 to 1877.

The only known instruments by Schleip are a decorative form of **upright piano** called a *Lyraflügel.* This design, which seems to have originated in Berlin, utilizes a lyre-shaped outline for the vertical **case.** The lyre is a common neoclassical motif in Biedermeier-style furniture; indeed, the significance of Schleip's pianos may be as a reflection of taste in interior design. His casework is usually veneered in nicely figured woods, such as mahogany or jacaranda, and the fancier examples have gilded trim, sometimes elaborate. Most of Schleip's pianos are supported by four legs, either simple turned and tapered ones or gracefully curved ones that terminate in a carved lion's paw. In a few examples the upper lyre-shaped portion rests on casework that extends to the floor, allowing the use of longer **strings** and sometimes the addition of a pedal board to play the lowest notes. This case configuration also permitted Schleip to use a hanging Viennese **action,** although the more common action in his pianos is an upright type derived from English models. Knee levers are often employed instead of **pedals** and a bassoon stop is frequently included. Schleip typically employed one of three different ranges (FF to f^4, DD to g^4, and CC to a^4), which may generally reflect three successive working periods.

Darcy Kuronen

Bibliography

Haase, Gesine. "Der Berliner Pianofortebau." In *Handwerk im Dienste der Musik: 300 Jahre Berliner Musikinstrumentenbau* (Dagmar Droysen-Reber, ed.), pp. 67–90. Berlin: Staatliches Institut für Musikforschung Preussischer Kulturbesitz, 1987.

Heyde, Herbert. *Historische Musikinstrumente des Händel-Hauses.* Halle an der Salle, 1983.

Koster, John. *Catalogue of Keyboard Instruments.* Boston: Museum of Fine Arts, forthcoming.

Sachs, Curt. "Der Berliner Instrumentenbau auf den Ausstellungen der Königliche Preussische Akademie der Künste 1794–1844." *Zeitschrift für Instrumentenbau* 32, nos. 29 and 30 (July 11 and 21, 1912): 1087–1089 and 1128–1130.

SCHMAHL FAMILY

Many members of the Schmahl family were prominent builders of various types of keyboard instruments in Swabia. Johann Matthäus Schmahl (1734–1793) of Ulm and his cousin Christoph Friedrich Schmahl (1739–1814) of Regensburg enjoyed the greatest fame. The former specialized in organs and a small **square pianoforte**, known as a *liegende Harfe*, a recumbent harp or harp-shaped piano. This instrument, as its name implies, looks exactly like a harp placed on its side and slipped into a piano **case**. It has four-and-one-half octaves and a Viennese *Prellmechanik* action. Most surviving examples of the *liegende Harfe* are neither dated nor signed.

Christoph Friedrich Schmahl began his career in his native Regensburg and achieved his greatest fame in 1774 as the partner of his father-in-law, Franz Jakob **Späth** (1714–1786). Together Späth and Schmahl developed a **grand piano** with a **tangent** action, the *Tangentenflügel*. The earliest surviving example of one of Schmahl's tangent pianos, dating from about 1780, is in the Württembergisches Landesgewerbemuseum in Stuttgart. Others can be found in public collections in the Bachhaus in Eisenach and in the German National Museum in Nuremberg.

Martha Novak Clinkscale

Bibliography

Clinkscale, Martha Novak. *Makers of the Piano: 1700–1820.* Oxford: Oxford University Press, 1992.

Hermann, Heinrich. "Die Regensburger Klavierbauer Späth und Schmahl und ihr Tangentenflügel." Dissertation, University of Erlangen, 1928.

Ripin, Edwin M. "Tangent piano." *The New Grove Dictionary of Music and Musicians.* 18: 562f.

SCHMIDT-FLOHR

The founder of this company, Johann Andreas Gottfried Flohr (1798–1872), was born in the Harz mountains, in Strassberg, Germany. As a nineteen-year-old cabinetmaker, he set out on his *Wanderschaft* and worked in Leipzig, Frankfurt, Bern, and Paris before finally settling in Bern and receiving Swiss citizenship. Flohr started producing pianos in 1830 under the name "A. Flohr & Cie," with an annual output of about thirty-five instruments up to 1890. After Flohr's death in 1872, his son-in-law, August Schmidt (d. 1904), took over the company, which was renamed Schmidt-Flohr. The company experienced a steady growth, reaching a production of nearly 700 instruments in the 1920s; however, the depression and World War II cut the output in half. The Schmidt-Flohr pianos were highly regarded abroad, winning the Grand Prix at a world exhibition in Barcelona, 1929. After World War II the company continued to grow but never quite reached its peak production of the 1920s. In 1975 the manufacturing of pianos came to an end in Bern. However, the "Schmidt-Flohrs" have been produced since 1977 under a license to Kemble in England.

Werner Iten

Bibliography

Europe Piano Atlas. Revised by H.K. Herzog. Frankfurt am Main: *Das Musikinstrument.* 4th ed., 1978.

Rindlisbacher, Otto. *Das Klavier in der Schweiz.* Bern and Munich: Francke Verlag, 1972.

Schmidt-Flohr AG. *Flügel- und Pianofabrik Bern, Biographie-Sammlung Schweizer Musterbetriebe.* Vol. 38, Basel: Max Glättli, 1941.

Schmidt, Hansjörn, Bern, verbal communication, 1991.

SCHÖFFTOSS, DONAT (C. 1773–1811)

Donat Schöfftoss (Schöftos) was probably born in Philippsburg am Rhein (c. 1773) and died in Vienna (15 February 1811). He was the younger son of the *Bataillonsfeldscher* [military medical officer] Franz Schöfftoss. After the early death of his father, his mother, Anna Elisabeth Schöfftoss, née Reisinger, (1748–1818) from Olmütz, Moravia, married (27 January 1780) the slightly younger organ and instrument maker **Anton Walter** (1752–1826) in Vienna. Donat was trained as an instrument builder in the workshop of his stepfather and worked there together with his brother Joseph Schöftoss (1767–1824) until 1804, when he acquired the *Meisterbrief* and the *Bürgerrecht* and opened his own workshop—apparently right after his brother had officially become Walter's partner. From then onwards he built excellent **fortepianos**, often with additional stops such as bassoon stop and "turkish music" stops. His instruments were also remarkably beautiful furniture pieces (Empire style). He signed them with "Donat Schöfftoss, Stiefsohn von Walter in Wien." When he died, his brother Joseph inherited his property, which included one finished and eleven unfinished pianos.

Eva Badura-Skoda

Bibliography

Haupt, Helga. "Wiener Instrumentenbauer von 1791 bis 1815." In *Studien zur Musikwissenschaft, Beihefte der Denkmäler der Tonkunst in Österreich* Vol.24, 1960.

Ottner, Helmut. *Der Wiener Instrumentenbau 1815–1833.* Tutzing: Verlag Hans Schneider, 1977.

SCHRÖTER, CHRISTOPH GOTTLIEB (1699–1782)

Christoph Gottlieb Schröter was the first German to propose designs for hammer **actions** for harpsichords, capable of being played loud or soft in response to finger **touch**. He was not an instrument maker but pursued a career as an eminent organist, composer, and music theorist. References that show him as an instrument maker have confused him with Johann Georg Schröter (1683–c.1750), a prominent contemporary organ builder.

Christoph Gottlieb Schröter began music study at an early age, first with his father, who was a music scholar, and then with prominent music educators in Dresden. By 1715, Schröter had started to teach music in Dresden to students who came from aristocratic families.

According to later published accounts that Schröter wrote himself, comments from his students aroused his interest in investigating what could be done to make the harpsichord more responsive in loudness to differences in touch. The idea of striking harpsichord strings with hammers occurred to him after he attended a performance in 1717 at which **Pantaléon Hebenstreit** played a large dulcimer using hand-held hammers. By the end of the year, Schröter completed two new hammer action designs for harpsichords, one up-striking, the other down-striking. To secure financial backing, in 1721 Schröter submitted a two-**key** action model illustrating each design to the Court of Saxony at Dresden.

Disappointed after waiting and not receiving the help promised him, Schröter left Dresden in 1724. He spent several years in Jena and then in Minden before settling in Nordhausen in 1732, where he remained as chief organist for the rest of his life.

Late in the 1730s, as **Gottfried Silbermann** pianos began to attract public interest, Schröter wrote his first letter giving a brief account of the hammer action designs he had submitted. He claimed credit for the invention, which he implied had been stolen from him. The letter, sent in 1738 to the Leipzig music journal *Neu-eröffnete Musikalische Bibliothek*, but not published until 1747, received little attention. Schröter repeated his claims and provided more details of his designs in a later letter published in the Berlin music journal *Kritische Brief* in 1763. In addition, he provided a diagram of an up-striking action, the first and only action drawing known to be the work of Schröter. (Edwin Good's volume contains Schröter's drawing.) Schröter's design—with the hammer mounted on a **rail** and lifted by a straight **jack** support on an intermediate lever—has some resemblance to the 1711 **Scipione Maffei** drawing of **Bartolomeo Cristofori**'s early action, although there are differences in proportion and placement. Schröter's drawing does not show a **damper**, **backcheck**, or **let-off** details. The only innovative feature of Schröter's design is his use of an iron **downbearing** bar across the **strings**, just in back of the **pinblock** bridge, to prevent the strings from moving up under the force of hammer blows. In modern pianos, the downbearing bar used for the same purpose is known as the *capo tasto* bar.

Rosamond E. M. Harding shows other drawings of museum models of Schröter actions. Their authenticity is questionable, however, since these models were constructed according to later interpretations of his writings. Whether any instrument with a Schröter hammer action has ever been built is doubtful. Schröter's most important accomplishments were his career as an outstanding organist, his ecclesiastical musical compositions, and his writings—essays in music journals and books on music theory, harmony, composition, and temperament.

Jack Greenfield

Bibliography

Arnold, F. T. *The Art of Accompaniment from a Thorough-Bass.* New York: Dover, 1965. (Reprint of Oxford 1931 edition).

Barbour, J. Murray. *Tuning and Temperament.* New York: Da Capo Press, 1972. (Reprint of Michigan State University Press 1951 edition).

David, Hans, and Arthur Mendel, eds. *The Bach Reader.* New York: Norton, 1972. (Revision of 1945 edition).

Good, Edwin M. *Giraffes, Black Dragons, and Other Pianos.* Stanford, Cal.: Stanford University Press, 1982.

Harding, Rosamond E.M. *The Piano-Forte: Its History Traced to the Great Exhibition of 1851.* Cambridge: Cambridge University Press, 1933. Reprints, New York: Da Capo Press, 1973; Old Woking, Surrey: Gresham Books, 1978.

Marcuse, Sybil. *A Survey of Musical Instruments.* London: David and Charles, 1975.

Rimbault, Edward B. *The Pianoforte.* London: Robert Cocks, 1860.

SCHUMANN, ROBERT AND CLARA (1810–1856) AND (1819–1896)

As a composer, Robert Schumann significantly contributed to the expansion of piano sonority and balanced the use of the whole range of the new iron-framed instruments after 1830 (e.g., his Toccata, Symphonic Etudes, Phantasie, Paganini-Studies). He was also one of the first composers to use a general mark *mit Pedal* [with **pedal**], establishing pedal effects as a continuous ingredient in the texture, rather than as a special effect. Overall, Schumann considered that the piano restricted his thoughts too much. Until 1845 he composed only at the piano, but not very idiomatically. He transferred string techniques and textures to the piano, enriching the articulation and phrasing palette. Aware of specific differences between instruments, he recognized Franz Schubert as an idiomatic writer (on Viennese instruments), but recommended imagining orchestral colors when playing works of **Ludwig van Beethoven**, who composed on instruments such as **Erard** and **Broadwood**.

Before he became a student of his future wife's father, Friedrich Wieck (1785–1873), Schumann had longed for a **Stein** piano. Wieck himself appreciated more the **Clementi** school (Broadwood), but his daughter Clara, being only eight in 1827, was happier with a lighter **action**, so he ordered for her a Stein (six-octave range, two pedals for different levels of soft **tone** as well as a third sustaining pedal). Wieck himself had a small business in pianofortes, and sold contraptions like *Handleiter* [hand leaders], trill machines, finger stretchers, and silent fingerboards. Clara herself received her first lessons with the help of Johann Bernhard Logier's *chiroplast*, and at the age of eighteen she was already compared to Sigismond Thalberg, Adolf Henselt, and **Franz Liszt**. In 1839 Clara wrote to Robert from Paris, complaining about the stiffness of the Erard she had to play, mentioning that the **Pleyel** was just a touch lighter. In 1840 Clara married Robert Schumann and brought with her her **Graf** piano (range CC–g^4, **leather**-covered **hammers**). For their wedding Schumann gave Clara a new Härtel **grand**. In the mid-1840s Robert preferred **uprights**, which Clara had always mistrusted. In 1845 the Schumanns acquired a **pedal piano**, primarily to practice organ, but Robert also composed for it (Etudes in Form of Canons). For their wedding anniversary in 1853 he again presented Clara with a grand piano, this time a Klems. After Schumann's death Clara gave the Graf to **Johannes Brahms** (the leather meanwhile having been replaced with **felt**).

After Robert's death, Clara was always surrounded by good pianos. She now preferred the **Grotrian-Steinweg**, which, with its "homogeneous **soundboard**," combined bass depth with a bright treble. During her stay in Baden-Baden in 1863, for example, she had three grands at her disposal. In 1870 in London, the Broadwoods gave her a **boudoir grand** to send to her daughter Julie (1845–1872) in Turin. In the summer of 1895 she rented a chalet at Interlaken, installing a Steinweg semi-grand piano; on getting a new cover for it from her children, she got so enthusiastic that she ordered a new Steinweg for herself. Praised as a pianist mostly for her serious approach, perception of composers' ideas, and a subtle but rich touch, Clara Schumann displayed a characteristically traditional attitude in a letter to Johannes Brahms (Interlaken, 27 August 1894). In it she approved rejection of a *Harfen-Klavier* acquisition for a Beethovenfest in Basel. This 1891 Ignaz Lutz instrument, a Viennese model, was intended to replace a harp in the orchestra and be played by a pianist. Clara had previously asked Brahms to acquire a professional evaluation of it from Eusebius Mandyczewski, curator of the Gesellschaft der Musikfreunde in Wien. In regard to the instrument's rejection, she wrote "I am glad that the people show good taste."

Robert Andres

Bibliography

Chissell, Joan. *Clara Schumann: A Dedicated Spirit.* London: Hamish Hamilton, 1983.

Litzmann, Berthold. *Clara Schumann: An Artist's Life.* Translated by Grace Hadow. London: Macmillan, 1913. Reprint. New York: Da Capo Press, 1972, 1979.

Plantinga, Leon B. *Schumann as Critic.* New Haven: Yale University Press, 1967.

Reich, Nancy B. *Clara Schumann: The Artist and the Woman.* Ithaca: Cornell University Press, 1985.

Schumann, Robert and Clara. *Briefe und Notizen Robert und Clara Schumanns.* Edited by Siegfried Kross. Bonn: Bouvier, 1982.

Walker, Alan, ed. *Robert Schumann: The Man and His Music.* London: Barrie & Jenkins, 1972.

SCHWEIGHOFER, MICHAEL (C. 1771–1809)

One of Vienna's earliest piano makers, Michael Schweighofer, a native of Bavaria, became a Viennese citizen in 1801. Receiving a dispensation for his foreign birth, Schweighofer won permission to build pianos in Vienna. Johann Michael Schweighofer (1806–1852) followed his father's profession and opened his own workshop in 1832. The only surviving instrument by Michael Schweighofer, a six-octave walnut **grand** from 1808, is in the collection of the Kunsthistorisches Museum in Vienna.

Martha Novak Clinkscale

Bibliography

Clinkscale, Martha Novak. *Makers of the Piano: 1700–1820.* Oxford: Oxford University Press, 1992.

Haupt, Helga. "Wiener Instrumentenbauer von 1791 bis 1815." *Studien zur Musikwissenschaft* 24 (1960): 120–184.

SCOTLAND, PIANO INDUSTRY IN

Piano-making in Scotland flourished between about 1785 and 1850. For much of the period, activity was centered in Edinburgh, although a few makers worked in Aberdeen. During the latter two decades, Glasgow assumed a prominent role.

Over twenty firms were active in Edinburgh between 1785 and 1835; after London, the Scottish capital was the most important piano-making center in Britain. The overall scale of production is difficult to assess. The largest firm, Muir, Wood & Co., achieved over one-tenth of Broadwood's output of almost 20,000 **square pianos** over the same twenty-year period; the other Edinburgh businesses were considerably smaller.

Although some were apprenticed to local craftsmen, many involved in the Scottish piano trade received their training within leading London houses. **John and Archibald Watson**, Robert Marr, Robert Allen (Aberdeen), and some of those employed by Muir, Wood & Co., **Rochead & Son**, and **Paterson, Mortimer & Co.**, were enticed from the English metropolis. John Broadwood and **Robert Stodart**, being Scots and therefore mistrustful of the English, preferred to employ men from their native land: the growing industry in Scotland subsequently drew some of these home again. For high-quality casework, Edinburgh firms could draw on the city's fine tradition of cabinetmaking.

The demand for pianos for the daughters of socially aspiring families provided local businesses with a reliable and growing market. The typical firm had a showroom or shop in the fashionable New Town, and a factory or workshop in the Old, where rents were lower. Although a few makers advertised **grands**, most restricted themselves to square and (later) **cabinet** and **cottage upright pianos**, reflecting the demands of domestic music-making.

The advantages over foreign counterparts lay in price and provenance. A combination of lower labor costs, no shipping or insurance charges, and economies in the technical design of instruments enabled undercutting of the London prices. The furniture appearance of most Scottish pianos imitates contemporary London fashions, while their mechanical characteristics represent the cheapest available options. Some intricate parts were probably obtained from London subcontractors, for example, brass under-**dampers**, damper **wires**, **nameboard** frets, and ready-cut and finished **ivories**. However, differences in **case** dimensions and manufacturing techniques confirm that most Scottish instruments were not simply relabelled imports.

In their advertisements, manufacturers frequently appealed to nationalist sentiment. This was a period in which the wealthier parts of Scottish urban society sought to balance expressions of national identity with a desire to keep apace with the latest London fashions. Scottish pianos can be seen as a metaphor of this phenomenon.

Although at least two Edinburgh firms established shops in London, the market for their pianos lay largely at home, or in cities in the north of England, Ireland, Russia, and the Americas.

Piano-making in Edinburgh went into sharp decline during the latter 1820s, following a disastrous economic depression, increasingly aggressive marketing by London firms, and the introduction of iron **plates** into square pianos. Although the growing industrial wealth of Glasgow fostered a lesser continuation of the trade during the following two decades, the mass production techniques of southern firms eventually priced the indigenous product out of the market.

John Cranmer

Bibliography

Newspapers–numerous advertisements and editorials from:

The *Edinburgh Evening Courant* 1760–1835

The *Caledonian Mercury* 1750–1780

The *Edinburgh Advertiser* 1770–1830

The *Scotsman* 1830–1840

The *Scots Magazine, or Edinburgh Literary Miscellany* 1818

The *Harmonicon*

Edinburgh Street Directories 1773–1850

The letters of John Muir Wood 1825–1828 (unpublished)

The Broadwood Archive (Surrey Record Office, U.K.)

SEILER

In 1849, in Liegnitz (Silesia), Germany, thirty-five-year-old cabinetmaker and musician, Eduard Seiler (1814–1875) founded the Seiler Pianofortefabrik. Piano production continued to the extent that by 1870 Seiler had built 1,000 pianos. Moreover, just two years later, in 1872, piano number 2,000 was ready for shipment.

After Eduard Seiler's death in 1875 his son, Johannes Seiler, took charge of the company. In 1896 the factory was enlarged, to provide extra space for production. Two years later, Seiler Pianofortefabrik had built its 25,000th instrument. Again, in 1907, the factory was enlarged.

In 1923 Johannes Seiler's son-in-law, Anton Dutz, took over management of the Liegnitz-based company, where 435 employees produced 3,000 pianos a year. As with virtually all European piano manufacturers during World War II, the Seiler company endured great economic hardship. After World War II the plant was occupied and the Seiler-Dutz family fled. In 1951 piano maker Steffan Seiler-Dutz, son of Anton Dutz, reestablished Seiler production in Copenhagen, Denmark.

In 1957, the Seiler piano was again made in Germany, first under license, and in 1962 Steffan Seiler-Dutz purchased the premises for a new factory location in Kitzingen, Germany, where Seiler pianos are currently manufactured. In 1963, Seiler-Dutz purchased a piano factory founded in 1837, the Zeitter & Winkelmann firm. Although this firm was based in Braunschweig, the actual manufacture of the Zeitter & Winkelmann piano was done in Kitzingen. After the above acquisition, Seiler's expanded production and sales necessitated further increase in plant space. In 1977 a concert hall and a training workshop for apprentices were added to another expansion of the plant.

Seiler apparently specialized in making **upright pianos** from the start. It was only later that Seiler manufactured a **concert grand** with a sound approaching that of the 9-foot pianos of better-known manufacturers such as **Steinway** and **Bechstein**. The company makes three "concert" **grand** sizes: the 180 cm (5 foot, 11 inch) Solon Grand, the 206 cm (6 foot, 9 inch) Semi Concert Grand, and the 240 cm (7 foot, 9 inch) Concert Grand. All three grands feature the **patented** "Membrator Soundboard System," which serves to disperse sound over a larger area than with previous designs. The Concert Grand has the addition of an "Amplivox" **scale design** that is said to produce "the sound of a full-size concert grand piano beyond its relatively short scale." In addition, all Seiler uprights and grands contain provision for **MIDI** compatibility.

Frederic Schoettler

SELF-PLAYING PIANO

Pianos that could be made to play without requiring the skill of a pianist marked a logical progression from the self-playing organ, in existence from at least as early as the beginning of the seventeenth century. The application of the pinned wooden barrel (as described under **Barrel Piano**) to the piano posed a complicated problem in mechanics. While with the barrel organ the pins on the barrel surface had only to move a lever (the keyframe key), which opened and closed an organ-chest pallet, in the case of the piano the pin was required to apply sufficient force to a **hammer** to strike the **strings**. This called for mechanical ingenuity and the use of stiffer pins in the barrel surface than the brass ones generally used in barrel organs.

In 1816 William Simmonds of London was granted British **Patent** Number 4030 for a barrel-type mechanism that could play a pianoforte, harpsichord, or organ. The barrel was designed along the same principles as the Flanders-style carillon barrel in that it could be repinned at will.

The first production barrel piano was a barrel-and-finger instrument by Thomas Hall **Rolfe**. However, John **Longman** made vertical pianos that had no **keyboard**: these were used for accompanying dancing and providing domestic musical entertainment. Other makers in Europe made similar keyboardless pianos in numbers: Imhof & Mukle in Germany continued to make large-compass, ornately cased cabinet barrel-only pianos until around 1865.

Arthur W.J.G. Ord-Hume

Bibliography

Harding, Rosamond E.M. *The Piano-Forte: Its History Traced to the Great Exhibition of 1851.* Cambridge: Cambridge University Press, 1933. Reprints, New York: Da Capo Press, 1973; Old Woking, Surrey: Gresham Books, 1978.

Ord-Hume, Arthur W.J.G. *Barrel Organ—History of the Self-Playing Organ.* London: Allen & Unwin, 1978.

———. *Pianola—History & Development....* London: Allen & Unwin, 1984.

———. *Player Piano—History of the Mechanical Piano.* London: Allen & Unwin, 1970.

SERIAL NUMBERS

At the conclusion of the manufacturing process, each piano is assigned a serial number, which is usually stamped on the **plate** or imprinted in some wooden surface. Although usually found in the **tuning pin** area, serial numbers may be located in various places, including large **action** parts such as the **keyframe**. These numbers identify each piano and correspond

with permanent records kept at the factory, which show the date of manufacture. Piano serial numbers are also listed in piano atlases that contain the names and dates of manufacture of various brands of pianos.

Serial numbers, usually containing six or seven digits, should not be confused with job numbers, used at the factory during manufacturing to identify the many parts of each individual piano.

Danny L. Boone

Bibliography

Herzog, H[ans] K[urt], comp. *Europe Piano Atlas: Piano-Nummern.* Frankfurt am Main: Bochinsky, 1989.

Michel, Norman Elwood. *Michel's Piano Atlas.* Rivera, Cal.: N.E. Michel, 1957.

Pierce, Bob. *Pierce Piano Atlas.* Long Beach, Cal.: Bob Pierce, 1990.

Taylor, S.K. *The Musician's Piano Atlas.* Macclesfield, Cheshire, Eng.: Omicron Publishing, 1981.

SEYTRE, CLAUDE FÉLIX (FL.MID–NINETEENTH CENTURY)

Claude Félix Seytre was a French engineer-mechanic from Lyon who on 24 January 1842 was granted a French **patent**, number 8,691, for a means of playing pianos and organs automatically, as well as accompanying them on another instrument such as an accordion, using either a perforated card strip or a perforated disc. He called his attachment the *Autopanphones* and claimed it could be built into instruments or attached to existing examples. **John McTammany** suggests that the ideas described in the patent were never realized, but Marie Pierre Hamel describes such an instrument with the comment that a piece of music comprising 80 measures (bars) cost no more than 1 franc 50 centimes. Rosamond Harding, translating this, misreads "measures" as "metres."

Arthur W.J.G. Ord-Hume

Bibliography

Hamel, Marie Pierre. *Nouveau Manuel Complet du Facteur d'Orgues.* Paris: Encyclopédique de Roret, 1849.

Harding, Rosamond E.M. *The Piano-Forte: Its History Traced to the Great Exhibition of 1851.* Cambridge: Cambridge University Press, 1933. Reprints, New York: Da Capo Press, 1973; Old Woking, Surrey: Gresham Books, 1978.

McTammany, John. *The Technical History of the Player*. New York: The Musical Courier Co., 1915.

Marcuse, Sibyl. *Musical Instruments: A Comprehensive Dictionary*. Garden City, N.Y.: Doubleday and Co., 1964.

Ord-Hume, Arthur W.J.G. *Pianola*. London: Allen & Unwin, 1984.

Wright, Rowland. *Dictionnaire des instruments de musique*. London: Battley Brothers, Ltd., 1941.

SHIMMING

Shimming is the process by which cracks in **soundboards** are filled. A wedge-shaped strip of spruce is glued into the soundboard crack, which, in turn, has been cut out to accept the strip.

Philip Jamison, III

SHUDI, BURKAT (1702–1773)

Burkat Shudi played a seminal part in the development of the pianoforte and the piano industry in London and, even if only indirectly, was responsible for founding the famed manufactory of **John Broadwood**.

Burckhardt, Burckat, or Burkat Tschudi was born in Schwanden, near Glarus in Switzerland, on 13 March 1702, the son of a prominent wool merchant, councilman, and surgeon and part of a family whose origins can be traced back to the year 870. Trained as a joiner and cabinetmaker, the young Burkat decided to travel to London, where skills such as his were in demand. He made the journey at the age of sixteen in 1718.

Hermann Tabel, who brought the Ruckers tradition of harpsichord-building to London, took the young Tschudi as an apprentice early in the 1720s and the youth seems to have blossomed quickly in his new profession. By 1728 he had left Tabel and set up in business on his own.

Tschudi, who anglicized his name to Shudi, lived at No. 1 Meards Street, Soho, close to the home of Johann Christoph Schmidt (John Christopher Smith), Handel's friend and amanuensis. The young Handel spoke no English at that time and so spent most of his spare time with the German-speaking community, which included the young Shudi. Thus began a profitable relationship for Shudi that culminated in Handel's presenting one of Shudi's harpsichords to the soprano Anna Strada in 1731.

Within a short while, Shudi was making harpsichords and spinets for the nobility: an account exists in the Royal Library at Windsor Castle showing that he charged £8.10s to make a new spinet for Prince George (later King George III). He made several improvements to the harpsichord, among these being a pedal to bring in preset registers without the player having to move his hands from the keys, and in 1769 the "Venetian Swell."

John Broadwood, who had joined him as an apprentice, quickly became one of his most trusted craftsmen. On 2 January 1769 the thirty-six-year-old John Broadwood married Shudi's second daughter, Barbara, then not yet twenty-one.

Although Burkat Shudi never made pianofortes, John Broadwood took a keen interest in the developments being carried out by another former Shudi worker, **Johannes Zumpe**. There is inconclusive family evidence that John Broadwood may have built or otherwise have owned a pianoforte as early as 1770.

Burkat Shudi made over his premises in Great Pulteney Street and Bridle Lane to John Broadwood in March 1771, giving his son-in-law right and title to his stock and trade and moving to a new house in Charlotte Street, Tottenham Court Road. It was here that he died on 19 August 1773 at age seventy-one.

The Shudi business made nearly twelve-hundred harpsichords in the sixty-five years of activity from 1729.

Arthur W.J.G. Ord-Hume

Bibliography

Boalch, Donald H. *Makers of the Harpsichord & Clavichord, 1440–1840*. Oxford: Oxford University Press, 1974.

Russell, Raymond. *The Harpsichord & Clavichord*. London: Faber, 1973.

Wainwright, David. *Broadwood by Appointment: A History*. London: Quiller, 1982; New York: Universe Books, 1983.

SIENA PIANO

The Siena Piano, Harp of David Piano, and Immortal Piano are the various names that have been given to a much-traveled Italian **upright**, whose construction was begun in the late eighteenth century and completed over a period of several decades by Sebastiano Marchisio of Turin and his sons, Giacomo and Enrico. Work on the instrument actually spanned four generations, as Enrico's grandson, Nicodemo Ferri, and his cousin, Carlo Bartolozzi, carved the piano's elaborate casework in their studio in Siena.

This upright piano was adorned with elaborate carvings of the Harp of David guarded by heraldic griffins, tablets of the Ten Commandments, and other biblical themes. There were also twenty cherubs in a classic festival pose as well as much scrollwork, fruits, and leaves. The sculptors even included small likenesses of five composers: Handel, Mozart, Guido Aretino, Cherubini, and Gluck. Stately lions served as support posts for this ornate instrument.

In 1867 the piano was sent by the city of Siena to the Paris Universal Exposition, where it was used for concerts in the Italian pavilion. Camille Saint-Saëns was among those who played it. The following year, the Siena town officials persuaded the Ferri family to donate the piano as a wedding gift to Crown Prince Umberto (later Humbert I) and Princess Margherita. **Franz Liszt** is said to have played "La Campanella" on the Siena Piano during the wedding festivities. Later the piano was inherited by King Victor Emmanuel III and was sometimes played by touring musicians.

During World War II, the instrument was stolen by members of General Erwin Rommel's Afrika Korps. It was encased in a thick layer of protective plaster and taken by the army to the Libyan Desert, where it eventually was buried in the sand near El'Alamein, Egypt. The piano was discovered in 1942 by a group of British soldiers using a mine sweeper. As they approached the buried piano, their equipment pulled magnetically on the **strings**. When the sweeper moved away, the strings produced harplike sounds as they sprang back into place. The British soldiers were curious about this music and somehow decided not to destroy the abandoned piano.

In 1943 the British Salvage Depot sold the Siena Piano, still in its bulky protective case, to a junk merchant in Tel Aviv. He, in turn, sold the plaster heap to the family of Avner Carmi, a local piano technician, who had been trained in Berlin. Much to the surprise of Carmi, he discovered that underneath that layer of plaster was the piano his grandfather, the Russian pianist Mattis Yanowsky, had so often talked about playing during a tour of Italy. Carmi had even made two trips to Italy before the war in an effort to study this instrument. Both times he had failed to see the object of his research.

In 1960 Avner and Hannah Carmi published *The Immortal Piano*, an account of the saga of the Siena Piano. Here they reported that the piano had special musical qualities because the **soundboard** was constructed from wood that was once a part of King Solomon's Temple. Two pillars from the razed temple were reported to have been taken from Jerusalem to Rome in A.D. 70 and were later recycled in Siena by some local churches. The piano's initial builder acquired some of this fabled wood after an earthquake demolished the church that had last used the temple pillars.

It took over three years' work for Avner Carmi to go through the tedious and expensive process of removing the plaster from the carved casework and then restoring the Siena Piano with spare parts from other instruments that had been sold as postwar salvage in Tel Aviv. He completed his work on 30 November 1947, the day the United Nations declared the independence of Israel.

In 1953, Avner and Hannah Carmi brought the Siena Piano to the United States, where it received much attention. For seventeen years, the piano was featured in concerts, radio shows, television specials, and recordings. The Carmis wrote *The Immortal Piano* during this period and it was translated into German and Japanese, as there was international interest in the instrument. They returned to Israel with the piano in 1970.

An article about the Siena Piano was published in the Israeli journal, *Yedkihot Aharonot* on 19 September 1990. Daphna Fischer has provided this translation from Hebrew: "Ten years ago Carmi died of pneumonia. He died while working on a recording of the piano. He was 80 years old. Today, the piano is in Hannah's house in Peth-Tikvah. Many people from around the world who read the book call and ask if the piano is real and still exists. Hannah invites them to come and see it and they do." The article further states that she often receives offers to buy the instrument (it was long ago given to the Carmis by the exiled king of Italy) but she refuses to sell it. Some have valued the instrument at over a million and a half dollars.

Peggy Flanagan Baird

Bibliography

Carmi, Avner, and Hannah Carmi. *The Immortal Piano*. New York: Crown Publishers, Inc., 1960.

Slonimsky, Nicolas. *Music Since 1900*. Fourth Edition: 843–844. New York: Charles Scribner's Sons. 1971.

SILBERMANN, GOTTFRIED (1683–1753)

Gottfried Silbermann was born 14 January 1683 in Kleinbobritsch near Meissen in Saxony and died on 4 August 1753 in Dresden. Silbermann got his training as an "organ and instrument builder" from his elder brother, Andreas (1678–1734), in Strassburg, Alsace. For some years after 1703 his brother was absent from the workshop and Gottfried was responsible for the business as well as for the construction of an organ in Strassburg. In 1711 he returned to Saxony and settled in Freiberg near Meissen as an organ and instrument builder. He soon became famous, mainly for building some of the most beautiful organs in Saxony; but he also became quickly known as a creative inventor of new stringed **keyboard** instruments. For his wingshaped *Cembal d'amour*, which he finished in 1721, he received a Royal **patent**. According to the description by Johann Friedrich Agricola, copied by E.L. Gerber in his *Historisch-Biographisches Lexikon der Tonkünstler* (1790–1792), this instrument was supposed to have been a kind of clavichord, large, wingshaped, and relatively loud. However, our knowledge of it is very limited, since not one *Cembal d'amour* instrument is known today. There are good reasons to believe that the known descriptions are erroneous and that the *Cembal d'amour* was not a kind of clavichord but rather an early type of **tangent piano**.

In Strassburg, around 1703–4, Gottfried Silbermann had helped build an extremely large **cimbalom** (dulcimer) instrument for the virtuoso **Pantaléon Hebenstreit**. With this instrument Hebenstreit travelled to Paris and played for Louis XIV with such success that the king named the instrument *Pantaléon* in his honor. For Silbermann, his association with Hebenstreit and the experience of hearing Hebenstreit's cimbalom, with its possibilities of all dynamic shadings from pianissimo to fortissimo as well as the intermingling of undamped sounds, certainly made an unforgettable impression and was important to his future invention of *Hammerklavier* stops for lifting **dampers** (see below).

Hebenstreit, who in 1714 became a highly paid Saxon court musician, commissioned Silbermann, by then also living in Saxony, to build another *pantaléon* instrument for him; and it seems that it was Silbermann who first equipped these large cimbaloms, now generally called "pantalone," with removable keyboards to make the playing of them easier, thus creating an instrument *che fà il piano e il forte*, like the new *cembali con martelli* of **Bartolomeo Cristofori** but equipped with different **action**. This would explain not only why Hebenstreit initiated a lawsuit against Silbermann, but also why in Saxony and Thuringia during the first half of the eighteenth century *hammer-harpsichords* or *cembali con martelli* often were called "pantalone," if the **hammers** fell on the **strings** from above. **Christoph Gottlieb Schröter**, who in 1721 demonstrated hammer actions at the Court in Dresden, reported later:

> More than twenty cities are known to me in which instead of the usual harpsichords since 1721 such instruments with hammers and hoppers are made which, if the hammers fall from above on the strings, are called pantalons by makers and buyers.

Most probably Gottfried Silbermann experimented even prior to this date (1721) with various kinds of hammer actions. **Johann Sebastian Bach** may have seen one of these early Silbermann instruments. But it was apparently only after Silbermann had an opportunity to study carefully the hammer action of an original Cristofori *cembalo con martelli* instrument during the 1720s that he managed to finish—probably in 1732—his first **grand piano** that worked successfully. According to an article on *"Cembal d'amour"* in Volume 5 of Zedler's *Universal Lexikon*, which appeared in 1733 in Leipzig, he called this new instrument "Piano-Forte," a name for the hammer-harpsichord, which combined the adjectives *piano* and *forte* as a compound substantive, one which is now used all over the world. Though the name "Piano-Forte" is an invention of Gottfried Silbermann's, Silbermann later signed his pianos (those preserved in the castles Sanssouci and Stadtschloss [in Potsdam] and in Nuremberg) less courageously with "Instrument: Piano et forte genandt," an expression that **Johann Sebastian Bach** also used when acting as Silbermann's agent in 1749.

It appears that in 1732 Silbermann finished at least two new pianoforte instruments, one of which he presented to the Crown Prince of Saxony while the other he sent to Leipzig. This might have been the *Hammerflügel* with which J.S. Bach declared himself satisfied in 1733; and there are good reasons to believe that Bach played it in his Collegium musicum concert on 17 June 1733 (*see* Bach, Johann Sebastian).

Today three Silbermann *pianoforte* instruments are still known (two in Potsdam, one in Nuremberg), and their action is strikingly similar to those of Cristofori. However, an important difference has to be noted: Cristofori's pianos have no mechanism to lift all dampers, which Silbermann's have. Thus, Silbermann is in principle the inventor of the modern piano **pedal**, though his damper mechanism was still operated by hand levers. Since the duration of the tones is much shorter on Silbermann's wingshaped pianos than on modern **concert grands**, a piece like the first Prelude of the Welltempered Clavier by Bach can easily be played throughout with lifted dampers.

Silbermann also invented other mutational stops. One consists of a row of ivory plates mounted over the strings right above the strike line of the hammers. When they touch the strings, a bright, almost harpsichordlike sound is produced. (The Sanssouci piano uses a brass plate in the extreme treble rather than ivory). As Stewart Pollens described it in his informative study:

All the stops in Silbermann's pianos must be operated with both hands—that is, the dampers have to be lifted from both ends simultaneously. This is also true for the mutational stops. Thus, it is not possible to operate the stops in the midst of playing, but only at pauses.

Silbermann's fame as a builder of excellent pianoforte instruments spread all over Germany. A reflection of it is found in an article in Hiller's *Anhang zum Dritten Jahrgang der Wöchentlichen Nachrichten und Anmerkungen die Musik betreffend* from 24 July 1769, praising a compound (**combination**) harpsichord-piano of Johann Andreas **Stein**. Here we read:

The instrument, which has been named Fortepiano and which only Silbermann could construct on such a high level of perfection, belongs to a class by itself and should not be put into the same category as the great number of instruments of the new kind which are either [badly] copied or self-manufactured

[home-made]; it is of special delight for most amateurs, particularly if it is played with dampers. . . .

Contrary to the prevailing common perception, probably soon after 1733 and in any case prior to 1740, J.S. Bach was not only acquainted with Silbermann's pianos but valued and played them and probably acquired one. When he visited the Prussian king in Potsdam in 1747, he had no problems whatsoever in playing the pianoforte on which he improvised on a theme given to him by **Frederick the Great**—an indication of his familiarity with the instrument.

Johann Nikolaus Forkel reported that King Frederick was such a great admirer of Silbermann's pianofortes that he bought fifteen of them. While this might well be an exaggeration, at least one more Silbermann pianoforte existed in Potsdam prior to World War II than the two instruments now preserved there. According to a newspaper advertisement of 1764, still another Silbermann piano was put up for sale in Leipzig that year (Heyde).

Eva Badura-Skoda

Bibliography

Badura-Skoda, Eva. "Besaitete Tasteninstrumente um und nach 1700: Hammer—Pantalone und Lautenwerke," (unpublished, in preparation).

———. "Komponierte Johann Sebastian Bach 'Hammerklavier-Konzerte'?" In *Bach-Jahrbuch 1991*, p. 159f.

———."Zur Frühgeschichte des Hammerklaviers." In *Florilegium Musicologicum, Festschrift für Hellmut Federhofer zum 75. Geburtstag*. Tutzing, 1988.

Heyde, Herbert. "Der Instrumentenbau in Leipzig zur Zeit Johann Sebastian Bachs." In *300 Jahre Johann Sebastian Bach*. Ausstellungs-Katalog, Tutzing, 1985.

Müller, Werner. *Gottfried Silbermann. Persönlichkeit und Werk*. Leipzig: Deutscher Verlag für Musik, 1982.

Pollens, Stewart. "Gottfried Silbermann's Pianos." *Organ Yearbook* 17 (1986): 103–22.

SKINNING

When skinning a **hammer**, the technician removes an amount of **felt** with sandpaper in order to remove the worn or overly hard outer layer. This may be a part of the **voicing** process, or may be done in order to remove grooves cut into the hammer by the **strings** after hard use.

The latter process is called "shaping." A similar technique may be used on the **damper** felts to remove the crusty outer layer that may cause unwanted **action** noise.

See also Voicing.

Philip Jamison, III

SKIVING

Skiving describes the process of cutting **felt** for **hammer** heads. A strip of woolen felt, long enough to cover an entire set of hammers, is cut ("skived") with a knife into a triangular shape in cross section. High-pressure gluing onto the wooden molding produces the familiar teardrop shape.

Philip Jamison, III

SOFT PEDAL

See Pedals and Stops

SOHMER PIANO COMPANY

The origins of the American piano-making firm of Sohmer predate 1860. Hugo Sohmer (1846–1913) was born in Dunningen, Germany, immigrating to the United States at the age of sixteen, where he apprenticed himself to the piano-making firm of Schuetze & Ludolf. In 1868 he returned to Europe, visiting the principal piano makers and studying their methods, returning to the United States in 1870. In 1872, in association with the Bohemian-born piano maker Joseph Kuder, he purchased the firm of Marschall & Mittauer, itself a successor to the J. H. Boernhoeft piano shop. From a small beginning of only a few pianos a week, the company grew in quality and productive capacity, receiving an award from the Centennial Exposition held in Philadelphia in 1876. Another factory was added in 1883, and the firm moved to yet another factory at Astoria, Long Island, in 1887. The company took out several **patents**, including one for a **scale** in which an auxiliary **string** for each unison was excited by sympathetic vibration. Of more lasting influence was the invention of the **baby grand** piano, the prototype of which, the "Bijou Grand," was patented in 1884.

In the early 1920s the company built a large plant in Long Island City, which became the center for all Sohmer manufacturing activities. Eschewing instruments for the concert stage, the company concentrated on the production of high-quality vertical pianos and small and medium-size **grands**. The Sohmer Company remained in the hands of the Sohmer family until 1982, when it was purchased by **Pratt, Read & Company** (est. 1798), then the world's largest manufacturer of piano **keys** and **actions**. Harry (d.1990) and Robert Sohmer, grandsons of the founder, remained with the firm in managerial positions, and production was moved from the Long Island City facility to the Pratt, Read factory at Ivoryton, Connecticut.

In 1986, Sohmer was purchased by a group of shareholders headed by Robert McNeil, former chief of McNeil Laboratories. Simultaneously, the company announced the acquisition of the **Mason & Hamlin, Knabe**, and George Steck trademarks, along with the corresponding tooling, designs, and works-in-progress formerly owned by the defunct **Aeolian Corporation**. Sohmer was thought to be one of the few companies in the United States capable of restoring the prestigious Mason & Hamlin line to its former state of excellence. In 1987, the company also acquired the Charles Ramsey Corporation, then the country's largest manufacturer of piano hardware; and in June 1989, Sohmer itself was purchased by the **Falcone Piano Company** (est. 1984) of Haverhill, Massachusetts, a small maker of high-grade grand pianos. Production was then transferred to a new plant in Ellysburg, Pennsylvania. Somewhat earlier, in June 1988, a controlling interest in the Falcone Company had been purchased by Bernard G. Greer of Bellevue, Washington; and in August 1989, Greer also acquired the Sohmer/Mason & Hamlin/Knabe/Steck conglomerate. In 1989 Sohmer was manufacturing a limited quantity of **upright pianos** at the Ellysburg plant, and in the fall of 1990, the first of the reconstituted Mason & Hamlin grand pianos were shipped from the Haverhill plant. The firm has since changed its name to the Mason & Hamlin Corporation, under which Mason & Hamlin and Falcone, as well as Sohmer, will be manufactured.

James Howard Richards

Bibliography

Dolge, Alfred. *Pianos and Their Makers.* Covina, Cal.: Covina Publishing Company, 1911. Reprint. New York: Dover Publications, Inc., 1972.

Fine, Larry. *The Piano Book*. Boston: Brookside Press, 1987.

"Mason & Hamlin Corporation." *The Purchaser's Guide to the Music Industries 1991*. New York: The Music Trades Corporation, 1990.

The New Grove Dictionary of Musical Instruments. Edited by Stanley Sadie. S. v. "Sohmer, Hugo," by Nancy Groce.

"New Mason & Hamlin Grands Ship." *The Piano Technicians Journal* 33 (October 1990):9.

"Pratt, Read Acquires Sohmer & Co. Piano Makers." *The Music Trades* 130 (August 1982): 18, 20.

"Pratt Read Sells Sohmer; Campbell Remains As Pres." *The Music Trades* 134 (June 1986): 34.

"Recreating the Famed Mason & Hamlin Piano." *The Music Trades* 138 (November 1990): 64–66.

"Sohmer Acquires Chas. Ramsey Corp." *The Music Trades* 135 (April 1987): 22.

"Sohmer, Mason & Hamlin Piano Sold to Washington Investor." *The Music Trades* 137 (August 1989): 42, 43.

"Sohmer Production Moves to Pennsylvania Plant." *The Music Trades* 137 (January 1989): 35.

Spillane, Daniel. *History of the American Pianoforte*. New York: By the Author, 1910. Reprint, New York: Da Capo Press, 1969.

SOSTENENTE PIANOS

Sostenente (or *sostinente*) piano is the name given to keyboard instruments on which the duration of sound is artificially lengthened. This can be done by (a) an endless bow, (b) compressed air, (c) repeated and quick striking of **hammers**, (d) free sounding reeds, (e) electric and/or electronic devices. The name *sostenente* is derived from the *sostenente piano* invented by Henry Robert Mott of Brighton (1817). A *sostenente* piano is by no means exclusively a piano.

(1) *Endless bow instruments*, also called wheel cymbals. The earliest example of one of these instruments is the *Geigenwerk* or *Geigen-Clavicymbel*, invented between 1550 and 1575 by Hans Haiden in Nuremberg. Haiden made in total some twenty-three of these instruments, none of which has survived. Instruments were ordered by August, Elector of Saxony, by Emperor Rudolf II, by Hans Leo Hassler, and many others. The *Geigenwerk* had the outline of a harpsichord. A pedal made wheels rotate against **strings**, which were pulled down by depressing the **keys**. A drawing of the *Geigenwerk* can be found in volume II of the *Syntagma Musicum: De Organographia* by Michael Praetorius (1619). The instrument of the Elector was seen and described by Johann Georg Schröter (1683–c.1750) at the beginning of the eighteenth century. Hans Leo Hassler bequeathed his instrument to the Elector Christian II.

The *Geigenwerk* was imitated abroad, e.g., by Fray Raymundo Truchado in Spain (1625); it also inspired many similar instruments built later. All were based upon the principle of the endless bow. It is not known whether the "arched viall," quoted by Samuel Pepys (1664), was an instrument made by Haiden or one constructed on similar principles by an English maker.

During the eighteenth century numerous makers tried their hand at endless bow instruments. One such was the *Clavecin-vielle* by Cuisiniér in 1708, which was similar to a large hurdy-gurdy. The wheel was moved by means of a pedal. There were twenty-nine keys and the instrument rested on four legs.

Similar were the instruments built in France by Le Voir (1742) and Le Gay (1762). Le Voir's instrument had twenty-five strings, but fifty tones could be obtained. The endless bow was activated by means of two pedals. The instrument made by Le Gay resembled an ordinary harpsichord with an additional set of strings that could be bowed by a wheel, as in a hurdy-gurdy. Gerli tried to improve this in 1789 without success.

The *Clavier-Gamben* constructed by the Germans Georg Gleichmann (Ilmenau) and Friedrich Ficker (Zeitz), c.1720, seem to have been inspired by Hans Haiden.

The Dutchman Roger Plenius constructed (Paris, 1741) a *Lyrichord*, in which the strings were tuned by leaden weights so as to continually keep equal tension. Several wheels rotated at varying speeds (as in the Truchado *geigenwerk*-styled instrument), thus setting the strings into vibration. As with Truchado's instrument, dynamics and vibrato were also obtainable with the *Lyrichord*. The *Épinette à archet* by Renaud of Orléans (1745) was a spinet with an endless bow. In 1779 Karl Greiner (Wetzlar) built a *Bogenhammerklavier*, similar to Le Gay's instrument, but with a **Hammerklavier** instead of a harpsichord. Haiden's *Geigenwerk* was again revived in the *Bogenflügel* by Johann Hohlfeld (Berlin, 1753). His instrument is mentioned by C.P.E. Bach (*Versuch über die wahre Art das Cla-*

vier zu spielen). Other *sostenente* instruments of this first category were devised by Garbrecht (Königsberg, 1792), von Mayer (Görlitz, 1794), Thomas Kunz (Prague, 1799). Mention should be made also of the *Xänorphika* by Carl Röllig (1801). **John Isaac Hawkins** constructed the *Claviol* in Philadelphia (1802), inspired by Le Voir's instrument. The *Claviol* had twenty-five strings and three **bridges**. Papelard (Paris, 1847) also built a *Claviol*, but this instrument was not a *sostenente* piano; its name is misleading. Father Grégoir Trentin took out a **patent** in 1824 for the *Metagofano*, a device with an endless bow to be placed inside the piano.

The *Polylectrum* (Dietz in Paris, 1827) was a bowed **upright piano**. The *Piano à sons prolongés* by Herman Lichtenthal (Paris, 1830) used gut strings, thereby producing a softer sound.

In the twentieth century, Henry Müller-Braunau built a *Pentaphon*, shaped like a zither (Hamburg, 1903). The instrument had twenty-eight frets. A **leather** band-bow was pressed onto the strings by holding down the keys. The *Streichharmonium* by Karl Beddies (Gotha, 1909) was never commercially produced, since it was surpassed almost immediately by Ludwig Hupfeld's *Geigenklavier*.

Sometimes a patent was obtained for an instrument that was never actually built. Such is the case with the *Celestinette* by the Englishman William Mason (c.1761) and the *Celestina*, a bowed piano by Adam Walker (1784).

With his *Euphon* (1789) and his *clavicylindre* (1793) the German acoustician Ernst Chladni (1756–1827) inspired a number of inventors to experiment with a rotating cylinder instead of an endless bow. Different sound producers were tried out: tuning forks in the *Melodikon* by Pierre Riffelsen (Copenhagen, 1800), metal rods in the *Melodion* by Johann Christian Dietz (Emmerich, 1805) and brass rods upon a brass cylinder in the *Euphonia* by Louis Klatte (Erfurt, 1812).

Other instruments guided by the idea of a rotating cylinder were built by Franz Leppich (*Panmelodikon*, 1810), Emile Vanderburg (*Odeophone*, 1818), Hubert Cyrille Baudet (*Piano-violon*, and *Piano Quatuor*, both c.1865).

Wooden rods rubbed by a cloth-covered cylinder were used in the *Xylosistron* (1808) and the *Xylharmonicon* (1810) by Johannes Andrea Uthe from Sangerhausen, also in the *Uranion* (1810) and the *Terpodion* (1816) by Johann Buschmann in Friedrichroda, and the *Harmonichord* by Friedrich and Johann Kaufmann in Dresden (1809), which should be mentioned especially because of Carl Maria von Weber's composition *Adagio und Rondo für das Harmonichord* (1811). Wooden teeth were still used in David Loeschman's *Terpolian* (c.1820). The *sostenente* piano by Goldsworthy Gurney (patent in 1825) used glass rods and tubes or bells to reinforce the sound obtained when the rods were bowed with a wet ribbon. In 1817 Henry Mott (Brighton), after whose instrument this series of *sostenente* pianos was named, constructed a piano wherein a series of rollers activated silk threads, which in turn transmitted their vibration onto the strings.

A rather round and pleasant timbre was possible on the *Piano enarmonico* constructed in Paris by Luigi Russolo. He used an endless bow (no cylinder) and coiled springs instead of strings. The original instrument has disappeared, but a copy, made by Russolo, is now on display in the Russolo-Pratella collection in Varese (Italy).

(2) *Compressed air*. Reduced to their simplest mechanism, instruments using this technique are in fact aeolian harps. In these instruments a jet of compressed air (obtained by means of bellows moved by pedals or eventually by a motor) is directed upon already vibrating strings in order to prolong the vibration. The first instrument of this subdivision seems to be the *Aéroclavicorde* (1778), of which almost nothing is known. It inspired Johann Schnell, in Paris to conceive his *Anémocorde* (1789), which was presented to Queen Marie Antoinette. Due to the political situation she could not afford to pay its inventor, and the instrument fell into other hands. The *Anémocorde* was similar in shape to a **grand piano**. Each note had three strings, two of which were struck by hammers; the third was subjected to a jet of air. Knee levers made dynamic changes possible. The bellows were worked with pedals. It seems that the *Anémocorde* inspired Isouard (Paris, 1837) with his *Piano éolique*. Here a movable box, divided into compartments, each of which was connected to a windbox through a valve, was placed underneath the strings. The *Piano éolique* must have had some success, for in 1851 its mechanism was improved and patented by Henri Herz. Similar instruments were made by **Jean-Henri Pape** (1840, 1850), Johnson & Anderson (1861), and Tongue (1871). Gustave Baudet (Paris, 1875)

constructed a *Piano chanteur* in which air-jet-influenced strings were replaced by vibrating steel rods. Previous to these metal rods, Schortmann (Buttelstedt, 1820) attempted to use upright wooden rods in his *Aeolsklavier.*

(3) *Repeated and quick striking of hammers.* This technique also suggests sustained tones. The first *sostenente* piano of this subdivision is the *Piano trémolophone* by the Parisian maker Philippe de Girard. His idea of a fast rotating cylinder with projecting tabs that engaged the hammers to strike (more or less the principle used in automatic carillon playing) was used by John Isaac Hawkins of Philadelphia (1800), **Sébastien Erard** (Paris, 1812), and Jean-Henri Pape (Paris, after 1825).

It was also possible to place a device in the piano that produced a quickly repeated action. All these appliances used springs fixed onto the hammers. The most reputed of these were the *Melopianos* by Caldera & Bossi (Torino, 1873), Henri Herz (Paris, c.1850), and Kirckman & Son (London, c.1850). Sometimes two sets of hammers were used, as in the *Armonipiano* by Ricordi & Finzi, and by Vaclav Hlavac (both c.1900).

(4) *Free sounding reeds. Piano à prolongement* was a generic name given in French-speaking countries to any piano in which a continuous sound was obtained by means of vibrating reeds. The name was derived from Edouard Alexandre's *Piano à prolongement* (c.1840). The acoustical principle used here is the **aliquot** vibration of reeds when a given string is struck.

Apart from the above-mentioned instrument by Alexandre, the *Piano scandé* by Houdart & Lenz (Paris, 1853), the *Piano à sons soutenus à volonté* by Jean Louis Boisselot (Marseille, 1843), and the *Piano à sons prolongés* by Schayrer (Paris, 1846) all belong to the same category. About 1927 Marcel Tournier & Gabriel Gaveau invented the *Canto*, a device that transmitted the vibrations of the strings by electromagnetic means to a set of reeds placed inside a grand piano.

Additional wooden resonators, in which the reeds were placed, were used in the *Eolodikon*, constructed in 1840 by Hanz Baltzer (Frankfurt/Oder). Since the sound produced was too loud, a volume-control system had to be added. This instrument was not successful.

(5) *Electric and electronic devices.* Although electricity is somewhat of a newcomer in application to musical instruments, an early example can be found in the *Clavessin électrique* invented by the Jesuit Jean-Baptiste Laborde in 1759. In this instrument static electricity was used to make two bells sound, alternately struck, as long as the key was held down.

Richard Eisemann used electromagnets in his *Elektrophonisches Klavier* (c.1890). Inducing strings into vibration by means of electromagnets is a technique applied in the *Choralcero* (1909), the *Crea-tone* (1930), and *Variochord* (1937).

Ordinary pianos in which the sound can be altered and/or amplified at will by electricity are the *Elektrochord* by the Förster firm (1933) and the *Pianotron* by Everett Piano Co. (c. 1934).

The *Sostenente-piano* of Vladimir Djemenjuk (Moscow, 1960), uses an electric motor to rotate a cylinder. Benjamin Meissner (Millburn, N.J.) took out a patent for an electric piano without **soundboard** but with electrostatic pickups. His system was eventually improved by Walter Nernst and Oskar Vierling of Berlin in the Neo-**Bechstein** (1934). In the Berlin instrument, electromagnetic pickups were placed above grouped strings that were struck with ultralight hammers.

Since World War II numerous electric and electronic pianos and devices labelled *sostenente* have been introduced to the public. Among them *Compac Roadracer* by Crumar Co., (since 1970), *Pianet* by Bierl & Zacharias (1962), *Beleton* (1954), and *Clavinet* (1960) by Hohner Company. Interesting, though unfortunately undeveloped due to their creation during the prewar era, were the *Piano électrique* by Jean Béthenod (Paris, 1928), the *Minipiano* by Hardman, Peck & Co. (New York, 1935), the *Dynatone* by Arthur Ansley (New York, 1938), and the *Storytone* by Story & Clark (New York, 1939).

F.J. de Hen

Bibliography

Buchner, Alexandr. "Das Sostenente-Piano." *Revue Belge de Musicologie* (1980–1981): 130–146.

Halfpenny, Eric. "The Lyrichord." *Galpin Society Journal* III (1950): 46 ff.

Harding, Rosamond E.M. *The Piano-Forte: Its History Traced to the Great Exhibition of 1851.* Cambridge: Cambridge University Press, 1933. Reprints. New York: Da Capo Press, 1973; Old Woking, Surrey: Gresham Books, 1978.

Pontécoulant, Louis Adolphe de. *Organographie.* Amsterdam: Fritz Knuf, reprint 1972.

SOSTENUTO PEDAL

The *sostenuto* **pedal** is usually the middle pedal on modern **grands**; it allows sustaining of certain **tones** while others continue to be damped. A rod holds up only those **dampers** that have been raised by their **keys**. Blanchet et Roller in Paris tried the idea in the 1840s, and **Claude Montal** of Paris exhibited such a pedal in London, 1862. Albert **Steinway patented** it for **squares** in 1874 and for grands and **uprights** in 1875. Uprights seldom have *sostenuto* pedals nowadays, and most European makers of grands avoided them until after World War II. Interesting musical effects of the stop are called for by such contemporary composers as Elliott Carter, Luciano Berio, and Ellen Taaffe Zwilich.

See also Pedals and Stops.

Edwin M. Good

SOUNDBOARD

All stringed instruments contain by design a vibratory medium through which the excited motions of the **strings** can be given resonance and intensity. Be the instrument a violin, a harp, or a piano, the vibrating string, if not coupled with some sort of soundboard, cannot be adequately heard, since its surface area is too small to vigorously move sufficient amounts of air. But if the string can be harnessed with a flexible soundboard, the effects of its vibrational energy will be transferred to a much larger medium capable of exciting sizeable zones of air. Hence, the feeble efforts of the unaided string will be given a much larger voice—ample in both sonority and volume. To appreciate the behavior and function of the soundboard it is only necessary to grasp that it is primarily a mechanical amplifier. Although the cause and effect mechanism of string-to-soundboard might suggest a time lapse, the movements of both are understood to be in unison, instantaneous, and the single resultant motion of many complex motions.

If this coupling of vibration of string to soundboard seems to be the perfect solution to a problem, it comes at a cost. In mechanics and energy, as in the double-entry accountancy of all natural law, every advantage must be bought. As to vibrating strings, the louder tone due to soundboard enhancement is purchased at the expense of a contracted vibrational duration

time; that is, the assisting soundboard, although supplying voice and character to the once-mute string, acts also as a brake. As a result, the constant challenge of piano makers and piano technicians has been to overcome the difficulty of a too-rapid tonal decay, especially in the higher octaves. In the contemporary piano (i.e., from the late 1800s onward) the problem has been largely overcome due to **scale design** improvements, proper **bellying** techniques and materials, and the skilled adjustment of piano **hammer** elasticity.

The foregoing suggests that in the design and manufacture of piano soundboards a balance must be struck in producing a component that not only incorporates a generous amount of flexibility but a necessary degree of strength as well. A single piano string (steel **wire**) pressing on the soundboard with a force of four pounds presents no problem of structural engineering. But multiply that four pounds by the approximately 230 strings that comprise the eighty-eight notes of the average piano and the total force brought to bear on the soundboard approaches 1,000 pounds of compression, a magnitude of force not to be trifled with. Another of the many challenges in piano belly engineering is to design a soundboard and encasement system that at once can withstand the onslaught of **downbearing** compression while remaining flexible enough to respond to an almost unimaginable number of frequency excitations.

It would seem that in this technological age a plethora of mathematical expressions must have been boiled down to those few equations necessary to govern the exact ratio of soundboard strength-to-flexibility. But no such calculus has been derived, or if it has been, has not been made public. As they exist today, and have existed for the last hundred years, piano soundboards have evolved experimentally through a sort of corporate and eclectic alchemy, the imaginative outworkings of artificers drawing freely from science, experience, trial and error, intuition, and tradition.

The Theoretical Soundboard

The stringing scale design of a piano—string tensions, lengths, mass, and frequencies of vibration—is the starting point from which every subsequent design feature of piano manufacture gets its cue. Ideally, the **tone** quality of an instrument is built into that scale design. If it "sounds" good on paper the piano should be a good instrument, if other features are appropriately designed and built. As an oversimplification it can be said that pianos are practical applications of the theory of scale design. The degree of success of that application hinges on faithful follow-through and careful workmanship at the factory level.

Given a workable scale design, the primary function of the soundboard is to expand the complex vibration forms of the strings. Since a soundboard is a tone amplifier rather than a tone generator it can give out nothing that is not first supplied to it. The concept of amplification is one of enlargement, the principle being identical in nature to that employed in electronic-sound amplification. A typical cone speaker has attached to it small electric wires that deliver tiny electric signals causing the speaker to vibrate. The vibrating speaker, like the piano soundboard, then sets the air into motion, producing sound. What careful piano builders strive for is the theoretically ideal soundboard—one which perfectly responds to the energy conducted to it, a soundboard which is able to express the same frequencies that are given to it by the string. In addition, a soundboard must not only be responsive, but respond uniformly over as much of the piano's frequency range as possible. But here again scale design is paramount. A poor design coupled with an ideal soundboard will yield a poor tone quality, since the soundboard, acting primarily as a magnifier, will simply intensify the deficiencies of the design. Conversely, a superior scale design will go unrealized in coupling with a poor soundboard.

Considering that piano tones are complex rather than simple—that is, piano tones not only originate from the full length of the string but from vibrational segmentations existing as higher **partials** of the fundamental **pitch**—the ability of the soundboard to faithfully reproduce and amplify the incalculable number of vibrations of the strings during a piano performance is not only remarkable but renders impossible a truly accurate mental picture of the many interlacing motions, or the final resultant motion, of the soundboard surface. The exact vibratory modes of the working soundboard are not fully understood, since the surface and internal motions are quite small, perhaps in-definitely small regarding the high partials, and cannot be (or at least have not been) accurately gauged.

The Physical Soundboard

In order for a soundboard to fulfill its threefold duties of flexibility, strength, and longevity, it must be constructed of a suitable material and according to an established procedure.

Many different soundboard materials have been experimented with, but none other than wood produces a timbre or tone quality deemed appropriate for what has come to be recognized as piano tone. The reasons for this are many, but it is certain that tradition plays an important role. In general, the evolution of all stringed instruments can be traced to similar if not identical beginnings—a stretched string finding its amplification and voice through a wooden amplifier. The harpsichord—considered to be the prototype piano when originally fitted with hammers—contained a wooden soundboard, and the tones emanating from it eventually became uniquely identifiable in the evolving piano. Metal soundboards (which have been experimentally tried) of appropriate thickness and mechanical properties, although capable of responding to the vibrations of the string, yield a sharp, crisp, but thinner tone compared to the fuller and warmer tones of a wooden soundboard. Doubtless, a certain amount of conditioning colors these judgments but, whatever the reasons, a wooden soundboard has become the standard.

Of all the varieties of wood there is one species considered to be best suited for piano, harpsichord, violin, and guitar soundboards—spruce. Why this is so is not as clear as the modern mind would like it to be. There are, however, certain measurable and observable facts that indicate some answers. Microscopic observation of the structure of spruce reveals an interesting characteristic unique to the cone-bearing tree species. Throughout the wood fibers can be seen millions of little cup-shaped discs that contain tiny vibrating membranes or diaphragms. There are those who contend that it is this vibrating membrane that gives tonal value to spruce above other wood species. In the book, *Piano Tone Building*, Dr. F. E. Morton, chief engineer of acoustics for the American Steel and Wire Company, comments in 1919, ". . . a wood similar to spruce in every other particular, but lacking those little diaphragms isn't a sounding board."

The mechanical properties of this wood are also an important determining factor. Spruce transmits vibrations along the grain—which in the mature tree is long, staight, and closely spaced—with greater rapidity than most other woods (perhaps because the previously mentioned membranes lie in line with the grain). Although a soundboard is not primarily a transmitter, it is clear that the more rapidly vibrations are transmitted over the entire area of the board, the better it will function as a vibrator. Moreover, spruce wood is extremely lightweight, yet strong. In fact, spruce is considered to have the best strength-to-weight ratio of any wood. This single characteristic allows the material to be exceptionally responsive to the minute impulses communicated to it—a crucial criterion for soundboard material. In addition, spruce wood is at once very flexible and elastic. These terms are not interchangable: a flexible material can have its shape easily altered; an elastic material can recover its original shape after having been altered. Obviously, the structural and vibrational necessities of a soundboard demand all of these properties, and since spruce possesses all of them to a high degree, it long ago became the standard material for soundboards.

Quality soundboards are therefore constructed from quarter-sawn, solid, close-grained spruce. The assembly begins with the construction of a wide panel from several narrower (four to six inches wide) pieces. At this stage of the process the individual boards, which are about one-half-inch thick and very dry as to moisture content, are edge-glued together to form a homogeneous large sheet, or panel. The panel is then cut to the perimetrical shape and its surfaces are planed down to the specified thickness (about $^3/_8$ inch) called for in a particular instrument.

One of the most critical aspects of soundboard manufacture involves the process of "crowning the board"; that is, introducing an upward arch into the panel by means of reinforcing **ribs** that are pressed and glued to the backside, or underside, of the panel. These ribs, usually spruce or sugar pine, are spaced about six inches apart and oriented at right angles to the panel grain. Ribs, which average a bit less than one square inch in cross section, serve not only to impart **crown** to the panel, but to assist in the unity of soundboard cohesion and wholeness. Additionally, ribs function as cross-grain highways propagating vibrational energy over the entire area of the panel. The amount of crown that ribs introduce into the structure is relatively small: the arch found in a forty-eight-inch-long rib will be higher by 0.400 inch at the center of its span relative to its ends. Soundboard crown geometry is theoretically based on, and has been traditionally based on, a plus or minus sixty-foot circle. That is, the twelve or so different length ribs found in the average-sized **upright** or **grand piano** describe arcs of a circle containing a sixty-foot radius.

The primary purpose of soundboard crown is to resist the compressive force of downbearing brought to bear by the strings. Were soundboard crown not evident, the force of downbearing would collapse the soundboard assembly. Such a condition would destroy the positive connection of strings to **bridges** so necessary in producing and maintaining clear and definite tones. Soundboard crown, then, is vital from both a mechanical and acoustical standpoint. As soundboards age they tend to lose crown and resilience, the negative consequence being a noticeable deterioration in tone quality.

Soundboard Thickness

Piano builders and rebuilders are keenly aware of the importance of a responsive soundboard. Beyond the requirements of the soundboard's mechanical strength, there is significant leeway for other design factors such as perimetrical shape, thickness grading (tapering), rib placement, and crown geometry. All of these factors have, for the most part, been experimentally determined over many years of piano building and refinement, and the similarity of one soundboard to the next is more striking than any difference.

Of particular note, however, is the matter of panel thickness, which seems to have been one area of almost unlimited experimentation and builder prerogative, especially in the days when soundboard panels were built with relatively simple jigs and presses, and were planed by hand to varying (non-uniform) thicknesses within the same panel. The exigencies of modern mass production have long since eliminated the hand planing of panels. And, in general, the varying thickness gradings that accompanied this skilled process were eliminated, along with the highly skilled woodworkers, in favor of uniformly thick panels that could be quickly processed through industrial milling machines by semiskilled workers.

Regarding the thickness of piano soundboards, there are essentially two schools of thought which, although they overlap in theory and practice, are distinct. The first, which prevailed from the late 1800s to the mid-1930s, could be referred to as the "resonant wood theory." Basically, this theory suggests that, although the soundboard cannot originate any tones, it can affect, magnify, and modify the relative intensities of fundamentals and partials. In light of this concept, the tone quality could be experimentally determined by matching just the right mass of wood at a particular place in the scale with the appropriate string frequencies existing at that place in the scale. For this reason it was long thought that the soundboard should be stiffer in the treble area than in the bass. This belief prompted the former customary practice of planing the board thicker in the treble ($3/8$ inch), while gradually tapering toward the bass ($1/4$ inch) and certain edges of the soundboard, since short, stiff wood naturally vibrates at higher frequencies than does longer, thinner wood. Put another way, an increase in density and rigidity tends to respond to a waveform that naturally favors the higher harmonics. Moreover, a too-heavy soundboard cannot vibrate fully under light playing, while a too-light board will be overpowered by heavy playing. Again, a compromise in thickness grading seemed not only a practical solution but a happy one as well. Virtually all old, pre-World War II pianos (though not exclusively so) contained tapered soundboards.

The Steinway "Diaphragmatic" Soundboard

Although soundboard tapering in one form or another was the general practice of the time, and although it appeared, in theory, to be founded on acoustical principles, not everyone agreed that it survived on anything more than mere shop custom. In 1916 Samuel Wolfenden, writing in *A Treatise on the Art of Pianoforte Construction*, had this to say regarding the usual practice of his day: "it has been customary to make [the treble part of the soundboard] thicker than the bass portion in the proportion of 3 to 2. But this has been proved to be unnecessary, and that a board of regular thickness but of just the same weight, will serve quite well. . . . It might however be proved that a much larger difference in thickness, and therefore in stiffness, would be an advantage."

For all of his genius in melding the theory and practice of piano building, Wolfenden is not credited with advancing any radical changes in soundboard theory or construction. Still, his educated hunch—which has as its core the idea that flexibility rather than resonance is the predominant factor in soundboard efficiency—turned out to be the basis for the second school of thought regarding soundboard thickness. This theory suggests that, though spruce is a particularly resonant wood, the best tone quality is more a function of a freely moving and essentially unimpeded soundboard. Such a concept, which might be referred to as the "diaphragmatic" approach to soundboard design, aims to taper the board so as to allow maximum but controlled board movement, rather than to match string frequencies to wood mass.

During the mid- to late-1930s the celebrated house of **Steinway & Sons** conducted a series of experiments designed to discover the limits of soundboard mass relative to flexibility. In order to determine this, the experimenters, Paul Bilhuber from Steinway and C.A. Johnson of E.E. Laboratories, set out to uncover the soundboard's responsive behavior by mechanical measurement of existing Steinway soundboards. The particulars of these tests, along with the conclusions drawn, were originally published in a paper entitled "The Influence of the Soundboard on Piano Tone Quality" and subsequently published in 1940 in the *Journal of the Acoustical Society of America*. Early on in the experiments it became clear to Bilhuber and Johnson that "anything that could be done to encourage the diaphragmatic response of the board would result in better tone." In terms of improving soundboard design it appeared that any change that would increase soundboard responsiveness (that is, reduce unnecessary stiffness or rigidity) would improve tone quality and general performance of the piano. This, they reasoned, was especially true of shorter scaled instruments with reduced soundboard area. Significantly, the timeliness of these tests perfectly dovetailed with the public demand for a small grand that could demonstrate the greatest possible dynamic range.

It was thought that perhaps a board could be built that more nearly fulfilled its function of best possible response to string vibrations. The minimum mass-to-stiffness ratio in any soundboard is fixed by the mechanical requirements for strength and resistance to the compressive force of string downbearing. A structural analysis of the then-standard Steinway soundboard indicated that it would be possible to make a board that was thinner at its perimeter while still satisfying strength requirements. It was hypothesized that a soundboard that was thinner all around the edges would allow for greater board movement throughout and would, to some extent, counteract the effects of the unavoidable stiffness that existed in those areas where the board is glued to the piano **case**. (Incidentally, this reasoning was not unique to Steinway, as many piano manufacturers of the time had been thinning soundboards at the edges for years, just not in the specific shape that Steinway was about to introduce).

The birth of the Steinway "diaphragmatic soundboard" (registered trade name) resulted from the Bilhuber-Johnson tests and conclusions. This new soundboard assembly, the first of its type, has a parabolic taper cut into its top surface (as viewed in cross section), which by definition contains more mass at its central regions than at its edges. In a sense, this type of spruce panel comprises a rounded and inverted dish shape. The designation of "diaphragmatic" is descriptive not so much of the physical characteristics of the soundboard—the parabolic shape roughly resembles the diaphragm under the human lungs as well as other natural and organic systems—but according to its intended mechanical action, that of a vibrating membrane. In practice, the parabolic tapering reduced the weight of the standard Steinway board by 7 percent, but the stiffness was reduced by 20 percent according to static load tests; that is, the stiffness decreased by three times the weight reduction.

Bilhuber and Johnson's conclusions of the tests were essentially summed up as follows:

(1) The changes in structure of the soundboard and its mounting have increased its tendency to vibrate like a diaphragm, with the maximum amplitude (movement) near the center of the board.

(2) A systematic method of adjusting the downward pressure of the strings permits an optimum equalization of the pressure, hence an equalization in the tone quality, for different sections of the bridge.

(3) The increased response of the board has resulted in a small increase in the intensity level (volume) of the airborne sound. The pianist can produce slightly louder tones with a given force.

(4) The enhanced response of the board has definitely increased the duration of a tone for a given force of strike. This is a major factor in producing what the musician calls the "liveliness" or singing ability of the piano.

The patented Steinway diaphragmatic soundboard has been standard equipment in most models of Steinway pianos since the late 1930s.

Although there have been many and varied refinements introduced into both piano design and (especially) manufacturing processes on a worldwide basis, pianos have remained essentially unchanged for more than a century. In fact, a grand piano built in 1895 much more closely resembles its modern counterpart than does a Model T Ford, a contemporary automobile. Until there exists a serious demand for the piano to do something significantly different than it has always done, or to do it more efficiently, the piano will go on in nature much the same as it always has. In the field of electronics, the transistor and the later computer chip are considered bonafide breakthroughs that revolutionized not only the industry but the way people live every day. No such claim can be made in the world of recent piano technology, not even if only those concerned with the piano are considered. As to piano soundboards and their attendant adjustments, there is probably not much room for radical change, although there is always room for experimentation, discovery, and refinement. Moreover, as the supplies of top-grade spruce continue to dwindle, the need for alternate woods (or even inorganic substances) will become sharper until, perhaps, a new materials science will of necessity dictate the directions of change. For the present, however, wooden soundboard assemblies, more or less built and adjusted in the traditional way, remain unchallenged as the choice amplification system for the vibrating piano string. (The author has previously published some of this material in the *Piano Technicians Journal*, and the *EKI* thanks the *PTJ* for its use here.)

Nicholas Gravagne

Bibliography

American Steel and Wire Company, Acoustic Dept. *Piano Tone Building*. (Proceedings of the Piano Technicians' Conference, Chicago, 1916, 1917, 1918). Pp. 117–129. Chicago: orig. pub. American Steel and Wire Co.; reprinted by Vestal Press, Vestal, New York.

Bilhuber, Paul, and C.A. Johnson. "The Influence of the Soundboard on Piano Tone Quality." *Journal of the Acoustical Society of America* 11; 3, (October 1940): 311–320.

White, William Braid. *Piano Tuning and Allied Arts*. Boston, Mass.: Tuners Supply Company, 1946.

Wolfenden, Samuel. *A Treatise on the Art of Pianoforte Construction*. Brentford, Middlesex: The British Piano Museum Charitable Trust, 1975. (Reprint of original 1916 edition published by Unwin.)

SOUTHWELL, WILLIAM (1756–1842)

William Southwell was a piano maker whose contribution to the development of the instrument cannot be underestimated.

Little is known of his origins or his life, other than that he arrived in London in 1794 from Dublin, where he had been in business for some years as a piano maker. In that year he was granted a British **patent** (no. 2017, dated 18 October 1794) for a piano with a "Single Action." Commonly called the "Irish Action," the **damper** stick was hinged directly to the **key** so that when the key was depressed the back end raised and lifted the damper from the **strings**. At the same time, to cater to the increasing demand for instruments with a wider compass upon which four-hand reductions of orchestral music might be played, Southwell increased the compass of the **square** pianoforte by a fifth from FF–f^3 to FF–c^4. He was the first maker to fit a square piano with what were then known as "additional keys."

He was granted a further British patent (no. 2264 of 8 November 1798) for an "**Upright Square**" pianoforte; he turned the instrument onto its side so that the strings formed a vertical plane. In so doing, he had to devise a new action. The result was the "**Sticker Action**" worked by a **jack** and, with it, the so-called Irish Damper.

In 1807 he was granted patent no. 3029 of 8 April for a **cabinet pianoforte** that stood six feet tall. The bass strings rose vertically from floor level. With this he also devised an improved action, called the "English Sticker Action," by adding an **escapement**. Four years later he was granted a patent (no. 3403 of 4 March 1811) for an upright piano standing just four feet six inches high. With the unusual but descriptive name of "Piano Sloping Backwards," this moved the player's face further from the strings and provided an angled **music desk**. This instrument was also fitted with a *volto subito* or automatic music-page turner worked by a foot pedal.

David Wainwright quotes from the **Broadwood** archives that "the vertical or cabinet piano was first produced by William Southwell from a sketch given to him by James Broadwood about 1804." Whether that is true or just malicious comment does not alter the fact that Southwell's action was the basis of the English Sticker Action used for almost a century by almost every upright-piano maker in Europe. Southwell was also the first maker to use silk as a decorative covering for the piano front.

The year of his birth and death are uncertain, although Philip James gives his dates as 1756 to 1842, suggesting he came to London in his late thirties. Rosamond Harding shows him in business in London's Lad Lane from 1794 to 1821, with his last address, between 1844 and 1857, in the Hampstead Road.

Arthur W.J.G. Ord-Hume

Bibliography

Good, Edwin Marshall. *Giraffes, Black Dragons, and Other Pianos: A Technological History from Cristofori to the Modern Concert Grand*. Stanford, Cal.: Stanford University Press, 1982.

Grove Dictionary of Music & Musicians. 1st ed. Edited by Sir George Grove. London: Macmillan, 1879.

Grover, David S. *The Piano: Its Story from Zither to Grand*. London: Hale, 1976.

Harding, Rosamond E.M. *The Piano-Forte: Its History Traced to the Great Exhibition of 1851*. Cambridge: Cambridge University Press, 1933. Reprints, New York: Da Capo Press, 1973; Old Woking, Surrey: Gresham Books, 1978.

James, Philip. *Early Keyboard Instruments*. London: Peter Davies, 1930. Reprint. London: Tabard Press, 1970.

Wainwright, David. *Broadwood by Appointment: A History*. London: Quiller, 1982; New York: Universe Books, 1983.

SPAIN AND PORTUGAL, PIANO INDUSTRY IN

Pianos were brought to Spain and Portugal early in the eighteenth century, among them, very likely, one or more instruments made by **Bartolomeo Cristofori**. Historical records and several early Spanish and Portuguese pianos modeled after Cristofori point in that direction.

Cristofori's first piano was made around 1698–1700 in Florence. Its association with the illustrious Medici court guaranteed that European aristocracy and musicians heard about the new invention. **Domenico Scarlatti** may have played on the Cristofori piano during a brief stay in Florence in 1702. When Isabella Farnese, duchess of Parma, married King Felipe V of Spain (r. 1700–1746) in 1714 she took Italian personnel with her to Madrid. Spanish and Portuguese aristocracy followed suit and hired large numbers of Italian courtiers and musicians. Among them was Scarlatti, who, in 1719, moved to the royal court in Lisbon to teach keyboard skills to Princess Maria Barbara, daughter of King João V, and to the king's brother, Don Antonio. When Maria Barbara married the crown prince of Spain in 1729, Scarlatti followed her to the Spanish court, where he stayed until his death in 1757. In 1732, **Lodovico Giustini** wrote a set of sonatas specifically for the pianoforte, which he dedicated to Don Antonio of Portugal. This raises the interesting conjecture that Scarlatti, since his royal pupils had access to pianos, may have composed some of his Sonatas for that new instrument.

The queen's inventory of 1758 lists no less than five Florentine pianos. The following year the famous castrato Farinelli, after twenty-two years of service at the courts of Felipe V and Fernando VI, received from the Spanish Queen a farewell present of three keyboard instruments. One of these was a Florentine piano made in 1730 by Cristofori's pupil **Giovanni Ferrini**.

With royalty interested in the new pianos, it is to be expected that local craftsmen made copies. One such copy is in the Bibliotheca

Nacional in Lisbon. It was built in Lisbon in 1763 by Henrique van Casteel, a Flemish instrument maker who worked in Lisbon between 1757 and 1767. Another very similar Portuguese piano is in London, in the private collection of Harold Lester. A very fine Cristofori-type Portuguese **grand** pianoforte by Manuel Antunes (1760–1789) from the last quarter of the eighteenth century appeared at Sotheby's in London in 1990. It is now in the United States, in the Shrine to Music Instrument Collection in Vermillion, South Dakota.

A Spanish-made piano modeled after Cristofori is on display in the Casa Murillo museum in Seville. A second one, in the collection of Sr. B. March in Madrid, is almost identical to a now lost instrument that was inscribed "Me Fecit Francisco Perez Mirabal en Sevilla, 1745." Mirabal, a prominent organ and harpsichord builder in Seville, probably was the first Spaniard to construct a piano. Pianos came into widespread use among the aristocracy in the 1770s, when **square pianos** (*pianos de mesa*), imported from England, became available. The rapid acceptance of square pianos in Spanish society was due in part to the long-standing popularity of the clavichord, which was, along with the guitar, almost a national instrument. The square piano, similar to the clavichord in shape, size, cost, and playing technique, and equally easy to transport, but with a cleaner and stronger **tone**, became the natural successor to the clavichord in palaces, homes, and churches. In church services where the organ could not be used, as during Holy Week and for funerals, the sound of the piano was thought to be more appropriate than that of either the harpsichord or clavichord. At the Cathedral of Palencia in 1799 the purchase of a **fortepiano** for the organist was justified because "it is suitable for funeral ceremonies." The square piano gradually replaced the clavichord also as practice instrument for organists and for pupils in the cathedral schools.

On the whole, Spanish and Portuguese piano builders were content to follow trends and ideas developed in Italy, Germany, France, and England. Most eighteenth-century makers worked after the English models from **Johannes Zumpe**, **Johannes Pohlmann**, **Longman and Broderip**, Gabriel Buntebart, Sievers, and **John Broadwood**. Francisco Florez (d.1824), active in Madrid, received a stipend from King Carlos

IV (r. 1788–1808) to visit London and train in the important ateliers there. Upon his return to Madrid in 1795, he was given the title of "Fortepiano builder to the Court of His Majesty."

As a result of this royal patronage, Florez received many commissions from the aristocracy in Madrid. Among his duties at the court was **tuning** the keyboard instruments of the Countess of Bonavente, a lady whose salons set the tone of Madrid fashion. She gave commissions to the most famous composers of her time, among them **Joseph Haydn**. We know that Haydn wrote a letter to Florez in 1785 from his residence in Vienna. It is not known if anything resulted from this contact.

Florez used the simplified action of Zumpe. However, this was an age of piano development and experimentation. Piano manufacture consisted of one-man ateliers, and those so inclined, or commissioned, occasionally worked on special projects. In the Palacio Real in Madrid stands a vertical piano by Florez in the form of a chest, dated 1807, which has a **janissary** stop, as was customary with Viennese instruments.

Another important harpsichord and piano builder in Seville was Juan del Marmol, who was born there in 1737 and trained in the workshop of Mirabal, also working according to Zumpe's model. But in 1779 he presented to the princess of Asturias, Dona Maria Luisa de Parma, a harpsichord-piano with fifteen registers. King Carlos III (r. 1759–1788), a patron of the arts, was so impressed that he gave Marmol a pension of 500 ducats per year, with the stipulation that he would always have two apprentices around him "to whom he will teach the theory and practice of his profession" (*Gaceta de Madrid*, 23 October 1779). It seems that Marmol was also an able pianist and composer who was invited to the fashionable salons, where he played his own compositions on the pianos he had built himself.

A very influential piano builder in the first half of the nineteenth century was Francisco Fernandez (1766–1852). Born in Asturias, he came to Madrid in 1792 and began constructing pianos in 1800, "imitating the instruments that came from abroad," as he said, and with which he soon had much success. He had a brilliant career. In 1806 he was named "Honorary Builder" at the royal court of Carlos IV. In 1813 he was recognized by the Real Sociedad

Economica for his services, and in 1816 he received a stipend for the position he held at the palace.

When Fernandez was appointed to the Court, to which Florez had already previously been appointed, competition between the two men developed. Florez, the darling of the upper aristocracy, made ornate instruments, using the finest woods. Fernandez pursued a simpler style and a wider market.

In this period of history, on the eve of the Industrial Revolution, guilds were declining and tradespeople were more and more educated in academies and economic societies, rather than through apprenticeships. Fernandez took the initiative in 1817 to found a school, where in addition to the regular curriculum, woodworking and piano building were also taught. He asked King Fernando VII (r. 1814–1833) for permission to take samples of all species of woods from the royal gardens for analysis. He proposed that the students should study English, French, and German pianos, and that in the school four different types of pianos should be built: a small, cheap instrument with five octaves and one single "thick" **string** per **hammer**; one of larger dimensions with six octaves and two strings per hammer; a third one of very large format for a big orchestra and for the use of advanced pianists, with six octaves and three strings per hammer; and finally one with a graceful shape, suitable for salons, with five and a half octaves and two strings per hammer.

Fernandez's advocacy of a national piano industry was in line with royal thinking; already Carlos III, although tone-deaf, had supported the piano industry within the context of building up the Spanish economy. Between 1800 and 1830 more than twenty piano ateliers opened in Madrid, about a fourth of them by foreigners, in order to meet the growing demand for pianos among the bourgeoisie.

The beneficial influence of the Court came to an abrupt halt with the death of Fernando VII in 1833. The Regent Queen Maria Christina modeled herself, in taste and manners, after Paris. As a result of her reforms all artisans attached to the Court in Madrid, and that included those in charge of musical instruments, lost their work and their wages. Bypassing national production, she ordered pianos for the royal palaces from the factories of **Erard** and **Pleyel**. Maria Christina's daughter, Queen Isabel

II (1833–1868) shared the French tastes of her mother. In addition to pianos, she acquired from abroad a great number of harmoniums and mechanical instruments.

The attitude of the queen was a sign of the times as much as it was a personal matter. To meet the growing demand for pianos from the bourgeoisie, enterprises with assembly-line methods were necessary. Around 1850 some firms in Madrid are known to have imported complete, ready-made actions from France. Gradually mechanical production was introduced. By the 1870s the one-man atelier had disappeared.

After 1850 Barcelona became the center of the piano industry on the Iberian peninsula. Spanish firms made attempts to enter the European market. Pianos from the factory of Lerch in Barcelona were exhibited at the Exposition of Paris in 1867 and at the World Exposition of 1888. The Spanish piano industry, however, lost out internationally and domestically against foreign competition. At present, the pianos found in Spain and Portugal are French, German, and Japanese imports.

The most interesting period of piano building in Spain and Portugal stretches from the 1740s into the second half of the nineteenth century. Musical life was rich and diversified, and every town of significance had one or more piano ateliers. Enough pianos have survived to give an idea of the great activity during that period.

Following is a listing of the more important piano builders in Spain and Portugal. Dates given are periods of known activity, unless otherwise indicated.

SPAIN

Madrid:

Francisco Florez. 1780s – d.1824

Francisco Fernandez. 1766–1852

Gaspar Ahrendt. c.1800–1850

Jose Colmenarejo. c.1800–1850

Juan Hosseschreuders. c.1800–1850

Julian Lacabra. c.1800–1850

Dionisio M. Martinez. c.1800–1850

Placido Martinez. c.1800–1850

Juan Puyol. c.1800–1850

Pedro J. Rodriguez. c.1800–1850

Miguel Slocker. 1831–1836

Montana. Business founded in 1864

Soler (and Sons). c.1860

Barcelona:

Joseph Franz Otter. 1800–1807

Josef Marti. 1805

Johannes Kyburz. 1800–1822

Pindo de Pedro Estela. Business founded in 1830

Josef Munné. c.1800–1825

Manuel Bordas. c.1800–1825

Raf. Car. Pons.

Giacomo Baldi.

Estela y Bernareggi. c.1850–1900

Puig y Ribatallada

Vernes y Vila.

Lerch. 1867–1879 (Factory taken over by Soler, Nogues, and Moliner in 1879)

Hermanos Guarra. Business founded in 1860

Louis Izabel. Business founded in 1860

Chassaigne frères. Business founded in 1864

Bernareggi & Co. Business founded in 1867

Nogues. 1860s–1870s

Moliner. 1860s–1870s

Mahon (Menorca):

Antonio Llado. c.1800–1850

Murcia:

Tadeo Tornel. 1770–1777

Seville:

Francisco Perez Mirabal. c.1700–1750

Juan del Marmol (father; pupil of Mirabal). 1739–1779

Juan del Marmol (son). b.1771

Manticio Piazza.

Valencia:

Rodrigo Ten y Co. 1902

Zaragoza:

Tomas Torrente. 1800

Antonio Enriquez.

PORTUGAL

Lisbon:

Henrique van Casteel. 1757–1767

Unknown Domicile:

Manuel Antunes. 1760–1789

Mary Louise Boehm

Bibliography

Bordas, Cristina. "Snaarinstrumenten met Klavier: Clavicordio, Monacordio en Piano." Brussels: *Catalogue of Europalia 85 España*, 1985.

Escalas, Roma. "Spaanse Muziekinstrumenten van de 16de tot de 19de eeuw." Brussels: *Catalogue of Europalia 85 España*, 1985.

Hirt, Franz Josef. *Stringed Keyboard Instruments 1440–1880.* Boston, Mass.: Boston Book and Art Shop, 1968. (1st ed. *Meisterwerke des Klavierbaus.* Olten, Switzerland: Urs Graf-Verlag, 1955); Also, *Meisterwerke des Klavierbaus—Stringed Keyboard Instruments.* Dietikon-Zürich: Urs Graf (distributed in the USA by Da Capo Press), 1981.

Michener, James A. *Iberia.* New York: Random House, 1968.

Pascual, Beryl Kenyon de. "Francisco Pérez Mirabal's Harpsichords and the Early Spanish Piano." *Early Music* 15 (November 1987).

———. "Un Desafio Musical." *Ritmo* (September 1983): 25–27.

———. "Diego Fernández—Harpsichord-maker to the Spanish Royal Family from 1722 to 1755—and His Nephew Julián Fernández." *Galpin Society Journal* 38 (1985).

———. "Carlos III: un rey protector de la música." *Reales Sitios* 25 (Third Trimester 1988).

Pollens, Stewart. "The Early Portuguese Piano." *Early Music* 13 (February 1985).

Schott, Howard. "From Harpsichord to Pianoforte: A Chronology and Commentary." *Early Music* 13 (February 1985).

SPÄTH

The Späth (Spath, Spaeth) family of organ and instrument builders had its most famous member in Franz Jakob Späth (1714–1786), who was born in Regensburg as son of the organ and instrument maker Johann Jakob Späth (1672–1760). Most biographical dates of older dictionaries and publications are not precise and contradict each other in details. The documentary evidence is sparse. We do not know whether Johann Jakob himself built early versions of **fortepianos**. It is possible that he constructed so-called pantaleons from the 1720s onward. These were instruments in the shape of harpsichords with **hammers** falling from above onto the **strings** and with **actions** that may have been removeable. He may have made only harpsichords and clavichords but there are reasons to believe that he somehow copied **Gottfried Silbermann's** *cembal d'amour* instruments (which originally were a special kind of large clavichord), altering them eventually into a kind of piano. Though it is possible that it was Johann Jakob who invented the so-called **tangent piano**, it is more likely that it was an invention of his son. Tangent pianos are instruments in the shape of a normal harpsichord with a mechanism that causes each tangent to come straight from below towards the strings, but in contrast to clavichords the tangent falls back immediately after having touched the strings, regardless of whether the **key** is pressed down for a longer or shorter time. According to Bossler's *Musikalische Correspondenz*, the tangent piano was invented by Späth in Regensburg "around 1750," but, unfortunately, Bossler did not mention the Christian name of this instrument maker. Of the older Johann Jakob Späth so far we know for certain only that he was the builder of an organ with nineteen stops for the Protestant Neupfarrkirche of Regensburg.

The tangent pianos that are known to be extant today are based on models invented by Franz Jakob Späth and built by him and his son-in-law Christoph Friedrich **Schmahl**, who was born in 1739 in Heilbronn and died 15 May 1814 in Regensburg. Bossler's report spoke of the great fame Späth's clavier instruments enjoyed "in all four parts of the world."

The remarkable reputation of the Späth instruments was probably the reason why **Johann Andreas Stein**, after finishing his apprenticeship years with his father(?), went not only to Strassburg to work for a while with the Silbermanns but then also to the Regensburg workshop of the Späths with the intention of learning more about his craft. He stayed in Regensburg from October 1749 to January 1750.

Wolfgang Amadeus Mozart was also one of the many admirers of the "spättischen Clavier" instruments and mentioned in his famous letter to his father from Augsburg (17 October 1777) that before he had seen the fortepianos of Stein he had considered Späth's pianos to be the best. (It is more than likely that by "spättische Clavier" Mozart meant wing-shaped pianos.) In connection with Mozart's remark it may be of interest to know that Elisabeth Haffner (for whose marriage festivities on 21 July 1776 Mozart composed the Serenade K. 250) married the Salzburg merchant Franz Xaver Späth, probably a relative of the Regensburg Späth family and an owner of a good Späth fortepiano. In Daniel Schubart's *Ideen zu einer Ästhetik der Tonkunst,* written in 1784, Späth (p. 288) is mentioned among the five "best makers of fortepianos," together with Silbermann, (Heinrich? Daniel?), Stein, Fritz, and Strouth.

In 1770 an announcement by Franz Jakob Spath [sic] appeared in Hiller's *Wöchentliche Nachrichten* in Leipzig. It advertised an instrument Späth called "Clavecin d'Amour," as well as pantaleons and compound instruments combining harpsichord with "Clavecin d'Amour"; the last may have been a misnomer for tangent piano, however the description is unclear and incomplete. Surprisingly, he claimed that his instruments could be built with so many stops that the sound could be altered fifty times.

In the last quarter of the century Späth's son-in-law Schmahl was regarded in the workshop of the Späth family as a member with equal rights, and the instruments were signed *Späth & Schmahl.*

Franz Jakob Späth was also active as an organ builder and was commissioned to construct the organs for two churches in Regensburg (Dreieinigkeitskirche and Oswaldkirche, for which he received 1,100 fl and 1,200 fl respectively). A draft that he submitted for a main organ of the prestigious Cathedral of Regensburg is known, but the decline of church music in the second half of the century diminished the interest in large organs and the plan was finally abandoned.

The reputation of Franz Jakob Späth was based mainly on his tangent pianos, his fortepianos, and **combination** instruments, though he also certainly built clavichords and normal harpsichords (Späth named all wingshaped instruments either "cembalo" or "clavecin" or "pantaleons"; this was usual prior to the 1780s but has caused confusion in the twentieth century).

Eva Badura-Skoda

Bibliography

Badura-Skoda, Eva. "Mozart and the Compound Keyboard Instruments." In *Festschrift für Warren Kirkendale* (in press).

————. "The Fortepiano in the Second Half of the Eighteenth Century." Paper read at the Mozart Symposium in Cardiff, July 1991 (to be published).

Bossler, Heinrich Philipp. *Musikalische Correspondenz der deutschen Filharmonischen Gesellschaft für das Jahr 1791, Nr.2.*

Herrmann, Heinrich. "Die Regensburger Klavierbauer Späth und Schmahl und ihr Tangentenflügel." Phil. diss. University of Erlangen, 1928.

Scharnagl, August. "Franz Jacob Späth." In *Musik in Geschichte und Gegenwart XII.*

Schubart, Chr. Fr. Daniel. *Ideen zu einer Ästhetik der Tonkunst.* Edited by Ludwig Schubart. Wien: 1806.

Sterl, Raimund W. "Musiker und Instrumentenbauer in den Bürgerbüchern Regensburgs." *Blätter des Bayerischen Landesvereins für Familienkunde* 30 (1967): 335 f.

————. "Musiker und Instrumentenbauer in den Totenregistern der Stadt Regensburgs." *Blätter des Bayerischen Landesvereins für Familienkunde* 36 (1973): 126 f.

SPINE

The spine is the straight side of a **grand piano case**, on the left or bass side of the instrument when facing the **keyboard**. This long, straight spine is opposite the treble or **bentside** of the grand piano.

Peggy Flanagan Baird

SPINET

Spinet is the name given to a modern small cross-strung **upright** about four feet high and similar in appearance to **Jean-Henri Pape's console** model of 1828. The modern spinet, or console, was developed as an answer to the problem of space limitation in twentieth-century living rooms.

See also Upright Piano; Console Piano.

Martha Novak Clinkscale

SPOON

In vertical piano **actions**, the "**damper** spoon" is attached to the **wippen** and lifts the damper from the **string** when the note is struck.

See also Actions.

Philip Jamison, III

SQUARE PIANO

The square piano is a horizontal piano deriving its shape from the clavichord. The **keyboard** on the long side of the rectangular **case** has the **strings** parallel to it. Because of their dimensions and fairly simple construction design, clavichords were used for experimentation with innovative devices that eventually facilitated the transition to the piano. For more than one hundred years the history of the mechanical improvements in the square piano and the development of the **grand piano** followed a parallel track. In Europe the square piano was the common domestic keyboard instrument until the 1850s, when the **upright** better answered the demand for an inexpensive instrument with good qualities of **tone** and suitable dimensions for the average house.

The Square Piano in Germany

The oldest surviving example of a square piano is in the Neupert Collection of the Germanisches Nationalmuseum in Nürnberg. It was made by Johann Söcher and is labeled "Johann Söcher im Obern Sonthofen Allgäu 1742." It has black **ebony** naturals, a compass from C to f³ and a decorated **lid**, as is often found on square pianos. The mechanism was a primitive Anglo-German **action** without **escapement** or checkpiece; this type of action does not allow much control of the **key**. The instrument has only one stop (lever) for damping. The combination of the simplified **Bartolomeo Cristofori** action, where a fixed **jack** lifts the **hammer** without an intermediate lever, and the German action, where the hammer head points towards the front of the instrument (with or without checkpiece), is found in the early years of Ger-

man piano making. Occasionally the complete Cristofori action was adapted to the square, as in the example by Johann Heinrich Silbermann in Stuttgart (Württembergisches Landesmuseum). On some square pianos one can find a design conceived to combine the traditional harpsichord or clavichord tone with the variation of expression offered by a pianoforte. A very old example of such an action is in the Germanisches Nationalmuseum (Nürnberg) in the Neupert Collection, where a piano with a compass of C to f³ has two hammers for each note. Each hammer can be separately engaged, one with a wooden head to give a cembalo tone, the other with a **leather** top to produce a pianoforte-type tone.

Other very simple devices, such as **tangents**, were installed in square pianos; with tangents the pressure of the key throws perpendicular cloth- or leather- covered hammers towards the strings. Other examples provide one solution to a problem often found in many square pianos—weakness of tone in the bass and treble—by adding another set of hammers that can be disengaged by a **pedal**. Many early German pianos did not have dampers, or were equipped with a stop to raise them.

Early experimentation with *Prellmechanik* was carried on by **Gottfried Silbermann** and developed by Johann Andreas **Stein** in the second half of the eighteenth century. The action featured a hammer-**butt** ending with a beak, to engage the *Prelleiste* (hammer **rail**). The hammer head pointed towards the front of the instrument; a kapsel, first made of wood, later of brass, can be found on the larger square pianos up to the 1840s.

The stops of the later square pianos were the same as for the grand (with the exception of the *una corda* pedal, which could not be installed in a square): basson, forte, Jeu d'Harpe, swell, lute, piano, and Turkish music. The casework was always very important: oak, walnut, cherry, and maple were often used. Developments in piano making attempted to satisfy the demand for a wider range and stronger tone; these needs were best met by the grand piano, and thus may be the reason for the decline of the square-piano industry in Germany.

The Square Piano in England

Even though the Rev. William Mason had introduced the first square piano in England in 1755,

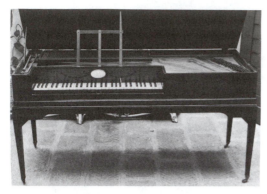

Square piano by Longman & Broderip c.1790–95 (marked: By Royal Patent - Longman & Broderip—Musical Instrument Makers—N° 26 Cheapside & N° 13 Haymarket—London). Property of Accademia Bartolomeo Cristofori, Firenze.

Square piano by Broadwood 1793 (marked: Johannes Broadwood—Londini fecit 1793—Patent—Great Pulteney Street Golden Square). Property of Accademia Bartolomeo Cristofori, Firenze.

the Cristofori tradition of piano making was brought to and developed in England by **Johannes Zumpe** in 1760. Zumpe made only square pianos and they shortly became incredibly popular, not only in England but also in France and Italy, because of their size, price, and loud and pleasant sound. The reputation of such instruments was enhanced by their sponsor: **Johann Christian Bach**, who was the queen's private music teacher in London and who used one of Zumpe's square pianos as a solo instrument in 1768. A few years later hundreds of square pianos were on the market. The earliest surviving Zumpe square piano dates from 1766 and is now in the Württembergisches Landesmuseum in Stuttgart. The mechanism,

which was later called English single action, is based on the Cristofori action. Zumpe also conceived square pianos with split black keys to facilitate mean-tone temperament tuning.

Johannes Pohlmann's square pianos, based on Zumpe's design, also gained renown. His pianos usually had hand stops for divided bass and treble dampers, lute, and occasionally a swell. Other improvements were gradually applied to the square piano. Schoene & Co. used a 1780 Zumpe variation of the single action, with a second jack fixed on an interposed lever, and called it a double action. Also at that time **Longman & Broderip** employed a type of damper called a crank damper, and in 1783 **John Broadwood** patented an under-damper mechanism made out of brass that was lifted off when the key was depressed. **John Geib** patented a modified double action in 1786 that used an escapement in the form of a spring hopper; shortly afterwards this invention became the common mechanism for the **English action.**

The early square pianos had a compass of five octaves, FF to f³, but the demand for a wider compass up to c⁴ required additional keys in the keyboard. In 1794 **William Southwell** solved the problem by conceiving an extension of the keyboard in the treble by cutting a gap in the back of the **soundboard,** in order to allow the strike of a new set of hammers placed on an additional **keyframe.** A few years later (1798) he devised a sort of upright piano by using a square piano turned on its side.

By the turn of the century the square piano had become more complex and its size had increased; however, the upright piano did not have the features to make it a potentially successful investment and was not yet ready to replace the square piano in the domestic market.

Many experiments were made on square pianos in order to control and solve the problem of the slackening of the **strings** due to humidity changes. The high **pitch** to which the strings were **tuned** (and the increased tension) made necessary the use of metal **braces** and iron **frame.** In 1820 **William Stodart** obtained the British **patent** for a metal "compensation" frame. Tubular bars that fluctuated along with the expansion or contraction of the strings were applied to square pianos after 1825. Broadwood, who was the first to use metal braces in the

1830s, produced an average of 1,650 pianos per year, of which 1,300 were squares. These numbers demonstrate the popularity of square pianos. Twenty years later, because of the development of the upright, the square piano was produced only for export; 90 percent of the English piano production was devoted to the upright and 5 percent to the grand.

The Square Piano in France

The French piano makers followed the English development of square pianos very closely and preferred the English instruments until the Erard firm influenced the market by the quality of its own square pianos. **Sébastien Erard**, before moving to London and leaving his brother Jean-Baptiste to continue their business in Paris, made square pianos that copied the Zumpe single action. Later on, Erard improved the action of his square pianos: by 1808 he patented the first repetition action for square pianos and in 1827 he designed a second one. **Pleyel** modified the fixed overdamping used in England, employing a separate frame easily removable for repair. Several pedals were used, such as forte, sordine, basson, and Jeu Celeste.

The Square Piano in America

The first square piano in America was built in 1775 by **Johann Behrent**, a German immigrant living in Philadelphia, and was followed by many copies of English instruments. In 1825 **Alpheus Babcock** patented the cast-iron frame for square pianos and in 1840 **Jonas Chickering** patented his own version of the iron frame for square pianos. By now pianos had grown to enormous sizes with a seven-octave compass. In 1855 **Steinway & Sons** exhibited a square piano with **overstrung scale** and full iron frame at the "Crystal Palace" New York Exhibition and strongly influenced the development of square pianos. The explanation for the much greater popularity of square pianos compared to grand pianos in the United States may partly be that before 1870 solo piano recitals were rare, and the market demanded from the piano industry instruments for domestic use only. In America the popularity of the square piano started declining at the end of the nineteenth century. In 1903 the Society of American Piano Manufacturers built a 50-foot-high pyramid of square pianos and set them on fire to publicize the danger of bankruptcy for the national industry of grand and upright pianos; at the same time the demonstration helped dramatize the demise of the square piano.

Donatella Degiampietro and
Giuliana Montanari

Bibliography

Baines, Anthony. *Storia degli strumenti musicali.* Milano: Rizzoli, 1983.

Barthold, Kenneth van, and David Buckton. *The History of the Piano.* London: British Broadcasting Corporation, 1975.

Colt, Alfred. *The Early Piano.* London: Steiner G. Bell, 1981.

Concise Oxford Dictionary of Music. Third edition, by Michael Kennedy. Oxford; New York: Oxford University Press, 1980.

Dizionario Enciclopedico Universale della Musica e dei Musicisti. Torino: UTET, 1985.

Dolge, Alfred, *Pianos and Their Makers.* Covina, Cal.: Covina Publishing Co., 1911. Reprint. New York: Dover, 1972.

Harding, Rosamond E.M. *The Piano-Forte: Its History Traced to the Great Exhibition of 1851.* Cambridge: Cambridge University Press, 1933. Reprints, New York: Da Capo Press, 1973; Old Woking, Surrey: Gresham Books, 1978.

Hirt, Franz Josef. *Stringed Keyboard Instruments 1440–1880.* Translated by M. Boehme-Brown. Boston, Mass.: Boston Book and Art Shop, 1968. Also, *Meisterwerke des Klavierbaus—Stringed Keyboard Instruments.* Dietikon-Zürich: Urs Graf (distributed in the USA by Da Capo Press), 1981.

Libin, Laurence. *American Musical Instruments in the Metropolitan Museum of Art.* New York; London: Norton, 1985.

Marcuse, Sybil. *Musical Instruments: A Comprehensive Dictionary.* New York: Norton, 1975.

New Grove Dictionary of Musical Instruments. Edited by Stanley Sadie. London: Macmillan Press; Washington DC: Grove's Dictionaries, 1984.

The Piano. (New Grove Musical Instruments Series.) New York: Norton, 1988.

Rimbault, Edward Francis. *The Pianoforte: Its Origin, Progress, and Construction.* London: Robert Cocks and Co., 1860.

Sachs, Curt. *The History of Musical Instruments.* New York: Norton, 1940.

Tintori, G. *Gli strumenti musicali.* (Vol.2) Torino: UTET, 1976.

STEIN FAMILY

The name Stein represented an important family of four generations of musicians and organ and piano builders. Stein pianos were among the most sought-after instruments in Central Europe during the last third of the eighteenth century and the first half of the nineteenth. Their elegant, silvery **tone** and feather-light, smooth-flowing **action**, known as the Viennese action, clearly influenced German-Austrian music during the Classical and early Romantic era, notably the writing of **Joseph Haydn**, **Wolfgang Amadeus Mozart**, and Johann Nepomuk Hummel.

Johann Georg Stein, the patriarch of the family, was born in Heimsheim near Heidelsheim on 6 October 1697 and died 12 September 1754 in Heidelsheim. He was probably a tailor at first, but as early as 1725 was active as an organ and piano builder.

The first important piano builder in the family was Johann (Georg) Andreas Stein (1728–1792), probably trained by his father. As a young man of twenty, seeking to perfect his craft, Johann Andreas did what was customary at that time: he travelled from town to town (on foot, no doubt) during the summer months, visiting other craftsmen and doing occasional jobs, and apprenticed himself to a master during the cold winter.

In his diary, kept throughout his itinerant apprenticeships, young Stein wrote down observations about instruments, persons, and places he visited. His arrival in Strasbourg, dated 4 August 1748, verifies the records of Johann Andreas **Silbermann** that Stein began working there under Johann Daniel Silbermann, another member of that renowned family of organ builders. The following winter he worked for Franz Jakob **Späth** in Regensburg. In the summer of 1750 he arrived in Augsburg, where an opportunity for employment had occurred following the death in 1749 of J.C. Leo, the city's only organ builder. By 1751 Stein became a permanent resident of Augsburg and remained there until his death. From 1755 to 1757 Stein was occupied with building the great organ of the Barfüsserkirche in Augsburg and on 19 August 1757 he was appointed organist there.

For a few months in 1758 Johann Andreas visited Paris with his friend, the pianist and painter, Johann Gottfried Eckard, and visited the Silbermann workshop in Strasbourg both enroute (19 October 1758) and on his return (6 January 1759). He then opened his own shop in Augsburg and in 1760 married Maria Regina Burkhardt of Augsburg.

There was such demand for Stein's pianos, with orders coming in from as far away as Salzburg, Vienna, Zürich, and Freiburg, that Stein phased out his organ-building activities to devote himself exclusively to pianos. His last large organ-building project, in the Holy Cross Church, was completed in 1766. It is interesting that on a concert tour in 1763, the Mozart family visited Augsburg and purchased a portable practice keyboard instrument from Stein.

The success of Stein's pianos was due to excellent craftsmanship and to new and improved parts in the action. Stein used the Viennese hopper, or *Prellmechanik* (escapement) action, which was similar to Silbermann's. However, a distinctive feature of Stein's instrument was the innovation (whether or not he invented it is uncertain) of replacing the stationary **rail** with individual spring-loaded escapement levers, one for each **key**. This device kept the **hammers** from jamming against the **strings**, thereby making rapid repetition possible. Also characteristic of Stein's pianos was his use of wooden *Kapseln* and posts covered with thick, flexible cloth to absorb the shock of the returning hammers. In the upper register Stein used round hollow hammers similar to those of the Silbermann pianos but made of hazelwood, and in the bass, short solid hammers made of pearwood and tapered on all sides (see *Prellmechanik*).

The typical Stein piano has a double **bentside case** with the inside liner sawn from solid wood. The inner **frame** is braced by two or three **rib**-like enforcements perpendicular to the **spine**, and several diagonal supports. The case is closed at the bottom by a thick board, with the grain running parallel to the straight part of the case. The outside of the case itself is usually veneered of plain walnut or cherry with a band of molding around the lower edge. The **soundboards** of Stein's pianos are made of quarter-sawn spruce carefully graduated in thickness. His pianos (at least those that survive) are usually double-strung, with the top octave triple-strung, though some examples exist that are double- or triple-strung throughout. The five-octave **keyboard** is generally made of spruce with **ebony** key facings for the naturals and dyed pearwood topped with bone or **ivory** for the sharps. To place the action in its proper position a "sled" or drawer about 5 cm deep is slipped under the keyboard. Individual **dampers** are fitted into a damper rail above the strings, which the player raises by means of knee levers under the keyboard. Stein was among the first to use wedge-shaped dampers between the strings.

Ernest Closson describes one of the rare, surviving Stein pianos (1786) in Brussels. "Its hammers are covered with chamois **leather** and are scarcely larger than peas; its **tone** is gentle, its timbre thin but clear and distinguished; the strings are of steel in the treble, and of unwrapped brass in the bass. Instead of pedals it is furnished with knee-levers, *organouillères*, which raise the dampers."

Stein's action allowed the lightness and responsiveness of **touch** and the rapid repetition of tones often impossible on earlier pianos. Mozart frequently mentioned Stein's pianos in his letters, as in the often-quoted letter to his father (17 October 1777), written after visiting Stein's workshop in Augsburg. (See **Mozart, Wolfgang Amadeus**), **Ludwig van Beethoven** is known to have played a Stein piano in 1783 while residing in Bonn, and in 1788 he may have received a Stein piano as a gift from Count von Waldstein, who had several in his palace.

Like other eighteenth-century instrument makers, Stein experimented with various inventions, generally action and register combinations, one being the "Poli-Toni-Clavichordium," a harpsichord and piano combined in a rectangular case, with keyboards at each end that could be coupled. In 1772 Stein described an instrument on which he had been working for fifteen years: the "Melodica," which combined a set of pipes with a compass of three and a half octaves and a type of swell built into the keys that provided a cantabile upper voice with the accompaniment of the key instrument on which it was placed. There was little interest in either of these instruments in Augsburg, so in 1773 he took them with him on a trip to Paris, where he managed to sell them.

At an exhibition in Augsburg in 1783 Stein displayed a "vis-à-vis Flügel" (now in the Naples Conservatorium) and a "Clavecin organisé," the latter being a **combination** organ and piano that was commissioned by a Swedish customer (the instrument is now in the Historisk Museum in Göteborg). Another combination-type instrument was the "Saitenharmonika" [string harmonica], which he sold to a customer in Mannheim in 1787 for 100 louis d'or and a barrel of Rhine wine (according to Harding). On this instrument a pedal-shift mechanism moved the action sideways so that the hammers played on an additional third string while the other strings vibrated sympathetically, thereby allowing a pianissimo to fade away to nothing. Stein called the instrument his "Spinettchen."

Johann Andreas Stein's most famous pupils were his children, Matthäus Andreas (1776–1842) and Maria Anna, known as Nannette (1769–1833). Another son, Andreas Friedrich (1784–1809), became a well-known pianist and composer. Maria Anna (Nannette) was an uncommonly talented and versatile woman. At age seven she began helping her father in his workshop and eventually became extremely knowledgeable in the piano-building craft. As a pianist, she played for Mozart at the age of eight, and in the same year (1777) performed the Mozart Triple Concerto in F Minor K242 with her father and Mozart. In a letter to his father (Augsburg, 23 October 1777) Mozart commented on her playing: "When she comes to a passage which ought to flow like oil and which necessitates a change of finger . . . she just leaves out the note, raises her hand and starts off again quite comfortably. . . . She will not make progress by this method." In spite of her bad habits, he said, "She may do well yet, for she has genius."

Nannette's father trained her from early on in the affairs of his business, so that on his death she continued it together with her brother, Matthäus Andreas. In 1794 she married **Johann Andreas Streicher** from Stuttgart (1761–1833), an excellent pianist and teacher, and the following year she, with her husband, mother, and brother, moved the firm to Vienna, where it became extraordinarily successful. Known as "Geschwister Stein," or "Frère et Soeur Stein," the firm of the Streichers and Steins continued from 1796 to 1802.

According to Hirt, Matthäus Stein's personality made it difficult for him to cooperate with his sister, and in 1802 he severed his partnership with Nannette and founded his own business under the name of "Andreas Stein" (or "André Stein"). Nannette's firm was then called "Nannette Streicher, geboren Stein" (or "Nannette Streicher née Stein"). Streicher, who up to then had handled the commercial side of the business, now took his full share of the work. Their firm became highly successful and their instruments were played by celebrated pianists throughout Europe.

Nannette Streicher was an energetic businesswoman, an excellent pianist, a model wife and mother. Socially she became prominent because of her ability to befriend important people, including Beethoven, with whom the Streichers were particularly close. It is well known that Nannette did much to alleviate the composer's housekeeping tasks, and even at times looked after him during his illnesses. Haydn and **Muzio Clementi** were other famous composer-pianists with whom the Streichers were closely associated. Concerts in their home became a rendezvous of the artistic, intellectual, and business elite of Vienna.

After 1825, Nannette Stein was in partnership with her son Johann Baptist Streicher (1795–1871), and the Streicher firm became famous for the finest Viennese pianofortes. Johann Baptist continued the business after Nannette's death, and from 1857 he was in partnership with his son, Emil (1836–1916), who then took over the historic business in 1871 after his father's death. When Emil retired in 1896 he dissolved the business.

Matthäus Andreas Stein (1776–1842), son of Johann Andreas and brother of Nannette, was also a pianoforte builder. He inherited the piano business along with his sister and the two were in partnership (constituted by imperial decree 17 January 1794) from 1796 to 1802, when the partnership was dissolved and he established his own piano-building firm in Vienna under the name of "Matthäus Andreas Stein" or "Andreas Stein" ("André Stein"). He married 12 November 1796. His son, Karl Andreas, eventually succeeded to the business.

Karl Andreas Stein (1797–1863), son of Matthäus Andreas, was trained as a piano builder and teacher. A pupil of Emanuel Förster in composition, he published a considerable number of piano pieces. He also wrote two piano concerti (still in manuscript), two overtures for orchestra, and a comic opera, *Die Goldene Gans.* Aside from giving a few concerts, he principally devoted himself to the piano business, travelling widely for the firm. In 1844 he was appointed "Piano Builder to the Court." His pianos were played by many artists of the day.

Mary Louise Boehm

Bibliography

Anderson, Emiy. *The Letters of Beethoven.* 3 vols. New York: St. Martin's Press, 1961.

Brinsmead, Edgar. *The History of the Piano: With an Account of the Theory of Sound and Also of the Music and Musical Instruments of the Ancients.* London: Novello, Ewer and Co., 1879. Reissue. Detroit, Mich.: Singing Tree Press, 1969.

Broder, Nathan. "Mozart and the 'Clavier.'" *Musical Quarterly* 27 (October 1941): 422–32.

Closson, Ernest. *La facture des instruments de musique en Belgique* [The manufacture of musical instruments in Belgium]. Bruxelles: Presses des établissements degrace à Hov, 1935.

Dolge, Alfred. *Pianos and Their Makers.* Covina, Cal.: Covina Publishing Co., 1911. Reprint, New York: Dover, 1972.

Gill, Dominic. *The Book of the Piano.* Ithaca, N.Y.: Cornell University Press, 1981.

Good, Edwin Marshall. *Giraffes, Black Dragons, and Other Pianos: A Technological History from Cristofori to the Modern Concert Grand.* Stanford, Cal.: Stanford University Press, 1982.

Harding, Rosamond E.M. *The Piano-Forte: Its History Traced to the Great Exhibition of 1851.* Cambridge: Cambridge University Press, 1933. Reprints, New York: Da Capo Press, 1973; Old Woking, Surrey: Gresham Books, 1978.

Hipkins, Alfred James. *A Description and History of the Pianoforte and of the Older Keyboard Stringed Instruments.* London: Novello, 1896. Reprint. AMS Press, 1977.

Hirt, Franz Josef. *Stringed Keyboard Instruments 1440–1880.* Boston, Mass.: Boston Book and Art Shop, 1968. (1st ed. *Meisterwerke des Klavierbaus.* Olten, Switzerland: Urs Graf-Verlag, 1955); Also, *Meisterwerke des Klavierbaus—Stringed Keyboard Instruments.* Dietikon-Zürich: Urs Graf (distributed in the USA by Da Capo Press), 1981.

Katalog der Sammlung Alter Musikinstrumente. Vol. 1—*Saitenklaviere.* Vienna: Kunsthistorisches Museum, 1966.

New Grove Dictionary of Musical Instruments. Edited by Stanley Sadie. London: Macmillan Press; Washington, D.C.: Grove's Dictionaries, 1984.

Newman, William S. "Beethoven's Pianos Versus His Piano Ideals." *Journal of the American Musicological Society* 23 (Fall 1970): 484–504.

Sumner, William Leslie. *The Pianoforte.* London: Macdonald, 1966. 3rd ed., rev. and enl. London: Macdonald, 1971.

Wainwright, David. *The Piano Makers.* London: Hutchinson, 1975.

STEINWAY & SONS

Steinway & Sons of New York, one of the world's best-known piano-manufacturing companies, has a long-standing reputation for the high quality of its products. Though its founder,

Heinrich Engelhardt Steinweg (later Henry Engelhardt Steinway, 1797–1871), made pianos in his native Germany in the 1830s, Steinway & Sons came into being in New York.

In 1850, Henry Steinway, Sr., and his wife, Julianne (1804–1877), brought seven of their nine children from Germany to New York and joined an eighth. The eldest son, C. F. Theodore Steinweg (1825–1889), remained in Seesen, perhaps intending ultimately to move to New York. The older sons and Henry, Sr., found jobs in several New York piano firms and learned the American trade. On 5 March 1853, Henry, Sr., and his sons Charles G. (1829–1865) and Henry E., Jr. (1830–1865) formed Steinway & Sons as a partnership, into which William (1835–1896) was admitted in 1856 and Albert (1840–1877) in 1866. Within a decade of the firm's founding it was second in the U.S. only to **Chickering** & Sons of Boston. The company was incorporated in 1876.

Steinway & Sons soon enjoyed local success. A Steinway **square** won a gold medal at a New York Mechanics Fair in the Crystal Palace in 1855, and Henry, Jr., received his first **patents** for improvements to the **grand action** (U.S. Patents 17,238 [5 May 1857] and 20,595 [15 June 1858]). These served notice that the company aspired to influence, since few American makers made grands, let alone improved them. Chickering was the major exception, and it is a permissible speculation that even by 1857, Steinway & Sons set its sights on the top ranking. In 1860, the company built a large factory at 4th (Park) Avenue and 52nd–53rd streets, leaving small shops and lofts downtown. The new company would not simply drift in a conventional current; Henry Steinway's sons were a vigorous, imaginative, ambitious lot.

Henry, Jr.'s major innovation was the design of a cross-strung grand (U.S. Patent 26,532, 20 December 1859). **Cross-stringing** was well

Concert Grand by Steinway & Sons, New York.

known for squares, but Henry's patent combined the one-piece iron **frame** (which Chickering had put into grands in 1843) with cross-stringing, which had not been done in grands. The new design won a first-rank medal at the London Exposition in 1862, and the first step toward an American hegemony in the piano trade was taken. In 1864, the company opened a building on E. 14th St. that housed offices and warerooms and, in 1866, added an important auditorium. Steinway Hall remained a major concert and lecture hall until it closed a year before Carnegie Hall was opened on 57th Street in 1891.

The company was threatened with collapse in March 1865, when Henry, Jr., and Charles died within three weeks of each other. Henry, Sr., was then sixty-eight years old and apparently not active in the company, and William, the only son we know was active, was only thirty. Heavy persuasion brought Theodore, the son who had stayed behind in Germany, to New York and into the partnership. A genius in design and invention, Theodore insisted on the most meticulous standards of construction. In 1867, Steinway and Chickering took the highest prizes (which was higher depends on which company is speaking) at the Paris Exposition, resulting in a growing American dominance of the worldwide industry.

One of Theodore's innovations was the determination to develop the **upright piano** at the expense of the square. By 1865, squares had effectively been replaced in Europe by uprights, which took less floor space. Though other companies made uprights, Theodore sought to bring them to a new standard of excellence. He succeeded to the extent that Steinway & Sons made its last square in 1888, and in time other American makers rejected the square and adopted the upright. That the ascendancy of the upright was the best thing that could have happened to the piano is debatable. The square had the advantage of access to better actions than are possible in the upright, whereas the upright could live in rooms too small for the massive squares to which American makers were addicted.

Theodore Steinway made several other improvements in piano design among his forty-odd patents. Perhaps the most important were the **duplex scale** (U.S. Patent 126848, 14 May 1872), in which the non-speaking lengths of **string** between the **tuning pins** and the *capo*

tasto and **agraffes** were proportioned as **partial** tones to the speaking lengths of the strings to allow some sympathetic enhancement of the **tone**; the "cupola frame" (U.S. Patent 127383, 28 May 1872), which was intended to allow freer distribution of the sound from the **soundboard** and to place the **bridges** closer to the center of the soundboard; and a **case** laminated of eighth-inch planks (U.S. Patent 229198, 22 June 1880), securely glued by use of an innovative **rim**-bending screw, which produces a lighter case that is claimed to improve tone by reflecting sound waves back across the soundboard. The patented screw, which holds the planks while the glue dries, is still used in the Steinway factory. One innovation, the *sostenuto* **pedal** (the middle pedal on modern instruments), was proposed by Theodore in 1873, but Albert made it work and was granted the patents (U.S. Patents 156388, 27 October 1874, and 164052–164054, 1 June 1875).

The company survived the depression of 1873–1877—perhaps in part through shrewd real-estate investment—and, by William Steinway's foresighted acquisition of land in Long Island City, the company moved part of the manufacturing process in 1873 from the Manhattan factory to the Astoria, L.I., location. The company built houses for workers and provided for stores, a church, a kindergarten, horse-car rail lines, a public bathing beach, and other amenities of community life, and the "Steinway" area of Queens, centering around Steinway Ave., still retains a distinct flavor. A mansion on one of the properties (now on the Register of Historic Buildings) provided the family with summer relief from Manhattan for many decades.

The latter part of the nineteenth century saw a tremendous expansion of international trade. William Steinway's financial acumen helped the company to reach a pinnacle of international reputation and of export success. A strong sales center in London, opened in 1875, assisted, and in 1880, William and Theodore opened Steinway's Pianofabrik in Hamburg, not as a Steinway & Sons property but as their own, though it assembled Steinway & Sons pianos from parts supplied by Astoria. This factory, destroyed in 1943, came into the company's possession after Theodore's death in 1889 and, with a later factory, has been the source of Steinway pianos sold in Europe. Its products have always been subtly different from New York Steinways, notably in a smoother, less brilliant sound than the typical American Steinway tone. Theodore Steinway, who hated New York, took the construction of the Hamburg factory as an excuse to move back to Braunschweig, Germany, where he lived until his death. The connection of Steinway & Sons with the Grotrian firm of Braunschweig has often been confusing. When Theodore Steinway came to New York in 1865, he sold out to Grotrian and his associates, allowing them for a period of time to call themselves "Th. Steinwegs Nachfolger" (Theodore Steinweg's successors). That is the only connection between the two companies, and, though the Grotrian company adopted the name **Grotrian-Steinweg**, a suit in the 1970s by Steinway & Sons led to an agreement that no pianos with the name "Steinweg" would be sold in the U.S. Grotrian has never had any connection with Steinway's Hamburg plant.

With Theodore's death, only William, who had become president when the corporation was formed in 1876, remained of the founding generation. Several men of the next generation had come into the company: Charles Ziegler (1854–1893), son of Dorette Steinway (1827–1900) and Jacob Ziegler (1825–1897), became manager of the London branch, and his brother Henry (1857–1930) was in charge of design and construction in New York under uncle Theodore's supervision, and later was vice president. Charles G. Steinway's three sons took positions: Henry W. T. (1856–1939) came to be factory manager (but was invited out of the company in 1892); Charles H. (1857–1919) became president on William's death in 1896; and Frederick T. (1860–1927) succeeded Charles H. as president in 1919.

William's two sons by his second marriage followed their older cousins in company management: William R. (1881–1960) managed the European ventures from 1919 until 1939, and Theodore E. (1883–1957) was president from 1927 to 1955, a very difficult time for the business. In the next generation, Frederick Vietor (1891–1941), grandson of Albert Steinway, Charles F. M. Steinway (1892–1967), son of Charles H., Frederick J. Ziegler (1886–1966), Henry Ziegler's son, and Paul Schmidt (1878–1950), son of Julia Ziegler and Constantin Schmidt, had positions with the firm. Other-wise, the company was mostly run by three of Theodore E. Steinway's sons, Theodore D. (1914–1982), who headed engineering until his death, John H. (1917–1989), who retired as chairman in 1982, and Henry Z. (1915–), who succeeded his father as president in 1955 until his retirement in 1980.

The twentieth century has had its ups and downs for the company. It closed for a time during World War I, suspended manufacturing for two years during the depression in the 1930s, and was deflected to making glider parts, coffins, and small upright pianos for military use during World War II. During the war, the Hamburg plant kept going until Allied bombing in 1943–1945 stopped production, and production of pianos resumed in 1948. After the war, the London sales establishment, which had not been seriously damaged, encountered some customs and tax difficulties because its pianos had always been supplied from Germany, but normalcy brought business back to something approaching profitability.

The New York establishment had moved all the manufacturing from 52nd St. to Long Island City in 1910 (the prime land on Park Ave. no doubt brought a handsome price), and the offices and salesrooms moved to 109 W. 57th St. in 1925. A flourishing concert management, resting on a tradition begun with Anton Rubinstein's famous North American tour under Steinway auspices in 1872 and continued with such artists as Ignacy Jan Paderewski in 1891, handled many of the best pianists in the world, and Steinway & Sons profited from commitments to play Steinways by many of the rest.

Like most piano companies, Steinway participated in the **player piano** boom during the 1920s, and like most, it was hard hit by the depression and the rise of the radio as the prime means of home entertainment in the 1930s. Toward the end of the 1930s, the company's sales were mainly of pianos built in the early part of the decade and stored in the meantime. Though business began to look better during the 1960s, the market was not really lively, and profitability was insufficient to produce investable capital. In 1972, the stockholders (still almost all family members) decided to sell the company to CBS, and, though Henry and John Steinway continued in high management, the direction of the company came from elsewhere. That the Steinway piano remained in all respects what it had traditionally been is a matter of debate. The use for some years of a Teflon plastic **bushing** was the cause of controversy, and it has more recently been abandoned. Significant design innovations have been few. Materials have changed somewhat, e.g., in the use of glues developed during World War II and the replacement of **ivory** by plastic key-covering, in accordance with U.S. law.

In 1985, a consortium of Boston businessmen, John P. and Robert M. Birmingham, and Bruce A. Stevens, purchased Steinway & Sons from CBS, and Mr. Stevens is the CEO. No evident modifications in design have been made, but there have been efforts to streamline the manufacturing processes.

Steinway & Sons has never given out production figures, but one can estimate them from **serial numbers**. In 1880, when the Hamburg factory was opened, total annual production was about 2,000. By 1900 it had reached about 5,000 combined, and that has been an approximate average during this century, with New York producing about 3,000 instruments to every 2,000 from Hamburg. The company presented its piano no. 100,000 to the White House in 1903 and no. 300,000 in 1938. The former is now in the Smithsonian Institution's National Museum of American History, and its impressive case paintings by Thomas Dewing have been restored. The latter remains in the East Room of the White House. In 1987, no. 500,000 was fitted in a case designed by Wendell Castle presented in a Carnegie Hall program in June 1988, where a number of Steinway pianists played it, and was then sent on a world tour.

In 1991, Steinway & Sons announced a collaborative effort with the **Kawai** company in Japan to produce a good-quality, medium-priced piano for the home. In its nearly 140 years of existence, the company has had an enviable name and a mixed commercial success. The future can only be guessed.

Edwin M. Good

Bibliography

Dolge, Alfred. *Pianos and Their Makers.* Covina, Cal.: Covina Publishing, Co., 1911. Reprint. New York: Dover Publications, Inc., 1972.

————. *Men Who Have Made Piano History.* Repr. of vol 2 of *Pianos and Their Makers,* 1913. Vestal N.Y.: Vestal Press, 1980.

Ehrlich, Cyril. *The Piano: A History.* 2nd ed. Oxford: Clarendon Press, 1990.

Good, Edwin M. *Giraffes, Black Dragons, and Other Pianos: A Technological History from Cristofori to the Modern Concert Grand.* Stanford, Cal.: Stanford University Press, 1982.

Groce, Nancy. "Musical Instrument Making in New York City During the Eighteenth and Nineteenth Centuries." Diss., University of Michigan, 1982.

Hoover, Cynthia Adams. "The Steinways and Their Pianos in the Nineteenth Century." *Journal of the American Musical Instrument Society* 7 (1981): 47–89.

The New Grove Dictionary of American Music. Vol. 4, 303–4. Edited by H. Wiley Hitchcock and Stanley Sadie, s.v. "Steinway" by Cyril Ehrlich. London: Macmillan, 1986.

Ratcliffe, Ronald V. *Steinway.* San Francisco: Chronicle Books, 1989.

Steinway, Theodore E. *People and Pianos: A Century of Service to Music.* New York: Steinway & Sons, 1953, rev. 1961.

STENCIL PIANO

The stencil piano is an instrument that bears a name (decal or "stencil") on its **nameboard** different from that of the company that actually manufactured it, the name instead being owned by a dealer or distributor. Such pianos were also known as "house" or "private label" brands. Better-grade pianos had their names cast in the iron **frame** of the instrument, but manufacturers of stencil pianos produced instruments for anyone who could purchase a given number of units, supplying them with whatever name the buyer desired. The way was thus opened to deceptive practices, for there was no way that the purchaser could determine the origin, and thus the quality, of the instrument. Frequently, identical pianos were sold under different names, thus allowing the manufacturer a broader market and the dealer the added prestige of his own "house" brand. Some names were deliberately formulated to imitate well-known brands, such as "Steinwebb" for **Steinway,** "Chicory" for **Chickering,** and "Brechstein" for **Bechstein.**

The stencil piano has been in existence for well over a hundred years, not only in the United States, but in Europe as well. **Alfred Dolge** attributed the stencil piano to Joseph P. Hale (fl. 1860–1890), who bought component parts in huge lots and assembled unpretentious instruments that sold for prices far below those asked by standard makers. Such pianos were excoriated on one hand on the grounds that, since they tended to be cheaply built, the average buyer, ignorant of piano quality, was being misled; and praised on the other by those who saw the stencil piano as a promotional instrument leading to the eventual purchase of a better, more expensive piano. In 1912 a bill was introduced in Congress that would make it illegal to offer pianos for sale that did not bear the name and address of their manufacturer, but it died in committee. In 1926 piano manufacturer William Tonk estimated that 70 percent of the pianos manufactured in the United States bore names other than that of their makers. Builders of stencil pianos in the United States in recent years have been **Wurlitzer**, **Kimball**, and **Aeolian**, the last named taking advantage of the many names accumulated in its various mergers. The stencil piano is produced worldwide, notably in the Far East.

James Howard Richards

Bibliography

Dolge, Alfred. *Pianos and Their Makers*. Covina, Cal.: Covina Publishing Co., 1911. Reprint. New York: Dover Publications, Inc., 1972.

Fine, Larry. *The Piano Book*. Boston: Brookside Press, 1987.

Roell, Craig H. *The Piano in America, 1890–1940*. Chapel Hill: The University of North Carolina Press, 1989.

STICKER ACTION

Also called the "abstract," the sticker is the part of a vertical piano **action** that connects the **key** to the **wippen**. The sticker may vary in length according to the height of the piano. From about 1798 to 1840, English **upright pianos** produced by George Wilkinson, **Broadwood**, and **Clementi** among others, used stickers three feet or more in length, as opposed to modern stickers which are less than six inches long. These actions with long stickers are called "sticker actions."

See also Actions.

Philip Jamison, III

STODART, ROBERT AND WILLIAM (1748–1831) AND (FL.1795–C.1838)

Robert and William Stodart represent a distinguished family of English piano makers and inventors who worked in London from 1775 to 1862. The founder was Robert, and key members were his son William and grandson Malcolm. The dynasty ended with the death of Malcolm Stodart in the 1860s.

Robert Stodart was a private in the Royal Horse Guards, a corps to which the private had to pay 100 pounds for admission. David Wainwright wrote that "having little duty, and consequently much leisure, he apprenticed himself for three years to John Broadwood." Robert Stodart appears to have been greatly talented; for, in conjunction with **Broadwood** and **Americus Backers**, he worked on the modification of the **Cristofori** action and perfected an **action** that included a check (**back check**) on the descending **hammer**. This obviated a failure of earlier pianos, where the hammer could sometimes bounce back and hit the **string** a second time. His check ensured greater clarity of **touch**. The Backers/Broadwood/Stodart action was first described in a **patent** for a combined piano and harpsichord designed by Robert Stodart in 1777. His invention came to be known as the **English** grand **action**. On completion of his apprenticeship, he became a significant piano maker in his own right.

Among Robert Stodart's inventions from the period of 1775 to 1796 were a patented **grand fortepiano** with an octave swell, and a combined piano and harpsichord. In 1795 he brought out an **upright** grand in the form of a bookcase.

In 1795, William Stodart took out a patent for an "upright grand." This was effectively little more than a grand piano simply turned upward ninety degrees and mounted on a stand at right angles to the **keyboard**. It stood between eight and nine feet tall. In 1820, two of William Stodart's workmen, **James Thom** and **William Allen**, invented a "compensating **frame**" in an attempt to eliminate the problem of the piano going out of **tune** in extremes of atmospheric temperature. This included tubes of brass and steel fixed above the strings. William Stodart immediately purchased their interest in it. What quickly became known as Stodart's compensating frame was shown in a grand piano exhibited at the Great Exhibition of 1851 staged in London.

Both Robert and William Stodart made fine instruments, including a large number of **square pianos** or table pianos. Their instruments were expensive (between 60 and 70 guineas) but for the purchaser represented a sound proposition because of their quality and hence durability.

When Malcolm Stodart, who had shown great promise, died, the interest of the surviving members of the family ceased, and the business, which had been declining, came to an end.

Arthur W.J.G. Ord-Hume

Bibliography

Grove, Sir George. *Dictionary of Music & Musicians.* 1st ed. London: Macmillan, 1879.

Harding, Rosamond E.M. *The Piano-Forte: Its History Traced to the Great Exhibition of 1851.* Cambridge: Cambridge University Press, 1933. Reprints, New York: Da Capo Press, 1973; Old Woking, Surrey: Gresham Books, 1978.

Wainwright, David. *Broadwood by Appointment. A History.* London: Quiller, 1982. New York: Universe Books, 1983.

STORY AND CLARK

Story and Clark was a major midwestern keyboard instrument manufacturer. In 1884, Hampton L. Story, a dealer in reed organs, Edward H. Story, his son, and Melville Clark (1850–1918), an expert organ builder, established the firm of Story and Clark in Chicago for the production of reed organs. The manufacture of pianos was started in 1895. Sales of Story and Clark instruments grew at a rapid rate and in 1901 the firm moved to a new factory in Grand Haven, Michigan. At this time, Clark left to form his own company in De Kalb, Illinois.

During the early decades of the twentieth century, Story and Clark produced **uprights**, **player pianos**, and **grands** in the moderate price range. The firm survived the unfavorable economic conditions of the late 1920s and then shifted to the manufacture of **consoles**. Except for the interruption by World War II, Story and Clark piano sales continued to climb.

In 1962, Story and Clark was acquired by the owners of the Lowrey Organ Company, who then added a new line of pianos under the Lowrey label. In 1965, the Hobart M. Cable label was acquired from the La Porte, Indiana, firm by that name, which dropped out of business that year. Except for a limited number of grand pianos, all of the firm's pianos were consoles with relatively minor differences in design.

Story and Clark/Lowrey piano sales began to decline slowly in the 1970s and continued downward until finally in 1984 production at Grand Haven was terminated. The piano manufacturing and Lowrey electronic keyboard businesses were then separated and sold to different groups of investors. The Story and Clark Piano Company became a division of Classic Player Piano Corporation, Seneca, Pennsylvania.

Jack Greenfield

Bibliography

Dolge, Alfred. *Pianos and Their Makers.* Covina, Cal.: Covina Publishing, Co., 1911. Reprint. New York: Dover, 1972.

"Norlin Sells Piano Manufacturing Plant." *The Music Trades* (September 1984): 28–30.

"M. H. Berlin." *The Music Trades* (September 1984): 91.

STOSSMECHANIK

Stossmechanik is the name given to the type of **action** used by many of the early English piano builders. It is based on the action invented by **Bartolomeo Cristofori** but reduced to its essential parts and thus simplified. Its basic elements featured a **hammer** head that pointed to the back of the instrument (the hammer assembly was hinged or pivoted to a blocked **rail**); the hammer's upward motion (initially activated by the **key** being depressed) is propelled by a **jack** or similar device fixed to the key lever without any intermediate lever, **escapement**, or check piece. This action principle was the forerunner of the **English action** and is commonly found on **square pianos**.

See also Actions.

Donatella Degiampietro and Giuliana Montanari

Bibliography

Dolge, Alfred. *Pianos and Their Makers.* Covina, Cal.: Covina Publishing Co., 1911. Reprint. New York: Dover, 1972.

Harding, Rosamond E.M. *The Piano-Forte: Its History Traced to the Great Exhibition of 1851.* Cambridge: Cambridge University Press, 1933. Reprints, New York: Da Capo Press, 1973; Old Woking, Surrey: Gresham Books, 1978.

Hirt, Franz Josef. *Stringed Keyboard Instruments 1440-1880.* Translated by M. Boehme-Brown. Boston, Mass.: Boston Book and Art Shop, 1968. Also, *Meisterwerke des Klavierbaus—Stringed Keyboard Instruments.* Dietikon-Zürich: Urs Graf (distributed in the USA by Da Capo Press), 1981.

Marcuse, Sybil. *Musical Instruments: A Comprehensive Dictionary.* New York: Norton, 1975.

New Grove Dictionary of Musical Instruments. Edited by Stanley Sadie. London: Macmillan Press; Washington D.C.: Grove's Dictionaries, 1984.

The Piano. (New Grove Musical Instruments Series.) New York: Norton, 1988.

STREET PIANO

A street piano is a mechanical piano made for use in the open. There are two principal forms, both played by a pinned wooden barrel rotated by a hand-turned crank so as to operate a simple **hammer** action against the musical **strings**.

First is the small portable instrument carried on the shoulder by itinerant musicians and supported, while playing, by a single wooden leg and a leather harness around the operator's body. Originating in Italy, the form was developed by the piano-making family of Hicks in Bristol, England, in the first quarter of the nineteenth century, and varieties were manufactured extensively in Britain and in America, almost exclusively in New York. The compass was never chromatic and covered around three octaves. Sometimes the instruments were provided with automated scenes showing a *tableau vivant* activated by special pins on the barrel.

Second is the larger instrument, normally mounted on a handcart and resembling in size a conventional **upright piano**. Again, although the compass was much larger than that of the smaller variety, the instrument was never fully chromatic. In these, eight tunes were played, and the barrels could be replaced. Over the years, many varieties were produced, and their production spans the period from about 1860 through to the outbreak of World War II.

See also Barrel Piano.

Arthur W.J.G. Ord-Hume

Bibliography

Harding, Rosamond E.M. *The Piano-Forte: Its History Traced to the Great Exhibition of 1851.* Cambridge: Cambridge University Press, 1933. Reprints, New York: Da Capo Press, 1973; Old Woking, Surrey: Gresham Books, 1978.

Ord-Hume, Arthur W.J.G. *Pianola—History & Development* . . . . London: Allen & Unwin, 1984.

STREICHER FAMILY

Throughout the nineteenth century the Streicher family was one of the most important and prosperous piano manufacturers in Vienna. During the first half of the century their pianos were considered among the best Vienna had to offer. These pianos had a smooth, light, and responsive Viennese **action** and were especially well built and carefully crafted. Other makers looked to them for designs, and performers of the day supported the firm enthusiastically.

The Streicher dynasty was descended from the **Stein** family of piano makers. Anna Maria (Nannette) Stein (1769–1833) and her brother Matthäus Andreas Stein (1776–1842) learned the craft of piano building from their father Johann Andreas Stein (1728–1792) in Augsburg. The siblings began managing their father's shop, possibly as early as 1791. In 1794 Nannette married Johann Andreas Streicher (1761–1833), a virtuoso pianist, composer, and teacher, and she also moved to Vienna with her brother to reopen their father's workshop as "Geschwister Stein" or "Frère et Soeur Stein" (1794–1802). At first Nannette and her brother handled the business, but by 1801 Streicher also joined them. His booklet, *Kurze Bemerkungen über das Spielen, Stimmen und Erhalten der Fortepiano welche von Nannette Streicher. . .* (1801) [Brief Remarks on the Playing, Tuning and Maintenance of the Fortepiano made by Nannette Streicher. . .] was probably intended to be given to new owners. The workshop took Nannette's name when she and her brother separated the business. The firm "Nannette Streicher, née Stein" (1802–1823) made between forty-five and sixty pianos a year and was one of the best makers in Vienna during this period.

At first the pianos were not much different from her father's; they still had a five-octave range with a very light action. Nannette then added new features to the *Prellmechanik* action inherited from her father. Her action, now called the Viennese action, gained a **back check** to control the **hammer** and a screw for regulating the **touch**; these pianos were noted for their balance and purity of **tone**. Her pianos in this period had a five-and-a-half or six-octave range, FF–c⁴ or f⁴, and were mostly triple strung. There were brass **strings** in the bass and iron strings for the remainder. These pianos usually had four **pedals**: *una corda*, bassoon, pianissimo, **damper**; piano No. 1031 in the Neupert Collection, Germanisches Nationalmuseum, Nuremberg (1814) also has knee levers for the Turkish **janissary** bells and drums.

Both Carl Maria von Weber and **Ludwig van Beethoven** thought highly of the Streicher piano of this period. Beethoven may have owned Streichers between 1810 and 1817 and the

Streicher firm may have built a six-and-one-half-octave piano for him in 1816 or 1817, but the evidence is not conclusive, according to Edwin Good (pp. 77–78, 91). Good also finds no support for the idea that Beethoven influenced the Streichers' building of pianos (p. 80), even though Beethoven did know the couple personally.

The son Johann Baptist Streicher (1796–1871) joined the firm in 1823, and the firm was renamed "Nannette Streicher, geb. Stein und Sohn" (1823–1833). Production in the 1820s was about fifty pianos a year, and the company continued to experiment with design. Johann Baptist **patented** a workable downstriking action (1823) in which the hammer was returned by a spring, but that idea did not catch on. In 1824 he patented a new version of the Viennese action that became very popular with both German and Viennese makers. Artists who used and liked the Streicher pianos of this generation included Clara Wieck, Felix Mendelssohn, and **Franz Liszt**.

Johann Baptist took over the firm completely after Nannette and Andreas's deaths in 1833. The firm was renamed J.B. Streicher (1833–1859) and it carried on successfully. Johann Baptist made further changes of design. For example, in 1831 he began to experiment with an Anglo-German action for some of his pianos that combined features of both the English and Viennese actions. He continued to build the pure Viennese action, making it heavier than before. In 1835 he patented a design for struts of iron tubing, and he also increased the range of his pianos to CC–g⁴. By mid-century he was making piano actions in three different designs: English, Viennese, and Anglo-German.

He took his son Emil Streicher (1836–1916) into the firm as a partner in 1857, and two years later changed the name of the firm to J.B. Streicher und Sohn (1859–1896). Johann Baptist had studied carefully the American **Steinway** design exhibited at the London Exhibition of 1862, and as a result, at the 1867 Paris Exhibition, succeeded in exhibiting an almost identical **overstrung** piano with a one-piece cast-iron **frame**, and the firm won a prize for this piano. In the meantime, however, the fortunes of the company had begun a gradual decline; this prize was not enough to return the company to its former position of importance in the piano market. Streicher was making only about 150 pianos a year and could not compete with **Bösendorfer's** growing influence in Vienna.

The Streicher company continued to build the old-fashioned Viennese piano alongside pianos with English or Anglo-German actions. The pianos with Viennese action resembled Nannette's pianos of the 1820s and 1830s although they had a larger **soundboard**, a longer treble scaling, and heavier action. They were usually straight strung, with a wooden frame and **leather** hammers. The range was increased to seven octaves; two iron tension bars and an iron string **plate** improved the piano's strength, and a *capo tasto* bar increased the **downbearing**. **Johannes Brahms** was given such a piano built in 1868 (no. 6713, now lost). Surviving instruments at the Kunsthistorisches Museum, Vienna, and the Edmund M. Frederick Collection, Ashburnham, Massachusetts, show other examples of this type.

J.B. Streicher und Sohn was no longer keeping pace with the manufacturing methods and modern marketing of the more aggressive piano companies; after Johann Baptist's death in 1871 gradually fewer concerts were held at the Streicher Salon. By 1896 Emil, sixty years old and comfortably wealthy, liquidated the firm because he could not interest his son Theodor Streicher (1874–1940) in continuing it. The Streicher firm's demise brought to an end the era of the Viennese action piano. For almost one hundred years it had been the dominant piano type for composers of the German-Austrian sphere.

Camilla Cai

Bibliography

Bolte, Theodor. *Die Musikerfamilien Stein und Streicher*. Vienna: Ludwig Schönberger, 1917.

Dolge, Alfred. *Pianos and Their Makers*. Covina Cal.: Covina Publishing Co., 1911. Reprint. New York: Dover Publications, 1972.

Edwards, Lynn, and E. Michael Frederick. "Two Nineteenth-Century Grand Pianos." *Early Keyboard Studies Newsletter* I (September 1985): 1–2.

Fuller, Richard A. "Andreas Streicher's Notes on the Fortepiano." *Early Music* 12 (1984): 461–470.

Good, Edwin M. *Giraffes, Black Dragons, and Other Pianos*. Stanford, Cal.: Stanford University Press, 1982.

Harding, Rosamond E.M. *The Piano-Forte: Its History Traced to the Great Exhibition of 1851*.

Cambridge: Cambridge University Press, 1933. Reprints, New York: Da Capo Press, 1973; Old Woking, Surrey: Gresham Books, 1978.

Hirt, Franz Josef. *Meisterwerke des Klavierbaus.* Olten: Urs Graf-Verlag, 1955. Also as *Stringed Keyboard Instruments 1440–1880.* Translated by M. Boehme-Brown. Boston: Boston Book and Art Shop, 1968. Also, Dietikon-Zürich: Urs Graf (distributed by Da Capo Press), 1981.

Luithlen, Victor. *Kunsthistorisches Museum: Katalog der Sammlung alter Musikinstrumente.* Part 1: *Saitenklaviere*, pp. 51–56. Vienna: Kunsthistorisches Museum, 1966.

Lütge, Wilhelm. "Andreas und Nannette Streicher." *Der Bär.* (Jahrbuch von Breitkopf & Härtel). Leipzig: Breitkopf & Härtel, 1927, pp. 53–69.

STRIKE POINT

The strike point in a piano is the point on the **string** that is struck by the **hammer.** This point on the string is usually determined to be $1/_7$ to $1/_9$ distance from the front termination point of the vibrating section of the string. The strike point is set so that no one **partial** (harmonic), is accentuated by the blow of the hammer. Studies of the vibrating nodes of a string have found that $1/_7$ to $1/_9$ from the termination will provide the strongest presence of the fundamental tone.

Kent Webb

STRINGS/STRINGING

Strings on a piano fall into two categories: plain and wound. Plain **wire** comes in various diameters and a specific wire size is chosen by the piano designer for each note, taking into consideration such factors as the speaking length, overtone structure, tension, and a wire stretch factor, all measured when that string is **tuned** up to **pitch.** Therefore it is important, when a string is replaced in a piano, that the replacement string is the same size in diameter as the old string. Wire diameter typically gets larger along with speaking length as the pitch gets lower. There is a point, however—dictated by the size of the piano—where a longer string is not possible and a thicker string would not sound good.

Wound strings, consisting of a steel core wire with a wrapping of heavier metal, are used in the lower tenor and bass for these reasons. Because of its high specific weight and its malleability, copper is typically chosen to be wound around the core wire, allowing the lower frequencies to be produced but keeping the length of the string within **case** design boundaries. The steel wire core of a wound string is similar, if not identical, in composition to plain wire.

There are two forms of core wire in use today: round and hexagonal. The common, round form of steel must be flattened slightly for short lengths where the copper winding is to begin and end, in order to provide an area onto which the copper can be fastened. The length along which the copper will be spun is usually roughed up with a file to improve the hold of the copper on the core. A core wire that is hexagonal in shape does not need to be flattened; the copper will grip the core beginning at any point and all along the wound length.

In his comprehensive *A Treatise on the Art of Pianoforte Construction*, Samuel Wolfenden describes the manufacture of piano wire: "The billet of steel is first passed through a rolling mill, and by repeated rollings is formed into roughly round rods of suitable dimensions for the drawing process. It is then drawn through the series of holes, each one decreasing its diameter and increasing its length. During this operation it has to be frequently annealed, because of the increase of hardness, and the drawing goes on until the required gauge is attained."

Professor W. V. McFerrin describes piano wire in *The Piano—Its Acoustics* as follows: "It is made of imported Swedish steel with a carbon content of .88% to .95%, and is low in manganese, sulfur, phosphorus and other elements." Later he points out that the dies through which the steel is cold drawn "may be of hardened steel at first, then tungsten carbide, and finally diamond dies are used for small sizes of wire."

In a sense, steel wire has had a dominating role in the development of the modern pianoforte. When steel piano wire replaced iron wire as the material of choice for nineteenth-century piano makers, it led to many of the improvements that were necessary for the evolution of the instrument into the piano we know today. With additional tension possible, the quality and projection of the piano sound, as well as the stability of the tuning, were reported to be much improved.

As early as the fourteenth century, iron wire had been used for musical instruments. In 1834, a cast-steel piano wire was developed in Birmingham, England, that was acknowledged as the most superior of that time.

Official tests held at the World's Exhibitions from 1867 to 1893 in Paris, Vienna, Philadelphia, and Chicago sparked competition among the many musical-instrument wire manufacturers and helped improve the quality of the material substantially. One manufacturer, Moritz Poehlmann of Nuremberg, Germany, was noted for improving size gradation and the polish of the wire, which protects against rust. The Poehlmann wire's tensile strength at breaking point improved by as much as 44 percent during the time records were kept.

As steel wire allowed the increase of tension needed for the greater amount and quality of sound, it became obvious that the wholly wooden case would not be able to bear the resultant load. Metal bars, their ends screwed into the wooden case, were added. These were placed above the strings to strengthen the case and prevent it from buckling. As this procedure proved beneficial, it led to still higher-tensioned **scales**, needing another metal bar or two. Soon it was evident that the bars could be connected within an iron **frame** and cast as one piece. **Alpheus Babcock** of Boston was granted a **patent** for this invention in 1825. Substantial improvements by **Jonas Chickering**, also of Boston, earned him a patent for a full iron frame in 1840.

To offset the added weight and tension developed by the improved **plates**, the case itself had to be strengthened and supported by its wooden beams underneath. It was after the above-mentioned developments of the steel wire and cast-iron plates that heavier **felt hammers** and the **actions** to control those hammers were developed.

Stringing refers to installation of the strings into the piano in the correct placement. One end of the string is positioned in the hole of the **tuning pin**. The string then winds around the tuning pin three or four times, forming coils. Then the path of the string is from the tuning pin, over a V-bar cast into the plate, through the **agraffe** (or under the *capo tasto*), over the **bridge** to a **hitch pin**. The most common design for plain wire is that where the string bends around that hitch pin and continues along a similar path all the way back to where it ends, positioned in the hole of the next tuning pin.

Some designs of European origin (for example, **Bösendorfer grands** and the **Bechstein concert grand**) choose to end each individual string in its own noose-like eyelet at its own hitch pin. This necessitates many more hitch pins in the plate. One advantage is that, especially in a concert situation, if a string breaks, it affects only that one note, and diminishes the sound by only about one-third. If a string that bends around the hitch pin breaks, it either diminishes a particular note by two-thirds, or affects two adjacent notes. There are other technical reasons having to do with the tunability and tuning stability that determine which method a scale designer will use. Naturally, each wound string will end in its own eyelet.

The speaking length (the main vibrating segment of the string) is established from the agraffe or *capo* to the forward bridge pin. Some designs—in the USA, most notably those of **Steinway & Sons** (patented in 1872) and **Baldwin** (patented in 1969)—have measured segments beyond the bridge and in front of the *capo* that are not struck by the hammer of the action, but are intended to vibrate sympathetically (**Duplex Scaling**). For those segments of string that the designer does not wish to vibrate, either the string rests securely on a fairly dense piece of felt or else a stringing braid—a vibration-eliminating strip of cloth or felt—is woven through those string segments.

Joel & Priscilla Rappaport

Bibliography

Dolge, Alfred. *Pianos and Their Makers.* Covina, Cal.: Covina Publishing, 1911. Reprint. New York: Dover Publications, 1972: 51, 123–124.

McFerrin, W.V. *The Piano—Its Acoustics.* Boston: Tuners Supply Co., 1971 (originally published in 1925); 90.

Wolfenden, Samuel. *A Treatise on the Art of Pianoforte Construction.* Old Woking, Surrey, England: Unwin Brothers Ltd., The Gresham Press, 1977, (originally published 1916): 6, 8.

STUTZFLÜGEL

Stutzflügel is the German name for the **baby grand** piano.

See also Grand Piano.

Camilla Cai

SWITZERLAND, PIANO INDUSTRY IN

Cultural and Economic Aspects of Historical Development

Piano building in Switzerland usually started in small workshops, and their success or failure depended on the general economic and political situation of the times. While no aristocracy supported the arts, an active music scene was patronized by the wealthy burghers in the larger cities such as Zürich, Basel, Bern, Fribourg, and Geneva. Compared with a rather small harpsichord-building tradition, the manufacturing of **fortepianos**, and in particular of **square pianos**, found its way into many small workshops from the late eighteenth through the first half of the nineteenth century. Noteworthy makers for this period are: Aloyse Mooser (1770–1839) in Fribourg, Johann Jacob Brosy (b.1748; fl.1764–1815) in Basel, and several members of the Hauert family from Bern, including Joseph (1749–1824) and Carl Ludwig (1785–1863). The name "Hauert" was anglicized to "Howard" for marketing reasons.

Economic aspects played a role in the development of the Swiss piano. In 1848 taxes were still applicable for merchandise crossing from one canton to another. High export taxes and low import taxes often encouraged the acquisition of a foreign piano, possibly with a renowned name like **Erard**. Because it was never a very attractive profession financially, few native Swiss could be found among the piano makers; approximately half of the Swiss builders emigrated from Saxony, Thuringia, Schwaben, and Alsace.

As to technical innovations, Switzerland played a small role; new developments were imported from abroad. Native Swiss makers or second-generation offspring of immigrant craftsmen often spent their apprenticeships with a Parisian or a Viennese master. Their later work usually shows the hand of their teacher.

The trend in the mid-nineteenth century away from the smaller square pianos to bigger, heavier ones, and the new form of the **upright piano**, required larger manufacturing facilities. This demand seems to have been best met by several companies in Zürich: Hüni & Hübert, in the 1860s the largest factory in Switzerland, with an annual production of about 300 instruments; Sprecher & Söhne, with a yearly output of 200 pianos; Hüni & Rordorf; Rordorf & Cie;

Kölliker & Grammer; and Goll. Other successful entrepreneurs set out in Thun: Heinrich Christian Jacobi (1817–1879); and in Burgdorf (canton Bern): Christian Burger (1842–1925). Christian Burger and H. C. Jacobi's son, Hermann Emil (b.1852), joined their companies in 1875 in Biel, where the firm was known as **Burger & Jacobi**. In Bern, A. Flohr was an important company; after 1872 the company was known as **Schmidt-Flohr**. In the eastern part of Switzerland, Bonifaz Bieger (1820–1870) founded a firm of the same name; this firm, in Rorschach, was known after 1919 as **Sabel**.

In the years 1870 to 1880 Swiss piano manufacturing experienced a boost due to lower export taxes. Swiss pianos came into demand in the greater part of Europe and even overseas. However, before the turn of the century, new economic obstacles led to the closing of many companies. Among the seven or more firms in Zürich, only Rordorf & Cie carried on. It moved later to Stäfa and then to Rapperswil, finally closing in 1922. In 1910 the firm's production was about 250 pianos. Companies that experienced a steady growth culminating in the 1920s were: Burger & Jacobi (720), Schmidt-Flohr (660), Sabel (460), and a newcomer, Wohlfart (460), founded in Grenchen in 1902 (figures in parentheses indicate annual production in the early 1920s).

The depression of the 1930s and World War II resulted in a drastic decline. After the war a general upward trend in production did not reach prewar levels. Competition from abroad, mainly from Japan and other Asian countries, became too overwhelming. Schmidt-Flohr ended its production in Bern in 1975. Burger & Jacobi closed its factory in Biel in 1986; the company was sold and instrument building continued under the same name, using mainly cheap foreign parts. Sabel made the last piano in June 1991. A long, colorful tradition had come to an end.

Technical Development

Regarding the earlier stages of the development of the piano **action**, Switzerland lies geographically between two completely different solutions: the **English action** (*Stossmechanik* and *Stosszungenmechanik*) and the Viennese action (*Prellmechanik* and *Prellzungenmechanik*). Both actions were used and there seems to be no correlation with an otherwise culturally significant border, namely, the one between the French- and the German-speaking parts of the country. The earliest and latest dates for the simple *Stossmechanik* found in a Swiss square piano are 1780 and 1806 respectively. Similarly, the *Stosszungenmechanik* had a later appearance, 1824–1855. For the *Prellmechanik* the earliest date is 1793, the latest 1804, and the advanced *Prellzungenmechanik* occurred 1795 to 1835. The earliest upright piano dates from 1830 and was made by Johann Andreas Gottfried Flohr (1798–1872) of Bern. In the earlier models, **strings** were arranged vertically and in parallel order, and later slanted, but still parallel. In their final development in the latter half of the nineteenth century, strings were crossed.

After 1825 cast-iron **frames** became common. Johann Jacob Goll (1771–1855) of Zürich received an Austrian **patent** in 1826 for a complete cast-iron frame for square pianos, a year after the first patent of this kind was issued to **Alpheus Babcock** in Boston. Another invention by Goll, patented in Zürich in 1820, had the **soundboard** of a square piano mounted on top of the strings. The striking **hammer** hits the string in a direction toward the soundboard instead of away from it, resulting in greater **tuning** stability. In the general trend of narrowing down types of pianos, experimentation became rarer, and small shops made way for larger ones. These in turn started to import prefabricated parts like iron frames, **keyboards**, and actions.

Werner Iten

Bibliography

Burkart, Josef. "Beim Klavierbauer." *Schweizerische Schreinerzeitung* 30 (26 July 1990): 691–697.

Europe Piano Atlas. Revised by H.K. Herzog. Frankfurt am Main: *Das Musikinstrument* Ed.4, 1978.

Hirt, Franz Josef. *Meisterwerke des Klavierbaus.* Olten, Switzerland: Urs Graf-Verlag, 1955.

Rindlisbacher, Otto. *Das Klavier in der Schweiz.* Bern and Munich: Francke Verlag, 1972.

SYNCLAVIER

Synclavier is the brand name for a sophisticated polyphonic digital **synthesizer** developed by Sydney Alonso and Cameron Jones in conjunction with Dartmouth composer, Jon Appleton. Manufactured by New England Digital of White River Junction, Vermont, since 1976, it was the first commercially produced digital synthesizer. The original *Synclavier* was based on the studio *Dartmouth Digital Synthesizer* designed by the same team during 1972–74 with modifications to adapt to live performance and typical studio needs. In 1980, the *Synclavier* was updated into the *Synclavier II*. The newer instrument consisted of a splittable five-octave, velocity-sensitive polyphonic **keyboard**, a console including 129 controls, a fingerboard ribbon controller, a disc drive, and eight foot controls. Up to sixteen synchronized tracks could be recorded in the sequencer memory.

In 1982, the *Synclavier II* was brought into line with other digital synthesizers through the addition of a computer monitor capable of a full range of graphics and an alphanumeric keyboard. Floppy discs may be replaced by hard discs with greater storage capacity. External inputs can also be stored. In 1990, two basic models of the *Synclavier* were available, the entry-level model *3200* and the high-end model *9600*. According to New England Digital, there were some 600 *Synclaviers* in studios, universities, and private ownership worldwide in 1990.

See also Electronic Pianos.

Samuel S. Holland

Bibliography

Alonso, S., J.H. Appleton, and C. Jones. "A Special Purpose Digital System for Musical Instruction, Composition, and Performance." *Computers and the Humanities* 10 (1976): 209.

Additional information provided by New England Digital, White River Junction, Vermont.

SYNTHESIZER

A synthesizer is an instrument that generates and processes electronic signals that can be converted into sound through an amplifier/speaker system. In principle, a synthesizer can create any sound whose properties can be specified in acoustical terms, from simulations of conventional musical instruments to uniquely electronic musical sounds. A synthesizer operates by generating an electronic waveform and allowing separate control of the frequency, amplitude, envelope, and other parameters of the waveform that characterize a particular sound. Early synthesizers were developed as sophisticated compositional tools for use in electronic-music studios. Throughout the 1970s and 1980s, synthesizers also played an increasingly significant role as performance instruments, particularly in popular music. During this period, manufacturers in the United States, Europe, and Japan developed a large number of synthesizer models that varied significantly in capability, mode of operation, size, appearance, and cost.

Synthesizers are broadly classified according to their basic method of tone generation as analog or digital. An analog synthesizer uses continuously varying voltages in its internal tone-generating and controlling devices. A digital synthesizer uses a microprocessor and discrete electronic units. This distinction also provides a convenient historical perspective, since analog synthesizers predated their digital counterparts by approximately two decades.

Analog Synthesizers

While devices for creating electronic sound can be traced back at least as far as the 1920s, the first synthesizer of practical consequence was the *RCA Electronic Music Synthesizer, Mark I,* 1951–52. It was installed at the Columbia-Princeton Electronic Music Center in New York City. This room-sized instrument used punched paper tape to control oscillators, noise generators, and filters. While it offered extraordinary potential to the composer and remains histori-

cally significant, the *Mark I* was rapidly superseded in the 1960s as inexpensive, solid-state electronic technology became available. By the end of 1964, **Robert A. Moog** (b. 1934) had developed and marketed a relatively small voltage-controlled synthesizer. Other significant instruments were developed concurrently by Donald Buchla (b. 1937) and Paolo Ketoff. Still oriented to studio use, these first voltage-controlled synthesizers were modular, that is, they were groups of individual devices (modules) that could be interconnected (patched), using direct cable connections in a variety of different configurations.

The modules of a typical analog synthesizer included: (1) *oscillators*, electronic devices that produce regular fluctuations in electrical current that can be switched on or off by a **keyboard** or other trigger; (2) *amplifiers* (sometimes *VCA* for voltage-controlled amplifier), which regulate the loudness of oscillator signal through a variety of methods; (3) *filters* (sometimes *VCF* for voltage-controlled filter), which remove selected frequencies in signal to alter timbre; and (4) *envelope generators* (*EG*), which produce changes over time in loudness and timbre by controlling both the amplifiers and filters. Analog synthesizers employ "subtractive" synthesis—a process of regulating and filtering already

Yamaha DX1 Programmable FM Digital Synthesizer.

complex signals to create different timbres. Voltage-control allowed complex interaction between modules and permitted synthesis of sounds whose properties could be controlled automatically. Synthesizers of this type were accessible to studios throughout the world and were used extensively in composition and recordings, for example Walter Carlos's (b.1939) landmark *Switched-On Bach* (1969). Modular synthesizers remained impractical in live performance since most were monophonic and reconfiguring the cables of the instrument for a new sound was complex and time-consuming.

During the 1970s, many new models of synthesizers designed as performance instruments were developed and aggressively marketed in increasing numbers. The *Minimoog*, developed by Robert Moog, was a landmark among them. Still smaller and simpler to operate than modular synthesizers, the new generation involved fewer components built into a single cabinet. Internal wiring and control-panel knobs replaced patch cords. The scope and flexibility of the instruments were restricted by this design, but the practicality was increased and cost was reduced. Polyphonic keyboard synthesizers were developed by 1975, further encouraging their use as performance instruments.

In 1978, Sequential Circuits introduced the *Prophet V*, a polyphonic analog synthesizer in which an onboard microprocessor was first used to store and retrieve complex patch settings. This increased performance facility, since the musician could instantly change the sound of the instrument among numerous predetermined patches (programs) with the touch of a single control switch. Other manufacturers including **Korg**, **Yamaha**, and **Roland** soon entered the market with comparable polyphonic, programmable analog synthesizers.

Digital Synthesizers

A digital synthesizer uses a microprocessor to store patch data as above, but more important, it uses the microprocessor to control and combine the signal generating and processing components, using discrete bits of information. This is in contrast to the continuous voltage control of an analog synthesizer. Ranging from systems that outwardly resemble analog keyboard synthesizers to standard microcomputers, digital synthesizers have been used widely in recording studios and in live performance.

Significant prototypes of studio digital synthesizers were developed in the early 1970s. The first commercially manufactured digital synthesizer was the **Synclavier** developed by New England Digital in conjunction with Dartmouth composer Jon Appleton (1976). During the second half of the 1970s, a number of digital synthesizers were developed in various research centers, including the *Samson Box* installed at Stanford University, the *SSSP* built by Bell Laboratories, and systems constructed by IRCAM in Paris and at Massachusetts Institute of Technology.

From the early 1980s, several low-cost, commercial digital synthesizers were rapidly developed—most notably the *Yamaha DX7*, which concurrently with the standardization of **MIDI** became a revolutionary industry standard for a number of years. The *DX7* used Frequency Modulation (FM) digital technology developed by John Chowning (b. 1934) at Stanford, which became proprietary to Yamaha International. In contrast to the analog subtractive synthesis, the *DX7* uses a process of additive synthesis. Pure sine waves are combined and manipulated to create complex musical sounds. Other notable digital synthesizers include the *Fairlight CMI* and the *Roland D50*.

In the late 1980s, a variety of hybrid synthesizers appeared. These instruments combined the features of analog and digital synthesizers and, in many cases, also incorporated sampled waveforms stored in ROM. Hybrid synthesizers include the Korg *M* series, the Yamaha *SY* series, **Kurzweil** *K* series, and several products made by Ensoniq. After the standardization of MIDI (1983), many synthesizers again were available in a modular form. Now all of the functional parts would be incorporated into a single, rack-mountable unit that could be controlled from a remote keyboard via a MIDI interface. Another significant development following MIDI is the polytimbral synthesizer, in which a single module is capable of producing several (2–16) different voices that are simultaneously controlled on different MIDI channels.

Samuel S. Holland

Bibliography

Bacon, Tony, ed. *Rock Hardware: The Instruments, Equipment and Technology of Rock*. New York: Harmony Books, 1981.

Contemporary Keyboard (1975–) [continued as *Keyboard*].

Darter, Tom, and Greg Armbruster, eds. *The Art of Electronic Music.* New York: GPI Publications, 1984.

De Furia, Steve. *The Secrets of Analog and Digital Synthesis.* Pompton Lakes, N.J.: Third Earth Productions Inc., 1985.

TAFELKLAVIER

The German name for a **square piano** is *Tafelklavier*, or table piano. Since the instrument is actually a rectangular box sitting upon a stand, it resembles a table when the **keyboard** is covered. Another explanation for the term *Tafelklavier* is that the piano may also be lifted from the supporting legs and placed on a table for playing (like the clavichord).

The French equivalent of *Tafelklavier* is *piano carré* and the Italian term is *pianoforte a tavola*. The term "table piano" is not common in English.

See also Square Piano.

Peggy Flanagan Baird

TAIL

The tail is the part of the **grand piano**'s casework that is at the opposite end of the instrument from the **keyboard**. On modern pianos, the tail is curved to correspond with the **bentside**. The early grand pianos usually had straight tails, as was also the design of harpsichords.

Peggy Flanagan Baird

TANGENTENKLAVIER/TANGENTENFLÜGEL

Tangentenklavier or *Tangentenflügel* is the German term for **tangent piano**.

R.P.

TANGENT PIANO

A tangent **action** consists of vertically-suspended **hammers** housed in a harpsichord-type box slide that are jacked up by the back ends of the **key** levers (usually with the intermediate levers) just like harpsichord jacks. The name (tangent action) is derived from the clavichord action, but the harpsichord affiliation is very clear and the sound of tangent pianos is similar to that of harpsichords. Tangent action is connected to the oldest prototypes of piano action, for example the *dulce melos*, described by Heinrich Arnold von Zwolle around 1440. The Metropolitan Museum of Art in New York possesses an Italian spinet from the mid-sixteenth century, made probably by Franciscus Bonafinis, which was remade into a tangent piano (**jacks** replaced with wooden tangents) probably in or prior to 1632.

Jean Marius presented to the Paris Royal Academy of Sciences in 1716 designs of four harpsichord hammer actions. Construction plans of one of them referred directly to the clavichord (wooden hammers attached vertically to the ends of the key levers). Another two designs referred to the harpsichord action and were a kind of tangent action also, one with a small wooden bar replacing the harpsichord jack, the second with a simple wooden **bridge** attached to the jack. **Christoph Gottlieb Schröter** of Dresden designed a tangent action in 1717 and another one with intermediate levers in 1739. In 1759 Weltman of Paris (?) invented a clavecin with jacks ("marteaux") that strike the **strings** instead of plucking them.

There are a few preserved Italian tangent **grands** from the last quarter of the eighteenth century. One is in Museo Belliniano at Catania, Sicily, probably invented c.1767–1773 in Catania by a Neopolitan priest, the other in private possession in Florence. In a private collection in Milan there is a harpsichord from the last quarter of the seventeenth century remade into a tangent piano at the end of the eighteenth century. Museo Nazionale degli Strumenti Musicali in Rome possesses a Carlo Grimaldi of Messina *clavecin brisé* with hammer-shaped tangents remade from jacks. Also, two Italian tangent pianos were listed for sale in Madrid at the end of the eighteenth century. One offered in May 1787 was similar to the Catania piano; the second, offered in July 1797, may have been similar to the Grimaldi instrument: a small, travel model in three folding segments. In 1774, **Joseph Merlin**, the maker of mathematical instruments in London, **patented** a harpsichord with a second set of tangent hammers capped with **leather** or cloth. At the same time Franz Jakob **Späth** of Ratisbon (Regensburg) constructed a tangent action; however, the date remains imprecise because the only preserved tangent grands made by the Späth and **Schmahl** firm were made after 1790 by Späth's son-in-law and former partner Christoph Friedrich Schmahl.

In the Diocesan Museum (Muzeum Diecezjalne) in Sandomierz, Poland, there is a square piano with tangent action, made in 1774 by Jan Skórski of Sandomierz (see illustration), and in the National Museum (Muzeum Narodowe) in Cracow there is a similar piano made around 1780–1790, probably by Skórski or his pupil. In Austad Gård, Drammen Museum, Norway, there is a harpsichord combined with a tangent piano, made in 1786 by Haucken

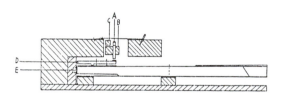

Tangent action by Jan Skórski (1774), Sandomierz, Poland. A = Hammer (tangent); B = Slide box; C = Lute (harp) stop; D = Intermediate lever; E = Guiding projection of the key lever.
(Drawing by Benjamin Vogel)

at Carl Gottlob Sauer's workshop in Dresden. In 1787 Humphrey Walton in England patented a tangent action for a grand. In 1792 **John Geib** of London patented an instrument with two **keyboards**, which could play as a pianoforte, a spinet, or a clavichord.

Germanisches Nationalmuseum in Nürnberg, Germany, possesses an **upright piano** with tangent action made at the end of the eighteenth century by Hepp in Amberg. The Bachhaus in Eisenach, Germany, owns a claviorganum from around 1804–1814 with a square tangent piano made probably by Christoph Friedrich Schmahl from Regensburg. Tangent pianos were made generally in Italy, Germany, and Poland, primarily in the last

three decades of the eighteenth century. Many of the German instruments made by Späth and Schmahl have been preserved in various collections. There was no affinity in construction between tangent grands from Germany and from Italy.

In Poland only **square** tangent pianos were made (with no similarities to those constructed at other centers). Bonafinis' spinet from the Metropolitan Museum of Art seems to be the oldest surviving tangent piano (unless it was remade into a tangent piano at the end of the eighteenth century, like many other Italian instruments). Because of their weak sound, tangent pianos soon went out of use.

See also Actions.

Benjamin Vogel

Bibliography

Cohen, Albert. "Jean Marius' *Clavecin brisé* and *Clavecin à maillets* Revisited: The `Dossier Marius' at the Paris Academy of Sciences." *Journal of the American Musical Instrument Society* 13 (1987): 23–38.

Harding, Rosamond E.M. *The Piano-Forte: Its History Traced to the Great Exhibition of 1851.* Cambridge: Cambridge University Press, 1933. Reprints, New York: Da Capo Press, 1973; Old Woking, Surrey: Gresham Books, 1978.

Heyde, Herbert. *Historische Musikinstrumente im Bachhaus Eisenach.* Eisenach: Bachhaus, 1976: 161–163.

Kenyon de Pascual, Beryl. "The Five-Octave Compass in Eighteenth-Century Harpsichords." *Early Music* 15 (February 1987): 74–75.

Meer, John Henry van der. "A Curius Instrument with a Five-Octave Compass." *Early Music* 14 (August 1986): 397–400.

———. "Observations." *Early Music* 15 (February 1987): 75–76.

Pollens, Stewart. "The Bonafinis Spinet: An Early Harpsichord Converted into a Tangent Piano." *Journal of the American Musical Instrument Society* 13 (1987): 5–22.

Vogel, Benjamin. "Fortepiany tangentowe w Polsce" [The Tangent Pianos in Poland]. *Muzyka Fortepianowa* 7 (1987): 291–302.

TANGENTENKLAVIER/ TANGENTENFLÜGEL

Tangentenklavier or *Tangentenfl̈gel* is the German term for **tangent piano.**

TAPE-CHECK ACTION

See Actions; Wornum, Robert

TASKIN, PASCAL (JOSEPH) (1723–1793)

Pascal Taskin, born in Theux, Belgium, was a harpsichord and piano maker who spent most of his life in Paris. He married the widow of his former employer, François-Etienne Blanchet (c.1730–1766), a well-reputed Parisian harpsichord maker, and took over the business. In 1774 he became keeper of the King's Instruments, a position he passed on to his nephew Pascal-Joseph Taskin (1750–1829) in 1777.

In 1791, Pascal Taskin (the elder) was probably tuner of instruments at the Ecole Royale de Chant (which later became the Paris Conservatory). Although he apparently took a lively interest in politics toward the end of his life, he was never actually taken seriously in that endeavor. A possible portrait of Taskin by an anonymous painter is reproduced by Ernest Closson.

Taskin is credited with the invention of the *peau de buffle* stop, which became very popular due to its delicate timbre. The *peau de buffle* stop was added to the *clavecin mécanique* by **Sébastien Erard** in 1776 and was placed on the very first pianos made by Taskin, the oldest of which is dated 1768 (Closson gives 1776). Taskin's pianofortes, built in ever-increasing numbers after 1770, show excellent, albeit very traditional, craftsmanship. The **actions** have no **escapement** or repetition mechanics and thus are no match for the instruments made by his younger rival, Sébastien Erard. It is also said—but not confirmed—that Pascal Taskin constructed the very first **grand** pianoforte in France.

Worth mentioning is Taskin's invention of the *crochet d'accord*, in which a single **string** is looped on a **hitch pin**, thus producing two perfectly unison-tuned strings (see also *Clédi-Harmonique*). Apart from the above quoted *peau de buffle* stop (soft **leather** instead of quill on the **jack**), he also improved the knee lever mechanism for changing stops on the harpsichord.

In addition, Taskin adapted many Flemish harpsichords (mostly Ruckers) by enlarging their compass to five octaves (so-called *ravallement*), at times leaving little of the original instrument.

F.J. de Hen

Bibliography

Boalch, Donald H. *Makers of the Harpsichord and Clavichord, 1440–1840*. London: G. Ronald, 1950.

Closson, Ernest. *La Facture des Instruments de Musique en Belgique*. Huy: Degrace, 1935.

Harding, Rosamond E.M. *The Piano-Forte: Its History Traced to the Great Exhibition of 1851*. Cambridge: Cambridge University Press, 1933. Reprints, New York: Da Capo Press, 1973; Old Woking, Surrey: Gresham Books, 1978.

Laborde, Jean-Benjamin de. *Essai sur la Musique ancienne et moderne*. T.I. Paris: Fr. D. Pierre, 1780.

Wangermée, Robert, and Philippe Mercier. *La Musique en Wallonie et à Bruxelles*. Bruxelles: La Renaissance du Livre, 1980.

TECHNIC—A SURVEY

The beginnings of pianoforte technic can be traced back to **Carl Philipp Emanuel Bach**. Part One of C.P.E Bach's *Versuch über die wahre Art das Clavier zu spielen* was published in 1753; Part Two appeared almost a decade later in 1762. The work deals with general problems of musicianship, from the points of view of correctness and expressivity in execution. It also functions as a practical theoretical treatise. In these respects it is companion to related works of Johann Joachim Quantz, Daniel Gottlob Türk, Friedrich Wilhelm Marpurg, Franz Anton Maichelbeck, and others. The essay is aimed primarily toward the clavichord or harpsichord player, with secondary mention of the organ and pianoforte, and in this respect might not be considered relevant to a discussion of mechanics specific to pianoforte playing. The pianoforte had appeared some fifty or more years prior to his writing the treatise, but his serious interest in it did not fully materialize until well after he published the essay, when in the 1780s he began composing sonatas designated for the piano. Nonetheless, there are matters in C.P.E. Bach's text for the modern pianist to contemplate, even though the treatise was not intended first and foremost for pianists.

Through C.P.E.'s discourse, it is possible to see two basic approaches in early piano technic, each markedly different from the other, one stemming from the school of harpsichord playing, the other from clavichord playing. C.P.E. felt one's true artistry was best judged by clavichord skill. The clavichord was his instrument of preference. At the same time, he understood the advantage of the harpsichord when clarity and projection were required. Distinguishing between the two instruments, he says: "The clavichordist grows too much accustomed to caressing the keys; consequently, his wonted touch being insufficient to operate the jacks, he fails to bring out details on the harpsichord. In fact, finger strength may be lost eventually, by playing only the clavichord. On the other hand, those who concentrate on the harpsichord grow accustomed to playing in only one color, and the varied touch which the competent clavichordist brings to the harpsichord remains hidden from them." To be sure, Emanuel himself saw the two approaches as interdependent and not necessarily mutually exclusive, but such statements presage the escalating conflict between the strong-fingered, brilliant, "pearly" mode of piano playing, versus the caressing, singing, expressive style that would continue to unfold long after C.P.E.'s death.

Mozart regarded C.P.E. Bach as the father of piano playing, saying that whatever pianists did right they owed to him, and those who failed to admit it were scoundrels. Emanuel's playing technic involved a light, fluid, *non-legato* **touch**, similar still to the harpsichord technic Johann Nicolaus Forkel describes of **Johann Sebastian Bach** a curved-finger technic which the finger tips glide from **key** to key with equal pressure producing "sounds brilliant, rolling and round, as if each note were a pearl." (It should be noted here that J.S. Bach would have had separate methods for harpsichord and clavichord playing, aiming for *cantabile* on the latter. In fact, the art of **fingering** to produce *legato*, codified by Emanuel but previously developed in generations of the Bach family, was brought to culmination in J.S. Bach. As Edith Hipkins points out, the title of the Two-Part Inventions as pieces " for acquiring a *cantabile* art of playing" indicates this.)

Mozart's style often included singing *legato* in melodic passages, and always demonstrated the finest taste, superb elegance in phrasing, without affectation. He criticized his competitor **Muzio Clementi** as having "not a farthing's worth of taste or feeling; he is a mere *mechanicus*." (Clementi, who defeated Mozart in a piano competition, and from whom Mozart borrowed the opening allegro subject of the *Magic Flute*

overture, had more kindly feelings toward his rival.) Mozart warned his sister not to practice Clementi's sonatas, which contained passages in thirds, sixths, and octaves, on the grounds that she would lose her natural lightness and flexibility in the effort. Though swift and exalted playing came naturally to him, Mozart always espoused the most sensible and down-to-earth advice to students, counseling them to practice slowly, with hands alone at first, listening for evenness from note to note and maintaining a steady pulse throughout. He would rather hear pieces played slowly and carefully by a student than at a fast and irregular tempo by a professional grappling to make a virtuoso impression. For him it was unmusical to play a piece faster than it could be played correctly. It was equally intolerable to him to use excessive *rubato*; he employed only the most judicious and delicate nuances of tempo fluctuation. Above all he demanded beauty, grace, and precision in performance.

Despite Mozart's misgivings about him, Clementi was actually the first to approach the pianoforte on its own terms, and not from a harpsichordist's standpoint. Departing from *non-legato* or *leggiero* playing, he sought to adhere chiefly to *legato*, instructing pupils to "keep down the first key till the next has been struck." This marked a definite departure from harpsichord technic as passed down from J.S. Bach, which prescribed that releases be executed by gliding "off the fore part of the key, by gradually drawing back the tip of the finger towards the palm," the flick of one finger then answered immediately by the snapping down of the next onto its key. Clementi's business position as a seller of pianos set the stage for promoting his pianistic concepts through technical exercises (notably the *Gradus ad Parnassum*, 1817, 1819, 1826) and compositions in various forms written for the new and developing instruments it was his livelihood to market. Further, he employed pianists in his firm to assist, among other things, in demonstrating the instruments. In this way he directly influenced John Field and Johann Baptist Cramer, the latter of whom followed Clementi in formulating written technical studies. Both Clementi's and Cramer's studies formed an essential part of **Beethoven's** technic and teaching. While Clementi's studies mainly developed digital prowess, his sonatas also cultivated **pedal** technics that Beethoven adopted in his work. Beethoven's celebrated continuous **pedal** passages, such as those in the *Tempest* Sonata (Op. 31, No. 2; 1802), are anticipated in Clementi. Clementi's programmatic Sonata in G Minor Op. 50, No. 3, entitled *Didone abbandonata*, offers a clear example. With the indication *continua il Pedale*, Clementi asks that the pedal be held down an entire eight and a half bars through changing textures and harmonies during the opening of the slow movement. The finale of Clementi's Sonata Op. 39, No. 3 — which compares closely with the trio section of Beethoven's Bagatelle Op. 126, No. 4—provides another extreme example in which the composer requires the sustaining pedal to remain unchanged for thirty-one full measures. Beyond this, Clementi gave Beethoven an awareness of textural extremes and dynamic possibilities, and introduced him to purely compositional innovations such as beginning movements *in medias res*, on harmonies remote from the tonic.

Beethoven, like Clementi, used principles of fingering set forth in C.P.E. Bach, and was particular about the use of the thumb. He called upon all the fingers, including the thumb, in sixteenth-note passages and, disapproving of the Mozart school's pearly, light **hammer** touch, sought a "different kind of jewelry." He avoided *staccato* and insisted upon *legato*. In a group of four sixteenth notes, he taught that "to obtain the strictest *legato*, the finger must not be lifted off the first note of each group until the fourth note is to be struck." As a rule the hands should be placed over the **keyboard** so the fingers need not be raised more than necessary. "Finger dancing" and "manual air sawing" were intolerable to him. He faulted Carl Czerny's lack of *Bindung*, or sustaining power, and his tendency toward the still-fashionable detached style—remnants of the mistaken transfer of harpsichord technic to pianoforte playing.

Occasionally erratic in performance himself, he frowned upon Czerny's histrionics. For Beethoven, true pianoforte technic was rooted in singing (C.P.E. Bach had proclaimed this in his treatise) and wind playing (Clementi had alluded to this notion)—the fingers must generate rather than strike **tones**, "hand and keyboard must be one." To achieve a fullness of tone, he discovered using the power of the arm for reinforcement. At one point Beethoven proposed a method book, sketches for which are in the British Museum. Reginald Gerig prints a

selection of examples and among these are exercises for dynamic range, leaps thrown from the hand, carriage of the arm, *legato* double notes, double-trills, and chord release in which notes drop out in measured fashion one by one from bottom to top.

In Beethoven's music, certain situations involving tied notes—e.g., in the Scherzo of the Cello and Piano Sonata in A Major Op. 69 and the Sonata Op. 110—raise the question whether Beethoven was calling for *Bebung*, or *vibrato*, available on the clavichord. As Beethoven asks for finger changes in such cases (e.g., 4–3), Edward Dannreuther suggests that such effects should be emulated on the piano by quietly restriking the tied note; Heinrich Schenker and Artur Schnabel discuss how to render at least a psychological impression of change in inflection on the tied note. Paul Badura-Skoda claims that, inasmuch as Beethoven had little or no contact with the clavichord, "a tie is just a tie," but since Alfred James Hipkins (not recognized by Badura-Skoda) establishes that a clavichord tradition still existed even until the mid-nineteenth century, citing examples in Field and **Chopin**, the issue and its controversy remain unresolved.

Beethoven wanted strength of expression in piano playing. Often he recommended putting words to troublesome passages to achieve communicative effect. Ernst Pauer said he "painted with tones," he "recited." His remarkable phrasing is well noted; he brought out melodic accents and especially shaded half steps. Ultimately he voiced worry about piano "gymnasts," and warned that "the increasing mechanism of pianoforte playing will in the end destroy all truth of expression in music."

Czerny, Beethoven's protegé, veered from his master in several ways. He had little affinity for Clementi, and as a result, Beethoven withdrew his nephew from Czerny's tutelage. Without doubt Czerny admired, even revered Beethoven's pianism, but despite his earnestness as Beethoven's student, tended, as his own virtuoso career developed, toward a brilliant manner of playing not sanctioned by his mentor. His prolific pedagogical opuses sought to develop finger strength, dexterity and speed, and his concert works were designed to display his unmatched mastery of these aspects of technic. Czerny's immediate and most prominent heirs were **Franz Liszt** and Theodor Leschetizsky.

Johann Nepomuk Hummel, Czerny's senior by thirteen years and in equally great demand as a pianist, was the principal exponent of the pearly Mozart tradition. He had studied with Mozart, who early on predicted he would become a better pianist than himself. Upon hearing Beethoven, who made a tremendous impression on him, Hummel was compelled to ask himself, "Was I to try to follow in the footsteps of such a genius?" but soon concluded that "it was best to remain true to myself and my own nature." Czerny observed that in some ways Hummel had synthesized the styles of Mozart and Clementi. Hummel's clarity and perfectionism were an inspiration to Czerny. Franz (son of Theodor) Kullak asserts in his volume on Beethoven's playing that Czerny's explanation of trills was influenced by Hummel's treatise. Followers of Hummel disapproved of Beethoven's dynamic and coloristic innovations, while Beethovenites found Hummel unimaginative and thought his fingers resembled spiders. The arch rivalry that developed between Hummel and Beethoven seems actually to have sprung up through a petty social misunderstanding. Hummel's exhaustive *Méthode Complète* (1828) contains exercises ranging from one-bar finger drills to complete sets of variations, and includes intricacies such as chromatic double-note turns and experimental fingerings. Hummel stressed playing by feel and sight rather than by ear.

Theodor Kullak, a pupil of Czerny, founded Germany's largest private institute for music education, the Neue Akademie der Tonkunst in Berlin. It specialized in piano instruction. Along with Liszt, who also spent time under Czerny's guidance, Kullak ranked as one of the nineteenth century's greatest pedagogues. Among Kullak's students were Moritz Moszkowski and Xaver Scharwenka. Hans von Bülow succeeded Kullak as the institute's director in 1855. Adolph Kullak, Theodor's brother, felt that Czerny's method books "closed an epoch" in the development of piano technic. His own work, *The Aesthetics of Pianoforte Playing* (1861), contains in its 320-some pages only a minimum of finger exercises. It concentrates rather on thorough explanation of the mechanics involved in making various finger strokes, wrist and arm movements, etc. Kullak shows how the thumb can be used on black notes in arpeggios, and describes the consequential angling of the other fingers

when employing the thumb in this way. Part II is "on the beautiful in pianoforte playing," and considers styles and colors of tone and touch, the share of technic in the rendering, and unity amid the diversity of nuances. The majority of illustrations are drawn from works of Beethoven and Chopin. The treatise continues to have relevance today. Nine years before A. Kullak's book appeared, Carl Engel in 1853 published his *Pianist's Guidebook*.

Throughout this period, alternate developments in piano technic were being made elsewhere outside the Austro-German arena. The first great French piano pedagogue was Louis Adam. Adam, who was self-taught, had a pupil of distinction in Friedrich Wilhelm Kalkbrenner. Variety of expression, not *bravura*, was their interest. Kalkbrenner had entrepreneurial enthusiasm for a piano pedagogical device, of which many came into vogue, invented and patented in 1814 by Johann Bernhard Logier, called the "Chiroplast." This contraption, clamped to the arm, was worn during practice to set and maintain the student's proper playing position. Kalkbrenner himself invented a hand-guide for similar purposes. Henri Herz, active in Paris, constructed a machine called the "Dactylion" to force the fingers to lift high. **Robert Schumann's** foray into the application of such mechanical aids may have cost him the effective use of his fourth finger.

In Bohemia, Ignaz Moscheles had made an impact on piano technic. He was renowned for purity, clarity, and astonishingly round and full tone. Jan Ladislav Dussek in 1796 published *Instructions on the Art of Playing the Pianoforte or Harpsichord*. He was an originator in placing the piano sideways on the stage. Václav Tomàschek, like Adam largely self-taught, said that Dussek's tone was "delicious yet empathetic," and referred to the sounds emanating from his fingers as voices of ten singers. Tomàschek himself disliked the virtuoso aesthetic of his time and sought other directions. In 1824 he started a music school in Prague to rival the established institutions. The school attracted among its students Alexander Dreyschock and the critic Eduard Hanslick. Tomàschek's piano concertos have a special personality, owing much to a knack for effective orchestration.

Chopin and Liszt contrasted considerably. Chopin was from the start a composer; even as a child, much of his lesson time was devoted to having his first teacher, Adalbert Zywny, take down his melodies. At the piano he was a prodigy. Though his next teacher, Josef Elsner, composer of twenty-seven operas, had stature in Warsaw both at the opera house and conservatory, he was renowned neither as a piano virtuoso nor a pedagogue. The power of Chopin's playing resided in its beauty, subtlety of nuance, and singing tone. It was intensely intimate; he drew the listener into the sound and the music. His pupils came from the ranks of the aristocracy and gentry, and generally studied as amateurs.

Liszt was the foremost virtuoso of his day, descended from the Czerny school. He blossomed later as a serious composer. His playing was forceful, brilliant, varied, declamatory, and not without show. The students who flocked to him mostly sought and often attained important careers themselves: Alexander Siloti, who later taught Sergei Rachmaninoff; Rafael Joseffy, Hans von Bülow, Carl Tausig (who had been his favorite), to name a few.

In Chopin's case it is difficult to say that the man founded a school of technic through pedagogy; he was not inclined to teach fundamentals or discuss mechanics. Lessons with Chopin often consisted of him doing most or all of the playing, without significant comment. Chopin intended near the end of his life to bring out a book describing his method and his theories. On his deathbed he ordered the notes for it burned. Except through speculating over recordings of Teresa Carreño, who studied with Chopin's pupil Georges Mathias, it is only through written accounts of students and admirers, as presented for instance in Edith J. Hipkins' *How Chopin Played* (1937, a compilation of A.J. Hipkins' diaries) and *Chopin: Pianist and Teacher as Seen by his Pupils* (1987) by Jean-Jacques Eigeldinger that we begin to imagine how he himself approached the piano. Of all things, Chopin loved singing. He taught that "everything must be read cantabile, even my passages; everything must be made to sing; the bass, the inner parts, etc." A.J. Hipkins reported after meeting Chopin: "He abhorred banging; his *forte* was relative, not absolute; it was based upon his exquisite *pianos* and *pianissimos*. He kept his elbows close to his sides, and played only with finger-touch, no weight from the arms. He used a simple, natural position of the hands."

As recorded by Mme. Auguste Boissier, Liszt in his early years of teaching privately gave much attention to basic technic. He wanted the body straight with the head bent slightly backward; preferred to use the flat of the finger tip to produce tone; prescribed at least two hours a day of scales and studies; above all, he asked for patience and slow practice: "when you think you are practicing very slowly, slow down some more." Amy Fay, the American pianist who toured Europe to study with several reigning *virtuosi* there, left descriptions of Liszt's later Weimar seminars in letters. At this point he spoke nothing of technic, only of interpretation, intricacies and subtleties of pedalling, mental control, and so on.

Of touch, Friedrich Wieck had strong opinions. "The blow of the finger upon the key should never be audible, but only the musical sound—no jingling or banging." He taught relaxation and a loose wrist, and castigated practitioners of the stiff, high-finger Stuttgart school. Fay claimed "the Wiecks think nobody can teach touch but themselves." She held Clara Wieck's sister Marie to have the "perfect touch," but found Clara herself unanalytical and cold. Eugenie Schumann, daughter of Robert and Clara, studied with **Brahms**. By her reports, Brahms created finger exercises from the piece itself, turning passages inside out, upside down, varying accents, etc., a practice later taken up in editions published by Alfred Cortot. Brahms' use of the thumb was idiosyncratic; he would sometimes fling it onto a note with his fingers clenched. He deplored *staccato*, and insisted that it not be used even in Bach. Brahms compiled a volume of *Fifty-One Exercises* (1893) that present patterns in uneven groupings, cross rhythms, and cross articulations. Such patterns occur in his compositions—to cite one example, the rapid runs three-against-two with the right hand in the Finale of the Op. 99 F Major Cello and Piano Sonata accompaniment.

Theodor Leschetizsky was born three years after Beethoven's death and lived until 1915. His concerts brought him great renown and his teaching career spanned the longest stretch yet in the history of piano pedagogy. Arthur Rubinstein remarked that had the circumstances permitted it, he would have rushed in his youth to study with Leschetizsky, whom he considered the greatest teacher alongside Ferruccio Busoni. During his life, close to 2,000 students would pass through the doors of his studio, Ignaz Paderewski, Ossip Gabrilowitsch, Vassily Ilyitch Safonov, Benno Moiseiwitsch, Isabelle Vengerova, Mieczyslaw Horszowski, among them. His second wife, Annette Essipov, also a pianist of distinction, taught concurrently, and Artur Schnabel and Sergei Prokofiev numbered among her pupils. The principal locations of Leschetizsky and Essipov's teaching were Vienna and St. Petersburg, at the new conservatory there.

Leschetizsky's father was an eminent pianist and teacher. He gave Theodor his first instruction, and at ten sent him on to study with Czerny. Presumably under Czerny, Leschetizsky would have perfected the high, curved-finger technic and brilliant hammer-stroke style with which he remains associated today. However, it was shortly after he began with Czerny that Leschetizsky heard the Bohemian pianist and friend of Chopin, Julius Schulhoff, who profoundly changed his concept of technic. While Leschetizsky always believed in developing finger strength, his approach became sound and singing oriented. He "began to foresee a new style of playing . . . a new and entirely different touch . . . striving to attain firm fingertips and a light wrist." The influence upon Leschetizsky of Schulhoff's wonderful tone, his melody in bold relief, should not be neglected.

Leschetizsky refuted the notion that he used a method. He said, "it is impossible to have a method, for every hand is different. It is far better to leave your mind a blank for the pupil to fill in." However, a book authored with his approval by Malwine Bree (*The Groundwork of the Leschetizsky Method*, 1902) summarizes the pianistic principles he taught. It contains useful exercises for passing under of the thumb and photos showing hand positions and finger angles. One chapter is devoted to pedalling. Of dynamics, the practice of making *crescendo* on a rising line, *diminuendo* on a descending line is suggested. Tone gradations according to a numbering system perhaps originate here. Leschetizsky said "tempo is not the treadmill of everyday monotonous routine." His description of a style of *rubato*, in which the melody notes are broken from the bass, is included. Other topics range from using the thumb on black keys, aphorisms for practicing, and memorization, to stage fright and the role of brainwork and reflection in building security. At age

seventy-six, Leschetizsky recorded for the **Welte-Mignon** reproducing mechanism. At least two performances, of the Mozart Fantasy K.475 and the Chopin D-flat Nocturne, Op. 27, No. 2, have been available on LP. These provide a precious opportunity to compare the written legend and the reality, and gauge with some confidence what tastes actually were.

Another great figure of the day was Anton Rubinstein, who taught Josef Hofmann, Arthur Friedheim, and Gabrilowitsch as well, and influenced Josef Lhévinne, Carreño, Busoni, and many more. Rubinstein was hailed for his fat-fingered tone and abandon in performance. He called the pedal "the soul of the piano." Rubinstein subscribed to no method, telling students who inquired about fingering to "play it with your nose." Neither would he demonstrate at the piano. As temperamental a teacher as he was an impassioned player, he stressed mental preparation for the character of the piece. His students learned to dig into themselves for answers, and expected to be driven like slaves. As Hofmann recounts, Rubinstein would exclaim, "The Lord helps those who help themselves." With Rubinstein and his colleague Safonov, and Safonov's pupil Maria Levinskaya, the so-called Russian school of piano playing began. This style of playing sought vividness of tone and encouraged elasticity in dropping arm weight into the keys. Levinskaya's system combined the best of the old finger methods and the weight-relaxation principles put forth by Rudolph Breithaupt.

Only studying as a child with his parents, Ferruccio Busoni emerged as one of the most eminent pianists of his age. Hanslick marvelled at his youthful polyphonic improvisations on given themes. The playing of Anton Rubinstein made a significant impression on Busoni. In his maturity, Busoni taught many pupils in composition and piano, among them Edgard Varèse, Kurt Weill, and Egon Petri. Beethoven and Liszt he esteemed as the composers who truly penetrated the piano's capabilities. He himself developed a unique manner of playing that involved coloristic pedalling, use of the **sostenuto pedal**, and harmonics. His touch became based on *staccato*; his book of technical studies he entitled *Lo staccato* (1921, Part III of the *Klavierübung*). Yet his playing, preserved on roll recordings, seems perfectly *legato*. He was known for a very pure tone, and this, combined with a careful measuring in quality of the beginning of each note, one to the next, through his peculiar *staccato* treatment led him to achieve connection in melodic playing and also passage work, with an uncommon clarity and evenness added. Busoni is frequently remembered for his "12 Maxims for Practising," set down in his essay *Piano Playing and Piano Music* (1910). Larry Sitsky's book *Busoni and the Piano* (1986) is a principal reference work for this anomalous figure.

Foreshadowed by Beethoven, and necessitated at least in part by the increasingly resilient double-repetition **actions** introduced in pianos in the last quarter of the nineteenth century, the use of arm weight and muscle relaxation became a widespread and primary concern. Breithaupt, through his assistant Tony Brandman, traced this idea back to Busoni's classes in Weimar. But before this, Ludwig Deppe already had approached the subject. Deppe in the early 1870s was teaching that tone-producing power lies in the palm of the hand. The wrist should revolve as on a pivot. The wrist is a feather, the elbow is lead. His approach was one of caressing the keys. Deppe determined that much arm strain was due to being seated too high, and advised people to sit lower. He called upon muscular synergy to avoid fatigue. Deppe formally documented some of his ideas only once, in the article "Armleiden des Klavierspielers" (1885), but Elisabeth Caland has preserved much of his thinking in her book *Die Deppesche Lehre* (1893). Deppe's teachings also influenced William Mason's four-volume work *Touch and Technic*, Op. 44.

Breithaupt was something of a cult figure and published widely on the topic of weight-relaxation. He was greatly inspired by Teresa Carreño, who practiced relaxation in a way that affected all her movements at and away from the piano. It was said that her avoidance of unnecessary contraction could often cause her to drop objects she held or carried. Breithaupt also admired Leopold Godowsky for his free and natural use of the arm. Godowsky himself was not conscious of these attributes and believed the best method must be eclectic. Breithaupt acknowledged Deppe, but differed with the idea that fixation of the joints and pronation of the hand were desirable. He described a supported swing of the arm and believed in retaining the arch of the hand. He insisted that "all conscious

pressing, spreading, seizing, clutching wastes time, exhausts energy and is therefore wrong." He dealt with low and high "fall," "rotary motion," "shoulder participation," "transmission of weight," "active carriage," and he assessed Friedrich Adolf Steinhausen's concepts on "passive hanging" and "passive weighting." Breithaupt saw himself as the main proponent of the weight school. In practice, he carried his principles to extremes, sacrificing accuracy and beauty of tone for relaxed, drop weight movement.

Just prior to Breithaupt's book *The Natural Piano Technique* (1905), Tobias Matthay published *The Act of Touch*. Matthay shared resonance with William Townsend, who had published an antecedent essay on balance of the arm, but his work shortly eclipsed Townsend's and that of Breithaupt and fulfilled the culmination of the weight-relaxation approach. His influence was wide-ranging. Matthay schools were founded in Britain and America, and his methods were absorbed by the Royal Conservatories. Myra Hess, Matthay's most famous protegé, derived enduring inspiration from him.

Matthay believed that separating technic from musical expression was impossible. "The *placing* (both as to Time and as to Tone) of each and every note, will be *directly prompted* by our Musical Feeling and Intelligence." The act of touch involved four components: inward musical attention determining Time—where each note should begin—and Tone—how each note should sound; and outward physical attention reacting to resistance experienced from each key, and the place in the key descent where each sound begins. He said that light *resting* and accurate ceasing of the act of key depression were the secret of agility. Rebound was also a crucial factor. He was opposed to squeezing the key into the bed, as sound is given off before the key reaches its full depression. He found key-hitting equally objectionable.

In his system, Matthay divided touch construction and formation into three species: tones made with finger exertion only; with hand weight reinforcement; and with arm support. In all cases, roundness of tone was desired, hardness and harshness were to be avoided by "playing only to the sound," and not too far down in the key descent. Matthay abhorred Breithaupt's manner of applying weight, and full arm weight at that, into the **keybed**, and transferring it from one keybed to the next, warning that this leads to "the utter destruction of Music-sense, and risk to limb and Piano!" The scope of Matthay's work is vast. His writing style, although he masterfully organized material, presented difficulties for many readers, so much so that his colleague Ambrose Coviello was moved to write a volume entitled *What Matthay Meant, His Musical and Technical Teachings Clearly Explained* (1948).

In 1929 Otto Ortmann published *The Physiological Mechanics of Piano Technique*. This classic work was a first in that it approached the subject entirely from a scientific viewpoint. Ortmann, director of the Peabody Conservatory, called upon physicians, physicists, and engineers from neighboring Johns Hopkins University and elsewhere for guidance and assistance. He himself took courses to better enable him to carry out his research. Slow-exposure photography was used, and special machines such as the dynamograph were built to assist Ortmann's experiments. Ortmann dealt with the structure of the skeleton, muscles, neural and circulatory systems, gravity, geometrics, coordination, and the piano action and anatomy as a unified continuum of levers. He was thoroughly conversant with the theories of Breithaupt, Matthay, Arnold Schultz, Steinhausen, et al. The concept of *Rollbewegung* to transfer weight he found illusory, and thought Reinecke placed undue emphasis on relaxation. He favored a combination of weight and contraction as the basis for technic, the wrist acting to eliminate percussion. He pointed out that the tone control developed in a number of methods was only imaginary, the eye determining the quality rather than the physics of the situation really producing the desired quality. He reached back to Beethoven's words about "gliding legato," and the desirability of this, as opposed to "pearly non-legato," in contemporary piano technic. An elliptical stroke of extreme lightness described by Ortmann shares similarity with the *carezzando* of Antoine de Kontski, in which the key, very gently depressed, is stroked from the middle to the front edge. Ortmann went on to discuss performance style, and referred to James Lange's theory of emotions. The book includes an extensive bibliography.

Ortmann's *Mechanics* was the last formal and comprehensive treatise on piano playing.

Its scientific orientation had been anticipated in works of James Ching, an English pianist who had studied with Matthay. Ching shaped his theories according to what he discovered from consultation with university physiologists. More vehemently than Ortmann, Ching differed with weight-relaxationists. The basis of his technic lay in the control of tension and specific measures of tension and relaxation. He called rotary movement "nonsense." He felt proper rotation consisted in correct adjustments in tension. He proposed reverse and oblique whole-arm touches, and examined curvilinear finger movement. Exercises away from the piano figure into Ching's method. The most interesting aspect of Ching's work is his concern with unconscious motivations in playing. In two case studies he tells of applying principles of Freudian analysis to overcome obstacles to help one student technically paralyzed in performance and another suffering from memory lapses. He exhorted others to pursue the bearing of psychology on learning and performance, opening the door on a dimension of musicianship formerly veiled.

As we near the turn of the century, an ever-increasing number of writings devoted to problems like memorization, performance anxiety, and learning deficiencies are being published. The range encompasses Luigi Bonpensiere's psychophysiological notion of ideokinetics, a process wherein the diffraction of volition transmutes into motor acts; the neurophysiological, Pavlovian ideas in *The Art of Piano Playing: A Scientific Approach* (1967) by George Kochevitsky; Charlotte Whitaker and Donald Tanner's short volume *But I Played It Perfectly in the Practice Room* (1987) that owes much to Leo Buscaglia's teachings on self-appreciation; *Anxiety and Musical Performance* (1984) by Dale Reubart; and *Tone Deaf and All Thumbs* (1986) by Frank Wilson, a neurologist who took up piano as an adult and analyzes the fears, tensions, and obstructions common to most pianists.

The application of Alexander Technique to musical practice and performance, and the use of various types of meditation to help musicians find psychological balance and inner peace that will lead to greater control in execution also join the picture. Many teachers today (Claudio Arrau was among them) recommend books like *Zen and the Art of Motorcycle Maintenance* (1974) by Robert Pirsig; *Zen in the Art of Archery* (1953) by Eugen Herrigel; and *The Inner*

Game of Tennis (1974) by Timothy Gallwey; as part of the student's technical education. Further contributions to modern-era piano technic were made by Béla Bartók/Sándor Reschofsky, Ernst Bacon, Percy Buck, Ernst von Dohnányi, Josef Gát, Guy Maier, William S. Newman, Isidor Philipp, Ruth Slencynska, and Abby Whiteside.

A number of books by concert artists that either record interviews with them or chronicle their lessons or classes richly add to the literature. These are represented in titles such as *Piano Technique* (1972, originally 1932 and 1938) by Walter Gieseking; *Great Pianists Speak with Adele Marcus* (1978); *Great Pianists Speak for Themselves* (1980), both by Elyse Mach; *The Teaching of Artur Schnabel* (1972), Konrad Wolff; *Conversations with Arrau* (1984), Joseph Horowitz; *On Piano Playing* (1981), György Sándor; *The Vengerova Method of Piano Playing* (1982), Robert Schick; *Basic Principles of Pianoforte Playing* (1972), Josef and Rosina Lhévinne; *I Really Should Be Practicing* (1981), Gary Graffman. An important source of new technical means is Dorothy Taubman. She declines to commit her method to print but gives regular classes in Amherst, Massachusetts, and around the country, training instructors in her method, which is based largely on rotation and relaxation.

See also Pedagogy—A SURVEY; Touch.

Curt Cacioppo

Bibliography

Bach, C.P.E. *Essay on the True Art of Playing Keyboard Instruments*. Edited by William Mitchell. New York: Norton, 1949.

Chasins, Abram. *Speaking of Pianists*. New York: Knopf, 1961.

Gerig, Reginald R. *Famous Pianists and Their Techniques*. Washington: R.B. Luce, 1974.

Hinson, Maurice. *The Pianist's Reference Guide: A Bibliographic Survey*. Los Angeles: Alfred Publishing Co., 1987.

Loesser, Arthur. *Men, Women and Pianos*. New York: Simon & Schuster, 1954.

Schonberg, Harold. *The Great Pianists*. New York: Simon & Schuster, 1964.

TEMPERAMENT

See Tuning

TENSION RESONATOR.

It is well understood in structural engineering that a downward force applied to an arched member will partially translate into outward thrusts at each end of the arch. The more flexible the arch the greater the magnitude of outward thrust (also called the horizontal component of the force) for a given applied load. In the case of a typical arched bridge designed to carry pedestrian or automobile traffic these outward thrusts must be reacted against by large (oftentimes massive) concrete and steel abutments; hence, as the outward thrusts are countered in kind by these abutments equilibrium is maintained and the structure survives. The arch, along with its reacting supports, is a mainstay in structural design work.

In the case of the crowned, or arched, piano **soundboard** receiving an aggregate force of **downbearing** from the **strings**, the structural requisites of arch and supports operate in like manner. Assuming the typical angle of downbearing to be 1.5 degrees, and the aggregate string tension to be 36,000 pounds, the downbearing force acting vertically on the soundboard computes to be about 1,000 pounds of compression. Were the relatively shallow-arched soundboard (only 0.400 inch high at the center of the longest 48-inch **rib**) not supported at its perimeter by a heavy and rigid **case**, it would flatten out or even collapse under the load. It is for this reason that piano makers, especially **grand piano** makers, construct the inner and outer **rims** of many laminations of hardwood. Hence, piano rims, or cases, supply a threefold function: as rigid, and hopefully immovable, abutments to counter outward thrusts; as a massive **frame** to which the soundboard can be rigidly affixed, thereby maximizing vibratory action of the soundboard; and as an esthetic surround in the form of pleasing wooden furniture.

Most piano manufacturers design, or try to design, cases of sufficient strength and mass that will remain stable against the outward thrusts applied to them. But it was for one inventor, Richard Gertz, to take out a **patent** in the U.S. in 1900 for a device consisting of an assembly of turnbuckles and rods spaced radially around a rigid iron hub. The layout and concept is not unlike that of an ordinary bicycle wheel, where the spokes are rods of small diameter that can be tensioned by means of small turnbuckles at the wheel's rim.

In the celebrated **Mason & Hamlin** piano, the one and only home for Gertz's brain child, the "tension resonator," as the device is called, lives underneath the soundboard and out of view. The hub is roughly centrally located and the outward extensions of the rods are securely attached to the piano rim. As tension is applied to the rods, the case is considerably strengthened against the outward thrusts it will receive when the piano is strung. It is obvious that in the manufacturing process, tension in the rods must increase beyond their installed tension after the piano has been strung and pulled to **pitch**. Englishman Lawrence M. Nalder, writing in 1927 in his book *The Modern Piano*, had this to say regarding the possible dynamic nature of the tension resonator insofar as it might be used as an adjusting mechanism for soundboard **crown** and downbearing: "It was claimed that by tightening up the rods the original arched form of the soundboard could be restored when age or other influences had caused a sinkage. The downbearing could be increased or decreased at will . . . . . [T]he rods could be screwed up simultaneously to bring pressure on the entire board; or individually if any part of the soundboard had sunk and the bearing lost." Be this as it may in theory, very little practical talk is exchanged among piano technicians regarding the use of the tension resonator as a dynamic adjustor.

It is sometimes supposed that only a part of the 1,000 pounds of downbearing acts in the form of outward thrusts tending to push apart the case. Actually the combined thrusts of, e.g., ten soundboard ribs in the small grand piano are considerably higher than the simple, vertical force of downbearing. Although the mechanical and mathematical analysis is complicated, it can be intuitively grasped that a mechanical advantage exists, since a force acting at a distance is the product of the force and distance. It is for this reason that levers employed to lift heavy objects through the application of a relatively small force will remain popular for all time. It must be realized that although 100 pounds of vertical force might be acting on each of the ten ribs, its point of action is more or less centrally located on each rib; for example, the point of application on a three-foot-long rib will be 18 inches from the case. Were piano soundboards designed flat instead of arched, 100 pounds of downbearing acting at a distance of one-and-a-half feet would tend to rotate each half of the rib, along with that portion of the

case it is attached to, by a force (again due to mechanical advantage) of 150 foot-pounds (called the "turning moment"). Turning-moment magnitudes in crowned soundboards are considerably more for given distances than in a hypothetical flat one. By similar reasoning it can be imagined that outward thrusts from a flat soundboard do not exist, but for an arched soundboard they do. Moreover, these thrusts in the arched board are not simple fractional parts of the downbearing load, but multiplications of it.

Piano rebuilders often find deformed conditions in old pianos' rims of both widening and rotation. And although it is generally conceded that no restorative process can undo the deformations (which are not gross in any event), new and resilient crowned soundboards can be made and installed, thereby significantly benefiting tonal characteristics and piano performance in general.

Piano technicians, like many others of all walks of life, are fond of renaming articles, devices, and processes according to their own fancy, particularly when the original name either overtly smacks of pretension, or, worse, is suspected of having been sifted through the thinktanks of clever marketing departments. Hence, the higher sounding name of tension resonator has been unofficially scrapped by many in piano technology in favor of the shorter, and more visually descriptive one of "the spider." At worst, the tension resonator has been criticized as merely a marketing device—the technically misleading word "resonator" acting as a tip-off—ostensibly designed as a critical component of piano frame stability; at best, it has been considered brilliantly conceived but, alas, unnecessary. But whether essential or not, the forces that the tension resonator are supposed to resist are not only quite real, but quite large.

See also Soundboard.

Nicholas Gravagne

THEATER PHOTOPLAYERS

A photoplayer is the generic term for the automatic orchestra used in cinemas to accompany silent movies. The name is taken from The American Photo Player Company, which was a leading maker of instruments under the brand name "Fotoplayer." This company had factories in Berkeley, California, and later at Van Nuys, while showrooms were situated in Chicago, New York, and San Francisco.

The Photoplayer is an **orchestrion** or small automatic orchestra developed from the **player piano** and in its simplest form comprised an upright **expression piano** with mandoline effect, plus manually controlled sound effects and percussion. Models were made that incorporated small pipe organs. The music was provided from a perforated paper roll.

Special music rolls, sometimes arranged in pairs so that selections could be played from either roll to suit the movie, were provided, and a skilled operator could be a positive asset to a picture-house.

Production of photoplayers began around 1910, peaked in the period 1915–1920, and virtually died with the onset of talking pictures. Of the dozen or so leading manufacturers, mostly based in America but with a few in Germany, most had shut down their lines by 1925. Bowers estimates that between 8,000 and 10,000 instruments of various kinds were made between 1910 and 1928. They were an instant box-office success, and picture-houses provided with a photoplayer became more popular with the then-large cinema audiences.

Although the name is associated with the company already mentioned, the best-selling instruments were the Reproduco (made by the Operators Piano Company of Chicago), and the products of Seeberg and **Wurlitzer.**

Largely because of their considerable size, bulk, and pneumatic complexity, very few survive today; those that do are mostly in the hands of collectors.

Arthur W.J.G. Ord-Hume

Bibliography

Bowers, Q. David. *Encyclopedia of Automatic Musical Instruments*. Vestal, N.Y.: Vestal Press, 1972.

Roehl, Harvey. *Player Piano Treasury*. Vestal, N.Y.: Vestal Press, 1961 and 1973.

THOM, JAMES AND WILLIAM ALLEN (fl. 1820) and (fl. 1800–1840)

According to Hipkins, James, Thom and William Allen, respectively foreman and tuner in the London firm of **William Stodart,** jointly authored an important invention (English **Patent** No. 4431, 1820) for a "compensation frame." Allen was also responsible for a patent (English no. 6140, 1831) for a cast-iron frame and the means of fitting a wooden wrest plank (**pin block**) to it.

The object of the 1820 patent was to lessen the tendency of pianos to go out of tune through humidity and temperature changes. The **string** tension was taken off the wooden frame by parallel metal tubes (brass above brass strings, iron above iron). One end of each tube was fastened in the wrest-plank area and the other end fastened to one of two (normally two) **plates** to which the strings were hitched, thus allowing the two metals to expand separately. Strong wooden cross-bars attached to the wooden frame prevented the tubes from buckling under the strain. Thus with variations of humidity and temperature the wooden frame was able to move independently from the metal frames, the slackening of strings at higher temperatures was compensated for by the lengthening of their bars and vice versa, and the area of freely moving **soundboard** became greater, as it was not so rigidly fixed to the frame.

The patent was immediately taken up by the firm of Stodart, and the principle was used until at least 1851. Modifications were very soon made, as follows. (1.) The varying of the metal used: already on no. 5821 (c. 1821) the iron tubes are fixed to a brass **hitch pin** plate, which negates something of the principle of the patent. (2.) An iron bracket across the action gap fixed on models ranging from nos. 5759 to 9458 (c. 1820–1833). (3.) The patent had four brass plus nine iron tubes, but one meets with a wide variety of schemes, e.g., nos. 5759, 5821, 8066, and 8708 (c. 1820–1831) have 3+7; 8976 and 9127 (c. 1832) have 3+6; 9458 (c.1833) has 2+5; 9772 (c. 1834) has 7 iron only; 10399 (c. 1837) has 8 iron only. (4.) No. 9772 has a *capo tasto* bar for the top thirty notes. (5.) Although not mentioned in the patent, Hipkins says "metal plates grooved to slide on balls fixed to the **bentside**," but no. 8066 has sliders, not balls, and the soundboard is allowed extra freedom by not being fastened to the **spine** in the **tail** area (e.g., on no. 8708 by around 67cms).

Kenneth Mobbs

Bibliography

Harding, Rosamond E.M. *The Piano-Forte: Its History Traced to the Great Exhibition of 1851.* Cambridge: Cambridge University Press, 1933. Reprints, New York: Da Capo Press, 1973; Old Woking, Surrey, U.K.: Gresham Books, 2nd ed., 1978: 202–205.

Hipkins, Alfred James. *A Description and History of the Pianoforte*. 3rd ed. Detroit Reprints in Music, 1975: 16–17.

Kibby, Bill. *Piano Archives*. Lowestoft, U.K.

Mactaggart, Peter and Ann Mactaggart, eds. *Musical Instruments in the 1851 Exhibition*. Welwyn, U.K.: Mac & Me Ltd., 1986: 41–42.

New Grove Dictionary of Musical Instruments. Edited by Stanley Sadie. S.v. "Pianoforte." London: Macmillan Press. Washington, D.C.: Grove's Dictionaries, 1984.

Patents for Inventions. *Abridgments of Specifications Relating to Music and Musical Instruments*. London 1871, facs. pub. Tony Bingham, London, 1984: 86, 112–113.

TOMKISON, THOMAS (FL. 1798–1851)

Thomas Tomkison was an English piano maker who established a small but distinguished firm at 55 Dean Street in the Soho area of London. Although he provided his instruments with **serial numbers**, Tomkison rarely dated them. One exception is a lavishly decorated **grand** that is part of the Colt Clavier Collection. This instrument was built for King George IV and was placed in the Brighton Pavilion (along with a grand by each of the firms of **Kirkman** and **Broadwood**). It is signed "For the King, December 21st 1821" in India ink on one of the **keys**. This eight-foot grand has a compass of six octaves and a Broadwood-type **English action**. The **case** is rosewood with elaborate designs of brass inlay. There are three decorative legs carved like inverted lyres. This piano is illustrated in an architectural rendering by John Nash entitled "Interior View of the Entrance Hall in the Brighton Pavilion."

It is known that Tomkison made **square pianos** with six turned legs by 1820. He added metal **plates** to these instruments for reinforcement and they were sold even in America. In all, his firm produced over 9,000 **uprights**, squares, and grands, and Tomkison was able to retire about 1840 to enjoy his fine art collection.

Peggy Flanagan Baird

Bibliography

Colt, C. F., with Anthony Miall. *The Early Piano*. London: Stainer and Bell, 1981: 76–79.

The New Grove Dictionary of Musical Instruments. Edited by Stanley Sadie. S.v. "Thomas Tomkison," by Margaret Cranmer. London: Macmillan Press Limited, 1989. Vol. 3., p. 605.

Harding, Rosamond E.M. *The Piano-Forte: Its History Traced to the Great Exhibition of 1851*. Cambridge: Cambridge University Press, 1933. Reprints, New York: Da Capo Press, 1973; Old Woking, Surrey, U.K.: Gresham Books, 1978.

Loesser, Arthur. *Men, Women and Pianos*. New York: Simon and Schuster, 1954: 459.

TONE

The human body can experience and distinguish various kinds of sensations by means of the sense organ that is stimulated and the nature of the stimulus employed. For example, the skin receives sensations of touch, the eye receives sensations of light, and the ear sensations of sound, each being totally distinct from the sensation of all other senses. The sensation of sound occurs as a reaction to the external stimulus sensed by the ear, which is capable of recognizing and distinguishing between various sounds. The sensation of musical tone is due to a rapid periodic motion of the sonorous body; the sensation of a noise, to non-periodic motions. The atmosphere conducts the motions coming from the sounding body to the ear.

It is difficult to give a verbal definition of tone. If one wants to know what a tone is, one must hear one. But if a tone cannot be defined, at least the physical cause of its sensation can be described. Sound travels to the auditory organs by means of the vibration of air which, in turn, is caused by some vibrating substance; in the case of musical tone, this is caused by the periodic motions of a **string**, a metal **plate**, or a vibrating air column within a pipe, as in the case of all wind instruments.

The word "tone" has several meanings. In the case of a musical sound it may be a "loud" or "soft" tone, poor or good tone, thick or thin tone, high or low tone, short or long tone. It may also refer to the distance between two **pitches**, known as "interval."

Every tone has five different qualities: volume, duration, loudness, pitch, and tone color (which is sometimes called "timbre"). Volume is a combination of pitch and loudness and represents the quality by which a tone seems to fill space. Duration and loudness are self-explanatory. Pitch generally refers to the difference that we express by means of the words "lower" and "higher." In other words, it refers to space relationships in a metaphorical sense.

The words "flat" or "sharp" are sometimes used to define lower and higher pitch too. Tone color is the distinguishing mark between the same tone played by a number of different musical instruments such as a piano, violin, flute, trumpet, etc.

One of the most important factors in producing a good musical tone is the blending of harmonics. If a string is perfectly flexible, and is struck with a hard **hammer**, it will produce the same value for each harmonic. The great number of harmonics produced by each sound would have to be divided equally. But because no string is so perfect in flexibility, the upper harmonics sound weak. As most of the higher harmonics are discordant with both the fundamental note and with one another, the tone produced will be a metallic kind.

In the piano each string passes over a **bridge** that is glued to a **soundboard**; this is a vital part of the instrument. When the hammer strikes, the string vibrates and these vibrations travel from the bridge to the soundboard. The hammer rebounds immediately, leaving the string free to vibrate.

The hammers are covered with **felt**, using various formulas (e.g., combinations of wool, silk, and hair). The hammers striking in the upper half of the piano are harder and thinner than those used in the lower part. The hammers are so felted to reduce the discordant harmonics created by the seventh, ninth, and higher partials. When the hammer leaves the string, a good part of the string will already be set in motion. Predominance is felt on higher harmonics (overtones) by means of a hard hammer, while a soft hammer will predominate over the fundamental tone and its octave.

The volume of every single note of the piano depends on the velocity with which the hammer travels to the string. Differences in the velocity of striking will not only produce loud and soft tones but will also produce different proportions of harmonics. This in turn alters the quality of tone, which varies with the volume. The more precise the piano, the more unified the tone from the softest to the loudest and the lowest to the highest note. In a piano, tonal beauty requires consistency in quality. A fine piano will have its tone equally beautiful and matched throughout the entire **keyboard** range. The blending of pitches and colors will also be artistically unified. Tone quality may be

affected by humidity, temperature, condition of the hammers, the size of the studio or room where it is placed, the amount and size of furniture surrounding the piano. The timbre of the piano, on the other hand, depends on factors such as the kind of wood used, iron **frame**, **scaling**, convexity, stringing, lamination, grain, age, weight of the instrument itself, shape, level, pressure and thickness.

A good piano will have complete balance between the sonority of the bass register, the rich *cantabile* tone of the middle, and bell-like quality of the upper register. All this depends on the vibrations absorbed and transmitted by the soundboard, which, by means of its large surface, is heard clearly. For such reasons, the soundboard is made of a special type of wood through which sound travels rapidly.

The piano offers an enormous range of tone and an endless variation in sound combinations. It can also offer an unlimited quality of blending and balance of tonal intensities from the softest to the loudest possible sounds. A tone may be greatly influenced by the use of the sustaining **pedal**, as it allows sympathetic vibrations to enrich the sound. The difference in sound is easily discernible when the **damper pedal** is depressed immediately after sounding a chord, because sympathetic vibrations are added to those already sounding, thereby creating a wider spectrum of sound.

See Acoustics; Partials.

Charles Zammit

Bibliography

Helmholtz, Hermann L. F. *On the Sensations of Tone as a Physiological Basis for the Theory of Music.* New York: Dover, 1954. Reprint of 1885 London edition.

Jeans, Sir James. *Science and Music.* New York: Dover, 1968. Reprint of 1937 Cambridge edition.

Zammit, Charles. *Sound Methods in Piano Pedagogy.* Ann Arbor, Mich.: University Microfilms International, 1990.

TONE REGULATION

See Voicing.

TOUCH

As applied to the piano, the word "touch" has two meanings: in connection with the instrument itself it means the responsiveness of the **keys** and **action**, which offer resistance to the fingers; it can also mean the manner in which the player applies the fingers to the keys, i.e., in a heavy or light manner, varied or not. The evolution of the piano saw many changes and advances in many parts of its mechanism, including the system of key **dip** and weight. In fact, the touch of the piano steadily became heavier as more power was sought, until it reached two to three ounces to depress a key.

To the performer, piano touch depends largely on the fundamental principles of finger **technique**, which should be developed from the very beginning of piano instruction. One of the most important aspects of study that should be at the command of the serious pianist is a mastery of finger technique.

The piano has two distinct components: the instrument itself, i.e., **strings** and **soundboard**; and the "machine" or mechanism, comprising keys and action. The most important parts of the piano mechanism are the **hammers** and the **dampers**. The hammer reaches the string after the finger has depressed the key, then falls back immediately afterwards. Thus the sound cannot be influenced in any way after the key is down. Therefore, the **tone** and quality of each sound is determined before the hammer touches the string. After the hammer produces the sound it falls back from the string, leaving the string free to vibrate. When the key rises (is released), a descending damper stops the vibrations, hence the sound is discontinued. The difference between loud and soft tones is caused by key-speed. Therefore, if the keys are pushed swiftly, they produce loud tones; when pushed slowly, soft tones will result. The important factor here is that one must always "feel" how much pressure the key needs to produce every tone. The key should be made to rebound very quickly, otherwise the damper will not descend sharply enough to prevent prolongation of the sound. The only way by which one can tell what weight is required to keep a key depressed is by carefully "weighing" the key and feeling the resistance offered by it. One can weigh (or push) the key down by allowing the whole arm to relax (from the shoulder) until the key is just overbalanced (dropped to the **keybed**). A controlled touch is most important, as it enables one to play legato with ease and certainty, to play passages in the softest possible manner, and to be able to judge key-resistance and weight-

control in order to produce various shades of tone.

Piano touch can be grouped into three types depending on which muscles are involved: in the first type, the sound is produced by finger exertion only, the hand lying loosely upon the keys, which are moved by the use of the finger alone (the hand can move swiftly across the **keyboard** in this type but not much tone can be obtained). With the second type, sound is produced by the exertion of the finger combined with the exertion of the hand. Here, the arm is supported by its own muscles and no arm-weight is used. Although it reduces agility, this type offers more tone than that using fingers alone. In the third type, tone is produced by a combination of the weight of the arm, exertion of the hand, and exertion of the finger. This type is capable of giving a full range of tone but cannot be used in very agile passage work because of the added weight. Within these three main types of touch there are various combinations and mixtures that result in a variety of descriptive labels. However, it must be remembered that every kind of "descriptive" touch is the result of muscular movement. Muscular involvement is used for all types to obtain brilliancy, while the arm-weight-touch covers the third type only and is employed for a singing (*cantabile*) tone. This "singing tone" can be aided further by the use of a "clinging touch," where the fingers are flatter and straighter. There is also the "thrusting" touch, in which the fingers should be well bent to aid brilliancy.

Two of the most important kinds of touch are the staccato and the legato. There are various ways to perform staccatos on the piano keyboard: one method is to keep the finger rigid and throw it from the wrist, bouncing off the keybed; another method is done without wrist involvement, where the finger snaps the key surface, sliding off in pinwheel fashion; and finally, combinations of both methods, including arm-weight involvement for added power (*martellato*). In "pure legato" touch the pressure of the fingers must be transferred neatly from key to key, making sure that each new tone is connected to the previous one without overlapping. "Legatissimo" (the superlative of legato) indicates that the player must focus full attention on the connection of tones to bring about a harmonious effect, which is achieved in this case by the overlapping of tones.

The "portato" (or "portamento") touch is considered a compromise between staccato and legato. The "non-legato" touch is similar to the "portato" in that the tones are not connected. In the portato, there is a greater pause between tones than there is in the non-legato touch. Portato is generally used in tone progressions of a quiet nature while the non-legato is used in livelier progressions as a means of separation. Both modes are not practical in very quick runs.

Another kind of touch is that known as "rotation" (or "roll"), where there is a change in the position of the forearm; the hand is tilted either toward the thumb or toward the little finger and there is a visible rocking motion of the hand. In this case, the wrist partially revolves on its own axis.

The "free fall" is a gravitational attack that is produced by the raising of the hand and forearm from the elbow and dropping the hand (and forearm) to the keyboard.

Sensitivity to touch and tone develops through years of playing and practicing, with attention to careful listening and a keen awareness of the physical aspects of the playing mechanism, i.e., fingers, hand, wrist, arms, etc., as well as the physical aspects of the instrument itself, and the crucial integration of both.

See also Technic—A Survey.

Charles Zammit

Bibliography

Kentner, Louis. *Piano*. New York: Macmillan, 1976.

Leimar, Karl. *Rhythmics, Dynamics, Pedal and Other Problems of Piano Playing*. Reprint. New York: Dover, 1972.

Matthay, Tobias. *The Act of Touch*. London; New York: Longmans, Green & Co., 1903.

Sándor, György. *On Piano Playing*. New York; London: Schirmer/Macmillan, 1981.

Schultz, Arnold. *The Riddle of the Pianist's Finger*. New York: Carl Fischer, 1949.

Seashore, Carl E. *Psychology of Music*. New York: McGraw-Hill, 1938.

Zammit, Charles. *Sound Methods in Piano Pedagogy*. Ann Arbor, Mich.: University Microfilms International, 1990.

TOUCHWEIGHT

The forces required to maintain **key** movement are collectively called touchweight. These forces include downweight—the minimum force required to make the key go down—and upweight—the minimum amount of force the key can lift once depressed.

The pianist can gauge the speed of the key stroke and the resulting volume of the musical **tone** produced by sensing the resistance, or touchweight, in the key during the downward portion of the stroke. If the touchweight is too high or too low the pianist may have difficulty controlling the **action**. This is complicated by the fact that there are actually three variables whose combined effect determines how much pressure the pianist feels in each key. These variables are gravity, inertia, and friction.

Gravitational **touch** resistance in a piano key is felt as the net difference of weight between the front and the back of the key. Its value is determined by the amount of **leads** set into the key during the key-balancing process. Its value remains constant no matter at what speed the key is struck.

Inertial touch resistance in the piano key is proportional to both the total weight on both sides of the key and the speed at which the key is thrown into motion when struck. Technically speaking, inertia is the tendency of matter at rest to remain at rest, and matter in motion to remain in motion at the same velocity and in the same direction, unless acted upon by an outside force. For this reason, a note played at pianissimo may have a touch resistance on the order of fifty grams but that same key when played at fortissimo will have a touch resistance of hundreds or thousands of grams. Also, since piano **hammers** are heavier in the bass and lighter in the treble it takes more keylead to counterbalance the parts in the bass than in the treble; therefore, inertia is higher in the bass and lower in the treble.

Frictional touch resistance in the piano key results from parts that move against each other within the action. Its value is determined by the pressure that sliding surfaces exert against each other. Friction values are also influenced by the quality of construction of the action parts as well as by environmental factors. In high humidity friction is higher and in low humidity friction is lower. Like inertia, friction increases as the key is struck harder but the effect is not so dramatic. As the key is struck harder inertial effects within the action cause sliding surfaces to be pushed harder against each other, thus increasing friction between those surfaces.

Piano technicians have two measurements at their disposal for measuring touchweight: downweight and upweight. Downweight is the minimum amount of weight that will cause a piano key to go down at the front. Upweight is the maximum amount of weight a key will lift at the front upon being released. Downweight and upweight are measured in grams. To measure downweight, a gram weight is placed on the key at the front and a rap or thump is given to the shop bench, **keybed**, or action stack with one's fist to break the starting friction. If the gram weight chosen is too light, the hammer will not rise (and the key will not drop) or will barely do so. If the gram weight is too heavy, the hammer will rise without the rap or will rise too swiftly. When the hammer rises and the key falls with a slow, controlled motion following the rap, it indicates that the gram weight with the correct weight value has been found. The measurement of upweight is done in a similar, but reverse, sequence: the correct gram weight has been found when the hammer drops and the key rises in a slow, controlled motion to a point just above its rest position and a rap then causes it to drop the remaining fraction of an inch. Slight variations in this technique are permissible as long as the chosen method is used in a consistent manner.

These measurements are taken between rest position and a point just prior to **escapement**, when the **jack** just touches the **let-off** button and the **repetition lever** just touches the drop screw, but the internal movements of the jack, repetition spring, etc., have not yet begun. These measurements are also taken without the **damper** system engaged, since the weight and timing of the dampers would otherwise exert a significant influence on the touchweight measurements. The action and **keyboard** are normally removed from the instrument and placed on a bench or table when taking these measurements.

The downweight and upweight measurements have both a gravity component and a friction component, but since these measurements are taken with the key slowly moving, inertia is not a consideration.

When measuring downweight, enough weight must be placed on the front of the key to equally counterbalance the extra weight on the backside of the key. To start the key moving, additional weight must be added to overcome friction in the key. So downweight equals gravity plus friction. When measuring upweight, the key is released and gravity pulls the back of the key back down, thereby causing the front of the key to rise. Friction robs from gravity's ability to cause the key to return. So upweight equals gravity minus friction.

Friction in the action alters the relationship between upweight and downweight. If the amount of friction changes anywhere in the action so does upweight and downweight. The difference between upweight and downweight is determined by total action friction.

As friction is decreased in the action, downweight and upweight approach each other. It is impossible to completely eliminate friction in piano actions, but if we could, downweight and upweight would meet at a single point. This theoretical point represents the gravity component of the touchweight measurement. It is also referred to as the "balance weight," literally the amount of weight it takes to counterbalance the effect of gravity in the key. The balance weight value is independent of, and unaffected by, friction, and can be altered only by changing the net difference of weight between either side of the key. Compared to friction, which changes seasonally or with use, balance weight remains relatively stable and can be precisely set by positioning keyleads.

In the modern piano with the Herz-**Erard** type action, a downweight value higher than about 55 grams is likely to be too heavy, and one lower than 45 grams is likely to be too light. Keys with an upweight value of less than 20 grams may be prone to sluggishness, while those over 30 grams may snap back with too much force. Notes with extremely low friction are difficult to control. Since inertia does not show itself in the touchweight measurements, one can only make qualitative estimates of its value. If there are too many keyleads in the key then it would be reasonable to assume that inertia will be high. High inertia can also result from hammers that are too heavy. Because of their longer key length, **concert grand pianos** tend to have higher inertia.

Variations in the proportions of these touchweight factors to each other cause considerable variation in the quality of touch found in individual pianos. As a result, pianists must adapt to the particular piano on which they are performing. It is very important to a pianist that the pressure required to depress the piano keys be consistent across the keyboard. For example, if every key feels alike, a pianist can easily play a series of notes at the same tonal volume by applying the same pressure to each key. When touch is uniform the piano is easier to play and the musical result more satisfying. If, on the other hand, each key requires a different pressure to play at a given volume, a pianist has the difficult task of learning how much pressure to apply to each key. In addition to problems with touch uniformity, pianists also encounter variety in the overall feeling of the action in different pianos ranging from heavy to light.

The tonal quality of the piano can also affect the way the piano feels. Consider a piano in which the hammers are too soft: in order to attain a higher volume the pianist compensates by hitting the key harder. Since inertia is proportional to the acceleration of the key and its associated action parts, hitting the key harder results in higher inertia, thus making the keys feel heavier. For the same reason, if the tone is uneven the touch will feel uneven.

David C. Stanwood

TRANSPOSING KEYBOARDS

A transposing **keyboard** allows the player to easily render a piece of music *prima vista* in a different key than it is written. The idea of transposing keyboards is not limited to pianos; indeed it is much older. As early as 1537, Hans Müller (Leipzig) made a harpsichord with a sideward-shifting keyboard. The advantage was that the instrument could accompany instruments in another key; however, it should be remembered that there were rather drastic limitations to the use of transposing keyboards as long as equal **tuning** was not accepted.

Since the keyboard was shifted beneath the **jacks** or **hammers**, enharmonic problems arose, resulting in disagreeable chords. The first solution given to this problem was to add pipes or strings. Another solution, found in the Antwerp harsichord-building school, required a small metal hook upon which the **string** could be shifted, thereby raising it a comma. This is particularly the case with a two-keyboard harpsichord on which the lower keyboard, for the same key, sounds a fifth higher than the upper keyboard. Hence the difficulty in changing G-sharp with its fifth, D-sharp, for E-flat. To overcome this difficulty all sorts of experiments were made with keyboards, such as the harpsi-

chords by Nicolà Vicentino and by Giovanni Battista Boni, or the *clavicymbalum universale* described by Michael Praetorius (1619). However, instruments with broken keys, as proposed by Boni, or several rows of keys (as with Vicentino) cannot be considered as transposing keyboards. Their aim was to find a solution to tuning problems, not to render playing easier. The closer tuning got to equal temperament, the more devices for transposing came into use.

Pianos made by Torenberg in Amsterdam (1788), Johann Schmahl in Regensburg (last quarter of the eighteenth century), and Edward Ryley (1801) all had keyboards that could be shifted to the right or to the left for one or more half-tone(s). The piano produced by the Parisian firm Roller-Blanchet could move up to five half-tones, whereas Edward Barry's transposing device (1855) allowed for four half-tones to be shifted.

A breakthrough came when a separate keyboard could be placed upon the real one, although here it also took some time before all tonalities became transposable. Edward Ryley **patented** such a device in 1801, and he was soon followed by an increasing number of inventors and imitators, such as Maurice Henry (1861), William Evans (1865), Vincent Newton (1866), Henry Kleinsjasper (1869), and Auguste Wolff (1872). Although the Biancandini firm still tried to improve the separate keyboard in 1923, the separate transposing keyboard by **Pleyel**, Wolff & Cie (Paris, 1883)—a many-levered device placed upon the ordinary keyboard with the ability to transpose down seven half-tones and up five half-tones—put an end to experiments.

Other types of transposing keyboards were introduced by Henry **Broadwood** in 1844. In these devices the **keys** did not move, rather the **frame** and strings were shifted laterally. Other experiments with transposing pianos include the instruments by **John Conrad Becker** (1801) and John George Thompson (1862). Both these instruments allow playing in natural temperament (not equal temper). Becker's piano could be tuned in quarter, half, three-quarter, and whole tones. For this purpose each **tuning pin** was made to pass through a socket with a lever upon which slid a quadrant. Hereupon were fixed links, kept stationary by a regulating screw. These links connected with **pedals** by the interposition of a crank. Holding down a pedal made it possible to transpose (at least theoretically) into any key. Thompson's instrument was technically easier but at the same time it required a stronger frame, since his piano had to be tuned all the way up in an enharmonic scale. A pedal allowed the keyboard to shift laterally.

Since the keyboard invented in 1882 by **Paul Jankó**, a Hungarian engineer, allows all major scales to be played with the same **fingering**, as are all minor scales, it can also be considered as some sort of transposing keyboard. This is not the case with the different enharmonic keyboards, intended more for obtaining a just intonation than for rendering playing more easy.

F.J. de Hen

TUNING

Tuning is the actual realization of **pitch** of a musical instrument: in other words, it is the determination of the actual frequency of every note the instrument produces. As such, tuning comprises two levels: (1) theoretical systems (called tuning systems and temperaments) that determine the content of musical intervals; and, (2) the preparation of an instrument to make the sounds it produces coincide with or match the frequencies of the chosen tuning system or temperament.

Tuning Systems and Temperaments
The difference between a tuning system and a temperament is not always easy to outline. In general we might say that a tuning system is a mere theoretical proposal based on arithmetical considerations. Temperament, on the other hand, is the "tempering" of a tuning system. This means that some intervals are widened and others narrowed in terms of their frequency ratios. This is done either to "soften" the original intervals or to deal with shifts and gaps that may arise from the stringent theoretical design of a tuning system. For instance, the concatenation of twelve pure fifths (ratio 3:2) does not produce seven octaves, as one might expect, but seven octaves plus 23.5 cents (100 cents is one semitone). One way to solve this shift is to temper each fifth with c. 2 cents (about 0.28%).

Of course, the number of tuning systems and temperaments that were developed during the history of Western music is great. The systems that have been in use for piano tuning fall into three categories: mean-tone, equal, and microtonal temperaments.

Mean-tone Temperaments
Mean-tone temperaments were found in various keyboard instruments from the middle ages to the nineteenth century. For pianos it is especially found on early instruments, since it was quite popular for harpsichord tuning in the seventeenth and eighteenth centuries.

The term "mean-tone" is derived from the fact that the major third is tuned pure (ratio of 5:4) and then divided in two equal whole tones. A pure third is only obtained if the fifths and fourths are tempered (they no longer have ratios of 3:2 and 4:3). The tempering implies the narrowing of the fifths and the widening of the fourths with one-fourth of the syntonic comma (a small interval with ratio 81:80, appearing in

---

Fig. 1
Number of beats per second for fifths, fourths, and thirds

Frequency of the lower note	Fifth	Number of beats per second Fourth	Third
440	0.74488616	0.662869215	2.50973797
466.163	0.789179564	0.702285528	2.65897465
493.883	0.836106539	0.744045496	2.81708574
523.251	0.885823965	0.788288593	2.9845984
554.365	0.938497782	0.835162878	3.16207171
587.329	0.994303942	0.884824038	3.35009813
622.253	1.05342841	0.937438727	3.54930544
659.255	1.11606836	0.993181706	3.7603581
698.456	1.18243313	1.05223942	3.98396063
739.988	1.25274467	1.11480856	4.22085905
783.990	1.32723665	1.18109846	4.47184443
830.609	1.40615797	1.25133038	4.73775434
880	1.48977232	1.32573843	5.01947594

the system of Didymos, first century BC). This common temperament is referred to as quarter-tone mean-tone. In some instances, the third is not pure but small fractions of the syntonic comma are used to widen or narrow it (e.g., one-seventh, one-ninth, one-third).

Since mean-tone temperaments very often lead to wolf fifths (fifths that are tempered too much and therefore sound unpleasant), gradually the thirds were widened and the mean-tone systems were abandoned, though they sound very warm when playing major chords, due to the pure major thirds. A gain of importance for just intonation (every interval is expressible in simple ratios) for keyboards did not arise, due to technical problems: the construction of divided **keyboards**, where several **keys** are divided into two or more separate working parts, each with their own **strings**, and proper tuning (just intonation implies different frequencies for notes with the same name for different tonalities). One of the few examples of pianos in just intonation was built in 1864 for Prince Odoevsky.

Equal Temperament

In the development of equal temperament for pianos, there probably was some use of irregular temperaments, though **Broadwood** pianos were tuned equal from about 1850. Irregular temperaments are those where some intervals (mostly fifths) are not equal throughout the compass, or certain ranges of the compass.

Of much greater importance, and nowadays omnipresent, is equal temperament. In equal temperament only the octaves are pure, and the notes in between are tempered so that every semitone has the same ratio $\sqrt[12]{2}\!:\!1$. In other words, the octave is divided in twelve equal parts, each of them comprising 100 cents. This makes equal temperament fundamentally a system of mistuning, but the mistuning is equalized throughout the octave and, as such, sounds pleasing. Typically, actual realizations of equal temperament never attain mathematical accuracy, and impressions of key color (see below) are present.

Microtonal Temperaments

As early as the sixteenth century, theorists began constructing microtonal divisions of the octave. Application of microtonal systems to the piano, however, did not arise before the twentieth century. A major exception was the

Telio-chordon, built by Charles Clagget of London in 1788. The Clagget instrument uses **pedals** to determine which of the three strings of a key will be struck.

The first microtonal system that was favored to some extent in piano construction was the quarter-tone temperament. One of the earliest examples is the quarter-tone piano constructed by Maison Diderichs in St. Petersburg (1913–1914) following the ideas of Arthur Lourié. Famous also are several instruments constructed for Alois Hába (a piano with three manuals constructed by **Grotrian-Steinweg** in 1924, the Förster pianos from 1924, 1925, and 1931, etc.).

In recent times, several experiments were pursued. Among these are innovations by Harry Partch and A.R. McClure in the 1940s, Lou Harrison in the 1950s, Ervin Wilson in the 1960s, the *pianos metamorfoseadores* (a series of pianos each in a different microtonal tuning) of Julián Carrillo (planned in 1927, built from 1947 to 1958), and Augusto Novarro.

Worth noting is the return to mean-tone and just intonations (both systems can be considered as microtonal strategies) in contemporary music, for example the Piano Sonata of 1963 by Ben Johnston (just intonation) or the Well-Tuned Piano (1964) by LaMonte Young (just intonation).

Tuning

As explained above, tuning is the actual realization of the pitch of musical instruments. Whatever system one chooses, there are two possible ways to pursue the process of tuning. One either uses some mechanical or electronic device that gives the desired pitch for every note or one works empirically using only the ear. Most experienced tuners use the latter method. With this method, the appearance of beatnotes is very important.

Tuning with Beats

The simultaneous sounding of two notes may, under specific circumstances, give birth to the phenomenon of beatnotes. The major condition for the rise of this beating effect is that the two frequencies lie close together or that certain of their **partials** have approaching frequencies. Beats are very regular (periodic) events and are therefore easily recognized and very useful in tuning.

Suppose one wishes to tune the fifth a–e¹ in equal temperament. The two notes have of course different frequencies. However, the second overtone of a (= e²) has the same frequency as the first overtone of e¹ (= e²), namely 1320 Hz. Since the two overtones have the same frequency, no beats will arise. However, if no beats arise the interval a–e¹ is a natural (pure) fifth and does not fit in our tempered scale. e¹ has a tempered frequency of 1315,510 Hz. The difference between the natural frequency of e¹ and the tempered e¹ is 1.490 Hz. This number represents the number of beats in one second. Consequently, one needs to lower the beatless e¹ till c. 1.5 beats per second are heard, and the desired tempered fifth is the result.

The example clearly illustrates that the number of beats per second is nothing other than the absolute value of the difference between the tempered frequency and the natural frequency of coinciding partials. There exist several publications listing the number of beats per second for fifths, fourths, and thirds. There is no problem if such lists are not available. Indeed, simple formulae express the number of beats:

for the fifth: $b = \left| \left(f \sqrt[12]{2^7} - \frac{3}{2} f \right) \right|$

for the fourth: $b = \left| \left(f \sqrt[12]{2^5} - \frac{4}{3} f \right) \right|$

for the major third: $b = \left| \left(f \sqrt[12]{2^4} - \frac{81}{64} f \right) \right|$

where b stands for the number of beats per second, and f for the frequency of the lowest note in the interval.

Every possible interval can be dealt with using analogue formulae but there is no need to do so: for intervals other than the fifth, fourth, or major third, the number of beats will be either too high or too low to be useful. The same problem may arise for the mentioned intervals, since the number of beats per second doubles with every ascent of one octave. (See fig. 1).

The Process of Tuning

There are several common procedures. Many of them focus on tuning in fifths. Why fifths are so predominant is easy to guess: in an equal temperament they are the first intervals to be tem-

pered, and their relation to the octave is very simple. Whatever the sequence of intervals one follows while tuning, the general strategy consists of tuning most of the notes in the interval between C and c¹ (the two octaves neighboring the middle c), and the subsequent tuning of all other notes of the compass, using octaves.

"Laying the bearings," as the fixing of the pitch is sometimes called, can be done in several ways. A very popular and indeed very satisfying method is to work round the circle of fifths. The tuning of the circle of fifths encompasses two movements. At first instance there is the gradual ascending of the scale. The tuner may start with a at 440 Hz. Using this note the lower A is tuned. The next step is to lay the bearing of the e in between. The determination of this e is done via the beating of the tempered fifth (see above). Once e is established, E is tuned, preferably a bit too narrow, for any widening of this octave will have disastrous results for the subsequent tuning. From this E on, a general ascending progression is followed, consisting of ascending fifth—ascending fifth—descending octave. The descending movement starts with c², and follows the general policy of subsequent fifths and octaves. It is important to check thirds whenever they become available (or rather tenths, for they are easier to listen to), sixths, and major chords. Of course several sequences of octaves and fifths are imaginable (see fig. 2).

Since this technique depends upon the evaluation of the presence or absence of beats, it deals very elegantly with the inharmonicity of the piano strings. The stretched **scaling** resulting from this inharmonicity has as its main feature the gradual widening of the octaves towards bass and treble. Sometimes tuners tend to widen even more the high octaves for the sake of brilliancy and because of the tendency of treble strings to lose their tension more quickly than bass strings.

The same degree of mathematical inaccuracy is present in tuning in general. One has to

Figure 2: An example of a tuning sequence

bear in mind that experienced tuners work empirically, and that the resulting irregularities are favored by both piano players and audiences. This explains also why the impure tuning of trichords (the three strings are "mistuned" c. 0.09 % compared to each other, in order to strengthen the intensity of the sound) has never provoked any protest. The mistuning of the trichords is done by inserting a strip of felt in between the three strings. The middle string is tuned pure. The right and left strings are then tuned till about one beat per three seconds appears.

Key Color

The system of equal temperament, when applied strictly, prevents the coloring of keys. Key color is the difference in general impression between different keys, e.g., keys with flats sounding closed and veiled compared to keys with sharps. The impression of key color may have to do with **fingering** and playing **technique**, but more probably it has to do with the judgment of the tuner. Besides, there are tuning principles that take into account the desire for key color. A fine example is the tuning principle of A.L. Leigh Silver, published in 1957, where the narrowing of each fifth in equal temperament by c. 1.95 cents (= one twelfth of the Pythagorean comma [an interval with ratio 531441:524288]) is proposed. Besides providing distinct coloring for keys, the principle of Leigh Silver allows very easy tuning.

Tuning Devices

The most popular tuning device is the tuning fork. Tuning forks with different frequencies circulate, but nowadays the standard is the fork of 440 Hz. Tuning forks (invented by John Shore in 1712) are very useful because fairly rapidly after striking only the fundamental tone is left.

Besides the tuning fork and some rare mechanical devices from the past (such as the Sonomètre of Etienne Loulié) in recent times several electronic tuning devices were developed, such as the Conn Strobotuner (with rotating stroboscopic disc), the Widner Accutone tuner (using computer circuits), and more recently, several types of electronic tone generators.

See also Acoustics; Partials.

Peter G.C. van Poucke

Bibliography

Askill, John. *Physics of Musical Sounds.* New York: D. Van Nostrand Company, 1979.

Campbell, Murray, and Clive Greated. *The Musician's Guide to Acoustics.* New York: Macmillan, 1987.

Meffen, John. *A Guide to Tuning Musical Instruments.* London: David & Charles, 1982.

Palmieri, Robert. *Piano Information Guide: An Aid to Research.* New York: Garland Publishing Inc., 1989: 112–117.

White, Harvey E., and Donald H. White. *Physics and Music: The Science of Musical Sound.* Philadelphia: Saunders College, 1980.

White, William Braid. *Piano Tuning and the Allied Arts.* Boston: Tuners Supply, 1946.

TUNING HAMMER

The tuning hammer is a special wrench of T or L shape with a wooden handle and a star-type metal socket that fits over the square head of the piano's wrest pins (**tuning pins**) in order to adjust the tension of the strings. This tool may also be called a tuning key.

Peggy Flanagan Baird

TUNING PIN

Tuning pins, which are found in most stringed keyboard instruments, are cylindrical pins made of steel or iron to which the **strings** are attached for the purpose of **tuning**. The upper half of the tuning pin, which protrudes above the **pinblock**, is often blued or nickel-plated to prevent rust. During manufacture, the top of the tuning pin is swagged into a square or oblong shape that allows a **tuning hammer** to be fitted to the pin. The serrated bottom half of the pin is fitted into a hole in the pinblock, which has been drilled slightly smaller than the diameter of the tuning pin. The tuning pin is set firmly in place in the pinblock, but it can still be turned with a tuning hammer. Tuning pins of various diameters, lengths, and configurations are found in instruments from different historical periods. In the nineteenth century various attempts were made to eliminate the tuning pin by attaching piano strings to mechanical machine screws. Although the experiments turned out to be impractical, successful "screw-stringers" were made by **Mason & Hamlin** in the United States and **Brinsmead** in England.

Edward E. Swenson

Bibliography

Bielefeldt, Catherine C. *The Wonders of the Piano: The Anatomy of the Instrument.* Melville: Belwin-Mills, 1984.

Mason, Merle H. *Piano Parts and Their Functions.* Second edition. Seattle: Piano Technicians Guild, 1981.

"TWELVE APOSTLES"

"Twelve Apostles" was the name given to a group of twelve German piano craftsmen who fled to England during the Third Silesian or Seven Years' War (1756–1763).

This war was to become responsible for the single most important event in the design and manufacture of the pianoforte in England: the emigration of Germany's most renowned craftsmen. In August 1756, when **Frederick the Great** invaded Saxony and took Dresden, **Gottfried Silbermann**'s workshop at nearby Freiberg was effectively closed down. The subsequent war between the Empire and Frederick II meant that craftsmen all over the country became uncertain of their futures.

The Twelve Apostles included apprentices trained by Silbermann. They were forced to flee Germany and settled in England to look for work in London, which was virtually the only European city still at peace. Of the group, several ultimately became renowned manufacturers. The first to reach London was a Dutchman, **Americus Backers** (fl. 1763–1781), who set up in business in Jermyn Street. Others followed, among them **Johannes Zumpe** (1726–1791), who brought with him the **Cristofori-Silbermann** tradition, **Johannes Pohlmann** (fl. 1767–1793), **Adam Beyer** (Bleyer) (fl. 1774–1795), Gabriel Buntebart (Buntlebart) (fl. 1769–1795), and Georg D. Schoene (Schoene & Co., 1784–1820). With them were harpsichord makers **Christopher Ganer** (fl. c. 1774–c. 1809) and Thomas Garbutt (fl. 1770–1776), the latter concentrating only on harpsichords.

The full list of the names of the Twelve Apostles is nowhere recorded, but exhaustive research by Edwin M. Good suggests the following list of men: Americus Backers; **Frederick Beck** (fl. 1756–1798); Adam Beyer; Gabriel Buntebart; Christopher Ganer; George Garcka (fl. 1783–1792); **John Geib** (1744–1818); Meyer, a partner of Zumpe in 1778; Johannes Pohlmann; Schoene, who advertised himself as "successor to Johannes Zumpe"; Sievers, a partner of Buntebart in 1788 and later; Johannes Zumpe. Some of the dates for these makers, particularly those who are more obscure, are conjectural, based where possible on known, surviving instruments.

Arthur W.J.G. Ord-Hume

Bibliography

Boalch, Donald H. *Makers of the Harpsichord & Clavichord, 1440–1840.* Oxford: Oxford University Press, 1974.

Good, Edwin Marshall. *Giraffes, Black Dragons, and Other Pianos: A Technological History from Cristofori to the Modern Concert Grand.* Stanford, Cal.: Stanford University Press, 1982.

Harding, Rosamond E.M. *The Piano-Forte: Its History Traced to the Great Exhibition of 1851.* Cambridge: Cambridge University Press, 1933. Reprints, New York: Da Capo Press, 1973; Old Woking, Surrey: Gresham Books, 1878.

Russell, Raymond. *The Harpsichord & Clavichord.* London: Faber, 1973.

Wainwright, David. *Broadwood by Appointment: A History.* London: Quiller, 1982.

TWO-KEYBOARD PIANOS

The usual aim of two-keyboard pianos is to allow easier playing, although new playing possibilities can also be the goal. Thus Mangeot Frères of Nancy **patented**, in 1876, a double piano (one **grand** reversed upon the other) with two **keyboards** (one reversed). This piano was designed by Joseph Wieniawski (1837–1912). In 1917 Pierre Hans, a Belgian engineer living during World War I in Maastricht (Holland), invented a double-keyboard piano in which the second keyboard shifted half a tone (so that the **fingering** for all the scales remained exactly the same). Another type of two-keyboard piano was the piano with rollover keyboard made by Carel Goetze (Berlin, about 1900), where the player could choose between a normal keyboard and (by rolling it over) a **Paul von Jankó** (1856–1919) keyboard. **Emanuel Moór** (1863–1931) introduced a pianoforte, c. 1920, in which the upper keyboard could be coupled with the lower one, thus producing its octave.

Other two-keyboard pianos were invented by **Pleyel** & Vishnegradsky (1922), Moritz Stoehr (1924), Alois Hába & Förster (1925), Hans Barth (1928), the Franscani firm (1930), and Abdul Hak (1974).

F.J. de Hen

UNA CORDA PEDAL

The *una corda* pedal is usually the left **pedal**, which shifts the **keyboard** to the right so that the **hammer** strikes fewer than all the **strings**. Also known as the "soft" pedal, the stop rather thins the **tone** than softens it.

Bartolomeo Cristofori made manually-operated keyboard shifts. A pedal was first used in England perhaps as early as 1770. On double-strung instruments, the hammer struck one string (*una corda*). With early triple-strung **grands**, the hammer struck one string, and the pedal could be partially raised for it to strike two strings, an effect for which **Beethoven** calls in the A-Major Sonata, Op. 101.

On modern grands the pedal makes the hammer strike two strings. **Uprights,** with stringing at an angle to hammers, cannot use a keyboard shift.

See also Pedals and Stops.

Edwin M. Good

UNITED STATES,
PIANO INDUSTRY IN THE

The history of the piano industry in the United States is less a story of technological development than one of commercial enterprise. This is not to depreciate such significant American contributions to piano technology as the full iron **frame**, the **overstrung scale**, and improvements in **soundboard** construction and piano **actions** (especially **player-piano** mechanisms). These accomplishments have been long recognized and properly acclaimed. But the interna-

tional strength of the American industry, and its critical role in business history, lies with its commercial development and the pioneering business strategies of leading firms.

Progressive factory organization, management practices, and mechanization technologies allowed for mass production. Organized dealer networks sustained national and international product distribution. Financing strategies permitted business expansion, the creation of large corporations with significant capital investment, and credit purchasing for consumers. National advertising and progressive merchandising cultivated brand-name recognition and loyalty. Organizations like the National Piano Manufacturers Association, the National Bureau for the Advancement of Music, and the Music Industries Chamber of Commerce promoted musical culture and instruction in the United States, as did various companies' promotions of player pianos, performing artists, and concert halls. It is upon this commercial foundation that the technological developments of the piano industry in the United States rest.

The art of piano building should properly be considered a craft rather than an industry during the sixty-five years after **Johann Behrendt** manufactured the first instrument, a **square piano**, in Philadelphia in 1775. (Notably, American makers concentrated on the square piano until the late nineteenth century, when the **upright** became the piano of choice among American consumers.) Significant among these craftsmen were **Charles Albrecht**, established in Philadelphia in 1789, and **Benjamin Crehore**, whose Boston shop founded in 1792 inspired **Alpheus Babcock** and **Jonas Chickering** to become leaders in the development of the full iron frame. By the early nineteenth century Boston (inspired by English designs), New York (influenced by German technology), Philadelphia, and Baltimore became centers of piano manufacture. Prominent among these early houses were Chickering & Sons and Hallet & Davis of Boston; Hardman, Peck & Co. and **Hazelton Bros.** of New York; **William Knabe & Co.** and Charles M. Stieff of Baltimore; and Schomacker Piano Co. of Philadelphia. By the 1840s these makers formed the core of the budding piano industry in the United States.

This industry was greatly encouraged at the first World's **Exhibition** in London in 1851. In an increasingly competitive industrial market-place, such fairs and expositions communicated technological leadership. "The beginning of the piano industry in America, *as an industry*, can historically be dated from the first World's Exhibition," wrote **Alfred Dolge** in the second volume of his work on the piano in America (1913). He appropriately considered the London Exhibition as foundational because the pianos of Chickering & Sons and Timothy Gilbert & Co. of Boston, **Nunns & Clark** of New York, and Conrad Meyer of Philadelphia attracted the attention of European makers and were awarded distinctions. (This was two years before the establishment of **Steinway & Sons.**) German immigrant craftsmen were a strong element in the trade. Among the significant houses established during the 1850s and 1860s were **Decker** & Sons, **Kranich & Bach**, George Steck & Co., Steinway & Sons, and **Weber Piano Co.** of New York, and **Mason & Hamlin** of Boston. During these decades piano manufacture also moved west into Illinois and Ohio. Important Chicago houses were W. W. **Kimball** Co., Lyon & Healy, J. P. Seeburg & Co., and **Story & Clark**. Cincinnati firms include D. H. **Baldwin & Co.** and Rudolph **Wurlitzer Co.**

The Paris Exposition of 1867 was even more of a turning point because innovative American piano technology conquered Europe and became the model for the future. Chickering and Steinway both reportedly spent $80,000 to promote their pianos and both claimed to have received highest honors from the panel of judges. They carried the battle home to fight it out in local newspapers and the trade press, benefiting greatly from the increased publicity. Nevertheless, as Dolge further noted, the beginning of the *modern* American piano industry dates to the Centennial Exposition held in Philadelphia in 1876. The industrial magnitude of the trade was evident in the display of hundreds of different makes, which incorporated the revolutionary innovations collectively called the "American system"—industrial production, the full iron frame, overstringing the bass, high-tension **wires**, and other construction to produce a powerful **tone**. Dolge emphasized that the exposition "established once for all the superiority of the American piano as an *industrial* product, in comparison with similar products of other countries," and that these products clearly showed that "the piano industry was equal in

importance to any other American industry, and, of course, far in advance of that of any other nation." Significant eastern houses established during the 1870s and 1880s were the **Aeolian Co.**, Jacob Doll & Sons, and **Sohmer & Co.** in New York, and Ivers & Pond in Boston. Western firms include Starr Piano Co. of Richmond, Indiana; Jesse French & Sons of New Castle, Indiana; Steger & Sons and Hamilton (as a division of Baldwin) of Chicago.

Although no radical technological changes marked the products displayed at the Chicago World's Columbian Exposition in 1893, the development of the American piano industry was striking in three ways. First, the supply industries, which specialized in the manufacture of actions, soundboards, iron frames, **cases**, **hammers**, **keys**, **strings**, and other parts, revealed a widening market for affordable instruments. Significantly, the supply industries allowed smaller companies with limited capital and production potential to compete in a market increasingly dominated by large firms able to manufacture parts in-house. Among the major piano supply manufacturers were **Pratt**, **Read & Co.**; Strauch Brothers; Wessell, Nickel & Gross; and Wood & Brooks Co. Second, the Chicago Exposition clearly showed that the East no longer monopolized the trade. Western manufacturers, especially those in Cincinnati and Chicago, offered viable competition (even to the point that many eastern manufacturers boycotted the fair). And third, the factory organizer and piano distributor received recognition for the first time because efficient production, management, marketing, and distribution techniques were considered vital to the industry's growth—as exemplified by Steinway, Baldwin, and Kimball.

Reflecting general business trends in the U.S., large firms increasingly dominated the piano industry in the 1890s and early 1900s. These highly capitalized corporations and holding companies, which absorbed by merger dozens of companies and then manufactured pianos under a variety of brand names, became leaders in production as well as in distribution and advertising. Thus, the great number of mergers that took place made the name on a piano's **fallboard** almost meaningless, in that the name, while it denoted a trademark and often a respected history, did not necessarily denote the real maker. Three types of business mergers were common in the piano trade. A *combination* usually maintained a company's individuality, executive officers, and factories. A *consolidation* absorbed a company's identity completely in the new parent corporation. An *amalgamation* resulted when several companies together formed a new corporation. Sale of a trademark did not necessarily devalue the piano name, but neither did it guarantee historical quality.

Intensive brand-name advertising generally kept the public ignorant of real ownership and offered buyers the illusion of greater choice than really existed. The piano brand name supplied a crucial distinction to products that by the late nineteenth century were physically similar in appearance, and offered the purchaser an expression of individuality through the purchase while obscuring the extent of industrial merger and bureaucratic complexity. This situation was made even more intricate by the piano supply industry and by the popularity of "stencil" pianos, which were low- to- medium-grade instruments manufactured anonymously by many piano houses and sold to dealers, who applied fanciful names to the fallboard. The acknowledged leader in the stencil trade was Joseph P. Hale, a pioneer in mass production as well as in progressive methods of mass distribution and merchandising. Dolge called him the "father of the 'commercial' piano of America."

The merger movement and the rise of the affordable commercial piano, as well as the educational and concert promotions by the makers of high-grade instruments (notably Steinway and Baldwin), created an unprecedented market for pianos in the United States. This market was additionally fed by piano sales through mail-order catalogs (Montgomery Ward and Sears, Roebuck were especially successful among the nation's rural folk), and through the new department stores (notably Wanamaker's and Grinnell Bros., who even manufactured their own instruments). Foreign markets, especially in Latin America and Australia, further produced growth through export trade. Yet an analysis of the industry's merger movement reveals that this growing market was not as open as it appeared. For example, although the census listed 255 so-called separate firms in 1914, in reality twenty-five corporations and holding companies produced 74 percent of the total output of some 320,000 pianos.

The most powerful holding companies were also connected to various banks that helped to finance floor planning and expansion. **American Piano Co.** (the largest trust in the industry and the brainchild of George C. Foster and W. B. Armstrong), controlled Knabe and Chickering, among others. Aeolian, Weber Piano & **Pianola Co.** (a multinational holding company under Harry B. Tremaine's [1866–1932] leadership) controlled Pianola, Weber, Steck, and others. **Kohler & Campbell** Industries' vast holdings annually produced almost 26,000 instruments under some twenty brands. Continental Piano Co.'s most famous brands were Jesse French and Smith, Barnes & Strohber. Conway Musical Industries controlled Hallet & Davis. The **Cable Co.** owned Conover-Cable, Cable, and Mason & Hamlin. The enormous Rudolph Wurlitzer Co. was the largest producer of mechanical instruments and player pianos. The most powerful corporations outside these holding companies include Steger & Sons, W. W. Kimball Co., the Baldwin Co. (under Lucien Wulsin I), Jacob Doll & Sons, **Gulbransen**-Dickinson, M. Schulz Co., Starr Piano Co., Hardman, Peck & Co., Steinway & Sons, and Story & Clark. Significantly, these leaders lobbied the U.S. government through the Music Industries Chamber of Commerce in 1916, and were able to convince the War Industries Board to declare pianos to be essential to winning World War I. As a result, American production was not curtailed and by 1918 the United States replaced Germany as the leader in the world piano trade.

The enormous increase in output of the American piano industry from only 25,000 instruments in 1869 (when square pianos still dominated) to 365,000 in 1909 (the peak year for uprights) and 344,000 in 1923 (the peak year for player pianos) would not have resulted without the progressive business practices already noted. But after 1900, the industry enjoyed unprecedented success also because of its connection with the "Tin Pan Alley" songwriting business through the player piano. Almost every American piano company manufactured player instruments. Among the leaders were Aeolian (maker of the famous "Pianola"), Wurlitzer, Seeburg, Gulbransen-Dickinson, and Kohler & Campbell. Progressive advertising campaigns by these leaders enticed Americans to purchase pianos that automatically played music with no effort or musical training. They offered consumers a *musical democracy* that, especially given the used piano trade, would deny the joys of music making to virtually no one. In close connection with music publishers (Tin Pan Alley and the Music Publishers Association), they pioneered the music-recording industry. With **coin-operated** player pianos and **orchestrions**, Wurlitzer and Seeburg fostered the jukebox culture that brought popular songs to the general public for a nickel. Wurlitzer and Seeburg also brought sound to silent movies with the "photoplayer," an automatic piano designed especially for theaters. Significantly, player pianos composed 56 percent of all pianos manufactured in the United States by 1923.

This concentration on automatic instruments proved disastrous. The public, thrilled with the instantaneous musical experience of the player piano, eagerly embraced the less expensive phonograph and radio (sold through many piano stores, ironically). The advent of sound movies ruined the photoplayer industry, also. Alternative entertainments such as the affordable automobile increasingly took the interests of young people away from the piano. Unsound retail sales practices and used pianos, which outsold new instruments by perhaps three-to-one, also hurt the piano industry. By 1926 most companies were experiencing financial problems; by 1929 the industry as a whole suffered a production loss of $67.3 million (retail losses would be about double this figure), of which $49.8 million represented player and reproducing pianos. The National Piano Manufacturers Association worked diligently with the Music Industries Chamber of Commerce and the National Bureau for the Advancement of Music (under Charles Milton Tremaine) to promote piano study in the home and school.

Unfortunately, the success of these efforts was soon lost in the trials of the Great Depression. By 1933 giants in the industry like Wurlitzer, American Piano Co., Aeolian, Baldwin, Kimball, Kohler & Campbell, and Steinway faced unprecedented financial strains, even bankruptcy. Only 34,300 pianos were shipped in 1933. The two men who carried the industry through the depression were Lucien Wulsin II of Baldwin and Theodore E. Steinway, who provided leadership in the New Deal's National Recovery Administration and in the National Piano Manufacturers Association. Their

efforts, together with the introduction of the modern **console piano** in 1935 amid intensive advertising and the nation's return to traditional values (including piano playing) during hard times, restored stability and growth to the industry by 1937—a trend interrupted only briefly by World War II.

Although only a few dozen companies survived the 1920s and 1930s, those that did enjoyed continued growth after 1945 into the 1970s. Annual production in the 1950s averaged almost 172,000 and topped 245,000 by 1965. Then, despite a twelve-year decline, production exceeded 250,000 by 1979. New companies emerged within this prosperity, notably in the South and West, and the industry increasingly became multinational. The decade of the 1980s, however, marked another downturn. Between 1980 and 1989 overall sales of traditional acoustic pianos declined from 233,000 to about 140,000 (though like the 1920s, the 1980s witnessed a slight increase in **grand piano** sales). An unsound domestic economy, severe competition from Japanese, Korean, and other imported pianos, alternative entertainment offered by video games, computers, television, and nontraditional values, and most recently, rivalry with **electronic** keyboards and digital pianos have been calamitous. Earnestly studying the lessons of the past and encouraged by the leadership of Baldwin, Steinway, Kimball, and *The Music Trades* (the industry's historic journal), the trade in 1991 was amid its worst crisis since the 1920s. Time will tell.

See also Loud and Company.

Craig H. Roell

Bibliography

Ayars, Christine Merrick. *Contributions to the Art of Music in America by the Music Industries of Boston, 1640 to 1936.* New York: H. W. Wilson, 1937.

Carson, Gerald. "The Piano in the Parlor, When There Was a Parlor." *Timeline, A Publication of the Ohio Historical Society* 7 (December 1990–January 1991):42–56.

Dolge, Alfred. *Pianos and Their Makers.* Vol. 1. *A Comprehensive History of the Development of the Piano from the Monochord to the Concert Grand Player Piano.* Covina, Cal.: Covina Publishing Co., 1911. Reprint, New York: Dover, 1972. Vol. 2. *Development of the Piano Industry in America Since the Centennial Exhibition at Philadelphia, 1876.* Covina, Cal.: Covina Publishing Co., 1913.

Davis, Robert M. *History of the Code of Fair Competition for the Piano Manufacturing Industry, 19 February 1936*. Washington, D.C.: National Archives Microfilm Publications, Document Series of the National Recovery Administration, 1933–36, microcopy no. 213, roll no. 127, Code no. 91.

Ehrlich, Cyril. *The Piano: A History*. London: Dent, 1976.

Good, Edwin M. *Giraffes, Black Dragons, and Other Pianos: A Technological History from Cristofori to the Modern Concert Grand*. Stanford, Cal.: Stanford University Press, 1982.

Loesser, Arthur. *Men, Women and Pianos: A Social History*. New York: Simon and Schuster, 1954.

The Music Trades. Englewood, N.J.: The Music Trades Corporation, 1890–present.

Ord-Hume, Arthur W. J. G. *Player Piano: The History of the Mechanical Piano and How to Repair It*. London: George Allen & Unwin, 1970.

"Pianofortissimo: In 1935 the Piano Industry Discovered Style." *Fortune* 20 (August 1939): 44–49, 118–20.

Roehl, Harvey N. *Player Piano Treasury: The Scrapbook History of the Mechanical Piano in America as Told in Story, Pictures, Trade Journal Articles and Advertising*. Vestal, N.Y.: The Vestal Press, 1961; 2nd ed., 1973.

Roell, Craig H. *The Piano in America, 1890–1940*. Chapel Hill: University of North Carolina Press, 1989; trade paperback edition, 1991. Extensive bibliography.

————. "The Rise of Tin Pan Alley, 1890–1940." In *America's Musical Pulse: Issues and Aspects of 20th Century American Popular Music*. Edited by Kenneth Bindas. Westport, Conn.: Greenwood Press, 1992.

Spillane, Daniel. *History of the American Pianoforte: Its Technical Development and the Trade*. New York: Daniel Spillane, 1890. Reprint. New York: Da Capo Press, 1969.

White, William Braid. "The Decline of the American Piano Industry." *The American Mercury* 28 (February 1933): 210–13.

UNUSUAL PIANOS

Unusual pianos exist in profusion. The pecularity can consist in the outline of the instrument, in the **soundboard**, in the size, in items related to the **keyboard**, in the portability, in the fact that **strings** are replaced by reeds, metal, glass, or wooden rods, metal springs, etc., in notation possibilities, and even in their combination with other instruments.

Pianos converted as pieces of furniture were frequently made in the nineteenth century.

Sébastien Erard made *pianos-secrétaire* (desk-pianos) in the early nineteenth century. **Square pianos** with desks for conductors existed even earlier in Germany (last quarter of the eighteenth century). During the same period many tea-table pianos were made for the ladies. **Upright pianos** were usually combined with bookcases. Rather unusual was the convertible piano with music stool, which Charles Hess patented in 1866. Inside the base of the piano is hidden a couch on rollers. On the side of the instrument there is a bureau with drawers and a closet fitted with toilet articles. The music-stool contains a workbox, a looking glass, a table, and additional drawers. More recently, in 1933, **Pleyel** designed the *Cortolette* (after the virtuoso Alfred Cortot). This was a small, upright piano with concealable keyboard, a radio, and a phonograph.

Portable pianos are less common. The best known is the **Orphica** invented by Carl Leopold Röllig (Vienna, 1795). The orphica was a single-strung portable piano. The frame was shaped like a harp and extended freely out of the soundbox. A shoulderstrap allowed one to use the instrument for serenades. More common as portable pianos were the small square pianos with folding legs. Giacomo Meyerbeer always took such an instrument with him on his journeys.

Unusual keyboards are of all sorts: curved keyboards, double keyboards, levelled keyboards, transparent keyboards, etc. Curved keyboards are intended to render playing at the extremes of the keyboard easier, since the distance from the body always remains the same. Similar keyboards were invented by Elias Schlegel as early as 1794, by Samuel Hallett (1857), and more recently by Monique de la Brucholerie (195?). She added **keys** in bass and treble so as to extend the compass to the limits of audibility. Mention should also be made of the **Ferdinand Clutsam** keyboard of 1907, which is based upon similar principles.

Pianos with all the keys on the same level were made by Johann Rohleder (Friedland, 1791), Charles Clagget (London, 1789), and Daniel Hewitt (London, 1844). The aim of levelled keys was to avoid uneven depression between the chromatic keys. A transparent keyboard was made by Fournier (Paris, 1971) to allow the placement of the score under the keys.

In 1843 Phiquepal d'Arusmont introduced a

piano with two parallel keyboards: the first had only the white keys, the second only the chromatic keys. Since these uninterrupted rows of keys might lead to confusion, the inventor introduced colored keys at regular intervals.

Pianos in which the strings are replaced by or combined with spring-activated reeds, rods (wooden, glass, metal) are mentioned in the article, *Sostenente* **pianos.**

Pianos with organ pedal added were made by Bellmann (Dresden, 1800), Father Gregoir Trentin, (1817), Pierre Erard (Paris, 1839 and 1844), Loddé (Orléans, 1855), and Guérin (Paris, 1863). **Robert Schumann** composed the *Esquisses pour le piano-pédalier* (Opus 58) for the instrument made by the Pleyel firm (Paris). This pedal could be removed at will.

Pianos with double rows of **hammers** were made by Wilhelm Schiffer (Cologne, 1793) and by **Chappell & Co.** (London, c.1815). The idea was that the second hammer struck the upper octave. Octave couplers were also foreseen with double hammers—or even divided hammers—by Erard (Paris, c.1812), Johann **Streicher** (Paris, 1824), Charles Lemoine (Paris, 1824; here not the upper but the lower octave was struck), Mme. Girard-Romagnac (Paris, 1842), Jean-Louis Boisselot (Marseille, 1843), and S.Warren (Montreal, 1845).

Very unusual is the **grand** pianoforte made by **Robert Wornum** (1830): here the **action** rests upon the bottom of the **case.** The soundboard, with **frame** and strings, is hinged onto the lower part of the case so that the strings are below the soundboard. This makes the action—which is of the **downstriking** type—in fact strike upwards. The **touch** of this instrument is very light.

There have been some unusual soundboards. Elliptical soundboards were made in 1825 by Ernst Eulriot. Double soundboards with soundposts (as in a violin) were experiments by **John Broadwood** (London, 1783), John Anders (1824), and Robert Wolfe (Paris, c.1840). A cylindrical soundboard was made by Erard in his **duoclave piano.** There have also been experiments to replace the wooden soundboard with a drumhead (Charles Clagget, 1788, and Rolfe & Davis, 1797) and to add and adapt the copper bowl of the kettledrum (examples by George Frederic Greiner, 1834; **Jean-Henri Pape,** 1834; Pierre Frederic Fischer, 1835). Samuel Hallett adapted the soundboard to the curve he had given his keyboard (see above).

Pianos that notated the music while it was being played were made by François Joseph Endrès as early as 1864. His idea was taken up again and improved by Baumgarten & Block (Paris, 1870) with the *notographe*, by Landrien in 1874 with the *Landriëno*, by Decuir (Paris, 1894), and by Barthelet (Paris, 1908) with the *pianographe*.

See also Combination Pianos; *Sostenente* Pianos.

F.J. de Hen

Bibliography

Barli, Olivier. *La Facture Française du Piano*. Paris: La Flûte de Pan, 1983.

Bingham, Tony, ed. *Patents for Inventions. Abridgments of Specifications Relating to Music and Musical Instruments. A.D. 1694–1866*. Reprint. London: The Sign of the Serpent, 1984.

Pierre, Constant. *Les Facteurs d'instruments de Musique*. Reprint. Genève: Minkoff, 1976.

UPRIGHT PIANO

Among the various other designations by which this style is known are vertical, **cabinet,** cabinet **grand,** *Ditanaklasis,* dog kennel, cabinet upright, *pianino,* **giraffe,** and pyramid. Appreciated for its compactness, the upright piano has proved itself to be more than merely a convenience for the conservation of floor space. Since its invention more than two centuries ago, it has been built consistently by most major makers and continues to be the most widely sold model today.

Earliest Types in Italy, Germany, and Austria

The first upright piano built was undoubtedly the "pyramid," a tall triangular box that was intended to be placed on either a table or a matching stand. Like its plucked companion, the clavicytherium, this early upright was derived from the familiar grand piano, or *Hammerflügel,* and the harpsichord, or *Kielflügel.* It was simply a grand tipped upward from its keyboard side and placed on a four-legged stand. The height of these earliest pyramids together with their stands could attain as many as an astonishing 274 centimeters, about 9 feet.

The earliest extant example of the upright piano is the pyramid of 1739 built by **Domenico Del Mela** in Florence. This early pyramid now belongs to the Conservatorio di Musica "Luigi

Cherubini" in that city. It has diagonal **stringing**, light-colored wooden naturals, and black-stained sharps, but no hand or knee registers or **pedals**. There are similar examples by Del Mela's German contemporary **Christian Ernst Friederici** in the Goethe Haus in Frankfurt-am-Main, the German National Museum in Nuremberg, and the Musée Instrumental of the Conservatoire Royal de Musique in Brussels. All three of the extant Friedericis date from between 1745 and 1750 and have a *Stossmechanik,* or primitive single **action**.

Later examples of the pyramid style became extremely elaborate. A highly ornate walnut-veneered example by Caspar Schlimbach, built in Königshofen about 1835, is nine feet high; its keyboard is supported at each side by two gilded Moors. Now in the Musikinstrumenten-Museum of the University of Leipzig (No. 192), it formerly belonged to Paul de Wit, an important late-nineteenth-century collector of keyboard instruments.

A new upright style became the fashion in Vienna during the first decade of the nineteenth century. This was the "giraffe," named after its gracefully curving upper **case**, which narrows toward the top and ends with the flourish of a scroll. The upper case of the giraffe was outlined by a tall, wide **frame** decorated by molding. This frame achieved its greater height to the left side of the keyboard and sloped gracefully downward toward the right. The noble expanse of upper case served as a shield for the strings and provided an opportunity for builders to add elaborate decorations to the instruments. Most giraffes had between four and seven pedals, which could demonstrate a remarkable range of sounds, including Turkish **Janissary** effects and the bassoon.

Giraffes remained popular even longer than pyramids and continued to be built until well past the middle of the nineteenth century. Perhaps the earliest maker of giraffes was the brother of Nannette Stein **Streicher**, Matthäus Andreas **Stein**, who frequently signed his name André. Other prominent Viennese builders to produce the new giraffe upright were Joseph Wachtl with his partners Bleyer and Martin Seuffert, and also Johann Jacob Könnicke. In Berlin J. F. Schwarzlose built giraffes, and Christoph Ehrlich produced elaborately detailed examples in Bamberg. The Smithsonian Institution boasts a fine example of this style by Johann Jacob Könnicke (No. 299,844), and the Metropolitan Museum of Art owns a fine André Stein giraffe (No. 1980.218).

The *Lyraflügel*, or lyre piano, is an upright pyramid named for the resemblance of its upper case to a large and grandiose lyre. The Berlin maker **Johann Christian Schleip**, many of whose pianos in this gracious and artistic form are still extant, may have been the inventor of the *Lyraflügel*. Surviving examples of his instruments, which date from the early nineteenth century, can be found in most major collections, including the Württembergisches Landesgewerbe Museum in Stuttgart, the Cincinnati Art Museum, the Musikinstrumenten-Museum in Markneukirchen, Germany, and the Colt Clavier Collection in Bethersden, Kent, England.

England

British builders also sought to develop a piano that could be placed against a wall, thus taking up less floor space in a parlor. The Irishman **William Southwell** invented an unusual and very personal variation of the upright in 1798; he simply tipped a **square** over onto its keyboard side and offered his upright square for sale in his London shop. In 1812, Frederick William Collard **patented** yet another version of the upright square. However, it was the **cabinet piano**, or cabinet upright, that would become the triumphant solution to the problem of placing a long concert instrument in the home. Like the makers of the pyramid before them, builders of this cabinet grand, as it was also called, turned the case upward toward the ceiling and rested the instrument on its wider keyboard side. The instrument was then placed in this seemingly precarious position on a four-legged stand. As a result of this shift, the **hammers** now struck the strings from the rear instead of from beneath. In England this form of upright met with its most successful public response.

Two variants on the original cabinet principle were built. The first was the invention of **William Stodart** in 1795. **Haydn** is said to have been curious enough about this new piano to pay a visit to Stodart's shop especially to see it. The piano contained two shelves to the right of the strings, and the entire upper case was backed with silk pleated into either a gathered rose or a gilt medallion at the center. The second and later model of the cabinet upright had the appearance of a tall armoire with two cupboard doors. The door on the right invariably shielded two or three shelves, convenient for the storage of books or musical scores. Outstanding extant examples of the cabinet upright are one by Stodart from the year 1795; it belongs to the Art Galleries and Museums of Dundee, Scotland. Another by Jones, Round & Co. from about 1810 is part of the Finchcocks Collection, Goudhurst, Kent, England.

In England the cabinet grand continued in popularity well into the nineteenth century. William Southwell took out an English patent for his own new cabinet in 1807. Subsequently he brought out several versions of his original design; some of them, uniquely his own, were never duplicated by other makers. **John Broadwood & Sons,** London, built cabinet uprights for about half a century, discontinuing their production only in 1856. Other eminent London makers of the cabinet grand were **Muzio Clementi** and **Collard & Collard.**

Thomas **Loud** of London not only made cabinet grands but about 1800 was one of the first makers to experiment with the novel idea of extending the strings to the floor. Almost simultaneously, **Matthias Müller** designed his sleek Viennese *Ditanaklasis* on the same principle. This new variation on the upright theme approximates a style that would become the norm before the middle of the nineteenth century. It is the type familiar to us today.

One especially interesting style of the new upright was that designed and patented about 1802 by the London and Philadelphia maker, **John Isaac Hawkins.** This compact little piano was barely 54 inches high. Hawkins called his new invention a **"portable grand pianoforte."** With a keyboard that folds into the case and carrying handles on either side, the portable grand when closed presents a compact, lightweight package that is easily picked up and moved. It is assumed to have been intended to carry aboard ship. The only two known surviving examples of Hawkins's portable are in the Smithsonian Institution (No. 313,619) and in a private collection in Massachusetts. The latter piano was formerly part of The Broadwood Collection, London.

Another type of English upright was the small, low **cottage piano** patented by **Robert Wornum** in 1811. He began manufacturing it in London about 1814. Like Hawkins's portable, the cottage piano is distinguished by vertical stringing that reaches all the way to the floor. It has an English double action of the hopper, or **jack,** type, which is also called the **"sticker" action.** John Broadwood & Sons, Muzio Clementi, Knowles & Allen, and Collard & Collard were among the several other important London makers of the cottage piano. In 1828, Wornum further refined his upright action with an improved **check,** later called a "birdcage" in the United States. According to Rosamond E. M. Harding, small uprights continued to be known in England as cottage pianos until 1836.

France

The French *piano droit* is an upright piano with oblique stringing: the bass strings begin at the upper left corner and extend to the lower right corner near the floor. Although this method of stringing had first been mentioned by Thomas Loud in his patent, London, 1802, it had been used much earlier by Christian Ernst Friederici in his pyramid piano of 1745. Despite the early recognition of the oblique stringing method, the practice did not come into general use until nineteenth-century Paris makers brought it into fashion.

Erard, the great rival to **Pleyel et Cie** in Paris, concentrated more effort on grands although not entirely dismissing the upright model. Pleyel, on the other hand, borrowed Wornum's idea for the cottage piano. Renaming it *pianino,* Pleyel quickly won the approval of the French public in 1815, after bringing out his imitation, complete with Wornum's upright action. The Pleyel factory continued to develop the pianino upright, including an adaptation of Wornum's **tape-check action,** throughout the nineteenth century.

In the year 1828 in Paris, **Jean-Henri Pape,** recently arrived from Alsace, patented his **console,** a low upright model whose upper case was virtually non-existent, the lower case containing action and strings. Pape's instrument was the first to be cross-strung, the bass strings passing over the treble. This meant that the strings could be longer than if straight-strung. **Cross-stringing,** an invention adopting a principle in general use up to the present day, gives considerably more sonority to the **tone** of the instrument. As on the *pianino,* the pedals of the console were attached at the bottom of the lower case itself, instead of to a lyre.

Pape's console, or *piano-console*, was only about 40 inches high. The console model was especially popular in France during the middle of the nineteenth century and was made not only by Pape but in similar versions by Pleyel and Erard as well. Also important as mid-nineteenth-century manufacturers of consoles were Blanchet et Roller and François Soufleto. The latter produced an unusual design known as a "dog kennel" because of the arched opening at the bottom center of the lower case. An early German maker of consoles during the 1830s was Bernhard Klinkerfuss in Stuttgart.

Many European upright pianos built during the latter part of the nineteenth century were extremely elaborate. Some cases were veneered with exotic rosewood, burl walnut, amboyna, or curly mahogany and decorated with generous gilded brass scrolls, medallions, and acanthus leaves. Natural **keys** were sometimes covered with mother-of-pearl, while sharps might be veneered with tortoise shell. Also practical and therefore popular were candle sconces or candlesticks, which were attached to the extreme right and left sides of the upper case. In England a broken pediment in the style of Thomas Chippendale was frequently placed at the top of the upper case; or a heavy carved molding might be set around the upper edge of an instrument.

United States

In the United States the square and, to some extent, the grand dominated commercial production until the latter part of the nineteenth century. Not until the 1870s, when **Steinway** began extensive manufacture of an American cross-strung upright, did American builders begin the trend that eventually resulted in the overwhelming preference of the upright in the United States.

New York was the first major center for the construction of the American upright piano. Indeed, the New York maker Joseph P. Hale, a leader in the race, was acclaimed by **Alfred Dolge** as the "father of the 'commercial' piano of America." His shrewd attention to the business of selling his instruments convinced the public that the piano—the upright piano—was an indispensable cultural asset to nearly every American home. By 1900 his list of **serial numbers** had reached 70,000; this meant that he was

building at least a thousand uprights per year. Other manufacturers were not to be outdone. Steinway & Sons ceased production of squares altogether in 1888, and, constantly concerned with the advancement of quality, had filed twenty-three upright patents by 1900.

Among other early successful builders of cheap uprights were the **Decker Brothers**, George Steck, and **Kohler and Campbell** in New York, and **Frederick Mathushek**, first in New Haven and from 1871 in New York. Makers in Philadelphia and Boston were concerned more with the square and the grand during the early and middle nineteenth century. However, later Chicago builders, such as William Wallace **Kimball**, H. D. **Cable**, and George P. Bent, established companies that became important manufacturers of upright pianos late in the century. In Cincinnati the **Baldwin Company's** production of what had become a ubiquitous model reached dynamic proportions by the turn of the twentieth century.

A modern small cross-strung upright about forty inches high and similar in appearance to Jean-Henri Pape's 1828 console appeared on the market in the 1920s. This model, usually called either console or **spinet**, was first presented by Winter & Co. and the Haddorff Piano Co. During the 1930s many other makers, including Baldwin and **Gulbransen**, seized the opportunity to develop the market potential of the new console. Later acquisition of such companies as Acrosonic, Hamilton, and Howard allowed Baldwin to dominate American spinet production, and thus the world's market for them in the twentieth century.

Twentieth-century consoles usually boast decorator cases with delicately carved moldings. Conveniently sized for a small sitting room, this little piano has enjoyed tremendous sales success. However, as a musical instrument, it suffers from a limited dynamic range and inadequate tone. Its low music stand is placed at a correct angle for a child's eyes, doubtless a factor in its popularity as a practice piano for the young.

Latest trends in uprights from the most important world makers, including **Yamaha** in Japan, Steinway and Baldwin in the United States, and the Korean and Taiwanese firms that anonymously supply dealers worldwide, include the studio upright, a vertical piano of about four to five feet in height. Although simple in de-

Upright Piano by Baldwin Piano & Organ Company.

sign, its compact case houses a better mechanism and larger **soundboard** than its cousin, the spinet. Altogether more satisfactory in tone and action, this current manifestation of the upright principle is cleanly designed, serviceable, comparatively cheap, and easily regulated. It has found a place in the music school and conservatory, the home, and the theater as a practice or rehearsal instrument.

The modern upright is no longer intended as an instrument of visual wonder. Its case is rather prim in appearance, and its comparatively inexpensive veneers are usually limited to stained fruitwood or an even more sober ebonized finish. The keys are covered with plastic, which is in itself almost a symbol of its present unpretentious and humble status.

Martha Novak Clinkscale

Bibliography

Barli, Olivier. *La Facture française du piano de 1840 à nos jours.* Paris: La Flûte de Pan, 1983.

Bonaventura, Arnaldo." Domenico Del Mela e il primo pianoforte verticale." *Bolletino della Società mugellana di studi storici*, anno IV, n.1, 1928: 1–10.

Dolge, Alfred. *Pianos and Their Makers. A Comprehensive History of the Development of the Piano from the Monochord to the Concert Grand Player Piano.* Covina: 1911; New York: Dover Publications, Inc., 1972.

Ehrlich, Cyril. *The Piano: A History.* London, Toronto and Melbourne: J. M. Dent & Sons Ltd., 1976.

Good, Edwin M. *Giraffes, Black Dragons, and Other Pianos. A Technological History from Cristofori to the Modern Concert Grand.* Stanford, Cal.: Stanford University Press, 1982.

Groce, Nancy Jane. "Musical Instrument Making in New York City during the Eighteenth and Nineteenth Centuries." 2 vols. Ph.D. dissertation, University of Michigan, 1982; rev. ed. New York: Pendragon Press, 1990.

Haine, Malou. *Les Facteurs d'instruments de musique à Paris au XIXe siècle: Des artisans face à l'industrialisation.* Brussels: Editions de l'Université de Bruxelles, 1985.

Harding, Rosamond E.M. *The Piano-Forte: Its History Traced to the Great Exhibition of 1851.* Cambridge: Cambridge University Press, 1933. Reprints, New York: Da Capo Press, 1973; Old Woking, Surrey: Gresham Books, 1978.

Ratcliffe, Ronald V. *Steinway.* San Francisco: Chronicle Books, 1989.

Roell, Craig H. *The Piano in America, 1890–1940.* Chapel Hill & London: The University of North Carolina Press, 1989.

Spillane, Daniel. *History of the American Pianoforte: Its Technical Development, and the Trade.* New York: D. Spillane, 1890. Reprint. New York: Da Capo Press, Inc., 1969.

UPWEIGHT

See Touchweight

VERSCHIEBUNG

Verschiebung is the German word for "displacement," meaning the **una corda** stop.
   See also Pedals and Stops.

Edwin M. Good

VERTICAL PIANO

See Upright Piano

VIENNESE ACTION

See Prellmechanik; Actions

VIENNESE PIANO, THE

Unlike the piano industries of Paris and London, Viennese piano building does not seem to have come from a strong tradition of harpsichord building. Whereas English and French **grand pianos** show survivals of harpsichord construction techniques even in the late nineteenth century, Viennese construction was conceived in terms of piano requirements from the late eighteenth century onwards.

The typical Viennese grand of circa 1790 had a range of five octaves from FF to f^3 or g^3, and had a Viennese **action**. It was duple strung except for the top octave and a half or so, which was frequently triple strung. The wooden **frame** consisted of a thick inner **rim** extending from the **soundboard** to the bottom with various **braces** running from the **bentside** to the **belly-rail**, the **spine**, and the bottom. The bentside of the rim was made by joining pieces of wood so that the grain ran more or less parallel to the

curve at any point. This made possible a thick rim without the difficulties inherent in bending a straight piece to a curve. This design is not a part of harpsichord building; the lower tensions of harpsichords make such heavy construction unnecessary. The outer bentside of Viennese-style pianos was usually quite thin and had little structural importance. This thin bentside makes Viennese pianos look frail compared to their English contemporaries, which were built like harpsichords and as such required massive bentsides.

The early Viennese instruments show a number of characteristics that were to remain typical of Viennese piano building in the nineteenth century. The Viennese action is one; it remained in production until well into the twentieth century. The early instruments with their small, light **hammers** have a very shallow, light action. In much of the literature about pianos, one gets the impression that this lightness is somehow inherent in the Viennese action *per se*. This is not the case. Heavy hammers inevitably are harder to move than light ones, and as hammers increased in weight throughout most of the nineteenth century, so did the **touch** grow heavier. The Viennese action was relatively easy to make in a small shop, and if properly designed and executed, it was as good as or better than the other types of single-**escapement** action.

The heavy full-depth rim also survived, and it grew heavier. Whereas it was difficult to increase the strength of harpsichord-derived frames past a certain point without metal reinforcement, the Viennese type of construction could readily be made heavier to withstand the tension of heavier **strings**. Consequently, iron bars did not become common in Viennese pianos until about 1845. The heavy inner rim of the modern grand piano is derived from the old Viennese construction.

The wedge-shaped **dampers** the Viennese used to damp bass strings are still with us, and not only in Vienna. As bass strings grew heavier in the course of the nineteenth century, wedge dampers became the standard for bass dampers outside Vienna. Around 1850 **felt** wedges replaced the earlier **leather**-covered wooden wedges.

Musically it is noteworthy that from the late eighteenth century on, the Viennese piano makers seem to have concerned themselves

427

with sustained, "singing" trebles. As obvious an ideal as this may seem today, it was not so entirely obvious in the late eighteenth century; English grand pianos of the period are much less "singing" in the upper register.

Finally, the commercial organization of the Viennese piano industry should be noted. Whereas in England and France the production of grand pianos was mostly by two or three leading makers, in Vienna there were dozens of makers of grand pianos. Three or four eminent makers had the greatest prestige, but their production was only a small part of the total output. The outlook of these makers was in good part that of traditional craftsmen rather than that of corporate businessmen. Viennese nameplates sometimes describe the maker as the pupil of a famous maker, and if the pupil took over the master's shop, he described himself as successor to his master. This is in contrast to the modern notion of a maker's name as a trademark that can be sold to someone of a different family.

The changes in Viennese piano-building from around 1790 to around 1840 involve the musical characteristics of the instrument rather than new mechanisms or materials. The most obvious change was the expansion of the **keyboard** range: from five octaves (FF–f^3 or g^3) it expanded to six octaves (FF–f^4) by 1808, and pianos with a range of six and a half octaves (CC–f^4) were available on order during the 1810s. This latter range gradually became more common and was standard on large grands (often with two additional notes to g^4) until about 1840.

From about 1815 on, most pianos were triple-strung throughout, except for the lowest few notes (usually only CC to EE). At the same time string diameters increased considerably, particularly in the treble. To withstand the higher tension, pianos were built much heavier; a large Viennese grand of about 1825 was about twice the weight (or more) of the instruments of thirty years earlier. The hammers, striking heavier strings on a larger, heavier soundboard, were growing heavier too, and while the key **dip** remained shallow, the resistance became considerably greater.

By the mid-1840s a seven-octave range from AAA was appearing on the large grands; brass bass strings were replaced by overspun steel strings, and the wooden **frame** was being rein-forced by iron bars, usually two in number, from wrest plank to bentside. By 1850 *capo tasto* bars were commonly used in the treble. Metal **hitch pin plates** were available as options from the 1840s on, but most grand pianos, particularly the large ones, did without them until about 1870. The heavier strings of these later pianos required larger, heavier dampers, especially in the bass. Earlier, the dampers had been mounted on thin strips of wood, shaped a little like dog-leg harpsichord jacks, and guided by a box-shaped construction with slots in the top. The later pianos have dampers that are hinged to a wooden frame above the strings.

The later type of Viennese piano here described was made as late as the 1920s by minor makers. The inherent cheapness of the design made it survive even long after other styles of piano had become common. It will be observed that this type of instrument had evolved directly from the Viennese piano of **Mozart**'s day, but as a musical instrument it is very much suited to the music of **Brahms**'s era, not Mozart's. The hammers had become large and heavy; the outer covering was still leather, but there was usually a thick layer of felt underneath. Although the **touch** of such pianos is heavy, the mechanism is very responsive, and the better instruments can produce very faint *pianissimos* without the use of the *una corda* **pedal**. There is a fair range of **tone** color available with the different dynamic levels. The tone tends to be rather dark and sustained even in the top register. The articulation at the beginning of the tone is fairly pronounced.

At the same time that makers were producing these late developments of Viennese piano making, there was also experimentation with other possibilities. While the usual Viennese grand piano had a Viennese action, some makers, Johann Baptist **Streicher** in particular, offered other choices. Some of these, such as Streicher's **downstriking** action, were oddities that led nowhere, but a fair number of pianos with Anglo-German actions survive, and J.B. Streicher also made a few pianos with English-derived actions. Viennese work in French and English styles was exhibited at the 1845 Viennese **Exhibition**. Impressed by **Steinway** pianos and their success at international exhibitions, Streicher produced a Steinway-style instrument for the 1867 Paris Exhibition, although the bulk of the firm's production continued along more traditional lines for years afterward. **Schweig-hofer, Ehrbar, Bösendorfer,** and others were also interested, and by the late 1870s **overstrung** pianos were a commercially available option in Vienna. "Option" is the key word in understanding this situation; in 1892 Schweighofer offered overstrung pianos with one-piece cast-iron frames and double escapement actions. They also offered overstrung one-piece frame instruments with Viennese actions and straight-strung composite plate instruments with Viennese actions.

The Viennese action continued to be commonly manufactured after World War I, but it increasingly was regarded as obsolete. It, of course, lacked double escapement, and the touch was markedly different from that of the double-escapement actions that had become the international standard.

World Wars, depressions, and the dismantling of the Austro-Hungarian Empire were all damaging to the Viennese piano industry, and today only Bösendorfer remains of all the Viennese makers of concert quality pianos.

Edmund M. Frederick

Bibliography

Haupt, Helga. "Wiener Instrumentenbauer von 1791 bis 1815." In *Studien zur Musikwissenschaft, Beihefte der Denkmäler der Tonkunst in Österreich,* 24 Bd., Graz-Wien-Köln 1960, S.120 ff.

Luithlen, Victor, ed. *Katalog der Sammlung alter Musikinstrumente. Part 1: Saitenklaviere.* Kunsthistorisches Museum, Vienna, 1960.

Ottner, Helmut. *Wiener Instrumentenbau 1815–1833.* Tutzing, 1977.

VIOLIN PIANO

The violin piano was a self-acting piano combined with a violin, the whole played automatically from a music roll or barrel.

The different techniques required to strike piano **strings** and to bow and finger the violin's strings were complexities that attracted several inventors. Around 1907, a man named Wauters, who worked for the Automatic Musical Instrument Company of Binghamton, New York, experimented with a pneumatically operated solo violin that he called the *Royal Violista*, but the first practical automatic violin piano was made in limited numbers by the German firm of Hegeler & Ehlers in 1908 and called the *Geigenpiano*. This was an **upright piano** with a violin placed horizontally on top and played as a unison with the upper register of the piano using a **sticker action.**

There were several other similar inventions, including a barrel-operated piano violin, but the first maker to achieve unquestionable success was **Hupfeld** & Co. of Leipzig, which in 1910 introduced the Phonoliszt-Violina. Developed from the company's successful upright **expression piano** called the *Phonoliszt,* a separate cabinet on top of the instrument housed three violins mounted vertically and encompassed by a rotating horsehair bow. Pneumatic fingers played one string on each violin and specially arranged music rolls produced a highly sophisticated piano-violin combination. The instrument was made in large numbers.

In 1905, a Swedish emigre, Henry Sandell, working for the Mills Novelty Company in Chicago, produced the Automatic Virtuoso, an electro-mechanically played violin, thought to have been inspired by the Swedish folk instrument, the *nykelharpa* or keyed violin. By 1909, Sandell had added a piano to the violin, renaming it the Violano-Virtuoso. This was to be the most renowned of all American mechanical musical instruments and one that was sold worldwide between 1912 and 1930. The automatic, keyless piano was distinctive in having a symmetrical iron **frame** with the bass notes in the center.

A late violin piano was the Violinovo made by Popper & Company of Leipzig and marketed in a limited manner during 1930. This was a roll-operated piano **orchestrion** with a horizontally mounted violin played by pneumatic action.

Arthur W.J.G. Ord-Hume

Bibliography

Bowers, Q.David. *Encyclopedia of Automatic Musical Instruments.* Vestal, N.Y.: Vestal Press, 1972.

Ord-Hume, Arthur W. J. G. "The Violano-Virtuoso and Its Swedish Origins." In *Music & Automata,* 1 (London, 1984.): 134–142.

VIRGIL PRACTICE CLAVIER, THE

The Virgil Clavier refers to several models of toneless keyboard instruments devised and **patented** by Almon Kincaid Virgil (b. Erie, Pa., 13 August 1839 or 1842; d. St. Petersburg, Fla., 15 October 1921) and Amos Cole Bergman (b. New York, N.Y., 15 September 1865; d. Bergenfield,

"Virgil Perfected Practice Clavier" by A.K. Virgil Company, New York City c. 1905. Owned by Dorothea A. Nahm.

N.J., 10 July 1948). Unlike various other practice keyboards, the Virgil instruments incorporated adjustable simulated piano **action** and were devised principally in support of a very specific teaching method. The Virgil method and clavier manufacturing operation flourished during the late nineteenth and early twentieth centuries with relative success, but is now essentially forgotten.

Almon Virgil had considerable training in voice and piano as a youth and later continued studies of voice and organ with Samuel Jackson and piano with William Mason. After gaining experience giving private instruction, Virgil founded a music conservatory in Fort Wayne, Indiana (July 1871), followed by another in Burlington, Iowa (1877).

In Burlington he met Antha Minerva Patchen (b. Elmira, N.Y., 6 February 1852; d. Park Ridge, N.J., 4 February 1939), a private piano teacher who became interested in his method of group piano instruction and joined the Conservatory faculty. In 1878 she and Virgil were married. The following year they moved to Peoria, Illinois, and opened a music school that continued until 1883. That fall they moved to New York City, where teaching activities stopped for a while and Mr. Virgil concentrated on the development of a practice keyboard instrument, first called the *Techniphone*. His Techniphone Co. began in 1884 with limited success for about four years. *The Virgil Clavier Method: Foundation Exercises* Book 1 was published in 1889, but Virgil devoted most of his time to improving his Clavier. The Virgil Clavier Company was formed in 1890, and Antha opened his Virgil Piano School in New York in 1891. In 1895 Virgil traveled abroad to England and Berlin where he founded schools and published *The Virgil Clavier Method: Foundation Exercises* Book 2 (1896). Other schools were to follow in

Chicago (late 1896), Boston (1899), and other cities, including St. Petersburg, Florida, where he died in 1921.

Over a twenty-seven-year period (1883–1910) Virgil obtained eight U.S. patents for an "exercising keyboard for musicians," which by the early 1890s became a relatively successful practice instrument marketed as the "Virgil Perfected Practice Clavier." More to the point, it was a necessary part of the very specific teaching method developed by the Virgils.

The Virgil Clavier available in the 1890s through c. 1920 offered three main features in addition to being a neighbor-friendly practice instrument. First, it supposedly simulated piano action. In particular, by the use of lead weights suspended a few millimeters over the rear end of the **keys**, it simulated the faint first impact of the **jack** slipping off the **hammer knuckle** followed by the immediate stronger impact of the key front contacting its **felt**. A second feature offered weight-of-touch control from two to twenty ounces, although the Method exercises specify no more than five ounces. A handle positioned on the **nameboard** operated a steeply pitched $3/8$ machine screw (eight threads to the inch), which advanced a **leather**-faced wooden batten against coiled springs mounted vertically on the rear of the keys. A poor design, it made a heavier action by intro-

An advertisement of the Virgil Practice Clavier offering various forms of relief.

ducing friction and not weight, thus tending to slow the return. A third feature was a clicking sound available on the down-and/or up-stroke of each key to develop proper timing and key release. This involved a pair of adjustable machine screws perforating each key to strike two brass click rails mounted on battens on the **case** bottom. Either up or down clicks could be set to on or off by moving levers at either end of the **keyboard**, which would raise or lower the click rails by a sliding reverse wedges system. The down and up click levers were at the treble and bass ends of the keyboard respectively.

The Virgil Clavier was equipped with folding legs and therefore declared portable, although the seven-octave model weighed between 90 and 100 pounds. Portability was emphasized by the manufacturer, and an advertising circular from around 1900 includes an item called "The Clavier in Camp," with a sketch of a clavier and folding camp stool in an inviting outdoor setting. The factory also offered a five-octave model, and various wood **finishes** were available, including solid oak with light stain and poplar finished to appear as mahogany or other woods. Two- and four-octave models in fibre carrying cases were eventually offered with or without clicks. The key covers for all models were generally made of celluloid.

The Virgil Clavier was first marketed in 1884 under the trade name "Techniphone." A July 1886 advertisement in *The Etude* states:

> The Techniphone is no longer an experiment. During the past two years it has been put to the severest tests of daily use in schools and conservatories, and by the most distinguished musicians, and no [*sic*] one has ever been returned.

The ad included testimonials from artists such as Julie Rivé King (1857–1937), with a drawing of the instrument positioned to suggest that it be placed at a right angle or at least adjacent to one's piano.

No example of the Techniphone has apparently survived, and it is therefore assumed that its click mechanism involved a bizarre device described in the first four of Virgil's eight patents. Virgil called his original click mechanism a "speaking spring." A batten at the rear of the case contained a row of spring steel tabs, each with its free end originally making constant tension contact with a screw perforating the rear end of the key and later with a **capstan** mounted on each key for better adjustability. Each spring was flexed by its key in either direction to the point that it would yield a snapping or clicking sound similar to the metal cricket toys that were once popular. The up and down clicks were always engaged, and the timing, maintenance, and adjustability were problematic at best. Virgil's sixth and seventh patents in 1888 and 1892 claim authorship of the direct striking click mechanisms to which he reverted in his "Perfected Clavier."

A third form of the Virgil Clavier appeared soon after Mr. and Mrs. Virgil's separation in 1900 or 1901. She retained their Virgil School in New York City while his company retained the branch schools in London and Berlin plus the New York factory and a smaller branch factory in Berlin. However, he quickly enlarged his operation with the installation of a competing school in New York and others in several eastern and midwestern cities. Mrs. Virgil countered by publishing her own version of the Virgil Method (Vol. 1, 1902; Vol. 2, 1905), followed by nearly 250 of her own graded piano compositions. She also set up a competing clavier factory in Bergenfield, New Jersey (1901), under the management of Amos C. Bergman, a New York area piano technician and inventor whom she married in 1902.

Between 1901 and 1912, Bergman obtained eight U.S. patents for practice-clavier design. The new Mrs. A.M. Virgil instrument designed by Bergman was marketed under the intentionally different trade name "Tekniklavier" and quickly nicknamed the "Tek." Its action was superior, with a more stable feeling, having the two striker screws for the click effect perforating a rocker arm element positioned above each key. The click rails were elevated in the case and swiveled in or out of position by levers at either end of the keyboard as on the A. K. Virgil instruments. The system was not only easier to adjust but rendered the up-click and down-click actions roughly equal to each other. The up-click motion on the A. K. Virgil instrument had a tendency to bounce and required a light hold-down spring at the rear of each key.

The Tekniklavier weight-of-touch mechanism was similar to the Virgil instruments but with springs attached to a swiveling batten on the **spine** of the case exerting a down pressure on the rear of each key. Bergman's actions take better advantage of gravity than the earlier attemps by Virgil. The Tekniklavier was similarly offered in the seven- or five-octave folding leg models and two- or four-octave suitcase models.

Mrs. Virgil's advertising late in the first quarter of the century displays an attempt at marketing an economy model called the "New Bergman Clavier." Illustrations of it show a case design similar to the A. K. Virgil instrument, although it probably had one of Bergman's patented actions. No example is known to have survived. It likely arrived too late to realize much production during the final, waning phase of Virgil Method teaching.

The Virgil operations were relatively immense, with three clavier factories between them (the branch in Berlin also made pianos), Virgil schools on both sides of the Atlantic, two separate publishing operations, correspondence courses, and numerous certified Virgil teachers advertising as far from the home operations as Sydney, Australia, and Madras, India. Several thousand claviers were manufactured, and want ads seeking to sell or buy used claviers were not uncommon after 1900. Those relatively few that surface today are usually A. K. Virgil instruments. Some are still in limited use, although few owners are aware that they were meant to be more than merely practice instruments. The Virgil Claviers were praised by period luminaries such as Vladimir de Pachmann, Moritz Moszkowski, and Mrs. H. H. A. Beach, but with the death of Almon Virgil's second wife, Florence Dodd in 1945, the Virgil Method was curiously soon forgotten.

See also Keyboard Practice and Exercise Aids.

Dorothea A. Nahm and Robert E. Sheldon

Bibliography

Brower, Harriette. *Piano Mastery.* 2 vols. New York: Frederick Stokes Co., 1915 –1917.

Nahm, Dorothea Agnes. "The Virgil Clavier and Keyboard Pedagogy Method." D.M.A. dissertation, Catholic University of America, 1983.

———. "The Virgil Clavier Pedagogy Method" *The Piano Quarterly* 129 (Spring 1985): 48–55.

———. "Etudes, The Virgil Method." *Keyboard Classics* (May–June 1985): 38–9.

Virgil, Almon Kincaid. *Education In Music: Lessons to Teachers in the Instruction of Parents.* New York: A.K. Virgil, 1907.

———. *The Virgil Clavier Method: Foundation Exercises in Pianoforte Playing; To Be Used on the Practice Clavier or Pianoforte.* Book 1, 1st ed. New York: Edward Schuberth and Co.; 6th ed. New York: Virgil Practice Clavier Co., 1895; 9th ed. New York: A. K. Virgil, 1904.

———. *The Virgil Clavier Method: Foundation Exercises.* Book 2, 1st ed. New York: The Virgil Piano School, 1896; 3rd ed. New York: A.K. Virgil, 1906.

———. *Step By Step: Text-Book in Piano Playing; Handbook for Teachers.* New York: A. K. Virgil, 1904.

Virgil, Mrs. A. M. *The Virgil Method of Piano Technique.* Book 1, New York: Mrs. A. M. Virgil, 1902; rev. 1931.

———. *The Virgil Method of Piano Technique.* Book 2, New York: Mrs. A. M. Virgil, 1905.

VOICING

Voicing, sometimes called **tone** regulating, is the practice of adjusting the timbre and dynamic range of a piano. Unlike **tuning**, which is mostly a precise and objective craft, voicing is unavoidably subjective. The technician must rely heavily on personal taste and experience to decide what kind of timbre is possible and desirable for a given piano and what techniques to use to bring about the desired results.

Before a piano can be voiced properly it must be well tuned and regulated. The **hammer** heads should be free of **string** grooves, and hammers should be well aligned to their corresponding strings in all respects.

For the modern piano, voicing is done mostly by manipulating the hammer **felt**. To achieve a louder or more brilliant tone, lacquer or other hardeners are applied. To achieve a mellower tone, needles are used to soften the felt (liquid hammer softeners are also an option, although few technicians experiment with them). The shape of the hammer itself can also be changed to affect the tone, although most technicians prefer to keep the hammers as close as possible to their original shape.

Discriminating pianists routinely make their tastes known to their technicians, who try, to the extent that it is practical, to favor their clients' wishes when doing the job.

Steven R. Manley

WALTER, ANTON (1752–1826)

Anton Walter was born in Neuhausen a. d. Fildern/Swabia in south Germany (5 February 1752) and died in Vienna (11 April 1826). Though baptized Gabriel Anton, Walter apparently never used the name Gabriel. His father was a carpenter and *ludimagister* [organist], his mother of Italian origin. Anton Walter probably came to Vienna already trained as a piano builder in 1778 (?), settled in one of the suburbs, and quickly won a name for himself as an instrument restorer. In January 1780 he married the widow of Franz **Schöfftoss**, Anna Elisabeth, *née* Reisinger (1748–1818). In February 1781 he was called to castle Esterháza, where he stayed for twelve days repairing the castle's keyboard instruments, for which he received twenty-four Gulden.

From 1780 until 1790 he built and sold 350 **fortepianos**, according to his own statement in his letter to Emperor Leopold II. Between 1782 and 1784, **Wolfgang Amadeus Mozart** purchased one of Walter's fortepiano **grands**. Prior to May 1785, this instrument was reinforced by a *pianoforte pedale*, which Mozart probably also acquired from Walter, and its use was announced in an advertisement of a concert in the Burgtheater on 10 May 1785. While the *pianoforte pedale* instrument was lost after Mozart's death, his original grand fortepiano remained in the possession of his widow Constanze and was given by her to their son Carl in 1810, "after it was repaired by Walter by whom it is" (according to a letter Constanze wrote to Carl in 1810). Today this instrument is in the posses-

sion of the Mozarteum in Salzburg, again restored and now exhibited in Mozart's birth house.

During the 1780s Anton Walter had worked without the official *Meisterrecht*, for which he could have been legally prosecuted under Empress Maria Theresa but was tolerated under Emperor Joseph II, who finally broke the power of the guilds in Austria in 1789. Prior to that year Walter may not have been officially allowed to build instruments and to sell them in the city of Vienna and, therefore, perhaps may have often refrained from signing his instruments. Only in 1791 did Anton Walter receive the *Meisterrecht* and perform the Viennese *Bürgereid*. By then he had delivered four pianoforte instruments to the Imperial Court. In December 1790 Emperor Leopold II granted him the title *k.k. Orgel- und Instrumentbauer*. Instruments built by Walter are signed *Anton Walter in Wien* (only after 1789?); instruments built after approximately 1800 are signed *Anton Walter und Sohn in Wien*, because by then Anton Walter worked together with his elder stepson, Joseph Schöfftoss (1767–1824).

In his application letter to Emperor Leopold II, dated December 1790, Walter claimed to have been the first in Vienna to build pianos "as they are now in general use," a phrase that is ambiguous but probably referred to the *Prellmechanik* or "Viennese action" as developed first in the 1770s by Johann Andreas **Stein**(?), which he slightly changed (*Metallkapseln*). He also stated in this letter that in spite of the fact that his instruments were the most expensive ones, he had sold 350 *Claviere* (a number which certainly also included **square pianos** and so-called *Giraffenclaviere*, though he may have built more grand pianos than anybody else in Vienna).

By 1790 he employed fourteen craftsmen; from 1804 onwards he employed twenty workers. Among his employees were the organ builder Ignaz Seuffert from Würzburg, Joseph Wachtl, and Jakob Bleyer. Seuffert was an especially talented creative instrument builder, who later founded a company with Wachtl and Bleyer but finally separated from the others and established his own workshop, which became a winner of a gold medal in 1845 at the World **Exhibition**. According to E. L. Gerber (*Neues historisch biographisches Lexikon der Tonkünstler*, Leipzig 1814, vol. 4, p. 192), as long as Seuffert worked for Walter it was mainly he who was responsible for the construction of an *organisiertes Querfortepiano*, a **combination** of a **Tafelklavier** and an organ, for which Walter received 3,000 fl. However, Anton Walter himself had also built at least one (small ?) organ, a fact that is documented in his letter to the Emperor published by Rice.

More than thirty fortepianos of Anton Walter are known to be extant today. Some of the older grand pianos show differences in **case** and **soundboard** construction as well as in the **action**, one of them being Mozart's fortepiano, another one the Walter piano now in the Burgenländisches Landes-Museum in Eisenstadt, proof of the creative mind of Anton Walter; it was not at all unusual for an instrument builder of his time to experiment in construction details. The sound of Walter's grand pianos was described in the eighteenth century as "singing and full" (Schönfeld), and prior to 1800 Walter's pianos sounded certainly more "romantic" and thus more modern than those of Johann Andreas Stein and his children. Not only Mozart, but also **Beethoven** considered Walter's instruments to be the best, and Beethoven wanted to own one when he was still able to act as a performing artist in Vienna. Walter's main competitor among Viennese piano builders was **Johann Schantz**, whose instruments had an equally voluminous but still more distinct **tone**.

A square piano signed *Anton Walter und Sohn* was used by Franz Schubert in the atelier of the painter Wilhelm August Rieder, who first had rented it for his friend. After Schubert's death Rieder decided to buy it. Later it was in the possession of Ludwig **Bösendorfer** and presently it can be seen in the Instrument Collection of the Kunsthistorisches Museum in Vienna.

During the 1790s Walter had been accused of sympathizing with revolutionary forces (*Jakobiner*) but was finally acquitted (the relevant documents in Viennese archives still need to be properly investigated). This event may well have been the reason why Walter preferred afterwards to live most of the time outside of Vienna.

Prior to approximately 1805, Anton Walter was no doubt Vienna's most successful piano builder and collected a considerable fortune; however, between 1815 and 1820 the fame of Walter's instruments diminished considerably, which may have embittered the ambitious man towards the end of his life.

Eva Badura- Skoda

Bibliography

Franz, Gottfried von. "Mozarts Klavierbauer Anton Walter." *Neues Mozart-Jahrbuch I.* Edited by Erich Valentin. Regensburg: Gustav Bosse, 1941: 211–217.

Haupt, Helga. "Wiener Instrumentenbauer von 1791 bis 1815." In *Studien zur Musikwissenschaft, Beihefte der Denkmäler der Tonkunst in Österreich* Vol. 24. Wien: 1960. P. 182.

Luithlen, Victor. "Der Eisenstädter Walterflügel." *Mozart-Jahrbuch* 1954, p.206f.

Meer, John Henry van der. "Mozarts Hammerflügel." In *Congress Report of the IXth International Congress of the International Musicological Society.* Salzburg: 1964. P. 273f

———. "Walter, Gabriel Anton." In *Die Musik in Geschichte und Gegenwart.* Vol. 14.

New Grove Dictionary of Music and Musicians. S.v. "Walter, Gabriel Anton," by Maribel Meisel and Philip R. Belt. Vol. 20, 1980.

Restle, Konstantin. "Mozarts Hammerflügel." In *Kongressbericht Salzburg 1991, Mozart-Jahrbuch 1989–1991* (im Druck).

Rice, John A. "Anton Walter, Instrument Maker to Leopold II." *Journal of the American Musical Instrument Society* 15 (1989): 32f.

Rück, Ulrich. "Mozarts Hammerflügel erbaute Anton Walter Wien." *Mozart-Jahrbuch* 1955. P.246f.

Schönfeld, Johann Ferdinand von. *Jahrbuch der Tonkunst von Wien und Prag 1796.* Im Schönfeldischen Verlag (Wien und Prag) 1796.

Steglich, Rudolf. "Studien an Mozarts Hammerflügel." In *Neues Mozart-Jahrbuch I,* Regensburg: Gustav Bosse, 1941, pp. 181–210.

WALTER PIANO COMPANY

This American firm of piano makers was founded by Charles R. Walter, head of Piano Design and Developmental Engineering at the C. G. Conn Company during the 1960s, when Conn was doing significant research in musical **acoustics**. In 1969 Walter, an engineer, bought the Janssen piano name (originally established in 1901 by Ben H. Janssen) from Conn, and in 1975 brought out the Charles H. Walter line of pianos. These pianos are a product of Walter's ongoing research and his extensive engineering background in acoustics as applied to the piano, as well as a devotion to high quality standards. To this end, on his purchase of the Janssen company, production was sharply curtailed, and currently the firm produces fewer than 2,000 pianos a year.

The company is unique in that it is family owned and operated, staffed by Walter himself, his wife, and various relatives. Walter currently produces a line of 43" and 45" studio pianos, termed "consoles" for marketing purposes. Each piano is inspected and signed by a family member. For a short period during the mid-1980s, some Walter pianos were equipped with player mechanisms by another company and sold under the name McDermed-Rouse. A few pianos were also sold under the names of **Story & Clark** and Janssen, inventory purchased from the old defunct Story & Clark Piano Company. The modern Walter company obviously has no connection with the early Walter Piano Company, a maker of **uprights** controlled by the James Munn Company of New York. The Walter Piano Company is located at 700 West Beardsley, Elkhart, Indiana. The firm plans to introduce a 6' 3" **grand piano**.

James Howard Richards

Bibliography

Dolge, Alfred. *Pianos and Their Makers.* 2 vols. Covina, Cal.: Covina Publishing Company, 1911; Vol. 2 repr. as *Men Who Have Made Piano History.* Vestal, N. Y.: The Vestal Press, 1980.

Fine, Larry. *The Piano Book.* 2nd edition. Boston: Brookside Press, 1990.

Pierce, Bob. *Pierce Piano Atlas.* 9th ed. Long Beach, Cal.: Bob Pierce, 1990.

"Walter Piano Co." *The Purchaser's Guide to the Music Industries 1991.* 94th annual edition. Englewood, New Jersey: The Music Trades Corporation, 1990.

WATSON, JOHN AND ARCHIBALD

Although a number of their surviving instruments bear the inscription "Makers from London," it is unclear both as to where and when the Watson brothers worked in the English metropolis, or why they left to start business in Scotland. They worked in Edinburgh between about 1786 and 1808, and were most prolific during the 1790s. During this decade they were the city's principal piano makers.

The firm made **square pianos**; there is no evidence that other types were produced. Since a system of **serial numbering** was not adopted, it is difficult to estimate the scale of production; it may have been as high as 500 pianos. The extant instruments follow a late-eighteenth-century design typical of smaller firms. Each has a **keyboard** compass of five octaves (FF–f^3), **English** single **action**, brass under-**dampers**, and **tuning pins** placed to the right-hand side. When present, the damper lift mechanism is operated by a single knee lever. The **cases** are veneered in mahogany and supported on a French **frame**.

John Cranmer

WEBBING

Webbing is a term that may be used to describe two different parts of a piano. The most common use of the word refers to the area of the cast-iron **plate** perforated by holes through which **tuning pins** are inserted into the **pinblock**. Webbing may also refer to **felt** or cloth strips that are braided through the non-speaking lengths of the **strings**.

Danny L. Boone

Bibliography

Mason, Merle H. *Piano Parts and Their Functions.* Seattle: The Piano Technicians Guild, 1977.

WEBER PIANO COMPANY

An American piano manufacturer, the Weber Piano Co. was founded in New York City in 1852 by German-born Albert Weber (8 July 1828–25 June 1879). Already an excellent pianist when he immigrated to the United States at age sixteen, Weber decided to become a piano builder. He apprenticed with the piano maker Charles J. Holden and later was employed in the D.J. Van Winkle piano factory. In 1851, at age twenty-three, Weber founded his own piano company, working with two assistants. His first piano was completed on 1 October 1851. By 1 January 1852, five additional pianos were completed.

Despite early difficulties, including the destruction of his workshop and equipment by fire in 1854, Weber was able to establish a large factory in New York in 1864 and to open his own lavish showrooms at Fifth Avenue and 16th St. in 1869. Weber pianos earned their excellent reputation more through the meticulous skill that went into their construction than through technical innovation. Weber was famous for employing only the best workmen and using only the finest materials. He inspired his workers to do their best and to take pride in their work. Moreover, he engaged in aggressive business and advertising practices, which brought his instruments to the public eye.

Although not a mechanical innovator, Weber did employ the inventor and piano builder Edward Stroud, who **patented** numerous improvements for use in Weber pianos. Albert Weber was the first to coin the term "**baby grand**" for a small, apartment-sized **grand piano**. Weber pianos were noted for their warm, lyrical **tone**, the famous "Weber sound," which was particularly admired by opera singers.

Albert Weber died at age fifty on 25 June 1879. His end was hastened by overwork induced by his insistance on running every aspect of the financial affairs of his large factory. His son, Albert Weber, Jr. (1858–c.1892), who succeeded him, was also a skilled businessman who continued the piano-building tradition of his father. Anticipating the geographical importance of Chicago, Weber was the first piano company to establish a large showroom there in 1880. A still larger Weber showroom and a Weber Concert Hall were opened in Chicago in 1883. Many eminent artists, including Madeline Schiller, participated in the grand opening of Weber Hall.

In 1887 Weber Pianos were shown at the American **Exhibition** in London and a factory was subsequently opened in England to satisfy the foreign demand for Weber pianos. Weber pianos were preferred by many leading virtuosi. Albert Weber, Jr., sought out well-known artists to endorse his pianos in concert. The beautiful Venezuelan pianist Maria Teresa Carreño was sponsored in concert by Albert Weber. The eleven-year-old Josef Hofmann made his first American tour, playing the Weber piano, in 1887. After a quarrel with **Steinway**, Ignaz Paderewski toured for two seasons using Weber pianos. Albert Weber provided the pits of New York theaters with his instruments, a fact that had to be featured prominently in the programs. Weber also specialized in the manufacture of pianos with art **cases**, including an elaborate Louis XIV style grand piano designed by W.P. Stymus, Jr.

In 1892, after the death of Albert Weber, Jr., the Weber Company was taken over by William

E. Wheelock (1852–?) and his partners, Charles B. Lawson (6 February 1855–?), and John W. Mason (1842–1919), and renamed the Weber-Wheelock Co. Through a merger, the firm was obtained by Harry B. Tremaine (20 July 1866–13 May 1932) in 1903 and renamed The **Aeolian**, Weber Piano and Pianola Co. Some excellent Weber pianos were manufactured by the Aeolian American corporation, which controlled the Weber name until the collapse of that company in bankruptcy in 1985. After the failure of Aeolian, the Weber name was sold to a South Korean manufacturer. Recent instruments bearing the Weber name have nothing in common with pianos designed in the United States by Albert Weber and his successors.

Edward E. Swenson

Bibliography

Dictionary of American Biography. S.v. "Albert Weber," by John Tasker Howard.

Dolge, Alfred. *Pianos and Their Makers.* Covina Cal.: Covina Publishing Co., 1911. Reprint. New York: Dover, 1972.

Groce, Nancy. *"Musical Instrument Making in New York City during the Eighteenth and Nineteenth Centuries."* Diss., University of Michigan, 1982.

Loesser, Arthur. *Men, Women and Pianos.* New York: Simon and Schuster, 1954.

New York Tribune. 26 June 1879.

Spillane, Daniel. *History of the American Pianoforte.* New York: D. Spillane, 1980. Reprint. New York: Da Capo Press, 1969.

Weber-Wheelock Co. *Greater and Lesser New York.* New York: Weber-Wheelock, 1897.

WELTE & SONS, M.

Edwin Welte, born in 1876, was the grandson of Michael Welte, who in 1832 founded M. Welte & Söhne, a renowned firm of **orchestrion** organ builders at Freiburg in Germany. Together with his brother-in-law, Karl Bockisch, Edwin Welte perfected the world's first successful **reproducing piano**. Known as the Welte Mignon, it was introduced in 1904 and produced in many styles. The earliest were purely reproducing-roll **player pianos**, which did not have a keyboard. Later models could also be played by hand. A special Welte product was a reproducing cabinet player or **push-up player** that was known as the *Vorsetzer* and could be used to play any ordinary pianoforte.

The chief inventor was Bockisch and he was the first to explore the possibilities of piano expression by varying degrees of suction power. Indeed, when **Aeolian** introduced its **Duo-Art** reproducing piano, Welte sued Aeolian for infringement of its **patents**. Subsequently, Aeolian was licensed to employ this system in its own patented **action** and paid Welte $2.50 for every Duo-Art it made.

The American market for Welte's instruments was so great that in 1907 a branch was opened at 18 East 17th Street, New York, under the name Welte Artistic Player Piano Company. Under the Alien Property Act, the company was confiscated on America's entry into World War I. In the 1920s the Welte-Mignon Corporation was formed at 297–307 East 133rd Street, New York, and an American-made, improved version of the original Welte-Mignon action was produced. This became known as the Welte-Mignon (Licensee) and the action was fitted to 112 different makes of American-made pianos.

See also Reproducing Piano.

Arthur W.J.G. Ord-Hume

Bibliography

Bowers, Q. David. *Encyclopedia of Automatic Musical Instruments*. Vestal, N.Y.: Vestal Press, 1972.

Ord-Hume, Arthur W.J.G. *Pianola*. London: Allen & Unwin, 1984.

WHITE HOUSE PIANOS

The White House, America's oldest showcase for the performing arts, has embraced a wide variety of piano styles and makers throughout its history. From its earliest days, these instruments were almost exclusively American made. They were either part of the first families' personal possessions, were purchased by the government, or were presented as gifts to the White House by their makers. Often four or five pianos have been part of the White House furnishings at one time—all lyrical barometers of the first families' lively interest in music for more than two centuries.

One of the first items George Washington bought for his "Presidential Palace" in New York City shortly after his inauguration was a piano, purchased from Thomas Dodds on 30 June 1789 for "16 Guineas, 4 Guineas being allowed for an old spinnett." Pianos may have graced the White House during the administration of the first two presidents who lived there—John Adams (from November 1800 to March 1801) and **Thomas Jefferson** (from 1801 to 1809)—but documentation is lacking. The earliest evidence that a piano was actually purchased for the White House is found in a letter of 17 March 1809 from the Surveyor of Public Buildings, Benjamin Latrobe, to Dolley Madison. Latrobe states that he purchased the piano for $450, but since the instrument was destroyed when the British set fire to the White House in 1814, the details may never be known.

On 15 September 1817, an elegant **grand piano**, made by **Erard** Frères of Paris, was shipped aboard the *Resolution* with other furniture for the White House during the administration of James Monroe. The instrument was purchased by the United States government through Russell and LeFarge of Le Havre for the "sitting room" (probably today's Red Room) and is described as being "decorated with bronze, having three legs, four **pedals** and a tambourin" (National Archives, RG 217, account #37.131, voucher #3). The tambourine effect was probably created by a "genouillère" or lever pushed sideways by the player's knee, which also worked a triangle and drum built into the base of the piano. With its potential for theatrical sound effects, President Monroe's Erard could render all the colorful **Janissary** music and descriptive piano pieces of the day.

The earliest White House piano still in existence belonged to Louisa Catherine Adams, wife of John Quincy Adams, and is now in the Smithsonian Institution. A small **square** of mahogany and rosewood, it was made by **Alpheus Babcock**, Boston, and dates from around 1825 to 1829. Mrs. Adams, a fine singer and amateur pianist, played this instrument often while in the White House. She undoubtedly acquired it after the Monroes' French tastes had been criticized and Congress had directed that the White House contain more American-made furnishings. Another American-made piano was purchased for the White House for President John Tyler from Emelius N. Scherr, a distinguished Philadelphia piano maker, for $600. It is described as a "concert piano with double grand **action** [double **escapement**], metallic **plate**, tablet front, large new-fashioned legs, iron **frame**, rosewood **case**, with a range of nearly 7 octaves" (National Archives, RG 217, account #87.086, voucher #1).

John Tyler's Scherr was undoubtedly a large American square, and as the nineteenth century progressed, the massive square became increasingly popular in the better American homes and concert halls. The White House of this period, however, was unique in that grand pianos were a regular part of the mansion's furnishings. The first American-made grand piano to be placed in the White House was made by the firm of **Jonas Chickering** and Sons. On 22 June 1857, John Blake, the commissioner of public buildings, requested for President James Buchanan a "first rate" instrument of "elegant appearance, but not elaborately carved or inlaid with pearl or papier mâché nor in any way decorated so as to give it a tinsel appearance" (National Archives, RG 42, Letters Sent).

Another important grand was brought to the White House in 1861 for Mary Todd Lincoln, wife of Abraham Lincoln, by the Philadelphia firm of William H. Carryl. Made by Schomacker and Company, Philadelphia (serial #1900), and now in the Chicago Historical Society, the piano bears a rosewood case, a one-piece cast-iron frame, and encompasses seven octaves plus a minor third. It remained in the White House throughout the administration of Ulysses S. Grant (1869–1877) until it was replaced two years later by another grand made by William **Knabe and Co.**, Baltimore. Grand pianos were presented to President William McKinley by W.W. **Kimball Company** of Chicago in 1897, and to First Lady Helen Taft by the **Baldwin Company** of Cincinnati in 1909. The Baldwin firm also gave President Harry S Truman an elegant ebony style K **concert grand** with a large, hand-wrought silver spread eagle on its **fallboard** in 1952.

During the last quarter of the nineteenth century, as ingenious Yankee mass-marketing techniques burgeoned, donating a piano to the White House was an honorable and coveted move. In March 1877, three weeks after President Rutherford Hayes took office, both the Bradbury and the Hallet and Davis piano companies vied for the honor of placing a piano in the Red Room. Bradbury apparently won, for on 22 March 1877 the firm gave a specially made **upright** with an American eagle inlaid on the case to President Hayes. Four years later, however, the new Hallet and Davis "**cabinet** grand upright" appears in photos of the Red Room during the Hayes administration, elegantly positioned under the Gilbert Stuart portrait of George Washington. But of the two competing

firms, Bradbury clearly was the favorite: after it's square piano was placed in the White House for Mrs. Ulysses Grant in 1871, the firm could boast eight other pianos used in the mansion before the end of the century—including the newly fashionable **baby grand** that graced the East Room for the Benjamin Harrisons' musicale on 18 April 1890.

Mrs. Harrison, a former music teacher, also had her own personal piano in the upstairs hall of the White House, for in 1889 during the family's first year in the mansion, Russell Harrison gave his mother, Caroline Scott Harrison, a fine upright made by J and C Fischer, New York, as a Christmas present. The piano's case is decorated with panels of incised gilt scrolls, foliage, and various musical instruments, and now stands in the Benjamin Harrison Memorial Home, Indianapolis, Indiana.

As the twentieth century began, the White House could count every variety of piano within its historic furnishings—small and wing-shaped pianos, massive squares, grands, and uprights. Even a **player piano** was enjoyed by the Herbert Hoovers, an A.B. Chase (#65864) with a **Welte-Mignon** reproducing action and 150 accompanying rolls. But the most important White House pianos of the twentieth century were made by **Steinway & Sons.** Before their famous concert grand was donated to the White House in 1903, Steinway had presented President and Mrs. Grover Cleveland with an elegant grand (#55,405) in 1886 as a wedding present, and it appears in photos of the family's quarters upstairs during the second Cleveland administration (1893–1897).

In January of 1903, during the administration of Theodore Roosevelt, Steinway presented to the White House the mansion's first concert grand piano (#100,000) on the occasion of the firm's fiftieth anniversary. The instrument, 8 feet, 11 inches long, was also the first piano made specifically for the East Room. Its case, designed by R.D. and J.H. Hunt, is decorated with coats of arms of the thirteen original states, and its lid, painted by the noted American artist Thomas Wilmer Dewing, is graced by dancing figures representing the nine Muses. Made of cherry with white lacquer and gold leaf, the instrument established the East Room as a focal point for the performing arts in America to the present day. During the Theodore Roosevelt administration, moreover, Steinway & Sons began to assist the first family in selecting and securing the artists who performed at the White House. In the early part of the century, they brought such luminaries as Ferruccio Busoni, Pablo Casals, Ernestine Schumann-Heink, Ignacy Jan Paderewski, and Sergei Rachmaninoff to the White House, and continued their role in bringing hundreds of famous artists to perform for the first family for well over half a century.

Another Steinway concert grand came to the White House when President Woodrow Wilson had his own nine-foot grand (#65,035) shipped from Princeton to the White House in 1912 shortly before his inauguration. But Margaret Truman's Steinway grand, given to her by her father when she was a child, made history when it broke through the White House upstairs floor, thus triggering extensive renovations of the entire mansion. Another grand (#290,498), loaned in 1937 by Steinway for family use upstairs, was (to the surpise of Steinway) later "donated" to the Harry Truman Library by President Nixon.

It was during the administration of Franklin Roosevelt, however, that the historic state Steinway currently in the East Room was donated to the White House, replacing the 1903 "Gold Steinway," which was then brought to the Smithsonian. The new piano (#300,000) was presented on 10 December 1938 at a program during which Josef Hofmann brilliantly performed several Chopin selections. Measuring 9 feet, 7 inches, the instrument is a standard concert grand with an extended case designed by the New York architect Eric Gugler. Its giant supporting gold eagles were molded by the sculptor Albert Stewart, while the gold-leaf decoration on the case was executed by Dunbar Beck. The motifs on the case represent important forms of American music—a Virginia reel, an Indian ceremonial dance, a New England barn dance, a black worker singing in the cotton fields, and a cowboy on the Western prairie.

Other pianos currently in the White House are a 5-foot, 7-inch ebony Steinway grand placed in the upstairs center hall, and a Steinway vertical used mainly by the U.S. Marine Band ensembles when they play for White House social functions, often several times a week. While some artists, such as Vladimir Horowitz and Rudolf Serkin, have preferred to bring their own instruments to the White House, the majority of artists use the state Steinway.

Elise K. Kirk

Bibliography

Cripe, Helen. *Thomas Jefferson and Music.* Charlottesville: University Press of Virginia, 1974.

Kirk, Elise K. *Music at the White House: A History of the American Spirit.* Champaign: University of Illinois Press, 1986.

———. "Pianos in the White House." *The Magazine Antiques* 75 (May 1984): 1164–1170.

WINKING

Winking is a procedure used in **regulating** piano **actions** to determine the interrelationship of various parts of the action. While one part is gently moved or tapped, another part is observed in order to detect very slight movement, or winking. For example, when adjusting the height of **repetition levers (balanciers)** to **jacks** in a **grand piano** action, each jack tender is moved up and down as the **hammer** is observed. When properly regulated, the hammer will "wink" and the jack will return freely to its rest position. Also, when regulating lost motion in a vertical piano action the keytop is gently tapped while the **back check** and catcher are observed. When properly regulated, there will be a very slight movement of the backcheck while the catcher remains motionless, and the jack will return freely to its rest position.

Other winking procedures involve the adjustment of **spoons** and **bridle tapes** in vertical pianos, and **dampers** in grand pianos.

See also Regulation.

Danny L. Boone

Bibliography

Mason, Merle H. *Piano Parts and Their Functions.* Seattle: The Piano Technicians Guild, 1977.

WIPPEN

The wippen is a rocking lever that transmits motion from the **key** to the **hammer** on vertical and **grand piano actions**. This device was first popularized by **Sébastien Erard**'s 1821 grand repetition action. Hermann Lichtenthal of Belgium devised a wippen for vertical actions in 1832.

See also Actions.

Philip Jamison, III

WIRE

It is assumed that even in antiquity wire was used for the **stringing** of musical instruments. The learned monk Rodkerus, called Theophilus Presbyter, provides the earliest description of wire-drawing by means of a drawing plate in his "Schedula diversarum artium" (c. 1100). The gold embroidery of the coronation robes of the German Kaisers indicates that it was possible by around 1180 to produce gold thread of .16mm diameter. The earliest illustration is contained in the *Buch der Mendelschen Bruderstiftung* in Nuremberg (1389 and 1418). Altena (in Westphalia) and Nuremberg were the centers of metal processing in Europe at the beginning of the modern era. A 1497 watercolor by Albrecht Dürer is considered the oldest example of a water-powered wire mill.

Music wire, made from copper, brass, and iron, occasionally even gold and silver, belonged to the highest quality wire products. Wires of copper alloys existed in the most varied compounds. "Red" wire for bass strings shows 86–99 percent copper content with tensile strength of maximum 500 N/mm² (MPa). "Yellow" wire, with a tensile strength of maximum 850 MPa, had a copper content of 70–78 percent. The major alloy was zinc, though traces of tin, silver, lead, and iron can be found. The quality of the strings was primarily determined by the property of the ore. The Westphalian foundries were favored by the presence of so-called rich Osmund iron. By contrast, for instance, France had to import music wire until the middle of the eighteenth century because of the lack of suitable raw materials and processing experience.

At the end of the sixteenth century, there is evidence that Johann Gerdes of Altena was producing "steel wire." It should not be assumed that this refers to modern carbon steel. Analysis of extant seventeenth- and eighteenth-century steel wire indicates a highly refined, nearly carbon-free iron with a high phosphorus content ("phosphorous steel") and a maximum tensile strength of approximately 1100 MPa. Tempered carbon steel for string wire was developed at the end of the eighteenth century in England, though it was rejected by the Viennese piano industry until around 1835 for reasons of **tone**.

At the beginning of the nineteenth century, Nuremberg lost its prime position because of high-quality production in Prussia ("Berlin wire") and in Austria. In 1819, W. Brockedon succeeded in drawing wire of consistent thickness and great strength by means of bored-through sapphire and ruby (English patent #4395). In 1834, Webster in Birmingham produced piano wire for the first time from crucible cast steel. In the middle of the nineteenth century the Vienna firm Miller & Sohn supplied piano firms in all of Europe, including **Broadwood** on the occasion of the World Exposition of 1851. In 1882, Bongardt founded the wire factory in Röslau (Bavaria), which remains the leading company today.

Modern steel piano wire has a tensile strength up to 2600 MPa. Individual string gauges are still indicated today by wire numbers. On the European continent a system was used primarily in which the number 1 had a diameter of .50–.60mm. The thinnest types, numbers 10–12, were drawn up to .15mm; their use is considered likely in the sixteenth century. Thicker strings were later marked 0, 2/0, 3/0— up to 12/0. At the end of the eighteenth century, half numbers were introduced as in-between sizes. In England and to some extent in France (Mersenne) the system still in use today was applied by which the numbers increased according to increasing thickness of the wire. String wires were not standardized until the end of the nineteenth century and, depending on the place of production, often deviated considerably in thickness and quality. The determination of the wire numbering system used by specific firms plays an essential role in the **restoration** of historic keyboard instruments.

Alfons Huber
Translated by David Anderson

Bibliography

Fischhof, Joseph. *Versuch einer Geschichte des Clavierbaues*. Wien: Wallishausser, 1853.

Goodwell, Martha, and Jay Scott Odell. "The Metallurgy of 17th and 18th Century Music Wire." *The Historical Harpsichord*. Vol. 2. New York: Pentagon Press, 1987.

Gug, Remy. "European Music-Wire Making Places." *Fellowship of Makers and Restorers of Historical Instruments Quarterly* 49 (October 1987): 45–48.

———. "Jobst Meuler or the Secret of a Nuremberg Wire-Drawer." *Fellowship of Makers and Restorers of Historical Instruments Quarterly* 51 (April 1988): 29–36.

Harding, Rosamond E.M. *The Piano-Forte: Its History Traced to the Great Exhibition of 1851.* Cambridge: Cambridge University Press, 1933. Reprints, New York: Da Capo Press, 1973; Old Woking, Surrey: Gresham Books, 1978.

Henkel, Hubert. *Beiträge zum historischen Cembalobau.* Leipzig: Deutscher Verlag für Musik, 1979.

Hubbard, Frank. *Three Centuries of Harpsichord Making.* Cambridge: Harvard University Press, 1965.

Huber, Alfons. "Saitendrahtsysteme im Wiener Klavierbau zwischen 1780 und 1880."*Das Musikinstrument* 37 (September 1988): 84–94.

Junghanns, Herbert. *Der Piano- und Flügelbau.* Frankfurt/Main: Bochinsky, 1984.

Karp, Cary. *The Pitches of 18th Century Strung Keyboard Instruments.* Stockholm:SMS-Musikmuseet, 1984.

Technologische Enzyclopaedie Vol. 4. S.v. "Draht," by Johann Joseph Prechtl. Stuttgart: Cotta, 1833.

Thomas, W.R., and J.J.K. Rhodes. "Harpsichords and the Art of Wire-Drawing." In *The Organ Yearbook* (1979): 126–139.

WOOD, SMALL AND COMPANY

In 1818, Wood, Small and Company, in Edinburgh, became the successor to **Muir, Wood and Co.**, which was the leading piano-making firm in Scotland. The partners were the two senior figures most active in the old firm: Andrew Wood and George Small. In 1822, following a period at the former firm's shop, business was transferred to Waterloo Place, Edinburgh. The old Calton Hill factory was retained. Trading continued until Wood's death in 1829.

Without John Muir's financial backing, piano making was continued on a reduced scale. Some 600 **square pianos** were produced over a ten-year period; these imitate contemporary London models, although none of the extant examples has a metal **hitch pin plate**. Each has a 5 $1/2$-octave compass and double **action**. The **cases** are square-fronted with six reeded legs. A number of 6-octave (CC–c⁴) **cabinet pianos** were also made, probably about one hundred. Substantial losses suffered during the economic depression of the latter 1820s greatly curtailed manufacturing activities. There were two successor firms: Wood and Co. and Small, Bruce and Co.

See also Scotland, Piano Industry in.

John Cranmer

WORLD WAR II AND AMERICAN PIANO BUILDERS

Survival of small business was paramount to the U. S. government in 1941, which feared that lack or deprivation of critical materials might force out of business the very manufacturers whose skill and expertise were so necessary for the war effort. The U.S.A. consisted of 2,750,000 small businesses in 1942, including some 169,000 manufacturers and 1,614,000 retailers, who, caught off guard on 7 December 1941, and greatly behind in materiel production, rose to supply not only its own fighting force, but that of its allies. America fought two enemies on two fronts, defeating them both, and the music industry played a significant role, providing equipment from file cabinets to hardware needed in the Manhattan Project.

Music was not only necessary for drills and parades in the military, it was essential for keeping up morale at home and in the barracks. The National Association of Music Merchants (NAMM) and the National Piano Teachers Association (NPTA) pledged support through resolutions sent to President Roosevelt and others; piano tuners volunteered their services to army bases; manufacturers turned to war work to help ends meet; and retailers emphasized service, repair, and rentals.

The first government agency a manufacturer dealt with was the Office of Production Management (OPM). The OPM was later closed and its function taken over by the War Production Board (WPB). The WPB contained many divisions, but the two most important to the music industry were the Production Division, directed by W.H. Harrison (formerly of A. T. & T.), and the Division of Industry Operations, headed by J.S. Knowlson (former president of the Stewart-Warner Corp.), which dealt with specific industries, including musical instruments. Knowlson's assistant, C.H. Matthieson, was in charge of the conversion of durable goods, including pianos. Tin was one of the first metals banned from use in instruments. Radio and phonograph production was cut, placing a greater premium on pianos as a source of musical entertainment.

On 18 February 1942, the WPB issued a limitation order: manufacturers could use 75 percent of their average 1940 consumption if the product contained 10 percent or less restricted materials by weight, 65 percent of average if containing 10–25 percent restricted materials by weight, and 50 percent if containing 25 percent or more by weight. Spare parts were limited to 75 percent of the 1940 average. Critical materials were restricted to 12.5 percent. Further and further restrictions trickled out of Washington until finally, on 1 June 1942, the WPB issued Limitation Order L-37-a: as of 31 July 1942 no more pianos or organs could be completed, and all production must cease on any instrument containing 10 percent critical materials by weight.

It appears that manufacturers were prevented from producing instruments even before the death-knell of L-37-a, due to the percentage of critical materials needed to turn out a piano. Henry Z. Steinway recalls, "I have a vague recollection that we were forbidden to make pianos at all effective April 15, 1942." The materials, in order of importance, were iron, steel, lead, zinc, magnesium, aluminum, rubber, copper, tin, phenol formaldehyde plastics, methyl methacrylate plastics, Neoprene, cork, nickel, and chromium. The WPB allowed the use of gold and silver as substitute metals, and ceramics were mentioned as possible alternatives. Piano makers were directed toward the manufacture of aircraft and gliders; organ manufacturers, blowers for link trainers, used in the ground training of pilots; and all other instrument makers (especially brass), precision instruments. Knowlson urged any industry with a war contract to find at least five sub-contractors. Dealers were urged to ferret out old pianos, rebuild them, and sell them to those who really wanted them.

A list (incomplete?) of piano makers in 1942 included: **Aeolian-American Corp.** (owners of **Mason & Hamlin**, **Knabe**, and **Chickering**); **Baldwin**; Estey; **Everett** (makers of Everett and **Cable-Nelson**); Jesse French; Haddorf; Hardman, Peck & Co.; Grinnell; **Gulbransen**; Charles W. House; Ivers & Pond; Janssen; **Kohler & Campbell**; **Kimball**; **Krakauer**; **Kranich & Bach**; Lester; **Mathushek**; National Piano Corp.; Schiller-Cable (makers of Conover, Cable, Schiller, Kingsbury, and Wellington); Shoninger; **Sohmer & Co.**; Steiff; **Steinway**; **Story & Clark**; Straube; Vose; Weaver; Weser; Winter; and **Wurlitzer**.

Some manufacturers produced a special **upright**, with a **frame** of plastic and plywood, using only 10 percent metal, claimed invented by C.D. Bond of Weaver Pianos for their Army Piano; Steinway made about 3,000 Victory Verticals, or G. I. Uprights, and Gulbransen, a War Model Upright. These pianos were small, light, and finished in a khaki color. All were sold only to those with WPB authorization. According to Henry Z. Steinway, "Our G. I. Uprights were ordered by the military, and we were given exception to the limitation order which we passed to Wood & Brooks, etc., to get the metal needed. Chauncey Bond's all wood piano was I think for general sales." Also of interest was a design patented by Louis Bromberg, Brooklyn, N.Y., called "**MirrApiano**," employing used upright stock and wholesaled by Gulbransen, Janssen, Weser, Perfection Piano Repair, Simonson, Wilking Music, and National Piano Corp. Forty-seven retailers nationwide sold them, with priority to naval stations, army bases, hospitals, etc. (see MirrApiano.)

Piano **wire**, possessing the greatest tensile strength of any plain carbon steel, was needed for springs in rifle and sidearm firing mechanisms. It also made an excellent garrote.

The CG-4A troop-carrying glider was designed by WACO Aircraft, Troy, Ohio, and manufactured by about fifteen firms; parts were interchangeable. It was used in Burma for the invasion and evacuation of wounded and in the "Over the Rhine" offensive, March 1945. Inspired by the Germans' use of gliders in their invasion of Crete, gliders were planned for use in the Normandy invasion, but American tank movement was so rapid that they were not deployed. Story & Clark made the glider nose, and Steinway was involved, sub-contracting to the General Aircraft Corp., to whom they leased one of their Astoria factories. Baldwin made a wing for a cargo plane. Aeolian-American was leased by the WPB Universal Moulded Products Corp. for manufacturing aircraft parts.

Wurlitzer was the most heavily involved in the war effort, with 406,400 square feet of factory space used in precision processing of woods, metals, plastics, glider production, and parts for the Corsair 122 Divebomber; it also worked on a specific weapon for the Navy. Its DeKalb plant won the first Army/Navy "E" pennant for excellence, and eventually won three of these awards.

Jesse French & Sons, the piano division of H. and A. Selmer Band Instruments, won an "E" pennant for its truck bodies and fuel-cell forms; it was the second "E" awarded to a piano maker.

Lyon & Healy, a harp manufacturer that at one time made pianos, won an "E" pennant for its oxygen valves, relays, remote-control circuits, and extension cords.

W. W. Kimball made bulkheads (partitions) of honeycomb construction (for lightness) for quad-engined warplanes, long seats for paratroopers, landing-gear doors, triangular wheel chocks, office equipment, deluxe custom workbenches for airplane engine factories, custom etching units with hoods for cleaning gun barrels, trays to hold engine parts for the B-29 and others, and custom lab tables with sinks and plumbing for a variety of applications, including the Manhattan Project (atomic bomb). Kimball used a special hot-gluing process for bonding wood to aluminum parts for the B-17 Boeing Flying Fortress, Lockheed Constellation, and Douglas C-54 Skymaster. It worked with M. I. T. and produced for a variety of big firms: GE, DuPont, Goodyear, and Chrysler, to name a few.

Gulbransen, in addition to its Army Piano, produced link training motors for ground training of pilots, holding the pilot plus a 600-pound plate, and moving the "plane" every which way to simulate all weather and flying conditions. The company also made a variety of wooden office equipment.

A number of piano makers began making caskets, Steinway & Sons and Everett among them.

Suppliers and subcontractors included: Tonk Manufacturing, makers of piano benches and cabinets for sheet music; S. E. Overton Co., makers of wood carvings and turnings for the piano industry, who made walnut gun stocks for the M-1 .30 cal. carbine; Wood & Brooks, makers of **ivory keys** and piano **actions**; Thayer Actions, who made parts for planes, bombs, tanks, and detection devices; Standard Felt Co., makers of **felt** piano **hammers**, who made felt for aircraft mechanized equipment and armaments (wadding, gunpowder bags, etc.); **Pratt, Read & Co.**, makers of keys and piano actions, who were a prime contractor for the CG-4A glider, converting their old Deep River plant to its production; Paragon Foundries, makers of piano **plates**; Chas. W. House, makers of woven felts; Schaff Piano String Corp.; and AMSCO-Wire Corp., makers of **tuning pins**.

In 1944, aluminum became available in quantity, and the wooden aircraft program was suspended practically in its entirety. Actually, war contracts provided little profit, and did nothing for the dealers; when they were completed, manufacturers became desperate. By mid-1944, the government asked manufacturers to substitute aluminum for brass and copper. Lumber shortages became serious. These conditions inspired Winter & Co. to produce an aluminum plate, called the "Alumitone," made for them by Alcoa, for their verticals; it weighed 45 lbs., and was 64 percent lighter than cast iron. Henry Steinway recollects: "The initiative came from Alcoa. We all tried them out, but only Winter went into them in a big way. The problem was creep: cast iron does not give under pressure of the **strings**, but aluminum does."

Although it is unfortunate that the war spelled the demise of many piano manufacturers, the industry can take pride in the great contributions it made to the allied victory. The role of the American piano builders is a remarkable example of the skill, craftsmanship, artistry, and dedication of thousands upon thousands of unsung heroes.

Daniel Barber

Bibliography

The Music Trades Magazine. New York, N.Y., 1941–45.

The Piano Trades Magazine. Chicago, Ill., 1941–45.

Ratcliffe, Ronald V. *Steinway*. San Francisco: Chronicle Books, 1989.

Personal recollections of Henry Z. Steinway.

WORNUM, ROBERT (JR.) (1780–1852)

There were two Robert Wornums: Senior and Junior. Born in 1742, Robert Wornum, Senior, originally Wornham, came from Berkshire in England. He worked as a music seller and musical instrument maker in Glasshouse Street, London, and from 1777 had premises in Wigmore Street. He died in 1815. Robert Wornum, Junior, was born in 1780 and was originally intended for the Church, but his mechanical bias led him to piano manufacture and design. It is he who is credited with the invention of the **upright** piano **action** and the **tape-check action**.

Initially he went into partnership with George Wilkinson in Oxford Street in 1810 and the following year, in the name of "Robert Wornum Junior," he was granted a British **patent** for an upright piano with "improved double **English action**" and diagonal **stringing** so as to make the piano smaller. In 1812 the factory burned, but a year later Wornum started up again in nearby Wigmore Street, this time on his own, describing himself as an "upright and horizontal pianoforte maker." He put forward some controversial theories at this time that he later revised; one patent granted in 1820 contains the assertion that all the strings in any one pianoforte should be the same **wire** gauge in order to produce an evenness of **tone**.

In 1826 came his first major invention—the form of the upright piano action, which was the basis of all subsequent upright piano developments. Combined with his improvements in reducing the dimensions of the upright, these inventions led to the production of what he called his "piccolo" or "**cottage**" **pianos**. As David Grover comments, Wornum's invention was to the upright piano what **Erard's** invention of 1821 was to the **grand piano**. **Pleyel** and certain other European makers were quick to adopt Wornum's improvements; ironically, for a long while this type of upright action was referred to erroneously as the "French action."

Next came his invention of the "tape-check" action, upon which the success of the upright action and its repetition was secured. Although Charles-François Wolfel of Paris had been granted a French patent for a form of tape-check action in 1840, Robert Wornum first used such a technique at least five years before the date of his own British patent—1842—thus predating the French claim. By 1844 he had invented a **down-strike action** with a tape-check for grands.

Some four years prior to this he had produced what he called his "Pocket Grand" piano, which had the **soundboard** above the strings; when the **lid** of the piano was raised, the soundboard and the strings rose with it, exposing the **hammer** action. While others were experimenting with up-strike grand actions, Robert Wornum still had faith in the down-strike action for grands and showed such an instrument at the Great **Exhibition** of 1851. Wornum was one of the last manufacturers of pianofortes to make his own piano actions and thus many varieties of Wornum actions may be found.

Robert Wornum died in 1852, the business falling under the control of his son, Alfred Nicholson Wornum, who continued to patent improvements up until his own death and the demise of the company at the turn of the century.

Universal acceptance of Wornum's upright action and his tape-check improvement was not immediate, and **William Southwell's** "**sticker**" **actions**, invented in 1798, were still being used into the 1890s, the decade in which they were finally superseded by Wornum's designs.

Arthur W.J.G. Ord-Hume

Bibliography

Ehrlich, Cyril. *The Piano: A History*. London: Dent, 1976.

Grove Dictionary of Music & Musicians. 1st ed. Edited by Sir George Grove. London: Macmillan, 1879.

Grover, David S. *The Piano: Its Story from Zither to Grand*. London: Hale, 1976.

Harding, Rosamond E.M. *The Piano-Forte: Its History Traced to the Great Exhibition of 1851*. Cambridge: Cambridge University Press, 1933. Reprints, New York: Da Capo Press, 1973; Old Woking, Surrey: Gresham Books, 1978.

Wainwright, David. *Broadwood by Appointment. A History*. London: Quiller, 1982.

WREST PIN

See Tuning Pin.

WREST PLANK

See Pinblock.

WURLITZER COMPANY

One of the great names in piano and organ trade history, the Wurlitzer Company was founded in Cincinnati in 1856 by Rudolph Wurlitzer (1831–1914) as a musical instruments retail organization. The company became the world's largest manufacturer of **player pianos, coin-operated pianos**, piano **orchestrions, theater photoplayers, barrel** and merry-go-round organs, and "Mighty WurliTzer" pipe organs. Along with J.P. Seeburg & Co., Wurlitzer dominated the coin-piano industry and introduced Americans to the jukebox culture.

Rudolph Wurlitzer immigrated to the U.S. in 1854 from a family of German musical-instrument makers. His Cincinnati firm became

Rudolph Wurlitzer & Bro. in 1872, and was the nation's largest musical instrument retailer, with branch stores in New York, Boston, Chicago, and other markets. The first pianos bearing the name Wurlitzer appeared in 1880. These were instruments manufactured to order by several midwestern firms. The company was incorporated under Ohio charter in 1890 as the Rudolph Wurlitzer Co., capitalized at $200,000. It enjoyed great success with piano sales and government contracts to supply the military with trumpets and drums. In 1899 Wurlitzer successfully introduced its "Tonophone," a coin-operated player made under contract by DeKleist Musical Instrument Manufacturing Co. of North Tonawanda, New York. This instrument won a gold medal at the Pan American Exposition in 1901 and convinced Wurlitzer to concentrate on the production of coin-operated player pianos and theater organs.

In 1904 the company launched the "PianOrchestra" line of coin players, which were automatic pianos instrumented with oboe, flute, clarinet, saxophone, and violin pipes, mandolin, xylophone, cymbals, and drums, and ranged in price from $1,000 to $60,000. These machines, equivalent to the large **Welte** and **Hupfeld** orchestrions of Europe, were called "The Most Wonderful Musical Instrument the World Has Ever Known" and "The Greatest Musical Wonder of the Age." The next year Wurlitzer became the national distributor of the renowned maker of player pianos, Melville Clark Piano Co., of DeKalb, Illinois. Surviving a fire at its Cincinnati headquarters, Wurlitzer increased its capital to $1 million in 1909 and opened its North Tonawanda Division by purchasing the DeKleist company, which was then renamed Rudolph Wurlitzer Manufacturing Co. and managed by Farny Wurlitzer (1883–1972), the youngest son of the founder. This plant, which manufactured hundreds of pianos daily, also made the perforated rolls for all Wurlitzer automatic instruments. By 1910, Wurlitzer's eighty-two page catalog of products listed fifty machines, including the Wurlitzer Automatic Roll Changer, a complex mechanical device able to interchange six music rolls that allowed up to thirty selections without repetition. A Wurlitzer roll catalog issued about 1923 listed some two thousand tunes available for its popular sixty-five-note player, offering more variety than any other manufacturer. The company

also published *The Wurlitzer Booster*, a monthly journal to dealers.

By the time Rudolph Wurlitzer died in 1914, leaving his sons Howard (1871–1928), Rudolph H. (1873–1948), and Farny in charge, the company was capitalized at $4 million (which was increased to $10.5 million by 1927), one of the highest capitalized firms in the industry, with retail stores in twenty-three cities nationwide. Significantly, the Wurlitzers gained control of about 26 percent of **American Piano Co.** stock and owned interest in other companies as well. In 1919 Wurlitzer purchased Melville Clark Piano Co. Other brand names acquired and used by Wurlitzer were Apollo Piano Co., Julius Bauer & Co., Schaff Bros., C. Kurtzmann & Co., and Hope-Jones Pipe Organ Co.

But the collapse of the player piano and photoplayer market in the late 1920s followed by the Great Depression of the 1930s forced Wurlitzer to reorganize in receivership under R. C. Rolfing (b. 1891), at which point the company ceased to be a single-family business. Rolfing liquidated the firm's musical-instrument divisions and retail operations (especially in furniture, radios, and refrigerators) and concentrated on vertical and **grand pianos**, electronic organs, and coin-operated phonographs. Rolfing guided Wurlitzer through World War II and in the 1950s transferred manufacturing operations to Holly Springs, Mississippi. Rolfing and his family took Wurlitzer into high profits in the 1960s and 1970s, including expansion into European operations. The firm introduced the world's first commercially available **electronic piano** about 1967.

The economic trials of the 1980s allowed Wurlitzer to purchase and produce the famous **Chickering & Sons** name and popular Aeolian player-piano line from **Aeolian Piano Corporation**, which went bankrupt in 1985. In an effort to stay profitable Wurlitzer also diversified into making billiard tables for Brunswick, as well as into office furniture and clock cases. Nevertheless, between 1980 and 1987 the firm lost $23.1 million. In February 1988 **Baldwin Piano & Organ Co.** purchased all assets, **patents**, and trademarks of Wurlitzer's piano and electronic keyboard business. In 1992 Wurlitzer continued to operate as an independent subsidiary of Baldwin.

Craig H. Roell

Bibliography

"Baldwin Acquires Wurlitzer Keyboard Business." *The Music Trades* 136 (February 1988):20, 116–18.

Bowers, Q. David. *Put Another Nickel In: A History of Coin-Operated Pianos and Orchestrions*. Vestal, N.Y.: The Vestal Press, 1966.

Dolge, Alfred. *Pianos and Their Makers* Vol. 1. *A Comprehensive History of the Development of the Piano from the Monochord to the Concert Grand Player Piano*. Covina, Cal.: Covina Publishing Co., 1911. Reprint, New York: Dover, 1972. Vol. 2. *Development of the Piano Industry in America since the Centennial Exhibition at Philadelphia, 1876*. Covina, Cal.: Covina Publishing Co., 1913.

Graham, Lloyd. "The Story of the Rudolph Wurlitzer Family and Business." 25 May 1955. Unpublished manuscript in possession of Mrs. Janet Wurlitzer Stites, Cincinnati, Ohio. (Typewritten.)

The Music Trades Corp. *Purchaser's Guide to the Music Industries*. Englewood, N.J.: Music Trades Corp., annually.

Ord-Hume, Arthur W.J.G. *Player Piano: The History of the Mechanical Piano and How to Repair It*. London: George Allen & Unwin, 1970.

Pierce, Bob, comp. *Pierce Piano Atlas*. Long Beach, Cal.: Bob Pierce, Publisher, 9th ed., 1990.

Roehl, Harvey N. *Player Piano Treasury: The Scrapbook History of the Mechanical Piano in America as Told in Story, Pictures, Trade Journal Articles and Advertising*. Vestal, N.Y.: The Vestal Press, 1961; 2d ed., 1973.

Roell, Craig H. *The Piano in America, 1890–1940*. Chapel Hill: University of North Carolina Press, 1989; trade paperback edition, 1991.

"Wurlitzer Acquires Aeolian Assets." *The Music Trades* 133 (July 1985): 18, 23.

YAMAHA

Yamaha is a major Japanese piano manufacturer with headquarters in Hamamatsu. Torakusu Yamaha (1851–1916), founder, began building reed organs in 1887. In 1889 the firm was incorporated under the name Nippon Gakki Co., Ltd. Torakusu Yamaha served as president until his death. In 1899, before beginning piano manufacturing, Yamaha travelled to the United States, researching the current technology. The company produced its first **upright piano** in 1900 and its first **grand piano** in 1902. In 1987 the corporate name was changed to Yamaha Corporation.

Yamaha is the largest producer of pianos in the world, with an extensive, worldwide sales division. Including a complete line of uprights and grands, over 150,000 pianos are manufactured every year. In 1986 a piano assembly plant was opened in Thomaston, Georgia, the first Yamaha facility in the United States.

The Yamaha Corporation is an enormous, diverse collection of corporate interests, both musical and non-musical. In addition to its piano manufacturing and sales, Yamaha is an important producer of band and orchestral instruments, including percussion instruments and an extensive line of brass and woodwind instruments, with models designed for use by musicians at beginner, intermediate, and professional levels.

Research and development at Yamaha have often been applied in a twofold manner, i.e., to existing Yamaha products and to other products in related fields. For example, in 1947 Yamaha began producing its own metal piano **frames**. The research for this product expanded and developed into related areas; now Yamaha markets alloys, electrode materials, and highly specialized metals.

In 1969 Yamaha began research in integrated circuits with a goal of making its own large-scale integration microchips for use in **synthesizers**. Now Yamaha produces electronic organs, digital synthesizers, and drum machines. Currently, Yamaha also markets integrated circuits and computers.

In other diverse corporate activities Yamaha sells home and professional audio and visual equipment such as loudspeakers, amplifiers, mixing consoles, CD players, and laser discs. The company produces a wide variety of sports equipment, including skis, archery bows, golf clubs, tennis rackets, and badminton rackets. Yamaha Motors produces motorcycles, golf carts, snowmobiles, motorboats, industrial robots, gasoline engines, and diesel engines. In 1964 the firm entered the leisure field by opening its first hotel. It also operates resorts, golf courses, and amusement parks.

In 1954 Yamaha initiated music classes in Japan that later developed into the Yamaha Music School, a network of classes and lessons for amateurs. The Yamaha Music School was first introduced in the United States in 1965 and in Canada in 1966. In addition, Yamaha now supports concerts and competitions throughout Asia, Europe, and the Americas.

Yamaha pianos have developed a considerable reputation for high quality. They have been selected for use by numerous prominent festivals and competitions in the United States, Europe, and Asia, including the Newport and Ravinia festivals, the Chopin International Piano Competition, the International Tchaikovsky Competition, and the Arthur Rubinstein International Piano Master Competition. Concert pianists Sviatoslav Richter and André Watts, among others, have endorsed instruments by Yamaha.

See also Japan, Piano Industry in.

Herbert Wise

Bibliography

Information provided by Yamaha Corporation of America.

YAMAHA DIGITAL PIANOS

Yamaha, founded in 1887 and incorporated under the name Nippon Gakki Co., Ltd. in 1889, is a highly diverse Japanese manufacturer of pianos, wind and percussion instruments, digital keyboards, audio equipment, and many other consumer goods. In 1987 the corporate name was changed to Yamaha Corporation.

The beginning of Yamaha's electronic musical instruments dates from 1959 when an all-transistor electronic organ was developed. The first Yamaha **electronic piano**—the *CP* series—was marketed in 1976. Now with one of the most extensive and varied catalogs and sophisticated marketing networks of any electronic musical instrument maker, Yamaha's digital pianos are available in various product lines depending on the targeted consumer. The *Clavinova* series, available in at least ten different models, is primarily designed for the home and educational markets. These instruments are built in a cabinet that is free standing and attractive, with onboard speakers, built-in drum machines, and sequencer memories. The *pf* series, designed for the touring professional musician, is built in a more durable and portable cabinet lacking some of the special features of the *Clavinova*.

Internally, the *Clavinova* and *pf* digital pianos use the same **tone**-generating devices. Early models, dating from 1983, utilized Yamaha's proprietary *FM digital synthesis*, originally designed for the *DX7* **synthesizer**. In 1985, the percussion sounds of the *Clavinova* were upgraded to PCM samples of actual instruments, and in 1986 Yamaha introduced *AWM* (Advanced Wave Memory), a method of tone generation based on digital sampling. In *AWM*, samples are processed according to **key** velocity so that attack, volume, brightness, decay, and modulation are all **touch**-controlled.

Clavinovas incorporate a **patented** *AE* (Action Effect) keyboard, which is designed to simulate the **action** of a **concert grand**. Models range from the highly portable *YPR* series with sixty-one unweighted keys to the more typical seventy-six or eighty-eight weighted keys of the *Pf* and *Clavinova* series. Each digital piano uses four to six high-efficiency speakers housed in a resonating cabinet. Some models are built with a variable digital reverb effect to enhance tonal ambience. Both professional and home products feature full **MIDI** implementation, a transposer that produces semitone transposition over an octave range, and stereo outputs. Professional models include sustain **pedals** and programmable soft or *sostenuto* **pedals**, while *Clavinovas* include pedals for these functions as well as a programmable pedal for starting/stopping sequences.

Low-priced *CLP* models feature five to ten preset keyboard sounds including acoustic piano, electric piano, vibes, harpsichord, and celeste. The more expensive *CVP* series incorporates twenty-two voices including various keyboards, bass, brass, string, and woodwind sounds. Some of these keyboards are splittable, allowing different sounds to be simultaneously specified for different registers. Most feature thirty-two-note polyphonicity. The *CVP* series includes preprogrammed rhythms as well as programmable drum machine, a ten-track sequencer or performance memory, and a floppy disk drive that can either store the musician's work or utilize Yamaha's *Disk Orchestra Collection*—a series of digital recordings of music in diverse styles designed to accompany the performer at the *Clavinova*.

Yamaha's *Disklavier* is the trade name for a **reproducing piano** that combines a Yamaha conventional piano with the full range of MIDI technology. Fiber-optic sensors convert all performance information—notes, duration, key velocity, and pedal movements—into digital data. This data is stored in an onboard sequencer and can be edited and/or saved to a 3.5-inch floppy disk. Playback operation utilizes a sophisticated solenoid system that reproduces the movements of the keys and pedals in complete detail. Available in the United States since 1988, the *Disklavier* has been used in significant creative, educational, archival, and research applications. It is available in a 50" **upright** model as well as grands of 5'3", 5'7", 6', and 7'6". The *Pianosoft Library* is a collection of recordings of performances by leading classical and popular artists for playback on any *Disklavier* piano.

Samuel S. Holland

YOUNG CHANG

Proclaiming itself "the world's second largest piano manufacturer," the Korean firm of Young Chang has distributed pianos in the United

States as Young Chang America, Inc., since 1979. In a comparatively short time the company has become a major firm in the manufacture of every piano type and model.

In addition to garnering a host of celebrity-owners of the instrument, the company boasts an array of institutions on its roster. The Cerritos, a California-based distributor, sponsors among other events: the Miss T.E.E.N. Pageant; The San Jose Symphony/Young Chang America Concerto Competition; and the Festival at Sand Point.

Young Chang represents a typical success story. Korea, ravaged by a war that ended in 1953, began to rebuild its economy. As Gunther Joppig writes, together with the rehabilitation of the economy, the South Korean musical-instrument manufacturers were to find a new impetus based on what Korean musicologist Yi Kang-Suk, considers three basic trends: (1) Western music, (2) traditional Korean music and, (3) experimental music containing elements from both cultures. However, it should be pointed out that emphasis on Western music had already existed in Korean schools for some ninety years.

Piano manufacture after the war was set in motion by three brothers Kim: Jai-Young Kim, Jai-Sup Kim, and Jai-Chang Kim, each an indispensable force in shaping the company: Jai-Young, an accountant; Jai-Sup, an engineer; and Jai-Chang, the youngest, an accomplished pianist as well as a piano technician.

After first importing **Yamaha** pianos to Korea, the brothers Kim began constructing their own **upright** instruments, importing only **frames** and **actions** from Yamaha. The first Young Chang factory was built in Seoul in 1964. Early obstacles relating to Korean imports forced the company to design and construct its own parts, e.g., **pinblocks**, metal components, and veneering.

After a ruinous fire in early 1976, the company made a comeback in the same year by reestablishing production at an Inchon manufacturing center. A second production facility was added in Inchon in 1979, and in 1984 **grand pianos** were added to production.

Larry Fine, writing in 1987, reports that when Korean pianos first arrived in the United States they deteriorated rapidly, due to inadequate seasoning of lumber used in the manufacture of frames (the same problem plagued the Yamaha company in its early years). They did, however, offer a presentable product with a good value for the price. Their **tone** resembled a neutral blend of American, European, and Japanese elements.

Yat-Lam Hong's 1989 report of his visit to the Young Chang factory in Seoul reveals a company with the most advanced and sophisticated production facilities available. Automated and computerized technology are used throughout the production process, especially in the final stages of warehouse shipping. Today Young Chang imports materials from all over the world, including Alaskan Sitka spruce (for **soundboards**), rock maple from Vermont and Michigan, mahogany from Indonesia, **hammer felts** from England, and steel **strings** from Germany.

Young Chang has a production work force of 5,400 employees that annually manufactures 100,000 verticals in seven sizes and 12,000 grands in six sizes (ranging from four feet, eleven inches to the nine-foot **concert grand**).

In common with other Asian piano manufacturers, Young Chang manufactures pianos under various labels (**stencil pianos**). One such name is Weber (the importer's name). Young Chang is one of a trio of present-day Korean piano manufacturers (Samick and Sojin are the other two) that produces a number of stencil pianos for export throughout the world.

See also Korea, Piano Industry in.

Frederic Schoettler

Bibliography

Fine, Larry. *The Piano Book*. Boston: Brookside Press, 1987.

Gill, Dominic. *The Book of the Piano*. Ithaca: Cornell University Press, 1981.

Hong, Yat-Lam. "The PTG Asian Tour: Part II." *Piano Technicians Journal*. (December 1989): 34–36.

Joppig, Gunther. "Young Chang Surge from Zero to 700,000 in Twenty Years." *Das Musikinstrument* 39 (February–March 1990): 224–228.

Wainwright, David. *The Piano Makers*. London: Hutchinson, 1975.

ZUMPE, JOHANN CHRISTOPH (1726–1791)

Johann Christoph Zumpe was a German crafts-man who was born in 1726 and died in his home country in 1791. Initially, he worked in the musical-instrument factory of **Gottfried Silbermann** and was thus fully conversant with the developments in the new **hammer-action** harpsichords (yet to be called "pianofortes") devised by **Bartolomeo Cristofori** and improved upon by Silbermann.

After the start of the Seven Years' War, Zumpe travelled to England as one of the "**Twelve Apostles,**" arriving in London sometime in the 1750s. He worked for a while with the harpsi-chord maker **Burkat Shudi** but in 1761 started up on his own at 7 Princess Street, Hanover Square.

While controversy remains over the true identity of the maker of the first real **square** pianoforte (Cristofori made **grands** based on the shape of the harpsichord), the oldest surviv-ing square piano is in the Germanisches Nationalmuseum in Nuremberg and is by Johann Söcher of Sonthofen in Bavaria. It is dated 1742. The claim that **Friederici** of Gera invented the square piano has no evidence to support it. It is likely that Zumpe made squares in Germany before emigrating to England. From this it can be deduced that his time with Shudi must have been no more than a stopgap, almost retro-grade, move until he was able to start his own business.

Once he had managed that transition, he flourished, for it was he who introduced the practical square pianoforte into England, and within a decade it was a popular instrument in great demand.

Contrary to the musical scene in the Ger-many he had left, Zumpe found to his un-doubted surprise that unequal temperament was customary in England. At first he was obliged to conform to it, but in a special pianoforte he built, dated 1766, he provided the necessary extra notes to offer a more equal temperament. This instrument, with a compass from GG to f^3 with the lowest GG$^\#$ omitted, divides its black keys from E$^\flat$ to a$^{\#2}$, leaving the top two black keys (c$^{\#3}$ and d$^{\#3}$) undivided.

Much of the early success of the square pianoforte came about through the genuine interest that the instrument generated. The first public performance in London took place at Covent Garden on 16 May 1767 when, at the end of the first act of the *Beggar's Opera*, one Miss Brickler sang a favorite song from Handel's *Judith* "accompanied by Mr. Dibdin [this was none other than Charles Dibdin, the composer-actor] on a new instrument call'd the Piano Forte." It is generally believed that this was a Zumpe instrument.

In the succeeding year, **Johann Christian Bach** performed a solo on a pianoforte, again in London, and for that occasion bought a Zumpe square pianoforte for which he paid 50 pounds. This compared with 73.5 pounds for a two-manual harpsichord from Shudi.

During the subsequent years, Zumpe was to become a major manufacturer of the instru-ment. So popular was the product that he was unable to supply the demand himself and passed on orders to his friend and compatriot, **Johannes Pohlmann**. His instruments were also in great demand abroad and he exported a good number of pianos to Paris.

To expand his production, in 1769 he formed a partnership with Gabriel Buntebart, but that was dissolved by mutual consent in September 1778. He was then joined for a while by another builder called Meyer. In 1780, he moved to Princes Street, Cavendish Square, remaining there until 1784, at which time he returned to Germany. One of his senior workers and a fellow "apostle" was [Georg D.] Schoene, who then took over the business. From that year onwards, instruments were marked Schoene, & Co "successors to Johannes Zumpe."

Zumpe brought numerous improvements to the development and subsequent perfection of the pianoforte **action**. He replaced Cristofori's wooden **jack** with a wire having a **leather**-covered wooden button at its upper extremity to set the **hammer** in motion. The system was known as the "English Single Action" and was either the invention of Zumpe or of his master Silbermann in Germany.

Zumpe's piano actions were practical but rather elementary, earning the nickname "mopstick" or "old man's head." Although subsequently revised by **John Broadwood**, the major improvement to Zumpe's action came from **John Geib**, who made pianos for the house of **Longman & Broderip**. His action, the subject of British **patent** number 1571 of 9 November 1756, added the "hopper" or "**escapement**," his action becoming known as the "grasshopper." Even so, it was some years before Geib's invention usurped the strong position held by the Zumpe action.

It was in an attempt to counteract the improvements being made by these other makers that Zumpe was inspired to revise his own action. This new model employed a second jack interposed between the jack and the hammer: this is called "Zumpe's Second Action" and was adopted by Schoene when he took over the business after Zumpe's return to Germany. For this reason, the earlier English Single Action is sometimes referred to as "Zumpe's First Action."

If Zumpe's actions were rudimentary at that time, so was the rest of the instrument. Hand-controlled levers were used to lift the **dampers** (not until John Broadwood's later revision of the instrument was a foot **pedal** substituted for controlling the dampers). However, to Zumpe goes credit for a major improvement in the development of the pianoforte: he invented a method of raising all the dampers at once using a form of what today would be called a damper **rail**.

Arthur W.J.G. Ord-Hume

Bibliography

Boalch, Donald H. *Makers of the Harpsichord & Clavichord, 1440–1840.* Oxford: Oxford University Press, 1974.

Harding, Rosamond E.M. *The Piano-Forte: Its History Traced to the Great Exhibition of 1851.* Cambridge: Cambridge University Press, 1933. Reprints, New York: Da Capo Press, 1973; Old Woking, Surrey: Gresham Books, 1978.

James, Philip. *Early Keyboard Instruments.* London: Peter Davies, 1930. Reprint. London: Tabard Press, 1970.

Contributors

David Anderson
Hiram College, Hiram, Ohio

Grotrian-Steinweg
Pfeiffer, Carl A.
Schimmel

Robert Andres
University of Kansas, Lawrence, Kansas

Clark (-Steiniger), Frederic Horace
Debain, Alexandre-François
Musicians and Piano Manufacturers
Schumann, Robert and Clara

Ben Arnold
Emory University, Atlanta, Georgia

Home, The Piano in the

Eva Badura-Skoda
Vienna, Austria

Bach, Johann Sebastian
Giustini, Lodovico
Haydn, Joseph
Pedal Piano
Scarlatti, Domenico
Schantz, Johann
Schantz, Wentzel
Schöfftoss, Donat
Silbermann, Gottfried
Späth
Walter, Anton

Peggy Flanagan Baird
Huntsville, Alabama

Bentside
Ebonies
Gaveau
Hebenstreit, Pantaléon

Ivories
Keybed
Keyblock
Keyboard Cover
Keyframe
Keys
Keyslip
Lyre
Merlin, John Joseph
Music Desk
Nameboard
Pape, Jean-Henri (Johann Heinrich)
Pedal Box
Rim
Siena Piano
Spine
Tafelklavier
Tail
Tomkison, Thomas
Tuning Hammer

Daniel Barber
Cleveland State University, Cleveland, Ohio

World War II and American Piano Builders

Patrizio Barbieri
University of Lecce, Italy

Italy, Piano Industry in

Jonathan Bellman
Stanford University, Stanford, California

Chopin, Frédéric François

Mary Louise Boehm
New York, New York

Astor & Co.
Böhm (Boehm), Joseph

Spain and Portugal, Piano Industry in
Stein Family

Danny L. Boone
Baylor University, Waco, Texas

Ancestors of the Piano
Burning Shanks
Leads
Maffei, Francesco Scipione
Serial Numbers
Webbing
Winking

Curt Cacioppo
Haverford College, Haverford, Pennsylvania

Fingering
Technic—A Survey

Camilla Cai
Kenyon College, Gambier, Ohio

Baby Grand
Boudoir Grand
Brahms, Johannes
Concert Grand
Falcone Piano Co.
Flügel
Graf, Conrad
Grand Piano
Hammerflügel/Hammerklavier
Living-Room Grand
Parlor Grand
Piano à queue
Piano à queue mignon
Piano de cauda
Piano de cola
Pianoforte a coda
Streicher Family
Stutzflügel

Seth A. Carlin
Washington University, St. Louis, Missouri

Beethoven, Ludwig van
Prellmechanik

Seunghyun Choi
EWHA Womans University, Seoul, Korea

Korea, Piano Industry in

Martha Novak Clinkscale
University of California, Riverside, California

Cabinet Pianoforte
Chappell & Co.
Claviharpe
Collections

Console Piano
Cottage Piano
Dettmer, George W. and Son
Edwards, William Henry
Geib, John Lawrence
Harp-Piano
Ibach
Lyraflügel
Pianino
Piano à buffet
Piano droit
Piano vertical
Pianoforte verticale
Portable Grand Piano
Schiedmayer
Schmahl Family
Schweighofer, Michael
Spinet
Upright Piano

John Cranmer
Nene College, Northhampton, England

Muir, Wood and Co.
Paterson, Mortimer and Co.
Scotland, Piano Industry in
Rochead and Son
Watson, John and Archibald
Wood, Small and Co.

Margaret Cranmer
Rowe Music Library, King's College, Cambridge, England

Allen, William

Edith M. DeForest
Chester, Connecticut

Pratt, Read & Co., Inc.

Donatella DeGiampietro
Accademia del fortepiano "Bartolomeo Cristofori," Florence, Italy

Adlung, Jakob
English Action
Escapement
Moderator
Square Piano
Stossmechanik

Brenda Dillon
National Piano Foundation, Dallas, Texas

National Piano Foundation

Carsten Dürer
Düsseldorf, Germany

Bach, Carl Philipp Emanuel

Euterpe Piano Co.
Germany, Piano Industry in
Giraffe/Pyramid Pianos
Grotrian-Steinweg
Sauter, C. Pianofortefabriken

Eszter Fontana
*Magyar Nemzeti Múzeum, Budapest,
Hungary*

Hungary, Piano Industry in

Edmund Michael Frederick
Ashburnham, Massachusetts

Erard, Sébastien (et frères)
Fortepiano
Viennese Piano, The

Larry Goldsmith
*Piano Technicians Guild, Kansas City,
Missouri*

Piano Technicians Guild

Edwin M. Good
Stanford University, Stanford, California

Babcock, Alpheus
Clutsam, Ferdinand
Cocked-hat Grand
Couplers
Damper Pedal
Dolge, Alfred
Forte Pedal
Janissary Stop
Jankó, Paul von
Keyboards
Loud Pedal
Moór, Emanuel
Pedals and Stops
Piano/Pianoforte
Querflügel
Sostenuto Pedal
Steinway & Sons
Una corda Pedal
Verschiebung

Nicholas Gravagne
Sandia Park, New Mexico

Acoustical Block
Acoustical Disc
Bellying
Soundboard
Tension Resonator

Jack Greenfield
Northfield, Illinois

Albrecht, Charles
Behrent, John
Cable-Nelson Piano Co.
Crehore, Benjamin
Everett Piano Co.
Friederici, Christian Ernst
Jefferson, Thomas
Marius, Jean
Schröter, Christoph Gottlieb
Story and Clark

Mary Ellen Haupert
LaCrosse, Wisconsin

Frame
Osborne, John

Florence Hayes
*National Library of Canada, Ottawa,
Canada*

Canada, Piano Industry in
Heintzman & Company Limited
Lesage Pianos Limited

Ferdinand J. De Hen
Rijksuniversiteit, Gent, Belgium

Apytholamprotérique
Bebung
Chirogymnaste
Cimbalom
Clédi-Harmonique
Combination Pianos
Duoclave Pianos
Low Countries, Piano Industry in the
Sostenente Pianos
Taskin, Pascal (Joseph)
Transposing Keyboards
Two-Keyboard Pianos
Unusual Pianos

Judith Ann Herd
Kokushikan University, Tokyo, Japan

Japan, Piano Industry in

David R. Hoehl
Rockville, Maryland

Challen and Sons
Patents
Purchasing a Piano

Samuel S. Holland
*Southern Methodist University, Dallas,
Texas*

Casio Digital Pianos
Electronic Pianos

Future of the Piano
Korg
Kurzweil
MIDI
Moog, Robert Arthur
Roland Digital Pianos
Sampler
Synclavier
Synthesizer
Yamaha Digital Pianos

Alfons Huber
Kunsthistorisches Museum, Vienna, Austria

Austria, Piano Industry in
Ditanaklasis
Leather
Müller, Matthias
Wire

Werner Iten
Tucson, Arizona

Burger & Jacobi
Sabel
Schmidt-Flohr
Switzerland, Piano Industry in

Philip Jamison, III
West Chester, Pennsylvania

Back Check
Balancier
Beats
Becket
Braces
Break
Bridge
Bridge Pin
Bridle Strap
Bushings
Butt
Capstan
Case
Chickering, Jonas
Chipping
Crown
Downbearing
Duplex Scaling
Fallboard
Felt
Hitch Pin
Jack
Knuckle
Lid Prop
Nose
Repetition Lever

Repinning
Shimming
Skinning
Skiving
Spoon
Sticker Action
Wippen

Keith T. Johns
Wollongong University, Wollongong, NSW, Australia

Australia, Piano Industry in
Czechoslovakia, Piano Industry in
Klavier
Scandinavia, Piano Industry in

Kerry Kean
Kent State University, Kent, Ohio

Hammer
Master Piano Technicians

Elise K. Kirk
Washington, D.C.

White House Pianos

John Koster
University of South Dakota, Shrine to Music Museum, Vermillion, South Dakota

Brodmann, Joseph
Montal, Claude

Lianli Ku
Shanghai Conservatory of Music, Shanghai, China

China, Piano Industry in

Darcy Kuronen
Museum of Fine Arts Boston, Boston, Massachusetts

Astor & Co.
Bach, Johann Christian
Cycloid Grand
Frederick the Great
Hancock, John Crang
Orphica
Schleip, Johann Christian

Michael Latcham
Haags Gemeentemuseum, 's-Gravenhage, Netherlands

Hofmann, Ferdinand

Steven R. Manley
University of Illinois, Urbana, Illinois

Pinblock

Pinblock Restorer
Voicing

Guy A. Marco
Rosary College, Chicago, Illinois

Periodicals

LLoyd W. Meyer
Renner USA, Weston, Connecticut

Renner, Louis GmbH & Co.

Daniele Mezzatesta
Pesaro, Italy

Del Mela, Domenico

Kenneth Mobbs
Mobbs Keyboard Collection, Bristol,
England

Euphonicon
Ganer, Christopher
Hervé, Samuel
Kirkman (Kirckman, Kirchmann), Jacob &
 Family
Longman and Broderip
Rolfe, William and Sons
Thom, James and William Allen

Giuliana Montanari
Reggio Emilia, Italy

Adlung, Jakob
English Action
Escapement
Moderator
Square Piano
Stossmechanik

Charles Mould
Bodleian Library, Oxford, England

Burney, Charles
Haxby, Thomas

Dorothea A. Nahm
Howard University, Washington, D.C.

Virgil Practice Clavier, The

Arthur W.J.G. Ord-Hume
Ord-Hume Library of Mechanical Music &
Horology, Guildford, Surrey, England

Aeolian Co.
Ampico Corporation
Backers, Americus
Barrel Piano
Beck, Frederick
Becker, John Conrad
Beyer, Adam

Brinsmead, John
Broadwood & Sons, John
Coin-Operated Pianos
Combination Pianos
Duo-Art
Enharmonic Piano
Expression Piano
Extemporary Recording
Fourneaux, Napoleon
Hawkins, John Isaac
Hupfeld A.G., Ludwig
Kirkman (Kirckman, Kirchmann) Jacob
 and Family
Loud and Company
Orchestrion, Piano
Pianola
Piano mécanique
Piano Player
Player Piano
Pohlmann, Johannes
Push-Up Piano Player
Reproducing Piano
Rolfe, William and Sons
Self-Playing Piano
Seytre, Claude Félix
Shudi, Burkat
Southwell, William
Stodart, Robert and William
Street Piano
Theatre Photoplayers
"Twelve Apostles"
Violin Piano
Welte & Sons, M.
Wornum, Robert
Zumpe, Johann Christoph

Steven Permut
Library of Congress, Washington, D.C.

Recordings

Peter G.C. Van Poucke
Rijksuniversiteit, Gent, Belgium

Acoustics
Partials
Tuning

Jan Rademacher
Berlin, Germany

Blüthner
Clavichord's Influence on the Piano

Priscilla and Joel Rappaport
Round Rock, Texas

Capo tasto/Capo d'astro/V-Bar
Pressure Bar

Scale
Scale Design
Strings/Stringing

James Howard Richards
Waco, Texas

American Piano Co.
Baldwin Piano and Organ Company
Kimball Piano and Organ Company
Krakauer
Kranich & Bach
McTammany, John
Mason & Hamlin
MirrApiano
Sohmer Piano Co.
Stencil Piano
Walter Piano Co.

Craig H. Roell
Georgia Southern University, Statesboro, Georgia

Gulbransen Incorporated
Kohler & Campbell, Inc.
United States, Piano Industry in the
Wurlitzer Co.

Sandra P. Rosenblum
Concord Academy, Belmont, Massachusetts

Collard & Collard
Overstrung

Sergei A. Rytsarev
University of Tel-Aviv, Tel-Aviv, Israel

Russia and the Commonwealth of
Independent States (formerly USSR),
Piano Industry in

Michael Saffle
Virginia Polytechnic Institute and State University, Blacksburg, Virginia

Chamber Music and Accompanying
Composers' Influence on the Piano
Exhibitions and World's Fairs
Liszt, Franz
Music for the Piano

Frederic Schoettler
Kent State University, Kent, Ohio

Bechstein
Bösendorfer
Clementi, Muzio and Co.
Prepared Piano
Seiler
Young Chang

Howard Schott
Boston, Massachusetts

Harpsichord to Piano, The Transition from
Mathushek, Frederick
Nunns, Robert and William

Robert E. Sheldon
Library of Congress, Washington, D.C.

Keyboard Practice and Exercise Aids
Virgil Practice Clavier, The

W. Richard Shindle
Kent State University, Kent, Ohio

Mozart, (Johann Chrysostom) Wolfgang
Amadeus

David C. Stanwood
Stanwood & Co., Vineyard Haven, Massachusetts

Touchweight

Ron Surace
Jacksonville State University, Jacksonville, Alabama

Cristofori, Bartolomeo
Ferrini, Giovanni

Edward E. Swenson
Ithaca College, Ithaca, New York

Agraffe
Aliquot Scaling
Care and Maintenance
Ehrbar Klavierfabrik
Decker Brothers
Hazelton Brothers Piano Company
Knabe & Co.
Restoration of Early Pianos
Tuning Pin
Weber Piano Co.

Tibor Szász
Duke University, Durham, North Carolina

Performance Practices—Stylistic Considerations (1700–1990)

Helen Smith Tarchalski
Gaithersburg, Maryland

Pedagogy—A Survey

Daniel E. Taylor
University of South Dakota, Shrine to Music Museum, Vermillion, South Dakota

England, Piano Industry in

Charles Timbrell
Howard University, Washington, D.C.

France, Piano Industry in
Pleyel, Ignace-Joseph (et Cie)

Benjamin Vogel
Warsaw University, Warsaw, Poland

Actions
Poland, Piano Industry in
Tangent Piano

Kent Webb
Baldwin Piano Co., Trumann, Arkansas

Aftertouch
Dip
Drop
Finish

Laying Touch
Let-Off
Pitch
Rebuilding
Regulation
Ribs
Strike Point

Herbert Wise
Monroe Community College, Rochester, New York

Kawai
Yamaha

Charles Zammit
Institute for Music, Malta

Tone
Touch

Index

Article titles and principal page entries are indicated in boldface; brand names and particular instruments are indicated in quotation marks.